D. O. Akpan
2/28/97

P.4   Memory Interleading

Practical Parallel Programming

Scientific and Engineering Computation
Janusz Kowalik, editor

Data-Parallel Programming on MIMD Computers, Philip J. Hatcher and Michael J. Quinn, 1991

Unstructured Scientific Computation on Scalable Multiprocessors, edited by Piyush Mehrotra, Joel Saltz, and Robert Voight, 1992

Parallel Computational Fluid Dynamics: Implementations and Results, edited by Horst D. Simon, 1992

Enterprise Integration Modeling: Proceedings of the First International Conference, edited by Charles J. Petrie, Jr., 1992

The High Performance Fortran Handbook, Charles H. Koelbel, David B. Loveman, Robert S. Schreiber, Guy L. Steele, Jr., and Mary E. Zosel, 1994

Using MPI: Portable Parallel Programming with the Message-Passing Interface, William Gropp, Ewing Lusk, and Anthony Skjellum, 1994

PVM: Parallel Virtual Machine—A Users' Guide and Tutorial for Networked Parallel Computing, Al Geist, Adam Beguelin, Jack Dongarra, Weicheng Jiang, Robert Mancheck, and Vaidy Sunderam, 1994

Enabling Technologies for Petaflops Computing, Thomas Sterling, Paul Messina, and Paul H. Smith, 1995

An Introduction to High-Performance Scientific Computing, Lloyd D. Fosdick, Elizabeth R. Jessup, Carolyn J. C. Schauble, and Gitta Domik, 1995

Practical Parallel Programming, Gregory V. Wilson, 1995

Practical Parallel Programming

Gregory V. Wilson

The MIT Press
Cambridge, Massachusetts
London, England

This book was set in Times-Roman by Windfall Software using ZzTEX and was printed and bound in the United States of America.

Library of Congress Cataloging-in-Publication Data

Wilson, Gregory V.
  Practical parallel programming / Gregory V. Wilson.
    p. cm.—(Scientific and engineering computation)
  Includes bibliographical references and index.
  ISBN 0-262-23186-7 (hc)
  1. Parallel programming (Computer science) I. Title
QA76.642.W553   1995
005.2—dc20

                                                                95-9800
                                                                CIP

This book is for my father,
who taught me how to write,
and that writing well is important

Contents

Series Foreword

The world of modern computing potentially offers many helpful methods and tools to scientists and engineers, but the fast pace of change in computer hardware, software, and algorithms often makes practical use of the newest computing technology difficult. The Scientific and Engineering Computation series focuses on rapid advances in computing technologies and attempts to facilitate transferring these technologies to applications in science and engineering. It will include books on theories, methods, and original applications in such areas as parallelism, large-scale simulations, time-critical computing, computer-aided design and engineering, use of computers in manufacturing, visualization of scientific data, and human-machine interface technology.

The series will help scientists and engineers to understand the current world of advanced computation and to anticipate future developments that will impact their computing environments and open up new capabilities and modes of computation.

Practical Parallel Programming introduces scientists, engineers, and students to four parallel programming techniques: data parallelism, shared variables, message passing, and generative communication, and illustrates how each approach can be used to solve various scientific and engineering problems. Parallel computing is not entirely new but only now are parallel computers becoming widely available as practical tools for solving large-scale problems. The aim of this book is to explain how one can develop parallel software and achieve good computational performance on the contemporary parallel hardware. All programs are written in a dialect of the well known programming language, FORTRAN.

Janusz S. Kowalik

Practical Parallel Programming

1 Introduction

In fact the advent of parallel programming may do something to revive the pioneering spirit in programming, which seems to be degenerating into a rather dull and routine occupation.
—S. Gill
Computer Journal, Vol. 1, 1958

Since the dawn of time (actually, the late 1940s), almost all electronic computers have had the same general form: a single processor, connected to a single bank of memory, appearing to execute a single program at a time. Since the late 1960s, however, physics, economics, and the Everest Syndrome[1] have led many computer architects to explore alternatives in which many processors work together on the same problem at the same time. Such computers are called *parallel* computers, and the subject of this book is how to program them.

As the quotation at the top of this page shows, the idea of parallelism has been around almost as long as computers themselves. However, parallelism only became practical with the advent of Very Large Scale Integration (VLSI) in the late 1970s. The few parallel computers constructed before that time were too expensive and unreliable to be competitive. Since then, computers containing a handful of processors have come to dominate the mid-range mainframe market, while others with hundreds or thousands of processors are now among the most powerful in the world.

Parallelism has become more popular because a large investment in one fast processor no longer buys as much performance as an equivalent investment in a dozen or a few hundred off-the-shelf microprocessors and some wires to connect them. Parallelism has become necessary because single-processor computers are not powerful enough to solve the so-called Grand Challenge problems of science, such as modelling global weather patterns, determining the mass of the proton or the structure of a protein molecule from first principles, or keeping track of the wealth of information which the Human Genome Project will produce.

Unfortunately, while parallel computer hardware has progressed rapidly since the late 1970s, parallel software has not. Every family of machines has a different operating system, and supports a different set of programming languages (or a different set of extensions to standard languages). Even worse, only a few general problem-solving techniques are well-known, even within the parallel computing community. The result is that achieving good performance on parallel machines is as much a black art as building multi-tasking operating systems once was on conventional machines.

---

1. "Because it's there . . . "

The aim of this book is therefore to explain and demonstrate the most useful parallel programming techniques. The first chapter introduces some of the problems parallelism has been used to solve, and some of the community's ideas and terminology. Each subsequent chapter describes a single parallel programming paradigm: data parallelism, shared variables, message passing, and generative communication. The examples in this book are written in dialects of a FORTRAN-based language called FORTRAN-K. The basics of FORTRAN-K are described in Appendix A, which also explains how you can get a compiler and emulator for it. The other four appendices contain a short history of parallel computing, a recommended reading list, a glossary of parallel computing terminology, and some tongue-in-cheek advice to designers of parallel programming systems.

No book like this can be written without support from many people. I learned most of what I know about parallel computing while working for the Edinburgh Concurrent Supercomputer Project, and its successor, the Edinburgh Parallel Computing Centre. I am grateful to its former director, Professor David Wallace, and to Neil Heywood for giving me so much freedom over the years. I am also grateful to Allen Malony (University of Oregon), Jonathan Schaeffer (University of Alberta), Richard Brent and Robin Stanton (Australian National University), Henri Bal (Vrije Universiteit, Amsterdam), and Ken Sevcik (University of Toronto), who supported me, financially and otherwise, during two years of writing, programming, and worrying. Finally, I would like to thank all of the students who have put up with my strong opinions over the years, the staff of Mamma's for keeping me fed, and my colleagues—especially Peter Bailey, Raoul Bhoedjang, Saniya Ben Hassen, Hugh Caffey, Lyndon Clarke, Paul Lu, Brent Gorda, Neil MacDonald, Tim Rühl, Mark Smith, and Brian Wylie—for keeping my head above water.

I have made every effort to ensure that the material in this book is correct and up-to-date, but I have written enough software over the years to know that mistakes inevitably creep in. If you find any, I would be grateful if you could let me know by sending email to PPP@mitpress.mit.edu.

Gregory V. Wilson

2 Fundamentals

It's not what you know, but what you can.
—Alexander Alekhine

A little bit of theory can go a long way; accordingly, this chapter presents just enough of the theory of parallel computing to get us through the rest of this book. The first section introduces some of the basic ideas of parallel computer architecture, while the next describes some ways of classifying parallel machines. Section 2.3 then describes some of the types of applications which have motivated the development of parallel computers. This discussion leads to the important notion of problem decomposition strategies, several of which are covered. The remaining sections then present some other key concepts of parallel computing, in no particular order.

2.1 Basic Architectural Ideas

The million-fold increase in computer speed since 1950 can be attributed in roughly equal measure to faster components, more efficient algorithms, and more sophisticated architectures. In many ways, the history of the last of these is the history of attempts to eliminate or circumvent the bottlenecks in the "classic" architecture which bears John von Neumann's name.

A computer's *architecture* is a specification of those internals of the computer which software must take into account. A pure von Neumann architecture consists of a single processing unit, joined by a single connection to a single memory bank which holds both instructions and data (Figure 2.1). The processor is responsible for fetching instructions from the memory, decoding each in turn, fetching whatever operands it requires, applying the instruction to the operands, and writing its results (if any) back to memory. These steps are done sequentially, with each being started only after its predecessor has completed. Such a computer is called a *uniprocessor*, to distinguish it from other architectures discussed later.

2.1.1 Memory Bottlenecks

A machine which behaves this way is relatively straightforward to build, but contains many potential bottlenecks. For economic reasons, a computer's memory is usually significantly slower than its processor (since many units of the former are needed for each instance of the latter), so a processor might often be stalled waiting on memory requests to be satisfied. Even if the memory is fast enough, the connection between it and the processor may not have enough bandwidth to support their interaction.

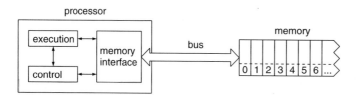

Figure 2.1
Von Neumann Architecture

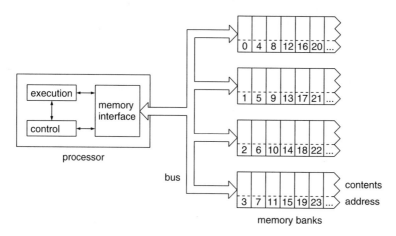

Figure 2.2
Interleaved Memory

Many architects have tried to eliminate the first of these bottlenecks by building a fast memory unit from slow components. The most common way to do this is to interleave several memory banks, as shown in Figure 2.2. Since memory access is usually sequential—i.e., since the chances are good that after fetching an instruction from address a a processor will fetch its next instruction from address $a + 1$, or that after fetching a particular array element a processor will then fetch the next one—addresses are usually mapped onto individual memory banks cyclically, to reduce the chances of an individual bank being the target of several successive requests. A k-way interleaved memory can therefore overlap up to k operations, and appear k times faster than a single uninterleaved memory of the same size, provided these operations reference different memory banks. To distinguish it from interleaved memory, memory built using a single bank is sometimes called monolithic.

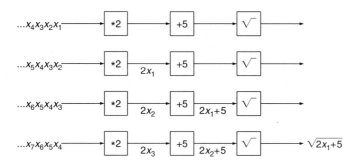

Figure 2.3
Pipelining

2.1.2 Vectorization

Computer architects frequently try to take advantage of the usually-sequential nature of processing in another way. In most numerical calculations, a single operation is carried out on many data values before any other operation is applied; examples include setting the values in an array to 0, adding a constant to every element of an array, adding corresponding elements of two or more arrays, and so on.

There are several ways to structure a computer to improve its performance on such calculations. The first, and most popular, speeds up the execution of operations by *pipelining* their execution. If, for example, a computer needs to calculate $\sqrt{2x_i + 5}$ for a vector of values $x_1, x_2, \ldots, x_N$, the time to do the entire computation can be reduced by using several arithmetic units to overlap separate calculations. In the first cycle, the first unit calculates $2x_1$, while the other two are idle. In the second cycle, the second unit adds 5 to the value $2x_1$, while the first unit calculates $2x_2$ (Figure 2.3). In the third step, the three calculations $2(x_3)$, $(2x_2) + 5$, and $\sqrt{(2x_1 + 5)}$ (where parentheses are used to show the input to each unit) are calculated simultaneously. After that, a single result appears every cycle, instead of the one every three cycles that a serial computer would produce. Just as an assembly line can speed up production in a factory, it is often possible to overlap the various stages of the processor's fetch-decode-execute cycle, particularly if the effects of successive instructions do not depend on one another. Pipelined machines are often called *vector processors*, since programs for them are usually phrased in terms of operations on vectors.

The time taken for a pipeline to produce its first result is called the pipeline's *latency*. In this example, the startup latency is 3, since the first result appears 3 timesteps after the first data value enters the pipeline. As the sequence of calculations becomes longer, the pipeline's latency becomes less significant, and the degree of concurrency comes to dominate its overall speed. To see why, consider a pipeline containing L stages, each of which operates in unit time, operating on a vector of N elements. At time 0, the first element of the vector enters the pipeline. At time L, the result corresponding to it leaves the pipeline, and one new result is produced at each time step thereafter. The total time to operate on the vector is therefore $N + L - 1$, and the effective rate of the pipeline $\frac{N}{N+L-1}$. As $N \to \infty$, this approaches 1, i.e. the latency L becomes less important.

Most pipelined computers do not actually overlap separate operations in this way. Instead, they break operations such as floating-point addition into separate steps, and then pipeline those steps. In order to add two floating-point numbers, for example, it is necessary to scale one or the other so that their exponents are the same, perform the addition, and then scale the result to re-normalize its exponent. Thus, given the calculation $\sqrt{2x_i + 5}$, a typical pipelined computer would pipeline the calculation of a temporary vector containing $2x_i$, then pipeline the addition of 5 to each element, and finally pipeline the square root operation.

Pipelined computers are well suited to solving large linear algebra problems, in which scaling a vector, finding the dot product of two vectors, or multiplying several large matrices together must be done millions of times. They are less well suited to irregular problems, such as compilation or running an operating system, for two reasons. The first is latency—compilers and operating systems do not operate on long vectors, but on scalars such as process IDs and file names. Secondly, performance is inevitably reduced by the bubbles caused by conditional branches. For example, suppose that every element in a vector is either to be multiplied by -1 or incremented by 3, depending on the result of some earlier calculation. Until that calculation's result becomes available, the multiplications cannot be started. As a result, the pipeline must empty and then be re-filled, which reduces the number of operations which can be overlapped.

A situation in which one calculation depends on the results of a previous calculation is called a *data dependence*. In scientific calculations, data dependencies most often arise in loops, as shown in the following fragment of FORTRAN-K[1]:

```
integer, constant :: Len = 8 * 1024
real :: x(Len)
   .
   .
   .
do i = 3, len
  x(i) = x(i-1) + x(i-2)
end do
```

1. A full description of FORTRAN-K can be found in Appendix A.

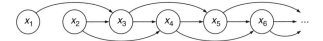

Figure 2.4
A Data Dependence Graph

Here, it would seem that the loop's iterations must be executed sequentially, since changes are rippling forward from x(1) and x(2) to x(3), from x(2) and the new x(3) to x(4), and so on. We can represent such dependencies using diagrams like the one in Figure 2.4, with circles showing data values and arrows showing dependencies. In fact, enormous progress has been made in the past two decades in automatically finding ways to pipeline, or *vectorize*, calculations such as these. By re-arranging the order of the computations and *unrolling loops* (i.e., replicating the body of the loop n times, and executing the replicated body $1/n$ times fewer) it is possible to vectorize many calculations which apparently need to be done serially. Some of these techniques will be discussed in Section 3.4.

Even using such magic, there are very sharp limits to what pipelining can achieve. For a start, values move through any pipeline only as fast as they move through that pipeline's slowest component. While the use of VLSI techniques and novel materials such as gallium arsenide (GaAs) have yielded components which are orders of magnitude faster than those used in the first commercial supercomputers in the mid-1960s, trying to make a single processor go extremely fast has proved to be less and less cost-effective. The alternative is to use several processors, and this is where parallel computing truly begins.

2.1.3 Bus-Based Multiprocessors

Putting several processors into a computer is much more complicated than interleaving several memories, just as having ten people saw the same piece of wood simultaneously is more hazardous than having one person stack ten pieces and saw them all at once. The simplest approach is to leave most of the computer's design alone, and just attach several extra processors to the memory through a single shared *bus* (Figure 2.5) to create a *multiprocessor*. This basic design has been used for everything from multiprocessor PCs and workstations through mainframes to machines in which each processor is a pipelined supercomputer in its own right.

The greatest strength of this design is that it allows a lot of pre-existing software to be recycled. In particular, *multi-tasking* operating systems such as VMS or UNIX are written so that processes may be executed and interleaved in an arbitrary order, i.e. may appear to run in parallel. They further assume that processes can communicate with one another, and with the operating system, by reading and writing special memory locations. Since

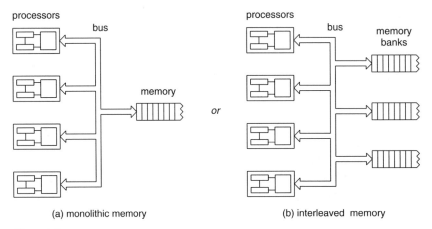

Figure 2.5
Bus-Based Multiprocessor Architecture

all of the processors in a multiprocessor share a single memory (either monolithic or interleaved), most multi-tasking operating systems can easily be modified to run processes on whatever processors are available. This idea can then be extended for use within individual programs. For example, if a program contains a loop which performs an operation on each element of an array, and there are no awkward data dependencies, then each of $\mathcal{P}$ processors can be given $(1/\mathcal{P})^{\text{th}}$ of the loop's iterations.

The greatest weakness of bus-based multiprocessor designs is that the bandwidth of this bus is finite. As the number of processors increases it becomes more and more likely that when one processor wants the bus, another will already be using it. This situation is called *contention*, and to date it has limited the practical size of bus-based multiprocessors to about two dozen processors. As will be discussed in Section 4.4, however, some new architectural ideas may be able to overcome this bottleneck.

2.1.4   Caching

Architects can use either or both of two strategies to try to reduce bus contention. The first, inherited from conventional uniprocessor designs, is to provide each processor with a small, high-speed memory of its own, called a *cache*. Uniprocessors use caches to exploit the fact that most programs exhibit both *spatial locality* and *temporal locality*. The former term means that if a process accesses address a, the odds are good that it will access addresses near a shortly thereafter. Similarly, once a process accesses a value, it will probably access that value again relatively soon. An example of spatial locality is access

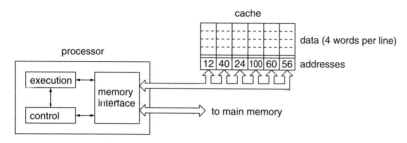

Figure 2.6
Cache Organization in a Uniprocessor

to the fields of record structures in high-level languages; an example of temporal locality is the repeated use of a loop index variable to subscript an array.

A cache is usually organized as an *associative memory*. In a normal computer memory, a word is accessed by specifying its physical address. In an associative memory, on the other hand, each word keeps track of its own logical address. When the processor tries to read or write some address A, each word checks to see whether it is supposed to respond. In practice, the words in caches are usually grouped into *lines* containing from four to sixteen words each (Figure 2.6).

Whenever a processor with a cache requires a value from memory, it first checks its private cache to see whether it has an up-to-date copy of the value it wants. If it does, it uses that copy rather than add to the traffic on the bus. If it does not, or if it is trying to write the value rather than read it, the processor waits for its turn on the bus and performs its transaction (Figure 2.7). As the frequency with which values are found in the cache, called the *hit rate*, goes up, the frequency of bus transactions goes down, and the bus becomes able to support a larger number of processors.

However, caches are a mixed blessing. Suppose that two processors P_a and P_b have copied the value at address a_x into their respective caches, and that P_a then modifies it. If this modification is not reflected in P_b's copy, processes running on P_a and P_b will have inconsistent views of the contents of memory. For example, if the variable stored at a_x is a pointer to the head of a linked list, then if both processors modify it independently, the list might split or become circular.

Memory inconsistencies such as these are exceedingly difficult to detect, and their effects are equally difficult to predict or analyze. As a result, most architects take steps to ensure *cache consistency*, i.e. that whenever a cached value is modified, other copies are either updated or marked as invalid. Some of the strategies used to do this are discussed

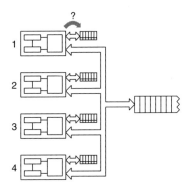

(a) processor 1 requests value from cache

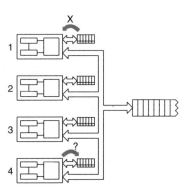

(b) processor 1's cache does not have value
processor 4 requests value from cache

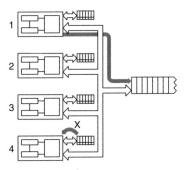

(c) processor 1 requests value from memory
processor 4's cache does not have value

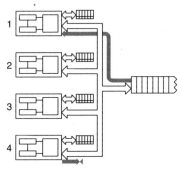

(d) processor 1 gets value from memory
processor 4 is stalled

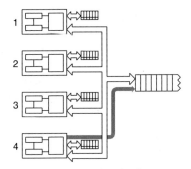

(e) processor 4 requests value from memory

Figure 2.7
Cache Operation

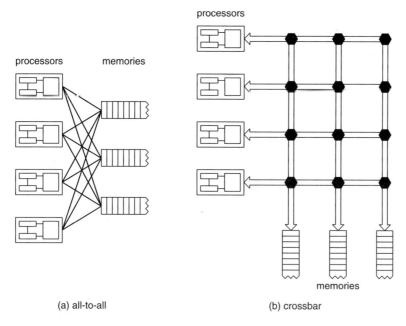

Figure 2.8
Loosely-Coupled Processor-Memory Connection Schemes

in Section 4.4; sadly, they all increase bus traffic, which again limits the potential size of bus-based multiprocessors.

2.1.5 Multiple Communication Paths

Another route which architects can take to ameliorate the single-bus bottleneck is to provide many communication paths between processors and memory. A machine with $\mathcal{P}$ processors and M memories could, for example, contain one bus to connect each processor to each memory (Figure 2.8a). Such a design would require $\mathcal{P}M$ buses, which would quickly become too expensive as the machine's size grew. Another expensive option would be a *crossbar*, in which $\mathcal{P}$ processor buses intersect M memory buses (Figure 2.8b), for a total of $\mathcal{P} + M$ buses and $\mathcal{P}M$ connections.

Affordable architectures tend to rely on sparser connections, which can be implemented using some kind of *multi-stage interconnection network (MIN)*. A MIN connects processors to memories through several layers of *switches* in such a way that any processor can interact with any memory unit indirectly. Each switch contains circuitry to route requests from processors to memories, and replies from memories back to processors. A typical

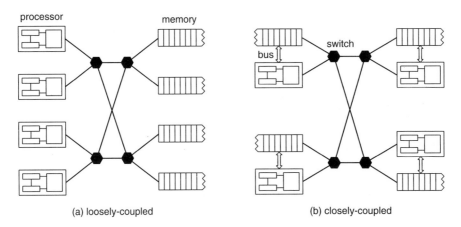

(a) loosely-coupled   (b) closely-coupled

Figure 2.9
Multistage Processor-Memory Connection Schemes

MIN design is shown in Figure 2.9a. The intermediate switches are typically very simple, containing only enough logic to select messages from their inputs and forward them to one of their outputs. (More complex switches capable of modifying or combining messages have been built, and will be discussed in Section 4.2.2, but to date have not proved cost-effective.) Typically, addresses are distributed cyclically amongst memories, just as they are in an interleaved memory, to try to prevent memory access contention.

MIN-based multiprocessors are an improvement over bus-based designs, since the bandwidth connecting processors to memories grows as machines get larger. However, they still have problems with cache values getting out of step. What is more, if every memory operation must traverse the MIN, it can still become saturated relatively easily. Caching can again be used to offset this, but so can another strategy: rather than placing the processors on one side of the MIN, and the memories on the other, an architect can connect each memory unit directly to one processor, and only use the MIN for requests which go outside that memory. This style of machine is shown in Figure 2.9b, and is sometimes referred to as a *closely-coupled multiprocessor*; designs in which all memories are equally far from all processors are in contrast called *loosely-coupled*. The basic unit of the design is a processor/memory pair, which usually operates like a conventional uniprocessor and its memory. Whenever a process tries to read or write, the operation's address is checked against the range of addresses represented by its local memory. If the address is in range, the operation is done locally. If not, a request is sent through the MIN to some other processor's memory, where it is serviced without that other processor being interrupted. So long as there is sufficient locality in programs—i.e., so long as most references are to local memory—

this scheme can deliver very high performance, while giving programmers the convenient illusion of having a single, shared-memory system. In order to help achieve locality, it is usual to distribute addresses between memories in blocks, instead of cyclically, so that (for example) adjacent elements of a data vector will usually reside in one processor's memory.

2.1.6 Multicomputers

It is worth mentioning the convenience of having a single memory which every processor can see because many designs go one step beyond MINs, and take it away. Rather than treating the close connection between each processor and a particular memory unit as just a way of improving performance, a *multicomputer* makes it a basic building block. A multicomputer consists of some number of processor/memory pairs connected to one another through *links* (which may themselves be joined through intermediate switches). Each processor can only access its own memory directly; to read or write values stored elsewhere, it must send a message to the processor connected to the memory holding those values (Figure 2.10). Putting it another way, rather than a single *address space*, or range of addressable memory locations, a multicomputer contains many disjoint address spaces, each of which is owned by a single processor. As a result, a pointer cannot safely be passed between processes which reside on different processors in such a machine, since the thing to which it points in the destination memory will be different from the thing to which it pointed at its source. Similarly, if a data structure such as an array has been decomposed, and its components spread across the available processors so that each may work on a small part of it, accesses to the local and remote portions of the array rely on different mechanisms, and may appear different to programmers.

All of this may sound bad enough, but in early multicomputers, the situation was even worse. If the destination of a message was not adjacent to (i.e., directly connected to) its source, then software had to forward the message somehow from processor to processor. All recent designs have done away with this by adding communication co-processors to each basic processor/memory pair. Such co-processors are not only responsible for forwarding messages, but also accept and sort incoming messages, and allow programmers to overlap computation (done by the main processor) with communication.

If multicomputers are so awkward to program, why have so many been built? The main reason has been that they are easy to scale up: given a basic component consisting of a processor, its memory, and a few links, it is possible to build a machine of arbitrary size, in which the ratio of computing power to communication and memory bandwidth stays constant. For some types of applications, such designs are very cost-effective, and can achieve very high performance.

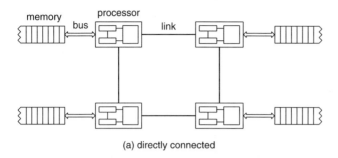

(a) directly connected

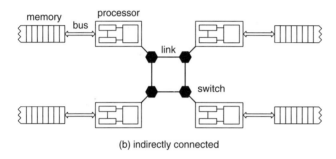

(b) indirectly connected

Figure 2.10
Multicomputer Connection Schemes

2.1.7   Symmetry, Hierarchy, and Balance

All of the discussion above has assumed that all of a machine's processors are identical. This is not necessarily true, and even when it is, a computer's processors may play very different roles. One example of this, which has been popular since the 1960s, is to incorporate one or more I/O processors into a design, so that the main processor is not held up by the sloth of secondary storage devices (Figure 2.11a). Another example is the use of *asymmetric operating systems*, in which some processors only run user-level processes, while others handle all operating system calls (Figure 2.11b).

Another important idea in parallel architecture has been that of *hierarchical architectures*. Such designs are typically classified as closely-coupled multiprocessors, but are different in important ways from the examples shown in Figures 2.8 and 2.9. Instead of each processor being connected to a single memory, and having to go through a MIN to reach other memories, a small number of processors are connected by a shared bus to a single memory, as in a bus-based multiprocessor (Figure 2.12). Several such units are then connected by a second-stage bus, which may or may not also be connected to some addi-

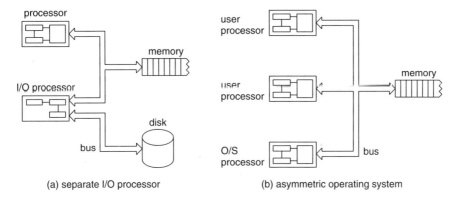

processor

memory

I/O processor

disk

bus

(a) separate I/O processor

user processor

user processor

memory

O/S processor

bus

(b) asymmetric operating system

Figure 2.11
Miscellaneous Architectural Uses of Parallelism

tional memory. These larger units can then be connected by third-stage buses, and so on. Again, provided the computation exhibits sufficient locality, i.e., provided most memory references are to the memory most closely coupled to the processor, the higher-level buses will not saturate.

The major difficulty with the ideas discussed in the preceding two paragraphs is achieving a workable balance: if a machine is to contain components of several different types, then how many of each should it have? If a mainframe has too many I/O processors, for example, then it will be unnecessarily costly; if it has too few, then its main processor will be idle too much of the time. Similarly, a processor dedicated to running an operating system will usually be either more or less powerful than is needed; even if it is just right for one application, it will be insufficient for another.[2] An old rule of thumb (first enunciated by Gene Amdahl in the 1960s) is that a "balanced" architecture should have an equal number of *megaFLOPS* (millions of floating-point operations per second), Mbytes, and Mbits per second of I/O bandwidth. A machine which is lacking in any of these respects will find itself bottlenecked on some types of operations.

2.2 Classifying Architectures

Before looking in more detail at the different computer architectures introduced in the previous section, it is worth developing a conceptual framework within which they can

---

2. As discussed in Section B.2, almost every multiprocessor built today uses a symmetric operating system, which treats all processors equally.

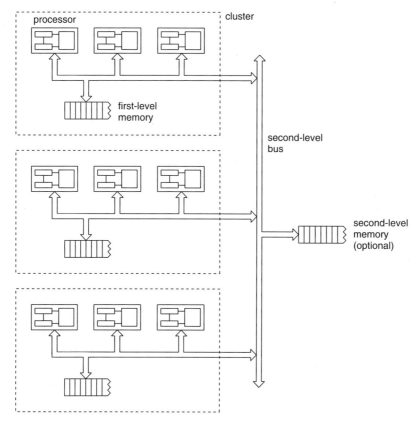

Figure 2.12
Hierarchical Memory Organization

be arranged. People working with parallel computers tend to think and talk more about architecture than people working with serial computers for the simple reason that parallel computers give them more to think and talk about. Here, "architecture" will be used to mean a description of the behavioral units in a computer which are visible to programmers. A computer's architecture defines the interface between the hardware in it and the software which runs on it by specifying which operations that computer can do directly, and which must be emulated using sequences of intrinsic operations.

2.2.1   Flynn's Taxonomy

The most influential paper on architectural taxonomy was [Flynn 1966]. According to Flynn, the two most important characteristics of a computer are the number of instruction

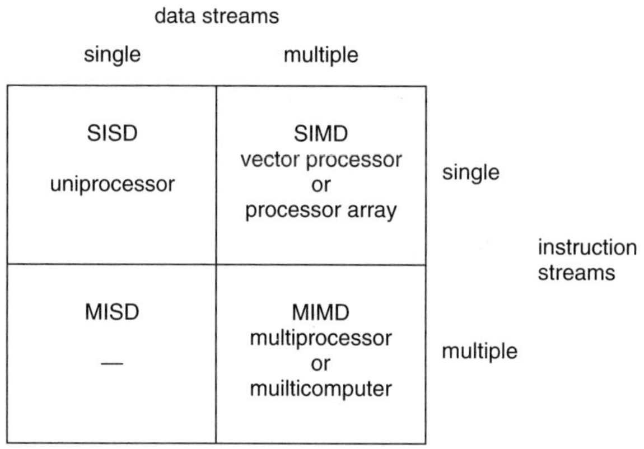

data streams

single	multiple	
SISD uniprocessor	SIMD vector processor or processor array	single
MISD —	MIMD multiprocessor or muilticomputer	multiple

instruction
streams

Figure 2.13
Flynn's Taxonomy

streams it can process at a time, and the number of data elements on which it can operate simultaneously (Figure 2.13). In a traditional von Neumann architecture, for example, a single processor steps through a single instruction stream, executing each instruction on a single datum. Architectures of this kind are accordingly classified as *SISD*, for single instruction, single data.

The next class in Flynn's taxonomy includes those machines which take advantage of the fact that many programs apply the same operation to many different data in succession. The traditional way to do this is to pipeline execution, as discussed in Section 2.1.2. However, some machines accomplish the same end by combining a very large number of slow, simple processors. In this style of machine, the whole of each operation is carried out by one processor, but each of the many processors applies the operation to a different datum. The most common example of this is found in designs in which most processors contain only the hardware needed to execute instructions, and cannot fetch or decode instructions themselves. Instead, a single master processor fetches instructions, executes branches, and so on, while broadcasting simple commands to the many execution processors (Figure 2.14).

A machine such as this is called a *processor array*, since the replicated processors are often organized as a regular two- or three-dimensional array. Typically, such machines contain a single *control processor* and a large number of *data processors*. The control processor, which is usually a conventional CPU, fetches, decodes, and broadcasts program instructions, and executes any serial operations in the program. The data processors, on the other hand, are usually extremely simple, containing only an arithmetic unit and some

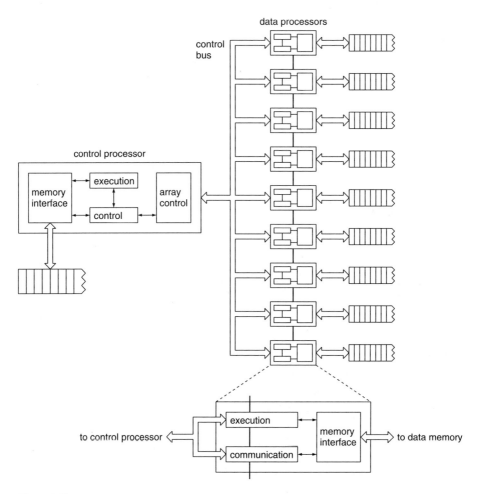

Figure 2.14
Processor Array

memory. (More complexity is usually not needed, since program instructions are decoded by the control processor, and in any case could probably not be afforded.) Each data processor accepts simple instructions from the control processor and applies them to data stored locally. Data processors may also exchange data with their neighbors, or choose to ignore certain instructions based on local conditions.

Both pipelined computers and processor arrays are classified as single instruction, multiple data, or *SIMD*, architectures, because they apply a single instruction to multiple data values before moving on to the next instruction. Such machines are very good at handling regular arithmetic problems but, as discussed in Section 2.1.2, their utility is limited by the fact that what a program does to its data often depends on the values of those data. Returning to the example of that section, suppose again that each element of a matrix is either to be multiplied by -1, or incremented by 3. Since the instructions broadcast by the control processor to the data processors are different in each case, this calculation must be done in two steps. In the first, only the data processors which are multiplying are busy, while in the second, only those which are adding are busy. In the general case, if each data processor is to execute exactly one of I different instructions, then the calculation requires I steps. As programs become more complicated, and I increases, a SIMD machine's efficiency necessarily decreases.

The usual solution is to build a multiprocessor or multicomputer in which each processor executes its own instruction stream, and works on its own data. This type of architecture is called multiple instruction, multiple data, or *MIMD*. It is now the most popular supercomputer architecture because of its flexibility, and because manufacturers can take advantage of economies of scale by building such machines by combining hundreds or thousands of standard, and relatively cheap, microprocessors. Unfortunately, their greater flexibility also makes MIMD computers more difficult to program than their SISD or SIMD counterparts. For practical purposes, most human beings cannot reason correctly about more than a few things happening simultaneously, but MIMD computers permit thousands or hundreds of thousands of different concurrent operations.

While Flynn's taxonomy has been very influential, it has several shortcomings. For example, it is difficult to imagine what a MISD (multiple instruction, single data) computer architecture would look like,[3] and architects have never been able to agree whether traditional vector processors are SISD, because the programmer sees a single program working on a single operation at a time, or SIMD, because each operation can be applied to many data values.

In addition, the boundaries between Flynn's SIMD and MIMD categories are in practice often blurred. Few programmers could or would write 10,000 different programs for a machine with 10,000 processors. Instead, many programmers implement an application by writing one program, and then replicating it as many times as their machine has processors. This model is often called the single program, multiple data, or *SPMD*, paradigm: each instance of the program works on its own data, and may follow different conditional branches or execute loops a different number of times, but basically performs the same

---

3. Some people apply this term to machines in which several processors mirror each other's actions in order to achieve fault tolerance, but since these processors usually execute the same instructions, the "MI" half of the classification is not really satisfied.

operations. In some systems, these program instances are further restricted in that they must all be either computing or communicating; it is not possible for some to be working on local data, while others are exchanging data. This crystalline model will be discussed in more detail in Section 5.2.

A further generalization of the SPMD category is the *FPMD* (a few programs, multiple data) model, in which replicated instances of a small number of different programs work together to process data, access the file system, display pictures, and so on. Most of the programs in Chapters 4 to 6 are either SPMD or FPMD.

2.2.2 Classifying Programming Paradigms

The greatest shortcoming of Flynn's taxonomy is that it describes architectures in terms of what hardware they contain, rather than what that hardware looks like to programmers. In practice, one of the most important characteristics of a parallel computer is how memory is organized. A computer with a *shared memory* architecture has a single address space, from which all processors read data, and to which they all write. In a *disjoint memory* architecture, on the other hand, there are many disjoint address spaces, usually (but not always) organized so that each processor has exactly one *private memory*. Processors only have direct access to their own memories, and must interact with others by sending messages or making requests in some way to access values in other address spaces.

Disjoint memory is often called *distributed memory*, because it usually results from distributing the total memory of the machine amongst the available processors. In this text, however, the term "distributed memory" refers only to the physical organization of memory; in practice, distributed memory may appear to be shared, as it is in MIN-based multiprocessors. In contrast, a memory which is physically organized as a single unit will be called a *centralized memory*. Memory organized in this way is almost invariably treated as shared memory, so the distinction is not as important.

Of course, the boundary between shared and disjoint memory is often blurred. The memory of a conventional mainframe, for example, appears to be shared, even when it is distributed among caches, several interleaved banks of main memory, and secondary (virtual) memory. On the other hand, many shared-memory systems are programmed as if they had disjoint memory—processes running on a multi-tasking operating system, for example, each appear to have their own address space. For our purposes, we will distinguish shared and disjoint memory by asking whether every process can access every memory location directly. If the answer is yes, the system has shared memory; otherwise, the memory is disjoint.

Most programmers find shared memory easier to work with than disjoint memory for two reasons. First, it is much easier to emulate disjoint memory on shared memory than vice versa. A programmer writing for a shared-memory machine can simply partition the available addresses and only allow each process direct access to one partition. A programmer working on a disjoint-memory machine, on the other hand, must have some way of trapping addresses which lie outside directly-accessible memory, determining what part of memory those addresses actually refer to, and sending a read or write request to some process responsible for that part of memory. During most of the 1980s, programmers had to write such software on a case-by-case basis; more recent designs provide intrinsic support for this, either in hardware, through the operating system, or in the programming system.

A second reason many programmers prefer shared memory is that many of the techniques developed since the 1960s for implementing multi-user operating systems and other concurrent systems can be re-used directly on shared-memory computers. These techniques, some of which are discussed in Chapter 4, are well-known to computer scientists and application programmers, and have been tested and refined over several working generations. Thus, one particularly attractive feature of support for shared memory is that it is easier for programmers to port applications originally written for conventional mainframes or supercomputers onto shared-memory machines than onto machines with disjoint memory.

As discussed in Section 2.1, the reason that most large machines have disjoint memory is that as a machine's size grows, the relative cost of providing or emulating shared memory also grows. A compromise which many architectures exploit is to provide a shared memory, but to implement it *hierarchically*. Thus, the key distinction between different shared-memory machines is whether access times for different parts of memory can differ. Architectures in which any part of memory can be accessed in the same time are called *UMA*, for *uniform memory access*; ones in which access times vary are called *NUMA*, for *non-uniform memory access*. In practice, the use of caches and virtual memory means that all modern computers, serial and parallel, have NUMA architectures. However, in most serial and shared-memory machines, programmers do not have to deal with this fact until the time comes to tune their programs, while programmers writing for disjoint-memory machines must include explicit code to handle the non-uniformity from the start.

In Chapters 4 to 6, we will primarily be concerned with parallel programming systems, rather than parallel computer architectures. The two key characteristics of such systems are how they manage communication between concurrent activities, and how they *synchronize*, or coordinate, these activities.

Figure 2.15 presents a taxonomy of programming systems which has three main categories: systems in which parallelism is implicit, *data-parallel* systems in which parallelism is represented by operations on aggregate structures, and *control-parallel* systems in

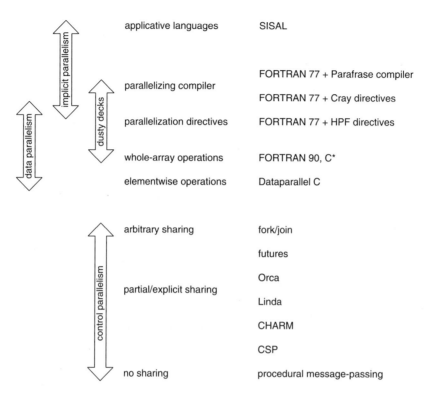

Figure 2.15
An Alternative Taxonomic Scheme

which users are given multiple threads of control (multiple instruction streams, in Flynn's terminology). Within each main category, several approaches can be taken:

• Implicitly-parallel systems can be based on entirely new languages, which have been designed with parallelism in mind, or on attempts to recycle existing sequential programs written in FORTRAN or some other language. The weakness of the latter approach is that parallelizing programs written in a sequential language has proved extremely difficult (Section 3.4); the weakness of the former approach is that few users are willing to discard their existing programs and skills.

• Systems which allow users to work on arrays or lists as if they were single items also take two forms. In the first, each item in the structure is thought of as a small actor, or agent, with a small amount of private data. Whenever an operation is ordered, each agent applies that operation to its own data. The second approach puts more emphasis on the structure as a whole; instead of asking each element of an array to add 5 to itself, for example, a program would add 5 to the array, and trust the compiler and run-time system to figure out exactly what this means. The difference between these two approaches may seem small, but in practice some programs are much easier to write using one or the other method.

• Finally, there are systems in which users are responsible for coordinating many different operations at once. These systems may be further differentiated according to the degree of data sharing seen by the user. Sharing can range along a continuum from completely arbitrary sharing, in which any structure of any size may or may not be shared between any number of processes, to no sharing at all, with limited sharing of some data values in between. Chapters 4 to 6 discuss these three sub-categories in turn.

2.3   Some Example Applications

As in the rest of science and engineering, researchers in parallel computing frequently think and talk in terms of a small number of well-understood problems. This section presents a few of these, and discusses ways in which they can be parallelized.

2.3.1   Odd/Even Transposition Sort

Sorting is one of the most fundamental problems in computing [Knuth 1981b]. While many parallel sorting algorithms have been developed [Akl 1985], one of the simplest is odd/even transposition sort, which is very similar to the standard bubble sort algorithm. Assume that $\mathcal{P}$ processors are connected in a line, such that each processor (except those at the ends) can communicate with only its left- and right-hand neighbors (Figure 2.16). Assume further that when execution begins each processor contains a single integer.

The algorithm is executed in discrete steps. In odd-numbered steps, every odd-numbered processor sends its value to the even-numbered processor to its right, then accepts a value back from it. Each even-numbered processor accepts a value from its odd-numbered neighbor and compares it to the value it currently holds. The even-numbered processor then keeps the larger of the two values, and returns the lesser to its odd neighbor. In the next (even-numbered) step, the same actions are repeated, with the even-numbered processors sending, then receiving, and the odd-numbered processors receiving, comparing, and replying.

It is easy to see how this algorithm shifts large values toward the right end of the processor array, and small values in the other direction. Since the largest value in the array moves at least one hop per iteration, it can move from the left-most processor to the right-most in at most $\mathcal{P} - 1$ steps. Thus, the worst-case running time for this algorithm is $\mathcal{O}(\mathcal{P})$,

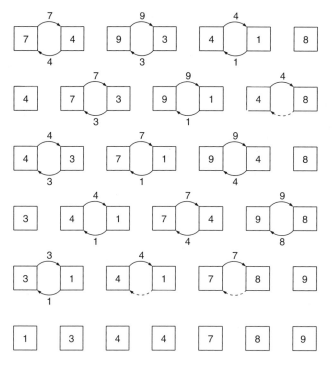

Figure 2.16
Parallel Sorting

i.e., the algorithm is linear in the number of values being sorted. This makes transposition sort seem an improvement on the best serial comparison-based sorting algorithms, which take $\mathcal{P} \log \mathcal{P}$ time to sort $\mathcal{P}$ values. However, if we consider the *time-processor product*, which is the product of the time taken and the number of processors required, we see that the cost of sorting serially is still $\mathcal{P} \log \mathcal{P}$, but $\mathcal{P}^2$ ($\mathcal{P}$ cycles on $\mathcal{P}$ processors) for odd/even transposition sorting.

Several of the assumptions made above are worth noting. First, not only is it assumed that there are as many processors as data values, but also that processors have some way to know where they are, i.e., that some labelling scheme has assigned each processor a unique integer in the range $1 \ldots \mathcal{P}$ so that each can tell if it is in an odd or even location. Second, the analysis of running time assumes that the processors are perfectly synchronized with one another. In many real parallel computers, this is not the case: processors may be unsynchronized, or may even run at different speeds, and algorithms may have to take this into account. Finally, while it may take fewer than $\mathcal{P} - 1$ steps to sort $\mathcal{P}$ values, we can be sure that if the algorithm is run for $\mathcal{P} - 1$ steps then the values will definitely be sorted. There is therefore a time after which the algorithm is certain to have completed. Once again, this is not the case for many other types of problems, in which the number of operations to be done depends on the values being manipulated.

Odd/even sorting may seem an unrealistic algorithm, since programs needing to sort a million values are much more common than machines containing a million processors. However, we can use this algorithm to sort any number N of values on a machine with $\mathcal{P} < N$ processors by introducing *virtual processors (VPs)*. To do this, we write the algorithm as if N processors were available, and then replace each group of $N/\mathcal{P}$ adjacent "processors" with a serial loop which executes on a single processor. Each loop iteration simulates the behavior of a single VP. When this VP needs to communicate with another VP which is being emulated by the same processor, it simply reads or writes memory; real messages are only sent when VPs communicate between processors. Thus, the code:

```
do parallel id = 1, N          ! for each processor
  do i = 1, N − 1              ! for each step
  .                            ! do single step
  .
  end do
end parallel
```

is replaced by:

```
do parallel id = 1, P          ! for each processor
  do i = 1, N − 1              ! for each step
    do p = 1, N/P              ! for each virtual processor
    .                          ! simulate single processor
    .
    end do
  end do
end parallel
```

In the general case, it may be simpler for a processor to emulate several VPs by time-slicing them, in the same way that an operating system time-slices processes by *context switching*, i.e., saving the state of one process and replacing it with another.. However, when the actions of the VPs are simple and predictable, a straightforward loop such as this is more efficient.

2.3.2 Cellular Automata

Cellular automata (CA) are simple systems which can be used to simulate physical processes whose behavior at any point depends only on the state of neighboring points. In a fluid flow simulation, for example, the temperature, pressure, and velocity at a point depend on the temperature, pressure, and velocity of neighboring points, but not on that of points located dozens or hundreds of sites away.

A cellular automaton is represented as a lattice of discrete values. Each lattice site may be in only one of a small number of states at any time. The states of all cells change simultaneously at fixed time steps. In each time step, each cell compares its present state with those of its neighbors, and then updates its state based on a deterministic rule. The most famous cellular automaton is Conway's Game of Life [Gardner 1983], which consists of a rectangular grid of cells with horizontal, vertical, and diagonal connections. Each cell can be in one of two states, alive or dead, and the update rule is simply:

	Number of Live Neighbors			
Present State	0 or 1	2	3	4 or more
alive	dead	alive	alive	dead
dead	dead	dead	alive	dead

The sequence of images in Figure 2.17 shows how a pattern of live and dead cells can change over time. The expanding cloud of cells in the upper-left corner eventually collides with the stable regions elsewhere in the world, erasing them and starting a new cycle of growth. More complicated patterns can be generated, including ones which can periodically generate gliders, reflect gliders at various angles, or change from one state to another and back as gliders collide with them. In fact, it has been shown that the patterns which Life creates are Turing-complete, i.e. can simulate any imaginable type of computer.

Cellular automata are obvious candidates for parallel implementation, since every cell's next state can be calculated at the same time as every other's. One CA which is somewhat more useful than Life was developed by Boghosian and Taylor to model particle diffusion [Boghosian & Levermore 1988]. In this CA, a set of particles (represented by particular cell states) diffuse from left to right across a 4-connected mesh, while another set of particles move up and down, colliding with one another and with the diffusing particles according to the rules shown in Figure 2.18a. These conserve the number of particles travelling in each dimension, so that diffusing particles never turn into obstacles, or *vice versa*. In order to model a region with low diffusivity, the program places many blocking particles in the region; a region of high diffusivity is modelled by providing fewer blocking particles (Figure 2.18b).

The easiest way to perform the updates required by this CA is to construct a 4-bit code simultaneously for each cell, in which 1's represent connections on which there

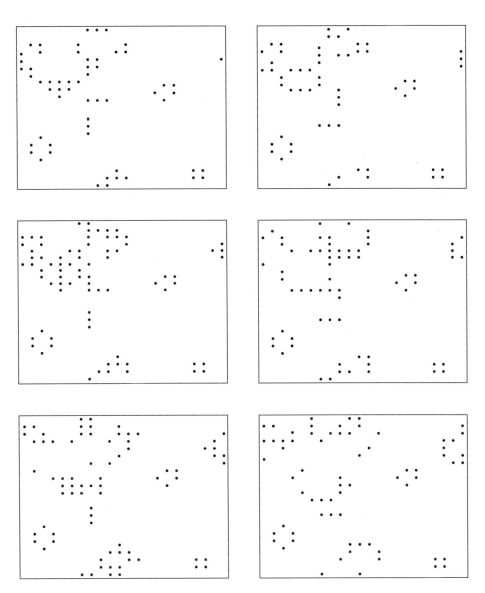

Figure 2.17
A Sequence from a Game of Life

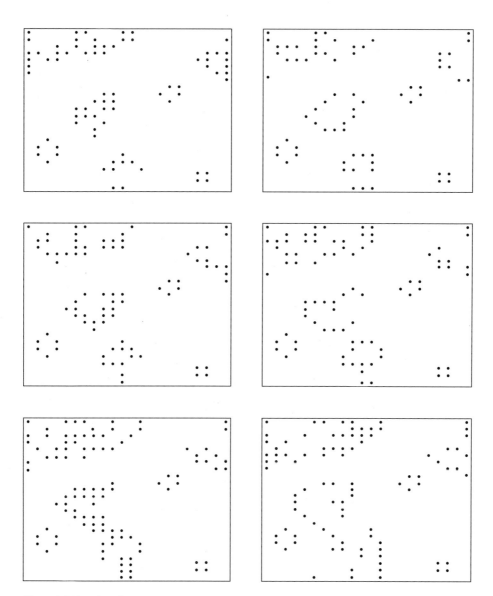

Figure 2.17 *(continued)*
A Sequence from a Game of Life

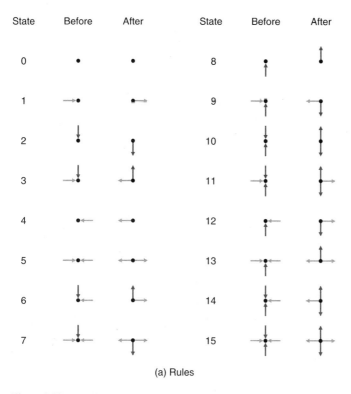

(a) Rules

Figure 2.18
Rules for a CA Simulation of Diffusion

are incoming particles, and 0's connections which are empty. The rules in Figure 2.18a are numbered to show the codes this method generates if links are numbered clockwise. The codes generated in this fashion are then used to index a 16-entry table to determine the next state of each cell. Note that this implicitly assumes that collisions only happen at intersections, and not along links. This simplifying assumption is made in most CA models.

The most important characteristic of cellular automata for parallel implementation is that while the lattice is a single structure, it can be divided into sub-structures which interact only occasionally. As Figure 2.19 shows, a rectangular lattice can split into one strip per processor, so that each processor only needs to access the values on the boundaries of its neighbors' patches. In a shared memory system, this splitting would be done by assigning a range of indices to each process, and having processes synchronize after updating their values. Such synchronization is necessary to ensure that a process does not

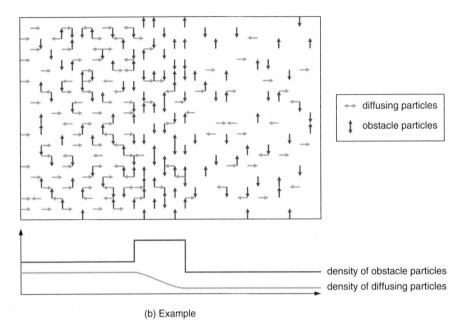

(b) Example

Figure 2.18 *(continued)*
Rules for a CA Simulation of Diffusion

start updating its cells for timestep $t + 1$ before its neighbor has read the values it needs for timestep t.

On a disjoint-memory system, the lattice would be divided in the same way, but the locations along the edges would be duplicated. Such duplicates are sometimes called *fluff*. Processes do not update their fluff; instead, after each process has updated the cells for which it is responsible, it sends a fresh copy of its border to its neighbor to overwrite its fluff. In this way, each process always has an accurate picture of its neighbors' values when it needs them. As with the version of odd/even sort in which there were more values than processors, each processor can update its internal sites without communicating with its neighbors, then swap some information. This strategy is so commonly used in parallel computing that many programming systems contain special support for it.

Another feature of cellular automata, which is not shared by most other mesh-based calculations, is that the workload at each point, and hence within each section, is the same. In a fluid-flow simulation, the work which has to be done to update a point in a turbulent region can be orders of magnitude greater than the work needed in a region of streaming flow. It is sometimes possible to guess in advance how much computation will be required at each point simply by examining the boundary conditions of the flow (there is likely

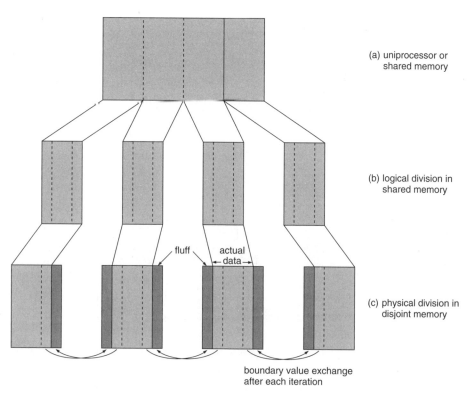

(a) uniprocessor or
shared memory

(b) logical division in
shared memory

fluff   actual
←data→

(c) physical division in
disjoint memory

boundary value exchange
after each iteration

Figure 2.19
Splitting Up a Cellular Automaton Mesh

to be more turbulence at a right-angle corner than along a smooth length of pipe), but
if the regions of heavier work change over time, there is a stark choice between finding
some way to re-balance the workload after every few iterations, or putting up with low
performance due to poor load balance. This problem will be re-considered several times in
this text.

2.3.3   Monte Carlo Particle Detector Simulation

A very different type of application is to determine how many of the short-lived particles
generated in a particle accelerator will be detected by sensors placed at particular locations. Particles may interact with the magnetic fields used to accelerate and contain them,
and with the materials making up the detectors, in many different ways. The designer's
job is to make sure that even after these interactions, most of what happens gets recorded
somewhere.

The technique most often used to determine the effectiveness of a given placement of detectors is to simulate many different experiments in order to determine the statistical behavior of a proposed design. This technique is called *Monte Carlo* because it relies on the statistical properties of repeated experiments, just as casino owners rely on the statistical profitability of roulette wheels.

Monte Carlo techniques are *embarrassingly parallel* (a term due to Geoffrey Fox), since separate experiments can be run on separate processors, and the overall results collected once all the experiments have been run. Once each processor has been told what trials to perform, it does not need to communicate with other processors until it has finished its tasks. Since time spent communicating is an organizational overhead, techniques which minimize it generally lead to better performance.

However, if the time required to simulate different experiments varies widely, the strategy of dividing tasks amongst the processors at the start of the program can lead to very poor performance. For example, suppose that four thousand experiments are to be run using four processors, and that, because of the choice of parameters, the last thousand will each take ten times as long to run as the first three thousand. If jobs are allocated in batches of a thousand at a time, three processors will spend at least 90% of their time idle, waiting for the fourth processor to finish its jobs. While this particular example could be improved by giving processor 1 the jobs numbered 1, 5, 9, . . . , 3997, processor 2 the jobs 2 to 3998, and so on, to ensure that each had a even mix of run-times, the general problem of balancing unpredictable workloads is much less tractable.

In practice, the best solution is not to allocate jobs to processors all at once, but to give each of $\mathcal{P}$ processors a few jobs, and then wait for it to come back and ask for more, as in:

```
initialize pool of jobs
do parallel id = 1, P
  get next job from pool
  do job
  save results
end parallel
```

This way, processors are kept busy so long as there is any more work to do. In the unevenly-balanced jobs above, each processor would probably do one quarter of the first three thousand jobs, and one quarter of the remaining thousand. If job lengths are variable, this scheme ensures good work distribution automatically (Figure 2.20). While each processor spends more time communicating in this scheme than if jobs are handed out all at once, the payback can be a large reduction in the overall running time if the time per job is highly variable.

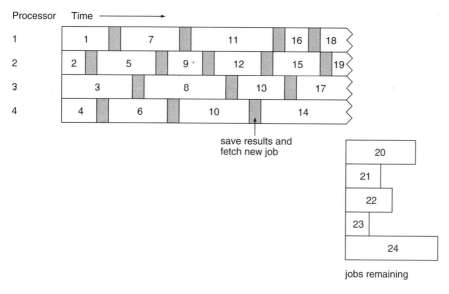

Figure 2.20
Load Balancing a Monte Carlo Simulation

A few general characteristics of Monte Carlo simulations are worth noting. First, since each processor can work at its own speed, Monte Carlo techniques can make use of machines containing different types of processors. In fact, workstation networks are increasingly being used to run simulations of this kind [Nakanishi et al. 1992, Schaeffer et al. 1993]. Second, in a disjoint-memory machine, each processor requires not only a complete copy of the simulation program, but also enough memory to run it. This sometimes caused problems on some of the multicomputers built during the 1980s, as their processors only had a few hundred kilobytes or a few megabytes of physical memory each, and no virtual memory. One way to get around such limitations is discussed in Section 2.4.2.

A third characteristic of Monte Carlo simulation is that there are special processes somewhere in the system to allocate work and collate results. These processes are usually called the "source" and "sink", while the ones which actually do the calculations are called "workers". Since the source and sink typically need very little CPU time, they can usually share a processor with one or more of the workers. The workers on that processor may run slightly slower as a result, but this will simply cause the job allocation algorithm to give more jobs to other workers.

Finally, it should be remembered that a Monte Carlo simulation is only as good as the random number generator it uses. As shall be seen in Section 3.3.4, generating $\mathcal{P}$

sequences of random numbers is easy, but making sure that the sequences generated by different processors are uncorrelated is not.

2.3.4   Steady-State Temperature Calculation

Explicit methods for solving problems like particle diffusion actually simulate the behavior of each point in space. By contrast, *implicit methods* turn the initial problem into a set of linear equations, and then solve those. The main advantage of this approach is that they allow one general technique—the solution of simultaneous equations—to be applied to a wide variety of problems.

As an example of how implicit methods are used, consider the problem of determining the temperature at each point in a metal plate, given the temperature along its boundary (Figure 2.21). While a direct simulation would actually model the diffusion of heat from the boundary into the plate's interior, a matrix-based method turns the problem into a set of finite difference equations. The two rules used are that the values on the boundaries must equal the values specified by the user, while the interior values must vary smoothly, i.e., the value of each interior point must be close to that of its neighbors. We can achieve this by requiring that:

$$t_{i,j} = \frac{t_{i-1,j} + t_{i+1,j} + t_{i,j-1} + t_{i,j+1}}{4}$$

for interior points, i.e., that each point's value is the average of its neighbors' values. In order to satisfy the boundary conditions, we must add the further constraint:

$$t_{i,j} = b_{i,j}$$

for boundary points, where $b_{i,j}$ is some problem-specific value. In the case of a 3×4 mesh, this leads to the set of linear equations:

$$
\begin{bmatrix}
1 & \cdot & \cdot & \cdot & \cdot & \cdot & \cdot & \cdot & \cdot & \cdot & \cdot & \cdot \\
\cdot & 1 & \cdot & \cdot & \cdot & \cdot & \cdot & \cdot & \cdot & \cdot & \cdot & \cdot \\
\cdot & \cdot & 1 & \cdot & \cdot & \cdot & \cdot & \cdot & \cdot & \cdot & \cdot & \cdot \\
\cdot & \cdot & \cdot & 1 & \cdot & \cdot & \cdot & \cdot & \cdot & \cdot & \cdot & \cdot \\
\cdot & \cdot & \cdot & \cdot & 1 & \cdot & \cdot & \cdot & \cdot & \cdot & \cdot & \cdot \\
\cdot & -\frac{1}{4} & \cdot & \cdot & -\frac{1}{4} & 1 & -\frac{1}{4} & \cdot & \cdot & -\frac{1}{4} & \cdot & \cdot \\
\cdot & \cdot & -\frac{1}{4} & \cdot & \cdot & -\frac{1}{4} & 1 & -\frac{1}{4} & \cdot & \cdot & -\frac{1}{4} & \cdot \\
\cdot & \cdot & \cdot & \cdot & \cdot & \cdot & \cdot & 1 & \cdot & \cdot & \cdot & \cdot \\
\cdot & \cdot & \cdot & \cdot & \cdot & \cdot & \cdot & \cdot & 1 & \cdot & \cdot & \cdot \\
\cdot & \cdot & \cdot & \cdot & \cdot & \cdot & \cdot & \cdot & \cdot & 1 & \cdot & \cdot \\
\cdot & \cdot & \cdot & \cdot & \cdot & \cdot & \cdot & \cdot & \cdot & \cdot & 1 & \cdot \\
\cdot & \cdot & \cdot & \cdot & \cdot & \cdot & \cdot & \cdot & \cdot & \cdot & \cdot & 1
\end{bmatrix}
\begin{bmatrix}
t_{11} \\ t_{12} \\ t_{13} \\ t_{14} \\ t_{21} \\ t_{22} \\ t_{23} \\ t_{24} \\ t_{31} \\ t_{32} \\ t_{33} \\ t_{34}
\end{bmatrix}
=
\begin{bmatrix}
b_{11} \\ b_{12} \\ b_{13} \\ b_{14} \\ b_{21} \\ 0 \\ 0 \\ b_{24} \\ b_{31} \\ b_{32} \\ b_{33} \\ b_{34}
\end{bmatrix}
$$

where $\cdot$ is used in place of 0 in the matrix for readability's sake.

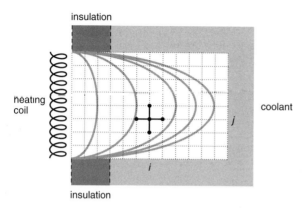

insulation

heating coil

coolant

j

i

insulation

Figure 2.21
Parallelizing a Boundary Value Problem

Two things about this matrix are immediately obvious. The first is that most of it is zero, and need not be stored; the second is that the non-zero elements occur in a very regular pattern. Such sparse diagonal matrices crop up so frequently in the description of physical systems that special techniques have been developed for storing and solving them. If the mesh is irregular, however, then the matrix will also be irregular; storing and manipulating it will then be much more difficult.

Parallelism can be used in at least two ways to solve general matrix problems, in which the matrix does not have a convenient banded structure. The first is to calculate the terms of the coefficient matrix and the boundary condition vector in parallel. While this is overkill in this situation (calculating $-\frac{1}{4}$ doesn't require very much effort), in real problems the points representing the lattice may be unevenly spaced, the material may be inhomogeneous, and the boundary conditions may be extremely complicated.

The actual solution of the matrix equation can also be parallelized, and this problem has probably been studied more than any other in parallel computing. The two main classes of solution technique are *direct methods*, which solve the matrix equation using the rules of linear algebra, and *indirect methods*, which solve the equation by successive approximation. One popular technique is a direct method called Gaussian elimination. The outer loop of the forward pass of this algorithm, shown in Program 2.1a, is executed once for each row in the matrix. In each loop, a different multiple of that row is subtracted from every row below it (Figure 2.22). Once these operations have been done, the solution to the original problem can be found by substituting values from the lower-right corner upward (Program 2.1b).

```
procedure gauss_fwd(A, B)
  real    :: A(:, :)                    ! matrix
  real    :: B(:)                       ! target vector
  integer :: i, j, k                    ! loop indices

  ! for each row . . .
  do k = 1, N
    ! calculate pivots in column k
    do i = k+1, N, 1
      A(i, k) = A(i, k)/A(k, k)
    end do
    ! update elements below row k
    do i = k+1, N, 1
      do j = k+1, N
        A(i, j) = A(i, j) - (A(i, k) * A(k, j))
      end do
    end do
    ! update element of solution vector
    do i = k+1, N, 1
      B(i) = B(i) - (A(i, k) * B(k))
    end do
  end do
end procedure
```

(a) forward pass

```
procedure gauss_bwd(A, B, X)
  real    :: A(:, :)                    ! matrix
  real    :: B(:)                       ! target vector
  real    :: X(:)                       ! solution vector
  integer :: i, j                       ! loop indices
  do i = N, 1, -1
    X(i) = B(i)/A(i, i)
    do j = i-1, 1, -1
      B(j) = B(j) - (A(j, i) * X(i))
    end do
  end do
end procedure
```

(b) backward pass

Program 2.1
Sequential Gaussian Elimination

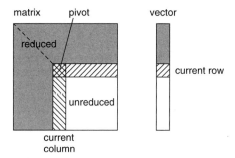

Figure 2.22
Gaussian Elimination

The other major class of matrix solution algorithms is represented by successive over-relaxation (SOR), which finds a solution vector by repeated approximation. In each iteration, the difference between the current best guess at the solution and the actual solution is estimated. The guess is then adjusted, and the algorithm applied again. The term "over-relaxation" is used because the algorithm usually converges most quickly when each successive guess tries to over-step the desired solution.

From a parallel programming point of view, SOR and Gaussian elimination are very different. The former is usually implemented in the same way as a CA, with each process being assigned a contiguous block of the matrix. In Gaussian elimination, on the other hand, operations are performed on whole rows at a time, while the pivot row must be broadcast globally during each iteration.

2.3.5   Simulated Annealing

The applications looked at so far either have not required global information (e.g., cellular automata), or have only required a little, and at known points. For an example of a problem in which globally-shared data is needed, but easily predictable, consider the optimization problem known as the Travelling Salesperson Problem (TSP). Given the coordinates of a set of N points in the plane, the aim is to find the lowest-cost closed path through those points which visits each point exactly once. Since there are $(N-1)!/2$ distinct possible tours, finding the one which is truly the shortest is impractical. As a result, most salespersons content themselves with reasonably short tours which can be found quickly. This is characteristic of most optimization problems—most users would prefer having a good solution today to having the best possible solution some time in the twenty-second century.

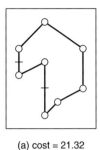
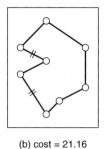

(a) cost = 21.32   (b) cost = 21.16

Figure 2.23
Travelling Salesperson Problem

One technique for solving optimization problems which has been widely studied is called simulated annealing. If a molten material is suddenly cooled, or annealed, the crystals which form are very small. If it is annealed slowly, on the other hand, its atoms have more opportunity to align themselves, and so larger, lower-energy crystals can arise.

Simulated annealing applies this same idea to optimization problems by making a random change to a configuration, and retaining the change based on a pseudo-random rule. The first step is to define an objective function, which measures the cost or value of a particular configuration of the system. In the TSP, a configuration is a tour (such as $AJDKWO...ZA$), and the objective function is the length of that tour. Given any tour, a program creates a new tour by transposing two of the connections, i.e., by changing the connections A_0A_1 and B_0B_1 to A_0B_1 and A_1B_0 (Figure 2.23). A new cost for this tour is then calculated. If the new cost is lower than the old, the program accepts the new tour unconditionally. If it is higher, the program accepts it with a probability:

$$p(\text{accept}) = e^{-\delta\ell/T}$$

where $\delta\ell$ is the change in length, and $T \geq 0$ is the present "temperature" of the system. T is initially given a high value, so that the system can accept high-cost changes. This rule gives the system a chance to make large moves through the search space. T is then gradually reduced to 0 to force the system to "make up its mind" and converge on a particular tour.

One way to use multiple processes in simulating annealing would be to have each process search independently, starting from a different (random) initial configuration. A more productive way is to have each process search for some number of steps, then gather their results together and start the processes off again using the best tour found so far as the initial point. Thus, each process repeatedly gets a tour and its associated cost, performs some number of changes, and then sends its current state to the controller. These messages

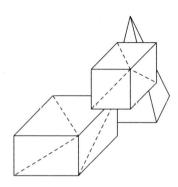

((3.0, 2.5, −1.3), (3.0, 2.9, −1.3), (3.4, 2.5, −1.3))
((3.4, 2.5, −1.3), (3.0, 2.9, −1.3), (3.4, 2.9, −1.3))
((3.4, 2.5, −1.3), (3.4, 2.5, −1.5), (3.4, 2.9, −1.3))
((3.4, 2.5, −1.5), (3.4, 2.9, −1.5), (3.4, 2.9, −1.3))
⋮

Figure 2.24
Rendering Polygons

are combined along the way, so that the controller eventually receives the best of the tours found by all processes. It then broadcasts that tour to the processes, and the cycle begins again. Between communication operations, each process runs at its own speed; it is only when intermediate results are gathered together and new starting points redistributed that processes must synchronize. A third approach is to share information about the shortest tour found so far. Only when a process finds a new tour which is significantly shorter than the shortest previously known does it broadcast a message to its peers. This approach is usually quickest at generating good answers, but is also the most complicated to implement, since it depends on some method of interrupting a process which might not be expecting a message.

2.3.6 Polygon Rendering

Our next example is drawn from computer graphics. Suppose that an application has generated a set of polygons, each of which is represented as a list of vertices in three-dimensional space (Figure 2.24). In order to display these, the program must transform them to take into account the viewer's location and direction of view, then remove those polygons, or parts of polygons, which appear to be behind others. This last step is called hidden surface removal, and may have to be done on thousands of polygons twenty or more time per second in order to generate a realistic image.

Transforming the polygons to take a particular view into account is relatively straight-forward, as it can be done by multiplying the vector representing each polygon vertex by a matrix. (In fact, for reasons which are discussed in most introductory texts on graphics [Foley et al. 1990], the vertices are usually represented using four coordinates, and the matrix multiplying them is therefore 4×4.) Removing the hidden surfaces is more complicated, as any polygon may potentially obscure any other. The standard serial algorithm, called z-buffering, does this by creating two arrays, each as large as the screen on which the image is to be drawn. The first of these records the depth of the shallowest polygon lying behind that pixel, while the second records the color of that polygon. Initially, the color of each pixel is black (or some other background color), and the depth array's values are all infinity. To render a polygon, the z-buffer algorithm determines its depth at each of the pixels which it overlaps, and compares that value to the depth value already recorded at that pixel's location. If the new polygon is shallower, its depth values overwrites the depth previously recorded, and its color replaces that pixel's color. This algorithm is also called the painter's algorithm, since each polygon is "painted over" the ones rendered previously.

This algorithm is more difficult to parallelize than our previous examples. For a start, several different operations are being done, and can potentially be overlapped (i.e., trans-formation of one polygon can begin while another is being painted over the existing buffer). Second, whatever code is produced will be expected to run as a library under the direction of some larger program. This requirement may constrain when the renderer's parts are allowed to communicate with one another. Third, if the renderer is to be run on a disjoint-memory machine, then all of the components performing z-buffering must have access to all of the z-buffer, since there is no easy way to tell in advance where a polygon will appear in a given scene.

One way to parallelize this renderer on a multicomputer is to create two cooperating sets of processes, as shown in Figure 2.25. Members of the first set accept polygons from the driving application and transform them into display coordinates, while each member of the second set is responsible for a single strip of the z-buffer. Once a transformer has calculated the display coordinates of a polygon, it sends a copy of that polygon to each z-buffer process which the polygon overlaps. Depending on the hardware available, the partial z-buffers which result may either be displayed directly (if a single video display bus is threaded through the processors running the z-buffer processes), or may be sent to a common collector, which in turn handles the display.

2.3.7   Symbolic Integration

As symbolic mathematics packages like Mathematica [Wolfram 1991] become more widespread, interest in symbolic mathematics is growing. One of the classic problems

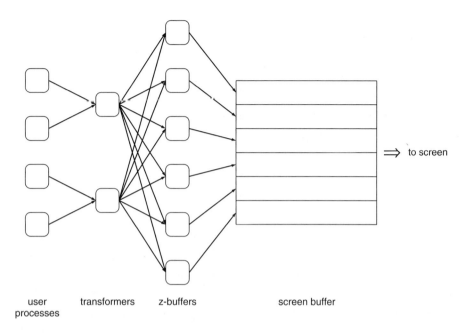

user   transformers   z-buffers   screen buffer
processes

Figure 2.25
Polygon Splitting

in the field is that of symbolic integration. Given an expression, such as:

$$\int\int 4\tanh x \cos\frac{y}{x}\,dy\,dx$$

there may be a dozen or more techniques which might yield its integral, each of which may involve finding integrals for several sub-expressions.

If many independent integrals are to be calculated, the best technique is probably the same as that used in the Monte Carlo simulation of Section 2.3.3, i.e., to have each processor take one job, work on it until it has finished, then take another. This solution is throughput-oriented, as it aims to calculate the greatest number of integrals per unit time. If, on the other hand, the system is to be used interactively, then minimizing response time will probably be the aim. In this case, it may make sense to treat the application of each technique as a separate job, and have as many processors as possible look for the solution in as many different ways as are known. As soon as one processor finds a solution, it returns it, and interrupts the other processors so that the next job can be started (Figure 2.26). This technique is called speculative decomposition, since all available techniques are being tried speculatively.

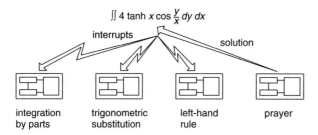

Figure 2.26
Speculative Parallelism

Speculative parallelism may seem wasteful at first, since the work of all but one processor thrown away. However, on average it reduces the time taken to find integrals to the shortest of the times required by each of the available methods. The payoff from speculative parallelism is even greater if some of the methods might never terminate. The main problem in implementing it lies in interrupting processes which are searching unproductive paths once an answer has been found; several ways of doing this will be examined in subsequent chapters.

2.3.8   Chess

Our final example is one for which a simple, but very inefficient, parallelization exists. People have been playing chess on computers almost as long as electronic computers have existed [Levy 1988]. Typically, the board is represented by an array of integers, in which 1 to 6 represent the white pieces, -1 to -6 the black, and 0 an empty square. The rules governing which pieces can move where are then encoded as a mixture of lookup tables and algorithmic code.

This is enough to allow a program to determine whether a move is legal, but not enough for it to play the game. In order to understand how computers do this, it helps to start with a simple game like tic-tac-toe. When a computer plays tic-tac-toe it can construct a tree below a given position, called a game tree, then look along all the branches from the root to see which ones lead to a won game, which to a draw, and which to a loss (Figure 2.27). It can then propagate what it has learned back up the tree in order to choose a move at the root.

The computer has to be careful how it does this in order to get the right answer at the root. In a two-player game like chess or tic-tac-toe, the only possible outcomes are a complete win for one or the other player, or a draw. If we say that a win is worth 1, a

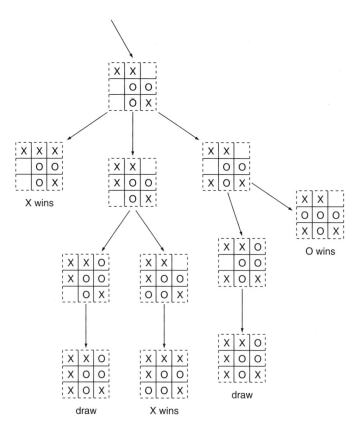

Figure 2.27
Searching a Game Tree

draw worth 0, and a loss worth -1, then the sum of the game's values to the two players is always 0. The interesting thing about such zero-sum games is that they are symmetrical: if one players gets 1 point from the game, the other must get -1, and vice versa. Thus, each player tries to maximize her own score, while her opponent tries to minimize it.

Knowing this, it is easy to propagate information up a game tree. We start by assigning scores to the leaf nodes of the game tree to show which end positions are won, drawn, or lost by the player whose turn it is to move. We then propagate values upward on the assumption that each player will always choose her best possible move. At each node, the values of the nodes below are negated, to take into account the fact that they represent the scores from the point of view of the opposing player. This procedure, called minimax, is guaranteed to select the move which restricts an opponent to the lowest possible score.

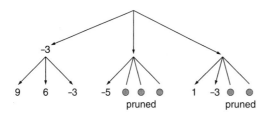

Figure 2.28
αβ Game Tree Search

In practice, it is impossible to construct and search game trees for interesting games. In chess, for example, there are typically 40 branches below each node in the game tree, so the width of the tree grows exponentially with its depth. Instead of searching all the way to the bottom of the tree, all programs search to some depth, such as 5 or 10 half-moves, and then use an *ad hoc* evaluation function to assess how good the position is at that point. These values are then propagated up the partial tree as before.

In the late 1950s, Alan Newell and Herbert Simon developed an algorithm which always returns the same answer as minimax, but on average does much less work. This algorithm, called αβ search, has been the basis of almost every chess program that has been written since. The basic idea behind it is that if a player discovers that a move M gives her opponent a better reply than some other available move, she will not choose M, no matter how good its other descendents might be (Figure 2.28). Once a program has searched one or more branches below a node, it may cut other branches without searching them completely. Using αβ instead of minimax can effectively reduce the branching factor of a chess game tree from 40 to 6. As a result, αβ can search about two moves more than minimax with the same effort (since 6^2 is approximately 40).

Game tree searching would seem to be an obvious candidate for parallelization, since the sequence of moves down one branch can be explored without reference to the moves down another. However, if every branch below a node is searched simultaneously, then the results of one search cannot be used to cut branches in another. The result is that a naive parallelization of game tree search effectively reduces αβ to its worst case, in which it runs exactly like minimax. The performance gained by parallelization is soon eroded by the extra work that is being done.

A related problem stems from the fact that in any given position there are usually only one or two good moves, and twenty or thirty bad ones. While it may not take very long to determine that a bad move truly is bad, it can take a lot of searching to find that a good move is not quite as good as the best one found so far. The distribution of work amongst the

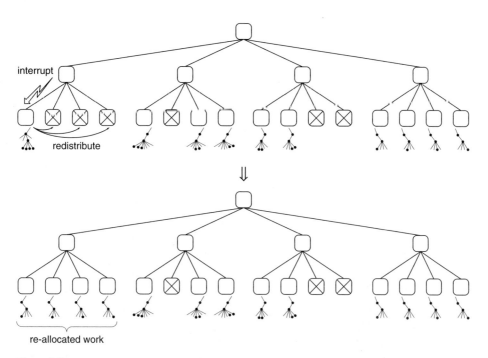

Figure 2.29
Work Reallocation in Waycool

jobs generated at each node is therefore very uneven, with one or two large jobs requiring more time than the other thirty or so put together. Even if jobs are farmed out on a demand-driven basis, as in Section 2.3.3, this can lead to most processors being idle most of the time.

The solution adopted by Ed Felten and Steve Otto, the authors of Waycool [Felten & Otto 1988], was to reallocate work to processors which had become idle. Suppose that four processors are searching the branches below a node, and that all but one has fallen idle (Figure 2.29). Waycool would halt the processor which was still running and distribute its work among the three idle processors. The search would then proceed until an answer was obtained, at which point the processor originally responsible for the search would resume from where it had left off. Waycool actually used this technique recursively, so that if only one of four teams of four processors was still working, their workload would be re-distributed among the other twelve processors in the super-team.

2.4   Decomposition Techniques

As the examples in the previous section have shown, there are a few general problem *decomposition* techniques which can be exploited to parallelize many applications. The four sections below discuss each of these in turn.

2.4.1   Geometric Decomposition

Programs which simulate the behavior of physical systems often contain data structures whose organization is similar to that of the system being simulated. The temperature and humidity at each point on a map, for example, are most naturally represented as dense arrays of real numbers, while the stress coupling between points in a metal object may be represented in a sparse array. The simplest way to parallelize operations on such structures is often to decompose the structures along physical lines, i.e., to divide up the data structures in the same way that the physical object being represented might be sub-divided. This process is called *tiling*; the parallelization method based on it is called *geometric decomposition.*

Geometric decomposition works best when the calculation to be done at each point in the data structure depends only on points within a relatively small radius around it. These points are called the *halo*; the larger the halo is, the more data must be moved around as calculations are done. For example, if a CA's update rules give each point a halo with a radius of 1, then only the outermost values of each processor's section of the mesh must be communicated to its neighbors (Figure 2.30). If the halo has a radius of 2, however, the amount of data to be communicated doubles.

Although geometric decomposition is usually used to simulate physical systems, it can be employed whenever the problem domain can be broken up into smaller domains, each of which interacts only with a few of its neighbors. For example, suppose that a network flow problem can be represented as a graph, and that the calculations performed for each graph node depend only on the values of neighboring nodes. If the graph is planar, then it can be divided into sub-graphs, each of which interacts only with neighboring patches. In order to calculate its own values, each processor only needs to communicate with a small subset of its peers. If the problem graph is non-planar, geometric decomposition might still be a good strategy, as long as the time required to find a decomposition which requires little communication is not greater than the time that would be required to solve the problem using a cruder decomposition.[4]

---

4. This can be an important consideration in some problems, since many optimal decomposition problems are computationally intractable.

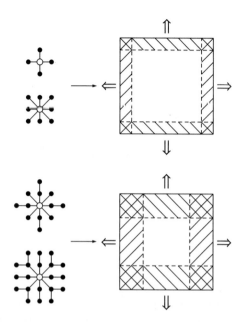

Figure 2.30
Halo Around Points in Regular Geometric Decomposition

2.4.2   Iterative Decomposition

A second common decomposition strategy is to take advantage of the fact that many serial programs contain loops, each iteration of which may do a different amount of work, or different work entirely. If the description of what a particular iteration is to do, and the values it needs, are stored in a central pool of tasks, then each processor can get its next job as soon as it finishes its previous one. Such *iterative decomposition* is often supported on multiprocessors, which maintain a central queue of runnable tasks, and hand them out to processors on a demand-driven basis. It is most effective whenever the number of iterations to be done is much larger than the number of available processors. If the work done in each loop is roughly the same, then pre-allocating loops to processors reduces administration costs; if the work done in each can vary widely, as in Monte Carlo simulation, then allocating loops (or jobs) on demand is probably most efficient.

Iterative decomposition is also commonly used on disjoint-memory machines, where it is usually called *task farming* because tasks are farmed out to processors on a demand-driven basis by a central source. The classic example of this is the parallelization of Monte Carlo simulations (Section 2.3.3), but many other problems lend themselves to this approach.

One drawback of task farming is its implicit assumption that the description of each task is small enough to fit in the memory of a single processor. If the world model of a simulation program is very complicated, and the parallel computer being used does not support virtual memory, the program may have to implement some form of explicit caching, in which each processor stores as much of the model as it can, and requests copies of other parts of the model from nearby processors when and as it needs them. One system which did this was KOAN [Badouel & Priol 1990, Badouel et al. 1990], which stored information about as many objects as possible in each processor's memory. Since the total memory of all processors was usually enough to hold several copies of the complete world description, most processors could get copies of objects they did not hold themselves from their immediate neighbors. The inclusion of this mechanism increased the complexity of the ray-tracing program while reducing its performance, but it or something like it was unavoidable in this case.

2.4.3   Recursive Decomposition

A third decomposition strategy, called *recursive decomposition*, starts by breaking the original problem into two or more sub-problems and solving these sub-problems concurrently. Each of these sub-problems may in turn be decomposed recursively. This technique is used in many sequential algorithms, such as quicksort and numerical quadrature; on a parallel system it may be implemented as a generalization of task farming, with each process acting as both a source of new jobs and a sink for results from previously-generated jobs.

One potential problem with recursive decomposition is that there is often an inverse relationship in a problem between the degree of parallelism and the amount of work. In the quicksort algorithm, for example, one process must initially partition the input vector V into two portion V_{lo} and V_{hi}. Two processes may then start to work in parallel, but each has only half as much to do as the first process. Their four children will each only have one-quarter as much to do, and so on. In numerical quadrature, on the other hand, the degree of sub-division required to get an accurate answer over some portion of the interval being integrated can be very data-dependent, so child processes may have just as much work to do as their parents.

2.4.4   Speculative Decomposition

In the symbolic integration example of Section 2.3.7, many different ways of finding a solution were run in parallel, with only the result of the first to finish being kept. This technique is called *speculative decomposition*, and its benefit comes from the expectation that trying N solution techniques simultaneously, and throwing away the effort of $N - 1$

of them as soon as one returns an answer, will result in a shorter overall solution time. As noted then, this is *not* less efficient than trying the available methods serially on a single processor.

Speculative decomposition can be viewed as a special case of iterative decomposition which is most applicable to search problems. It is best used when the time to complete a single task, rather than overall throughput on a set of tasks, is the primary concern. If many different problems are to be solved, and many solution techniques are available, then the most effective use of a parallel resource is usually to task-farm the tasks amongst the processors.

2.4.5 Functional Decomposition

The final parallelization strategy in common use is *functional decomposition*. Suppose that an application can be broken down into many distinct phases, each of which interacts with some or all of the others. In some conventional computing systems, the most natural way to implement such an application would be to write several co-routines. Each of these would execute as long as it could, then invoke another one, remaining suspended until it was in turn invoked again. If the calculations of such co-routines can be overlapped, it may be simplest to use one processor for each, in the same way that each member of a team of builders specializes in one task. One simple example of functional decomposition is the polygon-rendering example of Section 2.3.6. Here, the stages of the rendering pipeline are implemented as separate processes, and different numbers of each are run concurrently in order to balance throughput.

Functional decomposition is the simplest way to parallelize a problem if it can be implemented by turning its high-level description into a set of cooperating processes. However, balancing the throughput of the different algorithmic stages is a constant problem, particularly when dependencies between stages mean that one cannot begin its execution before its predecessors have generated at least partial results. In addition, the number of distinct functional steps in most programs is relatively small. Once these have been turned into concurrent units, the only way to increase parallelism further is to employ geometric, iterative, or speculative decomposition within one or more functional units.

2.5 Terms and Measures

This section describes some of the concepts which are commonly used in parallel computing, even though (or perhaps because) they are not precisely defined. A complete list of terms and definitions is given in Appendix D.

2.5.1 Locality

If processors have any local memory, then accessing values in it will be faster than accessing values stored in other parts of memory. We define the *locality* of a computation done on a multicomputer as the proportion of memory references which can be satisfied locally. A locality of 1 means that no processor needs to communicate with any other, and clearly cannot be achieved in any real computation (unless processors are running completely separate programs). A locality of 0, on the other hand, means that all memory references are being made to remote memory. Locality is harder to define for NUMA multiprocessors, such as the hierarchical architecture of Figure 2.12, but can be thought of either as a point in M-dimensional space, where M is the number of different levels in the hierarchy, or as a weighted sum of the proportion of references made to each level in the hierarchy.

While locality clearly depends on the architecture of the machine, as well as on the application itself, some algorithms are intrinsically local, while others are not. Most decomposition strategies are used because they increase or exploit locality. For example, geometric decomposition tends to deliver very high locality, since each processor only accesses the values in its own patch, and the values on the boundaries of its neighbors' patches. With iterative and speculative decomposition, once a processor has a task, it only communicates when it needs another task or has a result. Finally, functional decomposition is effective because it keeps all the data relevant to one portion of the overall algorithm (i.e., the variables which would be declared local to a particular subroutine in a serial program) in the memory most easily accessed by the processor executing that part of the algorithm.

2.5.2 Granularity

The *granularity* of a computation is the number of operations which are done between communication or synchronization events. Granularity may also be defined as the number of operations done between context switches, or between references to non-local memory in systems in which the memory hierarchy is visible to programmers. Programs with large grains are usually called *coarse-grained*, while those in which grains are only a few instructions long are *fine-grained*.

The granularity of a program decomposition is important because it influences how easily that program can be *load balanced*. The quickest way to complete a fixed amount of work given a fixed number of equally-fast processors is to give each processor an even share of the work (since if two processors have different amounts of work, one may finish before the other, and be idle for some time). If the amount of work done by each processor is roughly equal, that program is well-balanced; if the amount of work varies, the program is poorly balanced. One measure of this is $\mathcal{L}$, the load *imbalance* of a calculation. If τ_i is the completion time of processor i, and τ_{max} is the maximum value of τ_i (i.e., the overall completion time), then:

$$\mathcal{L} = \frac{\Sigma(\tau_{max} - \tau_i)}{\mathcal{P}\tau_{max}}$$

quantifies the load imbalance as the percentage of wasted processor cycles.

If a program is fine-grained, and its grains can be executed by any processor in any order with no set-up overhead, then it is relatively easy to load balance the computation by allocating grains to processors on a demand-driven basis, i.e., by task-farming. If the amount of work to be done for each element of the computation cannot be known in advance, and the amount of data which would have to be moved around in order to do task farming is prohibitively large, then an alternative strategy is to use a *scattered decomposition*, in which the work to be done is divided into many more fragments than there are processors, and each processor made responsible for many fragments. In a scattered geometric decomposition, for example, the mesh on which the calculation is being done is split into $k\mathcal{P}$ sections, and each of the $\mathcal{P}$ processors given k to work with.

Typically, sections are assigned either randomly or in a cyclic pattern in order to reduce the number of adjacent sections which each processor has (Figure 2.31). We do this because there is usually some correlation between the amount of work to be done at nearby points: if processors are given patches randomly, the odds are good that every processor will receive a similar number of "hard" and "easy" patches. The disadvantage of a fine-grained scattered decomposition is that if the values on the boundaries of patches must be communicated between processors, the amount of inter-processor communication which must be done is greater than that which would be done in a coarse-grained decomposition, since the ratio of total boundary to total area increases as the number of patches increases and the size of each patch decreases (Figure 2.32). In general, there will be some optimal tradeoff between load balance and communication cost.

This is one instance of the rule that the time required to communicate and synchronize determines how cost-effective it is to run a fine-grained program. If, for example, inter-processor communication has a high start-up time, i.e., if the time taken to do any communication has a fixed component which is large relative to the time required to do simple calculations, then the cost of sending one large message will be much less than the cost of sending several small messages. Since the size of the message which a processor can usefully send is usually proportional to the amount of work which it has done since the last time it sent a message, the most cost-effective way to use a system in which communication is relatively expensive is to give each processor relatively large grains. Of course, the larger the grains, the greater the potential for load imbalance. . . .

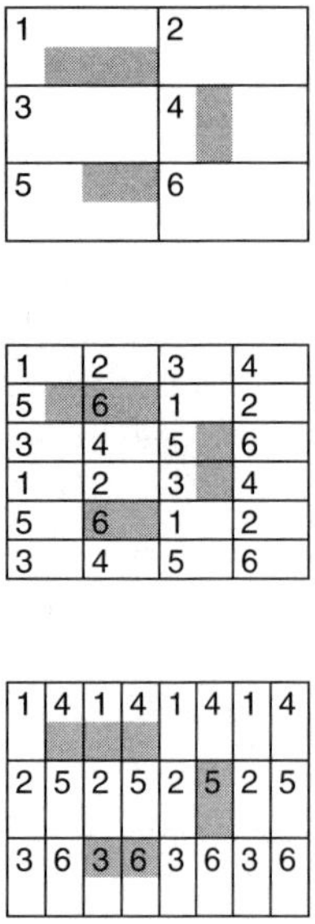

Processor	easy	hard	completion time
1	5	3	35
2	8	0	8
3	8	0	8
4	6	2	26
5	6	2	26
6	8	0	8

$L = 0.471$

Processor	easy	hard	completion time
1	8	0	8
2	8	0	8
3	7	1	17
4	8	0	8
5	6	2	26
6	4	4	44

$L = 0.708$

Processor	easy	hard	completion time
1	7	1	17
2	8	0	8
3	7	1	17
4	6	2	26
5	6	2	26
6	7	1	17

$L = 0.275$

Figure 2.31
Scattering and Its Effects

Similarly, if the time required to perform a context switch is high, then the most efficient way to use a processor is to have it run a single process. If, on the other hand, context switching is relatively cheap, it may be possible to use *processor overloading* to improve the modularity or the efficiency of a program. Processor overloading can improve the efficiency of a computation by hiding some of its communication costs. If several processes are running on each processor, then when one is waiting to send or receive a message, the processor can execute the others. Processor overloading is particularly attractive if the time required to do communication grows with the number of processors in the system, as it does in most multicomputers. In such cases, it may be possible to increase the number of processes per processor to hide the increased communication latency. For example, if the round trip time for messages is more than twice the context switching time, then a processor can usefully run one other process while waiting for a reply. If the round trip time is an order of magnitude larger than the context switching time, then it may make sense to run two or three other processes, each of which may generate messages in turn. The cost of this technique is an increase in memory requirements: since processes have to

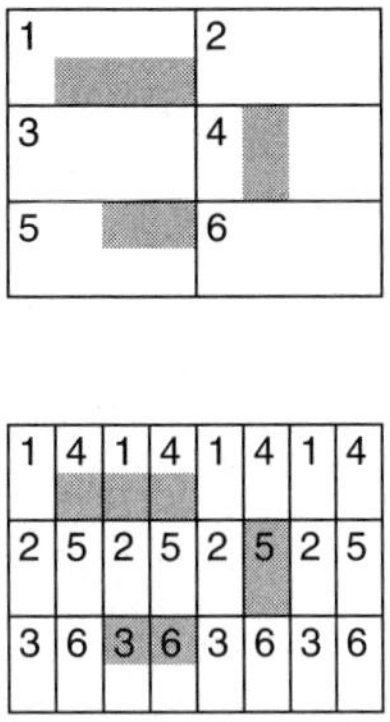

Processor	work time	communication time	total	
1	35	6	41	
2	8	6	14	
3	8	10	18	$L = 0.443$
4	26	10	36	
5	8	6	14	
6	8	6	14	

Processor	work time	communication time	total	
1	17	18	35	
2	8	22	30	
3	17	18	35	$L = 0.170$
4	26	18	44	
5	26	22	48	
6	17	18	35	

Figure 2.32
Boundary/Area Relationship in Scattered Decomposition

be stored somewhere when they are not executing, the memory required by each processor must grow in proportion to the number of processes it is running.

Scattered geometric decomposition can be viewed as a special case of processor overloading. While scattered geometric decomposition can be implemented by placing one process on each processor, and having that process perform calculations for several patches, a program which does this is usually much more complicated than a program in which every process handles exactly one patch. In effect, if a process is cycling amongst many patches, and handling incoming boundary values which are arriving in arbitrary order, that process is effectively doing the sort of context switching which an operating system kernel would perform automatically. Here, the tradeoff is between the simplicity of the program, and its efficiency.

Another influence on program efficiency is the startup latency of performing most operations. The time to send a message, for example, is normally the sum of a constant term representing setup costs, and a second term dependent on the length of the message. In many multicomputers, the startup latency is as great as the cost of sending hundreds or even thousands of bytes of data. As a result, there is often an incentive to make fine-grained operations more coarse-grained.

There are many ways to do this. Having one physical process emulate many logical processes (i.e., having one process work on several segments of a mesh in a scattered geometric decomposition) is the most common. This technique is used by many compilers for data-parallel machines, which allow programs to be written by an arbitrary number of virtual processors, and then generate code containing a mix of loops and data-parallel operations.

Another technique is to combine communication operations. Returning to the scattered geometric decomposition of Figure 2.32 again, we can see that mesh segments have been allocated to processors so that all neighbors across some axis of patches in one processor are located in another processor. Rather than sending one message for each patch, a program could concatenate boundary updates and send a single, larger message. Doing this effectively increases the grain size of the computation, while retaining the good load-balancing properties of a scattered decomposition.

By itself, knowing an application's granularity is not particularly useful, since a program could perform any amount of communication between grains. A measure which is therefore often associated with granularity is the *computation-to-communication ratio* of an application. This is simply the ratio of the number of operations a processor performs (measured in arithmetic instructions, total instructions, or whatever else is appropriate) to the volume of data that processor communicates. If this is large, the processors running the application perform many operations for each value they send or receive; if it is low, then the number of operations being done is roughly equal to the amount of data being exchanged.

While computation-to-communication ratio ignores the startup latency of messaging, it is often a good guide to the likely efficiency of an algorithm. For example, consider the problem of calculating the motion of a large number of stars, which interact with one another gravitationally. Each star exerts a force on each other; at each time step, these forces must be calculated and summed in order to determine the acceleration on each star, so that its position and velocity may be updated in the next time step.

The simplest parallel algorithm for doing this, described in [Fox et al. 1988], divides responsibility for the N bodies between $\mathcal{P}$ processors, which are logically connected in a ring (Figure 2.33). At the start of each iteration, each processor calculates the force on each of its bodies due to all of its other bodies. Processors then send copies of the information describing their bodies to their clockwise neighbors, while receiving information about other bodies from their counter-clockwise neighbors. After another round of force calculations, these body descriptions are shifted again; once they have been shifted all the way around the ring, each processor has calculated the total force on each of its bodies, and can update their positions and velocities.

Using this algorithm, the time taken by each processor to perform its calculations in each iteration is proportional to $N\frac{N}{\mathcal{P}} = N^2/\mathcal{P}$, while the total amount of communication each does is proportional to N. (The first cost is the time for each processor to calculate the interaction of its $N/\mathcal{P}$ bodies with N other bodies, while the second cost is the time for each processor to receive and then forward N bodies.) Thus, the computation-to-

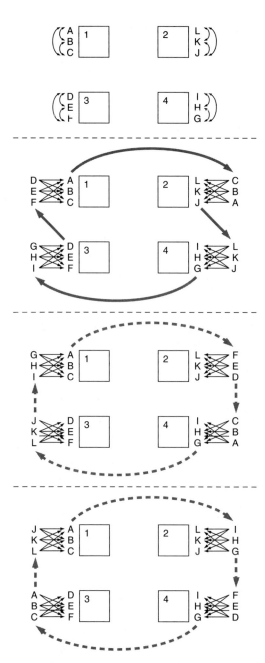

Figure 2.33
Parallelizing the *N*-Body Problem

communication ratio is roughly $N^2/\mathcal{P}N$, or $N/\mathcal{P}$. For a fixed number of processors, this increases with the number of bodies being simulated. Each processor therefore spends a larger proportion of its time doing calculations as the problem size increases, so the algorithm's efficiency improves as the simulation is scaled up.

2.5.3   Determinism and Reproducibility

Two adjectives which are often used to describe parallel applications are *deterministic* and *reproducible*. A deterministic program is one which always produces the same result when given the same input; a *non-deterministic* program is one which might not. Most serial programs are deterministic; even most serial random number generators will churn out the same sequence of values when given the same starting seed. However, because the order in which computations are performed in a parallel system can depend on timing effects and the allocation of data to processors, it is possible for a parallel program to produce a different result each time it is run. Ways of coping with, or avoiding, such indeterminacy will be discussed in subsequent chapters.

Even when timing effects are ignored, it is possible for parallel programs which do floating-point calculations to produce different answers than their serial counterparts. For example, suppose that every processor holds a value x_i, and that these values are to be summed. If this is done by sending the values to one processor, having it calculate the sum, and then distributing the result, every processor will get the same final value. If, on the other hand, the values are shifted cyclically, like the bodies in the N-body algorithm described above, then each processor will perform the additions in a different order. As will be explained on page 139, this could lead to different processors calculating different sums. If the next step taken by each processor depends on the value of this sum (i.e., whether it is positive or negative), the results could be disastrous.

2.5.4   Speedup and Efficiency

One simple quantitative measure of the benefit of parallelism is the *speedup* of an application. If $\tau(\mathcal{P})$ is the time required to run a program on $\mathcal{P}$ processors, then the speedup on $\mathcal{P}$ processors is:

$$\mathcal{S}(\mathcal{P}) = \frac{\tau(1)}{\tau(\mathcal{P})}$$

i.e., the ratio of the time taken to run the program on one processor to the time taken to run it on $\mathcal{P}$ processors.

Whenever speedup (or other measures) are quoted, it is extremely important to be clear what is being compared to what [Crowl 1994]. For example, if the odd/even sort of Section 2.3.1 is run on a single processor, its execution time is $\mathcal{O}(\mathcal{P}^2)$. Since its running time on $\mathcal{P}$ processors is only $\mathcal{P}$, it appears to achieve "perfect" speedup. However, any sensible programmer would use an $\mathcal{O}(\mathcal{P}\log\mathcal{P})$ sorting algorithm such as quicksort on a single processor; compared to this, the speedup of odd/even sort is only $\log\mathcal{P}/\mathcal{P}$. Similarly, while the N-body algorithm described on page 54 gets a speedup which is almost proportional to the number of processors used, most large-scale N-body simulations are done using recursive reduction algorithms which are much harder to parallelize. Thus, it is important to make clear whether speedup is being measured against the best known serial algorithm on a single processor, the parallel algorithm of interest running on a single processor, or the parallel algorithm running on two or more processors. Many programs have good speedup characteristics if measured in the second or third of these ways, but do very poorly when compared with a good serial program.

While speedup measures how much faster a program runs on a parallel computer than on a uniprocessor, it does not measure whether the processors in that parallel computer are being used effectively. Since few programmers would be happy if 100 processors were needed to make a program run twice as fast, *efficiency* is also commonly used to assess performance. The efficiency of a program on $\mathcal{P}$ processors is $\varepsilon(\mathcal{P})$, and is defined as the ratio of the speedup achieved and the number of processors used to achieve it:

$$\varepsilon(\mathcal{P}) = \frac{\mathcal{S}(\mathcal{P})}{\mathcal{P}}$$

$$= \frac{\tau(1)}{\mathcal{P}\tau(\mathcal{P})}$$

Another way to define efficiency is to say that the time taken to do a calculation on a parallel computer has two components: τ_C, which is the time taken to do the essential calculations, and $\tau_\|(\mathcal{P})$, which is the extra time required by a parallel program. $\tau_\|(\mathcal{P})$ includes such things as the time to do communication, the time processors spend waiting for messages to arrive, and the idle time of processors which finish before the entire calculation is completed. Since $\tau_\|(\mathcal{P})$ is zero for a uniprocessor, these terms can be used to give an equivalent definition of efficiency:

$$\varepsilon(\mathcal{P}) = \frac{\tau_C}{\tau_C + \tau_\|(\mathcal{P})}$$

$$= \frac{1}{1 + \frac{\tau_\|(\mathcal{P})}{\tau_C}}$$

Using this formulation, we can see that $\tau_\|(\mathcal{P})$ must decrease relative to τ_C as $\mathcal{P}$ increases in order for $\varepsilon(\mathcal{P})$ to approach 1. How quickly this happens can determine how effectively parallelism can be used to solve a particular problem; this point is discussed again below.

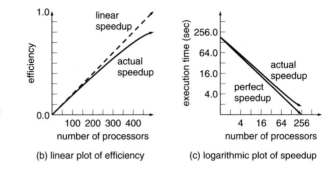

Figure 2.34
Speedup and Efficiency

One way to think about the relationship between speedup and efficiency is to draw a plot of speedup as a function of the number of processors used. If this is a straight line, then the parallel algorithm being used achieves *linear speedup*, i.e., it gains the same benefit from the $(\mathcal{P} + 1)^{\text{th}}$ processor used as it gained from each of the first $\mathcal{P}$ processors (Figure 2.34). In most cases, however, the speedup curve will be less than linear, and the difference will show how much efficiency is being lost due to parallel overheads.

Note that the third plot in Figure 2.34 is doubly-logarithmic, i.e., that it plots the logarithm of speedup versus the logarithm of the number of processors used. As [Crowl 1994] explains, this kind of plot is the least likely to mislead when large variations in the number of processors, execution times, or speedups are presented. It is also the best plot to use when comparing different systems, since the shape of a log-log curve is scale invariant.

Occasionally, claims are made of *superlinear speedup*, i.e., speedup which increases faster than the number of processors used [Parkinson 1986, Faber et al. 1986]. While it would seem impossible to speed a program up by more than a factor of $\mathcal{P}$ by using only $\mathcal{P}$ processors, some real programs do manage it. Usually, this happens because of differences in the nature of the hardware on which they are running. For example, if a serial program is run on one processor which has a C-byte cache, and is then decomposed and run on $\mathcal{P}$ processors, each of which has its own C-byte cache, then each processor in the parallel machine may have a higher cache hit rate, and hence run faster on an individual basis than its serial counterpart. Similarly, a speculatively-parallel program may show superlinear speedup because the order in which methods are being tried is different on a parallel machine than on a serial, and so a successful method may be tried earlier.

Disregarding cases such as this, no-one has found an algorithm which runs more than $\mathcal{P}$ times faster on $\mathcal{P}$ processors than on one. In all the examples which have been proposed, the reason for the superlinear speedup has been that the serial and parallel algorithms being

compared were not exactly the same. For example, suppose that a uniprocessor machine
and a multicomputer with $\mathcal{P}$ processors are both given the task of setting the $\mathcal{P}$ elements
of an array A to zero. The obvious serial algorithm uses a loop:

```
do i = 1, P
  A(i) = 0
end do
```

while the parallel algorithm simply gives one array element to each processor, and has it
set that element to zero.

If one counts cost only by counting assignment statements, then the efficiency of the
serial and parallel algorithms are the same. If one includes the cost of the loop construct
used in the serial algorithm, on the other hand, then its cost goes up, so that the time taken
by the parallel algorithm is less than $(1/\mathcal{P})^{\text{th}}$ of the time taken by the serial algorithm.

However, this is not comparing like with like. The most efficient serial algorithm does
not actually use a loop, but rather a sequence of assignment statements, as in:

```
A(0)    = 0
A(1)    = 0
A(2)    = 0
  .
  .
  .
A(P-1) = 0
```

Clearly, this program takes exactly $\mathcal{P}$ times as long to execute as the parallel one.

2.5.5   Limits to Efficiency

In all real programs, the law of diminishing returns eventually applies to processor utilization, and the speedup is sub-linear. In fact, for any given problem, the speedup will
eventually level off, as the time required to perform intrinsically serial parts of the program
starts to dominate the program's total execution time.

This rule was first formulated by the computer architect Gene Amdahl in [Amdahl
1967]. According to *Amdahl's Law*, a program contains two types of calculation: those
such as disk accesses, which must be done serially, and those which can be parallelized to
run on an arbitrary number of processors. Let the time taken to do the serial calculations
be some fraction σ of the total τ, $0 < \sigma \leq 1$, so that the parallelizable portion is $1 - \sigma$ of
the total. If we suppose that the parallelizable portion achieves linear speedup, i.e., that it
runs $\mathcal{P}$ times faster on $\mathcal{P}$ processors than it does on one, then the speedup on $\mathcal{P}$ processors
will be:

$$\mathcal{S}(\mathcal{P}) = \frac{\tau(1)}{\tau(\mathcal{P})}$$

$$= \frac{\tau(1)}{\sigma\tau(1) + (1-\sigma)\frac{\tau(1)}{\mathcal{P}}}$$

$$= \frac{1}{\sigma + \frac{1-\sigma}{\mathcal{P}}}$$

No matter how many processors are used, the speedup in this problem will be limited to $1/\sigma$. For example, even if only 1% of a program is sequential, the greatest possible speedup which can be achieved is 99 (Figure 2.35). Concomitantly, the efficiency, which is given by:

$$\varepsilon(\mathcal{P}) = \frac{1}{\mathcal{P}\sigma + (1-\sigma)}$$

will drop off to zero for large numbers of processors.

There are several ways to avoid the ugly conclusion of Amdahl's Law. One is to recognize that good serial algorithms are not necessarily good parallel algorithms, and to concentrate on parallelizing algorithms with small serial fractions. A more successful technique is to realize that Amdahl's formulation is incomplete, as it does not take the size of the problem into account. The amount of calculation done in the serial fraction of an algorithm is often independent of, or grows slowly with, the problem size, but the amount of calculation done in the parallel fraction usually increases in direct proportion to the size of the problem. One way to achieve higher efficiency is therefore to use parallel computers to solve larger problems.[5]

This conclusion is intuitively reasonable: the most effective way to use one hundred carpenters is not to have them build one house much faster, but to have them build many more houses in a fixed amount of time. Increasing the problem size to get better efficiency is also psychologically appealing—despite the million-fold increase in computer power during the last forty years, users still think in terms of waiting a few seconds,[6] a few minutes,[7] or overnight[8] to get their results. In practice, it often makes sense to use a faster machine to run a larger problem in the same time as the old machine ran the original problem, rather than trying to get the original problem to run faster.

---

5. This is sometimes called "cheating."

6. A sip of coffee.

7. A fresh cup.

8. Long enough to sleep off the effects of all that coffee.

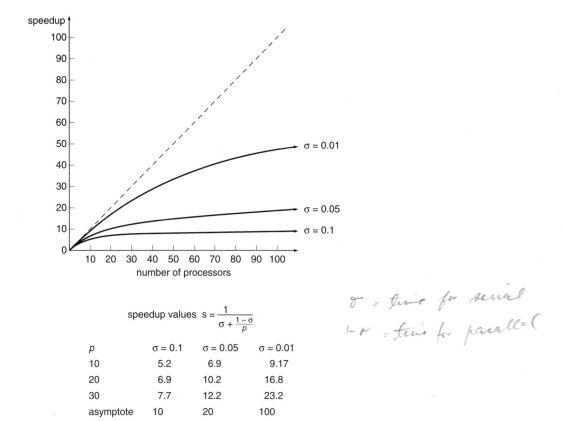

speedup values $s = \dfrac{1}{\sigma + \dfrac{1-\sigma}{p}}$

p	σ = 0.1	σ = 0.05	σ = 0.01
10	5.2	6.9	9.17
20	6.9	10.2	16.8
30	7.7	12.2	23.2
asymptote	10	20	100

Figure 2.35
Effects of Amdahl's Law

This line of argument leads to the notion of scaled speedup, which takes account of both the number of processors used and the size of the problem being solved. One of the first enunciations of this idea was in [Gustafson et al. 1988]. According to *Gustafson's Law*, if the size of the parallel portion of a problem is scaled up sufficiently, then any required efficiency can be achieved on any number of processors. Assume that τ_σ is the constant time taken to do the sequential part of the calculations on a problem, and $\tau_\parallel(\mathcal{N}, \mathcal{P})$ is the time taken to do the parallelizable part of the calculations for a problem of size $\mathcal{N}$ on $\mathcal{P}$ processors. The speedup achieved on $\mathcal{P}$ processors is then:

$$\mathcal{S} = \frac{\tau_\sigma + \tau_\parallel(\mathcal{N}, 1)}{\tau_\sigma + \tau_\parallel(\mathcal{N}, \mathcal{P})}$$

If we suppose that $\tau_\|$ increases with $\mathcal{N}$, but decreases with $\mathcal{P}$, then any desired efficiency $\varepsilon^\star$ can be reached by increasing the problem size. For example, if $\tau_\|(\mathcal{N}, \mathcal{P}) = \frac{\mathcal{N}^2}{\mathcal{P}}$ (as it does for some mesh-based applications), then:

$$\lim_{\mathcal{N} \to \infty} \mathcal{S} = \frac{\tau_\sigma + \mathcal{N}^2}{\tau_\sigma + \frac{\mathcal{N}^2}{\mathcal{P}}}$$

$$= \frac{\mathcal{P}\tau_\sigma + \mathcal{P}\mathcal{N}^2}{\mathcal{P}\tau_\sigma + \mathcal{N}^2}$$

$$= \mathcal{P}$$

and so the efficiency approaches 1 for a large enough problem.

Gustafson's Law is a better idealization of the way people actually use massively parallel computers, but is still just an idealization. In practice, the time taken to do the serial part of a program can increase with the number of processors, even if the time required to do the parallel portion decreases. The most illuminating way to think about *scalability* and efficiency seems to be to ask how the size of a problem must be scaled up, relative to the increase in the number of processors, in order to maintain some specified efficiency. This approach has led Vipin Kumar and others to develop the notion of *isoefficiency functions* [Rao & Kumar 1989, Kumar et al. 1993, Gupta & Kumar 1993, Grama et al. 1993] to measure the scalability of various combinations of algorithms and architectures. An isoefficiency function shows how the size of the problem being solved must grow as a function of the number of processors used in order to maintain some constant efficiency.

We can derive a general form for an isoefficiency function by re-considering the definition of efficiency:

$$\varepsilon(\mathcal{P}) = \frac{\tau_C}{\tau_C + \tau_\|(\mathcal{P})}$$

$$= \frac{1}{1 + \frac{\tau_\|(\mathcal{P})}{\tau_C}}$$

If we fix the efficiency at some constant value ε, and re-arrange the terms in this equation, we get:

$$\tau_C = \left(\frac{\varepsilon}{1 - \varepsilon} \right) \tau_\|(\mathcal{P})$$

Thus, if we wish to maintain a certain level of efficiency, we must keep the parallel overhead $\tau_\|$ no worse than proportional to the total useful calculation time τ_C. The function which relates these two values is the isoefficiency function for this problem, and depends on both the algorithm being used and the architecture on which that algorithm is implemented.

Like many things, this is easiest to understand from an example. Suppose we are trying to determine the heat distribution in a metal plate by approximating Poisson's Equation on a regular two-dimensional mesh (Section 2.3.1). During each iteration, we update each point in the mesh according to:

$$u_{i,j}^{t+1} = c_1 u_{i,j}^t - c_2(u_{i,j-1}^t + u_{i-1,j}^t + u_{i,j+1}^t + u_{i+1,j}^t)$$

where c_1 and c_2 control the rate of convergence. (Points on the boundary of the mesh are updated using the same formula, with values determined by the boundary conditions used in place of some of the mesh values.) After each update, we calculate the difference between the new values and the old, and then find the greatest absolute difference. If this is less than a certain tolerance, the algorithm terminates.

The total work which must be done in a single serial iteration of this algorithm is approximately $8Nt_c$, where N is the total number of points in the mesh (*not* the side length of the mesh) and t_c is the cost of a single arithmetic operation. The constant "8" is a count of the number of operations being done: each point update requires three additions, two multiplications, and a subtraction, which must be added to the cost of finding the absolute difference between the old and new values, and the pairwise comparisons to find the maximum absolute difference.

Now consider a parallel implementation of this problem, in which the mesh is decomposed geometrically into square patches on $\mathcal{P}$ processors. Each processor updates its portion of the mesh in $6\frac{N}{\mathcal{P}}t_c$ time, but must then swap boundaries with its neighbors and participate in finding the minimum absolute difference between old and new mesh values.

Let us assume that the time required to send a message of size M is $t_i + t_\ell M$, where t_i is the startup overhead of message transfer and t_ℓ is the transfer cost per unit of data. Assume also that processors are connected in a 4-way mesh, i.e., that there are no diagonal connections between processors, and that a processor may simultaneously send to and receive from all of its neighbors. The time required for swapping boundaries is then:

$$t_{boundary} = t_i + t_\ell \frac{\sqrt{N}}{\sqrt{\mathcal{P}}}$$

since each boundary of the mesh has length $\sqrt{N}$, and the processors are arranged in a $\sqrt{\mathcal{P}} \times \sqrt{\mathcal{P}}$ mesh.

Processors must then find the maximum absolute difference between old and new mesh values. Each processor can find the maximum value within its patch in a time:

$$t_{localmin} = 2\frac{N}{\mathcal{P}}t_c$$

These values can then be combined pairwise as shown in Figure 2.36. If we trace the path of the value contributed by the processor in the lower-right corner of the mesh, we find that it takes $2\log\sqrt{\mathcal{P}} = \log\mathcal{P}$ steps to reach the upper-left corner. The time for each step is:

$$t_{combinemin} = \log\mathcal{P}\,(t_c + t_i + t_\ell)$$

since each step involves sending a single unit of data, and performing a single comparison. Thus, the total time required to execute a single iteration in parallel is:

$$\tau(\mathcal{P}) = 6\frac{N}{\mathcal{P}}t_c + t_i + t_\ell\frac{\sqrt{N}}{\sqrt{\mathcal{P}}} + 2\frac{N}{\mathcal{P}}t_c + \log\mathcal{P}\,(t_c + t_i + t_\ell)$$

Now, if $\tau(\mathcal{P})$ is the time to execute the problem on $\mathcal{P}$ processors, τ_σ is the total serial work, and $\tau_\|$ is the parallel overhead time, then:

$$\mathcal{P}\tau(\mathcal{P}) = \tau_\sigma + \tau_\|$$

i.e., the total number of cycles used by the parallel program must be the total useful execution time plus any parallel overhead. Substituting from the previous equations, and eliminating the serial calculation time $8Nt_c$, we find that:

$$\tau_\| = \mathcal{P}\log\mathcal{P}t_c + (\mathcal{P} + \mathcal{P}\log\mathcal{P})t_i + (\sqrt{N\mathcal{P}} + \mathcal{P}\log\mathcal{P})t_\ell$$

In order for this problem to be scalable, i.e., in order for us to be able to keep the efficiency constant, this overhead must grow no faster than the total serial work being done. Thus, the isoefficiency function for this problem is:

$$8Nt_c = \mathcal{P}\log\mathcal{P}t_c + (\mathcal{P} + \mathcal{P}\log\mathcal{P})t_i + (\sqrt{N\mathcal{P}} + \mathcal{P}\log\mathcal{P})t_\ell$$

While it is impossible to simplify this equation significantly, we can easily find its dominant contributions. If we let τ_i and τ_ℓ be t_i/t_c and t_ℓ/t_c respectively, and get rid of the constant 8 by making the left and right sides proportional, we have:

$$N \propto \mathcal{P}\log\mathcal{P} + (\mathcal{P} + \mathcal{P}\log\mathcal{P})\tau_i + (\sqrt{N\mathcal{P}} + \mathcal{P}\log\mathcal{P})\tau_\ell$$

or

$$N \propto \mathcal{P}\log\mathcal{P}(1 + \tau_i + \tau_\ell) + \mathcal{P}\tau_i + \sqrt{N\mathcal{P}}\tau_\ell$$

Thus, we can see that N must grow as $\mathcal{P}\log\mathcal{P}$ in order to keep efficiency constant as the number of processors increases.

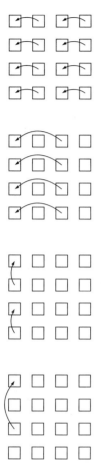

Figure 2.36
Finding the Global Maximum on a Mesh

This result is not unique to this problem. Almost every algorithm needs to synchronize occasionally; in the limit, the cost of such synchronization must somehow be paid for. In this example, the cost of updating mesh points may be so much greater than the cost of doing the global sum that the loss of efficiency as the machine is scaled up may be negligible. In general, there will be an optimal size of machine to use for any given problem. This is called the *parallel balance point* for a problem, which is the point at which adding more processors without increasing the size of the problem actually slows the calculation down (Figure 2.37). This is also one of the reasons that many parallel

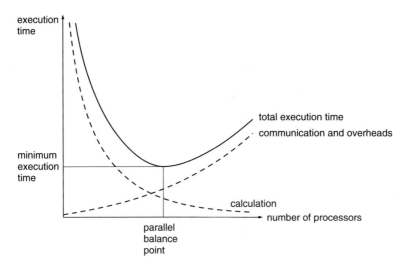

Figure 2.37
Parallel Balance Point

machines allow *space sharing*. In a *time sharing* system, such as a mainframe running a multi-user operating system, different programmers share individual processors; in a space-shared system, each program is allocated a subset of the available processors. If the efficiency characteristics of a program are understood, it may be possible to give each program the right number of processors.

2.5.6 r_∞ and All That

Speedup and efficiency measure the performance of a particular program or algorithm running on a particular machine; two other measures due to Hockney [Hockney 1982] are often used to characterize the intrinsic performance of machines, particularly pipelined supercomputers. These measures help to distinguish between the peak computation rate of a machine (which is the figure most often quoted by its manufacturers), and the rate which it can sustain on real computations (which is more interesting to most potential users).

The first of Hockney's measures is r_∞, which is the computation rate a machine could sustain on an infinitely long calculation. r_∞ is usually measured in megaFLOPS (*MFLOPS*), gigaFLOPS (*GFLOPS*), or teraFLOPS (*TFLOPS*). A multiplication pipeline with an r_∞ of 420 MFLOPS, for example, would perform 420 million multiplications per second on corresponding elements of two infinitely-long vectors.

A complementary measure is $n_{1/2}$, which is the length of vector on which the machine delivers half of its sustainable performance. As explained on page 5, there is always a lag between when a pipelined machine starts a calculation, and when it delivers its first result. The larger this latency, the larger a calculation must be in order to amortize it. For example, a pipeline with an r_∞ of 100 MFLOPS and a startup time of 100 μsec takes 100.01×10^{-6} seconds to do a calculation on a single-element vector, which reduces its effective speed to only 10 kFLOPS. In order to deliver at least 50 MFLOPS—half its potential performance—this machine would have to be given a vector containing at least 10,000 elements. The pipeline's $n_{1/2}$ is therefore 10,000.

These two values are related by a simple formula. Suppose that σ is the startup time for a pipeline, and that r_∞ is its ideal throughput. The time required to process n elements is then:

$$t(n) = \sigma + \frac{n}{r_\infty}$$

This makes the effective rate $r(n)$ on n elements:

$$r(n) = \frac{n}{t(n)}$$

$$= \frac{n}{\sigma + \frac{n}{r_\infty}}$$

If we set $r(n)$ equal to $r_\infty/2$, we find that $n_{1/2}$ is:

$$n_{1/2} = \sigma r_\infty$$

Substituting this into the formula for the effective rate gives:

$$r(n) = r_\infty \frac{1}{1 + \frac{n_{1/2}}{n}}$$

Figure 2.38 shows the general relationship between $n_{1/2}$ and r_∞. In general, a low $n_{1/2}$ indicates that fine-grained calculations will run well on a machine, while a large r_∞ implies that good performance will be achieved on large problems. An ideal machine would have both of these characteristics, but usually a tradeoff must be made between them and a machine's overall cost.

If $n_{1/2}$ is regarded as a measure of performance degradation due to filling and flushing a pipeline, then a third measure of machine performance, $f_{1/2}$, may be regarded as a measure of the degradation due to memory bottlenecks. Most arithmetic operations take two operands, and generate one result. A well-balanced machine should accordingly provide three times as much memory bandwidth as floating-point performance. In practice, most computers provide substantially less, and programs must therefore try to keep operands in registers for as long as possible.

$f_{1/2}$ is the number of floating-point operations which must be performed on each operand fetched from memory in order for a processor to achieve half of its peak speed. If $f_{1/2}$ is one, then the machine will deliver half its peak performance on an operation such

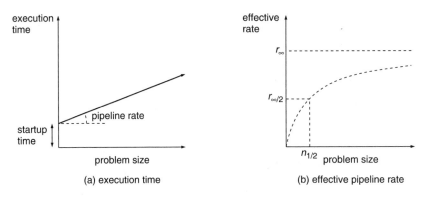

Figure 2.38
Relationship Between Startup Time and Maximum Performance

as multiplying every element of a vector by a scalar constant kept in a register (since one multiplication is done for each memory access), and less for pairwise multiplication of the elements of two vectors. If $f_{1/2}$ is greater than one, as it is on most modern microprocessors, then each operand must be used several times in order to justify fetching it from memory. This difference means that programs must be tuned in very different ways for these different architectures. To see why, consider the loop:

```
do i = 1, N
  y(i) = ((d * x(i) + c) * x(i) + b) * x(i) + a
end do
```

which uses Horner's Rule to calculate the value of a polynomial $dx_i^3 + cx_i^2 + bx_i + a = ((dx_i + c)x_i + b)x_i + a$ at each of a large number of points x_i. On a well-balanced pipelined machine, the best way to parallelize this might be to break the loop up into three independent loops, each of which could then overlap use of a pipelined adder and multiplier:

```
do i = 1, N
  y(i) = d * x(i) + c
end do
do i = 1, N
  y(i) = x(i) * y(i) + b
end do
do i = 1, N
  y(i) = x(i) * y(i) + a
end do
```

In an architecture with a high $f_{1/2}$, e.g., a *superscalar processor* containing both an adder and multiplier, it might be best to run the loop as originally given, in order to avoid fetching each vector element x_i three times.

A similar definition can be given for $s_{1/2}$, which is the number of operations which must be done between each synchronization point in order to achieve half of peak performance. This measure is most important in fine-grained systems which synchronize after every few instructions, but the basic idea can be applied to systems of any granularity. [Hockney 1991] discusses these parameters, and their relationship to some commonly-used computer benchmarks.

Finally, the measures *WARPS* and *WASPS* are sometimes used to quantify the performance of memory systems. The first means "words accessed randomly per second", and measures the worst-case throughput of a memory system. The second means "words accessed sequentially per second", and is the performance when the entire address range of the machine is stepped through in order. Because of caching effects, this usually gives the best possible throughput.

In practice, of course, it is difficult to predict the performance of real applications based solely on these values, since such things as the number of values fetched and the number of operations done on them depend on the problem size, data-dependent branching, and so on. However, these parameters do capture fundamental aspects of a machine's performance, and are a good way of thinking about what particular architectures are and are not good at doing. Low $n_{1/2}$ and $f_{1/2}$ values mean that the performance on scalar and vector portions of a program are likely to be similar, while large values imply that the payoff for vectorizing a program (or, more cynically, the penalty for trying to run unvectorized programs) will be large.

2.5.7 Topology

As explained in Section 2.1, the simplest way to connect the processors and memories making up a parallel computer is to use a single shared bus. However, since this is vulnerable to saturation, many multiprocessors, and almost all multicomputers, provide many independent connections. The pattern these form is called the *topology* of the machine.

Topologies are usually described using terminology taken from graph theory. A graph is a finite set of nodes, connected by edges. If an edge can only be traversed in one direction, it is called a directed edge; otherwise, it undirected.

Topological Measures   From a computer architect's point of view, the two most important characteristics of a graph are its *diameter*, and the degree, or *valence*, of its nodes. The valence of a node is simply the number of edges joining it to other nodes; the term *arity* is sometimes used to mean the same thing. While the nodes in a graph may have different arities, in most multicomputers the valence of all nodes is the same. This is not a sign of a lack of imagination among computer architects—in most cases, it is much simpler to build many identical nodes and connect them, and there is rarely any good reason to make one node different from another.

Valence is important because the amount of data which can get into or out of a processor is bounded by the bandwidth of the links connecting that processor's node to other nodes, and by the number of such links. While it is sometimes difficult to decide whether a few fast links are better than a large number of slow ones, it is always better (although more expensive) to have more links of a given speed than fewer.

The diameter of a graph is the greatest distance between any two nodes, measured by counting the number of links on a shortest path connecting them. Diameter is important because it helps determine how long it takes to send a message from any processor to any other: the greater the diameter of the graph, the further the message must travel. (Note that, for reasons described in Section 2.5.8, the time taken for a message to travel through a network in most present-generation parallel computers may not always be strictly proportional to the number of hops.)

Another important characteristic of a parallel computer's topology is whether it is *homogeneous* or *heterogeneous*. The nodes and links in a homogeneous graph are all identical; those in a heterogeneous graph may differ from one another. A ring of identical processors is a homogeneous topology, since every processor can behave in exactly the same way. A chain of processors, on the other hand, is heterogeneous, since the processors at the end of the chain must sometimes behave differently (i.e., not try to send data to their nonexistent neighbors). While most multicomputers consist of homogeneous processor-memory pairs, the individual computers making up a *distributed computer*—a cluster of workstations (or *COW*) being used together as a single resource—often contain several different types of processors. Dealing with this kind of heterogeneity is more an issue for software engineering than for parallel programming, as it involves such things as maintaining multiple versions of a program, translating between different data formats, and so on.

Two quantitative measures of graphs are *link loading* and *bisection bandwidth*. Link loading measures how evenly links are used. The simplest way to calculate it is to imagine that one message is being sent from each node in the graph to each other. Every time a message crosses an edge, a count associated with that edge is incremented; once all messages have been delivered, these counts form a histogram of the number of messages which have traversed each edge. If the computer's architect has done her job well, this histogram will show that message traffic is evenly distributed among the links. If it is not, then some communication patterns will leave some links idle while others are busy

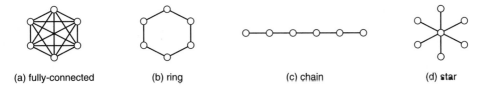

Figure 2.39
Fully-Connected, Chain, Ring, and Star Topologies

transmitting a disproportionate share of the total traffic. In a sense, some of the computer's link capacity will have been wasted.

Link loading is so important that it is often useful to think about *worst link loading*, which is how much traffic the most heavily loaded link in the graph must carry, or the *link loading ratio*, which is the ratio of the traffic carried by the most heavily used link to that carried by the least heavily used link. These two measures also have the advantage that they can be expressed as single numbers, rather than as histograms.

The concept of bisection bandwidth is related to that of link loading. Take an arbitrary graph, cut it into two connected halves, and measure the bandwidth between those halves (which is the product of the number of links connecting them, and the speed of an individual link). If the connecting bandwidth is low, then some patterns of communication will be very difficult, because some links will be very heavily loaded. If, on the other hand, any two halves of a graph are highly-interconnected, then messages will usually not have to contend with other messages for access to links. Finally, if the result varies widely depending on how the graph is bisected, then the speed of inter-processor communication will vary depending on which processors are trying to communicate with which others. In this case, the way data are mapped to processors, or equivalently the pattern of communication between processors, will be a critical factor in overall performance.

Popular Topologies   There are many different ways to connect processors. At one extreme is the *fully-connected network*, in which every processor is directly connected to every other (Figure 2.39). At the other are the *chain* and *ring*, in which processors are chained together in a (notional) line or circle. In between is the *star*, in which one central node is connected to all the other nodes, which are only connected to it.

Fully-connected networks seem to have a lot going for them: their diameter is low (always 1), and does not increase as the number of processors is increased. In addition, only two processors ever use any link, which keeps link loading low. The disadvantage of a fully-connected network is the number of links it requires: joining $\mathcal{P}$ processors to each other requires $\mathcal{P}(\mathcal{P}-1)$ links. Even if the 999,000 connections required to build a 1000-processor machine were affordable, physically connecting 999 wires to each processor would be quite a challenge.[9]

In a ring, on the other hand, each processor only has two connections, and the number of links is exactly the same as the number of processors. Unfortunately, the diameter of a ring grows proportionally to the number of nodes in it. This may not be a problem in geometrically-decomposed applications, in which processors only ever need to communicate with their immediate neighbors, but for most applications, the rapid growth of a ring's diameter is an unnecessarily high cost to pay. Finally, a chain adds heterogeneity to the disadvantages of a ring, while a star is only a slight improvement over a fully-connected network, since the central processor must still have an inordinate number of links.

Most large multicomputers use more sensible topologies than either of these. Two of the most popular are the *mesh*, used in Intel's Paragon, and *torus*, used in Cray Research's T3D. In a mesh, processors are laid out along the axes of a discrete $\mathcal{D}$-dimensional grid; a torus is simply a mesh whose edges wrap around (Figure 2.40). In practice, most meshes are two- or three-dimensional, while most tori are two-dimensional (although a ring can be regarded as a one-dimensional torus). Some reasons for the popularity of these topologies are:

• they are simple to construct out of nodes with a fixed valence;

• their diameter only grows as $\sqrt{\mathcal{P}}$, rather than as $\mathcal{P}$ for a ring;

• they can easily be enlarged by adding another row or column of processors; and

• geometric decomposition of many matrix and mesh-based calculations gives a good fit to this topology.

Another popular topology is the *hypercube*, which is used in NCube's multicomputers. A zero-dimensional hypercube is simply a point, i.e., a single processor. A one-dimensional hypercube is two zero-dimensional hypercubes joined together, i.e., a single line segment; a two-dimensional hypercube (or square) is made up of a pair of one-dimensional hypercubes, and a three-dimensional hypercube (or cube) is made by joining two two-dimensional hypercubes (Figure 2.41). Carrying on, a four-dimensional hypercube contains two three-dimensional cubes, and can be drawn either as one cube nested inside another, or as two cubes with corresponding nodes joined. A five-dimensional hy-

---

9. Not to mention finding and replacing the one that would inevitably have broken the day before the machine was supposed to be demonstrated for the first time.

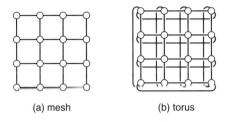

(a) mesh   (b) torus

Figure 2.40
Mesh and Torus Topologies

percube contains $2^5 = 32$ nodes and $5 \times 2^5/2 = 80$ edges,[10] and is more difficult to draw than to construct.

Note in Figure 2.41 how we construct a unique ID for each node. Each time two $\mathcal{D}$-dimensional hypercubes are joined to create a $\mathcal{D} + 1$-dimensional hypercube, identifiers for the new hypercube's nodes are created by prefixing a 0 to the IDs of one of the sub-cubes, and a 1 to the IDs of the other. As shall be discussed in Section 2.5.7, this recursive labelling scheme has many uses.

Hypercubes are interesting for three reasons. First, their diameter only grows logarithmically with the number of processors, rather than as the square root of the number of processors—a 256-node (square) mesh has a diameter of 16, but a 256-node hypercube only has a diameter of 8, and the difference becomes more significant in larger machines. Second, many other topologies can be embedded in hypercubes, including binary trees, tori, rings, and some of the more exotic topologies described below (Section 2.5.7). Third, hypercubes have lots of links, which gives them good link loading and bisection bandwidth characteristics. This is very important in applications in which message traffic is heavy and irregular.

The main drawback of the hypercube topology is the increase in the valence of each node as the hypercube's size increases. As with fully-connected networks, this means that the cost of the communication hardware required to build a hypercube grows faster than its size. It also means that it is not possible to use a single standard component to build a hypercube node. In theory, a $(\mathcal{D} + 1)$-dimensional hypercube can be built by joining two $\mathcal{D}$-dimensional hypercubes together, but in practice, either the nodes in the $\mathcal{D}$-dimensional hypercube must have been built with a fixed number of links, and not used some, or some

10. Each of its 2^5 nodes has 5 links, but each link connects two nodes.

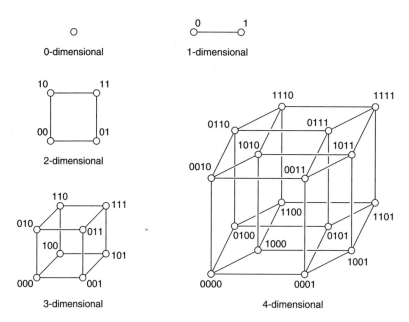

Figure 2.41
Hypercube Topology

extra links must be added on. The first option makes small machines unnecessarily expensive, while the second is expensive or impossible with present manufacturing technology.

Most of the commercial multicomputers built in the 1980s were meshes or hypercubes. As the development of new methods of routing messages (discussed in Section 2.5.8) has made graph diameter less important than it used to be, the popularity of hypercubes has peaked, and most new machines use some other topology. Two examples of this are Thinking Machines Corporation's CM-5 Connection Machine, and Meiko's CS-2 Computing Surface, both of which use a *fat tree*. A fat tree is one in which the thickness of the links between levels grows in proportion to the tree's height; equivalently, one can think of each node above the first level being replicated an increasing number of times, in order to increase the bandwidth near the tree's root (Figure 2.42). It can be shown that fat trees have many of the good properties of hypercubes and other logarithmic networks, but are more efficient in chip area and interconnection cost [Leiserson 1985].

An intermediate step between meshes and hypercubes which keeps the number of links per node constant but achieves a logarithmic growth in diameter is a topology called *cube-connected cycles (CCC)*. A $\mathcal{D}$-dimensional CCC is a $\mathcal{D}$-dimensional hypercube, each of

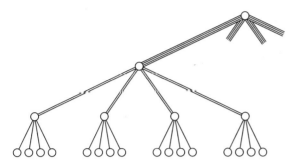

Figure 2.42
A Fat Tree

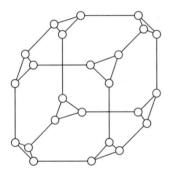

Figure 2.43
Cube-Connected Cycles

whose nodes actually contains $\mathcal{D}$ processors (Figure 2.43). These processors are connected in a ring, with one extra link per processor to connect the ring to other rings. If more links are available on each processor, each node can contain fewer processors (or equivalently the CCC can have a higher dimension). CCCs have good link loading and bisection bandwidth, low diameter, and are fairly straightforward to construct, but simpler topologies like meshes and rings cannot be embedded in them as easily as in hypercubes.

Another topology which deserves mention is the *random graph*: $\mathcal{P}$ processors with valence α, connected in a completely random way (but without two processors being connected twice). On average, the result is a graph whose diameter is proportional to $\log \mathcal{P}$, and which has the same loading and bisection bandwidth properties of a hypercube [Prior et al. 1990], but only uses a small, fixed number of links per node.

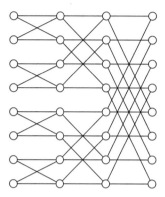

Figure 2.44
Butterfly Network

Random graphs are usually ignored for the same reason as CCCs. It is difficult to embed the regular meshes of most physical science applications in them, and difficult to analyze the performance of routing algorithms for them. However, on a computer whose topology can easily be changed, it may make sense to configure the available processors as a random graph for applications which do not have a natural geometric structure. A more significant drawback is that it is more difficult to construct provably correct algorithms for routing messages on random graphs than on regular graphs such as meshes, as will be discussed in Section 2.5.8.

The final class of topologies which are important to computer architects is the family of multi-stage interconnection networks which includes the Omega network [Lawrie 1975], the *shuffle-exchange network* [Stone 1971], and others; [Leighton 1991] is a good introduction to their similarities and differences. One example of this class is the *butterfly* network, shown in Figure 2.44. As with hypercubes, it is easiest to build butterflies recursively. Two nodes can be joined to two others in a single hop using two links per node. Four nodes can be joined to four others in two hops using one layer of intermediate nodes with two input and two output links each. Eight nodes can be joined to eight others in three hops using two layers of intermediate nodes, and so on. In practice, one set of nodes is usually the machine's processors, the other set its memories, and the intermediate nodes are simply switches.

The resulting graph has several interesting properties. First, there is a unique path from any node on the left to any node on the right. Second, while the number of links and intermediate nodes grows quickly, the number of hops only grows logarithmically. Third, the fact that the paths of all messages travelling to the same right-hand node eventually cross can be used to reduce contention by combining messages, as will be discussed in Section 4.2.2.

A butterfly in which interior nodes are simple switches has the same weakness as a hypercube: as the number of "useful" nodes increases, the proportion of hardware invested in communication also increases. One way around this is to make every node in the butterfly a processor-memory pair. The resulting topology has several interesting theoretical properties, which are mentioned in Section 2.5.9.

Several other topologies deserve mention. The first is the crossbar, discussed and discarded in Section 2.1.5. A crossbar connects M and N components of different types using MN switches. This large number of switches makes it too expensive to use in most large systems.[11] Another interesting topology is a generalization of the hypercube called the k-ary n-cube. Properly speaking, the hypercubes introduced above were binary hypercubes, in that they only had two processors along each axis. A k-ary n-cube extends this to k processors on each axis, in n dimensions.

Embedding Topologies   A central preoccupation of computer science is how to make one type of machine emulate another. In parallel computing, this often appears in a particularly specialized form: given a real machine with one topology, but a problem whose data structures naturally have a different topology, how can the latter be mapped to the former so that most operations are efficient? [Leighton 1991] contains considerable material on embedding; here, we will look at the particular case of embedding chains in meshes and hypercubes, and meshes in hypercubes.

A chain consists of a sequence of nodes $n_1, n_2, \ldots, n_N$, such that n_i is connected to n_{i-1} and n_{i+1} for $2 \leq i \leq N - 1$, and the left-most and right-most nodes are connected only once. A mesh, on the other hand, consists of a set of nodes $m_{x,y}$ for $1 \leq x \leq D_x$ and $1 \leq y \leq D_y$. Each interior point is connected to four others, each edge point to three, and each corner to two. As Figure 2.45 shows, it is easy to embed a chain in a mesh with the same number of nodes by repeated folding, so that adjacent nodes in the chain are still adjacent in the embedding. Provided the length of at least one of the mesh's axes is even, it is also possible to embed a closed ring in a similar manner.

Embedding a chain in a hypercube is a bit more complicated. The trick is to use a *Gray code* to order the hypercube's nodes. A Gray code is an ordering of the 2^n values from 0 to $2^n - 1$, such that each value differs from its predecessor and successor in exactly one bit location. Two possible 8-bit Gray codes are:

---

11. Although some machines, such as Fujitsu's VPP, take a "damn the expense" view and do employ a crossbar.

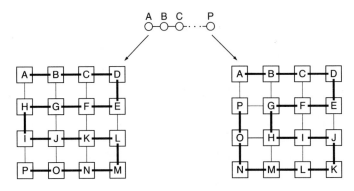

Figure 2.45
Embedding a Chain or Ring in a Mesh

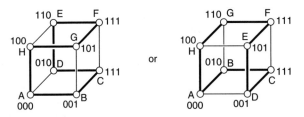

Figure 2.46
Gray Code Embedding in a Hypercube

000   001   011   010   110   111   101   100

and:

000   010   011   001   101   111   110   100

If each bit pattern is interpreted as an integer, then these values can be used to label a three-dimensional hypercube's nodes. What is more, since a hypercube node is connected to exactly those nodes whose addresses differ from its own in one bit location, any Gray code ordering of nodes is a list of adjacent nodes. Thus, a chain or ring of 2^n nodes can be embedded in a hypercube simply by threading it according to a Gray code sequence. Figure 2.46 shows the embeddings of an 8-node chain in a 3-cube which are generated by the Gray codes given above.

To see how to embed a mesh in a hypercube, we again start by arranging the hypercube's nodes in Gray code order. We then take advantage of the fact that if a Gray code is folded

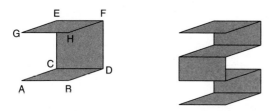

Figure 2.47
Embedding a 2-Dimensional Mesh in a Hypercube

in half, the values which are now adjacent always differ in exactly one bit position; for example, if the second of the Gray codes shown above is folded, the result is:

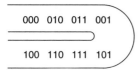

Thus, a 2×4 mesh can be mapped onto a 2^3 hypercube in such a way that nodes which were adjacent in the mesh are still adjacent in the hypercube (Figure 2.47). This technique generalizes to three dimensions; the trick is to impose a snake-like ordering on each layer, and then connect the end points of each layer's snake to those of the layers above and below, in such a way that the direction of traversal is reversed in each layer. Like hypercubes themselves, the result is harder to draw than to build.

2.5.8 Moving Information Around

Inter-process communication is relatively straightforward in shared-memory systems— one process writes data to a specified location, which one or more other processes subsequently read. There are many ways to ensure that reading does not happen until writing is finished; several of these are discussed in Chapter 4.

Inter-process communication is more difficult in disjoint-memory systems. In these cases, processes must explicitly send messages to one another, or to an intermediate mailbox of some kind. Again, this is relatively easy to do if the communication medium is shared, i.e., if some sort of bus or broadcast network is used, which sends every message to every possible destination. In a bus-based multiprocessor, for example, each processor (or a co-processor attached to it) can continually monitor the bus for messages which it is supposed to read, and copy them into its local memory.

As has been mentioned several times, the performance of such simple systems is eventually limited by the bandwidth of the bus. For this reason, almost all large parallel computers consist of a graph of point-to-point links through which messages can be forwarded. The sections below describe some of the techniques which have been developed for *routing* messages efficiently through such graphs.

Message-Passing Methods   The oldest and simplest message routing strategy is called *packet switching*. Using this strategy, the whole of the message is forwarded from its sender to the first intermediate node in its path, where it is stored in a temporary storage area called a *buffer* (Figure 2.48). Once the whole message has arrived, the intermediate node forwards it to the next node, and so on. Packet switching is used in many local-area and wide-area networks, including the Internet. Most early multicomputers, including first-generation hypercubic multicomputers and transputer-based machines, used it as well.

In the absence of other message traffic, the time taken for a packet-switched message of ℓ bytes to travel d hops can be represented as:

$$t_{ps} = \alpha + 2\beta\ell + \gamma d + \delta\ell d \tag{2.1}$$

where:

α is a fixed startup latency;

β is the message copying cost per byte;

γ is the overhead per link; and

δ is the transmission time per byte through each link

Here α represents the cost of initiating any messaging operation, i.e., of calling the message-passing system, creating whatever information that system needs in order to route the message to the correct destination, and so on. It can be thought of as the time required to send nothing nowhere. The term $2\beta\ell$ represents the time required to copy the message from the sending process into one of the message-passing system's buffers, and to copy it out again at the receiving end; β is therefore inversely proportional to the bandwidth between node memory and the communication network. In a sophisticated system, one or the other of these costs may be zero, as the system may be able to transfer the message directly out of a process's memory at one end, and directly into another process's memory at the other.

The third cost parameter, γ, is the time taken by the system at each hop to determine what to do next. This may involve choosing the next direction for the message, getting the attention of whatever piece of hardware is responsible for managing the appropriate link, and so on. Finally, δ is simply the reciprocal of the bandwidth of the communication links,

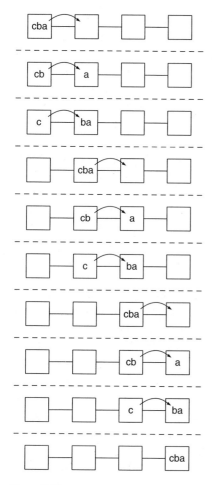

Figure 2.48
Packet Switching

so that $\delta\ell$ is the time taken to send the message across a single link, and $\delta\ell d$ the time to send it across d links.

Unfortunately, the time required to send a message in any real system is likely to be much larger than the time given by Equation 2.1. The main reason for this is that it is very rare for only one message to be in transit at a given time. In practice, messages will quite often have to wait for the link they need to become free before they can move forward. The time spent waiting depends on the amount and pattern of other message traffic, but quickly comes to dominate the total transmission time as the load on the system increases.

While this is a problem that all message-forwarding strategies face, packet switching has other drawbacks as well. One of the most important of these is the amount of buffer space needed at each intermediate node. To be safe, a system must provide enough buffer space to hold all of the messages which might be passing through it at any instant. The problem with this is that it may not be possible to put an upper bound on the number or size of messages the system might instantaneously contain.

One way to tackle this problem is to forbid a process from sending a second message until it has received some acknowledgment that its first message has been received. Such a transfer-acknowledge protocol automatically guarantees that the number of active messages in the system is bounded by the number of processes. However, protocols such as these increase the total time taken to complete a message transfer, since the distance information travels during the operation is effectively doubled from the sender's point of view (not to mention the increased likelihood of either the original message or the acknowledgment being delayed in transit).

The performance of TA can be improved by allowing the system to break each message into one or more packets of a fixed (and usually relatively small) size, so that it can forward the packets one by one. These can then be re-assembled once they reach the original message's destination. One advantage of doing this is that different packets can be sent in different directions in order to lessen the load on particular communication links. For example, Figure 2.49 shows how the four packets making up a message travelling across a mesh could be sent along four different paths to reduce the load on the most heavily-used link. An even more sophisticated approach is to route packets *adaptively*, i.e., to have the message choose its path as it goes along, based on the load it encounters at each intermediate node [Duato 1991]. While adaptive strategies often lead to packets arriving in an order different from the one in which they were sent, it is relatively straightforward to re-arrange them while copying them into the destination process's memory.

One way to reduce both the time required to send a message, and the amount of buffer space required while forwarding it in a lightly-loaded system, is to use *virtual cut-through* [Kermani & Kleinrock 1979] instead of packet switching. Consider the situation shown in Figure 2.50, in which a message has reached an intermediate node, and the link which it will use on its next hop becomes idle. Instead of putting the rest of the message into a buffer, the system can start to forward the front of the message while the tail is still arriving. If this is done at several intermediate nodes, it can lead to the message being strung out along several links simultaneously.

If every step is pipelined in this fashion, the time required to transmit the message is proportional to $\delta(\ell + d - 1)$ rather than $\delta\ell d$, i.e., to the sum of the message length and

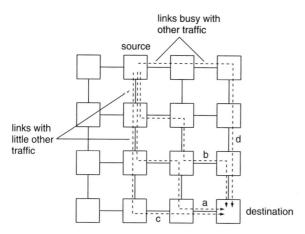

Figure 2.49
Adaptive Routing

the number of hops, rather than their product. However, in the worst case the time is still that given by Equation 2.1 since the message could be blocked, and need buffering, at each intermediate node. Thus, while virtual cut-through can deliver higher performance in lightly-loaded networks, a secure implementation requires as much buffer space as packet switching.

The most popular message-forwarding strategy today takes virtual cut-through one step further. A system which uses *wormhole routing* behaves like a system using virtual cut-through, except that messages are not allowed to accumulate at intermediate nodes. If a message is blocked at a node, and cannot proceed, then all of the links it is using are held, and none of the packets behind the head are forwarded (Figure 2.51). Only once the tail of the message has advanced through a link is that link freed for use by another message.

In a lightly-loaded system, wormhole routing performs just as well as virtual cut-through, i.e., the time taken to transmit a message is proportional to the sum of the message's length and the number of links traversed. In a heavily-loaded system, wormhole routing will tie up more links for a longer time than virtual cut-through, and thus the time lost due to link contention is likely to be greater. On the other hand, the buffering requirements of a system using wormhole routing are small, and can be determined in advance. What is more, these requirements do not increase as the number of processors in the system is increased, so that a single uniform implementation can be used in computers of arbitrary size. This uniformity is what has made wormhole routing so popular—from a VLSI designer's point of view, its needs are fixed, and can easily be accommodated on a

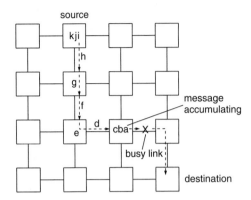

Figure 2.50
Virtual Cut-Through

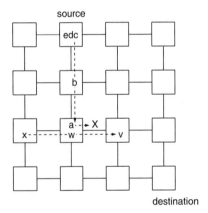

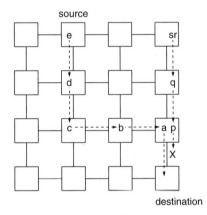

(a) message abcde blocked because next
    link is being used by message vwx

(b) message abcde now blocks
    message pqrs

Figure 2.51
Wormhole Routing

single chip, while the needs of virtual cut-through and packet switching may grow with the size of the computer being constructed.

The popularity of wormhole routing is one reason why the mesh topology has become more popular than the hypercube. Imagine two machines containing 16 processors each, arranged in either a 4×4 mesh or a 2^4 hypercube. Because of physical constraints, it is realistic to suppose that the connectivity of any two halves of each machine is the same,

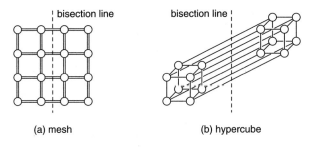

Figure 2.52
Comparing Meshes and Hypercubes

i.e., that the bisection bandwidth of each graph is constant. For the hypercube, this allows 8 processor-to-processor links, as shown in Figure 2.52. The mesh, on the other hand, only needs half as many links, so each can be made twice as thick. Thus, given the same packaging constraints, the processor-to-processor data rate of the mesh in this example can be twice that of the rate in the hypercube. The compensating benefit of the hypercube is its lower diameter, but, as we have seen, diameter is not particularly important in a wormhole-routed system. Thus, given a choice between many low-bandwidth links or a smaller number with greater bandwidth, many architects have used the latter.

Choosing a Path

The best way to cure deadlock is to pull the power cord out of the wall.
—Kevin Lind

All of the discussion of message routing so far has glossed over the problem of choosing a path to get a message from one processor to another. In fact, this has been one of the most intensively-researched subjects in parallel computing, because bad routing choices can lead not only to low performance, but also to system failure.

The reason bad routing decisions can lead to low performance is easy to understand. As they travel, messages compete with one another for buffers and for access to links. Such contention can arise coincidentally when two messages happen to be in the same place at the same time, or repeatedly because of some feature of the program which is generating those messages. For example, if every process in a program repeatedly needs to send a message describing its status to a single collection point, the links around that collection point are likely to be congested.

The reason why bad routing decisions can lead to system failure can be summed up in one word: *deadlock*. In any real multicomputer, both the amount of buffer space and the

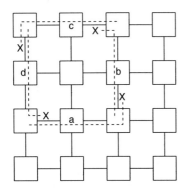

Figure 2.53
Deadlock in a Message-Routing System

number of links are finite. If either resource becomes saturated, it is possible for messages to "gridlock," i.e., for a situation to arise in which message A cannot move until message B moves, but message B is waiting for message C to move, and message C is blocked by message D, which is in turn blocked by message A (Figure 2.53). Once a single link is locked up in this fashion, messages which are supposed to use that link can start backing up on other links, until eventually the whole computer freezes.

To put this on a more formal basis, suppose that the routing system is described as a directed graph, in which nodes represent resources such as buffers and links, and edges represent possible dependencies. The edge (r_1, r_2) exists if and only if a message could need to acquire resource r_2 after having acquired resource r_1. In a wormhole-routed system, for example, the nodes of the dependence graph would represent the links connecting processors, while an edge would connect two links' nodes if a message arriving on one link could need to go out the other.

Given this representation, a necessary and sufficient condition for deadlock to be possible is that the dependence graph contains one or more cycles, i.e., that it contains one or more sequences of the form $\{(g_1, g_2), (g_2, g_3), \ldots, (g_N, g_1)\}$. If such a cycle exists, and if each resource on the cycle has been claimed at the same time, then none of the messages involved can move forward, and the system has deadlocked. For example, consider the 4-processor ring shown in Figure 2.54a. If the routing algorithm always sends messages clockwise, then the dependence graph is as shown in Figure 2.54b. As can be seen, if every processor tries to send a message to the processor two places clockwise from it, every link becomes occupied, and so no message can proceed.

The solution to this problem, first proposed in [Dally & Seitz 1987], is to impose an ordering on inter-processor links so that no cyclic dependencies can arise. On a mesh,

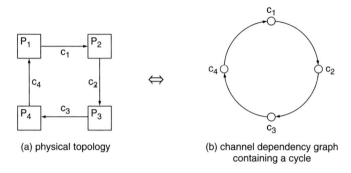

Figure 2.54
A Dependence Graph for a Message-Routing System

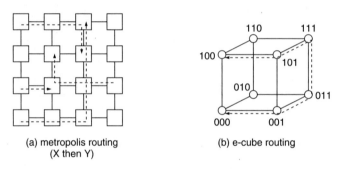

Figure 2.55
Dimensional Routing

this can be done by routing every message along the X axis, then along the Y axis (Figure 2.55a). This algorithm is usually called *Metropolis routing*. On a hypercube, a similar technique called *e-cube routing* orders the axes of the hypercube, and routes a message along those axes according to the bit-wise difference between the ID of its origin and destination. For example, if node 3 (011) in the 3-dimensional cube of Figure 2.55b wishes to send a message to node 0 (000), it first calculates the difference between the two node IDs (011), and then routes the message along axis 2 (010) and axis 1 (001) in that order. If node 3 wished to send a message to node 4 (100), it would route it along axis 3 (100), then axis 2, then axis 1.

But what about the 4-processor ring mentioned earlier? In cases such as this, it is often useful to make a distinction between the physical links which connect processors, and the logical *channels* which carry information through them. We can then multiplex two or

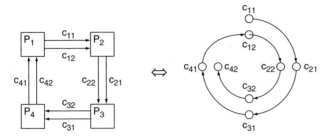

Figure 2.56
Eliminating Dependencies Using Virtual Channels

more *virtual channels*, over a single physical link, and break dependence cycles by constraining which messages can use which virtual channels. If every physical link in the ring carries two virtual channels, for example, then the dependence graph of Figure 2.54b can be replaced by the one in Figure 2.56. This has been made cycle-free by making the channel on which a message leaves a processor dependent on its final destination: messages to higher-numbered processors would use high-numbered channels, while messages to lower-numbered processors would use low-numbered channels. A message from processor 1 to processor 3, for example, would have to use channel $c_{1,2}$ and then channel $c_{2,2}$, while messages from processor 3 to processor 2 would use channels $c_{3,1}$, $c_{4,1}$, and $c_{1,1}$. Implementing virtual channels simply involves providing one buffer for each virtual channel, and interleaving individual *flits*, or message packets, across the link. Such interleaving does not generally make message transmission any slower, since if there is not a message waiting to use one virtual channel, the other can be given all the available bandwidth.

In order for these routing algorithms to be useful, it must be possible to translate them into simple rules which can be executed very quickly on each node as the head of a new message arrives. The e-cube algorithm for hypercubes can simply perform an exclusive-or between the node's own ID and the ID of the message's destination, find the most significant 1 bit, delete it, and send the message along that link. The Metropolis algorithm, on the other hand, can be implemented by comparing (x_d, y_d), the coordinates of the message's destination, with the coordinates (x_i, y_i) of the intermediate node when it reaches that node. If $x_d \neq x_i$, then the message is routed in either the positive or negative X direction; otherwise, it is routed in the Y direction until it reaches its destination. On more complicated topologies, more sophisticated strategies for selecting an outgoing link from an intermediate node may be necessary. [Ni & McKinley 1993] is a good survey of these, and of other routing-related issues.

One other routing technique which deserves mention is *two-phase random routing*. Rather than sending messages directly to their destinations, random routing sends each message to a randomly-selected intermediate node, from which it then travels on to its final destination. This might seem a silly idea, but it has been shown [Mehlhorn & Vishkin 1984] that the single level of indirection is enough to prevent contention from arising in all but the most improbable cases. On a hypercube of $\mathcal{P}$ processors, for example, random routing can deliver $\log \mathcal{P}$ one-to-one permutations of $\mathcal{P}$ values in $\mathcal{O}(\log \mathcal{P})$ time with overwhelming probability. Thus, provided there are more messages than processors, this technique yields optimal efficiency. One reason why this particular case is of interest is discussed in the next section.

All of the routing techniques discussed above are *oblivious*, which means that messages are always routed the same way, regardless of local conditions. On regular topologies, the routing decisions required by such methods can be encoded very compactly using a technique called *interval routing* [Van Leeuwen & Tan 1987]. This assigns integer IDs to nodes in such a way that each link out of a node can be labelled with a contiguous interval of ID values. Routing is then done at each node by finding which interval a message's destination ID falls into, and sending it through the corresponding link. A variety of adaptive routing techniques, which re-route messages to reduce network contention, have also been proposed [Duato 1991]; however, these tend to be more difficult to implement in hardware.

2.5.9   PRAM Emulation and Parallel Slackness

The final topic in this section is a theoretical model of parallel computation called the *parallel random access machine (PRAM)*. The PRAM is descended from the RAM (random access machine), a model used by complexity theorists to evaluate the efficiency of different algorithms. A RAM has two parts: a processor which can execute one operation, test, or branch per unit time, and an infinite, uniformly-accessed memory, each of whose cells stores a single value. A PRAM is simply a RAM containing an arbitrary number of processors, each of which can access the infinite shared memory in unit time (Figure 2.57).

Since its introduction in the 1970s [Fortune & Wyllie 1978], the PRAM has been a favorite vehicle for parallel algorithm designers; [Akl 1989] contains a good introduction to the design and analysis of algorithms for this model. Unfortunately, the relationship between the PRAM model and physically-realizable machines is at best tenuous. The reason lies in the assumption that every processor can access the memory simultaneously in unit time. Even in machines organized as hypercubes, or around multi-stage interconnection networks, the number of hops a message must take between its source and its destination

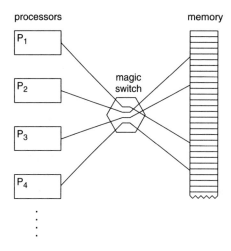

Figure 2.57
The Parallel Random Access Machine Model

grows logarithmically with the machine's size. As a result, any buildable computer experiences a logarithmic slowdown relative to the PRAM model as its size increases, even before the effects of link and memory contention are taken into account.

Parallel programmers often find that many of the algorithms developed by theoreticians cannot behave as promised on any hardware which can be built. As a result, many researchers have investigated ways of emulating PRAMs on more practical architectures. One of the most influential of these has been Leslie Valiant [Valiant 1988, Valiant 1990], whose arguments are summarized in [Skillicorn 1990]. Valiant advocates taking advantage of cases in which there is more parallelism in a program than in the hardware on which it is running, so that each physical processor emulates many virtual processors. He calls this *parallel slackness*, and proposes to take advantage of it through processor overloading (Section 2.5.2). The basic idea is that while one process is waiting for a reply to a message it has sent, other processes can be scheduled to do some useful work. Figure 2.58 shows an example in which one process, labelled A, sends a request for information to another processor, and is then taken off its own processor's scheduling queue for one hundred cycles. During that time, processes B to F each get twenty cycles of useful CPU time. If any of them were to generate messages during this interval, they would similarly be de-scheduled.

Valiant studied the efficiency with which various physically-realizable architectures could emulate the PRAM. In this, he relied on a theorem given in [Mehlhorn & Vishkin 1984] which states that:

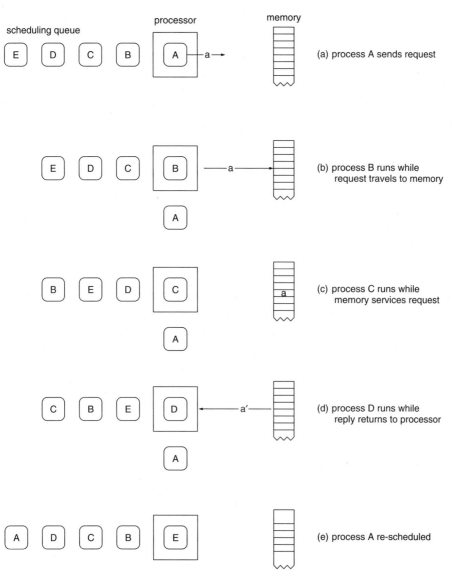

Figure 2.58
Exploiting Slackness in a Message-Passing System

1. if each of $\mathcal{P}$ processors sends a single message to a randomly-selected partner, it is highly probable that at least one processor will receive $\mathcal{O}(\frac{\mathcal{P}}{\log\log\mathcal{P}})$ messages, and some others will receive none; but

2. if each processor sends $\log\mathcal{P}$ messages to randomly-selected partners, then there is a high probability that no processor will receive more than $3\log\mathcal{P}$ messages.

Thus, it would seem that if problem size is increased at least logarithmically faster than machine size, efficiency can be held constant. Unfortunately, this result only holds for networks such as hypercubes and MINs, in which the number of communication links also grows logarithmically with the number of processors. Several ways around this limitation for this have been suggested. One is Valiant's own XPRAM model, in which the computation is broken up into steps, such that no processor may communicate more than a certain number of times per step. While programs which fit this model can be emulated efficiently on networks such as meshes, it is difficult to design algorithms in which the frequency of communication decreases as the problem size increases.

Other alternatives which have been proposed include restricting the allowed set of computations to those which can be emulated efficiently (e.g., the Bird-Meertens formalism suggested by Skillicorn in [Skillicorn 1990], or the scan-vector model of [Blelloch 1990]), and modifying the PRAM model to account for the relative distance of different portions of memory (as exemplified by [Vitter & Nodine 1993] and its antecedents). Another option is the scheme proposed in [Ranade 1991], which uses a butterfly network in which each node is a processor/memory pair, rather than just a switch. The protocol for routing messages is complicated—each message makes several passes forward and backward across the whole length of the network, and nodes must sort messages as they go by—but the end result is an optimal PRAM emulation. It remains to be seen which, if any, of these ideas will be adopted by the parallel computing community at large.

3 Data Parallelism

This chapter introduces data parallelism, which is one of the simplest forms of parallelism to understand and use. Data parallelism exploits the fact that many programs apply the same operation to each element of a composite data structure, such as an array or list, before applying any other operation to any other data structure. In a serial language, a programmer must specify not only the operation and the data structure, but also the form of repetition: loops over arrays, recursion over lists, and so on. In a data-parallel language, on the other hand, such repetition is done automatically, either by having multiple processors perform operations on different structure elements concurrently or by having the compiler or run-time system introduce serial repetition based on the nature of the operation and the size and shape of the data structure.

The main advantage of the data parallel programming model is that it can make programs easier to write and to read. In mathematics, for example, one simply writes $A = B + C$ to indicate that corresponding elements of the two arrays B and C are to be added together. As the order in which this is done is unimportant, it can be left unspecified. Data-parallel languages similarly allow programmers to concentrate on what is to be done, leaving the specification of how it is to be accomplished to automatic tools.

One consequence of this is that programs written in data-parallel languages are potentially more portable than ones containing explicit loops and other control structures. The reason for this is that such structures are always machine-dependent: where the single processor in a conventional workstation might need to loop 1000 times to update the elements of a matrix, the ten processors in a medium-sized multiprocessor might only loop 100 times each, while most of the 10,000 or more processors in a large processor array might actually have nothing to do until the next calculation started. By leaving such control structures implicit, programmers allow compilers and run-time systems to do whatever is most appropriate for a particular machine.

The main drawback of the data-parallel model is the difficulty of expressing irregular or heterogeneous computations in it. Algorithmic decomposition, for example, cannot be implemented, since a pipeline's different stages usually need to execute different operations at the same time. Similarly, as the computations to be carried out on the elements of a composite data structure become more dependent on the values of those elements, or their past histories, data parallelism becomes less and less helpful. Some examples of this will be given in later sections.

Despite these shortcomings, data-parallel dialects of traditional imperative languages are increasingly popular on uniprocessors as well as parallel computers. The original data-parallel language, APL [ISO/DP 8485], was never widely adopted (in part because it had to be read right-to-left, and used Greek characters and other specialized symbols), but FORTRAN is now well on its way to becoming an array-based data parallel language [Metcalf & Reid 1989]. Similar evolutionary extensions to imperative languages such as

Dimension: a particular coordinate range in an array. A(10, 12) has 10 unique index values in its first dimension, and 12 in its second.

Extent: the number of index values an array has in a particular dimension. A(10, 12) has extents 10 and 12.

Range: the extent of an array in a particular dimension. A(10, 12) has a range of 1...10 in its first dimension; an array like X(-5:5) (which isn't allowed in FORTRAN-K) would have a range of −5...5.

Rank: the number of dimensions in an array. A(10, 12) has a rank of 2, x(8) has a rank of 1. By convention, scalars have a rank of 0.

Shape: the cross-product of an array's extents. A(10, 12) has shape 10 × 12.

Table 3.1
Array Terminology

C [Hatcher & Quinn 1991] and C++ [Lee & Gannon 1991], and to functional languages such as LISP [Hillis 1985], have also appeared.

The first section below introduces the basic operations of the data-parallel paradigm. The next section describes two special operations called reduction and parallel prefix, which can be applied to the whole of a structure. The section following looks at how to control the layout of data in a machine's memory, and why programmers might want to do this. The final section then takes a step back, and looks at what current-generation compilers can do to find and exploit data parallelism automatically. Table 3.1 defines some of the terms that will be used in this chapter when discussing arrays.

3.1 Basic Operations

The basis of data parallelism is to allow operations to be applied to the whole of composite data structures in a single step, e.g. to allow programmers to add matrices using:

```
real :: A(100,100), B(100,100), C(100,100)
   .
   .
   .
A = B + C
```

instead of:

```
real    :: A(100,100), B(100,100), C(100,100)
integer :: i, j
```

```
real      :: A(100, 100), V(20)
integer :: i, j
  .
  .
  .
do i = 1, 100, 2
  do j = 1, 100, 2
    if A(i, j) >= 0 then
      A(i, j) = A(i, j) - V(i/5)
    end if
  end do
end do
```

Program 3.1
A Short Candidate for Data Parallelism

```
  .
  .
  .
do i = 1, 100
  do j = 1, 100
    A(i, j) = B(i, j) + C(i, j)
  end do
end do
```

If all the data structures in a program have the same shape, e.g. are 100×100 matrices, and all operations are to be done on every element of every data structure, then transforming a loop-based program into a data-parallel one is straightforward: one simply removes both the loops and the subscripts. However, consider Program 3.1. There is scope for data parallelism here, since only a single operation (subtraction) is being applied to a single data structure (the array A), but the use of a stride of 2 in both loops, rather than the default stride of 1, means that only one quarter of A's elements are actually affected by subtraction. The if enclosed in the double loop makes matters even more complicated, as it further restricts the domain of the subtraction operation in a data-dependent way. Finally, while the V value subtracted from a particular A value is chosen in a well-determined fashion, the mapping involves compressing the values of A within each row, or, equivalently, expanding V by replacing each of its elements with five copies of itself (Figure 3.1). Describing the selection of elements from A, and the mapping of elements of V to them, requires some fairly sophisticated machinery.

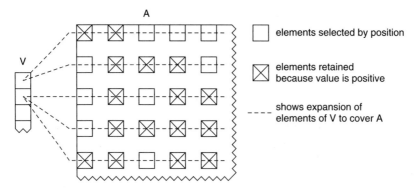

Figure 3.1
Operation of a Short Candidate for Data Parallelism

3.1.1   Describing Data Movement

If A and B are two arbitrary arrays with the same shape, then the assignment:

```
A = B
```

implicitly specifies an unambiguous one-to-one mapping of elements from B to A. Now suppose that A is a higher-dimensional structure than B, but that if one or more of A's dimensions were dropped, it would again have the same shape as B. While the direct assignment of B to A would not be meaningful, assigning B to a partially-specified component of A would. For example, suppose that A and B have been declared as:

```
real :: A(10, 20, 10), B(10)
```

By using a special symbol such as : to indicate that an array index has deliberately been left unspecified, a programmer could write:

```
A(4, 9, :) = B
```

or:

```
A(:, 17, 7) = B
```

since either would unambiguously select a single B-shaped portion of A (Figure 3.2). These assignments could obviously be turned around, and values copied from A into B with statements such as:

```
B = A(1, 3, :)
```

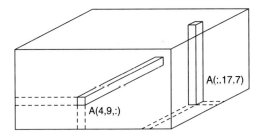

Figure 3.2
Selecting Columns out of a 3-Dimensional Array

```
B = A(:, 7, 9)
```

Such unspecified indices could also be used in arithmetic operations, as in:

```
A(2, 4, :) = A(:, 3, 1) + B
```

Here, the expression on the right-hand side selects a one-dimensional sub-structure from the matrix A, and adds the elements of B to it. The result is then put into another one-dimensional column of A which is oriented along a different axis. This operation is legal because the objects being manipulated all have the same shape, and the mapping between them is unambiguous. However, assignments such as:

```
A(1, 1, :) = A(2, :, 2) + B
```

are not legal because one of the objects being manipulated—A(2, :, 2)—has a different shape from the others. Another way to say this is that the two objects do not *conform* with one another.

Many operations can be expressed using nothing more than such implicit indexing. For example, consider the triply-nested loop of the usual matrix multiplication algorithm shown in Program 3.2a, which calculates $C_{i,j} = \sum_{k=1}^{N} A_{i,k} B_{k,j}$ in $\mathcal{O}(N^3)$ time. We can replace this loop nest with an $\mathcal{O}(N^2)$-time double loop whose inner-most operation is data-parallel, as shown in Program 3.2b. This operation effectively adds multiples of the rows of B to the rows of C.

Note the initialization expression C = 0 in the data-parallel code of Program 3.2b. This is an example of *scalar promotion*, and is allowed because a scalar can always be replicated to create something which conforms with any arbitrary array. The converse statement i = C, for some scalar i, is not allowed, because it does not contain a specification of how the multiple values in the array C are to be collapsed into a single value.

```
real    :: A(N, N), B(N, N), C(N, N)
integer :: i, j, k
  .
  .
  .
do i = 1, N
  do j = 1, N
    C(i, j) = 0
    do k = 1, N
      C(i, j) = C(i, j) + (A(i, k) * B(k, j))
    end do
  end do
end do
```
(a) sequential

```
C = 0
do i = 1, N
  do j = 1, N
    C(i, :) = C(i, :) + (A(i, j) * B(j, :))
  end do
end do
```
(b) data-parallel

Program 3.2
Matrix Multiplication

Most real applications require something more than just implicit indexing. To see why, consider Program 3.1 again. Neither the non-unit increments used in the two loops, nor the rule which matches every element of V against five adjacent elements of A, can be expressed just by omitting an array index. Another problem is that if arrays have the same size along several dimensions, there is no easy way for a programmer to specify which of the several legal mappings she wants. This problem is particularly acute when objects of different ranks are being manipulated together. For example, how should the assignment in:

```
real :: A(10, 10, 10), B(10, 10)
  .
  .
  .
A(5, :, :) = B
```

be interpreted? As Figure 3.3 shows, there are two ways of mapping B into the plane of A specified by fixing its first index. The first of these might seem the most natural, since it preserves the order of the axes within each array, but there is no reason to suppose that it

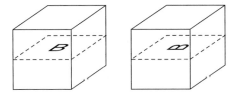

Figure 3.3
Mapping Planes into a 3-Dimensional Array

would always be the one desired. Trusting to the ordering of indices becomes even riskier in expressions such as:

```
real :: A(10, 10, 10, 10), B(10, 10, 10, 10)
   .
   .
   .
A(:, :, 1, :) = B(:, 1, :, :)
```

as it becomes less likely that the dimensions of the arrays involved correspond to the physical dimensions of some structure being modelled, and more likely that they are simply being used as a way of indexing the information in a table.

Striding and Shaping   Language designers have come up with many different solutions to the problem of mapping one array to another; [Sipelstein & Blelloch 1991] is a very good survey of the most important. However, many of the techniques it describes can only be used in very high-level languages. Data-parallel languages based on FORTRAN and C usually restrict themselves to providing two separate mechanisms. The first allows programmers to specify the *stride* which is to be used when indexing an array. Just as the control expression of a do loop may move from its initial to its terminal value in non-unit increments, so may a data-parallel array index be specified which selects a regularly-spaced subset of the elements along an axis. A program does this by separating the start, end, and increment values with colons, as in:

```
A(1:20:2, 2:20:4)
```

This expression selects the fifty elements of A whose first index is in the list $\{1, 3, 5, \ldots, 19\}$, and whose second is in $\{2, 6, 10, 14, 18\}$ (Figure 3.4).

It is important that the subscripts generated by such expressions are in fact ordered lists, rather than unordered sets. The reason is that without such ordering, the effect of operations combining elements from two or more structures would be unpredictable. This problem can arise even in minimalist examples such as:

Figure 3.4
An Example of the Use of Striding

```
integer :: X(2), Y(2), Z(2)
! X = (/1, 10/)
! Y = (/2, 20/)
  .
  .
  .
Z(1:2) = X(1:2) + Y(1:2)
```

If the indices generated by the 1:2 subscripts were not guaranteed to be ordered, this could lead to any of:

X indices	Y indices	Z indices	result
(1, 2)	(1, 2)	(1, 2)	(3, 30)
(1, 2)	(1, 2)	(2, 1)	(30, 3)
(1, 2)	(2, 1)	(1, 2)	(21, 12)
(1, 2)	(2, 1)	(2, 1)	(12, 21)
(2, 1)	(1, 2)	(1, 2)	(12, 21)
(2, 1)	(1, 2)	(2, 1)	(21, 12)
(2, 1)	(2, 1)	(1, 2)	(3, 30)
(2, 1)	(2, 1)	(2, 1)	(3, 30)

Since data-parallelism's greatest strength, compared to other programming models, is that it avoids non-determinism and unpredictability, almost all data-parallel systems would allow only the first of these eight cases to occur.

In general, any array index in FORTRAN-KDP may take the form:

start : *end* : *stride*

where *start* is one end of the range of values the "index" is to take on, *end* is the other, and *stride* is the stride to be used between them. If the stride is omitted, it is taken to be 1; similarly, if both the start and end values are omitted, they are taken to be the whole range of indices which are legal in that position. Thus, the expression:

```
integer :: A(20, 100)
  .
  .
  .
··· A(:, :) ···
```

selects every element of A, while:

```
··· A(:, 1:100:2) ···
```

selects half of those elements, and:

```
··· A(1:10:4, 1:100:2) ···
```

selects one eighth. A non-default stride field may only be included if both the starting and finishing values of the index range have been specified. The stride must be positive if the value of the end field is greater than that of the start field, and negative if it is less.

One key feature of the data-parallel model is that reading and writing are always indivisible, even when whole arrays are being read or written. To see what this means, consider the statement:

```
integer :: V(5)
! initialize V to (/100, 200, 300, 400, 500/)
V(2:4) = V(1:3) + V(3:5)
```

The intention here is clear: the middle values $(\cdots, 200, 300, 400, \cdots)$ in V should be overwritten to create $(100, 400, 600, 800, 500)$. However, if reading and writing on V were intermixed, the result could be equivalent to that produced by the serial loop:

```
do i = 2, 4
  V(i) = V(i-1) + V(i+1)
end do
```

This loop would fill V with (/100, 400, 800, 1300, 500/) because some values would be overwritten before they are read. Such overwriting does not happen in a data-parallel system; whenever a statement might modify variables, it behaves as though it had made a private copy of every value which it needed to read before it performed any writes. We will see examples in the next three chapters of what can happen when the programming system does not give this guarantee.

The second tool data-parallel languages provide for handling data movement is a way of re-arranging the layout of arrays. FORTRAN-KDP programs do this using the intrinsic function dp_shape. Its arguments are an array of rank R, followed by a list of R integers or strings (sometimes called a shape vector). The string elements of the shape vector must be a permutation of the integers in the range $1 \ldots R$; their order specifies that the contents of the array argument are to be re-arranged so that the values along the old axis i are now aligned along axis S_i. For example, if B is a two-dimensional matrix, then:

```
dp_shape(B, "1", "2")
```

would leave B unchanged, since it maps axis 1 to axis 1 and axis 2 to axis 2, but:

```
dp_shape(B, "2", "1")
```

would transpose B, since it maps axes 1 and 2 to each other (Figure 3.5).

Dimensional arguments to dp_shape are specified as strings because numerical arguments are used to indicate that an array is to be expanded by a specified amount along a new axis. Whenever a positive integer appears in a shape vector, it signals that the values of the dp_shape operator's array argument are to be replicated along the corresponding axis to create an object of a higher rank. For example, if V is a one-dimensional vector, then:

```
dp_shape(V, "1", 100)
```

and

```
dp_shape(V, 100, "1")
```

both create two-dimensional arrays: the first, by replicating the elements of V along rows, and the second, by replicating them along columns (Figure 3.6). The rule in such cases is that axes are re-arranged according to non-numerical values in the shape vector, and then replicated to create the larger object. Thus, in:

```
real :: A(40), B(100, 60, 40)
   .
   .
   .
B = dp_shape(A, 100, 60, "1")
```

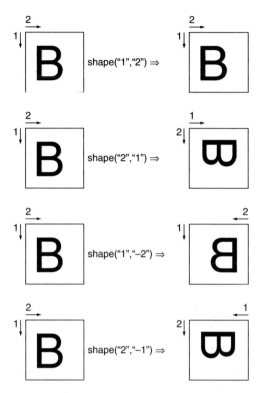

Figure 3.5
Reshaping Matrices Using `dp_shape`

A is aligned with B's third axis, then replicated by 100 in one direction and 60 in another, to create something which conforms with B. A negative axis index may also be specified. `dp_shape` interprets this to mean that the array is to be reversed along that axis. Note that the automatic promotion of scalars to arrays in expressions such as:

```
real B(100, 60, 40)
   .
   .
   .
B = 0.0
```

does not require a call to `dp_shape`, since such promotion is never ambiguous.

In practice, programmers do not change the ordering of an array's axes in most operations. By default, FORTRAN-KDP therefore maps objects in axis order in operations such as:

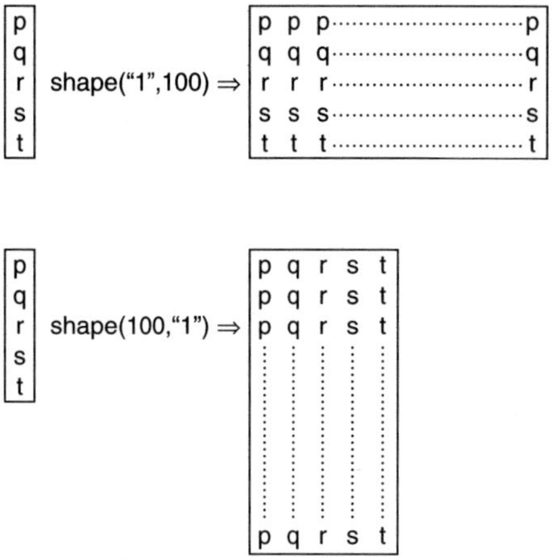

Figure 3.6
Replicating Values Using dp_shape

```
real :: A(10, 10), B(10, 10)
    .
    .
    .
A = A + B
```

The other useful default FORTRAN-KDP provides actually changes the rank of an array. If only a single index value is given along a particular axis, then that dimension effectively drops out, and the rank of the object being manipulated decreases by one. Thus, an expression such as:

```
real :: L(100, 64, 64), M(64, 64)
    .
    .
    .
L(37, :, :) = M
```

selects a two-dimensional plane from the three-dimensional array L, so that the assignment from M is conformant. Three-dimensional blocks can be selected from four-dimensional arrays, and so on, in the same fashion.

Striding and re-shaping can be mixed in many ways. For example, if a vector V and an array A are declared as:

```
real :: V(100), A(100, 100)
```

then:

- `A(1:100, 1:100) = dp_shape(V, 100, "1")` copies V into the rows of A;
- `A(:, :) = dp_shape(V, 100, "1")` has the same effect (since : on its own defaults to the entire index range);
- `A(1:100, :) = dp_shape(V(1:100), "1", 100)` copies V into the columns of A (note the change in the location of the value 100 in the shape vector given to dp_shape);
- `A(100:1:-1, :) = dp_shape(V(1:100), "1", 100)` copies V into the columns of A, but reverses the order of elements because of the downward stride specified in the subscript of A (remember, multi-valued indices are lists, rather than sets); and
- `A(1:100:2, 37) = V(1:50)` copies the first 50 elements of V into the odd-numbered elements of the 37th column of of A.

Because they can be so powerful, expressions involving both striding and re-shaping must be written carefully to ensure that they are correct and readable. For example, the two expressions:

```
A = dp_shape(A, "1", "2") - dp_shape(V, "1", 100)
```

and:

```
A = dp_shape(A, "2", "1") - dp_shape(V, 100, "1")
```

are both legal, and generate the same sets of values, but leave these values arranged in transposed order in A. The effect of more complicated expressions, such as:

```
real :: A(10, 5), B(10), thresh
    .
    .
    .
A(1:10:2, :) = (dp_shape(A(:, 2:10:2), "2", "1") .min. thresh) *
               0.5 * shape(B(6:10)**2, 5, "1")
```

can often only be worked out with the aid of a pencil and a piece of paper. This potential for obscurity is one of the prices of data-parallel languages' power; by compressing the notation used to describe operations, they can make those operations much harder to decipher.

Example 3.1 (Gaussian Elimination)   One of the most common operations in scientific programs is finding a vector x such that $Ax = b$ for some matrix A and some specified vector b. One efficient technique for doing this, called Gaussian elimination, was introduced in Section 2.3.4. The forward pass of this algorithm, given in Program 2.1a, is very simple to express in a data-parallel language. Each of the $N - 1$ iterations of the loop in the subroutine shown in Program 3.3a fixes another row and column of its input matrix, and

```
procedure gauss_fwd(A, B)
  real    :: A(:, :)                    ! matrix
  real    :: B(:)                       ! target vector
  integer :: i, j, k                    ! loop indices

  ! for each row . . .
  do k = 1, N-1
    ! calculate pivots in column k
    A(k+1:N, k) = A(k+1:N, k)/A(k, k)
    ! update elements below row k
    A(k+1:N, k+1:N) = A(k+1:N, k+1:N) -
                      (dp_shape(A(k+1:N, k), "1", N-k) *
                       dp_shape(A(k, k+1:N), N-k, "1"))
    ! update element of solution vector
    B(k+1:N) = B(k+1:N) - (A(k+1:N, k) * B(k))
  end do
end procedure
```
(a) forward pass

```
procedure gauss_bwd(A, B, X)
  real    :: A(:, :)                    ! matrix
  real    :: B(:)                       ! target vector
  real    :: X(:)                       ! solution vector
  integer :: i, j                       ! loop indices

  do i = N, 2, -1
    X(i) = B(i)/A(i, i)
    B(1:i-1:1) = B(1:i-1:1) - (A(1:i-1:1, i) * X(i))
  end do
  X(1) = B(1)/A(1, 1)
end procedure
```
(b) backward pass

Program 3.3
Data-Parallel Gaussian Elimination

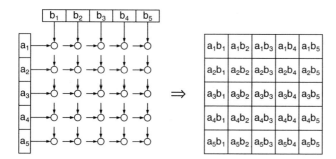

Figure 3.7
Outer Product

adjusts the values in the sub-matrix they dominate. Note how `dp_shape` is used to repli-cate the column and row values at right angles to one another, to create two $N - k$ matrices for element-wise multiplication (Figure 3.7). This operation is called an outer product, and creates a matrix M from two vectors x and y such that $M_{ij} = x_i y_j$. The backward pass of data-parallel Gaussian elimination is equally simple.

Shifting   The last indexing feature which a data-parallel language must support is *shift-ing*. This operation is like the bit-shifting found in some programming languages, but rather than moving the individual bits in a word to the left or right, it moves all the values in an array. As with bit shifting, array shifting comes in two flavors: *planar* and *circular*. The first of these moves values in one direction or another, throwing away values which have been shifted off the end of the array and filling the empty space at the other end with zeroes (Figure 3.8). A circular shift, on the other hand, uses the values which have spilled off one end to fill up the other.

As with alignment, there are many different ways of expressing shifting. One, which was used in earlier versions of FORTRAN-KDP but abandoned because of its implementation complexity, is to allow two more fields in every array subscript expression. These fields would specify the kind, direction, and amount of shifting along that axis. For example, the planar shift of Figure 3.8 would be expressed as:

```
A(1:4:1:p:2, 1:4:1:p:2)                ! no longer allowed
```

while the circular shift would be:

```
A(1:4:1:c:1, 1:4:1:c:-1)               ! no longer allowed
```

Here, p and c are used in field four of each index to indicate the type of shifting, while the direction is determined by the sign of the amount.

A second possibility would have been to provide separate functions to shift along each

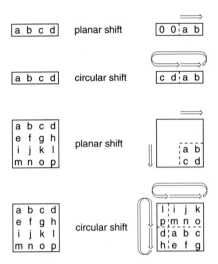

Figure 3.8
Shifting Operations

array axis, with names like `sh1c` (meaning "shift circular along first axis"). The obvious generalization of this is to provide one shifting function, which takes an array, an axis, a type of shift, and a signed value as arguments, and shifts the array along the specified axis. What FORTRAN-KDP actually provides is a generalization of this, in which shifting along all of an array's axes can be specified in a single call. The function `dp_shift` takes an array as its first argument, and returns an array of the same shape. `dp_shift`'s other arguments must be pairs made up of a `string` and an `integer`. The `string` must be one of:

"c" or "C"   circular shift

"p" or "P"   planar shift

"n" or "N"   no shift

The `integer` then specifies the direction and amount of shifting. The value given with a no-shift flag "N" is ignored; the absolute value of shift amounts given with circular or planar flags may be zero, but must be no greater than the extent of the array along that dimension. Returning once more to Figure 3.8, the two shifts shown there are expressed in FORTRAN-KDP by:

```
dp_shift(A, "p", 2, "p", 2)
```

and

```
dp_shift(A, "c", 1, "c", -1)
```

3.1.2 Parallel Conditional Statements

Even with the strides and shifts introduced so far, it is not possible to create a data-parallel implementation of Program 3.1. The problem is that the actions taken in this code fragment depend upon the values in the array A, but striding only takes into account the indices of array elements, not their values. What is lacking is a way to select array elements based on their value, and perform operations on them alone.

The where statement of most data-parallel languages does exactly this. A conventional if evaluates a logical expression, then executes a block of statements only if that expression is .true.. Similarly, a where executes a block of statements only in locations corresponding to .true. elements in an array of logical values. This behavior is sometimes called *masking*. For example, if A is an array of real values, then:

```
where A >= 0 do
  A = sqrt(A)
end where
```

only replaces an element of A with its square root if that element is non-negative. This statement is equivalent to, but much more elegant than, the conventional loop:

```
do i = 1, M
  do j = 1, N
    if A(i, j) >= 0 then
      A(i, j) = sqrt(A(i, j))
    end if
  end do
end do
```

Similarly, the values in A can be thresholded using:

```
where A < MIN_VAL do
  A = MIN_VAL
end where
where A > MAX_VAL do
  A = MAX_VAL
end do
```

In order to keep such code tidy, a `where` can be complemented with an `else`, or with `elsewhere`, just like an `if`. Thus, the thresholding example could be written:

```
where A < MIN_VAL do
  A = MIN_VAL
elsewhere A > MAX_VAL do
  A = MAX_VAL
end where
```

Going one step further, the elements of A could be updated depending on the values of a conformant array B:

```
where abs(A / B) < tolerance do
  A = epsilon * A + tolerance
else
  A = (A + (B / 2)) * epsilon
  where abs(A / B) < tolerance do
    A = tolerance
  end where
end where
```

In a nested `where` statement like this, the inner `where`'s effect is to narrow the domain on which the statement:

```
A = tolerance
```

takes effect, just as a nested `if` statement restricts the domain of the statements it controls. Nested `where`s always act cumulatively, each reducing the active set of array locations. For example, consider the pseudocode:

```
where X₁ do
  A₁
  where Y₁ do
    A₂
  end where
elsewhere X₂ do
  where Y₂ do
    A₃
  end where
  A₄
else
```

```
    A₅
    where Z₁ .or. Z₂ do
       A₆
    end where
end where
```

the actions A_1 to A_6 only take place where the following conditions hold:

A_1 X_1

A_2 X_1.and.Y_1

A_3 $(.not.X_1).and.(X_2.and.Y_2)$

A_4 $(.not.X_1).and.X_2$

A_5 $.not.(X_1.or.X_2)$

A_6 $(.not.(X_1.or.X_2)).and.(Z_1.or.Z_2)$

Determining what a parallel conditional expression actually does can be complicated if the arrays being manipulated have different ranks or sizes. For example, if A and B are declared as:

```
real :: A(10, 12), B(8, 8, 8)
```

then what is the effect of:

```
where A > 0 do
  B = 1.0
end where
```

FORTRAN-KDP resolves this by disallowing such operations whenever the arrays being manipulated do not conform to the mask set up by the where. However:

```
where shape((A(1:8, 1:8) > 0), "1", "2", 8) do
  B(1:8, 1:8, :) = 1.0
end where
```

is allowed, since the dp_shape converts the two-dimensional array of logicals resulting from the comparison into a three-dimensional mask which implicitly has the same size as B. The general rule in FORTRAN-KDP is that exactly one logical control value must correspond to each element of the arrays being manipulated. However, some other data-parallel languages allow non-conformant where controls, and either pad them with .false. when they are smaller than the arrays being manipulated, or select their least-significant elements when they are larger.

Now consider a slightly different case:

```
real :: A(10)
    .
    .
    .
where A(1:9:2) > 0 do
  A(2:10:2) = A(1:9:2)
end where
```

We could arbitrarily decide that a mask is always .false. for elements which have not been selected by striding. Such a default would mean that the elements A(2:10:2) in the example above would all be masked out, and that the operation would have no effect. However, such a rule would be a hindrance as often as a help. Instead, FORTRAN-KDP considers all masks to be normalized, i.e. compacted along each axis. This means that the where above generates the mask (/.true., .true., .true., .true., .true./), so all of the assignments to A(2:10:2) take effect.

The general rule in FORTRAN-KDP, as in most data-parallel languages, is that the masks created by where statements only disable writes and errors. Values can always be read from any part of any array, but the writing done by an assignment, or the occurrence of an arithmetic error, will only be visible where a where's mask is .true.. There is no deep theoretical justification for this convention; rather, it was a feature of the behavior of most first-generation processor arrays which survives in languages originally designed for such machines. While deeply-nested mixes of labelled striding and parallel conditional expressions can make programs unreadable, most programs do not nest wheres to more than one or two levels.

One last aspect of parallel conditional expressions which must be dealt with is their effect across function and subroutine call boundaries. Suppose that a program contains a subroutine flow_update, and that a call to it is nested inside a where, as in Program 3.4. The intention here is that the array flow should be updated only where the temperature is greater than freezing, but no information about the temperature has been explicitly passed to flow_update. In this case it would be helpful if conditional masks remained in effect across call boundaries; in other cases this would lead to very obscure bugs, as a mask set outside the body of a subroutine would affect the actions taken within that subroutine. In particular, leaving masks in place across function boundaries could make it very difficult to build robust, modular libraries.

In fact, FORTRAN-KDP and most other data-parallel languages do leave conditional masks in place across subroutine boundaries, even though this is annoying as often as it is

```
real :: flow(2000, 4000), temp(2000, 4000)
  .
  .
  .
where temp > Freezing_Point do
  call flow_update(flow, movement_thresh)
end where

procedure flow_update(flow, dx, dy, threshold)
  real :: flow(:, :)
  real :: dx, dy
  real :: threshold
  real :: flow_deriv(dx, dy)
  .
  .
  .
  call differentiate(flow, flow_deriv)
  where (flow < threshold) .or. (flow_deriv <= 0.0) do
    flow = 0.0
  else
    flow = flow * (1 + flow_deriv/flow)
  end where
end procedure
```

Program 3.4
Masking and Procedure Calls

helpful. A putative solution which some data-parallel languages offer is to allow programmers to re-set the activity mask arbitrarily at any point in their code, using a statement of
the form:

```
where .true. do
  statements
end where
```

However, this makes it difficult to define the effect of:

```
where A >= 0 do
  where .true. do
    B = 1.0
  end where
else
  B = -1.0
end where
```

An element of B corresponding to a negative element of A could be assigned either 1 or -1, depending on whether the initial where or the nested where executed last. Such non-determinism is exactly what makes parallel programming difficult, and is what data parallelism is supposed to preclude. A workaround which many programmers habitually use is to pass the current mask as a parameter to every subroutine, so that they can at least find out what its current contents are.

With where statements in our toolbox, we can finally parallelize Program 3.1. The original nested loops:

```
do i = 1, 100, 2
  do j = 1, 100, 2
    if A(i, j) >= 0 then
      A(i, j) = A(i, j) - V(i/5)
    end if
  end do
end do
```

operated on a matrix A(100, 100) and a vector V(20). The simplest thing to do is to move the conditional expression outside the loops, and turn those loops into strides. The expansion of V can then be handled using iteration, as in:

```
real     :: A(100, 100), V(20)
integer :: j
  .
  .
  .
where A >= 0 do
  do j = 1, 100, 20
    A(j:(j+20), :) = A(j:(j+20), :) - shape(V, "1", 100)
  end do
end where
```

Here, the j-indexed loop repeatedly selects 20 consecutive rows of A, while the dp_ shape call expands V to create a 20×100 object conformant with that selected block. If a program was doing this operation repeatedly, it would be more efficient to create a temporary matrix of the same size as A, and use repeated shifting to fill it with the values of B:

```
real :: temp(100, 100)
  .
  .
  .
```

```
temp(1:100:5, :) = shape(V, "1", 100)
temp(2:100:5, :) = temp(1:100:5)
temp(3:100:5, :) = temp(1:100:5)
temp(4:100:5, :) = temp(1:100:5)
temp(5:100:5, :) = temp(1:100:5)
```

It is tempting to try to make this code more compact by applying `dp_shift` to the left side of the assignments:

```
temp(1:100:5, :) = shape(V, "1", 100)
do i = 2, 5
  dp_shift(temp, "p", i) = temp(1:100:5)
end do
```

and in fact some systems would allow this, since `dp_shift` would not create a new array, but would instead return an alias of its argument. In FORTRAN-KDP, however, `dp_shift` is a proper function; storage for the result it returns is separate from the storage used by its argument. We achieve the desired effect by moving the stride to the left side:

```
temp(1:100:5, :) = shape(V, "1", 100)
do i = 2, 5
  temp(i:100:5) = temp(1:100:5)
end do
```

Note that the starting point for the subscript on the left is the loop index. Given this, the compiler and run-time system can shift data as required.

Example 3.2 (The Game of Life)   Data-parallel languages are good vehicles for implementing cellular automata, such as the Game of Life described in Section 2.3.2. In such implementations, the state of the CA at any time is represented by an array, each of whose elements corresponds to a single cell. In order to calculate the next state of the world, the program uses a sequence of shifts to align each cell's value with those of its neighbors. It then uses `where` statements to determine the next state of each cell. The code in Program 3.5 shows how this can be done.

Several features of Program 3.5 are worth noting. First, since each cell in the CA is either alive or dead, a `logical` array can be used to keep track of the world's state. In more complicated cellular automata, such as the fluid-flow CA described later, the number of cell states can be very large, and so the world would have to be represented using `integers`.

```
program
  logical :: world(N, N)                              ! world
  integer :: count(N, N)                              ! neighbor counts
  integer :: i, j, gen                                ! indices
  initialize world
  do gen = 1, Number_of_Generations
    call neigh_count(world, count)
    call world_update(world, count)
  end do
end program

procedure neigh_count(world, count)
  logical :: world(:, :)                              ! world to examine
  integer :: count(:, :)                              ! where to put counts

  count = 0
  where dp_shift(world, "c", 1, "n", 0) do   count = count + 1 end where
  where dp_shift(world, "c", 1, "c", 1) do   count = count + 1 end where
  where dp_shift(world, "n", 0, "c", 1) do   count = count + 1 end where
  where dp_shift(world, "c", -1, "c", 1) do  count = count + 1 end where
  where dp_shift(world, "c", -1, "n", 0) do  count = count + 1 end where
  where dp_shift(world, "c", -1, "c", -1) do count = count + 1 end where
  where dp_shift(world, "n", 0, "c", -1) do  count = count + 1 end where
  where dp_shift(world, "c", 1, "c", -1) do  count = count + 1 end where
end procedure

procedure world_update(world, count)
  logical :: world(:, :)                              ! world to update
  integer :: count(:, :)                              ! counts to use
  where (count == 3) .or. (world .and. (count == 2)) do
    world = .true.
  else
    world = .false.
  end where
end procedure
```

Program 3.5
Data-Parallel Life

Second, rather than writing out eight shifting expressions, this subroutine could store the required shifts in a table, and then loop over that table's entries:

```
type(string) :: shift_type(Number_of_Shifts, 2) =
               (/ "c", "n",
                  "c", "c",
                  .
                  .
                  .
                  "c", "c" /)
integer      :: shift_val(Number_of_Shifts, 2) =
               (/ 1,  0,
                  1,  1,
                  .
                  .
                  .
                  1, -1 /)
                  .
                  .
                  .
count = 0
do i = 1, Number_of_Shifts
  where dp_shift(world, shift_type(i, 1), shift_val(i, 1),
                        shift_type(i, 2), shift_val(i, 2)) do
    count = count + 1
  end where
end do
```

Shifting inside a loop could be less efficient than eight in-line shifting expressions, since the compiler might find it harder to optimize index expressions whose values are taken from arrays, but it would lead to more compact and readable code. We could make the code even more compact, with another slight loss of efficiency, using:

```
count = 0
do i = -1, 1
  do j = -1, 1
    if (i /= 0) .or. (j /= 0) then
      where dp_shift(world, "c", i, "c", j) do
        count = count + 1
      end where
    end if
  end do
end do
```

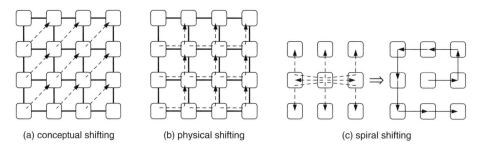

(a) conceptual shifting   (b) physical shifting   (c) spiral shifting

Figure 3.9
Removing Diagonal Shifts

Here, we rely on the fact that a circular "shift" of zero along an axis has no effect.

Optimizing a sequence of shifts such as this is best done after the program is working, and once the architecture of the target machine is known. For example, suppose that the target architecture is a processor array, whose processing elements are connected in a mesh or torus without diagonal connections. If the array `world` is mapped onto this in blocks (Figure 3.9a), every diagonal shift would actually require two shifting operations (Figure 3.9b). By making a copy of `world`, and shifting this in a spiral as shown in Figure 3.9c, the required number of physical (as opposed to logical) shifts can be reduced from 12 to 8. The subroutine in Program 3.6 shows how this is implemented. As before, these shifts can be represented in a variety of more compact forms.

Example 3.3 (Simulating Fluid Flow) The limits of pure data-parallel implementations of cellular automata, and of data parallelism in general, can be seen by looking at an implementation of a CA for modelling fluid flow. The first step in this is to represent the underlying 6-connected lattice of the CA using a 2-dimensional array, as shown in Figure 3.10, and to find a compact, efficient way to represent each cell's state. Inspection shows that the shifts required for cell (i, j) to get the values of its neighbors are:

	Even-Numbered Row	Odd-Numbered Row
up & left	$(i - 1, j)$	$(i - 1, j - 1)$
up & right	$(i - 1, j + 1)$	$(i - 1, j)$
left	$(i, j - 1)$	$(i, j - 1)$
right	$(i, j + 1)$	$(i, j + 1)$
down & left	$(i + 1, j)$	$(i + 1, j - 1)$
down & right	$(i + 1, j + 1)$	$(i + 1, j)$

```
procedure neigh_count(world, count)
  logical :: world(:, :)                          ! world to examine
  integer :: count(:, :)                          ! where to put counts
  logical :: temp(N, N)                           ! for constructing counts

  count = 0

  temp = dp_shift(world, "c", 1, "n", 0)
  where temp do count = count + 1 end where

  temp = dp_shift(temp, "n", 0, "c", 1)
  where temp do count = count + 1 end where

  temp = dp_shift(temp, "c", -1, "n", 0)
  where temp do count = count + 1 end where

  temp = dp_shift(temp, "c", -1, "n", 0)
  where temp do count = count + 1 end where

  temp = dp_shift(temp, "n", 0, "c", -1)
  where temp do count = count + 1 end where

  temp = dp_shift(temp, "n", 0, "c", -1)
  where temp do count = count + 1 end where

  temp = dp_shift(temp, "c", 1, "n", 0)
  where temp do count = count + 1 end where

  temp = dp_shift(temp, "c", 1, "n", 0)
  where temp do count = count + 1 end where

end procedure
```

Program 3.6
Data-Parallel Life with Fewer Shifts

(a) logical mesh

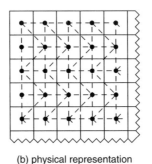
(b) physical representation

Figure 3.10
A 6-Connected Lattice for Fluid Flow Simulation

The obvious way to implement these shifts is to use a `where` statement to select even- and odd-numbered rows separately. The efficiency of this shifting will depend on the topology of the target machine (a mesh with diagonal links would clearly be better than one without), and on whether the compiler and run-time system can overlap shifting in different directions.

The next step is to decide how to represent each cell, and how to update its state given knowledge of the states of its neighbors. Once again, the most efficient representation depends on the nature of the target architecture. If it is made up of single-bit processing elements, like the DAP and CM-2 Connection Machine, the most sensible thing to do is to use six arrays of `logicals` (which can be implemented as single bits), and to store the state of each node's outgoing up/left link in one array, its up/right link in another, and so on. If the target machine is made up of conventional microprocessors, this could lead to each node requiring six bytes of storage, since `logicals` will probably be implemented using bytes. In this case, packing the state of several cells into a single `integer` and using bitwise operations on it may be the most space-efficient approach.

A second byte, or a second set of single-bit arrays, can then be used to accumulate each cell's neighbors' values. A subroutine to generate these values is shown in Program 3.7. This subroutine introduces a new intrinsic function called `dp_index`, which, when given an argument N, generates a vector containing the values $1 \ldots N$. Note that Program 3.7 has zero boundary conditions, i.e., no particles ever enter from the outside, since no values are ever shifted in to show particles arriving from "neighboring" cells outside the world. A real program would probably contain subroutines to introduce new particles at sources, and remove particles at sinks.

Once a code representing the relevant bits of each cell's neighbors' states has been generated, it is a simple matter to update the value of each cell using table lookup—simple,

```
integer, constant :: NX = world's x dimension
integer, constant :: NY = world's y dimension
integer, constant :: M_NW = Z'01'
integer, constant :: M_NE = Z'02'
integer, constant :: M_W  = Z'04'
integer, constant :: M_E  = Z'08'
integer, constant :: M_SW = Z'10'
integer, constant :: M_SE = Z'20'
    .
    .
    .
procedure neighbor_values(cells, neighs)
  integer :: cells(:,:)                          ! cells representing world
  integer :: neighs(_, _)                        ! neighbor values to fill
  logical :: mask(NX)                            ! activity mask

  ! set up masks and clear neighs
  mask = (dp_index(NX) .mod. 2) == 1
  neighs = 0

  where shape(mask, "1", NY) do                  ! odd-numbered rows
    neighs(2:NX, 2:NY)   = neighs(2:NX, 2:NY) .bitor.
                           (cells(1:NX-1, 1:NY-1) .bitand. M_NW)
    neighs(1:NX-1, 2:NY)  = neighs(1:NX-1, 2:NY) .bitor.
                           (cells(2:NX, 1:NY-1) .bitand. M_SW)
    neighs(2:NX, 1:NY)   = neighs(2:NX, 1:NY) .bitor.
                           (cells(1:NX-1, 1:NY) .bitand. M_NE)
    neighs(1:NX-1, 1:NY)  = neighs(1:NX-1, 1:NY) .bitor.
                           (cells(2:NX, 1:NY) .bitand. M_SE)

  else                                           ! even-numbered rows
    neighs(2:NX, 1:NY)   = neighs(2:NX, 1:NY) .bitor.
                           (cells(1:NX-1, 1:NY) .bitand. M_NW)
    neighs(1:NX-1, 1:NY)  = neighs(1:NX-1, 1:NY) .bitor.
                           (cells(2:NX, 1:NY) .bitand. M_SW)
    neighs(2:NX, 1:NY-1)  = neighs(2:NX, 1:NY-1) .bitor.
                           (cells(1:NX-1, 2:NY) .bitand. M_NE)
    neighs(1:NX-1, 1:NY-1) = neighs(1:NX-1, 1:NY-1) .bitor.
                           (cells(2:NX, 2:NY) .bitand. M_SE)
  end
```

Program 3.7
Data-Parallel CA Fluid Flow Simulation

```
!  do uniform operations
neighs(:, 2:NY)   = neighs(:, 2:NY) .bitor.
                        (cells(:, 1:NY-1) .bitand. M_W)
neighs(:, 1:NY-1) = neighs(:, 1:NY-1) .bitor.
                        (cells(:, 2:NY) .bitand. M_E)


end procedure
```

Program 3.7 *(continued)*
Data-Parallel CA Fluid Flow Simulation

but potentially very inefficient. Since each link either is or isn't carrying a particle into a cell, each cell can be in one of $2^6 = 64$ different states. A serial program could do the required updates using a 64-element table, as in:

```
do i = 1, NX
  do j = 1, NY
    cells(i, j) = table(neighs(i, j))
  end do
end do
```

Unfortunately, there is no simple equivalent to this loop in many data-parallel languages, including FORTRAN-KDP. To see why, consider what happens in a serial program when the expression:

```
table(neighs(i, j))
```

is evaluated. First, an index calculation is done to retrieve the value `neighs(i, j)`. Next, this value is used as an offset to the base address of the array `table` to generate the address of the new value for the cell. Finally, a value is loaded from this address and stored in the appropriate element of `cells`.

   This last step is the one that causes the problems. On SIMD machines such as the DAP or CM-2 Connection Machine, operand addresses are broadcast by the control processor in the same way as instructions. If different data processors are to access different values in their local memories, the control processor must broadcast each address separately; equivalently, the program must use a `where` statement to select appropriate processors, and loop over the possible addresses. As a result, the final step in this CA update must be:[1]

---

1. Note that while the table is indexed from 1, the possible states run from 0 to NUM_STATES-1, because the bit patterns generated by the shifting and or'ing shown earlier will lie in the range $0 \ldots (2^6 - 1)$.

```
integer, constant :: NUM_STATES = 64
integer, constant :: table(NUM_STATES) = (/ ··· /)
integer :: state
  .
  .
  .
do state = 0, NUM_STATES-1
  where cells = state do
    cells = table(state+1)
  end where
end for
```

The time to do each update this way is proportional to the number of states, no matter how many processors are used. If, on the other hand, a machine provides locally-calculated indirect addressing, it may be possible to use one vector as a subscript to another, i.e. to write:

```
Y = X(V)
```

where V, X, and Y are conformant. This expression uses the value of V at index i to determine which element of X to assign to element i of Y, and is equivalent to the loop:

```
do i = 1, N
  Y(i) = X(V(i))
end do
```

The Maspar MP-1 allows this because each data processor calculates its array addresses separately, and so can look up a different value in table. Many pipelined machines have special hardware support for this kind of indirection, and FORTRAN-90 allows one vector to be used as a subscript for another in some circumstances.

3.1.3 Permutation

Striding and re-shaping can describe regular data movements, but not arbitrary permutations of data. The shufflings required by the Fast Fourier Transform algorithm, for example, are very regular, but the rules describing them cannot be expressed in terms of counting from one value to another using a fixed increment [Kumar et al. 1993, Quinn 1994]. The shufflings required during sorting are not even regular, so some machinery is needed to allow programmers to specify completely arbitrary re-mappings.

In FORTRAN-KDP, *permutation* is done using the intrinsic function dp_push, which takes four arguments. The first is the name of the source array, from which values are read. The second is the array into which values are to be written, while the third is another

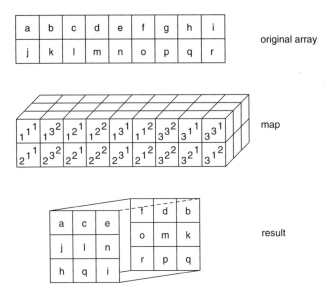

original array

map

result

Figure 3.11
Specifying a Mapping with an Array of Indices

array which specifies how those values are to be re-arranged. The final argument is a string specifying an operator, which tells dp_push what to do if several values are mapped into the same location in the destination. If this string is the assignment operator =, then values are simply copied from the source into the destination.

There are two ways in which the mapping from source locations to destination locations could be specified. In the first, which is more satisfying aesthetically, the map array would have the same shape as the source array, and each entry of the map array would completely specify the index of a location in the destination. The map array would accordingly either have the same rank as the source, if the destination was a vector, or a rank one greater than that of the source, so that the first R_s indices in the map array would correspond to the R_s indices in the source array, while the R_d values in the $(R_s + 1)^{\text{th}}$ dimension of the map array would specify the R_d co-ordinates of a location in the destination array. For example, to map the elements of a 2×9 array into a $3 \times 3 \times 2$ array would require a $2 \times 9 \times 3$ map array M: the value of M(i, j, k) would specify the kth co-ordinate in the destination matrix of the $(i, j)^{\text{th}}$ element of the source matrix (Figure 3.11).

The advantage of this method would be that interpreting the mapping matrix would be relatively straightforward. In order to generate a mapping from location $(s_1, \ldots, s_N)$ to location $(d_1, \ldots, d_M)$, a program would merely set mapvec($s_1, \ldots, s_N$, 1) to d_1, mapvec$(s_1, \ldots, s_N, 2)$ to d_2, and so on. The disadvantage would be the size of mapping matrices: unless the destination was one-dimensional, the mapping matrix would actually have more entries than the source. In Figure 3.11, for example, the source and destination arrays both contain 18 elements, but the map specifying their correspondence contains 54 elements.

To keep the size of maps reasonable, FORTRAN-KDP implements arbitrary mappings in a less intuitive way. As is described in Appendix A, a $d_1 \times d_2 \times \ldots \times d_N$ array is laid out in memory so that the first index varies most quickly, and the last most slowly.[2] FORTRAN-KDP mappings make use of this by considering both the source and the destination as one-dimensional arrays. This allows an arbitrary map to be a one-dimensional array, containing exactly as many entries as the source array. Each entry specifies that element's destination in the "flattened" version of the destination. This convention also allows programs to make calls of the form:

```
integer :: A(10, 10), B(100), M(100)
    .
    .
    .
call dp_push(a, b, m, "=")
```

in which the source A and the destination B are non-conformant. The map required for Figure 3.11 is therefore written as shown in Figure 3.12.

An intrinsic function which is often used with dp_push is dp_index, first introduced in Program 3.7. This function generates a vector containing the range of indices specified by its first argument. For example:

```
dp_index(5)
```

generates the vector (/1, 2, 3, 4, 5/). Using dp_index, it is straightforward to create simple one-to-one mapping between arrays with different shapes, as in:

```
integer :: source(4, 6), dest(2, 4, 3)
    .
    .
    .
call dp_push(source, dest, (4*6 + 1) - dp_index(4*6), "=")
```

This call re-arranges the values in source as shown in Figure 3.13. Such re-packings are often used to change the layout of data when crossing function and subroutine boundaries. While doing the arithmetic to create a mapping vector can be tedious if the source and

---

2. This layout is the reverse of that used in C and ALGOL-derived languages, but is consistent with most FORTRAN dialects.

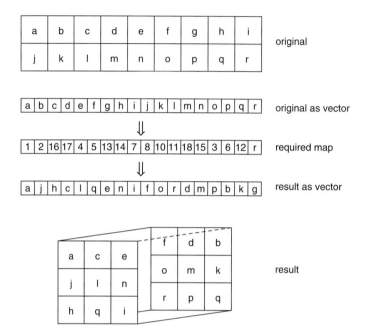

Figure 3.12
Specifying a Mapping with a Vector

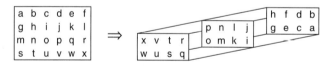

Figure 3.13
Rearranging Values in Memory

destination have high ranks, in practice most mappings map one vector into another. One common example, the use of re-mapping after a parallel prefix, will be discussed in Section 3.3.2.

Handling Collisions   As mentioned earlier, dp_push takes an optional fourth parameter, which controls what happens if several values are mapped to the same location. This parameter must be a string representing an intrinsic operation, such as "+", ".bitor.", or ".max.". During a mapping operation, all values sent to the same location are combined using the function specified. If two or more values are sent to the same location, and the

```
procedure histogram1(v, h)
  integer :: v(:)                              ! values
  integer :: h(:)                              ! histogram

  h = 0
  call dp_push(v, h, v, "+")
  h = h / dp_index(R)

end procedure
```

Program 3.8
A Data-Parallel Histogram Generator

specified operator was "=", then one of the mapped values is chosen arbitrarily and written into the destination.

The function specified must be both associative and commutative. These restrictions are necessary because the order in which values may arrive at their destination is non-deterministic; if the result of the function depended on the order of operations, the results generated by a mapping could vary from machine to machine, or even be unrepeatable on a single machine. This topic is discussed in more detail in Section 3.3.1.

Example 3.4 (Histogram Construction) One clever use of mapping with "+" is to calculate a histogram. Program 3.8 does this by using the values in a vector as a map for itself. Here, every occurrence of the value x in array is sent to location x in histogram. If there are n_x occurrences of x in array, then after the mapping histogram(x) holds xn_x. When these values are divided by dp_index(R), where R is the range of values in the source array, the result is simply the vector n_x. Implementing this technique if one of the values in the source array might be zero is left as an exercise.

A second approach makes use of another intrinsic function called dp_scalar. Where dp_index creates a vector containing the values from 1 to N, dp_scalar creates a vector containing N copies of the scalar i. This function is not normally needed for arithmetic, since scalars are automatically promoted to arrays when necessary, but can come in handy when passing arguments to functions which expect arrays, like dp_push. Program 3.9 uses dp_scalar to create a vector of 1's, which are then mapped as before using the input vector to create a histogram. This technique does not require a subsequent division, and works properly no matter what the input values are.

Note that the histogram vector h passed to Programs 3.8 and 3.9 must have at least as many elements as there are different values in the input vector v in order for dp_push to do its job properly. In the image processing and statistical applications in which histograms are most often constructed, such an upper bound is usually known *a priori*. It may, for

```
procedure histogram2(v, h)
  integer :: v(:)                          ! values
  integer :: h(:)                          ! histogram

  h = 0
  call dp_push(dp_scalar(1, size(v,1)), h, v, "+")

end procedure
```

Program 3.9
Another Data-Parallel Histogram Generator

example, be the range of different pixel values in an image, or the number of possible correct answers on an exam.

Permuting and Striding   If strides are being used to index the array being mapped, the map must have at least as many elements as the selected portion of the source array, i.e. the map must provide an index for every value being mapped (although as the histogram example shows, it may not necessarily conform to the result of the mapping). For example:

```
integer :: mapvec(10), source(20), dest(20)
   .
   .
   .
call dp_push(source(1:10), dest(1:10), mapvec)
```

is legal, since the portion of source being mapped, the mapping vector, and the portion of dest being overwritten all conform. However, the very similar statement:

```
call dp_push(source(:), dest(:), mapvec)
```

would cause an error, since it is trying to apply a 10-element map to a 20-element vector.

Example 3.5 (Matrix Multiplication Once Again)   Program 3.2 showed an algorithm which required $\mathcal{O}(N^2)$ loop iterations to multiply two $N \times N$ matrices. A more sophisticated algorithm which uses *skewing* can reduce this to $\mathcal{O}(N)$.

A skewed matrix is one whose elements have been shifted along one axis in a particular way. The first row (or column) is left alone; the second is shifted circularly by one place, the third by two places, and so on. For example, if the matrix:

$$\begin{bmatrix} a_{11} & a_{12} & a_{13} \\ a_{21} & a_{22} & a_{23} \\ a_{31} & a_{32} & a_{33} \end{bmatrix}$$

is skewed by 1 along its first axis, it becomes:

$$\begin{bmatrix} a_{11} & a_{32} & a_{23} \\ a_{21} & a_{12} & a_{33} \\ a_{31} & a_{22} & a_{13} \end{bmatrix}$$

Every element in the first column has been shifted forward by zero, every element in the second column by one, and so on. If the same matrix had been skewed negatively along its second axis, it would have become:

$$\begin{bmatrix} a_{11} & a_{12} & a_{13} \\ a_{22} & a_{23} & a_{21} \\ a_{33} & a_{31} & a_{32} \end{bmatrix}$$

In order to calculate $C = AB$, the $\mathcal{O}(N)$ algorithm skews A along its second axis and B along its first. The results are:

$$\begin{bmatrix} a_{11} & a_{12} & a_{13} \\ a_{22} & a_{23} & a_{21} \\ a_{33} & a_{31} & a_{32} \end{bmatrix}$$

and:

$$\begin{bmatrix} b_{11} & b_{22} & b_{33} \\ b_{21} & b_{32} & b_{13} \\ b_{31} & b_{12} & b_{23} \end{bmatrix}$$

The elementwise product of these two skewed matrices is:

$$\begin{bmatrix} a_{11}b_{11} & a_{12}b_{22} & a_{13}b_{33} \\ a_{22}b_{21} & a_{23}b_{32} & a_{21}b_{13} \\ a_{33}b_{31} & a_{31}b_{12} & a_{32}b_{23} \end{bmatrix}$$

The trick to the algorithm is that each of these values is a term in the proper matrix product. If the skewed copy of A is shifted left by one place, and the copy of B up by the same amount, a second direct contribution to the overall matrix product can then be calculated:

$$\begin{bmatrix} a_{12}b_{21} & a_{13}b_{32} & a_{11}b_{13} \\ a_{23}b_{31} & a_{21}b_{12} & a_{22}b_{23} \\ a_{31}b_{11} & a_{32}b_{22} & a_{33}b_{33} \end{bmatrix}$$

(I didn't believe it either the first time I saw it.) When this, and the result of multiplying another left shift of A with another upward shift of B, are added to the first term, the result is the product matrix C in which:

$$c_{ij} = \sum_{k=1}^{N} a_{ik}b_{kj}$$

The shifting needed to lay appropriate matrix values against one another after the matrices have been skewed is trivial. Skewing the matrices being multiplied, and un-skewing them afterwards if necessary, is a bit more complicated. Since each row or column must be shifted by a different amount, dp_shift alone cannot accomplish what is needed in a single go. A program could use an $\mathcal{O}(N)$ loop such as:

```
do i = 2, N-1
  A = dp_shift(A, "n", 0, "c", i-1)
end do
```

which would lead to code of the form:

```
! set up temporaries
A_t(1, :) = A(1, :)
B_t(:, 1) = B(:, 1)
do i = 2, N
  A_t(i, :) = dp_shift(A(i, :), "c", 1-i)
  B_t(:, i) = dp_shift(B(:, i), "c", 1-i)
end do
! multiply
C = 0
do i = 1, N
  C = C + A_t * B_t
  A_t = dp_shift(A_t, "n", 0, "c", 1)
  B_t = dp_shift(B_t, "c", 1, "n", 1)
end do
```

With a properly-constructed mapping vector, a call to dp_push can do the job of the setup loop in a single step. The first step is to write A as it is laid out in memory:

$$a_{11} \quad a_{12} \quad a_{13} \quad a_{21} \quad a_{22} \quad a_{23} \quad a_{31} \quad a_{32} \quad a_{33}$$

and then to write out the skewed matrix in the same fashion:

$$a_{11} \quad a_{12} \quad a_{13} \quad a_{22} \quad a_{23} \quad a_{21} \quad a_{33} \quad a_{31} \quad a_{32}$$

The map which must be applied to the first vector to get the second is:

$$1 \quad 2 \quad 3 \quad 6 \quad 4 \quad 5 \quad 8 \quad 9 \quad 7$$

We can break down the construction of the required mapping vector into two steps: generating the index of the first element in each row, and generating the offsets of the elements within each row. The first part is easiest. Suppose that N is 3, and that Nsq is N**2. The expression:

```
(dp_index(Nsq) - 1) / N
```

generates the values:

0   0   0   1   1   1   2   2   2

If we multiply by the number of elements per row, which is N, and then add 1 to account for FORTRAN-KDP's 1-based array index[3] we get:

1   1   1   4   4   4   7   7   7

Call this vector R.

Now, we need to generate the offsets within each column. This can be done with:

```
(dp_index(Nsq) - 1) .mod. N
```

which generates:

0   1   2   0   1   2   0   1   2

This vector C gives us the offset of each element from the start of its row; note that $R + C$ gives the actual index of every element.

The third intermediate vector we need is the amount of shifting within each row:

0   0   0   1   1   1   2   2   2

But we have seen this before during the generation of R; it is just:

```
(dp_index(Nsq) - 1) / N
```

Since we are shifting elements down within each row, we must subtract this from C to get:

0   1   2   −1   0   1   −2   −1   0

This vector shows where elements would go if there was no circular wrapping; in order to get wrapping, we can add back N and then use .mod. to adjust the values to:

0   1   2   2   0   1   1   2   0

---

3. One of the advantages of the 0-based indexing using in C is that array indexing calculations involving remainders don't need a corrective +1 afterwards. The advantage of the 1-based indexing used in most other languages is, er, well anyway, that's how FORTRAN indexes arrays.

If we write this out in matrix format, we can see that these values are simply the new indices of each element within its row:

0   1   2
2   0   1
1   2   0

Finally, we add the values in R, to turn these offsets into absolute indices, and get:

1   2   3   6   4   5   8   9   7

as required.

Essentially, this rather lengthy operation has added the index of the row containing each element to that element's vectorized index, then calculated the modulus of the result with respect to the length of each row. In a real program, a map such as this would probably be created once (by a carefully-tested and well-documented library routine) and then saved for repeated use. Calculating the skew mapping needed to shift B along its second axis is left as an exercise.

Pulling Instead of Pushing   The mapping function introduced above is called a *pushing map* since elements are "pushed" out of the source vector according to the map. The alternative way to do a mapping is to *pull*, i.e. to specify where elements are to come from, rather than where they are to go to. Pulling is particularly useful when some elements of the source array are to be mapped to many places in the destination. This idea is most easily explained by example. If the vector M contains the values:

4   1   3   2

and the vector src contains:

"one"   "two"   "three"   "four"

then dp_push(src, dst, M, "=") fills dst with:

"four"   "one"   "three"   "two"

i.e. the first element of src is sent to location 4, the second to location 1, and so on. In contrast, the call pull(dst, src, M) fills dst with:

"two"   "four"   "three"   "one"

i.e. location 1 is given the value that was at location 4, location 2 the value that was at location 1, and so on: values are pulled from locations, rather than pushed into them (Figure 3.14). A pushing map is therefore equivalent to:

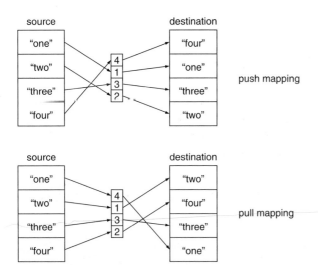

Figure 3.14
Pushing and Pulling

```
do i = 1, N
  dst(i) = src(map(i)
end do
```

while a pulling map is equivalent to:

```
do i = 1, N
  dst(map(i)) = src(i)
end do
```

To see why pulling maps are useful, consider once again the candidate data-parallel code of Program 3.1. Instead of using a loop to line up the values of V with the values of A, as the code on page 114 did, we could provide a map that showed which element of V each element of A needed. If we consider a single column of A, the desired pulling map is simply $((\text{dp\_index}(100)-1)/5)+1$, i.e. elements on row i of A map to the $i/5^{\text{th}}$ element of V (rounding up). We can then reshape the 100-element vector produced by this mapping to create the 100×100 matrix required, as in:

```
real    :: A(100, 100), V(20), temp(100)
integer :: j
```

```
      .
      .
      .
call dp_pull(V, temp, ((dp_index(100)-1)/5)+1)
where A >= 0 do
  A(1:100:2, 1:100:2) = A(:, :) - shape(temp, "1", 100)
end where
```

Note how this expands `temp` to cover the whole of A and appears to do the subtraction
everywhere, but only actually modifies A where elements are selected by stride and not
masked out.

3.2   An Inside-Out Syntax

The array-based syntax introduced so far is the most common way of expressing data
parallelism. An alternative notation based on parallel structures has also been employed,
most notably in the original implementation of C* by Thinking Machines Corporation,
and in Hatcher and Quinn's Dataparallel-C [Hatcher & Quinn 1991]. This approach makes
object shapes explicit by requiring programmers to declare them using a syntax like:

```
shape :: wide(300, 300), deep(20)
```

A shape can then be used to qualify the declaration of any variable. Its effect is to replicate
the variable as many times as there are "elements" in the shape. Thus, the two declarations:

```
integer, shape(wide) :: I
real, shape(deep)    :: V
```

create a 300×300 integer array I and a 20-element real vector V respectively.

The difference between the multiplicity introduced by a shape and normal array declarations is that operations on shaped elements are expected to be done in parallel. The
expression I+3, for example, would add 3 to each element of I concurrently. If J had been
declared as a normal array with the same extent using:

```
integer :: J(300, 300)
```

then the expression J+3 would *not* be parallelized, and might not even be legal.

This notation is most often used to group objects which are logically connected into
shaped parallel records. For example, a record definition such as:

```
type mesh_point
```

```
real    :: density, pressure, temperature, viscosity
integer :: look_ahead
logical :: last_turbulent
end type
```

could be combined with a shape definition to create a parallel array of records:

```
type(mesh_point), shape(wide) :: mesh
```

This declaration would create several sets of parallel variables, each of which would be notionally joined to the others at the same location (Figure 3.15a). Shapes and normal array declarations could be mixed:

```
type(mesh_point), shape(deep) :: edge(4)
```

Here, we have declared an array of four parallel vectors, each of which is notionally spread out over 20 processors (since deep is a 20-element shape). As Figure 3.15b shows, such a declaration might be implemented by putting each element of edge on a different processor, or by grouping them in twos or fours. However, parallel operations would only be allowed along the parallel axis defined by the shape; the sequential axis, with length 4, would have to be looped over as in a sequential program.

Parallel records such as these are manipulated using a with statement, as in:

```
with (mesh) do
  if .not. last_turbulent then
    viscosity = density * pressure / temperature
  end if
end with
```

Here, the with specifies a parallel record array, so that the compiler knows the shape it is dealing with. The if statement inside the with then acts as a parallel conditional expression, so that these statements are equivalent to:

```
integer :: i, j
  .
  .
  .
do i = 1, 300
  do j = 1, 300
    if .not. last_turbulent(i, j) then
      viscosity(i) = density(i) * pressure(i) / temperature(i)
    end if
```

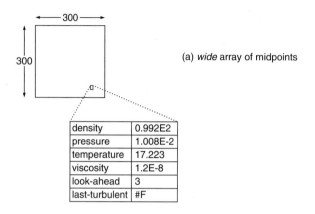

(a) *wide* array of midpoints

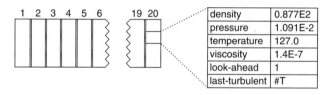

density	0.877E2
pressure	1.091E-2
temperature	127.0
viscosity	1.4E-7
look-ahead	1
last-turbulent	#T

Figure 3.15
Shapes Created by Inside-Out Syntax

```
    end do
end do
```

Proponents of this kind of syntax have argued that it leads to more structured programs. While it certainly eliminates some of the ugliness of complicated stride expressions, and of `where` statements whose nesting makes them difficult to understand, this notation makes it more difficult to express computations involving objects with different shapes. Operating on elements from both 200×200 and 40×1000 records at the same time, for example, can be just as tricky as expressing complicated strides.

Another problem is that decisions about which axes of arrays are parallel, and which are serial, are not localized. If a programmer wanted to change the layout of the 20×4 `edge` array shown above so that the shorter axis was parallel, and the longer one sequential, then every statement involving `edge` would have to be found and changed. A better mechanism for handling these software engineering issues, which is compatible with the array syntax used in FORTRAN-KDP and most other present-generation data-parallel languages, will be the subject of Section 3.5.

3.3   Other Data-Parallel Operations

The data-parallel operations introduced so far have worked on array elements one at a time. This section introduces three other types of operation which combine array elements to produce scalars, combine them to produce new arrays, or locate elements with known values.

3.3.1   Reduction

Floating point numbers are like sandpiles: every time you move one, you lose a little sand and you pick up a little dirt.
—Brian W. Kernighan and P. J. Plauger
The Elements of Programming Style

Combining the values in an array to create a scalar is called *reduction*. Reduction takes an array of any size or shape, and an operation, and uses that operation to combine all of the array's elements. If the operation is addition, for example, reduction adds the elements of the array; if it is `.or.`, reduction returns `.true.` if any of the values in the input array are `.true.`, while if it is `.bitand.` it returns a value in which bits are set only where they were set in every element of the array. These three operations would be written as `dp_reduce(A, "+")`, `dp_reduce(A, ".or.")`, and `dp_reduce(A, ".bitand.")` respectively in FORTRAN-KDP. `dp_reduce` is a true function; the type of the value it returns is determined by the type of its first argument. One simple example of reduction's use is the way it can sum the values contributing to each element of the result matrix in matrix multiplication:

```
do i = 1, N
  do j = 1, N
    C(i, j) = dp_reduce(A(i, :) * B(:, j), "+")
  end do
end do
```

In order to guarantee reproducibility, i.e. in order to ensure that the result of a reduction will always be the same, only operations which are associative and commutative can be reduced. If reduction with other operators such as subtraction were allowed, then the definition of reduction would have to include some specification of the order in which subtractions were done, in order to prevent one implementation returning:

```
(((A(1) - A(2)) - A(3)) - . . . ) - A(N)
```

while another returned:

```
A(1) - (A(2) - ( . . . - (A(N-1) - A(N))))
```

In fact, even with associative and commutative functions, different implementations of reduction (or different runs on the same machine, if that machine's execution can be non-deterministic), may yield different values. The cause of this is the round-off that occurs when floating-point values are being manipulated. In most 32-bit floating-point representations, the sum of 10^{10} and 10^{-10} is still 10^{10}, since there just aren't enough bits to hold a value whose most and least significant bits are so far apart. Such truncation can affect the result of reduction if the order in which terms are combined can vary from one machine to another, or from one run of the program to another.

For example, suppose that floating-point numbers have 3-bit mantissas and 2-bit exponents, and that all mantissas and exponents are interpreted as being non-negative. The values which this system can represent correctly are:

0 = 000.00	1 = 001.00	2 = 010.00	3 = 011.00
4 = 100.00	5 = 101.00	6 = 110.00	7 = 111.00
8 = 100.01	10 = 101.01	12 = 110.01	14 = 111.01
16 = 100.10	20 = 101.10	24 = 110.10	28 = 111.10
32 = 100.11	40 = 101.11	48 = 110.11	56 = 111.11

Now suppose that we are reducing a vector whose values are (/1, 5, 12, 24/). Adding the first two values gives:

```
      001.00
+     101.00
      ──────
      110.00
```

To add the second two (the 12 and 24), we first scale 24 to have the same exponent as 12, i.e. convert 110.10 to 1100.01, then do the addition and scale it back down to get:

```
      110.01      (110.01)
+     110.10      (1100.01)
      ──────────────────────
      100.11      (10010.01)
```

If we perform scaling, addition, and re-scaling in the same fashion, we find that:

	110.00	(110.00)
+	100.11	(100000.00)

	100.11	(100110.00)

so that adding 1+5 to 12+24 in our system leaves us with just 12+24=36. But suppose we do the addition in a different order, for example $((1 + 5) + 12) + 24$. The innermost sum gives 110.00 as before; adding this to 12 gives 100.10, and adding this to 24 (110.10) gives 101.11, or 40, instead of the 36 we had previously. None of this is random—if operations are re-done in the same order, as they probably would be in a sequential program, then the same answer is always produced. If the number of processors used in two program runs is different, however, then it is very unlikely that operation order will be strictly preserved.

While rounding effects are a problem on uniprocessors as well as on parallel computers, their effects are more noticeable on the latter. Suppose that global reduction has been implemented by repeatedly shifting the vector of values being reduced, and performing addition separately in each location. If the initial vector contains $(/a, b, c, d/)$, for example, this technique would first generate the sums $(/a + d, b + a, c + b, d + a/)$, then $(/a + d + c, b + a + d, c + b + a, d + c + b/)$, and so on. As hinted on page 56, this could lead to each location having a different final value for the sum. If these values are then used in an if statement—for example, if each processor is only to perform its next action if the global sum is less than some threshold—the result could be disastrous. The usual implementation technique, outlined below, avoids this problem by collecting the sum at a single location, and then broadcasting it again.

Reduction can be viewed as a special case of mapping, in which all elements of the source array are sent to the same location in the destination. Given any array A, a mapping vector M with the same number of elements, and a single-element array R one can perform a $\oplus$-reduction for any operator $\oplus$ using:

```
M = 1
call dp_push(A, R, M, "⊕")
```

Reduction is often used to control program flow, e.g. to determine whether a calculation has converged. For example, indirect methods like SOR (Section 2.3.4) repeatedly update the values in a matrix until the maximum difference between the old and new values falls below some threshold. Finding this maximum difference is a one-step process using dp_ reduce with .max..

The usual way to implement reduction sequentially is to run over the values of the array being reduced using nested loops, as in:

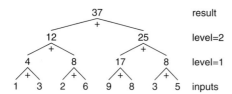

Figure 3.16
Reduction Tree

```
real      :: A(2000, 3000, 4000), r
integer :: i, j, k
     .
     .
     .
r = 0
do i = 1, 2000
  do j = 1, 3000
    do k = 1, 4000
       r = r + A(i, j, k)
    end do
  end do
end do
```

The time this takes is clearly linear in the number of elements in the array. In a data-parallel system, however, it is possible to do better than this. The trick is to combine values in pairs, then combine these results in pairs, and so on, as shown in Figure 3.16. Since the number of values contributing to each intermediate result doubles at each step, the number of steps required must be proportional to $\log N$, where N is the number of values in that dimension. The total time is thus proportional to the sum of the logarithms of the sizes, which is just the logarithm of the total size of the array. This idea was first seen for two-dimensional meshes on page 64.

For example, suppose that A has been declared as:

```
real :: A(16)
```

If the reduction operation being used is .min., then A could be explicitly reduced in-place in exactly 4 steps:

```
stride = 2
do i = 1, 4
  A(1:16:stride) = A(1:16:stride) + A((1+(stride/2)):16:stride)
```

```
    stride = 2 * stride
end do
```

which is equivalent to:

```
A(1:16:2)  = A(1:16:2)  + A(2:16:2)
A(1:16:4)  = A(1:16:4)  + A(3:16:4)
A(1:16:8)  = A(1:16:8)  + A(5:16:8)
A(1:16:16) = A(1:16:16) + A(9:16:16)
```

If A had more than 16 elements, but no more than 32, then only one additional step would be required.

3.3.2 Parallel Prefix

As mentioned above, reduction may be viewed as a special case of mapping, in which the map's combining function is more important than the data re-arrangement. Reduction may also be viewed as a special case of another powerful data-parallel operation called *parallel prefix*. Both practical experience and theoretical work, such as the *scan-vector model* described in [Blelloch 1989], have shown that parallel prefix greatly increases the power and expressivity of the data-parallel model.

In its simplest form, parallel prefix takes a vector V, and an operator $\oplus$, and calculates a sequence of partial results:

V_1

$V_1 \oplus V_2$

$V_1 \oplus V_2 \oplus V_3$

$\vdots$

$V_1 \oplus V_2 \oplus V_3 \oplus \ldots \oplus V_{N-1}$

$V_1 \oplus V_2 \oplus V_3 \oplus \ldots \oplus V_{N-1} \oplus V_N$

For example, if the operator is addition, then the parallel prefix calculates the sequence of partial sums of its input, while if the operator is .or. it creates a vector containing .false. up to the first .true., and .true. thereafter (Figure 3.17).

This type of parallel prefix is called *inclusive*, since the initial value of the first element is included in its final value. An *exclusive parallel prefix* generates the same values, except that the sequence is shifted up one place, and the identity element of the operator being used is written into the result's first location. Thus, an exclusive parallel prefix of V using + yields:

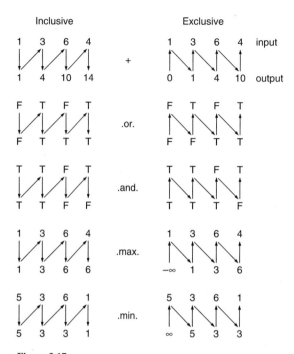

Figure 3.17
Examples of Parallel Prefix

$$0$$

$$V_1$$

$$V_1 + V_2$$

$$V_1 + V_2 + V_3$$

$$\vdots$$

$$V_1 + V_2 + V_3 + \ldots + V_{N-1}$$

since 0 is the identity element for addition. One can also do a parallel prefix by scanning down from the top element of the vector, rather than up from the first.

Parallel prefix is expressed in FORTRAN-KDP using the intrinsic function dp_scan, which takes four arguments: the vector on which the prefix is to be done, the name of the operator to be used, and two logical flags. The first flag determines whether the scan is inclusive (.true.) or exclusive (.false.); the second, whether the scan is to be done upwards (.true.) or downwards (.false.). Thus, the expression:

```
real :: A(1000)
  .
  .
  .
dp_scan(A, "+", .false., .true.)
```

would calculate the partial sums of the elements of A from lowest to highest, while:

```
dp_scan(A(1:1000:2), "+", .false., .false.)
```

would calculate the partial sums of the odd-numbered elements of A, from highest to lowest. Note that dp_scan is a true function, rather than a subroutine; it does not alter its argument, and its result must be assigned somewhere.

Example 3.6 (Data-Parallel Radix Sort) To see how useful parallel prefix is, consider the function shown in Program 3.10. Radix sort is one of the fundamental sorting techniques [Knuth 1981b]. It works by repeatedly splitting the values being sorted into two groups, based on whether a particular bit in their representation is 0 or 1. The first split is done on the least significant bit; the next is done on the next-highest bit, and so on (Figure 3.18). So long as each split maintains the order of values within each group created by previous splits, the result after b splits is that the values are ordered by their b least significant bits. After B splits, where B is the number of bits in the values, the values are completely ordered.

Program 3.10 does each radix split by constructing an index vector in two steps. First, each processor holding a value with a 0 in the current bit location marks itself by putting a 1 in the auxiliary vector M0. These marks are them summed using a forward prefix. Processors holding values with a 1 bit then mark themselves in M1, and these marks are summed using a reverse prefix. The values produced by this second prefix operation are then subtracted from the total length of the vector, so that they count down from the length of the vector, rather than up from one. These steps create two partial maps, one which compacts 0-bit values to the low end of the vector, the other of which compacts 1-bit values to the high end. These two maps are merged using a where, and the result used to re-arrange the values in the original vector. The loop is then repeated for the next most significant bit.

Example 3.7 (Load Balancing a Monte Carlo Simulation) As another example of how parallel prefix can be used, suppose a program is simulating the behavior of a collection of reactive molecules over an extended period of time. During the simulation, a single molecule may break down into smaller parts, or disappear entirely; meanwhile, new molecules may be introduced from outside the system.

```
procedure radixsort(orig)
  integer :: orig(:)                        ! to be sorted
  integer :: dim = size(orig, 1)            ! how large
  logical :: mask(dim)                      ! for choosing
  integer :: one(dim), zero(dim)            ! for copying
  integer :: i                              ! loop index

  do i = 1, Bits_per_Value
    mask = (orig .bitand. ishft(1, i-1)) == 0
    where mask do
      zero = 1 ; one = 0
    else
      zero = 0 ; one = 1
    end where
    zero = dp_scan(zero, "+", .true., .true.)
    one  = dim + 1 - dp_scan(one, "+", .false., .true.)
    where .not. mask do
      zero = one
    end where
    call dp_push(orig, one, zero, "=")
    orig = one
  end do
end procedure
```

Program 3.10
Data-Parallel Radix Sort

While the inter-molecular forces themselves may be very complicated, our interest at the moment is to ensure that the simulation remains load-balanced, by making sure that the molecules are always as evenly distributed as possible across the available processors. Here, we will assume that molecules are stored in a vector of structures, and that that vector is mapped cyclically onto the available processors (Figure 3.19). The key to doing the load-balancing efficiently is to use parallel prefix and re-mapping.

The first step is to decide on M, the maximum number of particles which any physical processor will be allowed to hold, and to allocate a vector of size $V = M\mathcal{P}$ to hold them, where $\mathcal{P}$ is the number of processors in the machine. The elements of this vector are then mapped cyclically across the physical processors, so that element i is on processor $i \bmod P$. N_I initial particles are introduced into the system by filling the low N_I elements of the molecule vector, and allowed to interact.

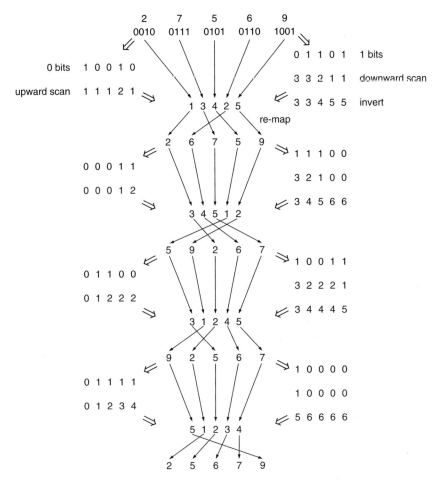

Figure 3.18
Operation of a Data-Parallel Radix Sort

After each set of interactions, the program calculates the difference between the greatest and least number of particles for which any physical processor is responsible. It does this by creating a V-vector of 1's and 0's, in which the 1's represent "live" molecules and the 0's represent unused slots in the vector. These values are then summed into another vector, load, using dp_push (Program 3.11).

If the greatest difference between processor workloads is above some threshold, or if any processor is close to having the maximum number of particles permitted, then the particles are "packed down" into the low end of the vector. The cyclic mapping of the

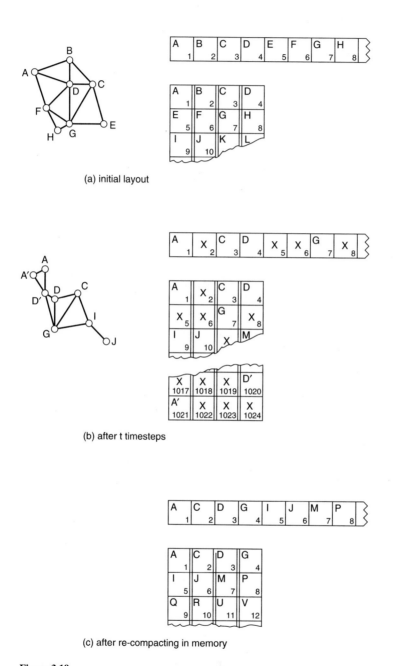

(a) initial layout

(b) after t timesteps

(c) after re-compacting in memory

Figure 3.19
Operation of Data-Parallel Load Balancing

```
do while simulating
  do an update
  ! mark live molecules
  where V_live(:) do
    active = 1
  else
    active = 0
  end where
  ! count load on each processor
  load = 0
  call dp_push(active, load, ((dp_index(V)-1)/M)+1, "+")
  ! find maximum load difference
  max_load_diff = dp_reduce(load, ".max.") - dp_reduce(load, ".min.")
  if max_load_diff >= load_diff_limit then
    ! relocate
    t1 = dp_scan(active, "+", .true., .true.)
    where active do
      t2 = dp_index(V)
    else
      t2 = -1
    end where
    num_live = dp_reduce(active, "+")
    call dp_push(t2, t1(1:num_live), t1, ".max.")
    call dp_pull(molecules(1:num_live), molecules, t1(1:num_live), "=")
  end if
end while
```

Program 3.11
Data-Parallel Load Balancing

vector across the available processors then ensures that the difference in load between any two processors is at most one. The first stage of packing relies on the vector `active` created earlier, which holds 1's where there are live molecules in the storage vector, and 0's elsewhere (Figure 3.20). An inclusive, upward, additive prefix is then done on this to generate the index of the location to which each live molecule is to be sent. However, this prefix calculation also assigns indices to locations in the storage vector which do not currently contain molecules. In order to make sure that only live molecules are re-mapped into the bottom portion of the storage vector, we use another `where` statement in conjunction with the intrinsic function `dp_index` to create a vector whose elements are either the result of the prefix (where there is a live molecule), or -1 (where there is not).

a		b	c		d	e	f			g		h				initial values
1	0	1	1	0	1	1	1	0	0	1	0	1	0	0	0	live markers
1	1	2	3	3	4	5	6	6	6	7	7	8	8	8	8	prefix of live markers
1		2	3		4	5	6			7		8				location markers
1	2	3	4	5	6	7	8	9	10	11	12	13	14	15	16	index vector
1	3	4	6	7	8	11	13									map of indices
a	b	c	d	e	f	g	h									result

Figure 3.20
Using Prefix to Pack Vector Values

```
integer :: t1(V), t2(V)          ! temporary index vectors
integer :: num_live              ! number of live molecules
    .
    .
    .
while (simulating)
  do an update
  mark live molecules
  ! remainder of load-balancing code
  t1 = prefix(active, "+", true, true) ! where things go
  where (active)
     t2 = index(V)
  else
     t2 = -1
  end
  num_live = reduce(active, "+")
  call dp_push(t1(1:num_live), t1, t2, ".max.")
  call dp_pull(molecules(1:num_live), molecules, t1(1:num_live))
end
```

Program 3.12
Packing Vector Values

The values created by the parallel prefix are then taken as a map on these index values. .max. is used to resolve conflicts so that the result is a vector whose lowest part is filled with the indices of live molecules. Finally, this vector is used as a pulling map to move live molecules to their final destinations. The code which does all of this is shown in Program 3.12.

Parallel prefix is implemented in almost the same way as reduction. Instead of discarding the intermediate results as reduction does, parallel prefix stores them in a tree

(Figure 3.21a). Once the root node has calculated its answer, it sends two different values to its descendents. Its left child gets the identity element of the operation (e.g. 0 for addition, 1 for multiplication, and .false. for .or.) while its right child gets the value produced by the left half-tree below the root. Each of these nodes then sends a different value to each of its descendents; the left child of each gets the value its parent received, while the right children receive that value combined with the value given to the parent by its left child. As Figure 3.21b–f show, this is much easier to do than it is to describe.

The result of this is that the left-most node in the whole tree always gets the operation's identity element, while the next node gets V_1, the next gets $V_1 \oplus V_2$, and in general element i receives the value $V_1 \oplus V_2 \oplus \ldots \oplus V_{i-1}$. (The implementation of inclusive scanning is left as an exercise.) The cost of this is only twice that of the cost of a simple reduction, but a great deal more information is created.

Segmented Prefixes   *Segmented parallel prefix* is an even more powerful extension of parallel prefix. In a segmented parallel prefix, each of the values in the input vector is accompanied by a logical flag, which indicates whether or not it is the beginning of a segment. When the segmented parallel prefix is done, accumulated values do not propagate values across segment boundaries. Instead, the values in each segment are treated as distinct, so the result is as if a separate parallel prefix had been calculated for each segment (Figure 3.22). Segmented parallel prefix is provided in FORTRAN-KDP by dp_scan_seg. This function takes the same arguments as dp_scan, plus a logical vector of the same length as the vector being operated on. Wherever .true. appears in this second vector, a new segment begins.

Segmented parallel prefixes are calculated in almost the same way as normal parallel prefixes. The only difference is that each value is accompanied by a *barrier bit*, which shows whether it is the beginning of a segment or not. Given the operator $\oplus$ which is to be used, we define a new operator $\overline{\oplus}$, which works exactly as $\oplus$ when neither of the barrier bits associated with its arguments is 1 [Leighton 1991]. When either or both of the barrier bits is 1, on the other hand, then only the value(s) to the right of the right-most barrier bit are included in the result. We can represent this by a table which looks like:

$\overline{\oplus}$	y	$\cdot y$
x	$x \oplus y$	$\cdot y$
$\cdot x$	$\cdot(x \oplus y)$	$\cdot y$

where x and y represent the normal operands, and $\cdot$ represents the barrier bit. Using this modified operator, a segmented prefix can be calculated in exactly the same way as a normal one.

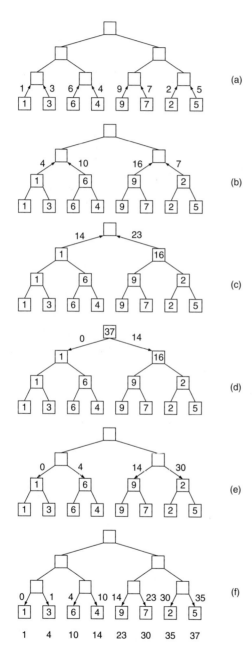

(a)

(b)

(c)

(d)

(e)

(f)

Figure 3.21
Implementing Parallel Prefix

5	3	4	6	2	8	values
F	T	F	T	F	T	segment vector
5	3	7	6	8	8	+-inclusive
0	0	3	0	6	0	+-exclusive
5	3	4	6	2	8	values
T	F	F	T	F	F	segment vector
5	8	12	6	8	16	+-inclusive
0	5	8	0	6	8	+-exclusive

Figure 3.22
Examples of Segmented Parallel Prefix

Example 3.8 (Data-Parallel Quicksort)   Segmented prefix is used to parallelize another standard sorting algorithm, quicksort [Knuth 1981b]. Quicksort works by splitting values into three sections, such that the values in the lower section are less than a chosen pivot value, while the values in the upper section are greater than the pivot. Each section is then sorted independently using the same rule. Eventually, sections contain only a single element, which implies that the whole array is sorted.

In a serial language, the recursive steps in quicksort are managed by recording and retrieving segment boundaries using a stack, a queue, or some other structure. (This recording may be done implicitly by function recursion, using the machine's intrinsic parameter stack.) In a data-parallel language, every level of the recursion can be handled at the same time using segmented parallel prefix.

A data-parallel quicksort routine consists of a loop, which is repeated until the whole array is sorted. (The test at the top of the loop can check for sortedness by comparing each element with its left neighbor, and then reducing the results with .and. to see if any pairs have failed the test.) If the values are not sorted, then the first element of each segment is chosen to act as that segment's pivot. This pivot value is copied to each other processor in the segment using segmented prefix with = as the operator.

Each element of the vector is then checked to see whether its value is less than, equal to, or greater than its pivot's value and a flag set to -1, 0, or 1 accordingly. The split operation introduced in the radix sort example earlier is then used to enumerate the elements in each segment, so that all the values in a segment tagged with -1 are numbered first, then all the values tagged with 0, and then all the values tagged with 1 (Program 3.13). dp_push is then called to move the values in each segment to their new locations, and new .true. values inserted into the segment boundary vector to control operation on the next loop.

j	x	g	i	n	f	d	k	
T	F	F	F	F	F	F	F	segment vector
0	1	–1	–1	1	–1	–1	1	comparison with "j"
–	–	1	2	–	3	4	–	enumeration of < values
–	–	1	2	–	3	4	–	adjusted enumeration
1	–	–	–	–	–	–	–	enumeration of = values
5	–	–	–	–	–	–	–	adjusted enumeration
–	1	–	–	2	–	–	3	enumeration of > values
–	6	–	–	7	–	–	8	adjusted enumeration
5	6	1	2	7	3	4	8	map
g	i	f	d	j	x	n	k	result
T	F	F	F	T	T	F	F	new segment vector

first iteration

g	i	f	d	j	x	n	k	
T	F	F	F	T	T	F	F	segment vector
0	1	–1	–1	0	0	–1	–1	comparison with {"g", "j", "x"}
–	–	1	2	–	1	2	–	enumeration of < values
–	–	1	2	–	6	7	–	adjusted enumeration
1	–	–	–	1	1	–	–	enumeration of = values
3	–	–	–	5	8	–	–	adjusted enumeration
–	1	–	–	–	–	–	–	enumeration of > values
–	4	–	–	–	–	–	–	adjusted enumeration
3	4	1	2	5	8	6	7	map
f	d	g	i	j	n	k	x	result
T	F	T	F	T	T	F	T	new segment vector

second iteration

Figure 3.23
Operation of Data-Parallel Quicksort

Figure 3.23 shows the operation of the first two passes of this algorithm on a vector of eight values. Note that in each successive loop, values will be sent shorter distances by the mapping described by the index vector, as every value remains within its new segment. Tracing the remaining passes is left as an exercise.

3.3.3 Location

The final type of operation commonly used in data-parallel programs is *location*, which determines where a particular value can be found. Suppose, for example, that a program needs to find the location of the maximum value in the array A. While dp_reduce(A, ".max.") will return the value being looked for, it gives no indication of where that value resides, or of how many times that value occurs. While the latter information can be found by replacing all occurrences of this value with 1, and then doing an additive reduction, as

```
procedure quicksort(v)
  integer :: v(:)                              ! values
  integer :: len = size(v, 1)                  ! number of values
  logical :: seg(len)                          ! segment boundaries
  logical :: ends(len)                         ! for re-segmenting
  integer :: pivot(len)                        ! pivot values
  integer :: base(len)                         ! base index of segment
  integer :: map(len)                          ! permutation
  integer :: greater(len), equal(len), less(len)
  integer :: less_off(len), equal_off(len)

  seg(1) = .true.
  do while dp_reduce(v(1:len-1) > v(2:len), ".or.")
    ! select and spread pivots
    where seg do
      pivot = v
    end where
    pivot = dp_scan_seg(pivot, "=", .true., .true., seg)
    ! choose direction for each
    where v < pivot do
      less    = 1
      equal   = 0
      greater = 0
    elsewhere v == pivot do
      less    = 0
      equal   = 1
      greater = 0
    else
      less    = 0
      equal   = 0
      greater = 1
    end where
    less    = dp_scan_seg(less, "+", .true., .true., seg)
    equal   = dp_scan_seg(equal, "+", .true., .true., seg)
    greater = dp_scan_seg(greater, "+", .true., .true., seg)
```

Program 3.13
Data-Parallel Quicksort

```
    ! create offsets
    ends(1:len-1) = seg(2:len)
    ends(len) = .true.
    less_off  = dp_scan_seg(less, "=", .false., .true., ends)
    equal_off = dp_scan_seg(equal, "=", .false., .true., ends)
    ! create vector of base indices
    base = dp_scan_seg(dp_index(len), "=", .true., .true., seg)
    ! add in
    less    = less + base - 1
    equal   = less_off + equal + base - 1
    greater = less_off + equal_off + greater + base - 1
    ! merge
    where v < pivot do
      map = less
    elsewhere v == pivot do
      map = equal
    else
      map = greater
    end where
    ! re-arrange
    call dp_push(v, v, map, "=")
    ! new segment vector
    ends = v < pivot
    where ends(1:len-1) .and. .not. ends(2:len) do
      seg(2:len) = .true.
    end where
    ends = v == pivot
    where ends(1:len-1) .and. .not. ends(2:len) do
      seg(2:len) = .true.
    end where
  end while
end procedure
```

Program 3.13 *(continued)*
Data-Parallel Quicksort

```
real function num_max_1D(A)
   real    :: A(:)                              ! array to examine
   integer :: temp(size(A, 1))                  ! storage

   where A == reduce(A, ".max.") do
     temp = 1
   else
     temp = 0
   end where
   return dp_reduce(temp, "+")

end function
```

Program 3.14
Finding the Number of Maxima in an Array

in Program 3.14, it would seem that the only way to find one of these maxima would be to search A using nested loops.

In fact, a single parallel prefix plus a binary search is enough to locate one of a set of values in any array in a logarithmic number of steps. Given an array A, with a total of N elements, a comparison is done between each element of A and the known value a, and the results mapped into a logical N-vector V. An .or.-prefix is then done, so that every element above and including the first occurrence of a is .true., while every element below the first a is .false.. Binary search can then find the location of the first occurrence of a in a logarithmic number of steps. Since the parallel prefix also took a logarithmic number of steps, the overall time for the calculation is $\mathcal{O}(\log N)$. Finally, the index of this first occurrence can be translated back into a set of indices which describe the same location in the original array A. Program 3.15 shows the steps between the initial mapping and the final index translation.

An alternative technique, which is the one actually used in most real parallel systems, is to define a new binary operator which takes as its arguments two structures, each of which contains a logical value and the index of the location in the source array from which that value comes. If the logical halves of both arguments are .true., the operator returns one or the other arbitrarily; if only one is .true., the operator returns it; and if both are .false., the operator returns a special value indicating that the desired value does not occur in the sub-tree below its arguments. As Figure 3.24 shows, the pairwise combining used in reduction can then be used to find an instance of the desired value, or determine that no such value exists.

```
integer function locate_1D(V)
  logical :: V(:)                           ! mask vector
  integer :: N = size(V, 1)                 ! length of vector
  logical :: temp(N)                        ! scan of V
  integer :: i, step                        ! indices

  temp = dp_scan(V, "or", .false., .false.)
  if V(1) then
    i = 1
  else
    i = N/2
    step = N/4
    do while .not. (V(i) .and. .not. V(i-1))
      if (V(i))
        i = i - step
      else
        i = i + step
      end
      step = step / 2
    end while
  end if
  return i

end function
```

Program 3.15
Using Parallel Prefix and Binary Search to Locate a Value

FORTRAN-KDP provides an intrinsic function dp_locate to do this calculation for arbitrary N-dimensional arrays. Its three arguments are the N-dimensional array being searched, the value being searched for, and a one-dimensional array of at least length N, into which the indices of an occurrence of the desired value will be put if such an occurrence can be found. dp_locate returns a logical value, which is .true. if the desired value was found, and .false. otherwise.

It is important to note that repeated uses of dp_locate on the same array will return the same set of indices—there is no notion of "stepping through" the occurrences of the specified value. If this is necessary, then each occurrence of the value must be replaced with some other value, or an auxiliary array of flags must be used so that masked-out occurrences of the value can be re-instated later. For example, the function ave_min_3D, shown in Program 3.16, calculates the average location of the minima of the array volume.

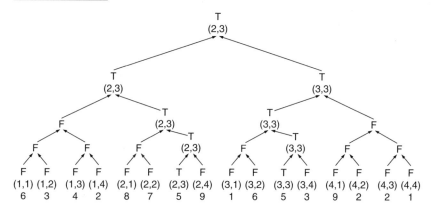

Figure 3.24
Data-Parallel Value Location

Example 3.9 (Invasion Percolation) Invasion percolation models the displacement of one fluid (such as oil) by another (such as water) in fractured rock. In two dimensions, this can be simulated by generating an $N \times N$ grid of random numbers in the range $1 \ldots R$, and then marking the center cell of the grid as filled. In each iteration, one examines all neighbors of all filled cells, chooses the one with the lowest value (i.e. the one with the least resistance to filling), and fills it in. The following shows the first few steps in this process:

26	12	72	45	38
10	38	39	92	38
44	29	X	29	77
61	26	90	35	11
83	84	18	56	52

26	12	72	45	38
10	38	39	92	38
44	X	X	29	77
61	26	90	35	11
83	84	18	56	52

26	12	72	45	38
10	38	39	92	38
44	X	X	29	77
61	X	90	35	11
83	84	18	56	52

```
procedure ave_min_3D(volume, indices)
  real    :: volume(:, :, :)                    ! volume to search
  integer :: indices(:)                         ! storage for indices
  logical :: loc(size(volume, 1),               ! location of minima
                 size(volume, 2),
                 size(volume, 3))
  integer :: next(3)                            ! index of next minimum
  integer :: num                                ! number of minima

  ! mark minima in loc array
  loc = (volume == (dp_reduce(volume, ".min.")))

  ! find and record minima
  indices = 0
  num = 0
  do while locate(loc, true, next)
    indices = indices + next
    loc(next(1), next(2), next(3)) = .false.
    num = num + 1
  end

  ! average
  indices = indices / num

end procedure
```

Program 3.16
Calculating the Average Location of the Minima of an Array

26	12	72	45	38
10	38	39	92	38
44	X	X	X	77
61	X	90	35	11
83	84	18	56	52

26	12	72	45	38
10	38	39	92	38
44	X	X	X	77
61	X	90	X	11
83	84	18	56	52

26	12	72	45	38
10	38	39	92	38
44	X	X	X	77
61	X	90	X	X
83	84	18	56	52

The simulation continues until some fixed percentage of cells have been filled, or until some other condition (such as the presence of trapped regions) is achieved. The fractal structure of the filled and unfilled regions is then examined to determine how much oil could be recovered.

```
! percolate
do i = 1, Number_to_Fill
  ! set up temporary
  where (patch /= Filled) .and.
         ((dp_shift(patch, "p",  1, "n",  0) -- Filled) .or.
          (dp_shift(patch, "p", -1, "n",  0) == Filled) .or.
          (dp_shift(patch, "n",  0, "p",  1) == Filled) .or.
          (dp_shift(patch, "n",  0, "p", -1) == Filled)) do
    temp = patch
  else
    temp = ∞  ! or some very large value
  end where
  ! find minimum neighbor
  min_val = dp_reduce(temp, ".min.")
  assert dp_locate(patch, min_val, coords)
  patch(coords(1), coords(2)) = Filled
end do
```

Program 3.17
Data-Parallel Invasion Percolation

The simplest way to parallelize invasion percolation in a data-parallel system is to use shifting to find all cells which have not yet been filled, but which are adjacent to filled cells, and then to use reduction to find the minimum of these values. Program 3.17 shows the code which does this.

It is important to note how the array `temp` is set up in Program 3.17. Reduction does not pay any attention to masks, since it is only reading the values from the source array. As a result, there is no way to reduce over only the element of `patch` which are adjacent to filled cells. Copying these values into `temp`, and filling the rest of `temp` with ∞ to ensure that they are thrown away during the `.min.`-reduction, has the desired effect.

A simple, but subtle, error was made in the first version of this invasion percolation program. Instead of shifting by ±1 along each axis, the first version shifted the first axis by -1 two times, and didn't shift the second axis by -1 at all. The percolation patterns this program produced were plausible for small tests, but appeared lopsided for larger ones.

One final note: while shifting, masking, and reducing is simple to implement, it is much less efficient than the best sequential implementation. This maintains a list of eligible boundary points, sorted in increasing order. In each iteration, the lowest-valued boundary point is taken from the head of the list and filled in; its neighbors are then added to the list (if they are not already in it). Since the list can be maintained as a binary tree, each iteration takes $\mathcal{O}(\log N)$ time on an N-point grid.

3.3.4 Random Number Generation

Many applications in both computer science and computational science rely on randomness in one way or another. The most common way to generate a stream of pseudo-random numbers is the linear congruential algorithm described in [Knuth 1981a]. Given an initial value x_0 (usually called a seed), and three suitable constants a, c, and m, a linear congruential generator produces the sequence:

$$x_{i+1} = (ax_i + c) \bmod m$$

For example, if $a = 3$, $c = 5$, and $m = 7$, and the initial value is 6, the sequence produced is 6, 2, 4, 3, 0, 5, 6, 2, ... More realistically, the three constants would be much larger, and the sequence produced would appear much more random.

It is tempting to use this algorithm directly on a parallel computer, and simply start each processor with a different seed, e.g. let the seed for each processor be $s + i$, where s is a user-specified value and i is the processor's ID. Unfortunately, the consequences of this can be disastrous, since it is very easy for the sequences of numbers on two processors to become highly correlated. In the simple sequence above, for example, three processors whose seeds started at 4, 5, and 6 would produce the sequences:

```
4   3   0   5   6   2   ...
5   6   2   4   3   0   ...
6   2   4   3   0   5   ...
```

Thus, if random numbers were being used to trigger events, then the event associated with 0 would always occur on processor p_2 two steps after it had occurred on processor p_0, and on processor p_1 one step later.

Choosing seeds so that every processor enters the random sequence at a point sufficiently far from that of its neighbors is difficult, since there is no easy way of measuring the distance of two values from one another except by tracing through the entire random sequence. A much better approach is to exploit the fact that if:

$$x_{i+1} = (ax_i + c) \bmod m$$

then:

$$x_{i+k} = (Ax_i + C) \bmod m$$

where $A = a^k \bmod m$ and $C = c \sum_{j=0}^{k-1} a^j \bmod m$. What this means is that if the constants used to generate the initial pseudo-random sequence are known, then constants can automatically be created to generate a sequence consisting of every k^{th} element of the original sequence.

Thus, in order to get an independent stream of random values on each processor, we start by creating a vector containing the first $\mathcal{P}$ random values x_i from the original sequence, where $\mathcal{P}$ is the number of processors in our machine. We then calculate the modified constants A and C, and copy them to each processor. Thereafter, the processor with index i calculates the elements $x_i, x_{i+\mathcal{P}}, x_{i+2\mathcal{P}}, \ldots$ from the original sequence using the modified formula (Program 3.18). Doing this gives the same effect as taking the original random numbers and distributing them cyclically amongst the processors.

3.4 Automatic Parallelization

Translating a data-parallel program into its serial equivalent is straightforward, albeit tedious. Translating a serial program into a data-parallel program, or *parallelizing* it, ought to be similarly straightforward. After all, a program is an exact specification of a function mapping input values to outputs. Given such a specification, it ought to be possible for a sufficiently clever compiler to determine which calculations depend on which other, and so find and exploit all of the parallelism the calculation contains.

In practice, the phrase "sufficiently clever" glosses over some immense difficulties. Programmers working with traditional imperative languages, such as FORTRAN and C, invariably save values from one calculation to use in another (i.e. perform assignments), use pointers or index vectors to access data structures, or use several different names to access a single data structure (such as segments of an array). Outlawing these practices makes programming more difficult; allowing them increases the difficulty of automatically producing efficient executables from arbitrary input.

In one special case, however, a great deal of progress has been made toward automatically finding and exploiting potential parallelism. Since the rise of vector supercomputers in the latter half of the 1960s, many researchers have developed techniques for transforming programs made up primarily of nested loops and operations on arrays into their data-parallel equivalents. The field of *compiler optimization* has been so active and productive that anything more than a brief overview is impossible in the space available here. For an in-depth look at the state of the art, see [Wolfe 1989] and [Zima 1990], or the more recent [Bacon et al. 1993].

3.4.1 Data Dependence

A program in an imperative language such as FORTRAN-K is a sequence of statements, some of which manage control flow and some of which assign values to memory locations. If we wish to parallelize such a program, the first question that must be asked is, "Which values depend on which others?"

```
program
  integer :: a, c, m
  integer :: seed, num, width, i, j
  integer :: state(:), a_prime, c_prime

  ! command-line arguments
  if argc /= 7 then
    write std_err, "usage: rng a c m seed num width\n"
    stop
  end if
  read argv(2), "%d", a
  read argv(3), "%d", c
  read argv(4), "%d", m
  read argv(5), "%d", seed
  read argv(6), "%d", num
  read argv(7), "%d", width

  ! initialize state
  call allocate(state, width)
  a_prime = a
  c_prime = 1
  state(1) = seed
  do i = 2, width
    state(i) = (a * state(i-1) + c) .mod. m
    c_prime = c_prime + a_prime
    a_prime = a_prime * a
  end do
  c_prime = (c_prime * c) .mod. m

  ! produce values
  do i = 1, num
    state = (a_prime * state + c_prime) .mod. m
    write std_out, "| "
    do j = 1, width
      write std_out, "%4d | ", state(j)
    end do
    write std_out, "\n"
  end do
end program
```

Program 3.18
Data-Parallel Random Number Generation

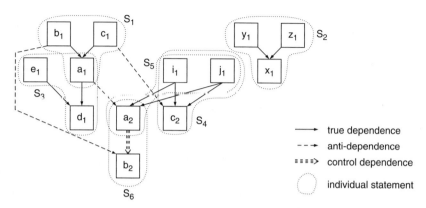

Figure 3.25
Data Dependence Example

To make this more concrete, consider the following sequence of statements:

```
a = 5 * b + c       ! S₁
x = (y + z)/2       ! S₂
d = (a + 2)/e       ! S₃
c = f(i, j)         ! S₄
a = i + j           ! S₅
if a < 0 then       ! S₆
  b = 0
end if
```

The *dependence graph* for this code is shown in Figure 3.25.

Clearly, S_1 and S_2 are independent of one another, since no variable appears in both. However, the result of S_3 depends on the result of S_1, since a appears on the right hand side of S_1. This relationship is called a *true dependence*, to distinguish it from the kinds of dependence which relate S_1 to S_4, S_5, and S_6. In the first of these, S_4 sets the value of the variable c which S_1 uses; clearly, this assignment must not take place before S_1 has read the previous value of c, and so there is an *anti-dependence* between these two statements. S_5, which also sets the value of a, has an *output dependence* on S_1, since S_1 must not perform its assignment after S_5's if the result of the program are to be unchanged. Finally, S_6 has a *control dependence* on S_1, which means that a value set in S_1 is used to control the behavior of S_6.

In this case it is easy to tell by inspection what the relationship between these statements is. However, it has been known since the mid-1960s that the general problem of determining dependencies among statements in the presence of branches is undecidable [Bernstein 1966]. The good news is that if all we want are sufficient, rather than necessary, conditions—i.e. if erring on the side of caution is acceptable—then the conditions which S_i and S_j must satisfy in order to be independent are relatively simple. Let $\mathcal{R}_i$ be the set of variables which S_i reads, $\mathcal{W}_i$ the set of variables which S_i writes, and $\mathcal{R}_j$ and $\mathcal{W}_j$ be the read and write sets for S_j. *Bernstein's Condition* for independence is that:

$$(\mathcal{W}_i \cap \mathcal{R}_j) \cup (\mathcal{R}_i \cap \mathcal{W}_j) \cup (\mathcal{W}_i \cap \mathcal{W}_j) = \emptyset$$

which simply means that S_i and S_j have no true dependence (S_j doesn't read anything S_i writes), anti-dependence (S_i doesn't read anything S_j writes), or output dependence (S_i and S_j don't assign to the same variable). Control dependence can be modelled by treating the condition variable as an input to subsequent statements. However, simple systems get away with only doing analysis inside *basic blocks*, which are sequences of statements which can only be executed in a particular order. Basic blocks have a single entry point, a single exit point, and do not contain conditional branches or loop-backs. While basic blocks are usually short in systems programs like compilers and operating systems, most scientific programs consist of basic blocks which do complicated sequences of calculations, and which are hundreds of instructions long.

The usual way to determine whether two statements violate Bernstein's Condition is to transform the program into a data dependence graph. The next step is to perform control flow analysis to find its basic blocks, and then dependence analysis to find the relationships between the variables used within each basic block. *Dead code*—statements which will never be executed—is then eliminated, and a variety of transformations applied to allow the program to take advantage of a particular computer's architecture.

To see how this works in practice, consider the following short piece of FORTRAN-K:

```
integer, constant :: Len = 256
integer           :: i, a(Len), b(Len), c(Len), c(Len)
do i = 3, Len/4, 2
  a(i+1) = 5*b(i) + c(i-1)
  if (i .bitand. 3) == 1 then
    d(i) = a(i) + 1
  else
    d(i) = a(i) - 1
  end if
end do
```

We begin transforming this by applying *constant replacement* and *loop normalization*. The first replaces expressions involving only constants with their known values, while the second makes every loop run from 1 to some upper bound by increments of 1, and adjusts indexing expressions within the loop accordingly. After these two operations, our example code becomes:

```
do i = 1, 31, 1
  a((2*1+1)+1) = 5*b(2*i+1) + c((2*i+1)-1)
  if ((2*i+1) .bitand. 3) == 1 then
    d(2*i+1) = a(2*i+1) + 1
  else
    d(2*i+1) = a(2*i+1) - 1
  end if
end do
i = 65
```

Next, assuming that the final value of the loop index i is not needed later on, the dead code i = 65 which has been added after the end of the loop can be removed, and the usual rules of algebra applied to simplify the indexing expressions:

```
do i = 1, 31, 1
  a(2*i+2) = 5*b(2*i+1) + c(2*i)
  if ((2*i+1) .bitand. 3) == 1 then
    d(2*i+1) = a(2*i+1) + 1
  else
    d(2*i+1) = a(2*i+1) - 1
  end if
end do
```

The last machine-independent step is to notice the dependence of the conditional statements on the calculated values of a, and to split the loop in two accordingly:

```
do i = 1, 31, 1
  a(2*i+2) = 5*b(2*i+1) + c(2*i)
end do
do i = 3, 63, 2
  if (i .bitand. 3) == 1 then
    d(i) = a(i) + 1
  else
    d(i) = a(i) - 1
  end if
end do
```

At this point, the first loop can be transformed into the data-parallel statement:

```
a(4:64:2) = 5 * b(3:63:2) + c(2:62:2)
```

The second loop can be transformed either by splitting it further into:

```
do i = 3, 63, 4
  d(i) = a(i) - 1
end do
do i = 5, 63, 4
  d(i) = a(i) + 1
end do
```

and then into the two data-parallel statements:

```
d(3:63:4) = a(3:63:4) - 1
d(5:63:4) = a(5:63:4) + 1
```

or by turning it inside out and using a where:

```
where (dp_index(256) < 64) .and. ((dp_index(256) .mod. 4) == 3) do
  d = a - 1
end where
where (dp_index(256) < 64) .and. (dp_index(256) > 4) .and.
      ((dp_index(256) .mod. 4) == 1) do
  d = a - 1
end where
```

Which approach is more efficient depends on how data are distributed, and on the architecture of the machine being used.

Much of the work which laid the basis for these techniques for finding dependencies, and then re-structuring programs to avoid them, was done by David Kuck and others at the University of Illinois in the 1970s [Kuck et al. 1972]. This work led to the development of tools such as Parafrase [Polychronopoulos et al. 1990], a re-structuring tool which allowed programmers to choose transformations from a catalogue and specify the order in which they are to be applied. Each transformation took a FORTRAN program and turned it into a different, but equivalent, program; while the order in which transformations were applied had no effect on the results the program produced, they could have a very large impact on the speed with which that program ran.

A similar project directed by Ken Kennedy at Rice University was the Parallel Fortran Converter (PFC). Like Parafrase, PFC applied transformations to a program after depen-

dencies had been analyzed; unlike Parafrase, however, PFC did not repeatedly translate
FORTRAN to FORTRAN, but instead converted programs into an abstract intermediate representation, and then applied its transformations to that. While PFC was not as "intelligent"
as Parafrase in some respects, its use of an internal representation made it faster, and allowed it to be adapted to other languages relatively easily. Both of these projects were
originally aimed at vectorizing code for pipelined supercomputers such as the Cray-1.
Later, both added features to exploit the potential of shared-memory machines, in which
loop iterations can be spread across several processors dynamically.

A key feature of these projects, and their many descendents, has been the use of *program transformation* to re-structure codes to make more vectorization and parallelization
possible. For example, the nested loops:

```
do i = 2, M
  do j = 2, N
    a(i, j) = a(i, j-1) + 1
  end do
end do
```

cannot immediately be vectorized, as there is a loop-carried dependence. However, inter-
changing the loops allows:

```
do j = 2, M
  a(1:N, j) = a(1:N, j-1) + 1
end do
```

which will yield much better performance on many architectures.

3.4.2   Linear Recurrences

The transformations used in the previous section to turn a looping serial program into a
data-parallel program relied on the fact that the original program did not contain any loop-
carried dependencies. Each iteration of each loop could be done independently, and so
their translation into a small number of data-parallel statements was relatively straightforward.

Unfortunately, loop-carried dependencies are common in real programs. One particular
class which is often encountered is linear recurrence, in which the value calculated by each
loop is a linear function of previously-calculated values. An example of such a recurrence
is:

```
integer :: a(N), x(N), y(N), i
```

```
   .
   .
   .
do i = 2, N
  x(i) = a(i) * x(i-1) + y(i)
end do
```

One way to parallelize such loops is to perform some extra computations in order to eliminate dependencies. To start with, the calculation done by the first iteration of the loop shown above is re-written as:

$$\begin{bmatrix} x_2 \\ 1 \end{bmatrix} = \begin{bmatrix} a_2 & y_2 \\ 0 & 1 \end{bmatrix} \begin{bmatrix} x_1 \\ 1 \end{bmatrix}$$

or, more concisely:

$$X_2 = M_1 X_1$$

The next iteration of the loop may similarly be re-written as:

$$\begin{aligned} X_3 &= & M_2 X_2 \\ &= & M_2 M_1 X_1 \end{aligned}$$

and in general:

$$X_i = (\prod_{j=1}^{i-1} M_j) X_1$$

where $M_i = \begin{bmatrix} a_i & y_i \\ 0 & 1 \end{bmatrix}$ for $2 \le i \le N$. The advantage of doing this is that the sequence of matrices M_j can be generated using parallel prefix, with matrix multiplication replacing the usual scalar multiplication.

This technique can be applied to many other linear recurrences. For example, the mutual recurrence relationship specified by:

```
integer :: a, b, c, d, e, f
integer :: X(N), Y(N), i
   .
   .
   .
do i = 2, N
  X(i) = a * X(i-1) + b * Y(i-1) + c
  Y(i) = d * X(i-1) + e * Y(i-1) + f
end do
```

can be transformed into:

$$\begin{bmatrix} X_i \\ Y_i \\ 1 \end{bmatrix} = \begin{bmatrix} a & b & c \\ d & e & f \\ 0 & 0 & 1 \end{bmatrix} \begin{bmatrix} X_i \\ Y_i \\ 1 \end{bmatrix}$$

Once again, the multiplications needed to generate successive powers of the coefficient matrix can be parallelized. In practice, a full matrix multiplication algorithm would not need to be used, since several of the operations it would carry out (e.g. multiplications by zero or one) would be known in advance to be unnecessary.

This technique allows multiple processors to be used concurrently on what initially seems like an inherently serial problem, but it has one serious drawback: it increases the total amount of work which must be done. In the last code fragment above, for example, the four multiplications and four additions per step of the serial code have been replaced by nine multiplications and six additions. Since the amount of extra work created grows more than linearly with the depth of the recurrence, one should always check that the extra work created by this technique will not overwhelm the speedup resulting from it.

3.4.3   Trace Scheduling

The greatest weakness of the techniques described above is the difficulty they have handling control dependencies. While some of these can be eliminated by using masks, many others are coarse-grained scalar branches, such as:

```
do while sum > 0
   ··· operations on v ···
   sum = dp_reduce(v, "+")
end while
```

Depending on the program's input data, the while loop might execute not at all, or thousands of times. If the compiler knew in advance how many loops were going to be done, it might be able to transform this code into a set of data-parallel statements, or pipeline the loop's operations to improve performance.

The need to wait for a variable's value to be set before testing it would seem to rule out pipelining such computations. However, suppose that hardware was free, so that a computer could contain an infinite number of independent processors. Whenever such a computer reached a branch, such as a conditional expression or a loop boundary, it would follow both paths until it knew which was the correct one. At that point, it would throw away the work done by one processor and keep the work done by the other. While no real computer can do this, the combination of a very smart compiler and some extra hardware can achieve much the same result. The basic idea is to compile the program as usual, but to guess the most likely direction each branch will take, and to pipeline the code as if this guess were guaranteed to be correct. Instead of writing results directly back to memory, however, the program which the compiler generates writes results into temporary locations. When the program is run, the computer waits until it is sure that the compiler had guessed correctly before saving the contents of those temporary locations in main memory. If the compiler had guessed incorrectly, the values in the temporary locations are discarded, and the computation re-started at the branch point (Figure 3.26).

Since a single path through a program is called a *trace*, this technique is called *trace scheduling* [Ellis 1985]. The traces produced by a compiler of this kind may be very long, so it makes sense to have the computer fetch many instructions at a time, or equivalently to make the machine's instructions very long and have each instruction do many things. Such *Very Long Instruction Word (VLIW)* architectures are logically the opposite of the RISC machines now in vogue, but share with them a dependence on large caches and sophisticated compilers to achieve maximum performance. Several companies, including Multiflow and Cydrome, brought VLIW machines to the market in the 1980s [Rau & Fisher 1993]. While these firms were not commercial successes, the idea of trace scheduling is still very much in vogue as a way to manage the complexity of superscalar processors.

3.5   Controlling and Exploiting Data Placement

The discussion of data parallelism so far has assumed that the compiler being used would be clever enough to allocate data to processors in a sensible fashion. In practice, programmers often want to be able to control *data layout* in order to improve efficiency. To see why, consider a simulation operating on a 400×400 mesh of points, running on a 16-processor machine. If we suppose those 16 processors are connected in a ring, then the most sensible way to implement geometric decomposition of the mesh is to give each processor a 25×400-element slice (Figure 3.27a). If we were to build that decomposition into our program, however, and then later move the code to a machine whose 16 processors were connected in a 4×4 grid, the extra distance being travelled by some messages would greatly reduce performance (Figure 3.27b). In fact, what we probably want is to be able to tell the compiler to change the array's layout so that (for example) each processor is responsible for a 100×100 patch (Figure 3.27c).

Optimizations such as these are necessarily machine-dependent, so the best way to express them is to embed them in programs as specially-marked comments, called *compiler directives*. Research in this area has recently culminated in the standardization of *High Performance Fortran* [Koelbel et al. 1994], a superset of FORTRAN-90 with a rich (some would say "fattening") set of directives for laying out data in memory and controlling parallel operations. It, and its predecessors such as Zima et al.'s Vienna Fortran [Benkner et al.

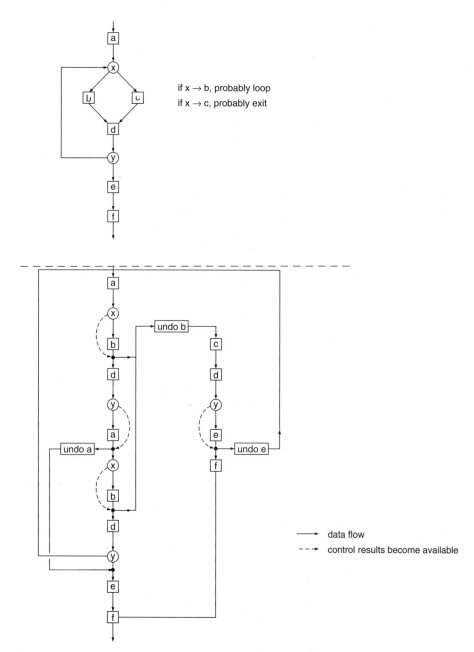

if x → b, probably loop

if x → c, probably exit

→ data flow

- - → control results become available

Figure 3.26
Trace Scheduling

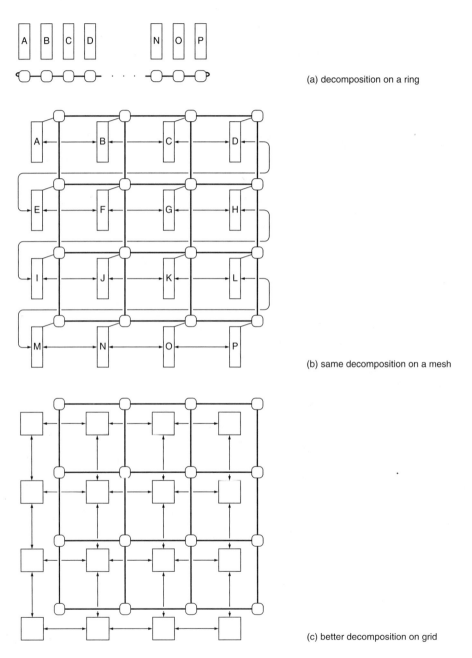

(a) decomposition on a ring

(b) same decomposition on a mesh

(c) better decomposition on grid

Figure 3.27
Data Placement

1990] and Kennedy et al.'s Fortran-D [Hiranandani et al. 1991], all provide more sophisticated tools than the ones introduced below for describing and controlling data layout, but
these will give the flavor of what HPF is about.

The first directive we introduce is the pseudo-variable $NP, which represents the number
of processors in the machine. Its value is not set until run-time, but it may be used to set
such static values such as array dimensions, as in:

```
integer, constant :: short_stride = 1000 / $NP
real              :: values(1000 * $NP)
```

Since the program may be executed on a varying number of processors, values dependent
on $NP are not actually set until run-time.

The second directive is a way of describing and naming arrangements of processors,
called *logical processor arrays*. We do this using the $pshape directive, which takes
one or more positive integer arguments. These values must be constants, or expressions
depending only on constants and $NP, and their product must be equal to $NP. Together,
they define a multi-dimensional array of processors which the compiler can then map onto
the physical processors in a particular machine. For example, the statement:

```
$pshape :: square_procs($np/2, $np/2)
```

defines a square array of processors called square_procs, while:

```
$pshape :: hypercube(2, 2, 2, 2, 2)
```

defines a hypercube of $2^5 = 32$ processors. A default shape called $pvec is provided,
which configures processors as a one-dimensional array. Its definition is equivalent to:

```
$pshape :: pvec($np)
```

Note that the names of logical processor arrays may be the same as the names of program
subroutines or variables, since there is no context in which both could be used. Overloading names like this is usually a silly thing to do, and should be avoided.

Once a logical processor array has been described, a program may align the axes of
any number of arrays with it using the $layout directive. Its single property must be the
name of a logical processor array which has previously been defined. The values in this
directive must be the names of arrays; each must be indexed by as many expressions as
there are axes in the logical processor array. Each axis specification must be an expression
whose value depends only on defined constants, the special constant $NP, and the special
variables $1, $2, etc. These refer to the values of the actual indices of the array being

Chapter 3

laid out. At run-time, these expressions are used to determine which processor holds a particular array element. Any array may only be aligned to one logical processor grid. Two example alignments are:

```
$pshape :: rectangle(4, 2)
$pshape :: cube(2, 2, 2)
integer :: A(40, 40), B(40, 40)
    .
    .
    .
$layout, rectangle :: A((($1 - 1) / 10) + 1,
                        (($2 - 1) / 20) + 1)
$layout, cube      :: B(((($1 - 1) / 10) .mod. 2) + 1,
                        (($1 - 1) / 20) + 1,
                        (($2 - 1) / 20) + 1)
```

Their effects are shown in Figure 3.28. The uses of $pshape define two ways of looking at the eight available processors. The first $layout then maps the array A onto one of these logical processor arrays by matching A's indices and those of the processors. The second $layout uses a more complicated rule to map segments of B onto a 3-dimensional hypercube.

Some types of mapping are so common that special support is provided for them. In fact, HPF only provides this special support, rather than the general index transformation described above. HPF layout directives take the form:

```
!HPF$ DISTRIBUTE(BLOCK, CYCLIC) ONTO rectangle :: A
```

which says that A is to be laid out in blocks along the first axis of the logical processor array rectangle, and cyclically along its second axis (Figure 3.29). Arrays can be collapsed along specified axes, so that all elements with a particular index value reside on the same processor, and layout directives can be parameterized by the size of blocks or the number of elements per cycle. [Koelbel et al. 1994] describes all of these facilities in detail.

The other way to specify a data mapping in FORTRAN-KDP is to use the $align function to specify that one array is to be laid out the same way as another of the same rank and size. $align is most often used in subroutines and functions, where aligning a locally-declared array with another array which has been received as a parameter may greatly increase a module's efficiency. $align takes at least two arguments: the first is the name of the template array, while the others identify the arrays which are to be laid out in the same way. An example of this is:

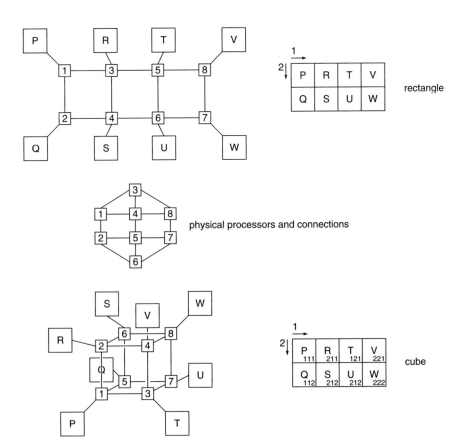

Figure 3.28
Effect of Data Alignment Statements

1	2	1	2	1	2	1	2
3	4	3	4	3	4	3	4
5	6	5	6	5	6	5	6
7	8	7	8	7	8	7	8

Figure 3.29
Block-Cyclic Data Layout

```
procedure smooth(image, margin)
  integer :: image(:, :)                         ! image to smooth
  integer :: margin                              ! tolerance on neighbors
  integer :: nx = size(image, 1),                ! dimensions
             ny = size(image, 2)
  integer :: temp(nx, ny)                        ! smoothed image

  $align, image :: temp                          ! map temp like image

  ! calculate smoothed image
  temp = 0
  temp(1:nx-1, :) = temp(1:nx-1, :) + image(2:nx,   :)
  temp(2:nx,   :) = temp(2:nx,   :) + image(1:nx-1, :)
  temp(:, 1:ny-1) = temp(:, 1:ny-1) + image(:,   2:ny)
  temp(:, 2:ny)   = temp(:, 2:ny)   + image(:,   1:nx-1)
  temp = temp / 4

  ! replace image with smoothed version where necessary
  where abs(image - temp) > margin do
    image = temp
  end where

end procedure
```

If this procedure is going to be put in a library, there is no way its author can know how image will be laid out. Thus, the best thing for her to do is to specify that temp is to be laid out the same way, in the hope that this will result in the least possible inter-processor communication.

Since the best way for a compiler to map processors and data onto a particular machine clearly depends on the machine's architecture, directives such as these give programmers a way of enforcing the things they are sure about, without constraining the compiler any more than necessary, or having to include code for every possible hardware platform. In a bus-based multiprocessor with a single bank of memory, layout directives usually don't make much difference; in an SIMD processor array, it obviously makes sense for the compiler to try to match the topology of the logical processor grid to the actual topology of the machine as closely as possible, e.g. by using the graph embedding techniques of Section 2.5.7. Finding a good mapping of a logical processor array to a less uniform architecture, such as one with a hierarchical memory (Section 2.1.7), can be quite a challenge.

One feature of these systems which FORTRAN-KDP lacks is a way of re-mapping data. It is quite common in large scientific computations for the best alignment of data to change over time. (The best layout for doing matrix multiplication, for example, may not be the same as the best layout for doing an FFT.) The only way to do this in FORTRAN-KDP is to declare two equal-sized arrays, lay them out in the desired ways, and then copy values from one to the other to achieve a re-mapping. This wastes a lot of memory, so HPF and its kin allow programs to change array mappings as a program executes with a `realign` directive. Each time this is done, the run-time system performs a one-to-one permutation on the array's elements, and then changes its notion of what function to use to calculate the actual index of the processor (or memory bank) holding the data, and the location of particular elements within that processor. So long as the alignments which might be used for an array are known during compilation, the compiler can optimize the required permutation, and in particular reduce the amount of buffering required to ensure that outgoing values are not overwritten by incoming values.

3.6 Discussion

The data-parallel paradigm has been the most widely used in parallel computing to date, both because it is the easiest to understand and because most of the things that the people who can afford to buy supercomputers want to do can be done using it. While expressions involving several parallel prefix, mapping, and shaping operations can be difficult to decipher, the loops required to achieve the same effects in a serial language are rarely any clearer. What is more, by constraining the way in which operations across multiple array elements are expressed, data-parallel languages make it easier for compilers to notice, and take advantage of, possible optimizations. However, many algorithms are difficult or impossible to express in a data-parallel fashion. In the next three chapters, we will explore some of the many alternatives.

4 Shared Variables

The *shared variables* model is the most widely used of the major parallel computing paradigms presented in this book. One reason for this is its origins in work on multi-user operating systems. Computer scientists began studying ways of running multiple processes safely and efficiently in a single physical address space in the mid-1960s, and since then a rich theory has been developed in which assertions about the behavior of interacting processes can be formalized and proved. [Andrews 1991] is not only an excellent introduction to this theory, but contains a great deal of historical information tracing the development of major ideas.

Another reason the shared variables model is widely used is that it is the "natural" model for many widely-available machines. Supercomputer architects adopted the shared-variables model as their machines evolved from uniprocessors to contain two or more independent processors. As described in Appendix B, manufacturers such as Cray Research Incorporated began replicating the processors in their machines in the early 1980s. At the same time, established minicomputer manufacturers such as DEC, and newcomers such as Sequent, began building smaller cost-effective multiprocessors in order to compete in the mainframe market.

This approach to parallelism has been extremely successful, both because well-constructed operating systems allowed most users to ignore the fact that the machines they were using contained multiple processors, and because the shared-variables model allowed those programmers who wanted to exploit parallelism explicitly to do so with a minimum of grief. The sections below describe some of the techniques suitable for shared-memory machines, and give examples of their use.

4.1 Creating and Coordinating Processes

Unlike a data-parallel program, a shared-variables program may contain many active processes, all of which may execute at the same time. In most shared-memory systems, these may be created dynamically, and are executed until they choose to terminate; disjoint-memory systems may require programs to create all processes in one go at the start of the program. This section presents a framework for thinking about shared-memory issues; the next two discuss practical programming mechanisms.

4.1.1 Fork, Join, and All That

In most modern operating systems, processes come in two types: heavyweight and lightweight. A *heavyweight process* consists of some code to be executed, an instruction pointer indicating what part of that code the process is to execute next, a stack for storing function parameters and temporary variables, a set of logical registers (which are

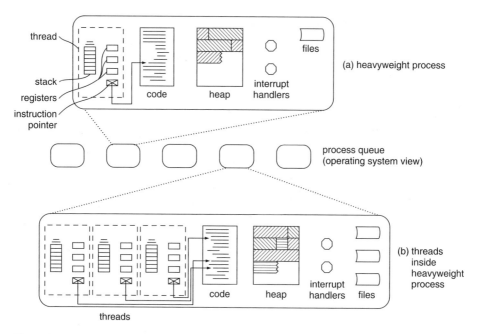

thread
stack
registers
instruction
pointer

files

code   heap   interrupt
                handlers

(a) heavyweight process

process queue
(operating system view)

code   heap   interrupt   files
                handlers

(b) threads
    inside
    heavyweight
    process

threads

Figure 4.1
Process Organization

mapped onto the machine's physical registers when the process executes), a heap from which dynamically-allocated memory is taken, memory management tables describing the process's view of the memory it is using, and other tables containing file descriptors, interrupt handlers, and the like (Figure 4.1a). As their name implies, heavyweight processes carry a lot of information around. This makes switching context an expensive operation. However, because all of this information is available, the operating system can protect heavyweight processes from one another, i.e., can ensure that one heavyweight process does not accidentally modify memory which is being used by another.

In contrast, a *lightweight process*, or *thread*, has only a set of registers and a stack; it borrows its code, its heap, and everything else from a heavyweight process. Threads require more user management than heavyweight processes, but are cheaper to create and context-switch.

Threads have become increasingly popular in the last decade as a programming tool on uniprocessors [Accetta et al. 1986]. For example, one way to handle operating system interrupts is to create a thread whose only job is to manage that interrupt. When the interrupt occurs, a lightweight context switch can be done very quickly to run the thread, and another done to return to the process's main thread once the interrupt has been serviced. The interactions between threads within a heavyweight process are usually managed in the same way as interactions between heavyweight processes, so the discussions in this chapter will be phrased in terms of the latter.

The first method we describe for creating concurrent processes is based on the *fork* and *join* operations used in the UNIX[1] operating system [Ritchie & Thompson 1974, Tannenbaum 1987, Schimmel 1994]. A brand-name UNIX fork copies the calling process to create a single new process; the versions of UNIX offered by manufacturers such as Sequent [Osterhaug 1989] and Alliant [Brawer 1989] offer slightly more functionality. In order to create one or more new processes, an existing process in one of these systems calls fork. This function takes a single integer argument, which is the number of new processes to create. These new processes are called the children of the calling process, which is (logically enough) called their parent. Each child has a complete copy of all of its parent's memory; any changes it makes apply only to its copy of memory, and are not visible to either its parent or its siblings.

After a call to fork(N) returns, the system will contain $N + 1$ identical processes. In order to distinguish between these, fork returns the value 1 to the parent, and $2 \ldots N$ to each of the children. Thus, if a process executes:

```
integer :: num_child, id
initialize num_child
id = fork(num_child)
if id == 1 then
   A
else
   B
end if
```

then only the parent process will execute the code section A; all the newly-created children will execute section B. If a program wants N processes to perform the same actions, it should call fork with $N - 1$ as an argument:

```
integer :: num_child, id
initialize num_child
id = fork(num_child-1)
operations
```

Here, the parent and children all execute the same operations.

---

1. UNIX is a registered trademark of AT&T.

A process terminates itself by calling the subroutine `join`. If the calling process has no children, it is allowed to proceed immediately. If the caller has any outstanding children, on the other hand, the call to `join` forces it to wait until they have all terminated. Only then is the calling process allowed to proceed. For example, if the code above is extended to:

```
integer :: num_child, id
initialize num_child
id = fork(num_child)
if id == 1 then
  A
else
  B
end if
call join()
C
```

then so long as no other processes have been created in either of sections *A* or *B*, each child will terminate when it calls `join`, while the parent will be suspended until all of the children have finished and then be allowed to proceed to section *C*.

But what if other processes had been created by either the parent or some of the children? In this case, the `join` would wait for them to terminate, rather than terminating the caller. For example, the `fork` calls in:

```
integer :: num_1 = 3, num_2 = 2, id_1, id_2
initialize num_child
id_1 = fork(num_1)
id_2 = fork(num_2)
call join()
call join()
```

create the tree of processes shown in Figure 4.2. Every process is uniquely identified by the pair of values in its copies of `id_1` and `id_2`. When each calls `join` for the first time, all those for whom `id_2` is greater than 1 terminate, while all those with an `id_2` of 1 are suspended. The second call to `join` is needed in order to clean up the children created by the first `fork`.

As presented so far, processes are not particularly useful, since there is no way for them to communicate. In particular, since a child's copy of memory is discarded when it terminates, the only way the work it has done can be used by its parent is if the child saves it externally, e.g., by writing it out to a file. This would not only be tedious to write,

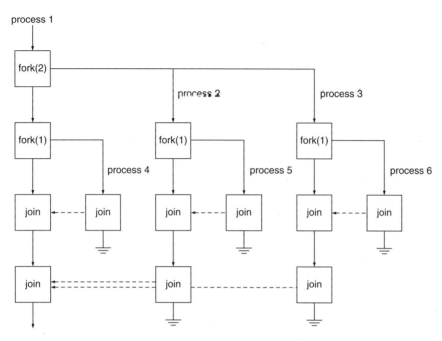

Figure 4.2
Creating Trees of Processes with Fork

but would be tremendously inefficient. To allow processes to communicate while running, many shared-variable programming languages allow programmers to mark variables using the keyword `shared`, which indicates that a variable is not to be copied when processes are forked. Instead, children inherit their parent's copy of the variable, so that any changes any child makes are seen by all other processes. For example, a program could initialize an array's values by making the array `shared`, and creating one process to assign zero to each element:

```
integer, constant :: Len = 1000
real, shared      :: A(Len)
integer           :: id
   .
   .
   .
id = fork(Len-1)
A(id) = 0
call join()
```

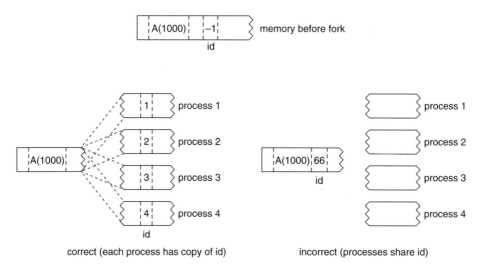

Figure 4.3
Correct and Incorrect Sharing

Because A is shared, the assignments made by the 999 processes created by the `fork` are all visible in the parent.

It is very important to note that the variable `id` in the example above is *not* shared. If it were, then each child process would write the value returned to it by the `fork` call into the same location in memory (Figure 4.3). The result would be chaos, since all processes would think they had the same ID. This problem is discussed in greater detail later in this section.

In almost all systems, it would be very inefficient to initialize an array in the manner shown above. Since the time required to create a single new process is likely to be several times greater than the time needed to initialize 1000 elements of the array using a loop, it would almost always be more efficient to have the main process assign zero to array elements itself. If the array contained one million elements, on the other hand, and the computer being used contained 100 processors, it could well make sense to have 100 processes initialize 10,000 elements each, as in:

```
integer, constant :: Len       = 1000000
integer, constant :: Num_P     = 100
integer, constant :: Elt_per_P = Len/Num_P
real, shared      :: A(Len)
integer           :: id, base, i
```

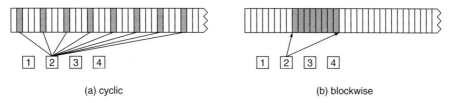

Figure 4.4
Memory Access Patterns Generated by Splitting Loops

```
     .
     .
     .
id = fork(Num_P-1)
base = Elt_per_P * (id - 1)
do i = 1, Elt_per_P
  A(base+i) = 0
end do
call join()
```

This loop is an example of *static scheduling*. Since the amount of work to be done is known in advance, we can build a load-balanced work allocation scheme into the program. Another common example of how static scheduling is used is shown by the function sum_ array in Program 4.1a. This function uses a user-specified number of processes to sum the values in a real array of arbitrary length. sum_array passes $P - 1$ to fork, rather than P, so that $P - 1$ new processes will be added to the one making the call. Once these have been created, the identifier returned by fork is used as the initial value of the index for the loop over the array elements, while the stride used in this loop is equal to the number of processes created. Figure 4.4a shows the memory access patterns this loop generates. Program 4.1b does the same calculation, but uses a blockwise allocation of work instead of a cyclic allocation (Figure 4.4b). The efficiency of each will be determined by the layout of the array A in memory, as described in Section 3.5. In general, a computation in a disjoint-memory machine will be most efficient if it follows the *owner-computes rule*: the processor in whose memory data are located should do the calculations involving that data.

While fork is the most common way to express process creation, it can be difficult in a large program to keep track of which join each fork corresponds to, and indeed whether all the forks and joins match up. Marking variables as shared can also lead to structural problems, as it may be convenient for processes to share a structure at one point, but have their own private copies at another.

```
real function sum_array(A, P)
  real, shared :: A(:)              ! array to sum
  integer      :: P                 ! number of processes to use
  integer      :: len = size(A, 1)  ! length of array
  real, shared :: sum(P)            ! temporary storage
  integer      :: id, i             ! identifier and loop index

  ! create processes
  id = fork(P-1)

  ! calculate partial sums (each process has different id here)
  sum(id) = 0
  do i = id, len, P
    sum(id) = sum(id) + A(i)
  end do

  ! restore single-process execution
  call join()

  ! calculate final result (only parent does this)
  do i = 2, P
    sum(1) = sum(1) + sum(i)
  end do
  return sum(1)

end function
```
(a) cyclic summing

Program 4.1
Summing an Array Using Fork

```
real function sum_array(A, P)
  real, shared :: A(:)                    ! array to sum
  integer      :: P                       ! number of processes to use
  integer      :: len = size(A, 1)        ! length of array
  real, shared :: sum(P)                  ! temporary storage
  integer      :: id, i                   ! identifier and loop index
  integer      :: base, num, lim          ! what to do

  ! create processes
  id = fork(P-1)

  ! calculate what to do
  num  = (len + P - 1)/P
  base = ((id - 1) * num) + 1
  lim = (base + num - 1) .min. len

  ! calculate partial sums (each process has different id here)
  sum(id) = 0
  do i = base, lim
     sum(id) = sum(id) + A(i)
  end do

  ! restore single-process execution
  call join()

  ! calculate final result (only parent does this)
  do i = 2, P
     sum(1) = sum(1) + sum(i)
  end do
  return sum(1)

end function
```

(b) blockwise summing

Program 4.1 *(continued)*
Summing an Array Using Fork

Prudent programmers therefore rely on more structured mechanisms for managing shared variables and concurrent processes. The one used in FORTRAN-KSV is the `create` statement, which allows an arbitrary number of processes of different types to be created at one time. The syntax of this is:

```
create
   num1 of subr1(params)
   num2 of subr1(params)
   .
   .
   .
end create
```

The first term in each branch must be a positive integer, and is the number of processes to create. The second term is laid out like a subroutine call. The parameters to this call are always shared between its instances, so that programmers can determine by examining the process creation code what structures those processes will share. All variables defined within the called subroutines, and any which they themselves call, are made private to each process. Global variables are always shared.

If a programming system does not support `create`, it is sometimes best to use nested `fork`s to create producers and consumers in two stages, as in:

```
type = fork(1)
if type == 1 then
   id = fork(Num_Type_1-1)
   operations
   call join()
else
   id = fork(Num_Type_2-1)
   operations
   call join()
end if
call join()
```

Nesting process creation like this is slightly more expensive than creating all processes in one go. However, it is conceptually much cleaner than creating all the processes in one `fork`, and then having each process compare its process ID with the number of processes of each type in order to determine what it should do next. This latter technique leads to error-prone code of the form:

```
id = fork(Num_A + Num_B + ··· + Num_Z)
```

```
if id <= Num_A then
  A
elseif id <= (Num_A + Num_B) then
  B
elseif id <= (Num_A + Num_B + Num_C) then
  .
  .
  .
end if
```

Note that `create` is a *blocking* operation. Once a process has created children, it cannot proceed until all of those children have completed execution.[2] Thus, if N worker processes are needed, N should be created, rather than $N - 1$ as with `fork`, since the parent process cannot participate in the work.

Note also that there is no automatic mechanism for copying data during process creation, as there is in the `fork`/`join` model. Instead, the intrinsic function `copy` can be used, as in:

```
create
  num1 of subr1( . . . , copy(x), . . . )
end create
```

so that each new process gets its own copy of x. `copy` can be applied to any scalar, array, or record. If it is applied to a record, it only copies that record, and not any other records the first record points to. Instead, pointers in the first record are nullified. This is called *shallow copying*, and is used for the sake of both efficiency and safety:

• Since linked structures can contain cycles (e.g., circular lists), some sort of traversal-recording algorithm would be needed to ensure that a process did not try to make an infinitely-large copy of an object. Such algorithms are common in languages such as LISP, where they are used to support automatic garbage collection, but represent a significant overhead.

• Shallow copying ensures that a process only gets what its parent explicitly gives it, and does not accidentally inherit pointers to other data. This is necessary in the disjoint-memory systems which are the subject of the next two chapters, but is good software engineering practice even when the hardware would allow pointers to be inherited.

---

2. This can lead to unexpected behavior if a function is being called to calculate how many descendent processes to spawn in a `create`, and that function itself creates children internally. Matters are even worse if the function performs any of the blocking operations described later, such as waiting on a semaphore.

```
real function sum_array(A, P)
  real     :: A(:)                              ! to be summed
  integer :: P                                  ! number of processes
  real     :: sum(P)                            ! scratch space
  integer :: i

  create
    P of summer(P, A, sum)
  end create

  ! calculate final result
  do i = 2, P
    sum(1) = sum(1) + sum(i)
  end do
  return sum(1)

end function

procedure summer(P, A, temp)
  integer :: P                                  ! number of processes
  real     :: A(:), temp(:)                     ! to be summed and scratch
  integer :: id = id_rel_self()                 ! own ID
  integer :: len = size(A, 1), i

  temp(id) = 0
  do i = id, len, P
    temp(id) = temp(id) + A(i)
  end do
end procedure
```

Program 4.2
Summing an Array Using Create

Program 4.2 shows how the array summing program can be re-implemented using create. In this version, sum_array is a shell which creates the desired number of processes,
and passes them a temporary storage vector into which they can write their partial results.

While this version appears more modular than its predecessor, the whole of the temp
array is still passed to each process. It is only by implicit agreement that each of the
summing processes only modifies its own element of the array. This lack of enforced
modularity is one of the most important weaknesses of the shared-variables model. Note

also that no variables or parameters are declared shared; this is decided automatically by the parameter-passing mechanism.

Three other aspects of these small programs deserve further comment. The first is the use of the temporary array sums to store the results calculated by each process, so that these can be totalled later by the parent. This might seem an unnecessary complication, as the code would be both simpler and more efficient if each process simply added a value to a single variable total. However, such an implementation would also be wrong; the reasons for this are the subject of the next section.

The second point is the use of the function id_rel_self. In the fork/join model, processes received IDs as a result of calling fork. In the create model, execution always starts at the top of a fresh procedure invocation. Processes must query the run-time system in order to find out who they are. An alternative approach would be to require that subroutines used inside create statements take an integer parameter as their first argument, and to have the run-time system assign each process's ID to a private copy of that parameter. However, this would make it difficult to write subroutines which could be called both normally and during process creation.

Third, while the cost of process creation varies from system to system, it is never cheap. Even with hardware support, creating a new thread of control can take hundreds of cycles. Thus, if the array to be summed in Program 4.2 only contains a few dozen elements, it will be much faster to add them sequentially, even on a multiprocessor. An extreme example of how *not* to use parallelism is code such as:

```
procedure zero_array(A)
  real    :: A(:)                        ! array to zero
  integer :: len = size(A, 1)


  create
    len of zero_element(A)
  end create


end procedure

procedure zero_element(A)
  real    :: A(:)                        ! array to zero


  A(id_rel_self()) = 0.0


end procedure
```

Example 4.1 (Mandelbrot Set I)   Program 4.3 shows a simple Mandelbrot Set generation program written in FORTRAN-KSV. This program assigns the calculation of each row of the Mandelbrot Set to a single process based on the process's ID and the row's index. While this is a simple strategy, it can be very poorly load balanced, since some rows require much more calculation than others. Later examples will show how to achieve better load balancing.

For some parameters, this program can produce a different result than its serial counterpart. As explained on Pages 56 and 139, changing the order in which floating-point values are added can change the result produced. If processes add (stride * Inc) to their copies of x independently, they will sample the complex plane at slightly different points than the serial program. For a fractal like the Mandelbrot Set, this can lead to noticeably different images being produced.

Example 4.2 (Quicksort)   Program 4.4 shows a simple parallel sorting procedure based on quicksort that uses nothing except create. Given a section of a vector v, it uses a (sequential) bubblesort if v has fewer than Qsort_Thresh values. Otherwise, it partitions v into two sections, and then quicksorts each. Since these subsections are disjoint, they can be sorted in parallel, so quicksort creates two children to do this sorting.

This program is an example of a strategy called *divide and conquer*: the initial problem is sequentially divided into parts, each of which can then be solved separately. The solution of the parts is then done concurrently. While simple, this strategy is very inefficient in this particular case. The reason is the inverse relationship between the amount of work to be done and the amount of parallelism being exploited. The first quicksort process must partition all N elements of the vector b on its own. If we assume that this takes time t, then we see that in the next stage of processing, two processes each take time $t/2$ (on average) to partition $N/2$ elements. If the next stage requires time $t/4$ and so on, the speedup achieved is at most 2. Example 4.4 describes a sorting algorithm which exploits parallelism much more effectively.

If several create blocks are nested inside one another, i.e., if a subroutine used in process creation itself contains a create, it may be useful to maintain a vector of IDs, so that each process can determine its parentage. An example of this is:

```
integer, constant :: Depth = 3
integer, constant :: Width = 3
integer           :: id_vec(Depth)
   .
   .
   .
```

```
create
  Width of tree(copy(id_vec), 1)
end create
  .
  .
  .
procedure tree(ident, d)
  integer :: ident(:), d

  ident(d) = id_rel_self()
  if d < Depth then
    create
      Width of tree(copy(ident), d+1)
    end create
  else
    do useful work
  end if
end procedure
```

This code creates a ternary tree of processes, as shown in Figure 4.5. Each process receives a copy of a vector of IDs which uniquely identifies its position in the tree. Note how copy is used to ensure that the variable id_vec (passed as the parameter ident inside tree) is not inadvertently shared between processes.

4.1.2 Atomicity, Exclusion, and Fairness

To understand why Program 4.2 needed to contain the temporary array sums, consider what happens when a conventional microprocessor executes a statement like:

```
x = x + y
```

First, the value of x is copied from memory into a register. Next, the value of y is copied into another register. The contents of this second register are then added to those of the first, and the result written back to memory. Thus, this simple operation translates into the lower-level instruction sequence:

```
LD  R1, x
LD  R2, y
ADD R2, R1
ST  R1, x
```

Now consider what could happen if a second process was executing:

```
integer, constant :: N = 21
integer, constant :: P = number of processes
real,    constant :: X0 = -1.5
real,    constant :: Y0 = -1.5
real,    constant :: Extent = 3.0
real,    constant :: Inc = Extent / (N-1)

program
  type(logical) :: patch(N, N)
  create
    P of worker(patch, P)
  end create
end program

procedure worker(patch, stride)
  type(logical) :: patch(:, :)         ! to fill
  integer       :: stride              ! offset between lines
  integer       :: id = id_rel_self()  ! own ID
  integer       :: i, j                ! traversal
  real          :: x, y                ! coordinates

  ! calculate
  x = X0 + ((id - 1) * Inc)
  do i = id, N, stride
    y = Y0
    do j = 1, N
      patch(i, j) = mandel(x, y)
      y = y + Inc
    end do
    x = x + (stride * Inc)
  end do
end procedure
```

Program 4.3
Simple Shared-Variables Mandelbrot Set Generation

```
integer, constant :: Qsort_Thresh = 4          ! bubblesort below this

procedure quicksort(v)
  integer :: v(:)                              ! to be sorted
  integer :: pivot, tmp                        ! pivot and swapping temporary
  integer :: lo, hi, lim                       ! indices and limit
  integer :: i, j                              ! traversal indices
  logical :: loop                              ! sorting control

  lim = size(v, 1)
  ! slowsort
  if lim <= Qsort_Thresh then
    call bubblesort(v)
  ! quicksort
  else
    ! setup
    i = 1
    j = lim
    pivot = v((i + j)/2)
    loop = .true.
    ! split
    do while loop
      do while v(i) < pivot
        i = i + 1
      end while
      do while pivot < v(j)
        j = j - 1
      end while
      if i <= j then
        tmp = v(i) ; v(i) = v(j) ; v(j) = tmp
        i = i + 1
        j = j - 1
      end if
      loop = (i <= j)
    end while
```

Program 4.4
Parallel Quicksort

```
    ! fork (or sort in-line)
    if 1 < j then
      if i < lim then
        create
          1 of quicksort(v(1:j))
          1 of quicksort(v(i:lim))
        end create
      else
        call quicksort(v(1:j))
      end if
    elseif i < lim then
      call quicksort(v(i:lim))
    end if
  end if
end procedure
```

Program 4.4 *(continued)*
Parallel Quicksort

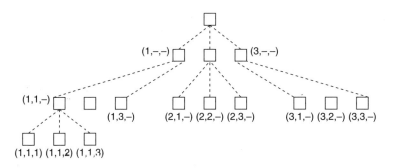

Figure 4.5
A Ternary Tree of Processes

```
y = 1
```

while the first was executing:

```
x = x + y
```

Assigning 1 to y only involves two low-level instructions—one to load the constant 1 into a register, the other to store the register's value to memory—but since the physical processor can only do one thing at a time, these instructions could be interleaved with the first process's instructions in an arbitrary fashion. One possibility is shown in Figure 4.6a,

P$_1$	P$_2$	x	y	R$_1$	R$_2$	R$_3$
		22	43	–	–	–
LD R$_1$,x		22	43	22	–	–
LD R$_2$,y		22	43	22	43	–
	LD R$_3$,0	22	43	22	43	0
	ST R$_0$,0	22	0	22	43	0
ADD R$_1$,R$_2$		22	0	65	43	0
ST R$_1$,x		65	0	65	43	0

(a) process 1 appears to run before process 2

P$_1$	P$_2$	x	y	R$_1$	R$_2$	R$_3$
		22	43	–	–	–
LD R$_1$,x		22	43	22	–	–
	LD R$_3$,0	22	43	22	–	–
	ST R$_3$,y	22	0	22	–	–
LD R$_2$,y		22	0	22	0	–
ADD R$_1$,R$_2$		22	0	22	0	0
ST R$_1$,x		22	0	22	0	0

(b) process 2 appears to run before process 1

Figure 4.6
Safe Interleaving

which loads the values needed by the first process, then executes the second process, and only then does the first process's addition and writes out its result. This sequence would have the same effect as running process 1, then running process 2. By contrast, the sequence of steps shown in Figure 4.6b would have the same effect as running process 2, and then process 1, since it writes out process 2's result before reading the second value required by process 1.

But consider what would happen if the statements:

x = x + 1

and:

x = x + 2

were run concurrently. Each involves four low-level instructions, but the order in which these are interleaved could make it appear as though only the first or the second statement had been executed, rather than both. For example, after the sequence shown in Figure 4.7a the value of x would have been incremented by 3, but after Figure 4.7b it would only have been incremented by 2, while after Figure 4.7c it would only have been incremented by

P1	P2	x	R1	R2	R3	R4	
		5	–	–	–	–	
LD R1,x		5	5	–	–	–	
LD R2,1		5	5	1	–	–	
ADD R2,R1		5	6	1	–	–	
ST R1,x		6	6	1	–	–	(a) x incremented by 3
	LD R3,x	6	6	1	6	–	
	LD R4,2	6	6	1	6	2	
	ADD R3,R4	6	6	1	8	2	
	ST R3,x	8	6	1	8	2	
		5	–	–	–	–	
LD R1,x		5	5	–	–	–	
	LD R3,x	5	5	–	5	–	
LD R2,1		5	5	1	5	–	
ADD R1,R2		5	6	1	5	–	(b) x incremented by 2
ST R1,x		6	6	1	5	–	
	LD R4,2	6	6	1	5	2	
	ADD R3,R4	6	6	1	7	2	
	ST R3,x	7	6	1	7	2	
		5	–	–	–	–	
	LD R3,x	5	–	–	5	–	
LD R1,x		5	5	–	5	–	
	LD R4,2	5	5	–	5	2	
LD R2,1		5	5	1	5	2	(c) x incremented by 1
	ADD R3,R4	6	5	1	7	2	
ADD R1,R2		5	6	1	7	2	
	ST R3,x	7	6	1	7	2	
ST R1,x		6	6	1	7	2	

Figure 4.7
Unsafe Interleaving

1. Only the first of these is a legal result; any sensible system would insist that x must appear to have been incremented by 3 after both processes have run. We say that x is a *live variable* in this context, since from the point of view of any single process its value can spontaneously change.

The root of these problems is that modifying a variable is not an *atomic* operation. Atomic actions are ones which are guaranteed to execute without interruption or interference; immediately after an atomic operation, the state of the system has been changed only by what that operation did. Reading a single scalar value from memory or writing a single scalar value back is atomic. Sequences of these operations are not, since a process could be suspended part-way through a sequence, and only re-scheduled after a second process had modified some of the values being used by the first. Such a situation is called a *race condition*, since the result of the operations is determined by a race between the two or more processes involved.

In order to ensure correct operation in such cases, the system must somehow be able to guarantee *mutual exclusion* between the operations that involve x, i.e., guarantee that while one process is manipulating x, no other process will be able to read or write its value. This can be done by introducing a new language construct, the when statement, which takes the form:

```
when logical condition do
    operations
end when
```

When a process encounters a when, it is suspended until the when's controlling condition, or *guard*, becomes .true.. At this point, the process is re-scheduled to execute the operations within the when. While this process is executing, no other process may read or write any of the variables which are read or written within the when. It is the compiler's job to make a list of the shared variables which are mentioned within each when, and the operating system's job to ensure that no other process which might access these is scheduled while the protected statements are being executed.

Using when, the double increment example shown above can be implemented very simply as:

```
integer :: x
    .
    .
    .
create
    1 of adder(x, 1)
    1 of adder(x, 2)
end create
    .
    .
    .
procedure adder(vbl, incr)
    integer :: vbl
    integer :: incr
    when .true. do
        vbl = vbl + incr
    end when
end procedure
```

Whichever process reaches its when first will add its increment incr to vbl. If the other process reaches its when while this is going on, it will be suspended until the first one has exited the when block, since only one process is allowed to execute a when involving vbl at any time. Since the rôle of the when is simply to block the execution of other processes, rather than to force a process to wait for a particular condition, the guard in each when statement is simply `.true.`.

Guarding whens with `.true.` is generally a bad idea, as it can block operations which might actually be safe. If, for example, several processes wish to read the value of a user-defined constant inside a when, they will be forced to take turns, even though it would be perfectly safe for them to read the constant's value concurrently. when therefore allows guards to be specified to control the degree of mutual exclusion around a region. An example that shows how this might be used is the *producer-consumer problem*, in which one process generates data which another process consumes. The two processes communicate through a shared queue; the producer adds items to the queue while the consumer removes them. For illustrative purposes, suppose that the queue has been implemented as an array of structures, as shown in Program 4.5. The subroutine enqueue copies the fields of its parameter item into the next free slot in the array queue%items, increments queue%count to show that an item has been added, and adjusts queue%tail to indicate the next free slot. For its part, dequeue copies the values in the record indicated by queue%head into its item parameter, then decrements queue%count and moves queue%head forward. When the head and tail indices reach the end of the array, they wrap around (Figure 4.8).

Now suppose that these routines are being used by two concurrent processes, as in:

```
type(queue_type) :: queue
logical          :: active = .true.
  .
  .
  .
queue = new_queue()
create
  1 of producer(queue, active)
  1 of consumer(queue, active)
end create
  .
  .
  .
procedure producer(queue, active)
  type(queue_type) :: queue
  logical          :: active
  type(item_type)  :: item

  do while items being produced
    produce(item)
    call enqueue(queue, item)
```

```
  end while
  active = .false.
end procedure
  .
  .
  .
procedure consumer(queue, active)
  type(queue_type) :: queue
  logical          :: active
  type(item_type)  :: item

  do while (active .or. (queue%count > 0))
    call dequeue(queue, item)
    consume(item)
  end while
end procedure
```

So long as the two processes work at roughly the same rate, and the queue never fills up or empties, everything will go well. However, if producing an item takes much less time than consuming one, or *vice versa*, then one or the other of the queue's assertions will soon fail. For example, if consuming an item takes twice as long as producing one, then after 200 items have been produced (and 100 consumed), the queue will be full, and the next attempt to enqueue an item will fail. Even if this were not the case, the two processes are incrementing and decrementing queue%count concurrently, which means that some of their operations could get lost, just as some of the increments on x were lost in the earlier example.

The solution is to enclose the actions on the queue in guarded when statements. For the producer, the guard condition is:

```
queue%count < Queue_Size
```

since the consumer should not attempt to add a value to a full queue. Similarly, the consumer's guard should be

```
queue%count > 0
```

so that it does not try to take items from an empty queue.

Adding these guards leads to the functions in Program 4.6. Here, when serves two purposes: it ensures that processes never try to enqueue when the queue is full, or dequeue when it is empty, and it ensures that operations on the head, tail, and count fields of the queue structure are atomic. This last guarantee is possible because, as mentioned earlier, a

```
integer, constant :: Queue_Size = 100

type queue_type
  integer       :: head, tail, count
  type(item_type) :: items(Queue_Size)
end type

type(queue_type) function new_queue()
  type(queue_type) :: result
  call allocate(result)
  result%head  = 1
  result%tail  = 1
  result%count = 0
  return result
end function

procedure enqueue(queue, item)
  type(queue_type) :: queue
  type(item_type)  :: item

  assert queue%count < Queue_Size
  call copy_item(queue%items(queue%tail), item)
  queue%tail  = mod1(queue%tail + 1, Queue_Size)
  queue%count = queue%count + 1

end procedure

procedure dequeue(queue, item)
  type(queue_type) :: queue
  type(item_type)  :: item

  assert queue%count > 0
  call copy_item(item, queue%items(queue%tail))
  queue%head  = mod1(queue%head + 1, Queue_Size)
  queue%count = queue%count - 1

end procedure
```

Program 4.5
Insecure Queue-Managing Routines

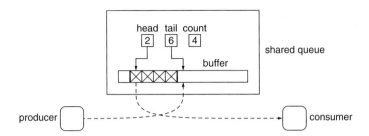

Figure 4.8
A Shared Queue

when determines which variables are manipulated inside each when, and tells the run-time system not to execute two or more whens concurrently if their variable accesses overlap.

However, this implementation is still incorrect, as it could lead to deadlock. Deadlock was first encountered in Section 2.5.8, and was defined as a situation in which two or more processes were suspended, and neither thought it had the right to continue before the other. To see how it can arise here, imagine that the two processes are interleaved so that events occur as follows:

1. The producer puts the last item in the queue, and exits its while loop.

2. The consumer is scheduled, and consumes the last queue item. It then checks active, finds that it is .true., and tries to execute its when statement. Since queue%count is 0, the consumer is suspended.

3. The producer is then re-scheduled, assigns .false. to active, and terminates.

4. At this point, the process which created the producer and consumer is waiting for the consumer to terminate. However, the consumer is waiting for someone to increment the queue's count, so that it can dequeue and consume another item. Deadlock has occurred.

This situation may seem very improbable, but that is precisely why it is dangerous. A program may run dozens or hundreds of times before such a time-dependent error occurs. What is worse, it may have to be re-run many more times before the error re-occurs. As a result, it can take much longer to find and fix errors in parallel programs than in serial ones.[3]

In this example, the problem of deadlock cannot be cured simply by guarding all reads and writes involving the variable active with whens, since the deadlock arises from

---

3. This is one of the reasons FORTRAN-K is an emulator, rather than truly parallel: because scheduling is controlled explicitly, every execution sequence is reproducible.

```
procedure producer(queue, active)
  type(queue_type) :: queue
  logical          :: active
  type(item_type)  :: item

  do while items being produced
    produce(item)
    when queue%count < Queue_Size do
      call enqueue(queue, item)
    end when
  end while
  active = .false.
end procedure
  .
  .
  .
procedure consumer(queue, active)
  type(queue_type) :: queue
  logical          :: active
  type(item_type)  :: item

  do while active
    when queue%count > 0 do
      call dequeue(queue, item)
    end when
    consume(item)
  end while
end procedure
```

Program 4.6
Improved Producer and Consumer Processes

scheduling order rather than from values being overwritten. Having the producer keep a count of the total number of items it has added to the queue, and the consumer a count of the total number it has removed, would also be incorrect. The idea behind this non-solution is to have the consumer stop as soon as it has dequeued all of the values the producer had created. However, since the consumer could catch up with the producer before the producer had finished executing, this could lead to a situation in which the consumer had terminated while the producer was waiting for someone to free up some queue space.

   The correct solution in this example is to modify the consumer so that it contains a single when, which can proceed either when an item is added to the queue, or when active becomes false:

```
procedure consumer(queue, active)
  type(queue_type) :: queue
  logical           :: active
  logical           :: loop = .true.

  do while loop
    when (.not. active) .or. (queue%count > 0) do
      if .not. active then
        loop = false
      else
        call dequeue(queue, item)
        consume(item)
      end if
    end when
  end while
end procedure
```

After the when has executed, the consumer must check its guard conditions one by one to see what it is supposed to do next. This wait-then-check technique is very common in shared-variable programming, but care must be taken to ensure that only one triggering condition in a guard could ever become true at any time, so that the process's subsequent behavior is deterministic. The when is not buried inside the queue manipulation functions for exactly this reason: if the queue-handling routines are used in other contexts, it may be unnecessary or simply wrong for them to wait in this way.

The producer-consumer program now seems correct, but its correctness depends on an assumption about the behavior of the system on which it is run. Suppose that the producer is de-scheduled immediately after finishing its while loop. When it is next scheduled, active will be set to .false., and the consumer will be able to terminate. However, what guarantee is there that the producer ever will be re-scheduled?

This objection may seem rather picky—after all, what kind of operating system would never schedule a process that was ready to run? In many cases, however, the correctness of many parallel programs depends on the *fairness* of the scheduling policy used. A system is said to be *unconditionally fair* if every process which could have continued executing when it was de-scheduled is eventually re-scheduled. Thus, a system only has to be unconditionally fair in order to execute the producer-consumer program correctly.

A system is *weakly fair* if it is unconditionally fair, and if every guarded action (i.e., every when statement) whose condition eventually becomes .true., and stays .true. thereafter, is eventually executed. A system is *strongly fair* if it is unconditionally fair, and if every guarded action whose condition is .true. infinitely often is eventually executed. The difference between weak and strong fairness is illustrated by the following example (borrowed from [Andrews 1991]):

```
logical :: a = .true., b = .false.
create
  1 of changer(a, b)
  1 of waiter(a, b)
end create
  .
  .
  .
procedure changer(a, b)
  logical :: a, b
  do while a
    b = .true.
    b = .false.
  end while
end procedure
  .
  .
  .
procedure waiter(a, b)
  logical :: a, b
  when b do
    a = .false.
  end when
end procedure
```

Each time changer goes around its loop it briefly sets b to .true.. If waiter is scheduled in one of these brief intervals, it will set a to .false.. Both processes will then terminate.

In a strongly fair system, this sequence of events is guaranteed to happen eventually. If it did not, then the condition on which waiter is waiting would be true an infinite number of times without ever being acted on. In a weakly-fair system, on the other hand, this program may or may not terminate, as it is possible that waiter might only ever check the value of b at moments when b is .false., e.g., at the end of each loop in the parent process. In fact, this latter behavior does occur on some systems, which only deschedule processes at conditional jumps. As a general rule, if there is any possible execution sequence which will make a program behave incorrectly, there is some computer out there which will choose that sequence at least once in a while. . . .

The distinction between weak and strong fairness is important because no efficient way of implementing strong fairness has ever been found. If a program is large, and if the conditional expressions which processes are waiting to become .true. are complicated, any modification of any variable could potentially allow some process to be re-scheduled. Checking these conditions repeatedly obviously puts a tremendous burden on the operating system. Thus, it is important that programmers satisfy themselves that their programs will always execute correctly, even on weakly-fair systems.

4.2   Practical Synchronization Mechanisms

Even in a weakly-fair system, evaluating the conditional guards in when statements would be so horrendously expensive as to be impractical. What is more, determining which whens had to be mutually exclusive would be practically impossible, since whens inside subroutines could depend on parameters, or on particular elements of arrays or linked structures. For these reasons, no practical parallel system provides this completely-general mechanism. Instead, most systems offer one of several simpler tools, which allow a process to wait on a single standard type of condition. These mechanisms are usually supported by special-purpose hardware, e.g., by one or more special instructions which are guaranteed to execute atomically.

4.2.1   Test-and-Set

The simplest practical synchronization mechanism is *test&set*. This function atomically copies the value of a logical variable called a *lock* into a temporary variable, assigns .true. to the lock, and then returns the value of the temporary variable. Test&set therefore behaves as the following function would, if its implementation were practical:

```
logical function testset(lock)
  logical :: lock
  logical :: temp
  when .true. do
    temp = lock
    lock = .true.
  end when
  return temp
end function
```

During each call to testset, the lock's value will be set to .true.. However, the value returned to the calling process will be either .true. or .false., depending on the lock's state before the call. Two or more processes can use this fact to ensure that only one of them enters a *critical region* at any time, simply by waiting until an agreed-upon lock is `.false.`:

```
logical :: lock = .false.
create
  N of worker(lock)
end create
  .
  .
  .

procedure worker(lock)
  logical :: lock

  do while loop condition
    non-critical operations
    ! spin until allowed to enter critical region
    do while testset(lock)
      skip
    end while
    critical region
    ! un-lock critical region
    lock = .false.
  end while
end procedure
```

The variable `lock` is shared, so changes to it are seen by every worker process. The inner `while` loop executed by each process, which waits until the lock is clear and then immediately sets it, is called a *spin lock* since each process "spins" in a tight loop until the lock becomes available. The code in the critical region guarded by the spin lock can be executed safely because any other process trying to enter the critical region has to spin until the lock becomes available. Once a process has done what it needs to do, it clears the lock by assigning `.false.` to it. The lock's new state will be noticed by the process whose own `testset` happens to be scheduled next.

It is important to understand why a special `testset` operation is needed, and why the spinning loop:

```
do while lock
  skip
end while
lock = .true.
```

could not be used in place of:

```
do while testset(lock)
  skip
end while
```

The reason is that if two or more processes were both waiting on the lock, one could see the lock become free, exit its `while` loop, then immediately be descheduled. If the other process was then scheduled, it too would see a free lock, and would exit its loop. Upon being re-scheduled, both processes would assign `.true.` to the lock, and then enter their critical regions concurrently.

Spin-locking using test&set is simple to use, and test&set itself is straightforward to implement in hardware. The main drawback of simple spin-locking is that it wastes both processor cycles and memory bandwidth. If a lock is held by one process for a long time, every other process waiting on that lock will repeatedly be scheduled, test the lock a few times, and be de-scheduled. Dozens or hundreds of cycles can be wasted restoring and then re-saving the process's state each time this happens. In addition, each test&set operation assigns a value to the lock. This necessarily involves accessing some part of shared memory, so spin-locking generates a very large number of memory operations. These increase contention for either the bus in a bus-based multiprocessor, or the communication network in a MIN-based multiprocessor or multicomputer. Thus, a process which is spinning for any length of time will indirectly slow down other processes, by interfering with their memory accesses.

The tight spinning implemented by:

```
do while testset(lock)
  skip
end while
```

should usually be avoided. If a lot of work is to be done in the region guarded by the lock, it may make more sense for processes which find the lock unavailable to put themselves to sleep for a while before re-testing the lock. This reduces both the number of wasted processor cycles and the load placed on the processor-memory interface. Most operating systems provide some sort of delay function for this purpose; a process calling this function is descheduled either for a specified period of time, or until a specified moment in time. In the Inmos transputer [Inmos 1988b], for example, waiting until a specified time is implemented by having a process add a record to a time-ordered queue. Each record in this queue contains the time to awaken a process, a pointer to the process itself, and a pointer to the next item in the queue (Figure 4.9). Special hardware continually compares the time

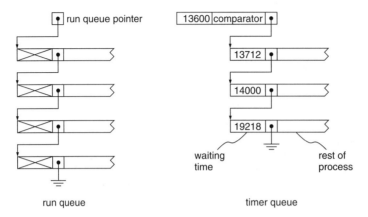

Figure 4.9
A Hardware-Based Process Pausing Mechanism

stamp in the record at the head of the queue with the value of the processor's internal clock; when the two became equal, the process in question is put back on the scheduling queue.

If processes are to be delayed, how large a delay should be used? If the delay is too small, it will have little or no effect, but if it is too large, processes will remain idle when they could acquire the lock they want. In the worst case, a process would be scheduled, test the lock, find that it was unavailable, and put itself out of action for a long interval, just before the process holding the lock released it. Another consideration is that if Π processes attempt to claim a lock at the same time, and those which fail wait the same length of time after failing, then when the time interval expires then $\Pi - 1$ processes will try to claim the lock almost simultaneously. Again, all but one will fail, leaving the remaining $\Pi - 2$ to collide again. Such inadvertent synchronization can greatly reduce system performance.

One solution to this, which is used in some local-area networks, is to have processes wait for random intervals whenever they fail to acquire a lock. Another, examined in [Graunke & Thakkar 1990], is to have processes wait a very short time initially, but to increase each process's delay each time it fails to acquire the lock. For example, a doubling delay schedule could be implemented by:

```
integer, constant :: Delay_Init = 64
logical           :: lock = .false.
  .
  .
  .
create
```

```
    N of worker(lock)
end create
    .
    .
    .
procedure worker(lock)
    logical :: lock
    integer :: delay = Delay_Init
    do while loop condition
        non-critical operations
        ! spin until allowed to enter critical region
        do while testset(lock)
            call pause(delay)
            delay = 2 * delay + 1
        end while
        delay = delay/2
        critical region
        ! un-lock critical region
        lock = .false.
    end while
end procedure
```

Figure 4.10 shows how this scheme works. While processes usually find the lock busy the first time they try to acquire it, the second time they try to enter the critical region they are delayed by staggered intervals. If a process's delay ever becomes too large, it will automatically be cut back by the halving which occurs after the test&set loop.

Another approach to making spin-locks more efficient is the test&(test&set) locking algorithm. This algorithm works best on machines with caches, in which only changes to variables are communicated. Such machines are the subject of Section 4.4. In a test&(test&set) lock, each process spins in an outer loop which reads the value of the lock without setting it:

```
acquired = .false.
do while .not. acquired
    do while lock                           ! wait until lock might be free
        skip
    end while
    acquired = .not. testset(lock)          ! check that lock is actually free
end while
```

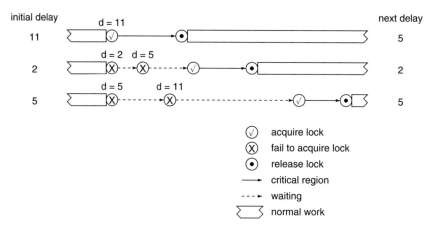

Figure 4.10
Avoiding Collisions by Delaying Processes

Only when a process thinks that the lock *might* be available does it execute a test&set. If many processes are contending for the lock, this can reduce the volume of communication significantly, since the reads required by the outer loop are satisfied in each processor's cache. Communication only takes place when one processor changes the lock's value, and sends news of its change to the main memory or to other processors.

A further refinement of spin-locking is described in [Mellor-Crummey & Scott 1991]. This algorithm creates a linked list of locking records, each in the cache or local memory of a particular process. Each process spins on its own locking record, so that no inter-processor communication is required. When the process at the head of the queue exits the critical region, it writes into the locking record of the process behind it. Thus, each process performs only a small, constant number of inter-processor communication operations each time it acquires and releases the lock.

4.2.2   Fetch-and-Operate

An extension of test&set which was supported by several machines designed in the 1980s [Gottlieb et al. 1983, Pfister et al. 1985] is called *fetch&add*. In its simplest form, fetch&add takes a single integer argument and increments it, while atomically returning its pre-increment value. Fetch&add is therefore equivalent to the (impractical) function:

```
integer function fetchadd(vbl)
   integer :: vbl
   integer :: temp
```

```
when .true. do
  temp = vbl
  vbl  = vbl + 1
end when
return temp
end function
```

If the value of `vbl` is 5 before a fetch&add on it, then the fetch&add will return 5, while setting `vbl` to 6. The next fetch&add will return 6, assigning 7 to `vbl`, and so forth.

Fetch&add can easily be generalized to allow any increment to be used, and further generalized to use a variety of operators, such as `.min.` or `.bitxor.`. [Kruskal et al. 1988]. To allow for this, FORTRAN-KSV's intrinsic function `fetchop` takes three arguments: the variable on which the operation is to be done, the operator to be applied, and the other argument to that operator. Thus, if `var` and `res` are integer variables, the sequence of operations:

```
var = 0
res = fetchop(var, ".max.",    1)
res = fetchop(var, ".bitxor.", 2)
res = fetchop(var, "+",        3)
```

would:

- return 0, setting `var` to 1 (0 `.max.` 1);
- return 1, setting `var` to 3 (1 `.bitxor.` 2); and
- return 3, setting `var` to 6 (3 + 3).

Spin-locks can easily be implemented using fetch&op with assignment as the operator. Each spin-lock is represented by a logical variable as before. A critical region is then protected by:

```
! spin lock
do while .not. fetchop(lock, "=", .true.)
  skip
end while
critical region
! release
lock = .false.
```

More interestingly, fetch&op can be used to implement fair resource allocation. For example, suppose that Π processes all require repeated access to a critical region, as in:

```
create
  num of worker( . . . )
end create
  .
  .
procedure worker( . . . )
  do while working
    non-critical region
    wait turn
    critical region
    exit region
  end while
end procedure
```

In order to ensure that every process gets its fair share of turns in the critical region, we can use a technique similar to the tickets handed out in delicatessens. A single integer variable, called `ticket`, keeps track of the number of the next ticket to be taken, while a second variable, called `turn`, keeps track of which ticket holder is currently being served. Both variables are initialized to 1.

When a process wishes to enter the critical region, it uses fetch&op with + and 1 as arguments to get a ticket and move the ticket counter on. It then spins, waiting for `turn` to be equal to its ticket's value. When this happens, it enters the critical region, performs whatever actions are required, and then increments `turn` to signal that the next process may now enter the critical region. The resulting code looks like:

```
integer :: ticket = 1, turn = 1
  .
  .
procedure worker(ticket, turn,  . . . )
  integer :: ticket, turn
  integer :: my_turn
  do while working
    non-critical region
    ! wait for turn
    my_turn = fetchop(ticket, "+", 1)
    do while turn /= ticket
      skip
```

```
      end while
      critical region
      ! exit critical region
      turn = turn + 1
   end while
end procedure
```

Adding 1 to turn does not have to be done inside the critical region, since only the process coming out of the critical region could be trying to modify it. In practice, the busy inner while loop in this example would probably be replaced with a variable-delay loop of the type discussed earlier.

Fetch&op can also be used to partition work among processes to achieve good load balance. Suppose that L loops are to be executed by Π processes, where L is much greater than Π and the amount of work to be done in each loop is highly variable. As described in Section 2.4.2, a good strategy for parallelizing this calculation is to task-farm the loop iterations. Before worker processes are forked, the parent process initializes the loop index variable to 1 (or whatever index the loop is to start at). Each child then repeatedly does a fetch&op on this variable, using + as an operator and whatever increment the loop requires, in order to get the index of the next loop to be executed. Once a process gets an iteration index larger than the termination index of the loop, it exits the loop. This leads to programs of the form:

```
integer :: index = initial index value,
           limit = upper iteration limit,
           incr  = iteration range
create
   N of worker(index, limit, incr)
end create
   .
   .
   .
procedure worker(index, limit, incr)
   integer :: index, limit, incr
   integer :: own_index, i
   logical :: continue = .true.

   do while continue
      own_index = fetchop(index, "+", increment)
      if own_index > limit then
         continue = .false.
```

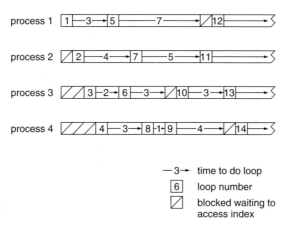

Figure 4.11
Allocating Loops Using `fetchop`

```
      else
         do i = own_index, own_index + increment
            do work
         end do
      end if
   end while
end procedure
```

Figure 4.11 shows how this technique might allocate a set of loop iterations among several processes. Note that no process ever has to spin in order to wait for its turn to access the shared variable `index`.

Much of the interest in fetch&op is due to the fact that it can be implemented in a way which helps reduce network contention. Suppose that several processors are connected to several memory units through a multi-stage interconnection network, and that two processes attempt to do a fetch&op on the same variable at the same time. If the two messages generated by these fetch&ops collide at an intermediate switching node in the MIN, then that node can *combine* the arguments in the two messages and forward a single message, saving one or the other of the original arguments. When the reply comes back, the node can use the saved argument to reconstruct the two original requests, and generate appropriate replies to them.

For example, suppose that process *A* calls `fetchop(x, "+", 3)`, while process *B* calls `fetchop(x, "+", 5)` (Figure 4.12). When these two messages collide, the node in

which they collide saves the value 3 locally, then forwards a single message requesting
fetchop(x, "+", 8). When this is serviced by the memory unit, it is as if the requests
by A and B had arrived immediately after one another. When the pre-increment value of
x returns to the intermediate node which stored the value 3, that node then sends the value
it receives to process A, adds 3, and sends the result to B. Clearly, this technique can be
applied recursively, with the values in the messages generated by intermediate nodes being
combined repeatedly.

Message combining of this kind is attractive because it reduces the number of messages
in the network, and the number of requests which memory units have to serve. In 1985,
Pfister *et al.* described an effect which they called *tree saturation* [Pfister & Norton 1985],
which made the need for combining even more pressing. Suppose that some fraction
h, $0 \leq h \leq 1$, of the memory requests made by each processor are directed to a single
memory unit (the "hot spot"), while the other $1 - h$ requests are made randomly. If there
are $\mathcal{P}$ processors and an equal number of memories, and each processor r memory packets
per cycle (where $0 \leq r \leq 1$), then total access rate for the hot spot will be $r(1 - h) + rh\mathcal{P}$.
As h increases, the buffers in the nodes close to the hot memory unit eventually fill up
(Figure 4.13). Once they do, the buffers in the nodes feeding into that node begin to fill,
and so on. Eventually, a tree of saturated nodes forms, with its root at the hot memory unit
and its leaves at the processors. Since the buffering at each intermediate node is limited,
requests to other memory units whose paths cross this tree will be significantly delayed.
The final result is that the performance of the system as a whole is dramatically degraded.

We can determine the limit on system performance by finding the point at which the hot
spot's memory unit is busy 100% of the time. This happens when $r(1 - h) + rh\mathcal{P} = 1$.
Re-arranging terms, we find that the sustainable memory access rate as a function of the
hot spot reference frequency and number of processors is:

$$R = \frac{1}{1 + h(\mathcal{P} - 1)}$$

The percentage of theoretical peak performance which a machine with hot spots can actually achieve is therefore:

$$T = pR = \frac{\mathcal{P}}{1 + h(\mathcal{P} - 1)}$$

This formula shows that for a very large number of processors, performance is roughly
bounded by $1/h$. Pfister *et al.* argued that combining was the only effective means of
avoiding the tree saturation that leads to this lost performance.

A later paper [Kumar & Pfister 1986] showed that tree saturation would have a significant impact on performance even in systems in which hot spots only exist for a short period

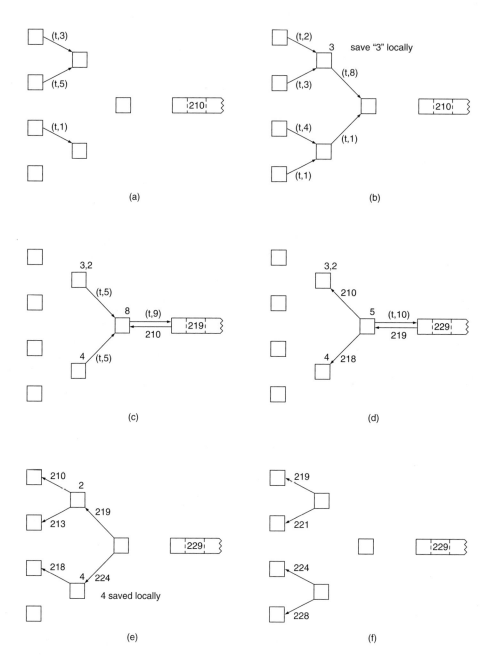

Figure 4.12
Combining in a Multi-stage Interconnection Network

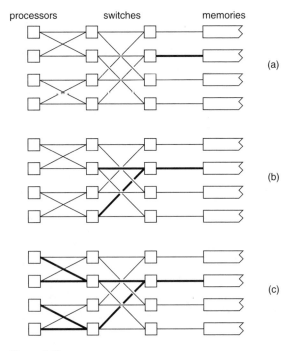

Figure 4.13
Tree Saturation

of time, e.g., systems in which processors work more or less independently, and must then all access the same memory location. Its onset was shown to be very sudden, while its effects took much longer to disappear. However, in the same year [Lee et al. 1986] argued that the pairwise combining which could take place in the IBM RP3 and the Ultracomputer at New York University would not be adequate to prevent degradation in throughput. This paper's authors claimed that since combining could only take place when two messages for the same memory location encountered one another in a switching node, the presence of uncombinable messages in that switching network would decrease the amount of combining which would take place. As system size increased, a performance asymptote would be approached. The solution, they argued, was to permit a greater amount of combining—rather than pairwise, they considered unlimited combining, and then limited k-way combining. Both of these would be implemented by allowing messages to combine with messages already queued for output, rather than just messages which happened to arrive in a switching node in the same switching cycle. The paper's authors determined empirically that the degree of combining needed in real situations would rarely exceed 3.

Another paper of the same period argued that combining hardware was unnecessary, and that combining could be done efficiently in software by distributing the memory locations at which combining took place among different memory units [Yew et al. 1986]. This would correspond to scattering the nodes of a combining tree randomly among the available processors in order to reduce contention near the node containing the variable being operated on. It is clear that this would increase latency, but given the probable extra cost of hardware to support combining, it might be cost-effective.

Despite its benefits, opportunistic combining has not been a feature of any commercial machine to date. The reason is simply its cost: a switching node which can detect the possibility of combination, store the values needed to undo combining, and match replies from memory units with stored values will inevitably be much more complicated, and hence more expensive, than a simple forwarding switch.

4.2.3 Semaphores

Whether locks are implemented with test&set or fetch&op, programmers are still required to write a sequence of instructions, including a properly-structured loop. It would obviously be better practice to standardize these operations and hide them in a couple of subroutines. The most popular construct used for this purpose is the *semaphore*, which was introduced by Dijkstra in [Dijkstra 1968].

Semaphores come in two flavors: binary and counting. Conceptually, both are structures on which only two operations are allowed. The first operation, called signalling, atomically sets the semaphore's value to 1. The second, called waiting, sets the semaphore to 0, but only when the semaphore's value is 1. If the semaphore's value is not 1 when the process invokes this operation, the process is suspended until someone else sets it to 1. Signalling is sometimes represented by the letter P, from the Dutch word "passeren", meaning "to pass", while waiting is represented by V, for "vrygeven", or "release".

Using semaphores, a repeated critical region can be implemented as follows:

```
type(semaphore), auto :: permission
  .
  .
  .
call sem_init(permission, 1, 1)
create
  N of worker(permission)
end create
  .
  .
  .
procedure worker(perm)
  type(semaphore) :: perm
```

```
      do while loop condition
          non-critical operations
          ! suspend until permission granted to enter critical region
          call sem_wait(perm)
          critical region
          ! allow other processes to get in
          call sem_signal(perm)
      end while
end procedure
```

The semaphore `permission` is first defined, then initialized by a call to the intrinsic function `sem_init`. The first argument to this function is the upper limit on the semaphore's value; the second is its initial value. After the semaphore has been initialized, the only operations which may be applied to it are `sem_wait` and `sem_signal`. It is illegal to assign a value directly to a semaphore, or to try to read its value.

The first worker to call `sem_wait` finds that the semaphore's value is 1, decrements it to 0, and enters the critical region. If other workers come along while the first is in the critical region, they find that the semaphore's value is 0, and are blocked. Once the first worker is through the critical region, it calls `sem_signal`. If there are no waiting processes, this increments the semaphore's value. If there are some processes waiting, on the other hand, this call releases exactly one of them instead, so that it can enter the critical region. Note that any number of processes can wait on a semaphore at once, but that only one is released each time the semaphore is signalled.

Another example of how binary semaphores are used is a re-implementation of the array-summing function of Program 4.2, shown in Program 4.7a. Here, each process saves the sum of its section of the array in the duplicated (i.e., non-shared) variable `temp`, then waits on the semaphore S before adding its `temp` value to `total`. This eliminates the need for the temporary array used to store partial sums in Program 4.2. In practical terms, this can make the whole program much faster, as there is no need to allocate and then free an intermediate array.

Processes sum their portion of the array into a local temporary variable so that they only have to wait on the semaphore once. While they could repeatedly add array values directly to the shared variable `total`, as shown in Program 4.7b, waiting on the semaphore would effectively *serialize* their operation, i.e., force them to occur sequentially rather than in parallel. This parallel code would be much slower than its sequential counterpart, since the additions would proceed no more quickly, and there would be the extra overhead of signalling and waiting. In general, it is good practice to do as many operations with private data as possible before trying to manipulate shared data, and then to spend as little time as possible in the critical region in which shared data are manipulated.

Two different types of errors are commonly made when using semaphores to manage critical regions. The first is to give each process its own semaphore instead of sharing it between processes. One way to make this mistake is to declare the semaphore as a local variable inside the subroutine called in a `create` block, instead of passing it as a (shared) parameter. In this case, processes are either never blocked or blocked forever, depending

```
real function sum_array(A, P)
  real                 :: A(:)              ! to be summed
  integer              :: P                 ! number of processes
  real                 :: total = 0.0       ! result
  type(semaphore), auto :: sem              ! lock on total

  create
    P of summer(P, A, total, sem)
  end create
  return total

end function

procedure summer(P, A, total, sem)
  integer       :: P                        ! number of processes
  real          :: A(:), total              ! to be summed and scratch
  type(semaphore) :: sem                    ! lock on total
  real          :: temp = 0.0               ! local sum

  do i = id_rel_self(), size(A, 1), P
    temp = temp + A(i)
  end do

  call sem_wait(sem)
  total = total + temp
  call sem_signal(sem)
end procedure
```
(a) Efficient Summing

Program 4.7
Summing an Array Using Semaphores

```
procedure summer(P, A, total, sem)
  integer         :: P                          ! number of processes
  real            :: A(:), total                ! to be summed and scratch
  type(semaphore) :: sem                        ! lock on total

  do i - id_rel_self(), size(A, 1), P
    call sem_wait(sem)
    total = total + A(i)
    call sem_signal(sem)
  end do
end procedure
```
(b) Inefficient Summing

Program 4.7 *(continued)*
Summing an Array Using Semaphores

on the semaphore's initial state. If this happened in Program 4.7, for example, the additions
to total would not be protected, and so the final value of total would be unpredictable.

The second common error is to call sem_wait when only one process has access to the
semaphore, i.e., to try to execute something like:

```
create
  N of worker(shared_variable, sem)
end create
call sem_wait(sem)
```
some operations on shared_variable
```
call sem_signal(sem)
```

In this case, the parent process creates N workers, and is then blocked while they happily
synchronize amongst themselves using sem. Once they no longer exist, the parent tries to
wait on the semaphore before manipulating one or more variables that had been shared by
its concurrent children. Since no-one is left to signal the semaphore, the parent could be
permanently stuck.

It is often impossible to capture the synchronization requirements of a program using
a single semaphore. In such cases, it may be possible to "split" a semaphore's value into
several parts. As an example of this, consider a producer-consumer program in which the
mediating buffer can only hold one value at a time. The producer may only write to the
buffer when the buffer is empty, while the consumer may only read from the buffer when
the buffer is full. A program could implement this by having each process test the buffer's

```
type(some_type), auto :: buffer
logical               :: full = .false.
type(semaphore), auto :: lock
   .
   .
   .
call sem_init(lock, 1, 0)
create
  1 of producer(buffer, full, lock)
  1 of consumer(buffer, full, lock)
end create
   .
   .
   .
procedure producer(buffer, full, lock)
  type(some_type) :: buffer
  logical         :: full
  type(semaphore) :: lock
  type(some_type) :: item
  logical         :: proceed

  do while producing
    produce(item)
    proceed = .false.
    do while .not. proceed
      call sem_wait(lock)
      proceed = .not. full
      if .not. proceed then
        call sem_signal(lock)
      end if
    end while
    call item_copy(buffer, item)
    call sem_signal(lock)
  end while
end procedure
```

Program 4.8
Spin-Locking with Semaphores

state repeatedly, as shown in Program 4.8, but this is just spin-locking in disguise. (Note that the consumer procedure in this example is symmetrical with the producer.)

A more efficient way to implement this is to use two semaphores, one to control the producer's write access to the buffer, the other to control the consumer's read access. Only one of these will ever be available at a time, so in a sense a single semaphore's value has been "split" between the two semaphores. In Program 4.9, the binary semaphore `empty` is initialized to 1, to show that the buffer can be written to, while the other semaphore `full` is implicitly initialized to 0. The producer repeatedly waits on `empty`, then signals the consumer using `full`; the consumer's behavior is symmetric.

This idea can be extended to a buffer containing N elements by providing a pair of semaphores for each element, plus head and tail indices guarded by a semaphore of their own (Program 4.10). Every time a producer (there may be more than one) wishes to add an element to the buffer, it waits its turn on the tail index, finds out which element of the buffer it is supposed to write to, then waits for that element to be empty before writing. Similarly, consumer processes take turns accessing the head index, then wait on particular elements of the queue becoming full. This leads to the situations shown in Figure 4.14, in which a different producer or consumer may be waiting to write or read each buffer element. Note that the queue no longer needs to keep an explicit count of the number of values it contains, as the semaphore controls on individual items ensure that no item is ever over-written or read multiple times. Note also that if the number of producer or consumer processes is greater than the number of slots in the buffer, this implementation's behavior depends on a strongly-fair scheduling policy. If such a policy is not used, producers could wait forever for buffer elements which are repeatedly being read by consumers, then immediately over-written by other producers.

It is tempting to try to implement this using one semaphore per element, but this is incorrect. Suppose the producer was implemented so that it waited on the single semaphore associated with a buffer slot before writing into that slot. If the slot was already full, the producer would see that the semaphore was 1, and would proceed to overwrite the slot's value. As a result, some of the items produced would be lost.

Another generalization of the problem of connecting producers and consumers through a single-element buffer is the *readers-writers problem*. Suppose that a database or other data structure is shared between Π processes which both write to it and read from it. In order to maximize throughput, we wish to allow any number of processes to read the structure's contents at the same time. However, we must ensure that no process tries to read from the structure while any processes are writing to it, and that no more than one process is writing at any time.

One possible solution to this problem would be to guard each section of the data structure with a separate semaphore, and have each process lock and unlock each section it

```
type(some_type), auto :: buffer
type(semaphore), auto :: full, empty
  .
  .
  .
call sem_init(full, 1, 0)
call sem_init(empty, 1, 1)
create
  1 of producer(buffer, full, empty)
  1 of consumer(buffer, full, empty)
end create
  .
  .
  .
procedure producer(buffer, full empty)
  type(some_type) :: buffer
  type(semaphore) :: full, empty
  do while producing
    produce(temp)
    call sem_wait(empty)
    call item_copy(buffer, temp)
    call sem_signal(full)
  end while
end procedure
  .
  .
  .
procedure consumer(buffer, full, empty)
  type(some_type) :: buffer
  type(semaphore) :: full, empty
  do while consuming
    call sem_wait(full)
    call item_copy(temp, buffer)
    call sem_signal(empty)
    consume(temp)
  end while
end procedure
```

Program 4.9
A Producer-Consumer Program with a Single-Element Buffer

```
integer, constant :: Queue_Size = 100
type queue_type
  integer              :: head, tail
  type(semaphore), auto :: indices
  type(some_type), auto :: items(Queue_Size)
  type(semaphore), auto :: full(Queue_Size), empty(Queue_Size)
end type

procedure init_queue(queue)
  type(queue_type) :: queue
  integer          :: i
  queue%head = 1
  queue%tail = 1
  call sem_init(queue%indices, 1, 1)
  do i = 1, Queue_Size
    call sem_init(queue%full(i), 1, 0)
    call sem_init(queue%empty(i), 1, 1)
  end do
end procedure

procedure enqueue(queue, item)
  type(queue_type) :: queue
  type(some_type)  :: item
  integer          :: index

  ! get index
  call sem_wait(queue%indices)
  index = queue%tail
  queue%tail = mod1(queue%tail + 1, Queue_Size)
  call sem_signal(queue%indices)

  ! wait for entry to become free
  call sem_wait(queue%empty(index))
  call copy_item(queue%items(index), item)
  call sem_signal(queue%full(index))

end procedure
```

Program 4.10
A Queue for a Producer-Consumer Program

```
procedure dequeue(queue, item)
  type(queue_type) :: queue
  type(some_type)  :: item
  integer          :: index

  ! get index
  call sem_wait(queue%indices)
  index = queue%head
  queue%head = mod1(queue%head + 1, Queue_Size)
  call sem_signal(queue%indices)

  ! wait for entry to become free
  call sem_wait(queue%full(index))
  call copy_item(item, queue%items(index))
  call sem_signal(queue%empty(index))


end procedure
```

Program 4.10 *(continued)*
A Queue for a Producer-Consumer Program

wished to read or write. However, if operations on the data structure were very coarse-grained, such sectional locking might not permit enough concurrency. A better, and simpler, solution is to solve the problem in two stages. First, a single semaphore is used to control read and write access to the structure. In order to make sure that this semaphore is set properly, a count of the number of reading processes can be maintained. This count, which is guarded by a second semaphore, is incremented each time a process begins to read, and decremented each time a read completes. The last process to decrement the count of readers then signals that the structure is no longer being accessed. A process may write to the structure only when this last semaphore is available. Program 4.11 shows this implementation.

The order in which processes wait and signal using the semaphores num_rd_sem and struct_sem is important. Suppose that no processes are accessing the structure, and then one process tries to read it. That process will first pass the sem_wait on num_rd_sem, which blocks other processes from trying to read, and then try to pass the sem_wait on struct_sem. If some other process has in the meantime managed to pass the writer's sem_wait on struct_sem, the reading process will be blocked until the read has completed. Because of this, other reading processes will also be blocked, since the first reader will not have relinquished num_rd_sem. As soon as the writer signals it is done, the

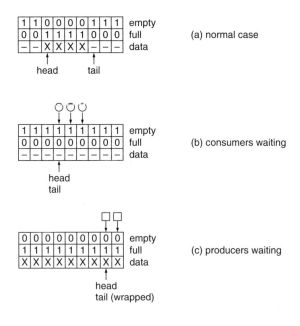

Figure 4-14

Figure 4.14
Producers and Consumers Waiting on Buffer Elements

first reader's `sem_wait` completes, increments the count of the number of readers to 1, and then signals to other readers that they may now enter the critical region (Figure 4.15).

At this point, any number of processes may take turns incrementing `num_rd`, reading the data structure, and then decrementing `num_rd`. None of these will attempt to `sem_wait` on `struct_sem` so long as more than one process is still reading. However, when the last process to read decrements `num_rd`, and finds that it has gone to zero, it signals to any waiting writers that they may now proceed.

This implementation will yield poor performance if the frequency with which processes try to read the structure is so great that writers are locked out for long periods of time by successions of readers. However, if individual processes read and write with roughly equal frequency, then the number of processes attempting to read will fluctuate over time, as processes enter the portion of the program in which they try to write to the shared structure.

```
type(semaphore), auto :: num_rd_sem, struct_sem
integer                :: num_rd
  .
  .
  .
call sem_init(num_rd_sem, 1, 1)
call sem_init(struct_sem, 1, 0)
create
  N of worker(num_rd, num_rd_sem, struct_sem)
end create
  .
  .
  .
procedure worker(num_rd, num_rd_sem, struct_sem)
  integer        :: num_rd
  type(semaphore) :: num_rd_sem, struct_sem

  do while reading and writing
    if need to read then                                          ! read
      ! increment reader count (and claim structure)
      call sem_wait(num_rd_sem)
      if num_rd == 0 then
        call sem_signal(struct_sem)
      end if
      num_rd = num_rd + 1
      call sem_signal(num_rd_sem)
      read
      ! decrement reader count (and release structure)
      call sem_wait(num_rd_sem)
      num_rd = num_rd - 1
      if num_rd == 0 then
        call sem_signal(struct_sem)
      end if
      call sem_signal(num_rd_sem)
    else                                                          ! write
      call sem_wait(struct_sem)
      write
      call sem_signal(struct_sem)
    end if
  end while
end procedure
```

Program 4.11
Concurrent Reading and Writing of a Shared Data Structure

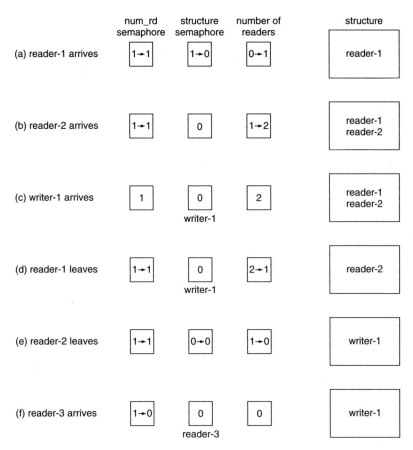

Figure 4.15
Operation of Readers-Writers Protocol

Example 4.3 (Mandelbrot Set II) Program 4.12 shows a refinement of the Mandelbrot Set program of Example 4.1. Instead of statically assigning rows to processors, this program assigns single cells on a demand-driven basis. The main program begins by initializing a semaphore and a set of four index variables. Two of these, x and y, give the real coordinates of the next location to be calculated; the other two, i and j, keep track of where the results of that calculation are to be written.

The main loop of each worker is executed until there are no more values to calculate. During each iteration, each worker uses sem_wait to get the lock on the shared index variables, then fetches their current values and increments them using the fetch_int subroutine. The worker then releases its lock on the indices, does the required calculation, and loops again.

A common mistake when writing a program like this is to try to use fetch&op to manipulate the index values. If each process's fetch&ops on the four indices are done in the same order, one would hope that each process would be left with x, y, i, and j values that corresponded to one another. However, this cannot be guaranteed, because process execution can be interleaved in arbitrary ways. If a process was descheduled immediately after getting its x value, for example, the next process to be scheduled might get the next x, but the y value belonging to the previous process. One way around this would be to keep a sin-

```
program
  type(logical)         :: patch(N, N)              ! to fill
  type(semaphore), auto :: sem                       ! lock on increment counter
  real                  :: x = X0, y = Y0            ! coordinates
  integer               :: i = 1, j = 1             ! location indices

  call sem_init(sem, 1, 1)
  create
    P of worker(patch, sem, x, y, i, j)
  end create
end program

procedure worker(patch, sem, x_shared, y_shared, i_shared, j_shared)
  type(logical)    :: patch(:, :)          ! to fill
  type(semaphore)  :: sem                    ! guard on counter
  real             :: x_shared, y_shared     ! x coordinate
  integer          :: i_shared, j_shared     ! location index
  integer          :: id = id_rel_self()     ! own ID
  integer          :: i, j                    ! traversal
  real             :: x, y                    ! coordinates

  call fetch_inc(sem, x_shared, y_shared, i_shared, j_shared, x, y, i, j)
  do while (i <= N) .and. (j <= N)
    patch(i, j) = mandel(x, y)
    call fetch_inc(sem, x_shared, y_shared, i_shared, j_shared, x, y, i, j)
  end while
end procedure
```

Program 4.12
Mandelbrot Set Generation with Better Load Balancing

```
procedure fetch_inc(sem, x_val, y_val, i_val, j_val,
                    x_out, y_out, i_out, j_out)
   type(semaphore) :: sem              ! guard
   real            :: x_val, y_val     ! variables to fetch and increment
   integer         :: i_val, j_val     ! location indices
   real            :: x_out, y_out     ! return here
   integer         :: i_out, j_out     ! return here

   call sem_wait(sem)                  ! wait for turn

   ! save values
   x_out = x_val ; y_out = y_val
   i_out = i_val ; j_out = j_val

   ! increment
   j_val = j_val + 1
   y_val = y_val + Inc
   if j_val > N then
     j_val = 1
     y_val = Y0
     i_val = i_val + 1
     x_val = x_val + Inc
   end if

   call sem_signal(sem)                ! someone else's turn
end procedure
```

Program 4.12 *(continued)*
Mandelbrot Set Generation with Better Load Balancing

gle shared index k, whose value ran from 1 to N^2. Each process would use fetchop(k, "+", 1) to fetch and increment its value, and then do some arithmetic to convert it back to a row and column index.

While Program 4.12 will definitely achieve better load balance than Program 4.3, there is no guarantee that it will run any faster. The reason is the cost of performing synchronization each time a process needs a new cell to calculate. In many applications, the total cost of performing N^2 signals and waits could be larger than the time that would be lost due to the poor load-balancing of a statically-scheduled implementation. The best approach is a hybrid scheme of the sort shown in Program 4.13. Like Program 4.12, this hands out work on a demand-driven basis, but instead of handing out single cells it hands out entire

```
program
  type(logical)          :: patch(N, N)  ! to fill
  type(semaphore), auto :: sem           ! lock on increment counter
  real                   :: x            ! x coordinate
  integer                :: i            ! location index

  x = X0
  i = 1
  call sem_init(sem, 1, 1)
  create
    P of worker(patch, sem, x, i)
  end create
end program

procedure worker(patch, sem, x_shared, i_shared)
  type(logical)       :: patch(:, :)            ! to fill
  type(semaphore)     :: sem                    ! guard on counter
  real                :: x_shared               ! x coordinate
  integer             :: i_shared               ! location index
  integer             :: id = id_rel_self()     ! own ID
  integer             :: i, j                   ! traversal
  real                :: x, y                   ! coordinates

  ! calculate
  call fetch_inc(sem, x_shared, i_shared, x, i, Inc)
  do while i <= N
    y = Y0
    do j = 1, N
      patch(i, j) - mandel(x, y)
      y = y + Inc
    end do
    call fetch_inc(sem, x_shared, i_shared, x, i, Inc)
  end while
end procedure
```

Program 4.13
Balancing Synchronization Overhead and Load Balancing

```
procedure fetch_inc(sem, v_val, i_val, v_out, i_out, v_inc)
    type(semaphore) :: sem              ! guard
    real            :: v_val            ! variable to fetch and increment
    integer         :: i_val            ! location index
    real            :: v_out            ! return here
    integer         :: i_out            ! return here
    real            :: v_inc            ! amount of increment

    call sem_wait(sem)                  ! wait for turn
    v_out = v_val
    i_out = i_val
    v_val = v_val + v_inc
    i_val = i_val + 1
    call sem_signal(sem)                ! someone else's turn
end procedure
```

Program 4.13 *(continued)*
Balancing Synchronization Overhead and Load Balancing

rows. This reduces the number of synchronizations required from N^2 to N, while reducing the cost of each synchronization. Program 4.13 will not be as well load-balanced as Program 4.12, but if the number of rows in the matrix is several times larger than the number of processes, the load imbalance will probably be very small.

Counting Semaphores   As was mentioned on page 220, a second type of semaphore called a counting semaphore also exists. While a binary semaphore may only take on the values 0 and 1, a counting semaphore may take on any value in the range $0 \ldots N$, where N is specified when the semaphore is initialized. Processes which wait on the semaphore are blocked until the semaphore's value is greater than 0, then decrement it and proceed. Processes which signal are always allowed to proceed, incrementing the semaphore along the way if its value is less than N. Thus, binary semaphores are simply counting semaphores whose maximum value is 1.

Counting semaphores can be used to control the number of processes active in a critical region at any time. If we consider once again a producer-consumer problem in which several processes communicate through a shared queue, then only two counting semaphores are needed to mediate their interaction correctly. Just as the two semaphores `full` and `empty` in Program 4.9 showed whether a single-element buffer could be read from or written to, the sum of the two counting semaphores of Program 4.14 is always equal to the total number of slots in the buffer. When the buffer is empty, any process which calls `sem_wait(full)` blocks until some other process writes to the buffer, and calls `sem_signal(full)`. Similarly, writes are blocked waiting on the semaphore `empty` whenever all slots in the buffer are full. As in the original implementation in Program 4.5, head and tail indices are maintained in order to keep track of where values should be put. Note that we still need a binary semaphore called `indices` in Program 4.14 to ensure that access to the head and tail indices is atomic.

```
integer, constant :: Queue_Size = 100
type queue_type
  integer :: head, tail
  type(semaphore), auto :: indices, full, empty
  type(some_type), auto :: items(Queue_Size)
end type

procedure init_queue(queue)
  type(queue_type) :: queue
  call sem_init(queue%indices, 1, 1)
  call sem_init(queue%full, Queue_Size, 0)
  call sem_init(queue%empty, Queue_Size, Queue_Size)
end procedure

procedure producer(queue)
  type(queue_type) :: queue
  type(item_type)  :: item
  integer          :: index

  do while producing
    produce(item)
    call sem_wait(queue%empty)
    call sem_wait(queue%indices)
    index = tail
    tail = mod1(tail + 1, Queue_Size)
    call sem_signal(queue%indices)
    call item_copy(queue%items(index), item)
    call sem_signal(full)
  end while
end procedure
```

Program 4.14
Producers and Consumers Using Counting Semaphores

```
procedure consumer(queue)
  type(queue_type) :: queue
  type(item_type)  :: item
  integer          :: index

  do while consuming
    call sem_wait(queue%full)
    call sem_wait(queue%indices)
    index = head
    head = mod1(head + 1, Queue_Size)
    call sem_signal(queue%indices)
    call item_copy(item, queue%items(index))
    call sem_signal(empty)
    consume(item)
  end while
end procedure
```

Program 4.14 *(continued)*
Producers and Consumers Using Counting Semaphores

4.2.4 Monitors

In almost all cases, semaphores are associated with particular data structures, such as
counters or queues. However, nothing forces programmers to respect this association. In
order to encourage better-structured programs, some programming languages provide a
construct called a *monitor*, which encapsulates one or more variables, and code to initialize
them, and procedures to operate on them [Andrews 1991]. A monitor is like a record
structure, except that its data fields can only be accessed by the procedures declared within
it, and (most importantly) only one process may operate on a particular monitor at a time.
Thus, monitors automatically guarantee the mutual exclusion which some of the examples
in the previous section took on trust. Section 6.7.2 describes a programming system based
on a monitor-like construct, and discusses the strengths and weaknesses of this kind of
programming model.

4.2.5 Barrier Synchronization

A *barrier* is a point in a program which every process must reach before any process is
allowed to pass. *Barrier synchronization* is often used in numerical programs to ensure that
one stage of a calculation has completed before the next stage is begun. While the same
effect can usually be achieved by repeatedly creating processes, synchronizing a fixed set
of processes with barriers is usually more efficient.

For example, consider the incorrect shared-variables implementation of the Game of Life shown in Program 4.15. Each process counts the number of live neighbors of the cells in its strip of the mesh, then updates those cells. Clearly, there is a race here—if one process begins updating the boundary of its section before the processes responsible for the adjacent sections have finished counting the number of live neighbors each of their cells has, the result will be incorrect.

This race condition can be cured by repeatedly spawning processes, so that all the processes which count neighbors are merged before any updating processes are spawned. This approach leads to the code of Program 4.16. However, if the number of processes being used is Π, this requires 2Π processes to be created and terminated during each iteration. Given the high cost of process creation, it will almost always be more efficient to modify the worker subroutine of the first implementation so that its instances synchronize with one another using a barrier in order to prevent racing. A complete implementation of this is shown in Program 4.17.

FORTRAN-KSV provides barriers as an intrinsic record type. After being declared, a barrier is initialized using:

```
call bar_init(b, N)
```

where N is the the number of processes which must meet at the barrier. Once it has been initialized, the only operation allowed on a barrier is a call to the procedure bar_arrive, which blocks its caller until $N - 1$ other processes have arrived at the barrier.

Note that two barriers are required in the loop in Program 4.17 to guarantee correct execution. The first prevents some processes from updating their cells' values before other processes have finished counting live neighbors, while the second prevents processes from starting to count live neighbors on the next iteration before updates on this iteration have finished. This sort of arrangement is sometimes called a *fuzzy barrier*: no process is allowed past the second synchronization point until all processes have passed the first.

There are many different ways to implement barrier synchronization; a good summary can be found in [Arenstorf & Jordan 1989]. The simplest is to have one process act as a manager. This process waits for all other processes to signal that they have reached the barrier, then tells them that they may proceed (Program 4.18). Client processes use one array of Π binary semaphores to signal their arrival, while the manager uses another array of equal size to tell them when they may proceed. Replacing these semaphore arrays with counting semaphores, and structuring the manager process so that barriers may be re-used, are left as exercises.

One reason for using a separate barrier manager is that it simplifies the construction of code in which some inherently sequential operation, such as prompting the user for new

```
integer, constant :: Num_Proc = number of processes
  .
  .
  .
program
  logical :: world(X, Y)
  integer :: count(X, Y)
  create
    Num_Proc of worker(world, count)
  end create
end program
  .
  .
  .
procedure worker(world, count)
  integer :: world(:, :)
  logical :: count(:, :)
  integer :: id = id_rel_self(), width = X/Num_Proc
  integer :: start = (id-1) * width + 1, end = start + width
  integer :: iter, x, y

  do iter = 1, num_gen
    do x = start, end                    ! count
      do y = 1, Y
        count(x, y) = neigh_count(world, x, y)
      end do
    end do
    do x = start, end                    ! update
      do y = 1, Y
        world(x, y) = world_update(world, count, x, y)
      end do
    end do
  end do
end procedure
```

Program 4.15
Incorrect Game of Life

```
program
  integer :: count(X, Y), iter
  logical :: world(X, Y)

  do iter = 1, num_gen
    create
      N of counter(count, world)
    end create
    create
      N of updater(count, world)
    end create
  end do
end program
  .
  .
  .
procedure counter(count, world)
  integer :: count(:, :)
  logical :: world(:, :)
  integer :: id = id_rel_self(), width = X/Num_Proc
  integer :: start = (id-1) * width + 1, end = start + width
  integer :: x, y

  do x = start, end
    do y = 1, Y
      count(x, y) = neigh_count(world, x, y)
    end do
  end do
end procedure
  .
  .
  .
```

Program 4.16
Slow Game of Life

```
procedure updater(count, world)
  integer :: count(:, :)
  logical :: world(:, :)
  integer :: id = id_rel_self(), width = X/Num_Proc
  integer :: start = (id-1) * width + 1, end = start + width
  integer :: x, y

  do x = start, end
    do y = 1, Y
      world(x, y) = world_update(world, count, x, y)
    end do
  end do
end procedure
```

Program 4.16 *(continued)*
Slow Game of Life

```
program
  logical            :: world(N, N)    ! world
  integer            :: count(N, N)    ! neighbor counts
  integer            :: num_gen        ! generations
  type(barrier), auto :: bar           ! to synchronize

  fill world
  call bar_init(bar, P)

  create
    P of evolver(world, count, num_gen, bar)
  end create
end program

procedure evolver(world, count, num_gen, bar)
  logical        :: world(:, :)        ! world to examine
  integer        :: count(:, :)        ! where to put counts
  integer        :: num_gen            ! how long to evolve
  type(barrier)  :: bar                ! how to synchronize
  integer        :: id = id_rel_self() ! own ID within group
  integer        :: num = id_grp_size() ! number of chares in group
  integer        :: gen                ! generation index
```

Program 4.17
Game of Life Using Barriers

```
   do gen = 1, num_gen
     ! count neighbors
     call neigh_count(world, count, id, num)
     call bar_arrive(bar)
     ! update world
     call world_update(world, count, id, num)
     call bar_arrive(bar)
   end do
end procedure

procedure neigh_count(world, count, start, stride)
...
do i = start, N, stride
   update count for row i
end do
end procedure

procedure world_update(world, count, start, stride)
...
do i = start, N, stride
   update world for row i
end do
end procedure
```

Program 4.17 *(continued)*
Game of Life Using Barriers

```
integer, constant      :: Num_Cli = number of clients
type(semaphore), auto :: at_bar(Num_Cli), pass_bar(Num_Cli)
integer               :: i
  .
  .
  .
do i = 1, Num_Cli                              ! initialize semaphores
  call sem_init(at_bar(i), 1, 0)
  call sem_init(pass_bar(i), 1, 0)
end do
  .
  .
  .
```

Program 4.18
Barrier Synchronization Using a Manager Process

```
create
  1 of bar_man(at_bar, pass_bar)
  Num_Cli of client(at_bar, pass_bar, other parameters)
end create
  .
  .
  .
procedure bar_man(at, pass)
  type(semaphore) :: at(:), pass(:)
  integer         :: i

  do i = 1, Num_Cli                              ! wait for arrivals
    call sem_wait(at(i))
  end do

  do i = 1, Num_Cli                              ! allow passage
    call sem_signal(pass(i))
  end do
end procedure
  .
  .
  .
procedure client(at, pass, other parameters)
  type(semaphore) :: at(:), pass(:)
  integer         :: id = id_rel_self()
  pre-barrier operations
  call arrive(at(id), pass(id))
  post-barrier operations
end procedure
  .
  .
  .
procedure arrive(at, pass)
  type(semaphore) :: at, pass
  call sem_signal(at)
  call sem_wait(pass)
end procedure
```

Program 4.18 *(continued)*
Barrier Synchronization Using a Manager Process

parameters, is to be executed by only one process before the other processes are allowed
to proceed. The manager can do this after all of the clients have arrived, but before any of
them are allowed to proceed:

```
procedure bar_man(at, pass)
  type(semaphore) :: at(:), pass(:)
  integer         :: i

  do i = 1, Num_Cli                                ! wait for arrivals
    call sem_wait(at(i))
  end do
  sequential operations                            ! all clients blocked
  do i = 1, Num_Cli                                ! allow passage
    call sem_signal(pass(i))
  end do
end procedure
```

Note that there is a significant security hole in this implementation, in that every client
is trusted to use the right elements of the two semaphore arrays, and only those elements,
in the right order. If many different types of client have been created, as in:

```
integer, constant      :: Num_A = number of type A
  .
  .
  .
integer, constant      :: Num_Z = number of type Z
integer, constant      :: Total_Num = Num_A + ··· + Num_Z
type(semaphore), auto :: at_bar(Total_Num), pass_bar(Total_Num)
integer                :: i
  .
  .
  .
do i = 1, Total_Num
  call sem_init(at_bar(i), 1, 0)
  call sem_init(pass_bar(i), 1, 0)
end do
  .
  .
  .
create
  Num_A of subr_A(at_bar, pass_bar, other parameters)
  .
  .
  .
```

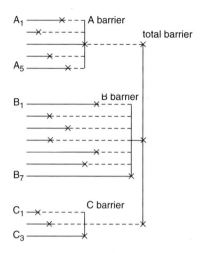

Figure 4.16
Barrier Managers Synchronizing in Stages

```
    Num_Z of subr_Z(at_bar, pass_bar, other parameters)
end create
```

then the members of group A must only use elements 1 . . . Num_A of the two arrays, while
the members of group B must only use elements $Num\_A + 1 \cdots Num\_A + Num\_B$, and so on.

Luckily, such multi-group synchronizations are relatively rare; when they do occur,
it is good practice to implement them in two stages. In the first, the members of each
group synchronize with one another under the control of a single manager process per
group. Those managers then synchronize with one another, as shown in Figure 4.16. Each
manager then signals its clients that they may proceed.

Figure 4.17a gives a timing diagram of the sort introduced in [Arenstorf & Jordan 1989]
for manager-controlled barriers. This diagram shows that if all processes begin to execute
the barrier at the same instant, the time taken to execute this barrier is linear in the number
of processes involved. The shaded area shows the amount of time wasted as processors
stand idle, waiting for others to arrive at the barrier. However, if processes were to reach
the barrier in the same order as their process IDs, then there would be no wasted CPU time
(Figure 4.17b). While such a fortuitous arrival order might seem unlikely, in practice the
repeated use of this kind of barrier would force processes into exactly such an order: if the
time required by processes to do their operations between barrier synchronizations is the
same, then since they leave the ith barrier in order, they will reach the $i + 1^{th}$ barrier in

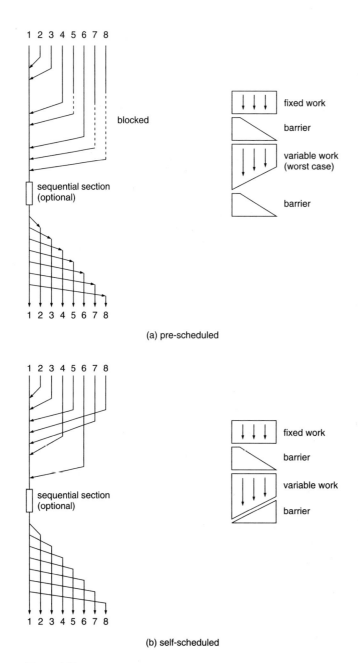

(a) pre-scheduled

(b) self-scheduled

Figure 4.17
Timing Diagram for a Linear-Time Barrier

the same order. This behavior is similar to the self-synchronization described earlier, but is beneficial rather than harmful.

An alternative implementation which does not have this linear worst-case running time is a generalization of the two-level barrier introduced above. This implementation uses a binary tree of semaphores, and is similar in concept to the binary combining tree used to implement reduction operations in data-parallel systems (Section 3.3.1). Pairs of processes synchronize with one another, then one member of each pair synchronizes with one member of another pair, and so on, until all processes have been synchronized. The sequence is then reversed in order to allow all processes to pass the barrier. In practice, this can be done with two semaphores per process, as shown in Program 4.19. Process 1 acts as the root of the tree, while the children of any process p are the processes whose IDs are $2p$ and $2p + 1$. Each process waits for its children (if it has any) to signal that they have reached the barrier, then signals its parent (if it has one). Exiting the barrier is done symmetrically; as before, a section of sequentially-executed code can be inserted between entering and exiting the barrier.

As the timing diagram in Figure 4.18 shows, this method has a running time which is logarithmic in the number of processes being synchronized. While in most cases this will lead to better performance, it is less likely to produce the self-synchronizing behavior noted earlier. [Grunwald & Vajracharya 1994] discusses the implementation of barrier synchronization on various types of hardware, and gives some guidelines as to which is best in particular cases.

Example 4.4 (Parallel Sorting by Regular Sampling) The parallel quicksorting procedure given in Program 4.4 was inefficient because it employed a maximum of parallelism when there was a minimum of work to do. Program 4.20 gives a much more efficient sorting program, which uses an algorithm called parallel sorting by regular sampling [Shi & Schaeffer 1992].

The idea behind this algorithm is to do the bulk of the sorting sequentially within each process, so that we can take advantage of good sequential sorting algorithms. Given a vector v of length N and $\mathcal{P}$ processes, the procedure psrs determines how many elements each process should be responsible for, and then creates $\mathcal{P}$ children. Each of these begins by sorting its own section of v (Figure 4.19).

The program must now merge these sorted sub-sections to create the required result. It does this by dividing each process's data into $\mathcal{P}$ sections according to the rules described in the next paragraph. Process 1 is then given the first section of each process's values, process 2 the second sections, and so on. These sub-sections are then re-sorted to create the final result.

```
integer, constant :: Num_Proc = number of processors
integer, constant :: Num_Cli  = number of clients
program
  type(semaphore), auto :: up(Num_Proc), down(Num_Proc)
  integer               :: i
  do i = 1, Num_Proc
    call sem_init(up(i), 1, 0)
    call sem_init(down(i), 1, 0)
  end do

  create
    Num_Cli of client(up, down, other parameters)
  end create
end program
  .
  .
  .
procedure client(up, down, other parameters)
  type(semaphore) :: up(:), down(:)
  integer         :: id = id_rel_self()
  pre-barrier operations
  call bar_arrive(up, down, id)
  post-barrier operations
end procedure
  .
  .
  .
procedure bar_arrive(up, down, id)
  ! wait for children (if they exist)
  if 2*id <= num_proc then
    call sem_wait(up(2*id))
    if 2*id+1 <= num_proc then
      call sem_wait(up(2*id+1))
    end if
  end if
  ! signal parent (if not root)
  if id > 1 then
    call sem_signal(up(id))
    call sem_wait(down(id))
  end if
```

Program 4.19
Tree-Like Barrier Synchronization

```
  !  signal children to proceed (if they exist)
  if 2*id <= num_proc then
    call sem_signal(down(2*id))
    if 2*id+1 <= num_proc then
      call sem_signal(down(2*id+1))
    end if
  end if
end procedure
```

Program 4.19 *(continued)*
Tree-Like Barrier Synchronization

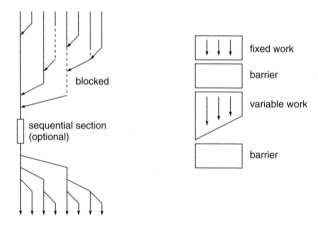

Figure 4.18
Timing Diagram for a Logarithmic-Time Barrier

```
procedure psrs(v)
  integer            :: v(:)                    ! to be sorted
  integer            :: len = size(v, 1)        ! vector length
  integer            :: slice, rslice           ! sizes
  integer            :: sample(P*(P-1))         ! store sample points
  integer            :: pivots(P-1)             ! pivot points
  integer            :: subsize(P*(P+1))        ! sub-list sizes
  integer            :: bucket(P)               ! bucket sizes
  type(barrier), auto :: bar                    ! for merging

  slice  = (len + P - 1)/P
  rslice = (slice + P - 1)/P
  call bar_init(bar, P)

  create
    P of child(bar, v, slice, rslice, sample, pivots, subsize, bucket)
  end create
end procedure

procedure child(bar, v, slice, rslice, sample, pivots, subsize, bucket)
  type(barrier) :: bar                          ! for synchronization
  integer       :: v(:)                         ! values
  integer       :: slice, rslice                ! sizes
  integer       :: sample(:)                    ! samples
  integer       :: pivots(:)                    ! pivoting points
  integer       :: subsize(:)                   ! sub-sizes
  integer       :: bucket(:)                    ! section sizes
  integer       :: id = id_rel_self()           ! own id
  integer       :: i                            ! generic loop index

  ! sort sub-array and select samples
  call sort_for_sample(id, v, sample, slice, rslice)
  call bar_arrive(bar)
```

Program 4.20
Parallel Sorting by Regular Sampling

```
! sort samples and select pivots
if id == 1 then
  call quicksort(sample)
  do i = 1, P-1
    pivots(i) = sample(((i-1) * P) + (P/2))
  end do
end if
call bar_arrive(bar)

! handle division into sublists
call sub_divide(id, v, slice, pivots, subsize)
call bar_arrive(bar)

! count partition sizes
call part_count(id, bucket, subsize)
call bar_arrive(bar)

! merge partitions in parallel
call merger(id, v, subsize, bucket, bar)
call bar_arrive(bar)
end procedure

procedure sort_for_sample(id, v, sample, slice, rslice)
  integer :: id                        ! own ID
  integer :: v(:)                      ! whole array to be sorted
  integer :: sample(:)                 ! where to put sample points
  integer :: slice, rslice             ! size parameters
  integer :: start, lim                ! limits on own partition
  integer :: base                      ! for pivot selection
  integer :: i, j                      ! loop index

  ! determine own limits
  start = (id - 1) * slice + 1
  lim = (start + slice - 1) .min. size(v, 1)

  ! sort own portion
  call quicksort(v(start:lim))
```

Program 4.20 *(continued)*
Parallel Sorting by Regular Sampling

```
    ! select samples and store for global use
    do j = 1, P-1
      i = start + j * rslice .min. lim
      sample((id - 1) * (P - 1) + j) = v(i)
    end do
end procedure

procedure sub_divide(id, v, slice, pivots, subsize)
    integer :: id                                  ! own ID
    integer :: v(:)                                ! whole list
    integer :: slice                               ! sub-list size
    integer :: pivots(:)                           ! pivot values
    integer :: subsize(:)                          ! sub-list sizes
    integer :: start, lim                          ! limits on own partition

    ! determine own limits
    start = (id - 1) * slice + 1
    lim = (start + slice - 1) .min. size(v, 1)

    subsize((id - 1) * (P + 1) + 1)     = start
    subsize((id - 1) * (P + 1) + P + 1) = lim + 1
    call sub_lists(v, start, lim, subsize, (id - 1)*(P + 1) + 1,
                   pivots, 1, P-1)
end procedure

procedure sub_lists(v, start, lim, subsize, base, pivots, first_p, last_p)
    integer :: v(:)                                ! values
    integer :: start, lim                          ! own region (inclusive)
    integer :: subsize(:)                          ! to be filled
    integer :: base                                ! base index in subsize(:)
    integer :: pivots(:)                           ! pivot values
    integer :: first_p, last_p                     ! pivot limits
    integer :: mid, pivot                          ! mid-point and pivot
    integer :: low, high                           ! bounds
    integer :: center                              ! for splitting
```

Program 4.20 *(continued)*
Parallel Sorting by Regular Sampling

```
  mid   = (first_p + last_p)/2
  pivot = pivots(mid)
  low   = start
  high  = lim
  do while low <= high
    center = (low + high)/2
    if v(center) > pivot then
      high = center - 1
    else
      low = center + 1
    end if
  end while
  subsize(base + mid) = low
  if first_p < mid then
    call sub_lists(v, start, low-1, subsize, base, pivots, first_p, mid-1)
  end if
  if mid < last_p then
    call sub_lists(v, low, lim, subsize, base, pivots, mid+1, last_p)
  end if
end procedure

procedure part_count(id, bucket, subsize)
  integer :: id                              ! own ID
  integer :: bucket(:)                       ! where to put sums
  integer :: subsize(:)                      ! what to sum
  integer :: j                               ! summing loop index

  bucket(id) = 0
  do j = id, P*(P + 1), P+1
    bucket(id) = bucket(id) + subsize(j + 1) - subsize(j)
  end do
end procedure
```

Program 4.20 *(continued)*
Parallel Sorting by Regular Sampling

```
procedure merger(id, v, subsize, bucket, bar)
  integer       :: id                              ! own ID
  integer       :: v(:)                            ! values
  integer       :: subsize(:)                      ! sub-list sizes
  integer       :: bucket(:)                       ! bucket boundaries
  type(barrier) :: bar                             ! for copying synchronization
  integer       :: lim = bucket(id)                ! how much data to handle
  integer       :: base                            ! base of own region
  integer       :: temp(lim)                       ! own scratch space
  integer       :: i, j, k                         ! loop indices

  ! setup (saves a barrier synchronization)
  base = 1
  do j = 2, id, 1
    base = base + bucket(j-1)
  end do

  ! copy values into scratch
  i = 1
  do j = 0, P-1
    do k = subsize(id + j *(P + 1)), subsize(id + j * (P + 1) + 1)-1, 1
      temp(i) = v(k)
      i = i + 1
    end do
  end do

  ! sort
  call quicksort(temp)

  ! synchronize
  call bar_arrive(bar)

  ! copy back
  do i = 1, lim
    v(base + (i - 1)) = temp(i)
  end do
end procedure
```

Program 4.20 *(continued)*
Parallel Sorting by Regular Sampling

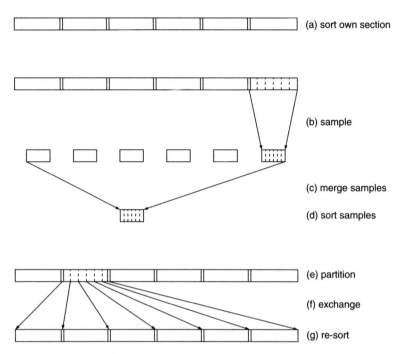

(a) sort own section

(b) sample

(c) merge samples

(d) sort samples

(e) partition

(f) exchange

(g) re-sort

Figure 4.19
Parallel Sorting by Regular Sampling

The boundaries for each process's sub-sections are determined by sampling the original data to produce an estimate of the distribution of values in the array. Since there are $\mathcal{P}$ processes, $\mathcal{P} - 1$ inter-process boundaries are needed. Each process therefore selects $\mathcal{P} - 1$ evenly-spaced values from its own data. These are collected by one process, which sorts them, selects the final $\mathcal{P} - 1$ dividing values, and distributes these to the sorting processes. [Shi & Schaeffer 1992] proves that this procedure places an upper bound on how much load imbalance there can be in the final division. In practice, as they report, the load imbalance is rarely greater than one or two percent.

4.3 Futures

Along with work on operating systems, research into networking has been a major current in computer science during the past two decades. One of the techniques which has come out of this is called *remote procedure call (RPC)*. The idea behind RPC is that it may sometimes be faster, and more modular, to have a function call executed by another processor somewhere in the network than to execute it locally. When a client process calls a server's interface functions in a client/server system, for example, the system may send the parameters to that call to the processor on which the server is actually running. The programming paradigm introduced in this section is in some ways a specialization of this model.

Consider a simple computation such as:

```
x = f(a, b) + g(c, d, x)
```

If f and g are both expensive functions to evaluate, it may make sense to create a second process to do part of the work, as in:

```
real, shared :: temp1, temp2
   .
   .
   .
id = fork(1)
if id == 1 then
  temp1 = f(a, b)
else
  temp2 = g(c, d, x)
end if
call join()
x = temp1 + temp2
```

If the calculations being done were more complicated, however, and several layers of processes were being created to do them, keeping track of what processes had been created, what they were supposed to be evaluating, and what values they were supposed to share would become difficult.

In [Halstead 1985], Robert Halstead described a simple and elegant construct called a *future* to handle situations such as this.[4] A future is simply a commitment by a process to use the result of a calculation at some later date. When a future is evaluated, a new process is created; when the parent of that process tries to read the future's result, it is automatically suspended until the child has returned a value. It is the runtime system's responsibility to decide whether to execute a future in parallel with its creator, or to use a *lazy evaluation* strategy, which only calculates values when they are needed. Consequently, programmers should not make assumptions about the state of variables which both might modify.

---

4. Although similar ideas had appeared earlier, notably in the synchronous variables of the Denelcor HEP.

There are several ways to implement futures and present them to users. The cleanest relies on having one extra tag bit for each word in memory. This bit is similar to a binary semaphore to control access to that word. If the bit is 1, the word is "full" and may be read. If it is 0, on the other hand, any attempt to read it is blocked. Such a full/empty bit is not exactly analogous to a semaphore, because all waiting processes are allowed to proceed with reading the word as soon as its bit is set.

The advantage of such a single-bit implementation is that any variable can be used as a future at any point in the program. The disadvantage is that most hardware does not provide the extra bit required. This is not a problem in most LISP-like languages, which normally use two or more words to represent each atomic value anyway. In a C- or FORTRAN-based language, however, it is simplest to require users to declare explicitly which variables might be the targets of futures, so that extra storage for them can be allocated, and their values tested at run-time to block reading processes correctly. Program 4.21 shows a recursive summation program written in an unimplemented dialect of FORTRAN-K called FORTRAN-KFT which takes this approach.

This pair of subroutines is typical of the way futures are used. `array_sum` itself is just a wrapper, which passes its parameters, plus an initial index, to `array_sum_f`. `array_sum_f` then does the real work recursively. If fewer than `Threshold` values are being summed, summing is done directly. (This test saves the expense of creating processes which do nothing except add two values and return.) If the number of values to be summed is larger than the `Threshold`, on the other hand, the values to be summed are split into two halves. A future is then created to sum the values in the lower half into the variable `temp`. The process which is to do this is handed the array, a base index into it, and a count of the number of elements to be summed. The parent process then sums the top elements itself. When the statement:

```
result = result + temp
```

is reached, the run-time system checks the status of the temporary variable which is the target of the child's future. If this is still empty, then the child must still be executing. In this case, the run-time system suspends the parent until a value for `temp` becomes available. Once this happens, the parent creates and returns the final sum.

To determine when creating a future for this purpose is economical, suppose that the cost of performing each individual operation is t_{op}, the number of operations to be performed is n_{op}, the cost of creating a new process is t_p, and the cost of waiting for a future to return (i.e., descheduling a process if a required value is not yet ready) is t_{delay}. Clearly, a perfect split will give a t_{delay} of zero, and so the times spent in the parent and child will be equal. Creating a future is only worthwhile if:

```
integer, constant :: Threshold = some small integer
  .
  .
  .
real function array_sum(A, N)
  real    :: A(:)
  integer :: N
  return array_sum_f(A, 1, N)
end function
  .
  .
  .
real function array_sum_f(A, start, num)
  real    :: A(:)
  integer :: start, num
  real    :: result = 0.0, temp
  integer :: i, n
  if num < Threshold then
    do i = start, start+num
      result = result + A(i)
    end do
  else
    n = num/2
    future temp = array_sum_f(A, start, n)
    result = array_sum_f(A, (start + n), num - n)
    result = result + temp
  end if
  return result
end function
```

Program 4.21
Recursive Summation Using Futures

$$t_p + \frac{n_{op}t_{op}}{2} \leq n_{op}t_{op}$$

or equivalently if:

$$t_p \leq \frac{n_{op}t_{op}}{2}$$

Futures are often simpler to use than semaphores because synchronization in futures-based programs is implicit. For example, if the values in an array must be be initialized before being used, it is simple to execute each initialization statement as a future, so that the program will automatically halt before trying to access any uninitialized values. Futures can depend on futures in order to chain calculations together, as in:

```
integer, constant :: Width = 1024
real              :: pressure(Width), temperature(Width)
real              :: strain, max_strain
integer           :: i, imax
  .
  .
  .

! initialize pressure and temperature
do i = 1, Width
  future pressure(i) = init_pres(i)
  future temperature(i) = init_temp(i)
end do

! calculate location of greatest strain
imax = -1
max_strain = - ∞ ! or some very negative value
do i = 1, Width
  strain = calc_strain(pressure(i), temperature(i))
  if strain > max_strain do
    max_strain = strain
    imax = i
  end if
end do
```

Here, the temperature calculations are automatically held back until the pressure values they refer to have been calculated, while the final calculation of the maximum point of strain is similarly delayed as much as it needs to be.

Two issues which users of futures must be careful with are when and where variables are copied, and whether futures can be prematurely terminated. The safest way to approach the first of these is to give each process its own private copy of every variable which it references. However, if large structures are being manipulated, as in the array-summing example above, this can lead to unacceptably poor performance. In addition, if a program uses pointer-based structures, it can be difficult or impossible to mark exactly the right set of variables.

A more efficient solution is to require a `future` to explicitly copy variables when it wants private copies of them, as in:

```
future z = f(copy(x), y)
  .
  .
  .
```

```
real function f(a, b)
  real :: a, b
  do while a > b
    a = ishft(a, 2)
  end while
end function
```

This kind of copying is usually required when futures are being created inside a loop. For example, consider:

```
do i = 1, N
  future array(i) = some_function(i)
end do
```

This code creates *N* futures, all of which share a single instance of the loop index variable i. As a result, most of these processes will probably behave incorrectly, since the creating loop will be updating i as they run. The right way to implement this calculation is:

```
do i = 1, N
  future array(i) = some_function(copy(i))
end do
```

Terminating futures prematurely is a thorny problem. At first glance, it may seem that this should never be necessary—after all, why would a process commit itself to using the value of a calculation, and then change its mind? However, if speculative parallelism is being exploited (Section 2.4.4), a process may want to initiate f futures, then terminate $f - 1$ of them as soon as any one returns a value.

If futures are given identifiers as they are created, this can be implemented by providing some explicit function to terminate a future, and any futures it might have created itself. A more structured approach is to have the system terminate a future when the variable to which it is to assign its result is assigned a value by some other calculation. For example, suppose that the functions depthwise and breadthwise both search a data structure D. If the speeds at which these functions complete the search is data-dependent, and either could be fastest, it may make sense to try both searches simultaneously using:

```
type(result_type), future :: result
future result = depthwise()
future result = breadthwise()
```
calculations involving result

Unfortunately, even this simple calculation contains a race condition. Suppose that an *eager evaluation* strategy is used, i.e., that whenever a future is created, its parent is immediately suspended, and the future's value calculated. (Such a strategy might be used when running a program containing futures on a single processor.) Under such a rule, the depthwise calculation of result would complete before the breadthwise calculation was started. The former's result would therefore always be over-written by the latter's.

For this reason, futures-based systems that support process termination should require all potentially-concurrent futures on a variable to be created in a single statement of the form:

```
future x = A, B, C
```

where *A*, *B*, and *C* are arbitrary function calls. Only the result of the first to complete is stored in x; the others are terminated, although any side-effects they have had will persist. For further security, it should be illegal to begin a future on x if one or more are currently outstanding.

One subtlety in the implementation and use of futures is the way pointers are handled. Suppose p is a pointer to a record of type T, which has fields f1 and f2, and that the following code is executed:

```
type some_type
  integer, future :: f1
  integer         :: f2, f3
end type
  .
  .
  .
type(some_type) :: p
  .
  .
  .
future p%f1 = func_a()
future p = func_b()
p%f2 = value
```

How should the process executing this code behave? In particular, is it legal for a process to access a field of a record if there is a future outstanding on the pointer through which the process is referencing the record?

In FORTRAN-KFT, the answer to the latter question would be "no." If there is a future outstanding on a pointer, then any references through that pointer are considered reads, and blocked until the future completes. However, consider the first assignment in the code above, which creates a future on a field of the record initially pointed to by p. This operation behaves like a future on any other scalar variable; in particular, it does not prevent

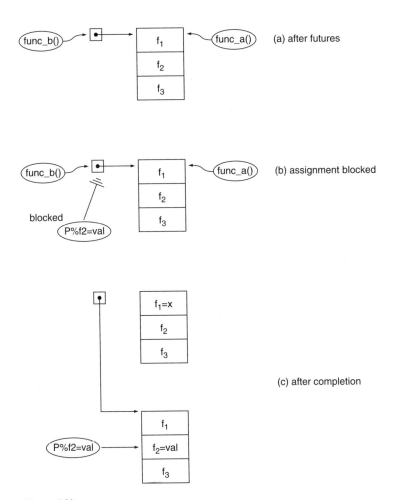

Figure 4.20
Futures on Pointers

the subsequent future on the pointer itself from being started. However, once the future on the pointer p completes, there might be no reference to its old record (Figure 4.20). In this case, even if the future on the field f1 runs to completion, its result will be lost, since nothing points to the original record any longer.

One final problem with futures-based systems is that synchronizing on aggregate structures is no easier with futures than with lower-level constructs like semaphores. Suppose that we want to create one future to initialize each row of a matrix, and block processes that are trying to read the matrix until its values are initialized. We cannot use something like:

```
real, future :: A(N, N)
integer      :: i
   .
   .
   .
do i = 1, N
  future A(i, :) = initialize(A(i, :))
end do
A(1, 1) = A(N, 1) + A(N, N) + A(N, 1)              ! should block for a while
```

because it would mark the rows of A, rather than its individual elements, as having outstanding futures. Just as the fact that a future was outstanding on a pointer to a record did not imply that there were futures outstanding on the record's fields, so having a future outstanding on a row of a matrix does not necessarily imply that there are futures on the elements in that row. The usual trick is to create a dummy vector of synchronization targets, and then explicitly test those elements with (for example) self-assignment:

```
real, future :: A(N, N)
logical       :: synch(N)
integer       :: i
do i = 1, N
  synch(i) = initialize(A(i, :))
end do
synch(1) = synch(1)                               ! make sure row 1 initialized
synch(N) = synch(N)                               ! make sure row N initialized
A(1, 1) = A(N, 1) + A(N, N) + A(N, 1)             ! no longer need to block here
```

Finally, nothing has been said about communication between futures. As was seen in the discussion of the Game of Life in Section 4.2.5, repeatedly creating and terminating processes is an expensive way to implement this application. However, it may be the only option in the futures model, as there is no way to create a group of peer processes which can then *swap boundary values* back and forth amongst themselves.

4.4 Caching

While it is relatively easy for a computer with only one processor to give many processes the impression that they are sharing memory, it is much more difficult to do this in a multiprocessor system whose processors have local data caches, or in a multicomputer whose memory is physically distributed. While these issues are properly the concern of computer architects and systems programmers, rather than application programmers, in many of today's systems it is necessary to understand how shared memory is implemented in order to use it effectively.

The origin of the consistency problem is the tension between keeping data local, so that they can be accessed quickly, and keeping them consistent, so that all processes see the same values at the same time. Consider a simple bus-based multiprocessor, in which several microprocessors are connected to a single memory. Every time a processor fetches an instruction or an operand, or writes a result back to memory, it must claim the shared bus. Because of this, the scalability of this system is sharply limited by the achievable bus bandwidth.

The universal solution to this problem takes advantage of the spatial and temporal locality of most programs (Section 2.1.4) by giving each processor a small, but extremely fast, memory unit called a cache. Unlike locations in main memory, cache elements do not have fixed addresses. Instead, whenever that processor references a memory location, it first checks to see whether it currently has a copy of the contents of that memory location in its cache. If so, it can read that value, or write to it, without accessing the bus. Only if its cache does not have a copy of that location's contents does the processor claim the bus and copy the value it needs from main memory. In practice, contiguous blocks of memory (typically a few bytes or words long) are read into the cache, and written out again, to amortize the overheads involved.

Of course, this glosses over some rather thorny issues. The most important of these is what happens when several processes have copies of the same variable in their caches at the same time, and are independently modifying them. For example, if S is a semaphore, and a process A calls wait(S), a copy of S will probably be brought into A's cache. If S is not currently set by another process, A can set it and enter the critical region it guards. However, if a process B subsequently calls wait(S) before A has written the semaphore's new value back to main memory, B will get the same ready copy of S that A got, and will think it has permission to enter the critical region. The mutual exclusion S was supposed to ensure will thus have failed. A similar situation will arise if S is initially zero, and that value is copied into A's cache. A will remain blocked even if some other process later sets the semaphore, since A will only be checking its cached value.

Most multiprocessor systems use some hardware-based protocol to ensure that problems such as these do not arise. Usually, these protocols are designed to allow as many processors as possible to keep local copies of variables, so long as those copies are only being read. Once a processor writes to its copy, the protocol must ensure that the effects of that write operation are felt by all other processors.

The two basic types of *cache protocol* are called *write-invalidate* and *write-update* [Stenström 1990]. When a processor writes to a block in its cache in a system using a write-invalidate protocol, a signal is sent to all other processors, telling each to invalidate its copy of that block (if it has one). The next time one of those processors tries to access data in that block, its request is serviced by the cache of the processor which most recently wrote to it, as shown in Figure 4.21. By contrast, a write-update policy does not render other processors' copies invalid, but rather sends them the information they need to make those copies consistent with the one belonging to the writing processor (Figure 4.22). While this would seem to be more sensible, it can also generate much more message traffic, and so lead to lower performance.

The problem with both types of protocol is that they seem to require processors to broadcast information to one another every time they perform a write. In systems which connect processors to memory units via a shared bus, this broadcast can be eliminated by having every processor's cache controller continuously watch the bus for write operations. This is called *snooping*; when a snoopy cache sees a write operation to a block of memory which it currently has copied, it marks its copy invalid, or updates it, automatically.

The update problem is much more difficult to solve if shared buses are not used, because there is no easy way for processors to know whether the values they are manipulating are out of step with those being manipulated by other processors. One approach is to make the memory responsible for handling updates. Suppose a bit-vector is associated with each block of memory, and that this bit-vector contains one bit for each processor in the system. Every time a processor takes a copy of a block, its bit in the vector is set. Whenever a processor writes to a block, it sends a warning message to the memory unit [Lenoski et al. 1992]. The memory unit then forwards this message to each of the processors marked in the directory as currently holding copies of that block. Provided most blocks are only referenced by a few processors, this method is much more efficient than simple broadcast on systems in which processors and memories are connected through a switching network.

The use of caching has several implications for application programming on parallel computers. First, caches are usually processor-oriented, rather than process-oriented. As a result, re-scheduling a process may cause a flurry of cache activity, as most of the values in the cache will have been brought there from the parts of memory referenced by the previously-scheduled process. For this reason, a program may sometimes run faster (or rather, less slowly) if it uses only one process per processor, and lets some processors be idle some of the time, than if it places many processes on each processor and continually moves data in and out of those processors' caches.

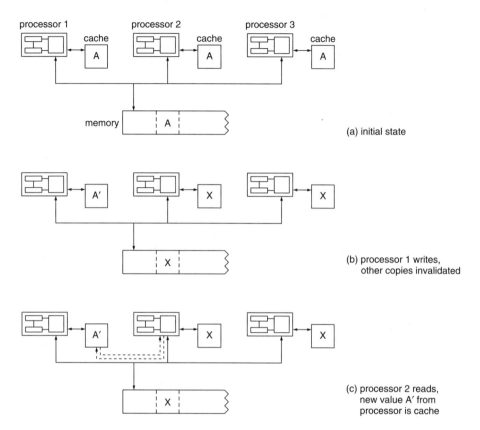

Figure 4.21
Write-Invalidate Cache Policy

A second implication of caching is that if even a single variable is frequently accessed by many different processes, the performance of the whole program will suffer. If a critical region is protected by a single semaphore, or a single counter variable is used to implement barrier synchronization, the speed at which the program runs may be completely determined by how quickly that variable's value can be tossed back and forth between the machine's caches. As tree-structured barriers and locks suffer from these problems less than their linearly-structured cousins, they should be used in most circumstances.

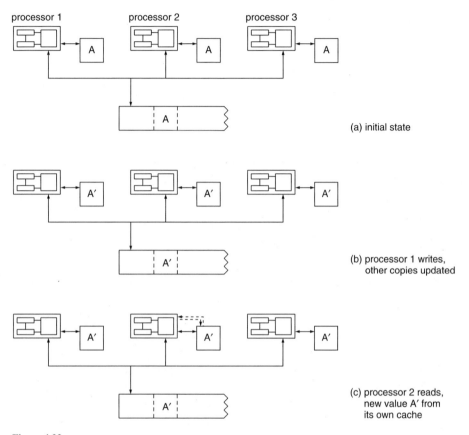

Figure 4.22
Write-Update Cache Policy

4.5   Scheduling and Mapping Parallel Programs

Thus . . . the model of the problem does not correspond well to reality, the solutions found are generally impractical, the performance analyses given are meaningless, and the proven results are frequently incorrect . . .   On a positive note, this is an area that offers great opportunities for improvement.
——Andrew S. Tannenbaum
Modern Operating Systems

Another issue which programmers working with control-parallel systems must deal with is how work should be mapped to the available memory. Consider a short program such as:

```
x = v/2
y = (3 * x) + 1
z = sqrt(y)
```

in which every statement uses the result of the previous statement. Clearly, there is little scope for parallelism in this—none of the operations can be started before the previous operations have completed. But if we consider a more typical program fragment, such as that shown previously in Figure 3.25, there is usually a great deal of potential parallelism.

This idea can be exploited in two related ways. The first is to develop languages and architectures which implement this *dataflow model* of computation directly. In this model, serialism and parallelism are not things the programmer worries about—once the computation has been specified, the system being used is responsible for ensuring that the dependence constraints are obeyed. A program written in a dataflow language like Id [Nikhil 1991] is merely a partial order which represents the dependencies between different calculations; the programmer does not specify the exact order of the calculations. Dataflow's advocates argue that this allows programmers to concentrate on what they want done, and leave the when and how up to the system; dataflow's critics point out that while this might be a laudable goal, no-one has yet managed to build a dataflow computer whose performance is competitive with that of conventional serial and parallel computers. [Arvind & Brobst 1993] describes the evolution of dataflow hardware over the last twenty years.

The other way to use the idea that programs can be described as dependence graphs is to take programs written in conventional languages, turn them into graphs, and then use those graphs to *schedule* and *map* processes, i.e., to find the most efficient order and location in which to do work. This subject has been studied since the late 1950s, and while most problems have turned out to be computationally intractable, some interesting approximate methods have been developed.

This section starts by describing what scheduling tries to accomplish, and what factors are usually taken into account. Some of the positive and negative results that have been produced are then laid out, and some of the heuristic techniques that have been developed are described.

4.5.1 The Rules of the Game

Suppose we represent a collection of computations as a dependence graph. Each node g_i in this graph has a weighting w_i, which shows the time required to execute it on a single processor. Each arc $a_k(i, j)$ between two nodes shows a dependence—the calculation represented by g_j cannot begin before the calculation represented by g_i has finished. Constructing such a *directed acyclic graph (DAG)* is straightforward for a program which contains neither loops nor conditional branches.

Now suppose the computer on which we wish to execute this computation contains $\mathcal{P}$ identical processors. While a processor is performing a calculation, it may do nothing else; equivalently, each processor does an entire task from start to finish, and only then begins the next task assigned to it. The scheduling problem can then be stated as:

Given a DAG ($\{g_i\}$, $\{a_k\}$) and $\mathcal{P}$ identical processors, what ordered assignment of DAG nodes to processors will minimize the time required to complete the whole computation?

This formulation of the problem characterizes both the problem of scheduling work within a single program, and the problem of scheduling separate programs, although there are usually only a few dependencies in the latter case.

Before looking at how the scheduling problem might be solved, it is worth pointing out that there are many variations on it. If the computer is being used by many people, for example, and their jobs do not interact, it might be more sensible to try to find a schedule which maximizes the throughput, or number of jobs completed per unit time. Alternatively, if processing time is very expensive, we could try to find a schedule which involves the least idle time. Since a program run on a single processor never wastes any time, the second question always has a trivial answer. In general, there will be some function describing the tradeoff between efficiency and time to completion, and the problem will be to get the best score possible. This last formulation of the scheduling problem is particularly interesting given that many parallel machines can be space-shared in the way described at the end of Section 2.5.5.

The scheduling problem could also be made more complicated by allowing some processors to be faster than others, or even by allowing some processors to be faster at some types of calculation, but slower at others. In a heterogeneous system containing many scalar integer processors and a few pipelined floating-point units, for example, an efficient schedule would probably concentrate numerical calculations on the floating-point units, while trying to keep everything else off them.

Finally, we could require that the optimal schedule be determined on the fly. While any particular execution of a program can be described retrospectively as a DAG, it may not be possible to construct such a DAG in advance for a program containing data-dependent conditional expressions or loops. Accordingly, we may want an algorithm which looks at the workloads on different processors as the computation is being done, and only chooses a node for the next task when that task is ready to run. Since collecting information from each processor and weighing it up each time a task had to be allocated would be very inefficient, most work on dynamic scheduling has concentrated on algorithms which use only local information, i.e., information that can be gathered from processors which are "near" one another. [Grunwald et al. 1990] describes the performance of some algorithms for doing this.

4.5.2   Solving Simple Cases

Returning to the original formulation of the problem, it turns out that optimal schedules can only be found efficiently in a few very restricted cases. If each task takes one unit of time to do, and the dependencies are structured as a tree, then an optimal schedule can be found in polynomial time [Hu 1961]. If dependencies are structured arbitrarily, but there are only two processors, a different polynomial time algorithm can find the optimal schedule [Coffman and Graham 1972]. In almost every other case, it can be shown that the time required to find the optimal schedule grows exponentially with the number of tasks, the number of processors, or both.

This is the bad news; the good news is that there are some algorithms which give good, though not necessarily optimal, solutions to the scheduling problem in polynomial time. One such heuristic, called Highest-Level-First (HLF), starts by assigning a level number of 0 to terminal nodes of the DAG, and a level of $\ell + 1$ to a node if its highest-numbered descendent has level ℓ. Those nodes with no predecessors are then put into a priority queue, with the highest-level node at the front. Other tasks are only added to the priority queue once all of their predecessors have completed. When a processor finishes a task, it is given the next task from the front of the priority queue.

A variation on Highest-Level-First, discussed in [Shirazi et al. 1990], is Heavy-Node-First (HNF). This algorithm starts by initializing a set S to contain all the tasks in the DAG without ancestors. It then constructs another set A of processors which are currently idle; initially, this set contains all the processors. The algorithm then assigns the heaviest task in S to a processor. If there are several equally-heavy tasks, as many are assigned as possible. The algorithm then steps forward in time to the first moment at which a processor

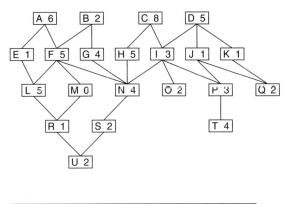

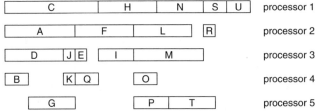

Figure 4.23
Heavy-Node-First Scheduling

finishes the task assigned to it, and adds any tasks which are made runnable by that task's completion to another set, S'. Another task from the original set S is then assigned to the processor. The algorithm continues in this fashion until the set S is empty, at which point it moves the tasks in S' into S. If there is ever a point at which a processor is ready to run a task, but no task is available, a dummy task is created to keep that processor "busy" until the completion time of the next processor due to finish.

The effects of this algorithm, whose running time is $\mathcal{O}(N \log N)$ for N processes, are shown in Figure 4.23. As [Shirazi et al. 1990] discuss, the quality of the schedules produced by this algorithm is comparable to that of schedules produced by more complicated algorithms based on finding and scheduling critical paths.

4.5.3 Taking Communication Delay into Account

While a model in which it takes no time for information to propagate from one task to another may be adequate for describing multiprocessors with shared memory, it is inadequate for disjoint-memory multicomputers, in which results may have to be transferred from one part of memory to another in order to be available to dependent computations.

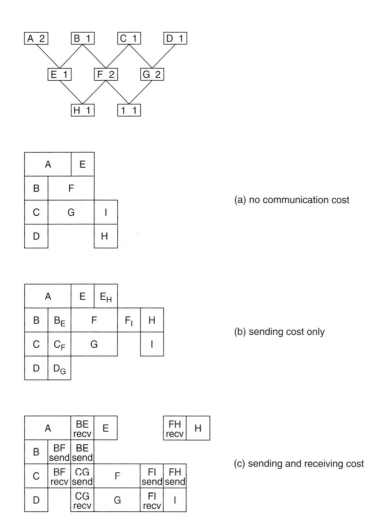

Figure 4.24
Schedules Taking Communication Delays into Account

Suppose that each arc $a_{i,j}$ of a DAG is labelled with a value that represents the time taken to move the results of task g_i from the processor it has run on to the processor on which task g_j is to run. As Figure 4.24 shows, even small changes in these delays can have a large effect on the optimal schedule for that DAG.

An example of a scheduling heuristic which takes communication delays into account is the Earliest Ready Task (ERT) heuristic proposed in [Lee et al. 1988]. ERT works by repeatedly finding the set of tasks which could be scheduled at the earliest possible time, selecting one (if there are several which could be scheduled simultaneously), and placing it on a processor. ERT is an example of a greedy algorithm, which repeatedly makes the choice which seems best in the immediate circumstances. It starts by setting the availability time of each processor to zero, and constructing a set of un-run tasks S, which initially contains every task. The algorithm then repeatedly constructs another set S', which is the set of tasks in S with no parents in S, i.e., the sets of tasks which can now be run. It then finds the earliest time at which each task in this set could be run on each processor p_i by summing the time at which each of the task's ancestors is due to complete, and the time required to communicate that ancestor's results to processor p_i. ERT then finds the times at which each runnable task could actually start executing on processor p_i. A task with an earliest runnable time is chosen, and removed from the set S of un-run tasks. The availability time of the processor on which it is to be run is then adjusted, and the steps above repeated. The total running time of this algorithm is $\mathcal{O}(N\mathcal{P}^2)$, and the schedule it produces is guaranteed to complete in a time less than $(2 - \frac{1}{N})\tau' + C$, where τ' is the time required by an optimal schedule, and C is the time of the longest chain of communication delays in the program.

While ERT uses a more realistic model of multicomputer behavior, simply labelling arcs with delays is still an inadequate description of how real machines work. In a real multicomputer, the time taken to send a message from one processor to another depends not only on the size of the message, but also on the distance between the processors and the amount of contention for inter-processor links. Modelling the first requires some knowledge of the physical topology of the multicomputer being used; modelling the second is extremely difficult, as delays introduced by contention in one part of the program will affect the order in which tasks are able to start, which will in turn affect the amount of contention at any time.

One of the things that makes scheduling such a difficult problem is that it often makes sense in a disjoint-memory system to perform *redundant computation*, i.e., to have two or more processes calculate the same value. Doing this is often cheaper than having one process calculate the value and send it to other processes.

4.5.4 Process-Based Models

All of the ideas described above assume that a program can be described as a DAG. As mentioned above, this can only be done retrospectively for programs which contain data-dependent branches and loops. Because of this, some work, such as [Stone 1977] has used process-based models instead. In a process-based model, each node in the program graph represents a long-lived process, while each arc represents a steady volume of traffic.

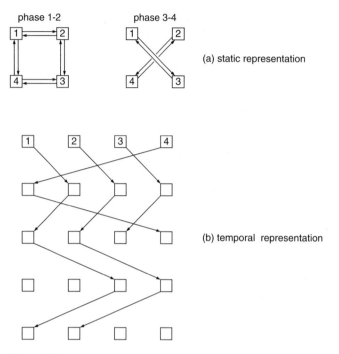

phase 1-2   phase 3-4

(a) static representation

(b) temporal representation

Figure 4.25
A Temporal Communication Graph

However, these models have their shortcomings as well, as they do not capture transient behavior which can be an important influence on performance.

A hybrid model combining the best features of both DAGs and static process graphs was proposed in [Lo 1992]. This model takes each process in a static process graph and expands it through time, as shown in Figure 4.25. The blocks in each column represent the evolution of a single process over time, while the arrows connecting columns show inter-process communication. Graphs of this form can be described in a simple language which captures the regularity of many communication patterns. Descriptions written in this language can then be fed to various automatic and semi-automatic mapping and scheduling tools, or used by the debugging and performance profiling tools described in Section 5.4 to transform low-level events into ones recognizable to users.

4.5.5   Guided Self-Scheduling

One special case of the scheduling problem which has received a lot of attention is that of scheduling iterations of nested loops. The naïve way to do this is to task-farm at the single-

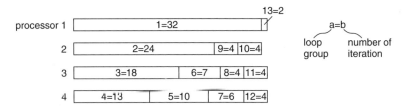

Figure 4.26
Guided Self-Scheduling

iteration level, but if the body of each loop is small, and the number of iterations is large, this can result in unacceptably high overheads. The next obvious strategy is to schedule the iterations in blocks of some fixed size. However, if the execution time for different iterations can vary, this can lead to poor load balance.

One strategy which is both effective and easy to implement is called *guided self-scheduling* [Smith 1981, Polychronopoulos & Kuck 1987]. It is best understood by taking the point of view of an individual processor p_i which wants to do its fair share of work, but wants to leave enough work for its peers. If there are N iterations left to be done when p_i is ready to claim some more work, the safest thing for it to do is to assume that its peers are also ready to claim some more work. Processor p_i should therefore claim $N/\mathcal{P}$ iterations, i.e., to take an equal share of the number of iterations remaining.

Guided self-scheduling can be implemented by maintaining two shared counters: one recording the base index of the next loop iteration, and one recording R, the number of iterations left to be done. Whenever a processor p_i is ready to claim some more work, it calculates $N_i = R/\mathcal{P}$, records the base index counter, increments that counter by N_i, and reduces R by the same amount. As Figure 4.26 shows, this leads to processors grabbing larger blocks of iterations early on, and smaller blocks later. Thus, synchronization and mutual exclusion costs are kept down during the early part of the loop, while a sufficient number of small loop blocks are left at the end to help maintain a good load balance.

4.6   Parallel I/O Systems

One definition of "supercomputer" is "any device which turns a compute-limited problem into an I/O-limited problem." This joke is only funny until one encounters programs which spend 90% of their time loading and saving data sets, or checkpointing long computations as insurance against a hardware error. To alleviate the frustration this can cause, most vendors now supply I/O systems with enough bandwidth to support concurrent access from multiple processors. Many of these are built using *RAIDs*, or redundant arrays of inexpensive disks, in which many small disks are combined to create a single fault-tolerant file system with good response and high bandwidth. [Gibson 1992] is an excellent study of the hardware that might underpin such a system. However, since there is little agreement on what such systems should look like to their users, this section looks at some of the design criteria and constraints for parallel I/O.

4.6.1   Visualization Systems

The I/O systems most often used with parallel computers are of two types: visualization systems, and file systems. The former usually consist of either video capture devices such as framegrabbers, or video output devices, such as television monitors, high-resolution RGB monitors, or video recording devices. The latter are usually made up of one or more disks, plus associated control processors and software.

The most common method of connecting a visualization device to a parallel computer is to thread a bus through several of the computer's processors. If the bandwidth of the visualization device is B_v, and the rate at which each processor can deliver data to the bus is B_p, then so long as parallel overheads are minimal, B_v/B_p processors can be put on the bus to drive the output device at its maximum rate. If the visualization device is a camera connected to a framegrabber, for example, and can produce 20 frames a second at 512×512 8-bit pixels per frame, then the total input bandwidth is approximately 42 MHz. If each processor is connected to the bus through double-ported memory (i.e., memory which can be accessed simultaneously by two devices), and the one-sided bandwidth of this memory is 8 MHz, then six processors would be more than enough to handle the incoming data—provided, of course, that they are not required to do anything else. If incoming frames are being divided equally amongst processors, and each processor needs one-tenth of a second to perform some image processing on its 85 lines of the image (assuming a simple strip-wise decomposition), then clearly more processors would be needed.

This simple calculation ignores the overheads of parallel processing which any such system would inevitably incur. If processors need to synchronize after processing each input image, for example, then the time to synchronize can also increase the number of processors required to handle incoming data. (System designers must of course ensure that adding more processors to offset the increased synchronization time does not increase that time even further . . .) Similarly, if many processors are collaborating to draw a sequence of output images on a shared screen, then the time to perform a barrier synchronization after each frame is drawn (in order to ensure that parts of the next frame do not overwrite it) must be taken into account.

4.6.2   File Systems

In contrast with visualization systems, parallel file systems may have an unlimited bandwidth, since they can be constructed by combining an arbitrary number of disks. So long as these are connected to separate processors, their raw overall bandwidth will simply be the sum of their individual bandwidths. Each of the disks in such a system usually has its own controlling processor, which (in most cases) runs a version of a standard operating system such as UNIX. While the input or output device in a visualization system provides a natural point to manage synchronization, the distribution of the disks in a parallel file system means that synchronization and control issues are more difficult.

Like everything else in an operating system, a parallel file system must try to be all things to all people. First, it is important that there be as few distinctions as possible between "standard" files, created and manipulated by sequential programs, and the files created by parallel programs. For example, if the parallel file system created a set of files output.1, output.2, ..., output.N to represent a single logical file output created by a program containing N processes, then programmers would have to write tools to concatenate (or split) files in order to allow the output of parallel programs to be manipulated by sequential utilities, or the output of sequential programs (such as parameter generators) to be read by parallel programs. Moving, deleting, and renaming such files would be both tedious and error-prone.

Using multiple physical files to represent a single logical file is even less acceptable if the number of processes manipulating the data in the logical file can change between (or during) runs of the program. If, for example, files are written by 20 processes on one computer, and then moved to another computer on which they are read by 22 processes, the system should manage the required mapping of physical storage to logical files. The simplest way to do this is to hide as much of the internal structure of the file as possible (e.g., disguise the fact that it has 20, or 22, components).

If a parallel file system is being used by a program which has a single thread of control, then it is reasonable to require that I/O be synchronous and uniform: whenever one process reads or writes, every other process must read or write the same volume of data. In this case, "all" the file system has to manage is the mapping of the indices identifying data values in the program (such as array indices) to the physical devices. This problem is similar that of mapping data to processors, as discussed in Section 3.5, and can be managed using similar mechanisms. (Note however that some systems might allow input or output operations of the form io_op(ptrs, counts), where ptrs is an array of pointers to blocks of data, and counts is an array of block sizes. This allows data-parallel systems to write records of differing sizes in a single operation; supporting this therefore requires the techniques described below. Alternatively, a system might allow active processing elements to enumerate themselves using parallel prefix (Section 3.3.2), and only read or write on behalf of active elements [Nickolls 1994].)

If the program using the parallel file system contains many threads of control, on the other hand, then managing their access to the file system is considerably more complicated. As [Best et al. 1993] points out, if four processes were to try to print "Hello", then either:

```
Hello
```

or:

```
Hello
Hello
Hello
Hello
```

might be what the programmer wanted. In fact:

```
HHHHeeeellllllllloooo
```

might also be desired in some cases, while:

```
HHeHeHeellllooloIllo
```

might be acceptable under other circumstances.

Thus, a parallel file system should be able to support both one-to-one access, in which each value is put in correspondence with exactly one process, and one-to-many access, in which each value read is given to all reading processes, and only one copy of duplicated writes is left in the file. Further, in the one-to-one case, programmers may want some control over interleaving, so that either of the second or third examples above could be produced, or they may want interleaving to be arbitrary, as in the last example.

In order to handle all of these cases, most systems require programmers to specify a file access mode when opening or manipulating a file. This mode determines how many independent file pointers are associated with the file, and how those pointers are updated after each operation. In the file system for the CM-5, for example, a file can be in one of four modes: local (L), synchronous sequential (SS), synchronous broadcast (SB), or independent (I) [Best et al. 1993]. Each process that opens a file in "L" mode maintains a separate file pointer; these pointers are updated independently after each read, write, or seek operation. If several processes have the same file open at the same time, it is their responsibility to ensure that operations are consistent.

In "SS" mode, on the other hand, all operations are synchronized, and appear to have been performed in an order determined by the IDs of the processes carrying them out. If 256 processes open the file state.2 in "SS" mode, for example, and then read a 1024 kbyte block from it, process 1 will get the first kilobyte, process 2 the second, and so on. Similarly, if processes write to the file, then it appears as if the writes are blocked until all are available, and then executed in process order.

While "SS" mode may be the one most commonly used for scientific and engineering programs, it is difficult to implement it efficiently in the case in which the records being read or written are of variable length. If record lengths are known in advance, then the file system can simply seek to the appropriate location, and then place data there. If record lengths are unknown, on the other hand, it would seem that the file system would have wait to execute operations in process order. One way around this is to use two physical files to represent each logical file, as shown in Figure 4.27. Entries in the first file are of fixed size, and are interleaved in process order. Each of these entries records an offset and size in the second file, which stores the actual data records. The strength of this method is that it allows quick access to particular records; its weakness is that the file cannot be read by standard serial system utilities.

The third mode supported by the CM-5's file system, "SB," is intended to handle cases in which it is simpler to have every process appear to do its own write or read than to require programmers to insert control code to block all but one process from doing the operation. For example, an input file might comprise a header containing scalar parameters which are to be distributed to all processes, followed by one or more arrays which are to be distributed. When processes read in "SB" mode, it is as if only one process actually read data, and then broadcast those data to the other processes. Similarly, when processes write in "SB" mode, only process 0's data are written. (This case is less common than the others, but may be used when parameters are saved while checkpointing long program runs.)

In the final mode, "I," each process has its own file pointer, and may read, write, or seek at will. The difference between this and simply opening the file many times becomes apparent if the program changes the file access mode while it is executing: when the mode changes from "I" to "SS" or "SB", the resulting single file pointer is set to the maximum of all the individual file pointers, so that subsequent operations begin beyond any of the operations done while the file was in independent mode.

A similar, but different, approach is taken in PUL-GF, the file system constructed at the Edinburgh Parallel Computing Centre [MacDonald 1993]. In PUL-GF, a set of processes signal that they wish to access the file system co-operatively by calling the function gf_join to join a particular file-access group. A single process may join any number of file-access groups; however, all file operations are done on a group-wide basis.

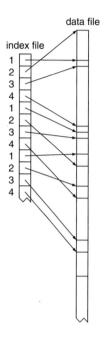

Figure 4.27
Two-Level Representation of Files

After processes have joined file access groups, they may use `gf_open` to open files in any of three modes: single (S), multi (M), or random (R). `gf_open` takes one of these modes as a parameter, along with the access mode of the file (i.e., read or write), the file's name, and the identifier of the group which will be manipulating it. `gf_open` (and the corresponding subsequent `gf_close`) is a synchronizing operation: it blocks its callers until all members of the file access group have called it.

PUL-GF's "S" mode has the same semantics as the Synchronous Broadcast (SB) mode of Best's system. Whenever the processes in a file group try to read the file it is as if a barrier synchronization occurs, after which each process gets a copy of the same single record from the file. (The actual implementation is more sophisticated, and only performs synchronization when necessary.) Similarly, when processes try to write, only one record is actually placed in the file. Note that this implies that all processes within the group must be trying to read or write the same sequences of values. This mode is most often used to read common parameter values from a file, or to write those back when creating an output file.

"M" mode corresponds to Best's Synchronous Sequential (SS) mode. Processes are again blocked until all are ready to perform I/O, and then the operation(s) are done in order, without overlapping. Initially, this order is determined by the order of processes within the file-access group. However, processes may use an auxiliary function `gf_setorder` to re-order themselves, so long as the new ordering is a one to-one permutation of the old values.

The biggest difference between PUL-GF and the CM-5's I/O system is the way they handle independent file access. In the latter, each process is given its own file pointer; in PUL-GF, by contrast, processes share use of a single file pointer. This behavior is particularly useful when processes are reading input data for a task farm, and may take records in an unpredictable order, or when they are writing the results from such a program. In order to allow processes to write several records at a time, PUL-GF supplies functions to begin and end an I/O block. While a process is within an I/O block it has exclusive access to the file; any other process which attempts to access the file while the block is active is suspended until the block is finished.

4.7   Discussion

The shared-variables model has always been the most widely used in parallel computing. While many researchers in the latter half of the 1980s believed that its prospects were limited because it could not be scaled up to very large systems, programmers like shared memory so much that vendors feel compelled to provide it. A combination of hardware support in microprocessor-based message-passing architectures (such as Meiko's CS-2 Computing Surface, NEC's Cenju-3, and Cray Research's T3D), novel cache coherence schemes (such as those used in the DASH project at Stanford University [Lenoski et al. 1992] and the Alewife project at MIT [Chaiken et al. 1990, Agarwal et al. 1993], or the Scalable Coherent Interface (SCI) standard [Gustavson 1992]), and a move toward parallel object-oriented software mean that shared memory will continue to be the most widely-used of parallel programming paradigms.

5 Message Passing

Message passing is the main alternative to shared-variable programming models on present-day parallel computers. In a *message-passing* program, processes do not communicate through shared data structures; instead, they send and receive discrete messages.

Like the shared-variables model, message passing can trace its origins to work on operating systems for uniprocessors, and to the development of computer networks in the 1970s. The original motivation for using message passing in the former context was modularity: by eliminating shared structures, and making both the reading and writing ends of communication explicit, operating systems designers hoped to make their software more robust. At much the same time, techniques for routing message packets and broadcasting messages to many destinations were being developed by groups working on local- and wide-area networks. As always, [Andrews 1991] contains a good summary of the historical development of many of these ideas.

Supercomputer message-passing systems also owe a great deal to pioneering work done at the California Institute of Technology (Caltech) in the early 1980s. As described in Appendix B, the Caltech Concurrent Computation Project built the first hypercube multicomputers, and (necessarily) the first software for such machines. Several of the message-passing systems in use today are direct descendents of that early work, and most others have been influenced by it.

This chapter introduces three of the principal variations on the message-passing model. In the first, anonymous processes are connected to one another through named channels. Two processes can only communicate if there is a channel between them. In the second, processes are arranged in a regular topology, and can communicate only with their immediate neighbors and with a special control process. This model can be viewed as a bridge between the data-parallel models of Section 3, and the third of the models introduced in this chapter. This last is very flexible: each process has one or more names, and any process may communicate with any other.

5.1 Channels

The channel-based programming model has its origins in ideas developed by Hoare [Hoare 1985] and others [Milner 1989] in the 1970s and early 1980s. Hoare's work is known as *communicating sequential processes (CSP)*; its most famous implementation is a language called OCCAM [Inmos 1988a], which was developed by May and others at Inmos. OCCAM was the first language available for transputers, and was promoted strongly during that chip's early years.

While it has many strengths, the CSP model of parallelism also has many weaknesses. This section begins with a discussion of how CSP programs are built out of processes and channels, and then describes some of the more advanced features of CSP-like languages. After some examples, the use of channel-based communication for large-scale software engineering is critiqued.

5.1.1   The Model

The fundamental idea in the CSP model is that independently-executing processes communicate with one another by sending messages through specially-identified communication channels. Processes themselves are unnamed, and two processes may only communicate if they are linked by a channel.

In order to create processes, CSP-based languages like FORTRAN-KCSP provide the same `create` construct used in the previous chapter:

```
create
  N_A of A( . . . params . . . )
  N_B of B( . . . params . . . )
  .
  .
  .
  N_Z of Z( . . . params . . . )
end create
```

The execution of these processes may be interleaved in any order; as before, their parent does not continue executing until all of its children have terminated.

Instead of using semaphores to control access to shared variables, the CSP model requires processes to communicate explicitly through channels. Channels are an intrinsic record type, like strings or devices. Channel variables are declared in the usual way:

```
type(chan) :: c, d, y(10)
  .
  .
  .
type handle
  type(chan), auto :: c
  real             :: buffer(128)
end type
```

Any process can both read from and write to any channel. In this sense, CSP channels are more like ham radio frequencies than UNIX-style pipes. However, programmers should always ensure (a) that any process only ever reads from or writes to a channel, and (b) that any channel is only ever shared by two processes. The reason for this is that the behavior of overlapping reads or writes on channels is undefined. If, for example, two processes try to write while one is reading, then the writers' messages may be interleaved in an arbitrary order, or one of the writers could become confused and try to read from the channel. If many processes in a program share a channel, or if a channel is used for two-way communication, then an error such as this will eventually occur as the program grows or is modified. Such errors are extremely difficult to detect and track down.

A process sends a message through a channel using the special operator <-, which takes a channel on its left, and a comma-separated list of expressions on its right. The expressions are evaluated, and their results are sent in order through the channel. Thus:

```
type(chan), auto :: c
real             :: a = 3.14159
  .
  .
  .
c <- 1, a, "frisbee"
```

sends the integer 1, a very crude approximation to π, and the string `"frisbee"` through the channel c. <- can be thought of as an indirect assignment operator, that assigns values through a channel to variables in some other process.

A process at the other end of the channel would receive this message by copying values out of the channel using ->:

```
integer          :: i
real             :: x
type(string), auto :: s
  .
  .
  .
c -> i, x, s
```

Here, values are "assigned" through the channel to the variables i, x, and s. Note the use of auto in the declaration of the string s. It is the user's responsibility to ensure that storage is allocated to receive values from a channel. Without this declaration (or an explicit call to allocate), the channel would find that s was unassociated, and a run-time error would occur.

CSP advertises itself as a disjoint-memory model, but in fact uses a mix of shared and disjoint memory. In most CSP-based languages, processes can be created out of arbitrary blocks of code, as in:

```
logical :: X, Y
real    :: M(100, 100)
create                          ! not allowed in Fortran-K
  begin                         ! process A
      . . . statements A . . .
```

```
   end
   begin                                    ! process B
      . . . statements B . . .
   end
   .
   .
   .
end create
```

Here, the two processes *A* and *B* would share the variables X, Y, and M. FORTRAN-KCSP uses subroutines to structure process creation in order to encourage modularity: FORTRAN-KCSP processes only share common parameters. This sharing is necessary, because if channel parameters could not be shared, processes would be unable to communicate. The examples given later in this section will show how the use of shared memory can be used to improve program performance.

Channels are intrinsically typeless, in that any message may be sent through any channel. However, the run-time system checks that the types of the values sent in a message conform to the types into which those values are being received. Thus, while:

```
type(chan), auto :: c
   .
   .
   .
create
   1 of sender(c)
   1 of receiver(c)
end create
   .
   .
   .
procedure sender(c)
   type(chan) :: c
   integer    :: a(3), i
   c <- a, i
end procedure
   .
   .
   .
procedure receiver(c)
   type(chan) :: c
   real       :: x, a(2)
   c -> a, i
end procedure
```

would compile, it would generate an error when executed, since the types and the shapes of the values being sent would not match those of the variables supplied at the receiving end.

One important feature of FORTRAN-KCSP, and most other message-passing systems, is that shallow copying is used when messages are sent. As explained on page 189, a shallow copy of a variable is one which does not contain copies of any recursively-nested structures contained by the original. Thus, if a process has built up a linked list, and sends the first element of the list through a channel, only that element reaches the receiving end; the system does not copy the whole list recursively. If processes wish to send linked structures to one another, they must send the components individually.

A simple example of the use of channels is shown in Program 5.1. This program models the activity of a pub; each of the three processes plays the part of a member of staff or the lone customer.[1] These processes pass "drinks" and "money" to one another as signals through channels (Figure 5.1).

The behavior of channels is defined so that they can play two distinct roles. The first is communication: once processes are started, they can only exchange information through channels. The second, which is equally important, is synchronization: messages are transferred only when both of the processes participating in the transfer are ready. If a sender reaches a transmission point first, it is blocked until some other process is willing to receive a message on that channel. Conversely, if a receiver is first, it is blocked until there is a message ready for it to receive.

Because of this, a channel can be used like a binary semaphore to synchronize a pair of processes. This is accomplished by having one process send, then try to receive, while the other receives, and then (after doing some work) sends an acknowledgement. Program 5.2 shows how this can be used to ensure that processes write values to the screen in a particular order. Note that the value the two processes are exchanging is unimportant; it is the presence of a message, rather than its contents, which forces synchronization.

Like previous examples, Program 5.2 shows that there is nothing explicit in the language to indicate whether a given process is supposed to read from or write to a particular channel. If by accident the pong process was to try to send on c(First), and read from c(Second), then both processes block forever, or one process could mistakenly send, over-writing the value the other process is trying to send.

To see why, consider one possible implementation of channels. Each channel is represented by a 3-word record in memory (Figure 5.2a). A process which wishes to send data through the channel starts by checking the first word in this record. If it is null, then

---

1. The operating systems mid-term is the next day.

```
program
  integer, constant :: Wtr_Bar = 1
  integer, constant :: Wtr_Cust = 2
  type(chan), auto  :: drink(2), pay(2), change(2)
  create
    1 of bartender(drink(Wtr_Bar), pay(Wtr_Bar), change(Wtr_Bar))
    1 of waiter(drink, pay, change)
    1 of customer(drink(Wtr_Cust), pay(Wtr_Cust), change(Wtr_Cust))
  end create
end program
  .
  .
  .

procedure bartender(drink, pay, change)
  type(chan) :: drink, pay, change
  integer    :: dollars, cents, num_beer
  do while customer is drinking
    pay -> dollars, cents
    num_beer = make_change(dollars, cents)
    change <- dollars, cents
    drink <- num_beer
  end while
end procedure
  .
  .
  .

procedure waiter(drink, pay, change)
  type(chan) :: drink(:), pay(:), change(:)
  integer    :: dollars, cents, num_beer
  do while customer is drinking
    pay(Wtr_Cust)    -> dollars, cents
    pay(Wtr_Bar)     <- dollars, cents
    change(Wtr_Bar)  -> dollars, cents
    drink(Wtr_Bar)   -> num_beer
    change(Wtr_Cust) <- dollars, cents
    drink(Wtr_Cust)  <- num_beer
  end while
end procedure
  .
  .
  .
```

Program 5.1
A Pub Program

```
procedure customer(drink, pay, change)
  type(chan) :: drink, pay, change
  integer    :: dollars, cents, num_beer
  do while not aware that exam is tomorrow
    pay <- dollars, cents
    change -> dollars, cents
    drink -> num_beer
  end while
end procedure
```

Program 5.1 *(continued)*
A Pub Program

Figure 5.1
Operation of a Pub Program

no other processes are ready to communicate. The sender therefore fills the record with a pointer to itself, a pointer to the data it wishes to send, and a count of the number of bytes it wishes to transmit. It then takes itself off its processor's scheduling queue to wait.

Some time later, another process tries to receive data through the channel. When it checks the channel's status record, it sees that a sending process is waiting for it. The receiver can then copy the data indicated by the second and third words in the channel record into its own memory, and re-schedule the sending process pointed to by the record's first entry. Both processes can proceed on their way.

Clearly, this scheme is symmetric: if the receiver arrived first, it would store a pointer to itself, a pointer to the buffer into which it wished to receive data, and a count of the number of bytes it was willing to receive in the channel's status record. The sender would then find a partner waiting, and would copy values as appropriate.

But what if two processes were to try to send on the same channel? The first would fill the channel status record as before. The second, however, would see a filled status record and assume that the process on the other end was a receiver (Figure 5.2b). It would therefore overwrite the data the first process was trying to send. Conversely, if two receivers were matched up, the second one to arrive would copy data from the buffer into which the first was trying to receive data.

```
integer, constant :: First = 1
integer, constant :: Second = 2
integer, constant :: Num = number of iterations
type(chan), auto  :: c(2)
  .
  .
  .
create
  1 of ping(c, Num)
  1 of pong(c, Num)
end create
  .
  .
procedure ping(ch, n)
  type(chan) :: ch
  integer    :: n
  integer    :: i, dummy
  do i = 1, n
    write std_out, "ping\n"
    c(First) <- 0
    c(Second) -> dummy
  end do
end procedure
  .
  .
  .
procedure pong(ch, n)
  type(chan) :: ch
  integer    :: n
  integer    :: i, dummy
  do i = 1, n
    c(First) -> dummy
    write std_out, "pong\n"
    c(Second) <- 0
  end do
end procedure
```

Program 5.2
A Ping-Pong Program

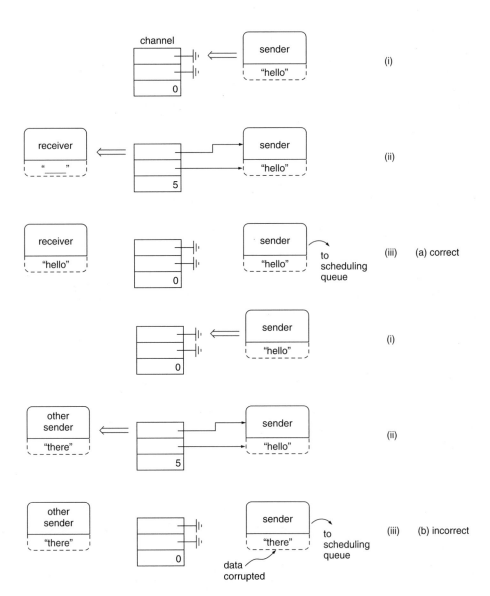

Figure 5.2
Implementation of Channels

There are two ways this problem can be dealt with. The first is to add one more field to the status record, to show whether the pending process is trying to send or receive. This would not prevent errors, but would at least allow the run-time system to detect some types of error. (FORTRAN-KCSP implements this, but OCCAM did not.) The second option would be to distinguish the reading and writing ends of channels, so that mistakes could be caught as type errors during compilation [Foster & Chandy 1995]. In this scheme, channels would actually be records having reading and writing ends, as in:

```
type chan
  type(chan_reading_end) :: rd
  type(chan_writing_end) :: wr
end type
```

The sending operator <- could then only be applied to the writing end of a channel, while the receiving operator -> could only be applied to a reading end.

The problem with this approach is that it can make software engineering more difficult. Suppose that a single process is acting as a server, and needs to be connected to many clients. In FORTRAN-KCSP, the required connections can be put in place using:

```
integer, constant :: Num_Cli = number of clients
  .
  .
  .
type(chan) :: c2s(Num_Cli), s2c(Num_Cli)
  .
  .
  .
create
  1 of server(c2s, s2c)
  Num_Cli of client(c2s, s2c)
end create
```

As it starts up, each client determines its ID using the `id_rel_self` function introduced in the previous chapter. It then sends requests to the server through `c2s(id)%wr`, and receives replies through `s2c(id)%rd`.

Ideally, we would like to modify the language so that the server process was only passed the receiving ends of the channels in c2s, and the sending ends of the channels in s2c, while clients were passed the opposite ends. However, neither FORTRAN-K nor most other procedural languages contains a way to select all corresponding fields of an array of records, and treat that as a new array. In some data-parallel languages, this could be accomplished by something like `s2c(:)%rd` or `c2s(:)%wr`, but no dialect of FORTRAN-K

permits this.[2] Sadly, programmers must pass the whole of every channel to each process
that uses it, rather than just the channel's reading or writing ends, and trust each process to
behave sensibly.

As mentioned earlier, the run-time system type-checks the values used at each end of
each communication operation. There are two cases in which this can be annoying. The
first arises when an array section whose length is not known until run-time must be sent
through a channel. For example, suppose a process wishes to send a patch of color values
to a graphics server. If the colors are represented as single integers, packed into an array,
then it would seem that the system would require users always to send a block of the same
fixed size, as in Program 5.3. Here, the array transferred in each message is always as large
as the largest possible message, even if the actual message is only a fraction of this length.
This policy avoids the error which would occur if the client process was to send a larger
patch than the server was prepared to read, or if the server was to try to read more values
than the client had sent.

To eliminate this inefficiency, FORTRAN-KCSP allows programmers to use multi-valued
subscripts to specify that a portion of an array is to be sent or received. This notation is the
same as the `start:end:stride` allowed in the data-parallel dialect, and leads to code of
the form:

```
! sender
integer :: a(X, Y), extent_x, extent_y
c <- a(1:extent_x, 1:extent_y), extent_x, extent_y
   .
   .
   .
! receiver
integer :: b(X, Y), received_x, received_y
chan -> b, received_x, received_y
```

The whole of b is provided for message receipt. Once the operation is complete, `received_x` and `received_y` show how much of b has been filled with new data. When arrays are
used in this fashion, the rule is that the receiving array must have the same rank as the
array which is being sent, and must be at least as large as the array being sent along each
of its axes.

The second case in which type and size checks on messages are annoying comes when
different types of messages might be sent down the same channel. For example, in order

---

2. Since it would allow users to create arrays of arrays by selecting an array-valued field of an array of records.

```
integer, constant :: Gfx_Circle = 1
integer, constant :: Gfx_Block = 2
  .
  .
integer, constant :: Gfx_Text = 99
integer, constant :: Gfx_Len = maximum length of graphics message
type(chan), auto  :: cli_2_gfx
  .
  .
create
  1 of gfx_server(cli_to_gfx)
  1 of client(cli_to_gfx, other parameters)
end create
  .
  .
procedure gfx_server(req)
  type(chan) :: req
  integer    :: buffer(Gfx_Len)
  .
  .
  do while running
    req -> buffer
    if buffer(1) == Gfx_Circle then
      draw_circle(buffer(2), buffer(3), buffer(4), buffer(5))
    elseif buffer(1) == Gfx_Block then
      draw_block(buffer(2), buffer(3), buffer(4), buffer(5), buffer(6))
  .
  .
    else
      report unknown message type
    end if
  end while
end procedure
  .
  .
procedure client(to_gfx, other parameters)
  type(chan) :: to_gfx
  integer    :: buffer(Gfx_Len)
  .
  .
```

Program 5.3
A Simple Graphics Server

```
    do while running
      do work
      if need to draw circle then
        buffer(1) = Gfx_Circle
        buffer(2) = center x-coordinate
        buffer(3) = center y-coordinate
        buffer(4) = radius
        buffer(5) = color
        to_gfx <- buffer
      elseif need to draw block then
   .
   .
   .
      end if
    end while
  end procedure
```

Program 5.3 *(continued)*
A Simple Graphics Server

to ask a graphics server to draw a circle, a client process might wish to send a structure of
the form:

```
type circle
  integer :: x, y, radius
end type
```

but to have the server draw a triangle, the client might wish to send an instance of:

```
type triangle
  integer :: x(3), y(c)
end type
```

One option would be to *marshal* each structure, i.e., to compact its values into an array, and
then send that array. This method is used in Program 5.3, and typically leads to programs
containing many small subroutines like:

```
procedure send_circle(ch, circ, col)
  type(chan)   :: ch
  type(circle) :: circ
  integer      :: col
  integer      :: temp(5)
  temp(1) = Gfx_Circle
```

```
   temp(2) = circ%x
   temp(3) = circ%y
   temp(4) = circ%radius
   temp(5) = col
   ch <- temp(1:5)
end procedure
```

and:

```
procedure recv_circle(buf, circ, col)
   integer      :: buf(:)
   type(circle) :: circ
   integer      :: col

   assert buf(1) == Gfx_Circle
   circ%x      = buf(2)
   circ%y      = buf(3)
   circ%radius = buf(4)
   col         = buf(5)
end procedure
```

Note that the buffer is not actually received by recv_circle, since that would require the receiving process to know in advance what type of object it was about to be asked to draw. Instead, the receiving process would probably accept a message, check its type, and then call the appropriate unmarshalling routine, as in:

```
do while running
   ch -> buffer
   if buffer(1) == Gfx_Circle then
     call recv_circle(buffer, circle, color)
     draw a circle of the specified color
   elseif ...
   .
   .
   .
   else
     report unknown message type
   end if
end while
```

Writing such message managers, and ensuring that their sending and receiving halves are consistent with one another, is tedious and error-prone. It is usually much simpler to have clients send a signal indicating the type of the following message, and then send the message, as in Program 5.4. In practice, messages of variant types are commonly handled this way: when a process sends a message, it first sends a tag to identify that message's type. Receiving processes first accept a tag, then branch on it in order to accept the message's contents into the correct type and size of structure. Some CSP-based languages, but *not* FORTRAN-KCSP, provide syntactic support for this sort of protocol by allowing programs to specify that any one of several message receipt operations can be allowed, depending on the first values of the message. This leads to code of the form:

```
procedure gfx_server(req)
    type(chan)    :: req
    integer       :: buf(Gfx_Len)
    type(circle)  :: circ
    type(block)   :: blk
    do while running
      req -> type == Gfx_Circle, circ
          -> type == Gfx_Block, blk
    .
    .
    .

    end while
end procedure
```

If the user sends Gfx_Block as a message type, but mistakenly follows it up with a circle, the run-time system can catch and report the error.

5.1.2 Selecting Inputs

Protocols such as the one described above allow processes to send messages with different *message tags* down a single channel, but no mechanism has been introduced so far to allow processes to select messages from different channels. To see why this is needed, consider once again the problem of implementing a general-purpose graphics server process. This server must clearly be able to service many clients, but if those clients were to share access to a single client-server channel, it would be possible for the message tag sent by one client to be followed by the message tag of another, rather than by the first client's data (Figure 5.3).

How can a process listen to many input channels at once? It cannot simply loop over an array of channels, trying to receive a message on each in turn, because input is a blocking

```
procedure server(req)
  type(chan)    :: req
  type(circle)  :: circ
  type(block)   :: block
  integer       :: msg_type, color
  .
  .
  do while running
    req -> msg_type
    if msg_type == Gfx_Circle then
      req -> circ, color
      draw circle
    elseif msg_type == Gfx_Block then
      req -> block, color
      draw block
  .
  .
  end while
end procedure
  .
  .
procedure client(to_gfx, other parameters)
  type(chan)    :: to_gfx
  type(circle)  :: circ
  type(block)   :: block
  integer       :: color
  .
  .
  do while working
    do work
    if need to draw circle then
      to_gfx <- Gfx_Circle
      to_gfx <- circ, color
    elseif need to draw block then
      to_gfx <- Gfx_Block
      to_gfx <- block, color
  .
  .
  end while
end procedure
```

Program 5.4
A Better Graphics Server

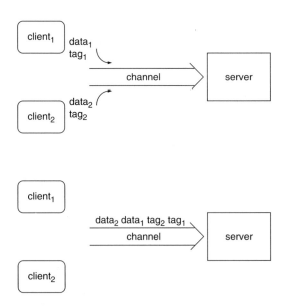

Figure 5.3
Data Confusion on Channels

operation. CSP-based languages therefore provide another construct, the `alt`, to handle
this.

An `alt` block lists one or more alternative input operations, and the statements to be
executed after each one. In its simplest form, each alternative consists of the keyword
`choose`, followed by a channel input operation and a block of statements terminated by
`end`. The receive operation is called the block's guard, because the block is only executed
if the receive occurs. A simple example of this is:

```
type(chan), auto :: a, b
integer         :: i
alt
  choose a -> i
    write std_out, "received %d on a\n", i
  end
  choose b -> i
    write std_out, "received %d on b\n", i
  end
end alt
```

When a process executes this `alt`, it is suspended until a message is available on at least one of the channels a and b. The process then selects one of the eligible operations, accepts the input on its channel, and executes the corresponding block of code. The other operation is left undisturbed. For example, if a program contained the `alt`:

```
type(channel), auto :: ch_a, ch_b, ch_c
real                 :: x, y, z(N)
  .
  .
  .
alt
  choose ch_a -> x
    A
  end
  choose ch_b -> x, y
    B
  end
  choose ch_c -> z
    C
  end
end alt
```

then either:

1. a value for x would be received through `ch_a`, and *A* executed;

2. values for x and y would be received through `ch_b`, and *B* executed;

3. n values would be received into the array z and *C* executed; or

4. nothing would ever be received through any of the channels.

Exactly one of these four events would occur each time the `alt` was executed; in most cases, the fourth would indicate some sort of error in the program. Note that as soon as one of the three guards has executed, i.e., as soon as a value has been received on any of the three channels, then the other input operations are immediately cancelled, and cannot occur. A given channel should only appear once in any `alt`, so that the system does not attempt to cancel an operation on the channel through which it has just received data. Finally, note that the branches of an `alt` can receive the same or different types of messages, and can safely put them into the same variables, since only one branch is executed.

   `alt` guards may be made more selective by joining logical expressions to their input operations using `when`. (Guards not containing logical expressions are treated as if they were guarded by the constant expression .true..) The logical components of all guards are evaluated before any of the channels in the alt block are examined. When the alt is executed, only those blocks whose guards were .true. are enabled. For example, if a process wanted to be able to receive messages alternately on channels ch_a or ch_b, but always wanted to be able to accept data on ch_c, it could use:

```
logical :: enable_a = .true.
   .
   .
   .
do while running
  alt
    choose ch_a -> variables when enable_a
      statements A
    end
    choose ch_b -> variables when .not. enable_a
      statements B
    end
    choose ch_c -> variables
      statements C
    end
  end alt
  enable_a = .not. enable_a
end while
```

As will be seen in later examples, logical guards are often used to turn off channels once certain events have occurred, or until certain conditions are met. For example, messages arriving through different channels could represent interrupts at different priority levels. When a process is at level L, interrupts from levels less than L are not to be accepted. Program 5.5 shows one implementation of this. (In practice, an interrupt handler would also need to be told who had caused the interrupt, and whether the interrupt level was to be re-set.) Alternatively, it is sometimes necessary to flush out the messages in a network of processes so that those processes may terminate cleanly. The task-farming pipeline shown later in Example 5.2 is an example of this.

FORTRAN-KCSP has two other forms of alt branch. The first is an iterated branch, which allows a program to choose between elements of an array of channels:

```
procedure root(c)
  type(chan) :: c(:)
  integer    :: i, j, k = 0
```

```
do while running
  alt
    any j = 1, N choose c(j) -> k
      write std_out, "root got %d in branch %d\n", k, j
    end
  end alt
end while
end procedure
```

The any construct in this `alt` is exactly equivalent to:

```
alt
  choose c(1) -> k
    operations
  end
  choose c(1) -> k
    operations
  end
    .
    .
    .
  choose c(N) -> k
    operations
  end
end alt
```

but automatically adjusts the number of branches to be equal to the size of the channel array. Inside the selected branch, the value of the index variable which accompanies the any shows which branch was selected. This index can also be used to guard iterated branches, as the following code shows:

```
alt
  choose scalar_chan -> x, y, z
    operations
  end
  any i = 1, N, 2 choose array_chan(i) -> x, y when control(i)
    operations
  end
end alt
```

```
integer, constant :: Num_Intr_Level = number of interrupt levels
  .
  .
procedure intr_handler(intr_chan, init_level)
  type(chan) :: intr_chan(Num_Intr_Level)
  integer    :: init_lovel
  integer    :: dummy, level = init_level
  alt
    choose intr_chan(1) -> dummy when level <= 1
      handle level-1 interrupt
    end
    choose intr_chan(2) -> dummy when level <= 2
      handle level-2 interrupt
    end
  .
  .
  end alt
end procedure
```

Program 5.5
Handling Interrupt Levels in the CSP Model

The final form of `alt` branch is one which does not contain a receive. Such branches allow programs to contain default actions, which are executed when no inputs are available:

```
procedure run_until_interrupt(intr, other parameters)
  type(chan) :: intr
  logical    :: signal
  logical    :: looping = .true.

  do while looping
    alt
      choose intr -> signal
        loop = .false.
      end
      when .true.
        do some work
      end
    end alt
  end while
end procedure
```

This construct is often used to support speculative parallelism. During each loop iteration, the procedure either sees an interrupt arriving through `intr`, and re-sets `looping` so that it exits the work loop, or does some more work on its current problem.

One annoying feature of `alt` statements is that messages cannot be selected on the basis of their contents. In the interrupt handler, for example, interrupts at different levels arrive on different channels because there is no way for the server to inspect a message, then decide whether or not to accept it. In practice, it would probably be preferable to have one channel per client, rather than one channel per interrupt level; building such a system is left as an exercise.

Another annoying but necessary feature of `alt` statements is that they may only contain receives, not sends. The reason for this restriction is that it allows processes to make decisions locally; if `alt`s could contain both sends and receives, some kind of global arbitration would be needed to ensure consistent operation. To see why, consider what would happen if alternative input and output were allowed, and the four processes connected as shown in Figure 5.4 were trying to do the operations shown. It is clear that either $A \rightarrow B$ and $D \rightarrow C$, or $A \rightarrow C$ and $D \rightarrow B$, but which should happen if all four processes try to communicate at the same time? If A and D both decide unilaterally to send to B, then B must tell one of them (say D) that it was mistaken, and that it must send to C instead. But C has already decided to accept from A, and has cancelled its receive from D. Matters would be even worse if C was also willing to accept from another process E, while D was also willing to send to F.

In practice, the absence of alternative output is rarely, if ever, a problem. Instances where it would be useful can usually be replaced with some form of handshake, in which the process which would want to do alternative output instead does a normal `alt`, and the processes to which it would send values explicitly signal that they are willing to receive. The load-balancing pipeline in the following example contains an instance of this.

5.1.3 Examples

Example 5.1 (Task Farming)   Section 2.4.2 introduced the use of task farming to handle iteratively-decomposed problems, such as ray tracing and Monte Carlo simulations. Examples 4.1 and 4.3 then showed how task farming could be implemented in a shared memory programming system. Implementations in disjoint-memory systems are more complicated, as they must explicitly move jobs to processes when they are required, and to move results to a sink process as they are produced.

Program 5.6 shows a simple task farm which uses one process as both source and sink, and an arbitrary number of workers. The protocol which connects these is simple: messages from the source to the workers contain a row index and a corresponding x

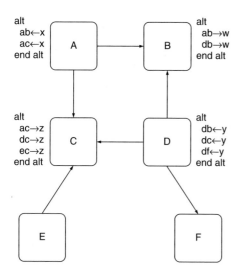

Figure 5.4
Attempting to Select on Output

coordinate, or 0 and 0.0 to signal that there are no more jobs. Messages from the workers to the source consist of a row index and a buffer of result values. If the message is the first message from that worker, its row index is 0, indicating that it is just a request for work.

This program puts the whole operation of the source into one main loop. One improvement would be to add a guard to the any branch in the root process's `alt` so that the root did not try to receive messages from workers which it knew were finished. This change is left as an exercise.

Another alternative would be to split its operation into three stages: one to send initial jobs to workers, one to keep workers busy while there were more jobs to do, and one to send end-of-job markers to workers once all the work had been done:

```
! send initial jobs
do i = 1, W
  job(worker) <- i, x
  x = x + Inc
end do
! send remaining jobs
do i = 1, N-W
  alt
    ! get message
```

```
    any worker = 1, W choose req(worker) -> j, buffer
      ! copy data
      do k = 1, N
        patch(j, k) = buffer(k)
      end do
      ! send new job
      job(worker) <- i, x
      x = x + Inc
    end
  end alt
end do
! send end-of-job markers
do i = 1, W
  job(worker) <- 0, 0.0
end do
```

However, this code would be incorrect if the number of workers was greater than the number of jobs. While one might argue that task farming would be an inappropriate strategy under such circumstances, programs should take such boundary cases into account. Modifying this triple-loop implementation to handle this case, and writing the corresponding worker code, is left as an exercise.

Example 5.2 (A Load-Balancing Pipeline)   In the previous example, every worker was directly connected to the source process. There are two reasons why this might not be done in a real system. The first is the cost of setting up and taking down `alt`s: if there are 144 workers in the task farm, then each pass through the main loop of the source involves testing up to 144 channels. This may not seem like much of an overhead, but in a system containing many workers the speed of the source will be the main performance bottleneck, so such overheads should be avoided.

The second reason why a task farm might not be structured this way is that some systems simply wouldn't permit it. On first- and second-generation transputer hardware, for example, each of the physical links between processors could support exactly one logical channel in each direction. Since there were only four links per processor, users either had to multiplex their communication through the links manually, or find a way to avoid a need for multiplexing. These constraints led to the notion of a load-balancing pipeline (Figure 5.5). Each unit of such a pipeline has three components: a worker, responsible for doing useful work, and two buffers. The first of these delivers jobs to the worker, or forwards them to other workers, while the second carries results away. These units can be

```
integer, constant :: N = array size
real,    constant :: X0 = -1.5
real,    constant :: Y0 = -1.5
real,    constant :: Extent = 3.0
real,    constant :: Inc = Extent / (N-1)
integer, constant :: W = number of workers

program
  type(chan), auto   :: req(W), job(W)        ! connections
  logical            :: patch(N, N)           ! to fill

  create
    1 of root(req, job, patch)
    W of worker(req, job)
  end create
end program

procedure root(req, job, patch)
  type(chan)        :: req(:), job(:)         ! channels
  logical           :: patch(:, :)            ! to fill
  logical           :: buffer(N)              ! for messages
  integer           :: worker, i, j, k        ! indices
  real              :: x = X0                 ! coordinate

  ! farming
  do i = 1, N+W
    alt
      ! get message
      any worker = 1, W choose req(worker) -> j, buffer
        ! copy if real data
        if j > 0 then
          do k = 1, N
            patch(j, k) = buffer(k)
          end do
        end if
        if i <= N then                             ! send new job . . .
          job(worker) <- i, x
          x = x + Inc
```

Program 5.6
Task Farming Using Channels

```
        else                              !  . . . or end-of-work signal
          job(worker) <- 0, 0.0
        end if
      end
    end alt
  end do
end procedure

procedure worker(req, job)
  type(chan)          :: req(:), job(:)        ! channels
  integer             :: id = id_rel_self()    ! which channels to use
  logical             :: buffer(N)             ! for messages
  integer             :: i, j                  ! indices
  real                :: x, y                  ! coordinates

  ! start farming
  req(id) <- 0, buffer
  job(id) -> i, x

  ! farm
  do while i > 0
    ! do job
    y = Y0
    do j = 1, N
      buffer(j) = mandel(x, y, label)
      y = y + Inc
    end do
    ! send result
    req(id) <- i, buffer
    ! get next job
    job(id) -> i, x
  end while
end procedure
```

Program 5.6 *(continued)*
Task Farming Using Channels

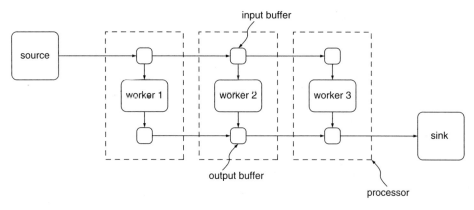

Figure 5.5
A Load-Balancing Pipeline

replicated without any need to increase the number of channels required at the source or sink.

Initially, all the buffers in the pipeline are empty, so the first job created by the source is delivered to the first idle worker. When the next job reaches this buffer, it flows through to the second worker's buffer, and then into the second worker. Once the workers have filled up in this way, jobs accumulate in the buffers until every worker has one job waiting for it. As soon as a worker finishes a job, it sends the result to its output buffer and takes its next job from its input buffer. The jobs behind the one in that buffer then bump down the input pipe, keeping it full, while results flow toward the sink in a similar manner. This pipeline is an example of a *systolic* system, in which local rules govern data movement to ensure efficient operation.

The code to implement this pipeline is shown in Program 5.7. The three application-dependent processes are `source`, `sink`, and `workcrew`. `source` takes a single channel as a parameter. Inside its main loop it waits for a request for a job, and then sends a description of the next bit of work to be done to the first unit in the pipeline. At the other end of the pipe, `sink` also takes a single channel as a parameter, from which it repeatedly reads results. As each arrives, `sink` saves it in `patch`.

Having decided how these processes will behave, it is only necessary to build buffers to support them. These are constructed from small, simple components, as shown in Figure 5.6. The first of these is the job-forwarding buffer `buf_job`, which repeatedly accepts a job and forwards it to either the worker process or the next job buffer. Because `alt` on channel output is not allowed, `buf_job` uses a handshaking protocol: its downstream partners send signals on `fwd_req` or `work_req` when they are ready to accept another job, and

```
program
  type(chan), auto    :: job(W), req(W), res(W)
  logical             :: patch(N, N)

  assert N >= 2
  create
    1 of source(req(1), job(1))
    W of workcrew(req, job, res)
    1 of sink(res(W), patch)
  end create
  call print_patch(patch)
end program

procedure source(req, out)
  type(chan) :: req, out                          ! where to send jobs
  integer    :: i                                 ! job index
  real       :: x = X0                            ! job value
  logical    :: ping                              ! signal

  ! send jobs
  do i = 1, N
    req -> ping
    out <- i, x
    x = x + Inc
  end do

  ! send termination
  req -> ping
  out <- 0, 0.0
end procedure

procedure sink(in, patch)
  type(chan)     :: in                            ! whence to receive results
  logical        :: patch(:, :)                   ! values
  integer        :: i, j                          ! indices
  logical        :: buffer(N)                     ! for receiving values
```

Program 5.7
Implementation of a Simple Load-Balancing Pipeline

```
  ! read until end-of-stream seen
  in -> i, buffer
  do while i > 0
    do j = 1, N
      patch(i, j) = buffer(j)
    end do
    in -> i, buffer
  end while
end procedure

procedure workcrew(req, job, res)
  type(chan)          :: req(:), job(:), res(:)    ! connections
  integer             :: id = id_rel_self()        ! to determine channel usage
  type(chan), auto :: req_w, job_w, res_w          ! internal connections

  if id == 1 then                                  ! front of pipeline
    create
      1 of buf_job(id, req(1), job(1), req(2), job(2), req_w, job_w)
      1 of worker(id, req_w, job_w, res_w)
      1 of buf_res(id, nullptr(chan), res_w, res(1))
    end create

  elseif id == W then                              ! tail of pipeline
    create
      1 of buf_job(id, req(W), job(W), nullptr(chan),
                   nullptr(chan), req_w, job_w)
      1 of worker(id, req_w, job_w, res_w)
      1 of buf_res(id, res(W-1), res_w, res(W))
    end create

  else                                             ! middle of pipeline
    create
      1 of buf_job(id, req(id), job(id), req(id+1), job(id+1), req_w, job_w)
      1 of worker(id, req_w, job_w, res_w)
      1 of buf_res(id, res(id-1), res_w, res(id))
    end create

  end if
end procedure
```

Program 5.7 *(continued)*
Implementation of a Simple Load-Balancing Pipeline

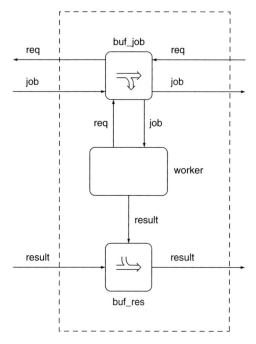

Figure 5.6
Buffers in a Load-Balancing Pipeline

`buf_job` then sends the job on `fwd` or `work`. In order to satisfy this protocol requirement for the job buffer upstream from it, each `buf_job` must send a signal upstream on `in_req` before trying to read a job on `in`. (This is why the source process waits to read a signal on `req` before sending a job on `out`.)

The main loop of `buf_job` is controlled by the condition:

```
do while (i > 0) .or. (num_live > 0)
```

which keeps the buffer going until it has seen the end-of-stream signal (a row index `i` equal to 0) and has forwarded it to its downstream partners. Once it sees the end-of-stream signal, it no longer tries to get more jobs from the buffer upstream from it. Instead, it executes its `alt` one more time for each downstream process, sending each the end-of-stream message in turn. `buf_job` then exits its main loop.

The one remaining feature of `buf_job` which deserves mention is the first test in its `alt`:

```
choose fwd_req -> ping when associated(fwd_req)
```

By definition, the last job-forwarding buffer in the pipeline does not have a downstream partner. `workcrew` therefore arranges for it to be passed an unassociated channel (created using the `nullptr` function). This test then ensures that the last buffer in the pipeline does not try to send anything through this null channel.

The result buffer `buf_res` is somewhat simpler than `buf_job`. This buffer simply merges its two input streams until it has seen an end-of-stream marker on both. There is no handshaking protocol because it is choosing between input streams rather than output streams. Since the forwarding input channel will be unassociated if this buffer is the first result buffer in the pipeline, `buf_res` starts by setting flags to control which channels it tries to listen to in its `alt`. When the buffer receives an end-of-stream marker on one of its active channels it does not send the marker on immediately; instead, it disables that channel. Only when both channels have been disabled, and the buffer is certain that it will not receive any more messages, does it send an end-of-stream to its downstream partner.

The most complicated part of this program (and the one where mistakes are most likely to be made) is not the design of the protocol, but the plumbing contained in the `workcrew` procedure. This code must connect each channel to exactly two processes; what is more, it must connect them all in the right order, so that (for example) a buffer does not try to signal its readiness to accept data using the channel from which it should read data, or try to read data from the channel connecting its worker to the worker's result buffer.

We can derive a simple performance model for this pipeline as follows. Let f_i be the proportion of all jobs completed by the processors $p_1 \ldots p_i$, for $1 \le i \le \mathcal{P}$. (We define f_0 to be zero to simplify the arithmetic.) The proportion of jobs done by processor p_i is $f_i - f_{i-1}$, since the proportion of results forwarded to p_i is f_{i-1}, and the proportion of jobs forwarded by it is $1 - f_i$.

If we assume zero idle time on each processor at equilibrium (a rather unrealistic assumption, but sufficient for present purposes), and define:

T_c calculation time (time to turn a job into a result)

T_j time to forward a job

T_r time to forward a result

then processor p_i spends its time as follows:

$T_c(f_i - f_{i-1})$ doing calculations

$T_j f_{i-1}$ forwarding jobs

$T_r(1 - f_i)$ forwarding results

If work is perfectly balanced, then the time spent by all processors must be equal. If we let

```
procedure buf_job(id, in_req, in, fwd_req, fwd, work_req, work)
  integer    :: id                           ! which work crew
  type(chan) :: in_req, in                    ! where to get jobs
  type(chan) :: fwd_req, fwd                   ! where to forward jobs
  type(chan) :: work_req, work                 ! connections to own worker
  integer    :: num_live                       ! number of live connections
  integer    :: i                              ! job index
  real       :: x                              ! job value
  logical    :: ping                           ! for handling requests

  ! set num live
  if associated(fwd_req) then
    num_live = 2
  else
    num_live = 1
  end if

  ! signal willingness and get first job
  in_req <- .true.
  in -> i, x

  ! forward jobs (including termination signal)
  do while (i > 0) .or. (num_live > 0)
    ! forward most recently received job
    alt
      choose fwd_req -> ping when associated(fwd_req)
        fwd <- i, x
      end
      choose work_req -> ping
        work <- i, x
      end
    end alt
    if i > 0 then                              ! ask for another . . .
      in_req <- .true.
      in -> i, x
    else                                       ! . . . or handle termination case
```

Program 5.8
Workcrew Components in a Load-Balancing Pipeline

```
      num_live = num_live - 1
    end if
  end while
end procedure
procedure buf_res(id, left, right, out)
  integer          :: id                     ! which work crew
  type(chan)       :: left, right, out       ! connections
  logical          :: left_live, right_live  ! activity controls
  integer          :: i                      ! result index
  logical          :: buffer(N)              ! result buffer

  ! setup
  left_live = associated(left)
  right_live = associated(right)

  ! buffer while either channel active
  do while left_live .or. right_live
    alt
      choose left -> i, buffer when left_live    ! one channel . . .
        if i > 0 then
          out <- i, buffer
        else
          left_live = .false.
        end if
      end
      choose right -> i, buffer when right_live  ! . . . or the other
        if i > 0 then
          out <- i, buffer
        else
          right_live = .false.
        end if
      end
    end alt
  end while

  ! terminate when both channels finished
  out <- 0, buffer
end procedure
```

Program 5.8 *(continued)*
Workcrew Components in a Load-Balancing Pipeline

```
procedure worker(id, req, job, res)
  integer            :: id              ! which work crew
  type(chan)         :: req, job, res   ! channels
  logical            :: buffer(N)       ! for messages
  integer            :: i, j            ! indices
  real               :: x, y            ! coordinates

  ! farm
  req <- .true.
  job -> i, x
  do while i > 0
    ! do job
    y = Y0
    do j = 1, N
      buffer(j) = mandel(x, y)
      y = y + Inc
    end do
    ! send result
    res <- i, buffer
    ! get next job
    req <- .true.
    job -> i, x
  end while

  ! termination
  res <- i, buffer
end procedure
```

Program 5.8 *(continued)*
Workcrew Components in a Load-Balancing Pipeline

this time be T, then:

$$T = T_c(f_i - f_{i-1}) + T_j f_{i-1} + T_r(1 - f_i)$$

or:

$$f_i - \frac{T_c - T_r}{T_c - T_j} f_{i-1} - \frac{T - T_j}{T_c - T_j} = 0$$

This formula is a recurrence relation of the form $f_i - A f_{i-1} - B = 0$, where $A = (T_c - T_r)/(T_c - T_j)$ and $B = (T - T_j)/(T_c - T_j)$. Its general solution takes the form $f_i = C A^i + D$. Since $f_0 = 0$, $D = -C$; substituting this into the recurrence expression for f_1 then gives $C = B/(A-1)$. Thus:

$$f_i = B\frac{A^i - 1}{A - 1}$$

where A and B depend on T, T_c, T_j, and T_r. We can now eliminate the arbitrary time T by using the fact that $f_\mathcal{P} = 1$ (since all jobs are processed somewhere) to get:

$$f_N = B\frac{A^\mathcal{P} - 1}{A - 1} = 1$$

or $B = (A-1)/(A^\mathcal{P} - 1)$. This finally gives:

$$f_i = \frac{A^i - 1}{A^\mathcal{P} - 1}$$

Note that this expression is valid only when A is not one, i.e., when the time to forward jobs and results are different. When A is one, f_i works out to be $1/\mathcal{P}$. This is the expected result: if message transmission is free, every processor does an equal amount of work.

Example 5.3 (Grid Decomposition)   Task farming is one thing message-passing systems are good for; solving iterative problems on regular meshes is another. Consider the Game of Life once again. Every process is assigned a patch of the mesh; in each iteration, each process updates the values in its patch, and then swaps boundaries with the processes responsible for neighboring patches. The shared-variables implementation of this worked by having processes iterate over their own patches, then copying boundary values from their neighbors. We can translate this directly into the channel model to give Program 5.9. Note how each worker declares its own `world` and `count` arrays, and how each of these has two extra columns. This simplifies the implementation of `neigh_count` and `world_update`, which can loop over all the interior points of these arrays uniformly, instead of handling the boundaries with special-case code.

Unfortunately, this program is simple, but is also wrong. Consider what happens when a long chain of processes connected by channels concurrently execute Program 5.9. Having done its update calculations, each process tries to send a boundary to its neighbor. Unfortunately, that neighbor is not willing to accept the boundary, as it is trying to send a boundary of its own to its other neighbor. If processes are configured in a ring, this program immediately deadlocks. If, on the other hand, they are configured in a non-cyclic chain, and the last process in the chain does not try to send its boundary to its non-existent neighbor, then communication is effectively done sequentially: the $(N-1)^{\text{th}}$ process sends its boundary to the Nth process, then accepts the boundary offered to it by the $(N-2)^{\text{th}}$ process. This process is then free to accept a boundary from the $(N-3)^{\text{th}}$ process, and so on.

```
integer, constant :: N = world size
integer, constant :: P = number of processes
integer, constant :: W = N/P
integer, constant :: W_Plus = W + 2

procedure evolver(clock, anticlock, num_gen, do_print)
  type(chan)   :: clock(:), anticl(:)    ! ring channels
  integer      :: num_gen                 ! how long to evolve
  integer      :: id = id_rel_self()      ! own ID
  integer      :: left_id = mod1(id-1, P) ! downwards ID
  logical      :: world(W_Plus, N)        ! own portion of world
  integer      :: count(W_Plus, N)        ! neighborhood counts
  integer      :: gen                     ! generation index
  integer      :: i, j                    ! traversal

  initialize world

  ! evolve
  do gen = 1, num_gen
    ! swap boundaries
    clock(id) <- world(W+1, :)
    anticl(left_id) <- world(2, :)
    clock(left_id) -> world(1, :)
    anticl(id) -> world(W+2, :)
    ! count neighbors
    call neigh_count(world, count)
    ! update world
    call world_update(world, count)
  end do
end procedure
```

Program 5.9
A Simple (But Incorrect) Mesh Program

There are several solutions to this problem. The simplest is to divide processes into odd and even sets, so that no process ever has to send and receive at the same time. This solution, shown in Program 5.10, is like that used in the odd/even exchange sort of Section 2.3.1. While workable, its performance is rather low, since only half of the links in the ring are busy at any one time.

A program can compensate for any inefficiency this might introduce by putting an even number of processes on each processor, so that the process at one end would al-

```
procedure evolver(clock, anticlock, num_gen)
   type(chan)   :: clock(:), anticlock(:) ! ring channels
   integer      :: num_gen                 ! how long to evolve
   integer      :: id = id_rel_self()      ! own ID
   integer      :: left_id = mod1(id-1, P) ! downwards ID
   logical      :: world(W_Plus, N)        ! own portion of world
   integer      :: count(W_Plus, N)        ! neighborhood counts
   integer      :: gen                     ! generation index
   integer      :: i, j                    ! traversal

   initialize world

   ! evolve
   do gen = 1, num_gen
     ! swap boundaries
     if (id .mod. 2) == 0 then
       clock(id) <- world(W+1, :)
       anticlock(left_id) <- world(2, :)
       clock(left_id) -> world(1, :)
       anticlock(id) -> world(W+2, :)
     else
       clock(left_id) -> world(1, :)
       anticlock(id) -> world(W+2, :)
       clock(id) <- world(W+1, :)
       anticlock(left_id) <- world(2, :)
     end if
     ! count neighbors
     call neigh_count(world, count)
     ! update world
     call world_update(world, count)
   end do
end procedure
```

Program 5.10
A Simple (And Correct) Mesh Program

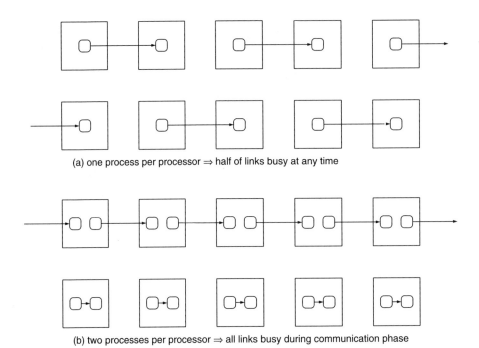

(a) one process per processor ⇒ half of links busy at any time

(b) two processes per processor ⇒ all links busy during communication phase

Figure 5.7
Odd/Even Process Placement

ways be reading when the other was writing (Figure 5.7). Another solution is to create sub-processes to handle the communication required to send and receive boundaries. As Program 5.11 shows, these processes exist exactly long enough to ensure that the required synchronization occurs. While it is neater than relying on the placement of processes to achieve efficient use of communication resources, setting up sub-processes repeatedly can be expensive.

It is important to note how hardware considerations have intruded into the programming level in this example. These programs exchange boundary values because they do not have shared memory, but then rely on shared memory within each processor to improve performance. Some programmers regard this sort of mixing as impure, and feel it should be relegated to the same historical scrap heap as the explicitly-managed paging in early virtual memory systems. Others argue that there is no reason why a programming system shouldn't reflect the memory hierarchy of the underlying hardware—after all, we make a distinction between core memory and files. A language like FORTRAN-KCSP could make the distinction between shared and disjoint memory clear by providing two different

```
procedure evolver(clock, anticlock, num_gen)
   type(chan)   :: clock(:), anticlock(:)      ! ring channels
   integer      :: num_gen                      ! how long to evolve
   integer      :: id = id_rel_self()           ! own ID
   integer      :: left_id = mod1(id-1, P)      ! downwards ID
   logical      :: world(W_Plus, N)             ! own portion of world
   integer      :: count(W_Plus, N)             ! neighborhood counts
   integer      :: gen                          ! generation index
   integer      :: i, j                         ! traversal

   initialize world

   ! evolve
   do gen = 1, num_gen
     ! swap boundaries
     create
       1 of sender(clock(id), world(W+1, :))
       1 of sender(anticlock(left_id), world(2, :))
       1 of receiver(clock(left_id), world(1, :))
       1 of receiver(anticlock(id), world(W+2, :))
     end create
     ! count neighbors
     call neigh_count(world, count)
     ! update world
     call world_update(world, count)
   end do
end procedure


procedure sender(c, vec)
   type(chan) :: c                              ! where to send
   logical    :: vec(:)                         ! what to send
   c <- vec
end procedure


procedure receiver(c, vec)
   type(chan) :: c                              ! where to receive
   logical    :: vec(:)                         ! what to receive
   c -> vec
end procedure
```

Program 5.11
A More Sophisticated Mesh Program

forms of `create`, one for creating parallelism within a processor and one for distributing processes across processors.[3]

If shared memory is relied upon within worker processes in order to get better performance, it is possible to get significantly more benefit from it. If synchronization is handled carefully, a process can overlap the updating of its interior points with the exchange of boundaries with its neighbors. This code could then be improved even further by creating the exchange and update processes once, and then synchronizing them using barriers or semaphores. Implementing this improvement is left as an exercise.

Example 5.4 (Sorting) Our final example of the channel model is a sorting program modelled on the odd/even exchange sort of Section 2.3.1, and described in [Fox et al. 1988]. Swapsort is designed for processes connected in a hypercube (Section 2.5.7). Each process begins by sorting its own values using a sequential quicksort. Processes which are neighbors along the first axis of the hypercube then exchange a few of their values: the low-numbered process along that axis sends its partner its uppermost values, while the high-numbered process sends its lowermost. These newly-received values are then merged with the process's original values. If, during merging, a process runs out of values, it performs another exchange with its neighbor. Once merging has been completed along the first axis, each process copies the merged values back into its original buffer and performs the same steps again along the next axis. The code that implements this is shown in Program 5.12.

Figure 5.8 shows the values held by each processor in a 2-dimensional hypercube after each step of sorting. One of the advantages of using a high-dimensional structure for sorting, rather than (for example) a ring, is that values can move a long way through the overall array in a single step. While it would take $\mathcal{P} - 1$ swapping stages for a value to move from the lowest-numbered processor to the highest-numbered processor in a ring, this can be done in at most $\mathcal{D}$ stages in a hypercube.

Program 5.13 gives the code for the two procedures which implement the high end of pairwise swapping in swapsort; writing the corresponding procedures for the low end is left as an exercise. `cmp_ex_hi` begins by swapping its lowest values for the highest values in its neighbor. It then copies values one at a time from the communication buffer and the original array into `new_list`. When the communication buffer is exhausted, it performs another swap. It is easy to show that if the high-end process needs more values, the low-end process will need them as well, so this exchange is guaranteed to take place. However, it is not guaranteed to be perfectly synchronized. In most cases, if one process needs a

---

3. This approach was taken by OCCAM, which provided both a `par` and a `placed par` statement.

```
integer, constant :: N = number of values
integer, constant :: P = number of processes
integer, constant :: B = buffer size
integer, constant :: Dim = logarithm of P
integer, constant :: Maxval = upper limit on values

program
   type(chan), auto :: hcube(P, Dim)        ! hypercube connections
   type(chan), auto :: ring(P)              ! ring connections

   assert (N .mod. B) == 0
   call rndm_init(Seed)
   create
     P of sorter(hcube, ring)
   end create
end program

procedure sorter(hcube, ring)
   type(chan) :: hcube(:, :)                ! hypercube connections
   type(chan) :: ring(:)                    ! ring connections
   integer    :: values(:)                  ! to generate and sort
   integer    :: result(:)                  ! where results are put
   integer    :: id = id_rel_self()         ! own ID
   logical    :: token                      ! for printing

   ! create values
   call random_int_vec(values, N + ((i - 1) * B), Maxval)
   call allocate(result, N + ((i - 1) * B))
   ! do sorting
   call swapsort(id, hcube, values, result)
   ! print results
   if id > 1 then
     ring(id) -> token
   else
     write std_out, "\n=== %d ===\n", i
   end if
   call print_integer_1(std_out, id, "...", result, Print_Width)
   if id < P then
     ring(id+1) <- True
```

Program 5.12
Swap Sort

```
    else
      write std_out, "\n\n\n"
    end if
end procedure

procedure swapsort(id, hcube, values, result)
  integer    :: id                      ! own ID
  type(chan) :: hcube(:, :)             ! hypercube connections
  integer    :: values(:)               ! to sort
  integer    :: result(:)               ! where results go
  integer    :: len = size(values, 1)
  integer    :: i, j, k                 ! loop indices
  integer    :: bit_i, bit_j            ! shifted bits
  integer    :: id_i, id_j, id_o        ! bitted IDs

  assert size(result, 1) == len

  ! sort values internally
  call quicksort(values)

  ! loop over dimensions
  do i = 1, Dim, 1
    bit_i = ishft(1, i)
    id_i = (id - 1) .bitand. bit_i
    ! loop over connections
    do j = (i-1), 0, -1
      bit_j = ishft(1, j)
      id_j = (id - 1) .bitand. bit_j
      id_o = ((id - 1) .bitxor. bit_j) + 1
      if (id_i == 0) /= (id_j == 0) then
        call cmp_ex_hi(id, hcube, j+1, id_o, values, result)
      else
        call cmp_ex_lo(id, hcube, j+1, id_o, values, result)
      end if
      do k = 1, len
        values(k) = result(k)
      end do
    end do
  end do
end procedure
```

Program 5.12 *(continued)*
Swap Sort

(1) before internal sort
15 11 13 14 0 12

(1) after internal sort
0 11 12 13 14 15

id 1 dim 1 connection 0 LO

(1) after swap_lo
7 7

(1) before cmp_ex_lo
0 11 12 13 14 15

(1) after swap_lo
8 8

(1) after swap_lo
10 11

(1) before cmp_ex_lo
0 11 12 13 14 15

id 1 dim 2 connection 1 LO

(1) after swap_lo
4 7

(1) before cmp_ex_lo
0 7 7 8 8 10

(1) after swap_lo
12 14

(1) after cmp_ex_lo
0 7 7 8 8 10

id 3 dim 2 connection 0 LO

(1) after swap_lo
1 2

(1) before cmp_ex_lo

---

(2) before internal sort
10 11 7 8 8 7

(2) after internal sort
7 7 8 8 10 11

id 2 dim 1 connection 0 HI

(2) after swap_hi
14 15

(2) before cmp_ex_hi
7 7 8 8 10 11

(2) after swap_hi
12 13

(2) after swap_hi
0 11

(2) after cmp_ex_hi
7 7 8 8 10 11

id 2 dim 2 connection 1 LO

(2) after swap_lo
1 2

(2) before cmp_ex_lo
11 11 12 13 14 15

(2) after swap_lo
2 3

(2) after swap_lo
4 4

(2) after cmp_ex_lo
11 11 12 13 14 15

id 1 dim 2 connection 1 LO

(2) after swap_hi
7 8

(2) before cmp_ex_hi

---

(3) before internal sort
4 4 1 2 7 3

(3) after internal sort
1 2 3 4 4 7

id 3 dim 1 connection 0 HI

(3) after swap_hi
14 15

(3) before cmp_ex_hi
1 2 3 4 4 7

(3) after swap_hi
12 14

(3) after swap_hi
2 4

(3) after cmp_ex_hi
1 2 3 4 4 7

id 3 dim 2 connection 1 HI

(3) after swap_hi
8 10

(3) before cmp_ex_hi
4 7 12 14 14 15

(3) after swap_hi
7 8

(3) after cmp_ex_hi
4 7 12 14 14 15

id 2 dim 2 connection 0 HI

(3) after swap_lo
11 11

(3) before cmp_ex_lo

---

(4) before internal sort
14 4 2 12 15 14

(4) after internal sort
2 4 12 14 14 15

id 4 dim 1 connection 0 LO

(4) after swap_lo
1 2

(4) before cmp_ex_lo
2 4 12 14 14 15

(4) after swap_o
3 4

(4) after swap_lo
4 7

(4) after cmp_ex_lo
2 4 12 14 14 15

id 4 dim 2 connection 1 HI

(4) after swap_h
14 15

(4) before cmp_ex_hi
1 2 2 3 4 4

(4) after swap_hi
12 13

(4) after swap_hi
11 11

(4) after cmp_ex_hi
1 2 2 3 4 4

id 4 dim 2 connection 0 HI

(4) after swap_hi
14 15

(4) before cmp_ex_hi

Figure 5.8
Operation of Swapsort

```
procedure cmp_ex_hi(own_id, hcube, d, other_id, values, new_list)
   integer     :: own_id              ! own ID
   type(chan) :: hcube(:, :)          ! hypercube connections
   integer     :: d                   ! swapping dimension
   integer     :: other_id            ! swapping partner's ID
   integer     :: values(:)           ! values to compare-and-swap
   integer     :: new_list(:)         ! where to put results
   integer     :: len = size(values, 1)
   integer     :: com_buf(B)          ! comms buffer
   integer     :: com_buf_len         ! number of values in buffer
   integer     :: c = 1               ! base of next block
   integer     :: i, j, k             ! indices

   ! setup
   i = len
   call swap_hi(hcube, d, own_id, other_id, c, values, len, &
                com_buf, com_buf_len)
   j = com_buf_len


                                       ! merge and swap
   do k = len, 1, -1
     if values(i) >= com_buf(j) then              ! take from old list
       new_list(k) = values(i)
       i = i - 1
     else                                          ! take from comms buffer
       new_list(k) = com_buf(j)
       if j > 1 then                               ! comms buffer not exhausted
         j = j - 1
       elseif (1 <= c) .and. (c <= len) then      ! comms buffer exhausted
         ! exchange
         call swap_hi(hcube, d, own_id, other_id, c, values, len, &
                      com_buf, com_buf_len)
         j = com_buf_len
       end if
     end if
   end do
end procedure
```

Program 5.13
High End of Swapsort

```
procedure swap_hi(hcube, d, own_id, other_id, c, values, len,
                  com_buf, com_buf_len)
  type(chan) :: hcube(:, :)          ! hypercube connections
  integer    :: d                    ! swapping dimension
  integer    :: own_id               ! own identifier
  integer    :: other_id             ! partner's identifier
  integer    :: c                    ! base of what to send
  integer    :: values(:)            ! what to send from
  integer    :: len                  ! number of values
  integer    :: com_buf(:)           ! incoming communication buffer
  integer    :: com_buf_len          ! incoming buffer length)
  integer    :: lim                  ! limit on sending

  lim = (c + B - 1)
  hcube(other_id, d) <- lim+1-c, values(c:lim)
  hcube(own_id, d) -> com_buf_len, com_buf
  assert com_buf_len == (lim + 1 - c)
  c = c + B

end procedure
```

Program 5.13 *(continued)*
High End of Swapsort

certain number of merging steps to exhaust its buffer, the other will need either more or fewer steps. Thus, one process will be idle, waiting for a buffer, while the other is still merging. This load imbalance can be reduced by sending larger buffers, but this increases the communication costs of the program.

5.1.4   Shortcomings of the Channel Model

Channel-based communication received a lot of publicity in the mid-1980s when OCCAM and the transputer first appeared, but the experience of many programmers since then has been that the model is not well-suited to large-scale application programming. While many of the criticisms that have been made of the model are in fact criticisms of its OCCAM implementation, rather than of the notion of channels, some are more substantial.

One frequent criticism of channels is their cost. Suppose a message M is being passed from process A, through process B (which may be a multiplexer or buffer of some kind), to process C. If A, B, and C are all on the same processor, then M may be copied two or more times, when it did not actually need to be copied at all. If many buffers, multiplexers, and filters are being used (as, for example, in the load-balancing pipeline), the cost of repeated copying can quickly become unaccceptable. It is tempting in these circumstances to allow processes to pass pointers to messages, rather than the messages themselves, but this forces programmers to know when messages are being passed within a single address space (i.e., between processes resident on the same processor in a multicomputer), and when they are passing between address spaces (i.e., between different processors).

Another expensive part of the CSP model is `alt`. In OCCAM, the time taken to start and terminate an `alt` is proportional to the number of branches in it. Only one of those branches will ever succeed, so the larger an `alt` is, the more of its setup effort is effectively wasted. Such considerations lead programmers to write code in which the main aim is not clarity, but minimizing the number of `alt`s. Typically, this was done by creating a tree of `alt`s by replicating an intermediate processes whose only role was to execute its `alt` statement indefinitely (Figure 5.9).

The greatest weakness of the channel model, however, is the amount of plumbing it requires. In most large systems, programmers want to be able to send messages *to* a destination, rather than *through* a channel. It may seem that this would not be difficult if direct point-to-point channels can be provided from anywhere to anywhere else, but in practice the burden of connecting processes correctly quickly becomes overwhelming. For example, consider a process which manages access to a filing system. This process must be able to accept requests from any number of other processes, perform file operations, and return replies. It is easy enough to pass an array of channels to this process so that it can receive and respond to messages, but how easy is it to ensure that each of those channels connects it to exactly one client? Program 5.14 shows the sort of thing which is necessary in even the simplest programs; real applications, consisting of hundreds or thousands of processes drawn from a dozen different libraries, are far more difficult. To see why, try drawing a picture of the connections created by this code.

This problem becomes even worse if processes need to reply to messages they have received. Suppose that a file system is in fact implemented using several co-operating manager processes, and a request reaches one of these. If that process forwards the message to a different manager to be dealt with, how is that second manager to send its reply to the originating process? The first manager is not allowed to pass its reply channel to the second manager (although it would be possible to extend the model to allow this, as has been done in some parallel dialects of ML [Reppy 1991]); neither can it pass the client's name to the second manager, because there are no names for processes in a channel-based system. The only solutions are either to create some *ad hoc* global naming scheme, and give every process a connection to every other (which is a plumbing nightmare), or to have the second manager pass its reply back to the first, which then returns it to the client. This not only complicates the implementation of the managers, but also increases the degree of unnecessary copying done in the system.

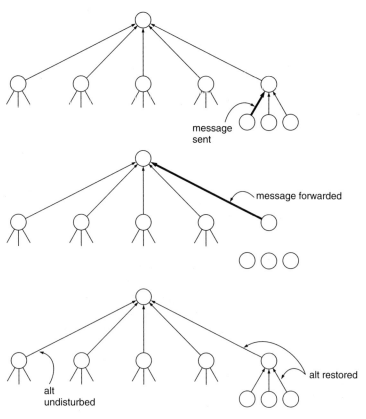

Figure 5.9
Using Trees to Select Messages

Barbara Liskov called this the problem of conversational continuity [Liskov 1979], and it is the greatest drawback of channel-based communication. In practice, most programmers who started with OCCAM developed or used general-purpose routers such as Tiny [Clarke & Wilson 1991], which allowed them to send messages between arbitrary processes. Unsurprisingly, these message-passing systems turned out to be very similar to those developed for non-transputer-based multicomputers. The features such systems should have, and how they can be implemented, are the subject of the next two sections.

```
integer, constant :: Worker_Per_Node = 4
integer, constant :: Output_Std_Out = 1
integer, constant :: Output_Std_Err = 2
integer, constant :: Output_Width = 2

procedure node(outside_to_node, node_to_outside)
  type(chan)        :: outside_to_node, node_to_outside
  type(chan), auto :: central_2_worker_buf(Worker_Per_Node)
  type(chan), auto :: worker_buf_2_worker(Worker_Per_Node)
  type(chan), auto :: worker_2_central(Worker_Per_Node)
  type(chan), auto :: std_out_in(Worker_Per_Node + 1)
  type(chan), auto :: std_err_in(Worker_Per_Node + 1)
  type(chan), auto :: output_chans(Output_Width)
  type(chan), auto :: central_2_std_err

  create
    1 of central(central_2_worker_buf, worker_2_central,
                 central_2_hash_table, hash_table_2_central,
                 output_chans, central_2_std_err)
    Worker_Per_Node of worker_buf(central_2_worker_buf, worker_buf_2_worker)
    Worker_Per_Node of worker(worker_buf_2_worker, worker_2_central,
                              std_out_in(1:Worker_Per_Node),
                              std_err_in(1:Worker_Per_Node))
    1 of hash_table(central_2_hash_table, hash_table_2_central,
                    std_out_in(Worker_Per_Node + 1),
                    std_err_in(Worker_Per_Node + 1))
    1 of std_out_mux(std_out_in, output_chans(Output_Std_Out))
    1 of std_err_mux(std_err_in, output_chans(Output_Std_Err),
                     central_2_std_err)
  end create

end procedure
```

Program 5.14
Plumbing a Large CSP Program

5.2   The Crystalline Model

In the early 1980s, a series of increasingly sophisticated programming environments were developed by physicists and computer scientists in the Caltech Concurrent Computation Project [Fox et al. 1988] While the techniques embodied in these environments were created with C^3P's hypercubes in mind, they were adopted by programmers working on a variety of other machines. The style of programming embodied in these systems is sometimes called *crystalline*, due both to the regular process topologies it uses, and the regular structures which it was designed to manipulate. A slightly more general form of the model is often called single program, multiple data, or SPMD (Section 2.2.2), in reference to the fact that all processes execute the same code, but may execute different branches within it.

5.2.1   Basic Facilities

In the crystalline model, processes are loosely synchronized: they are free to work independently between communication events, but when communication occurs, they must all participate. In addition, just as the forces acting in a crystal are short-range, so too is communication in a crystalline environment: processes are organized in a regular topology, and each process may only communicate with its immediate neighbors. In this sense, the model is similar to the CSP model of the previous section, with the constraint that process creation can only occur once, at the beginning of the program, and processes are always arranged regularly. Finally, in contrast with the shared variables model, there is no shared memory in a crystalline environment: every process has its own data, and cannot directly access that belonging to another process.

The crystalline model can be thought of as an inside-out data-parallel model. Instead of creating a data structure, and then imagining that a separate process is responsible for each element, the crystalline model creates a fixed number of processes, then gives each a portion of a larger data structure. When a data-parallel program would shift data, a crystalline program uses a combination of explicit sends and receives; when a data-parallel program would use `wheres`, a crystalline program uses conventional `if`s inside loops. This feature is one of the model's main strengths: while having to call procedures to move data around usually makes crystalline programs larger (and less readable) than their data-parallel equivalents, allowing different processes to execute different conditional branches concurrently can eliminate many efficiency headaches.

The crystalline model assumes that programs consist of Π identical worker processes, numbered $1 \ldots \Pi$, plus a single controller process. Worker processes execute independently, and can communicate with a subset of their peers; the controller also executes

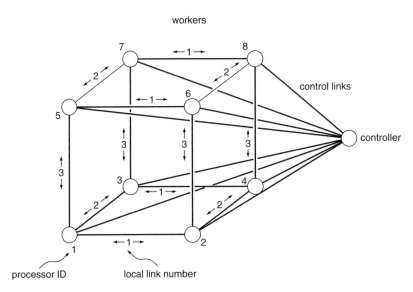

Figure 5.10
Structure of a Crystalline Message-Passing System

independently but can communicate directly with any of the workers (Figure 5.10). The
pattern of connections between workers is geometric, e.g., a ring, torus, mesh, or hypercube. A worker identifies communication partners by specifying the direction in which it
is sending, or from which it is receiving.

One important restriction of this model is that processes may not be created dynamically as programs execute. Once an initial arrangement of worker processes has been
chosen, they execute for the life of the program. This means that crystalline programs are
often similar to coarse-grained shared-variables programs written for machines on which
repeated barrier synchronization is used in place of repeated process creation and termination.

Sending and receiving are symmetric in the crystalline model, and are implemented by
a single intrinsic function called cr_comm. This function takes as arguments one of the
strings "send" or "recv" (to show whether data are being sent or received), a direction
identifier (which is simply an integer in the range $1...\mathcal{D}$ in an $\mathcal{D}$-dimensional process
graph), and one or more expressions or variables, laid out as they would be for a communication operation in the channel model of the previous section. Thus, if processes are
connected in a ring, processes could try to shift a single integer clockwise using:

```
integer, constant :: Anticlock = 1
```

```
integer, constant :: Clock = 2
   .
   .
   .
integer :: a
   .
   .
   .
call cr_comm("send", Clock, a)
call cr_comm("recv", Anticlock, a)
```

However, as with the boundary swapping of Example 5.3, this program would deadlock, since every process would be trying to send when none was willing to receive. The solution used here is the same: messaging is done in two stages, with half the processes sending before receiving, and the others receiving before sending. If each process uses id_rel_self to determine its ID, a clockwise shift can be implemented as:

```
integer :: i, temp
   .
   .
   .
if (even(id_rel_self())) then
  call cr_comm("send", Clock, i)
  call cr_comm("recv", Anticlock, i)
else
  call cr_comm("recv", Anticlock, temp)
  call cr_comm("send", Clock, i)
  i = temp
end if
```

Note the use of the auxiliary variable temp; without it, each odd-numbered process would overwrite its data value before transmitting it.

cr_comm calls come in pairs like this so often that a single routine cr_shift is provided to save programmers the trouble of determining a safe order in which to transfer messages. cr_shift takes two direction codes as arguments, and sends the values in its variable list in the direction indicated by the first while receiving from the direction indicated by the second. The uni-directional shift looked at above can therefore be implemented as:

```
call cr_shift(Clock, Anticlock, i)
```

It is the run-time system's job to allocate any temporary buffering required to execute this correctly, and the programmer's to remember that this will overwrite i.

While these functions are intrinsic to FORTRAN-KCR, they are provided as extrinsic library functions in most systems. As a result, programmers must usually marshal and unmarshal data explicitly when sending or receiving (page 295). For example, to send two integers and an array of floating-point values, and receive similar values, a program would have to contain something like:

```
procedure sender(dir, a, b, z)
  integer :: dir, a, b
  real    :: z(:)
  integer :: i, temp(size(z, 1) + 2)
  temp(1) = a
  temp(2) = b
  do i = 1, n
    call byte_copy(temp(i+2), z(i))
  end do
  call cr_comm("send", dir, temp(1:n+2))
end procedure
```

As with channels, programming at this level is considerably more complex, tedious, and error-prone than programming with higher-level functions, but sadly it is all that some systems provide.

5.2.2   The Control Process

One feature of data-parallel programming systems which the CA example above does not use is reduction. The examples in Chapter 3 showed that it is often necessary to gather information to a single point, or to scatter it from that point. In the crystalline model, that point is the control process. The code implementing this is written by a user along with the code for her worker processes, and is responsible for such things as I/O, the user interface, and any other operations which are best done serially.

One way to think about the relationship between the control process and the replicated worker processes is to think of the former as the control processor in a processor array, and of the latter as the array's processing elements (Section 2.2.1). The steps taken by worker processes between communication events are then analogous to macro-instructions coded by the user; similarly, the functions called by the crystalline controller correspond to the communication operations which the control processor would execute. In effect, a crystalline environment moves the bulk of the program to the PEs, and leaves only those operations requiring global synchronization at the controller.

In the simplest crystalline model, the controller can only execute one communication function: cr_all. Like cr_comm, its first argument determines whether data are sent or received. The second argument is not a direction, but rather an array containing one entry

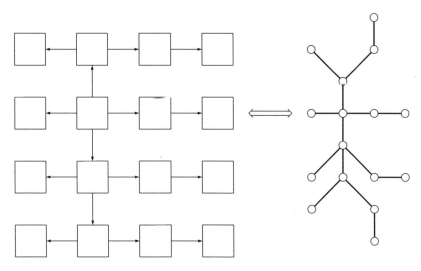

Figure 5.11
Spanning Trees

per process. When data are sent, process p receives element p of this array; when data are received, element p is filled with p's contribution. Crystalline processes interact with the controller using cr_comm as usual, but send to, or receive from, direction 0. cr_all is typically used to collect data for output, or to distribute data which have been read from input files.

An outbound cr_all is often called a *scatter*, or a *one-to-all personalized communication*, because each process receives a message from the controller, but the data sent to each receiver are different. An incoming cr_all is often called a *gather*, or an *all-to-one personalized communication*. In this case, each worker process sends a single message, and these are packed in order into an array as they reach the controller.

A useful variant on scatter is *broadcast*, or *one-to-all replicated communication*, in which every process receives the same message. A system could implement this using cr_all by having the controller copy the data to be sent into each slot of an array, and then call cr_all on that array, but most message-passing systems provide a separate broadcast function to do this. In FORTRAN-KCR, this function is called cr_bcast. It takes a single value as an argument, and sends a copy of it to each worker process. Broadcast is often implemented using *spanning trees*, which are branching paths that connect all nodes to an arbitrary root node (Figure 5.11). Each node in the tree forwards the message to all of its children, so that at any instant the message may be traversing many different links.

If the inverse of scatter is gather, the inverse of broadcast is reduction. Most systems implement this using pairwise combining, as introduced in Section 3.3.1. In FORTRAN-KCR, reduction is invoked when the controller and all of the workers call the intrinsic function cr_merge. Unlike FORTRAN-KDP, in which only one of the system-supplied functions can be used for merging, cr_merge may be passed the name of any function, including one defined by the user. This is feasible because the worker processes can all execute calls to this function independently. Thus, given any function f, if the workers and the controller all execute:

```
call cr_merge(f, a)
```

the values left in the controller's copy of a is the result of applying f in stages to some permutation of the worker processes' values. Note that cr_merge does not automatically copy this result to each worker; cr_bcast must be used explicitly to do this.

Many crystalline systems provide several other functions to allow workers to exchange data amongst themselves. Typically, these support *all-to-all replicated communication* and *all-to-all personalized communication*. In the former, each worker broadcasts a single message to every other worker; in the latter, each worker sends a different message to each other (Figure 5.12). Finally, some systems allow *one-to-one communication*, in which each worker sends one message to one other worker. This function is the basis for more general message-passing systems which will be discussed in Section 5.3.

5.2.3 Shortcomings of the Crystalline Model

Like the channel model, the crystalline model has as many weaknesses as strengths. Attempts to correct the former have led to the more sophisticated message-passing systems discussed in the next section, many of whose features can only be understood by looking at the problems they are trying to remedy. This section introduces some of these problems, and discusses ways of dealing with them.

Flow and Execution Control   One shortcoming of the crystalline model is that communication in it must be both blocking and synchronous. The first term means that a process cannot continue past a communication operation until that communication has completed; the second means that communication only takes place when both participants are ready. Its opposite, asynchronous communication, occurs when a process can send data unilaterally, without being sure that anyone is ready to receive it. As discussed in Example 5.3, the performance of boundary-swapping programs can be improved by overlapping calculations on interior points with boundary exchanges. Since the crystalline model insists on blocking, synchronous communication, programs based on it cannot exploit this idea.

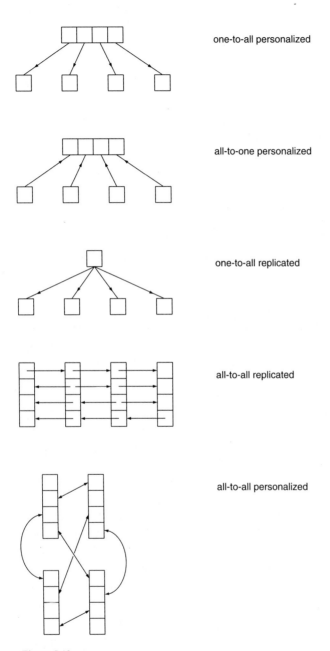

one-to-all personalized

all-to-one personalized

one-to-all replicated

all-to-all replicated

all-to-all personalized

Figure 5.12
Common Communication Patterns

Allowing asynchronous communication is not really an answer, as it is intrinsically unsafe. To see why, consider what happens if a message arrives before a receiver is ready to handle it. In such a case, the message must either be discarded, or the system must buffer it. If the former is done, users' programs become much more complicated, as they must be able to test for message receipt, and re-send old messages that failed to get through. The latter approach is also unsafe, since any real system will only be able to provide a finite amount of buffering. Once this has been filled, the programmer is faced with the re-send problem once again. Asynchronous communication is therefore best used at the systems implementation level, rather than at the user level [Culler et al. 1993].

Non-blocking operations, on the other hand, can be implemented safely. If a process initiates a non-blocking send, it is allowed to proceed with other calculations while the system waits for a buffer to be provided by the receiving process. Once this happens, the message's data are copied into the buffer, and a flag set to indicate that the sending process can now overwrite the variables whose values were sent. A non-blocking receive is similar: a process gives the system one or more variables to use as a buffer, and is given a tag in exchange. The process can later check the tag's value to see whether anything has been written into that buffer. This allows the receiving process to do other work (for example, to continue searching a problem space in a speculative application) while waiting for a message. Systems usually provide another function, which suspends the caller until a particular operation has finished. This function is used in situations in which processes want to continue working until there is nothing else they could usefully, or safely, do.

Non-blocking receives are particularly useful if processes can restrict the sources of messages which can be used to satisfy them. Consider, for example, a simple boundary-swapping program. Suppose each process were to use a non-blocking send to give its updated boundaries to its neighbors, then update its internal values and wait for incoming boundaries. Since it could not know the order in which boundary messages would arrive from its neighbors, it would have to set up as many non-blocking receives as its mesh patch had boundaries, wait for them to be filled, and then use some information about the sources of the filling messages to determine which boundary to fill with which buffer's data. (Alternatively, a process could receive its neighbors' messages directly into its boundaries, and then swap boundary values locally using a copying loop if necessary.) If, on the other hand, a process could specify who was allowed to write into a receiving buffer when that buffer was given to the message-passing system, then it could arrange for messages to be put directly into the correct places.

Message Selection   The boundary exchange example of the previous section is one instance of the more general problem of message selection. In the CSP model, a process may use `alt` to receive a message from one of a specified set of input channels. In other models, any (or all) of three different message selection mechanisms may be used:

Select by source: If each message carries with it some identification of its origin, then receivers can specify that they are willing to accept a message from a particular source, from a subset of possible sources, or from any source. Selecting by source helps solve the problem of conversational continuity: once a server process p_S has received a message from a client process p_C, it can elect to accept only messages from p_C until the transaction is completed.

Select by arrival: If processes are allowed to have several separate connections to the message-passing systems, similar to the multiple input channels allowed processes in the CSP model, then receivers can specify the connection or connections through which they wish to receive a message. Such connections are often called *message ports*.

Select by type: If messages have types, like the messages handled by the graphics server processes of Section 5.1.1, then processes might elect to receive a message of a particular type, or of a set of types.

Each of these schemes requires some sort of labelling mechanism, whether it be for processes, ports, or message tags. In some message-passing systems, processes are labelled by pairs made up of a processor ID and a local process ID. Each process's ports are then numbered from 1. Similarly, message tags are arbitrary integer values specified by users when sending and receiving messages.

The problem with such simple schemes is that they make it very difficult to construct large programs by combining smaller ones, as large serial programs are constructed out of libraries. Consider an implementation of the polygon rendering utility described in Section 2.3.6, shown in Figure 5.13. If the selection mechanism is based on process IDs, then each process in each particular *program configuration* of the utility must know the IDs of the others. However, there is no intrinsic connection between the logical identity of a process (i.e., the fact that it is the fifth of eight Z-buffers) and its physical ID in a given program. As a result, users must write programs which can cope with changing configurations. If a programmer makes a mistake at this level, it can be as hard to find as a plumbing mistake in a channel-based program.

Similarly, selecting messages by type or by arrival port is unsafe when programs are being built by combining separately-written libraries. Suppose the authors of two separate libraries had both used the values $1 \ldots T$ as message tags. If a process used both libraries, and received a message whose type was in the range $1 \ldots T$, it would have no way of knowing which library to give that message to. Separately-written libraries can also collide by trying to use the same port for messages. For example, one library might expect other processes to send it boundary values on port 3, while another library might use port 3 for receiving replies to file system requests.

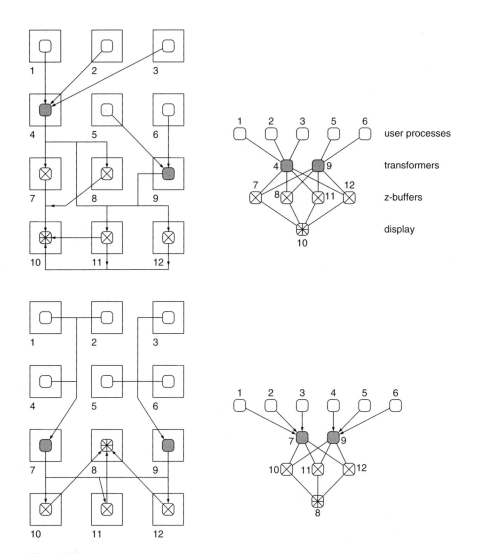

Figure 5.13
Possible Configurations of a Program

5.3 Procedural Message-Passing Systems

The best way to label processes in a real procedural message-passing system is to formalize what programmers do when they are given an unstructured message-passing system. Most real parallel programs consist of replicated instances of a few types of process. Programmers usually think of each of these *process groups* as providing a set of services which other processes can use, or as co-operating to carry out some computation. When they are required to label processes explicitly, they normally do so using names of the form `frisbee_1`, `frisbee_2`, and so on. For this reason, a structured message-passing system should be built around the notion of process groups, as indeed the recently-pseudo-standardized Message Passing Interface is [Gropp et al. 1994].

Supporting process groups directly has several useful consequences. One of these is that it separates the issues of process identity and program configuration. A process's name is not an absolute (integer) ID, or a (processor, process-on-processor) pair, but a label consisting of the name of a group of processes, and a numeric index in that group. A configuration, on the other hand, is a mapping of such names to physical processors. This process naming scheme can be thought of as a level of indirection, which obviates any need for changes in a program's source as it is re-mapped.

There are two ways of managing process groups: either processes are created as members of groups, or groups are created when and as processes join them. Figure 5.14 illustrates the difference between these two approaches. In the first, the programmer specifies the groups which are to be created, and the number of processes which are to belong to each. Each group specification includes information such as the number and type of ports owned by members of the group, and (for example) the type of processor on which members of that group can run. One advantage of this approach is that such specifications can be stored in libraries, and then instantiated when needed. Another is that the configuration specifies both what processes are being created, and what their roles are. However, describing complex configurations requires a very complex notation. For example, if programs are running on heterogeneous machines, programmers may need to specify that several different possible executables can be used to create members of a single group. This requires some way of expressing a hierarchy of super-groups and sub-groups. The notation becomes even more complicated if a single process needs to be a member of several groups; situations in which this is useful are described below.

In the second approach, groups do not exist before the program starts to run, and processes are not intrinsically members of any groups. Once it starts executing, however, a process may choose to join one or more groups. When this happens, the system checks to see whether the group already exists. If it does, the process is given a unique ID within the group; if it does not, the group is created, and the process becomes its first member.

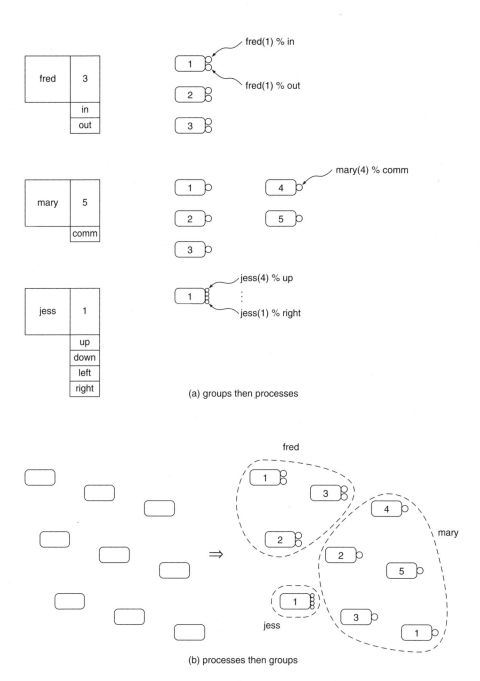

(a) groups then processes

(b) processes then groups

Figure 5.14
Process Grouping in a Message-Passing System

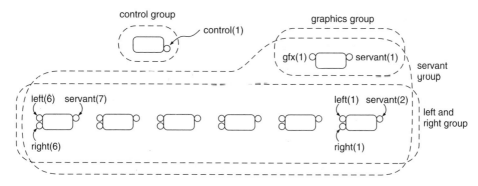

Figure 5.15
Multiple Grouping in a Message-Passing System

The main advantage of creating groups as processes execute is that libraries which an application program's processes use can create groups for their own use without the programmer having to know that they are doing so. This is why it is useful to allow a single process to belong to several different groups. For example, a worker process in a mesh decomposition program might be member 422 of two groups called "left" and "right" used for swapping boundaries, and at the same time member 38 of the group of file system clients. Similarly, all of the workers and the graphics management process might belong to a single group called "servant", which exists to receive broadcast messages from the control process (Figure 5.15). As this last example suggests, another advantage of the process-then-group approach is that processes of different types may belong to a single group. Finally, it is easier to program heterogeneous systems using the process-then-group model, since the fact that processes are running on different types of processors need not make any difference to group management at run time.

A serendipitous benefit of basing a process-labelling scheme on the notion of process groups is that it simplifies the implementation of *multicasts*, i.e., broadcasts in which the message goes to many, but not necessarily all, processes. Many applications perform broadcasts and multicasts almost as frequently as they do point-to-point communication. For example, processes managing an array in a numerical application may wish to exchange data with other processes in their row or column, or all the Z-buffers in a rendering package may want to exchange synchronization counts. In a heterogeneous network of processes, a broadcast must contain some mechanism for selecting the set or sets of processes which are to receive the message. Any scheme must clearly take into account the ability of the recipient to understand the message: there is no point sending a "clear screen" message to a file system process. If process groups are supported, then the sending process

can simply send the message to the group containing the processes capable of interpreting it.

One final issue which must be resolved when designing a message-passing system is
whether to use *run-time initialization (RTI)* or *static parameter binding (SPB)* to pass
information about the state of the system to processes. In an RTI-based system, processes
call functions in order to determine such things as their ID, how many processes there
are in a particular set, and so on. These functions are typically called once, during an
initialization phase, and the information returned by them stored in local variables. Note
that these functions are distinct from `id_rel_self` and its kin, which return processes'
system-specified IDs rather than their IDs within user-defined groups.

In an SPB-based system, the system automatically adds some variables to each process,
and stores configuration information in those variables directly.[4] The advantage of this
is that it eliminates the need for the user to include a (possibly lengthy) series of function calls in the source of each process. The disadvantage is that it requires compiler
support: the variables in which information is to be stored must be identified (e.g., by being included in the header of the code implementing the process class), and the compiler
and run-time system must be able to identify and manipulate these variables. Since most
message-passing systems are implemented as libraries called from serial languages, RTI is
almost invariably used. RTI is also a better fit with the dynamic group creation model.

5.3.1   The Interface

The text above described one model for a general-purpose message-passing system and
why that model has the features it does. This section describes the procedural interface to
one such system, which is available in the FORTRAN-KMP dialect of FORTRAN-K. Three of
the important features of these procedures are:

1. Processes can import information describing the configuration of the program which
they are part of.

2. There is no run-time searching for messages, i.e., the system is designed so that it does
not have to pay the setup and take-down costs of a FORTRAN-KCSP `alt` statement.

3. Once a process has set itself up, the interface puts as little burden on them as it can. In
particular, it is not necessary to make a dozen function calls in order to create and send a
single message.

---

4. In particular, if the compiler can recognize what libraries or software packages a particular process is linked to,
it could automatically generate code to make that process a member of the appropriate message groups (discussed
in the following pages). However, since the process might still want to specify its identity within each group, the
payoff from this approach does not justify its complexity.

It is important to remember that the model implemented by these functions does not have a clear theoretical basis like the data-parallel, shared-variable, and channel-based models of previous chapters, or the generative model of the next. Message-passing libraries like these are used simply because we know how to make them work efficiently on the hardware we have today. Section 6.7.1 describes one system which incorporates ideas like these into the syntax of the language, while putting a firmer basis underneath them.

It is also important to remember, when reading the sections below, that real message-passing systems are much more complex than the one described here. The most popular message-passing system in use today, called PVM [Geist & Sunderam 1992, Geist et al. 1994], contains many more calls than FORTRAN-KMP; the Message Passing Interface standard is even larger [Gropp et al. 1994]. This complexity is needed to deal with such things as fully-dynamic process spawning and the presence of heterogeneous processors and data formats that might co-exist in a distributed computer.

Initialization   The first step in a process-then-group system is to get processes into groups. Because processes run independently, and asynchronously, this is done in several stages. In the first, processes join one or more groups, and then call a function to indicate that they have done all the joining they are going to do. This function performs a barrier synchronization across all processes in order to ensure that the system has reached a stable point. Tables describing which processes are where, and which groups each process belongs to, are then constructed, and copied to each physical processor. (Since these tables are read-only, all the processes on a processor may share a single copy of them.) Finally, processes are allowed to continue execution, and may examine the system's configuration and send or receive messages.

This join-then-run approach is necessary to preclude race conditions. If processes were able to query the system before all group membership had been determined, or broadcast messages to groups which were still being constructed, the results would be unpredictable, and probably bad. While the barrier synchronization approach precludes truly dynamic process creation, it does make the behavior of the system much easier to understand.

The first two components of the message-passing interface are the startup functions:

```
integer function mp_join(group_name, desired_id)
   type(string)  :: group_name
   integer       :: desired_id
```

and:

```
procedure mp_synch()
```

The first, `mp_join`, makes the process a member of the group named by `group_name`, and returns the process's ID within that group. If this group does not yet exist, it is created by the call. If `id` is a positive integer, then the system understands that the process is specifying what its ID within the group is to be; if the ID is `MP_Any_Id`, on the other hand, the system chooses an ID for the process. (FORTRAN-KMP automatically defines the constant `MP_Any_Id` to be a negative number.) This convention is required because processes sometimes need to make sure that they have particular IDs within groups, but at other times do not care. Processes on adjacent processors in a mesh decomposition problem, for example, may want their IDs to be consecutive, but the numbering of workers in a task farm is probably unimportant. Note that a process may only join a particular group once, i.e., it may not have multiple identities within a single group. This restriction simplifies the implementation of message sending, as will be discussed later. Note also that it is an error for two processes to specify the same ID when joining the same group.

`mp_synch` is the barrier synchronization function alluded to earlier. Once a process has joined at least one group, and has called this function, it is suspended until all processes have made a similar call. After this synchronization is complete, any call to `mp_synch` is an error. Accordingly, any library initialization procedures which join groups must be called before `mp_synch` is called. In turn, this means that active libraries (i.e., libraries containing independently-executing processes) must often be initialized in two stages, one before the barrier and one after. Some of the consequences of this are criticized in Section 5.5.

After the system has been set up, processes may want to find out how large a particular group is. The function which does this is:

```
integer function mp_grp_size(grp_name)
   type(string) :: grp_name
```

Program 5.15 shows a procedure which joins several groups, and then records some information about them. A process may also call:

```
integer function mp_grp_id(grp_name)
   type(string) :: grp_name
```

to discover what its ID within a particular group is. The calling process must be a member of the named group; it can determine whether it is or not by calling:

```
logical function mp_grp_mem(grp_name)
   type(string) :: grp_name
```

```
program
  write std_out, "main before f\n"
  create
    1 of f()
  end create
  write std_out, "main after f\n"
end program

procedure f()
  integer :: a, b, z
  integer :: i

  write std_out, "f: about to join A as 1\n"
  a = mp_join("A", 1)
  write std_out, "..f: ID in A is %d\n", a

  write std_out, "f: about to join B as any\n"
  b = mp_join("B", MP_Any_ID)
  write std_out, "..f: ID in B is %d\n", b

  write std_out, "f: about to join Z as 3\n"
  z = mp_join("Z", 3)
  write std_out, "..f: ID in Z is %d\n", z

  write std_out, "mp_grp_id("A") is %d\n", mp_grp_id("A")
  write std_out, "mp_grp_id("B") is %d\n", mp_grp_id("B")

  write std_out, "mp_grp_mem("A") is %l\n", mp_grp_mem("A")
  write std_out, "mp_grp_mem("B") is %l\n", mp_grp_mem("B")
  write std_out, "mp_grp_mem("C") is %l\n", mp_grp_mem("C")
  write std_out, "mp_grp_mem("Z") is %l\n", mp_grp_mem("Z")

  write std_out, "mp_grp_size("A") is %d\n", mp_grp_size("A")
  write std_out, "mp_grp_size("B") is %d\n", mp_grp_size("B")
  write std_out, "mp_grp_size("C") is %d\n", mp_grp_size("C")
  write std_out, "mp_grp_size("Z") is %d\n", mp_grp_size("Z")
```

Program 5.15
An Example of Message-Passing Setup

```
  do i = 1, mp_grp_size("Z")
    write std_out, "Z%d is live: %1\n", i, mp_grp_mem_live("Z", i)
  end do
end procedure

main before f
f: about to join A as 1
..f: ID in A is 1
f: about to join B as any
..f: ID in B is 1
f: about to join Z as 3
..f: ID in Z is 3
mp_grp_id("A") is 1
mp_grp_id("B") is 1
mp_grp_mem("A") is #t
mp_grp_mem("B") is #t
mp_grp_mem("C") is #f
mp_grp_mem("Z") is #t
mp_grp_size("A") is 1
mp_grp_size("B") is 1
mp_grp_size("C") is 0
mp_grp_size("Z") is 3
Z1 is live: #f
Z2 is live: #f
Z3 is live: #t
main after f
```

Program 5.15 *(continued)*
An Example of Message-Passing Setup

Finally, because process IDs within a group need not be contiguous, FORTRAN-KMP
provides:

```
logical function mp_grp_mem_live(grp_name, member_id)
  type(string) :: grp_name
  integer      :: member_id
```

This function returns .true. if the named group contains the specified member, and
.false. otherwise.

Operation   Once processes have let the world know how they are to be addressed,
they can start sending and receiving messages. The simplest communication function in

FORTRAN-KMP is mp_send, which sends a message from one process to another. The specification of this function is:

```
procedure mp_send(src_grp, dst_grp, dst_id, msg_type, ···values···)
  type(string) :: src_grp
  type(string) :: dst_grp
  integer      :: dst_id
  type(string) :: msg_type
```

dst_grp and dst_id specify the message's destination. The former must be the name of a process group, while the latter must be either a positive integer, specifying a particular member of that group, or MP_All_Id, which specifies that the message is to be broadcast to all of the group's members. (The system automatically defines the constant MP_All_Id to be a negative number.) msg_type is used to distinguish messages of different types, and must always be present. It is followed by zero or more values, which make up the message to be sent. When the procedure is called, a shallow copy of these values is sent to each of the processes specified by dst_grp and dst_id. While it might seem odd to send a message with no data in it, in practice it is quite common to need to send only a signal, such as "ready" or "terminate", and this can be packed into the message's type.

The src_grp parameter identifies who is sending the message. Such identification is necessary because a process may belong to several groups; in order for the process which receives the message to be able to reply sensibly, it needs to know which of the sender's identities to talk to. This is the reason a process is not allowed to join a group twice: mp_send would then need an extra parameter to specify which of its aliases within a group the process wished the message to appear to have come from. What is worse, operations such as broadcast might then deliver multiple copies of the same message to a single process. Finally, transmission is always blocking, i.e., the caller is not allowed to proceed until it is safe to overwrite the values being sent.

Messages are received in two stages. In the first, one or more variables are passed to the run-time system to be filled with an incoming message. The function which does this is:

```
type(msginfo) function mp_pend(dst_grp, msg_type, ···variables···)
  type(string) :: dst_grp
  type(string) :: msg_type
```

dst_grp must be the name of a group to which the calling process belongs; it determines what kinds of messages the caller is willing to receive. The string msg_type specifies what type of message the receiver is willing to accept. This function allocates and returns a structure of a pre-defined type called msginfo, which has the following fields:

`dst_grp` a string identifying the destination group of the message

`src_grp` a string identifying the source group of the message

`src_id`   assigned process group ID of message sender

`msg_type` a string identifying the message type

Pending is a non-blocking operation; as soon as the run-time system has been made aware that another buffer has been provided, the calling process is allowed to continue executing. In order to determine when and whether the pending buffer has been filled, the process may pass the `msginfo` structure returned by `mp_pend` to the function `mp_test`:

```
type(msginfo) function mp_test(block, msg)
  logical       :: block
  type(msginfo) :: msg
```

If the `logical` parameter `block` is `.true.`, then `mp_test` blocks until the buffer identified by the message record `msg` has been filled, and then returns `msg`. If `block` is `.false.`, on the other hand, `mp_test` only returns `msg` if the transaction has completed; if it has not, `mp_test` returns a null pointer instead. Thus, a process may poll the status of the receive by setting the `block` parameter of `mp_test` to `.false.`, or suspend itself by setting `block` to `.true.`. Once message receipt has completed, a process may examine the transaction's message record to determine where the received message originated.

`mp_test` can also be used in two other ways. First, a process can pass the special message record `MP_Any_Id` to `mp_test` instead of a particular message record. Doing so indicates that the caller wants to know if *any* of its outstanding receives has completed. If `mp_test` is given `MP_Any_Id` as an input, and `block` is `.false.`, it will return either a null pointer (indicating that nothing has completed), or a message record identifying exactly one outstanding transaction which is now finished. If `block` is `.true.`, `mp_test` will block its caller until at least one outstanding receive has completed, and it can return a non-null value.

Second, `mp_test` can be given the special message record `MP_All_Id` as an input. This value specifies that *all* outstanding receive operations are to be completed. `block` must be `.true.` in this case, and the caller will be suspended until all pending communication operations are finished. This capability is not strictly necessary, but is often useful, as a process in (for example) a geometric decomposition may wish to send its boundary values, set up buffers to receive boundaries from its neighbors, do its interior calculations, and then block itself until it may safely proceed.

When using this message-passing library it is important to remember that `mp_pend` allocates a fresh `msginfo` structure each time it is called. To avoid leaking memory, programs

must free these when they are no longer needed. Some of this tedium can be avoided by
using the procedure:

```
procedure mp_recv(dst_grp, msg_type, ···variables···)
  type(string) :: dst_grp
  type(string) :: msg_type
```

`mp_recv` acts like an `mp_pend` inside a `mp_test`, and blocks its caller until a message
of the specified type has been received. Note that there is no way for the process calling
`mp_recv` to determine who sent the message.

5.3.2   Configuration

Having to configure programs manually is both tedious and a potential source of error.
However, if a message-passing system is implemented without compiler support, there is
no real alternative. Once again, this form of message-passing can be seen to be a lower-
level approach to parallelism than the data-parallel and shared-variables models, and even
than the channel model of Section 5.1.

Most existing multicomputer programming environments separate configuration from
the run-time use of the message-passing system. Typically, a tool is provided which reads
in a configuration file written by users, then creates and places the processes described
in this file. Each process must be written as a separate program; if a UNIX-like model is
being followed, the configuration tool may allow users to specify command-line arguments
for processes.

If it is to be able to handle arbitrary configurations, such a tool must provide the conditional expressions, loops, and array-like constructs of a full-grown programming language.
An alternative route is therefore just to provide a library of functions to allow programmers
to build up a data structure from within a normal serial program which describes what their
parallel program is to look like. For example, FORTRAN-KMP configuration could be handled by requiring users to write a serial FORTRAN-K program, in which calls were made to
the function:

```
procedure mp_place(arch, pid, exec, args)
  type(string) :: arch               ! architecture
  integer      :: pid                ! processor ID
  type(string) :: exec               ! executable
  type(string) :: args(:)            ! command-line arguments
```

The first argument to this function specifies the type of processor on which the process is to
run; this is needed to ensure that executables for one type of processor in a heterogeneous

```
program
  type(string)       :: worker
  integer            :: num_worker
  integer            :: i, j
  type(string), auto :: source_args(6), work_args(2), sink_args(2)

  worker = argv(2)
  read argv(3), "%d", num_worker

  source_args(1) = "source.exe"
  source_args(2) = "-t"
  source_args(3) = "unbuffered"
  source_args(4) = "-w"
  write source_args(5), "%d", num_worker
  source_args(6) = "test.out"

  sink_args(1) = "sink.exe"
  sink_args(1) = "test.out"

  work_args(1) = "worker.exe"

  call mp_place("banana", 1, "source.exe", source_args)
  call mp_place("banana", 1, "sink.exe", sink_args)
  do i = 1, num_worker
    do j = 1, num_worker
      write work_args(2), "%d", (i-1) * num_worker + j
      call mp_place("crayon", (i-1) * num_worker + j, "worker.exe",
                    work_args)
    end do
  end do
end program
```

Program 5.16
Example Configuration Program

system are not placed on a different type of processor. The second specifies which particular processor is to be used, while the third is the name of the process's executable, and the
fourth contains the command-line arguments which will be passed to that process when it
begins executing. Program 5.16 shows a program that would build the configuration shown
in Figure 5.16 for a mesh-configured Crayon multicomputer hosted by a Banana Junior
workstation.

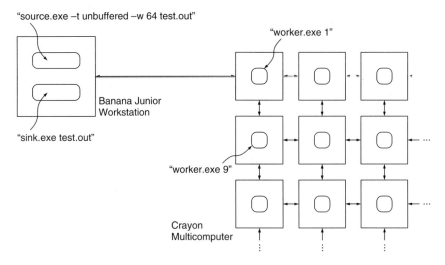

Figure 5.16
Example Configuration

5.3.3   Examples

Example 5.5 (A Simple Message-Passing Task Farm)   Our first example of how message passing is used is (yet another) task farm. The FORTRAN-KCSP implementation of the Mandelbrot Set discussed in Example 5.2 took advantage of the synchronous, blocking nature of communication through channels to ensure that tasks and results flowed properly. There was no need for the source to know where jobs were going: all it had to do was inject them into the pipeline, which would eventually deliver them to some worker process.

In contrast, the task farm implemented in Program 5.17 is more closely related to that of Example 5.1, in that every worker communicates directly with the source in order to get jobs and forward results. Since the source has no way of telling when a worker has finished its job, and needs another, workers must send requests for more work to the source. These requests must be tagged in some way to identify the sender, so that the source knows where to send its reply.

The program begins by creating one `root` process and some number of `worker` processes. `root` then joins a group called (logically enough) `"root"`, then calls `mp_synch` to show that it has finished its setup. `mp_grp_size` is then used to find out how many worker processes there are. `root` then goes into a loop in which it repeatedly pends and then accepts a buffer and a row index. If the message received is a real one (i.e., not the initial request from a worker) data are copied from `buffer` into the result array `patch`. A reply is

```
type(string) :: Root_Grp = "root"
type(string) :: Work_Grp = "worker"

program
  create
    1 of root()
    W of worker()
  end create
end program

procedure root()
  integer      :: id                    ! own ID in group
  integer      :: num_w                 ! number of workers
  logical      :: patch(N, N)           ! to fill
  logical      :: buffer(N)             ! for incoming
  integer      :: i, j, k               ! indices
  real         :: x = X0                ! coordinate
  type(msginfo) :: msg                  ! message information

  ! setup
  id = mp_join(Root_Grp, 1)
  call mp_synch()
  num_w = mp_grp_size(Work_Grp)

  ! calculate
  do i = 1, (N + num_w)
    msg = mp_test(.true., mp_pend(Root_Grp, "req", j, buffer))
    ! copy data if an actual buffer
    if j > 0 then
      do k = 1, N
        patch(j, k) = buffer(k)
      end do
    end if
    ! send job . . .
    if i <= N then
      call mp_send(Root_Grp, msg%src_grp, msg%src_id, "job", i, x)
      ! and move on
      x = x + Inc
```

Program 5.17
A Message-Passing Task Farm

```
    !  ... or termination signal
    else
      call mp_send(Root_Grp, msg%src_grp, msg%src_id, "job", 0, 0.0)
    end if
    ! tidy up
    call deallocate(msg)
  end do
end procedure

procedure worker()
  integer    :: id                          ! own ID in group
  logical    :: buffer(N)                    ! for messaging
  integer    :: i, j                         ! indices
  real       :: x, y                         ! coordinate

  ! setup
  id = mp_join(Work_Grp, MP_Any_ID)
  call mp_synch()

  ! calculate
  call mp_send(Work_Grp, Root_Grp, 1, "req", 0, buffer)
  call mp_recv(Work_Grp, "job", i, x)
  do while i > 0
    ! calculate this line
    y = Y0
    do j = 1, N
      buffer(j) = mandel(x, y)
      y = y + Inc
    end do
    ! send back to root (doubles as request)
    call mp_send(Work_Grp, Root_Grp, 1, "req", i, buffer)
    ! get next (or termination signal)
    call mp_recv(Work_Grp, "job", i, x)
  end while
end procedure
```

Program 5.17 *(continued)*
A Message-Passing Task Farm

then sent, containing either another job or an end-of-work signal (which is represented by a row index of zero). Finally, `root` tidies up by deallocating the `msginfo` structure. Note that `mp_recv` cannot be used in this loop, because `root` needs to know which `worker` sent the message in order to be able to reply correctly.

The `worker` process is roughly symmetrical. It begins by joining the group `"worker"`, giving `MP_Any_Id` as a parameter to `mp_join` to show that it doesn't care what ID it is given, so long as it gets one. After synchronizing with the other processes in the program, it sends a dummy buffer to signal that it is ready to start work. It then loops until it receives an end-of-work message from `root`. In each loop it processes the job it has been given, then sends `root` its results.

Note that this implementation does not rely on messages being delivered in the order in which they are sent. If this could be guaranteed, then the program could be made slightly more efficient by having the source broadcast a termination message immediately after handing out the last job, and then waiting for confirmation of receipt from each worker. However, if the termination message was able to overtake job messages, a worker might believe that it had seen its last job and shut itself down, only to have an orphaned job reach it a few moments later. The wider implications of this possibility are discussed in Section 5.4.1.

Given the small amount of work required to process each job in Example 5.5, it would be very inefficient to send jobs one at a time. In this application, it would be more appropriate to use a coarse-grained decomposition of the problem, i.e., to pack several job descriptions into each message sent to the workers.

Since "several" is not a precise measure, the best technique is to allow users to specify the granularity of the farm by passing a command-line argument to each process. Alternatively, since the sizes specified to different processes must be the same if the program is to behave correctly, it might be better to pass the granularity to the root alone, and have it send a preliminary message containing this information to the workers.

The worker process in this version would be similar to its predecessor, but would contain an extra loop to strip jobs out of messages once they had been received. The number of jobs contained in the message would be sent as a separate field in the message, as in:

```
call mp_send(Root_Grp, Work_Grp, id, "job", num_jobs, start_dex, job_buffer)
```

If jobs are large enough for it to be economical to send them singly, but network latencies are so large that it is uneconomic to have workers ask for jobs only once they become idle, some local buffering of jobs at workers may be useful. This is similar to the buffering implemented by the load-balancing pipeline, in which a "spare" job was held for every process so that its worker could be kept busy continuously. Here, we will consider three different ways of modifying our original task farm to produce one which does some local buffering.

The first way is to modify the behavior of the worker so that it initially asks for a job, then asks for another before listening for a reply to its first request. If the worker does this, the source will send it two jobs, only one of which will be internalized and processed immediately. Every time it finishes a job, the worker accepts the one which is pending, and, if it is not a termination signal, sends another request before starting to process the job. Thus, the code to send a request and accept a reply are put at opposite ends of the main loop, instead of being adjacent to one another.

But what if we want to have triple buffering, or quadruple buffering, or build the program so that each worker keeps a variable number of jobs in reserve at a time? Writing a single process which does this, as well as the calculations required to transform jobs into results, quickly becomes complicated. The best way to manage this complexity is to separate the communication requirements of the worker from its calculations by writing a separate communication manager process to accompany each worker. This communication manager's role is simply to send requests to the source, and buffer up the replies until the worker wants them. The worker can then use the simple request-response communication pattern it originally had. As messages arrive, they change the state of the manager, either by adding to its pool of jobs and signalling that it should not make any more requests, or by signalling that the worker wants another job. Once it knows its new state, the manager can take appropriate action, e.g., request another job, forward a job to the worker, or shut itself down.

It is tempting to try to mix the shared-variable and message-passing paradigms when writing programs like this one, e.g., to have a process and its communication manager execute independently, but share most of their data structures, and manage their one-to-one interactions using semaphores. The main obstacle to doing this is the difficulty of mixing semaphore operations with message handling. To take the obvious case, a communication manager would want to wait until either a new message arrived, or its client signalled that it wanted something. Designing a syntax for mixing such heterogeneous events, and giving that syntax efficient run-time support, is complicated. One approach is to define general "event" objects, which can be tied to semaphores, message receipt, or other events, and to allow processes to wait on these in the same way that they can wait on non-blocking receives in FORTRAN-KMP. However, implementations of this must usually pay the set-up and take-down costs associated with the `alt` construct of Section 5.1.2.

Example 5.6 (Gaussian Elimination) Our second example of the use of a structured message-passing system is Gaussian elimination. Program 5.18 gives the code for a simple version of this which uses $\mathcal{P}$ worker processes to solve an $N \times N$ problem, where, for

```
integer, constant :: N = matrix dimension
integer, constant :: P = number of processes
integer, constant :: W = N/P
type(string)      :: Work_Grp = "workers"

program
   real    :: A(N, N), A_o(N, N)              ! A and a copy
   real    :: B(N), B_o(N), B_c(N)            ! B, a copy, and a check
   real    :: X(N)                            ! solution
   real    :: max_diff                        ! maximum difference
   integer :: i, j                            ! loop indices

   assert (N .mod. P) == 0
   create
     P of worker()
   end create
end program

procedure worker()
   integer :: id = id_rel_self()              ! own ID
   real    :: A(W, N), B(W), X(W)             ! problem and solution
   real    :: A_o(W, N), B_o(W)               ! copies for checking
   real    :: B_c(W)                          ! also for checking
   real    :: max_diff                        ! error

   ! join group
   assert id == mp_join(Work_Grp, id)
   call mp_synch()

   ! setup
   call init(id, A, B)
   call copy_real_2(A, A_o)
   call copy_real_1(B, B_o)
   ! find solution
   call gauss_fwd(id, A, B)
   call gauss_bwd(id, A, B, X)
```

Program 5.18
Gaussian Elimination

```
  ! check
  call mat_vec_prod(id, A_o, X, B_c)
  max_diff = vec_dist_real(B_o, B_c)
  max_diff = real_reduce_max(P, id, max_diff)
end procedure

procedure gauss_fwd(id, A, B)
  integer :: id                              ! own ID
  real     :: A(:, :)                        ! matrix
  real     :: B(:)                           ! target vector
  real     :: pivot(N)                       ! pivot row
  real     :: pivot_b                        ! pivot vector element
  integer :: base = 1                        ! base of active section
  integer :: i, j, k                         ! loop indices

  ! for each row . . .
  do k = 1, N
    ! get (or fill) pivot row
    call get_pivot(id, k, base, A, B, pivot, pivot_b)
    ! update base?
    if mod1(k, P) == id then
      base = base + 1
    end if
    ! update elements
    do i = base, W, 1
      A(i, k) = A(i, k)/pivot(k)
      do j = k+1, N, 1
        A(i, j) = A(i, j) - (A(i, k) * pivot(j))
      end do
      B(i) = B(i) - (A(i, k) * pivot_b)
    end do
  end do
end procedure

procedure get_pivot(id, k, base, A, B, p_row, p_b)
  integer :: id, k                           ! where we are
  integer :: base                            ! current base index
  real     :: A(:, :), B(:)                  ! own values
  real     :: p_row(:), p_b                  ! to fill
  integer :: j                               ! copying index
```

Program 5.18 (*continued*)
Gaussian Elimination

```
      ! use own values
      if mod1(k, P) == id then
        call mp_send(Work_Grp, Work_Grp, MP_All_ID, "pivot",
                     k, A(base, :), B(base))
        do j = 1, N
          p_row(j) = A(base, j)
        end do
        p_b = B(base)
      ! use someone else's
      else
        call mp_recv(Work_Grp, "pivot", j, p_row, p_b)
        assert(j == k)
      end if
end procedure

procedure gauss_bwd(id, A, B, X)
  integer :: id                              ! own ID
  real    :: A(:, :)                         ! matrix
  real    :: B(:)                            ! target vector
  real    :: X(:)                            ! solution vector
  integer :: i, j                            ! loop indices
  real    :: x_elt                           ! X-vector element
  integer :: top = W                         ! top of range

  ! solve
  do i = N, 1, -1
    ! solve for solution, or get someone else's
    call get_soln(id, i, top, A, B, X, x_elt)
    ! update top?
    if mod1(i, P) == id then
      top = top - 1
    end if
    ! update preceding elements
    do j = top, 1, -1
      B(j) = B(j) - (A(j, i) * x_elt)
    end do
  end do
end procedure
```

Program 5.18 *(continued)*
Gaussian Elimination

```
procedure get_soln(id, k, top, A, B, X, x_elt)
  integer :: id, k                          ! where we are
  integer :: top                            ! top of range
  real     :: A(:, :), B(:), X(:)           ! own elements
  real     :: x_elt                         ! to fill
  integer :: k_other                        ! for checking

  ! use own element
  if mod1(k, P) == id then
    X(top) = B(top)/A(top, k)
    call mp_send(Work_Grp, Work_Grp, MP_All_ID, "soln", k, X(top))
    x_elt = X(top)
  ! get someone else's
  else
    call mp_recv(Work_Grp, "soln", k_other, x_elt)
    assert k_other == k
  end if
end procedure
```

Program 5.18 *(continued)*
Gaussian Elimination

simplicity, N is a multiple of $\mathcal{P}$. Each worker joins the program's one message group, initializes its portion of the matrix, and then makes copies of the matrix and the target vector so that the program can later check the correctness of its answer. worker then calls the routines gauss_fwd and gauss_bwd. The first of these does the work of reducing the matrix iteratively. In each iteration, the process either broadcasts the current row (if it holds the pivot row) or accepts a row into a temporary vector called pivot. In order to achieve good load balancing, rows are allocated to processes cyclically. A process then knows *a priori* that it holds the next pivot row by checking if the remainder of the row index and the number of processes is equal to its own ID.

Once every process has the pivot row, it reduces all of the other rows for which it is responsible in exactly the same way used in the serial code of Program 2.1. Once all of the rows have been reduced, gauss_bwd is called to do backward substitution, which constructs the solution vector X. Like gauss_fwd, this either sends or receives a single element, then updates the remainder of its portion of the vector.

Once the matrix-vector equation has been solved, the next step is to check the answer using prod_mat_vec (Program 5.19). Each process executes $\mathcal{P} - 1$ iterations. In each, it sends a portion of the putative result to one of the other processes, and receives a portion in reply. It then calculates part of the overall matrix-vector product using this

```
procedure prod_mat_vec(id, matrix, vector, result)
   integer :: id                              ! caller's ID
   real    :: matrix(:, :)                    ! left argument
   real    :: vector(:)                       ! right argument
   real    :: result(:)                       ! where to store result
   real    :: tmp(W)                          ! for other's sections of vector
   integer :: proc, i                         ! loop indices
   integer :: base = id

   ! initialize
   do i = 1, W
     result(i) = 0.0
     tmp(i) = vector(i)
   end do

   ! own section
   call mat_vec_partial(matrix, tmp, result, base)

   ! others' sections
   do proc = 1, P
     if proc /= id then
       call mp_send(Work_Grp, Work_Grp, proc, "vector", base, tmp)
       call mp_recv(Work_Grp, "vector", base, tmp)
       call mat_vec_partial(matrix, tmp, result, base)
     end if
   end do
end procedure

procedure mat_vec_partial(matrix, vec, res, base)
   real    :: matrix(:, :)                    ! left argument
   real    :: vec(:), res(:)                  ! right argument and result
   integer :: base                            ! offset in matrix
   integer :: i, j                            ! loop indices

   do i = 1, W
     do j = 1, W
       res(i) = res(i) + (matrix(i, base + ((j-1) * P)) * vec(j))
     end do
   end do
end procedure
```

Program 5.19
Checking Code for Gaussian Elimination

```
real function real_reduce_max(num_procs, id, own)
  integer :: num_procs, id              ! size and own location
  real    :: own                         ! own contribution
  real    :: result, tmp                 ! value returned and scratch
  integer :: left = 2*id,                ! left child's ID
             right = 2*id+1,             ! right child's ID
             parent = id/2               ! parent's ID

  ! accumulate
  result = own
  if left <= num_procs then
    call mp_recv(Work_Grp, "reduce", tmp)
    result = result .max. tmp
  end if
  if right <= num_procs then
    call mp_recv(Work_Grp, "reduce", tmp)
    result = result .max. tmp
  end if

  ! get answer
  if id == 1 then
    call mp_send(Work_Grp, Work_Grp, MP_All_ID, "reduce-solution", result)
  else
    call mp_send(Work_Grp, Work_Grp, parent, "reduce", result)
    call mp_recv(Work_Grp, "reduce-solution", result)
  end if

  return result
end function
```

Program 5.19 *(continued)*
Checking Code for Gaussian Elimination

temporary value. Finally, the workers perform reduction to find the maximum element-wise difference between the original vector B and the result of multiplying the original matrix against the proposed solution.

5.3.4 Application Constructors

As can be seen from the previous examples, procedural message passing leads to programs which are longer and less readable than their data-parallel or shared-variables counterparts. Procedural message passing may not have the plumbing problems of the CSP model, but its need for setup functions, group names, and synchronization after group construction can be just as bad.

The paradox is this: the only way to get good performance out of existing machines seems to be to use message passing, but message-passing systems are intrinsically low-level and difficult to use. The fact that message-passing systems are almost always used in one of a small number of ways (chiefly task farming, pipelining, geometric decomposition, and in client/server systems) only aggravates the situation: having built N task farms, most users come to believe that something else ought to build the $N + 1^{th}$. This section describes two systems which do this. The first is modelled after the Parallel Utility Libraries (PUL) software developed at the Edinburgh Parallel Computing Centre [Clarke et al. 1994]. These libraries provide a parallel *skeleton* around which users can build particular types of applications; similar systems include the templates developed at the University of Pisa [Bacci et al. 1994]. The second system is ENTERPRISE, which was developed by Schaeffer, Szafron, and others at the University of Alberta [Schaeffer et al. 1993]. ENTERPRISE hides its code skeletons from its users, and uses source-to-source program transformation to translate procedure calls into parallel activations. Much of what is in both systems was presaged by Cole's work on algorithmic skeletons, which is discussed in [Cole 1989].

Skeletons A skeleton is a procedure whose role is to call other procedures. The quick-sorting routine provided in the standard C libraries, for example, takes as input a pointer to a block of memory (which is presumed to hold an array of objects to be sorted), the number of elements, the size of each element, and a function. This function must take as its arguments two of the objects being sorted, and return a negative integer if the first is less than the second, zero if they are equal, and a positive integer otherwise. Packaging the essentials of an algorithm into a procedure, which then calls one or more object-specific procedures, is a common programming technique in functional languages. It is also very useful in parallel programming: if system builders provide functions which (for example) handle the job-request and -delivery protocols used in a task farm users are freed from writing endless variations on a theme. The resulting code is often more efficient as well, since it is more cost-effective to optimize a skeleton which is going to be used many times than one which will be used only once.

A simple example of a parallel skeleton is one which implements task farming. This skeleton takes five arguments, the first three of which are functions. These represent the source of the farm, which generates jobs; the worker, which transforms jobs into results; and the sink, which consumes those results. Each function take an integer count and an array of strings as its first two arguments; users can pass "command-line" parameters in these using the usual UNIX mechanism.

The last two arguments to the skeleton are the sizes of the data structures to represent jobs and results. (The `memory` function returns the size of a structure in bytes. It is not standard in FORTRAN-K, but analogous functions exist in many languages.) The source function must return a structure of the first type; the skeleton will call it each time a worker needs something to do, giving it an `integer` job ID as its third argument. The worker's extra arguments must be an `integer`, which in each call will contain the ID of the worker process, and a job structure, and return a result structure. (Workers are passed their IDs in case they wish to do error reporting.) Finally, the sink must take a result structure as its third argument.

A simple example will make this all more concrete. Program 5.20 shows the three functions required by a task-farming skeleton, along with a call to the skeleton itself. Note that each function re-parses its command-line arguments each time it is called. Most languages which are more sophisticated than FORTRAN-K (i.e., most languages) provide some way for a function to retain some state information between calls, like the `static` mechanism of C. In a real program, these functions could use such a mechanism to avoid repeatedly re-parsing their arguments.

While the task-farming example does not require users to include any calls to parallel library procedures inside their routines, other skeletons may not be so easy-going. A skeleton supporting regular geometric decomposition, for example, may not only require users to provide a procedure which takes a specific number of parameters in a specific order, but might also insist that users call a library procedure such as `skel_mesh_synch` after each complete mesh update. This procedure would then handle boundary-value exchange, while performing a barrier synchronization to ensure that updates stayed in step. A more sophisticated skeleton which allowed users to overlap boundary exchange and internal updates might require calls to two or more such procedures.

In order to be fully general, such a skeleton might also require users to create structures they might not otherwise have made explicit. For example, along with its many other parameters, the PUL-RD (Regular Domain) skeleton requires a *stencil* argument. This stencil must be an $h \times h$ `logical` array, where h must be odd. The central point of this array represents a single point in the mesh; `.true.` values in the array indicate points which are needed in the update of a central point, while `.false.` values represent points which are not needed. Using this, the skeleton can calculate how much data to swap along each axis of the mesh. By default, the system handles edge and corner points in the mesh by masking out parts of the stencil; a more elaborate skeleton would require users to specify separate stencils for these.

Enterprise Skeletal libraries such as those described above relieve users of most of the burden of constructing most types of parallel program. However, programmers must still

```
type job_type
  description of job
end type

type result_type
  description of result
end type

type(job_type) function source(argc, argv, next_id)
  integer      :: argc
  type(string) :: argv
  integer      :: next_id
  user code goes here
  return next job
end function

type(result_type) function worker(argc, argv, id, job)
  integer        :: argc
  type(string)   :: argv
  integer        :: id
  type(job_type) :: job
  user code goes here
  return result of doing job
end function

procedure sink(argc, argv, result)
  integer         :: argc
  type(string)    :: argv
  type(result_type) :: result
  record result
end procedure
.
.
.

program main
  type(job_type), auto    :: job
  type(result_type), auto :: result
  call task_farm(source, worker, sink, memory(job), memory(result))
end program
```

Program 5.20
Using a Task-Farming Skeleton

make certain changes in their code manually in order to use these libraries, and they do not directly support composition: it is not possible, for example, to create a task farm of mesh programs.

ENTERPRISE [Schaeffer et al. 1993] was designed to address exactly these issues, and the issue of code re-use. The system consists of an application-building interface and a run-time system. The latter contains many of the same facilities of PUL, and is structured in the same way. The former consists of a configuration tool, and a compiler which can perform source-to-source transformations. When the configuration tool is invoked, it presents its user with a box representing her parallel program (Figure 5.17a). She can then select from a menu of parallelization strategies, such as **pipeline** and **replicate**. The **pipeline** option, for example, prompts for a positive number, and then transforms the single box into a line of that many boxes, as shown in Figure 5.17b. If the **replicate** option is then applied to one of these, the user will be asked for the upper and lower bounds on replication; the box will then be replaced with a stack of boxes as shown in Figure 5.17c. Any transformation may be applied to any box, but users may not directly edit the results. Thus, it is possible to create pipelines of task farms, or task farms of pipelines, but not arbitrarily-connected structures.

As she is building up the configuration of the application, the user can associate particu-lar program modules with each box. When the configuration and source code are passed to the compiler, it can analyze them together to determine which function "calls" are actually to be inter-process communication. If the configuration identifies a particular function as a worker in a task farm, for example, then ENTERPRISE transforms the call in the control process from:

```
result(i) = worker(···params···)
```

to:

```
integer :: buffer(Required_Buffer_Size), transaction_id
    .
    .
    .
call marshall(buffer, ···params···)
call mark_as_future(buffer(i), .true.)
transaction_id = low_level_send(worker_processor_id, worker_process_id,
                                Work_Request_Tag, buffer, buffer_length)
call low_level_recv(transaction_id, buffer, buffer_length)
call unmarshall(result(i), buffer, buffer_length)
call mark_as_future(buffer(i), .false.)
```

Here, a buffer of the appropriate size (or of a size large enough to hold all of that process's

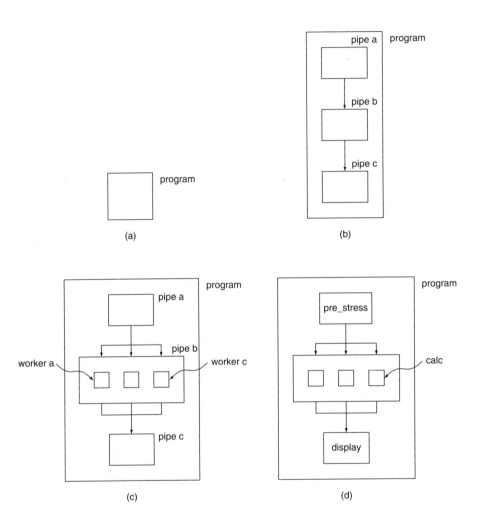

Figure 5.17
Using Enterprise to Construct a Parallel Application

interactions) is allocated, and then filled with the parameters to be passed to the worker. The structure into which the result is to be written is then marked as a future (Section 4.3), so that the controller will block if it tries to read the value of `result(i)` before such a value is received from the worker. Finally, the parameters are sent to the worker, and the controller waits for the response.

Since a practical program would probably contain many workers, the code actually produced by the transformer would be more complicated. It might, for example, have to be able to handle multiple outstanding messages. It might also want to be able to accept those results in any order, rather than in the order in which jobs were sent out. ENTERPRISE allows users to specify this during configuration; if a module is marked as unordered, then results from it are delivered to its caller in the order in which they arrive, rather than necessarily in the same order as calls were made. ENTERPRISE also allows users to mark the parameters to calls as IN, OUT, or INOUT. When a call occurs, the values of IN parameters are copied from the caller to the callee, but changes are not copied back. The reverse happens with OUT parameters: nothing is sent by the caller in its calling message, but new values for its variables are returned by the procedure being called. Finally, INOUT parameters are copied both ways. Using these tags helps to make the system more efficient, as it reduces the volume of data copied unnecessarily. More importantly, it enables use of procedures which work by modifying their arguments, e.g., procedures which overwrite part of an array during calculation.

One of ENTERPRISE's many strengths is the ease with which its users can exploit varying resources. As mentioned earlier, when a user chooses to replicate a program component, the system prompts her for upper and lower bounds on the degree of replication. The system can then decide dynamically at run-time exactly how many processes to use. This behavior is particularly useful on distributed computers, in which the number of nodes (usually workstations) available between one run of the program and the next may vary.

ENTERPRISE does have its weaknesses. One of these is that procedures must sometimes be restructured to match ENTERPRISE's calling conventions. Each of the functions used in a pipeline, for example, must call the next function as its last action, so that the system knows when to forward values. While the code this leads to is certainly readable:

```
type(type_X) function front(params)
   .
   .
   .
   return A(···actual params to A···)
end function
```

```
type(type_X) function A(formal params A)
```

```
   .
   .
   .
   return B(···actual params to B···)
end function

type(type_X) function B(formal params B)
   .
   .
   .
   return back(···actual params to back···)
end function

type(type_X) function back(formal params to back)
   .
   .
   .
   return something of type X
end function
```

it is not necessarily structured as it would have been if the programmer had not been intending to parallelize it.

This becomes more than a minor flaw when geometric decomposition is considered. The current release of ENTERPRISE does not support this parallelization strategy, primarily because it is difficult to specify that each process is to work on its own portion of the overall mesh, and to exchange boundaries with its neighbors, without introducing boundary-swapping calls of the kind seen in the previous section. Transforming a function which handles an arbitrary portion of a mesh, along with a specification of the halo around each point, into the required code, would be a feasible, though far from trivial, extension of the current system.

5.4 Watching Programs Run

So far, we have only looked at writing programs. Real programming systems, however, must support debugging and performance tuning as well. This section describes some of the problems that arise when one tries to do these things in an MIMD environment.

5.4.1 Time, Clocks, and Relativity

Suppose that three processes A, B, and C are running on separate processors in a multicomputer, and that each performs several broadcasts. As shown in Figure 5.18, even if the order in which each process's message reaches the other two processes is consistent

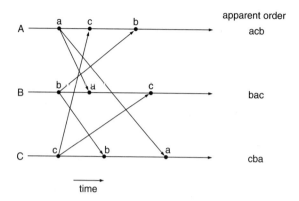

Figure 5.18
Possible Event Orderings in a Broadcast System

in *clock time*, it is possible for different processes to receive messages in different orders. In effect, different processors have different views of *logical time*, which is the order in which events appear to occur.

This phenomenon should be familiar to anyone who has studied the theory of relativity. If information can only travel as fast as light, then the order in which an observer sees events occur depends on the relative position of the events and the observer. As Figure 5.19 shows, this can be visualized using time-space diagrams, in which physical location is one axis (for a one-dimensional system) and time the second. The outward propagation of information about an event is shown by a "light cone." Only observers within an event's cone know that the event has occurred; the apparent order of events is determined by the overlap of different light cones.

One of the implications of this phenomenon is that it may not make sense to say that two events are *synchronous* or *asynchronous*, i.e., that they occurred at the same instant or at different instants in clock time. Instead, the best that can be done is to put them into some partial order, and say that event x happened before event y, after it, or that the two cannot be ordered.

The implications of this are important, particularly when we are trying to debug parallel programs, or trying to ensure the consistency of operations on shared data structures in a disjoint-memory machine. In his seminal paper [Lamport 1978], Leslie Lamport showed how a correct partial order on events can be constructed as a program executes. Suppose a program consists of a set of Π processes labelled p_1 to p_Π. Each process executes serially; no processes are created or destroyed during the program's active life. After the program terminates, we must try to determine which events could have influenced which others.

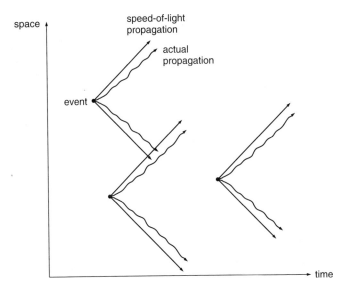

Figure 5.19
Space-Time Diagrams

We can do this by recording events locally in each process, and ordering them according to two rules. First, the actions of an individual process are ordered according to their local execution. This rule gives a set of orderings $\prec_i$, $1 \le i \le \Pi$, for the sets $\{e_{i,j}\}$ of events which occurred on processor i.

These orderings can then be related to one another by using the fact that a message cannot be received before it has been sent. If we use $s(p_i, m)$ to denote process p_i sending a message m, and $r(p_j, m)$ to denote process p_j receiving that message, then we can add $s(p_i, m) \prec r(p_j, m)$ to our partial order for all messages m. The partial order that results is shown in Figure 5.20, in which three processes perform calculations and send one another messages. This partial order is compatible with either of the total orders shown.

In order to construct this partial order on the fly, each process must maintain a single integer counter, which it uses as a logical (as opposed to real-time) clock. Each process initializes its clock to 0. Whenever it does something noteworthy, it increments the clock by one. In particular, whenever it sends a message, it includes the current value of its clock, and then increments the clock by 1. When a process receives a message, it sets its own clock to be the maximum of its previous value and the value included in the incoming message, and then increments that by 1. This guarantees that events within individual

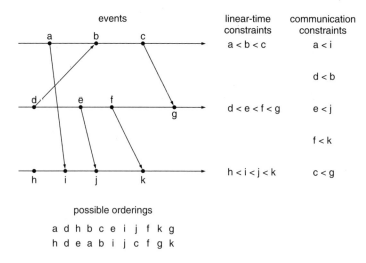

Figure 5.20
A Partial Order on Events

processes are ordered as they occurred, and that messages always appear to have been received after they were sent. [Fidge 1991] discusses this in greater detail.

Figure 5.21 shows how this works for the same example used in Figure 5.20. Once the program has completed, the clock values recorded by each process for the events that involved it can be used to construct a correct partial order for the entire set of events. Such partial event order graphs can then be used to visualize program execution.

5.4.2   Debugging

If you are as clever as you can be when you write [a piece of code], how will you ever debug it?
—Brian W. Kernighan and P. J. Plauger
The Elements of Programming Style

The fact that it is usually impossible to speak of "the" state of an MIMD system makes parallel debugging much harder than serial debugging. Serial debuggers typically allow programmers to do the following:

interrupt execution at any time;

inspect variable values (and possibly modify them);

set breakpoints so that execution is halted at particular statements;

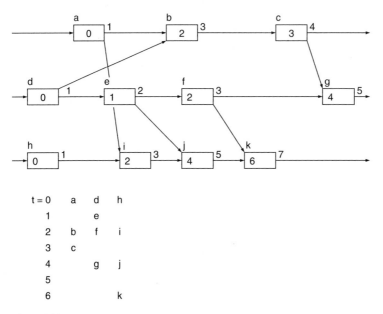

Figure 5.21
Constructing a Partial Order for Events

make assertions about process state so that execution halts when particular events occur; and

single-step so that critical portions of code can be examined in detail.

A parallel system which contains a global control mechanism capable of freezing all processes at the same moment in real time can provide these same facilities with relative ease. However, such mechanisms are typically found only on SIMD processor arrays, such as the CM-2 Connection Machine, and small bus-based multiprocessors, such as the Sequent Symmetry. As a result, such machines are presently the only ones which offer debugging tools as effective as those found on serial machines.

Large MIN-based multiprocessors, such as the BBN TC2000, and multicomputers such as the Meiko CS-2 Computing Surface, usually do not have a single clock, or a single global control bus. A message like "stop!" therefore takes a finite time to propagate through the system, just like any other message. This means that processes may stop in inconsistent states after an interrupt, i.e., some processes may execute a few or a few thousand more instructions than others. If any of these instructions modify private or shared data, it may be impossible to determine what state the system was in when the interrupt was issued.

Single-stepping programs on large parallel machines is similarly problematic. Quite often, bugs in parallel programs are due to race conditions; if processes are slowed down, those conditions may change or disappear. This problem is particularly annoying in message-passing multicomputers, in which there might not be any way to "single-step" messages. The problem is particularly pronounced when the occurrence of an error depends on contention for inter-processor links. If a program is single-stepped, and messages always proceed to completion once they are initiated, then contention which would have arisen in a real run of the program might not arise in a debugging run. In the worst case, the order in which messages reach a particular process can be consistent within both normal and debugging runs, but differ in the two kinds of runs.

While it is easy to make assertions about the internal state of concurrent processes, it is much harder to make assertions about their external state, i.e., about aspects of the program which are related to two or more processes. While one could certainly build a tool which allowed users to say "Stop when A is sending a message and B is not", the information needed to test this assertion cannot be collected reliably, due to the proscription on global knowledge discussed in the previous section.

As if these problems weren't enough, parallel debuggers inevitably suffer from a phenomenon called the Parallel Heisenberg Principle, or, more prosaically, the *probe effect*. This states that one cannot measure a process, or a parallel system, without affecting it. For example, unless separate hardware exists to timestamp and record communication operations and remote memory accesses, every processor will have to spend a few extra cycles creating and logging this information during each operation. Once again, this can easily change the timing of certain events, and alter the program's overall behavior.

Finally, there is the problem of information overload: human beings can usually keep track of two or three things at once, but tracking hundreds or thousands of concurrent events is simply impossible. Even if execution traces for thousands of processes could be collected, they would more probably be part of the problem than part of the solution.

One way to deal with these problems is simply to ignore them. Since the mid-1980s, many manufacturers have provided debuggers for their systems which look and feel like multi-window versions of dbx-style serial debuggers. Instead of a single window showing the state of a single process, these tools provide one window per process; in order to follow the interactions between processes, or inspect data, users must switch between windows manually. This burden is acceptable for small programs, or scaled-down prototypes of large programs, but limits the usefulness of such tools on real applications.

An obvious way to extend such a tool is to allow users to specify sets of processes, and then apply operations such as single-stepping or breakpointing to specified sets. Such sets may or may not correspond to the process groups set up by a `create` statement, or created dynamically by the message-passing system of Section 5.3. However, enabling users to manipulate groups of processes does nothing to ameliorate the probe effect. If data are being collected, analyzed, and displayed while a program runs, it is almost certain that its execution order will be altered beyond recognition.

A better approach is to always record events as they occur, and then inspect them after the program has finished executing. Storing event data locally can greatly reduce the probe effect, so much so that it may be feasible to specify that monitoring is always turned on, even if data are not being collected. In this case, the probe effect may disappear entirely, since there are no longer any un-monitored program runs against which to compare monitored runs. Performance will suffer slightly, but many users would happily trade a few percent of peak performance for debuggability.

Data can be collected in any of several ways. First, users may be required to instrument their code manually, e.g., by calling a different set of communication library routines, or by inserting calls to an event-recording library. At a slightly higher level, it may be possible to provide two versions of the run-time system, only one of which records data. This approach is taken in many sequential debugging systems, in which a user's code is linked either with a standard library, or with a version containing debugging hooks. Finally, compiler-level systems may take a high-level description of the information the user wishes to collect, and automatically generate and insert the instrumentation required. One strength of this approach is that the system can try to minimize the volume of data collected; a concomitant weakness is that a user who changes her mind about what to examine after the program has run may find that the system has not collected the data needed to answer that question.

Once data have been collected, the next step is to perform some filtering to select interesting events or sequences of events. This can be done by allowing users to specify patterns of events, and having the system replace each occurrence of that pattern with a single meta-event. Examples of interesting patterns include two different processes writing to a variable without synchronizing with each other, or a process reading from a message buffer before a message has been put into it. In an iconic display, each such occurrence might be directly represented by half a dozen icons, all of which could be replaced by a single higher-level icon. Filtering such as this is needed to reduce the volume of data to a comprehensible level (Figure 5.22).

After filtering, data can be visualized. There are two fundamentally different ways of doing this. The first is to represent time explicitly as in the lifeline scroll of Figure 5.23. In this, each process is represented by a bar, which is shaded to show where in its source it was at each point in its life. Communication between processes is shown by arrows, whose thickness indicates the size of the message. Users can scroll such a display forward and backward in order to determine the partial order of events.

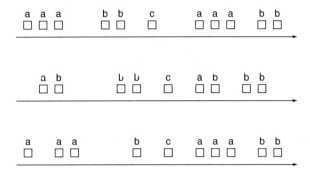

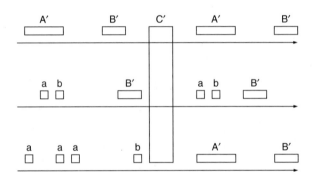

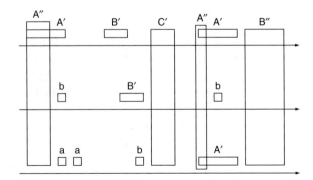

Figure 5.22
Iconic Representation of Parallel Program Behavior

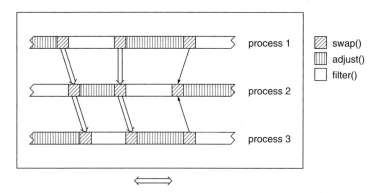

Figure 5.23
A Scroll Display of Process Lifelines

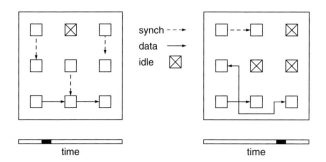

Figure 5.24
Animating Process Histories

A complementary approach is to represent time implicitly, by creating an animated cartoon showing events. A snapshot from such a cartoon is shown in Figure 5.24. The two spatial dimensions of the display screen are used to show the spatial arrangement of processes; this is particularly helpful when geometric decomposition is being used, as users almost always think of their processes as being arranged in some regular pattern. The slide at the bottom of the display is used to move the cartoon forward or backward through time; messages appear as arrows, and are visible for as long as it took to deliver the message.

One of the serendipities of collecting event traces for later visualization is that an execution trace may later be used to drive a simulation of the program [Netzer 1994]. Rather than recording everything that every process did (which typically requires enormous amounts of memory), a system can just record the interactions between processes. The programmer can then re-create that run exactly by re-executing the program and using the recorded interactions in place of any generated by the second run. Instead of recording the contents of every message received by a process, for example, such a system would simply record the order in which messages arrived. Any message that actually arrives out of order during the replay would then be buffered, so that they could be delivered in the "correct" order. Such a capability can also allow users to run programs until a particular state is reached, and then force a change in the order of the next few events in order to carry out "what if?" experiments.

More details about parallel and distributed debugging can be found in the survey article [McDowell & Helmbold 1989], or in [Miller & McDowell 1991]. These describe some of the filtering, event reconstruction, and display techniques which have been developed for parallel debuggers.

5.4.3   Performance Monitoring

Debugging a program involves examining it at a microscopic level; performance tuning, on the other hand, requires examination of a program's macroscopic performance properties. Debugging systems must be able to display discrete events, while performance monitoring systems are more concerned with its continuous, or time-averaged, behavior.

The performance of serial programs can be measured at two levels. The first is to instrument the operating system underneath the program to count such things as cache misses and page faults. This information can tell the programmer whether she is using the available hardware efficiently. The second level is the program itself: the compiler or the programmer can, for example, insert counters into the code to record the number of times each statement or procedure is executed, or the system can generate regular timer interrupts, and record where the program counter is at each. Both methods measure program coverage, i.e., the frequency with which each part of the program is executed; however, sampling under the control of a timer gives a better indication of where the program's hot spots are, since some statements may take much longer to execute than others.

Data can be collected on parallel systems in similar ways, although once again the probe effect means that the performance of the program being monitored will usually differ from the performance of an unmonitored version. In most performance monitoring systems, the run-time system on each processor records the behavior of the processes it is supporting, e.g., by recording the time of each message transmission or receipt, and the volume of data in each message. However, unlike a debugging system, a performance monitoring system can compress this data, e.g., by recording only the total volume of message traffic

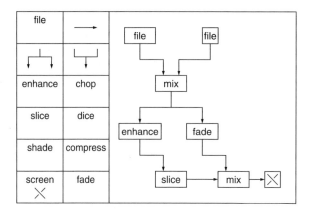

Figure 5.25
An Applications Visualization System

in a particular time interval. Compressing data in this way makes it more feasible to construct monitoring systems which display performance information as programs are running, since compressed performance data may represent only a small increase in the system's total message traffic.

As in parallel debugging systems, collecting performance data is often easier than interpreting it. While some researchers have tried to develop expert systems for doing this [Kohn & Williams 1993], visualizing performance has proved to be more tractable than visualizing behavior. The key has been the realization that a parallel computer system can be treated like any other large physical system [Rover & Wright 1993]. Many of the techniques used to visualize scientific data [Nielson 1991], and much of the software developed for this purpose, can therefore be recycled. In particular, systems designed to allow users to explore data have proved a very effective basis for further work [Reed et al. 1991]. These systems, such as AVS [Upson et al. 1989], allow users to build up a flow-graph in which nodes represent input and output, filtering, or statistical massaging, and arcs represent data paths (Figure 5.25). With these tools, users can quickly build a visualization program to display their input data in any of a very large number of ways. Inevitably, some of these displays will not be particularly informative, but others can highlight features of the data which then mean something to the user.

A useful classification of some of sources of inefficiency in parallel programs can be found in [Crovella & LeBlanc 1993]. This list includes:

Load imbalance: work is available, but some processors are idle anyway.

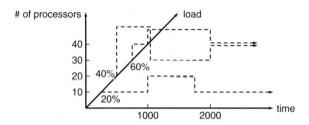

Figure 5.26
Load Display

Starvation loss: processors are idle because no work is available (i.e., there is not enough parallelism to keep all available processors busy).

Synchronization loss: processors are synchronizing with one another, e.g., at a barrier or by blocking on message receipt, rather than doing useful computation.

Braking loss: a solution to the problem has been found, but some processors are still doing calculations which will just be thrown away.

Memory loss: processors are stalled waiting for data (e.g., due to memory request collisions in a MIN-based multiprocessor, or while waiting on a reply from a server in a multicomputer).

Redundant computation: two or more processors are doing the same calculation.

A good performance monitoring system should not only show how often processors are idle, but also why they are not busy at those times. Ideally, such a tool should also be integrated with mapping and scheduling tools of the type discussed in Section 4.5, if such are available.

The easiest thing to visualize is the load on the system: how busy processors are, how close to saturation buses or communication links are, and so on. The crudest sort of display for this is a simple dial, whose pointer shows the average load in the system. Several such dials can be combined, and controlled by moving a slider (if the system is working from saved data) to see how performance changes over time.

A more informative version of this is a graph showing load as a function of time. One such display is shown in Figure 5.26. The horizontal axis represents time; the other axes represent the load on processors, and the number of processors loaded to that degree. A similar display can be used to show link loading, non-local memory accesses, or any similar machine feature.

What this display does not show, however, is interaction between the program's components. For this purpose, maps of the kind shown in Figure 5.27a–c are often used.

Figure 5.27a uses color to show the amount of data sent from each processor to each other; dark squares represent large volumes of communication, while light squares represent less. Note that this display is a total over the whole of the program's life; including time in it, e.g., by stacking maps showing message volume in discrete time intervals, would almost certainly make the picture less intelligible.

Figure 5.27a makes the pattern of communication in the program very clear: each processor primarily sends to its two neighbors. Figure 5.27b displays exactly the same data, but permutes the order of processors. This display makes the communication pattern much less obvious, and highlights one of the great failings of visualization systems in general. In most cases, such systems can only make patterns obvious if users already suspect that those patterns will be present, and structure their displays to highlight them. Figure 5.27c shows how using a different type of display can help find patterns. Each horizontal bar in this represents the messages sent by one processor; each bar contains one line for each other processor, and length is used to indicate load. This display does not make the nearest-neighbor communication pattern any clearer, but does make it plain that each processor is primarily talking to only two others.

Another useful kind of display is shown in Figure 5.28. The two axes represent the load on a processor, and the load on its communication links. The time interval over which load has been measured is shown by the slider at the top; the width of the bar on this slider shows the averaging interval. Each small dot in the display represents a single processor; where two processors' dots would be directly on top of one another, the system draws a slightly larger bubble.

As the slider is moved back and forth (or as the program runs, if the display is being used interactively), processor dots swim around the display. If a processor is primarily calculating, its dot spends most of its time in the display's lower right-hand corner; if it is also communicating a great deal, the dot will live in the upper right-hand corner, and so on. Using a long averaging interval makes tracking particular dots easy, but may give a misleading impression of what processors are actually doing—a dot might move smoothly from one part of the display to another, for example, when the processor it represents actually made the transition suddenly. If the averaging interval is very short, on the other hand, users can see short-lived transient behavior, but may find it difficult to follow individual processors. The limiting cases are an averaging interval equal to the whole life of the program, and no averaging at all. The former leads to a scattered bubble plot of processor and link loading, while the latter leads to a confusing mess.

There are of course many ways to augment a display such as this. Dots could be colored, for example, to represent the frequency of cache misses, although this would make it more difficult to merge processor dots to form larger bubbles. Dots could also be given luminous tails in order to make it easier to track their motion. One interesting variation on this is

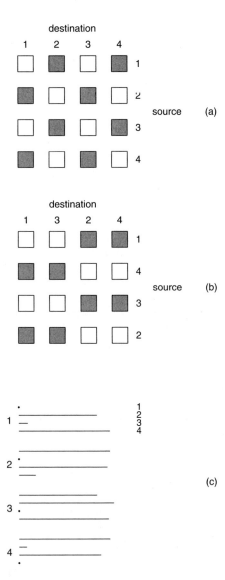

Figure 5.27
Mapping Process Interaction

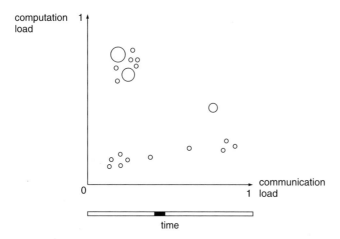

Figure 5.28
Representing Process Trajectories

to eliminate the dots entirely, and simply trace the trajectory of a process in load space. Figure 5.29 shows what such a display might look like; the ticks, which are equally spaced in real time, show how long it took the processor to traverse this path. [Tufte 1983] and [Tufte 1990] are essential reading for anyone interested in making displays of this form comprehensible.

All of the discussion above has been in terms of physical processors. While statistics related to these are usually easier to collect than statistics about particular processes, the latter are usually more interesting to programmers. One difficulty which performance visualization systems face is translating between these two types of data. If a processor supports several processes, for example, then it should be possible to display performance data separately for each, but still possible to determine the effect of competition between those processes for access to the processor's CPU and communication links. Similarly, if a process may have several different identities (as in the message-passing model outlined in Section 5.3), then users will almost certainly want sensible answers to questions like, "What percentage of the messages received by this process were replies to graphics requests?" Users might also want to visualize process performance in terms of program location, rather than real time. Systems which do not help users determine the coupling between behavior and code are much less useful than ones which do provide such information.

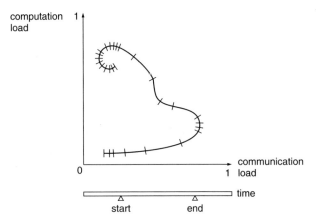

Figure 5.29
Tracing Processes in Load Space

5.5   Discussion

As should be evident by now, message-passing systems put a much greater burden on programmers than the systems examined in previous chapters. The use of channels forces programmers to do a lot of plumbing; the complexity has led some people to describe the CSP model as "the revenge of the goto." The need to call initialization functions in procedural message-passing systems, and the need to marshal and unmarshal data in most instances of them, makes programs which use them both larger and less readable than their data-parallel or shared-variable counterparts. It is only when channels are eliminated, and process-to-process communication handled either by application-building tools, or with compiler support, that this model becomes comfortable enough for application programming.

6 Generative Communication

Both of the control-parallel paradigms discussed so far have their weaknesses. Shared variables are relatively easy to use, but are difficult to support efficiently on large machines. Message passing, on the other hand, works as well on large machines as it does on small ones, but this does not actually say very much: for many application developers, message-passing programming feels all too much like systems programming, or assembly-level programming.

What programmers need is a paradigm which has the simplicity of the shared variables model, but scales like message passing. This chapter introduces one candidate for this role, called *generative communication*. Processes do not share variables in a generative system. Instead, processes all have access to a single shared space which is outside any of them. Generative communication takes its name from the fact that processes do not send messages to one another, but rather generate passive data structures in the shared space, which other processes may then read, alter, or delete. The generative model makes a distinction between local and non-local operations, but only just; the operations it allows on the shared space look very much like the operations normally found in a serial programming language.

The best-known implementation of the generative model is LINDA, which was developed by David Gelernter and Nicholas Carriero at Yale University [Carriero & Gelernter 1990b]. LINDA is not a new language, but rather a small set of operations which can be added to any serial language to produce a parallel dialect of it. This is one of the generative model's other strengths: it holds out the hope of recycling existing programs (and existing programmers) with a minimum of grief.

The sections below introduce the shared, associative memory which forms the basis for the generative model, and the operations which programs can perform in it. Mechanisms for creating processes are then described, along with some common ways of using the shared memory. Reasons why naive implementations of the generative model deliver poor performance are then discussed, along with ways of making implementations more efficient. Some variations on the basic model are then outlined. The chapter closes with a comparison between the generative model and three others which seek to achieve a similar mix of simplicity, expressivity, and efficiency.

6.1 The Generative Model

Generative communication, as implemented in FORTRAN-KGC, is a control-parallel paradigm. A generative system may contain any number of processes, but there are no direct connections between processes, and processes can never modify one another's internal states. Instead, processes communicate through a shared memory called a *tuple space*. Unfortunately, in order to understand how tuple space is used, it is necessary to know what it can do, but in order to understand what it can do, it is necessary to know how it is used. The description that follows introduces the "what", then the "how".

6.1.1 Tuples and Tuple Space

The generative model introduces only one new type of object, called a *tuple*. Like a FORTRAN-K record, a tuple is an ordered, finite collection of typed fields. Each field may either contain a particular value, called an *actual*, or be an unvalued place-holder, called a *formal*. Formals are used in the pattern matching described below; some examples of tuples containing only actuals are:

```
{ "fred" }
{ "jane", 3 }
{ "worker", "boundary", 42, 5.112, (/(/0.3, 0.5112/), (/(/0.017, .2221/)/) }
```

The first of these tuples has a single field, which contains the string `"fred"`. The second tuple contains the string `"jane"` and the integer value 3, while the third contains two strings, an integer, a real, and a 2 × 2 array of reals.

Tuples only ever exist in a shared memory called tuple space, which can hold nothing except tuples. Processes themselves are outside tuple space, as shown in Figure 6.1. A process adds a tuple to tuple space using out. This operation takes as arguments one or more expressions; out evaluates those arguments in an unspecified order, then creates a tuple containing the results of those evaluations. For example, the following fragment of code would create the three tuples described above:

```
type(string)        :: label_1 = "fred"
integer, constant   :: i = 3
type(string), auto :: label_2
integer             :: j
real                :: block(2, 2)
      .
      .
      .
label_2 = "jane"
j = 42
block(1, 1) = 0.3000 ; block(1, 2) = 0.5112
block(2, 1) = 0.0170 ; block(2, 2) = 0.2221
      .
      .
      .
out label_1
out label_2, i
out "worker", "boundary", j, 5.112, block
```

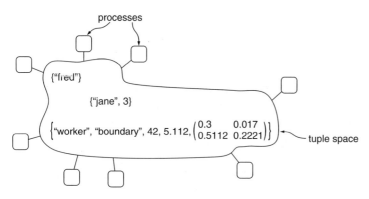

Figure 6.1
Tuple Space

A write-only memory is not particularly useful, so the generative model provides two operations for reading and removing tuples. The first of these is called rd. Like out, it takes one or more expressions as arguments, but rather than adding a tuple to tuple space, rd blocks its caller until a tuple whose fields match its arguments can be found in tuple space. Thus, a process which executed:

```
rd "jane"
```

when tuple space contained only the three tuples described above would be allowed to proceed, but one which executed:

```
rd "mary"
```

would not, since no tuple containing only the string "mary" could be found and matched in tuple space. This process would only be unblocked if and when some other process later added a tuple containing nothing but the string "mary".

The second generative input operation is in. This behaves exactly like rd, except that it deletes the tuple which it matches. A given tuple can therefore only be ined once, but may be rded any number of times. Processes can synchronize with one another by using tuples very much as they would semaphores. Suppose that a single copy of a tuple {"sem"} has been created. A process can do the equivalent of waiting on this "semaphore" by executing:

```
in "sem"
```

If the tuple is in tuple space at the time, the in will proceed, and delete the tuple. Any other process which then tries to claim it will block. The process which did claim it can later perform the equivalent of a signal operation by re-creating the tuple using out (Figure 6.2a). This technique can easily be extended to create a counting semaphore with a value of N, simply by putting N identical {"sem"} tuples in tuple space during initialization. The first N processes which wait on the semaphore these tuples represent will each erase one of the tuples; the $(N + 1)^{th}$ process to try to wait will then be blocked until one of its predecessors signals by putting a new {"sem"} tuple in tuple space (Figure 6.2b). Note that each tuple matches exactly one in, because this operation is destructive, but can match any number of non-destructive rds.

The problem with in and rd as presented so far is that a process must know exactly what it is looking for in tuple space before an operation can go through. This is rather like requiring processes to know the value of a variable before being allowed to look it up in memory, and just as restrictive. In order to allow processes to communicate with one another through tuple space, or to create shared data structures in it, the generative model allows them to specify incomplete tuples, or *anti-tuples*, when performing ins and rds. All of the fields in the tuples seen so far have been actual fields, i.e., they have had both a type and a value. An anti-tuple is one containing one or more formal fields. A formal field (or formal for short) has a type, but does not have a value. Formals are indicated in in and rd operations by prefixing the name of a variable or data type with a question mark (?), as in:

```
integer      :: i, b(4)
type(string) :: s
    .
    .
    .
in "fred", ?i                          ! field 2 is formal
rd ?s, 3, ?b                           ! fields 1 and 3 are formals
```

The nature of a field is called its *polarity*; an anti-tuple's fields may have any mix of polarities.

When a process uses an anti-tuple in an input operation, any tuple which matches the anti-tuple may be used to satisfy the operation. A tuple and an anti-tuple match if and only if:

1. they have the same number of fields;

2. the types of corresponding fields are the same; and

3. the values of corresponding fields which are both actuals are the same.

Table 6.1 shows several tuples and anti-tuples which match or fail to match, and explains

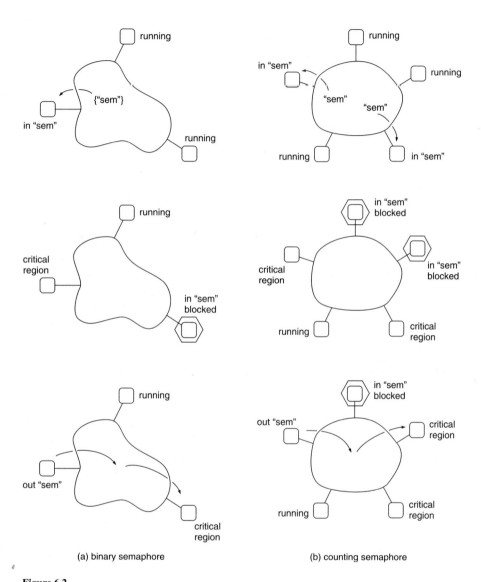

(a) binary semaphore   (b) counting semaphore

Figure 6.2
Building Semaphores from Tuples

Table 6.1
Tuple Matching Examples

```
integer :: i = 3, j = 4, X(3), Y(2, 2), Z(4)
logical :: b
```

Anti-Tuple	Tuple	Match?	Comments
{2}	{2}	yes	values match
{2}	{3}	no	values do not match
{i}	{3}	yes	types and values match
{i}	{2}	no	types match, but values do not
{?i}	{2}	yes	types match (i ← 2)
{?i, ?b}	{2, .true.}	yes	types match
{?b, ?i}	{2, .true.}	no	types do not match in order
{X}	{(/1, 2, 3/)}	error	actual-actual array matching illegal
{?X}	{(/1, 2, 3/)}	yes	types and shapes match
{?X}	{(/1, 2, 3, 4/)}	no	shapes fail to match
{?Y}	{Z}	no	shapes fail to match

the reasons in each case. As before, if no tuple matching the anti-tuple given in a `in` or `rd` operation can found, the process performing the operation is blocked until a match becomes available.

When the run-time system finds a match for an anti-tuple, it copies some or all of the values in the matched tuple into the memory of the process performing the operation. The rule governing this is simple: if a formal field was specified using a variable, that variable is assigned the corresponding value in the matched tuple. Table 6.2 shows the copying that would take place after each of the successful matches of Table 6.1.

Some implementations, but not FORTRAN-KGC, allow users to use type names as formals, as in:

```
real :: v
   .
   .
   .
in "matchstick", ?integer, ?v
```

Fields of this kind constrain what matching can take place without communicating information.

Three features of tuples and anti-tuples need mention here. First, if a field is a formal, then the whole of the field is a formal. There is no way to specify that part of an array-

Table 6.2
Copying After Tuple Matching

Anti-Tuple	Tuple	Bindings
{2}	{3}	none
{i}	{3}	none (i already has value 3)
{?i}	{2}	i = 2
{?i, ?b}	{2, .true.}	i = 2
		b = .true.
{?X}	{(/1, 2, 3/)}	X = (/1, 2, 3/)

or record-valued field is formal, and part of it actual. Second, a tuple may not contain pointers; the behavior of systems in which pointers are put into tuples is undefined (and usually disastrous). This rule prevents processes from modifying one another's internal state, either deliberately or accidentally. For this reason, FORTRAN-KGC uses shallow copying (page 189) when putting records in tuples. Finally, while every field of a tuple has a type, tuples themselves are untyped. There is no need to declare a tuple structure before using it, as there is with FORTRAN-K records.

Tuples are not stored inside processes like other data structures. Instead, as mentioned above, they are stored in a separate tuple space, which has four important properties:

1. It is shared: all processes work with the same tuple space, and tuple space can be accessed by any process.

2. It is a bag, not a set: tuple space may contain many identical tuples.

3. It is associative: items are removed from tuple space using the pattern-matching rules described above, rather than by being addressed directly. In this respect, tuple space is rather like a cache.

4. It is anonymous: once a tuple has been placed in tuple space, the system does not keep track of who created it or when. A program may include information in tuples to keep track of where they came from or where they are to be used, but managing this is the programmer's responsibility.

Note that if there are several tuples in tuple space which could match a particular anti-tuple, the system is allowed to choose an arbitrary match using any deterministic or non-deterministic rule. For example, suppose that a process has created two tuples using:

```
integer :: i = 5, j = 3
   .
   .
   .
```

```
out "single", i
out "single", j
```

After these operations, tuple space would contain the tuples {"single", 5} and {"single", 3}. The code:

```
integer :: k
    .
    .
    .
rd "single", ?k
```

would then assign either 3 or 5 to k, depending on which tuple the system "saw" first. If some other process had already executed:

```
in "single", 5
```

however, the rd call could only bind 3 to k, since the {"single", 5} tuple would have been removed from tuple space. If some process had executed:

```
in "single", ?k
```

then there would only be one value that the rd could match, but it could be either of 3 or 5, depending on which tuple the previous operation had *not* matched.

Some systems allow process to out tuples containing formals; however, formals in anti-tuples are never allowed to match formals in tuples. This rule ensures that in and rd can always bind values to their formal arguments. If, for example, one process created a tuple using:

```
out "fred", ?x, 25
```

then that tuple could not be ined or rded using:

```
in "fred", ?y, ?z
```

since that would leave y unbound. Since FORTRAN-KGC does not allow formals in out operations, this problem does not arise.

6.1.2   Process Creation

The last of the generative model's basic operations is eval. This has the same eventual result as out, i.e., it installs a tuple in tuple space, but it achieves this in a roundabout way. Instead of evaluating each field, and then creating a tuple to hold the results, eval creates a place-holder in tuple space called an *active tuple*, then creates one new process to evaluate each field of that tuple. Each of these processes runs until it returns a value, which then fills in the appropriate field of the active tuple. Once all of an active tuple's fields have been filled in, it turns into a normal tuple, indistinguishable from those created by out. As long as any of its processes are still running, an active tuple cannot be matched by an in or rd operation. Normal tuples are often called *passive tuples* in order to distinguish them from those whose fields are still being calculated.

For example, assume a program contains the functions:

```
real function f(a)
  real :: a
  .
  .
  return something
end function
real function g(b, c, d)
  real :: b, c, d
  .
  .
  return something
end function
```

and the variable definitions:

```
real :: x, y, z
```

Executing:

```
eval "example", x, f(x), g(x, y, z)
```

would then create four new processes: one to evaluate the constant "example", one to evaluate x, one to evaluate f(x), and one more to evaluate g(x, y, z). In practice, any sensible implementation would just install the values of "example" and x in the tuple directly, rather than creating new processes for this purpose.

The processes created by eval are peers of their creator—there is no intrinsic connection between them and their parent, and they may themselves use any generative operation, including eval. In this sense, eval has some similarity to the future construct of Section 4.3. It is quite common for a process to use eval to create processes which calculate values which it will need later on, and for it then to in the results, as in:

```
! process needs to calculate "z = f(x) + f(y)"
eval "result", f(x)                        ! f(x) will proceed concurrently
tmp_1 = f(y)
in "result", ?tmp_2
z = tmp_1 + tmp_2
```

Unlike the processes created by a `future`, however, the processes created by an `eval` do not have access to their parent's private memory, and cannot read or modify any of their parent's values. This rule can be difficult to enforce in a program which contains global variables. Suppose that a function which is `eval`ed at some point in a program not only references, but also modifies, a global variable x. When the `eval` takes place, the run-time system can:

1. make a copy of that global variable for the new process to use;

2. allow the new process to access its creator's copy of that variable;

3. signal an error; or

4. allow the effects to be undefined.

The first option will be expensive if the global variable is a large array or complex linked structure; however, some generative systems do support it. The second option is unsafe, as it would result in many processes performing unprotected operations on the same variable. The third option is the best, but to keep FORTRAN-KGC simple, it uses the fourth instead. As a rule, good generative programs do not contain global variables.

In order to simplify its implementation, FORTRAN-KGC only creates processes to evaluate tuple fields whose top-most operation is a function call. Thus, if a process executes:

```
eval "tag", 1 + f(a, b)
```

a new process will *not* be created to evaluate `f(a, b)`, since this call is nested beneath an addition. Note that processes created by `eval` in FORTRAN-KGC programs should *not* rely on `id_abs_self` and similar functions to determine their own identity. These functions are only guaranteed to return sensible answers for processes created by a `create` statement; the FORTRAN-KGC run-time system is free to assign arbitrary IDs to processes created by `eval`. In practice, it is always best to pass an explicit ID as a parameter to the `eval`ed function.

6.2   Managing Data Structures in Tuple Space

The description above of how tuples are manipulated does not convey the richness of the ways in which tuple space may be used. In general, programs add, copy, and remove tuples for three different reasons: to communicate information directly to other processes, to create shared data structures which other processes may access at their leisure, and to synchronize. One of the beauties of the generative model is that it reduces these operations to variations on a theme.

6.2.1   Simple Data Structures

The simplest data structure of all is a named scalar, whose value can be read or written atomically. Scalars can be implemented using binary tuples, in which the scalar's name is the first field, and its current value the second. Once the tuple has been created, its value can be read using:

```
rd "name", ?val
```

and written using:

```
in "name", ?val
out "name", new_val
```

Note that the in-out sequence automatically guarantees that this update is atomic. Any other process attempting to overwrite the same tuple using the same sequence of calls will block at its in call until the tuple becomes available again. This blocking can be exploited to implement both binary and counting semaphores, as discussed earlier.

One shortcoming of using tuples as semaphores is that the generative model does not guarantee fairness. If, after a single copy of the tuple {"sem"} has been put in tuple space, two processes both execute the code:

```
do while .true.
  in "sem"
  critical operations
  out "sem"
end while
```

there is no guarantee that the system will not *livelock*, giving the tuple to one process again and again while starving the other. This problem was discussed in Section 4.2.2, and can be tackled using something like a ticketing algorithm. Program 6.1 shows the two functions needed to signal and wait on a ticketed semaphore, as well as the structure of a process which might use these functions. Note that there is still no firm guarantee that this will be fair, since one process might repeatedly race through its work and grab the next ticket before a second process has a chance to claim its turn. However, in practical situations this behavior would probably only occur if there were more processes than there was work for them to do.

Tuples can represent indexed data structures such as arrays by storing indices along with values. To represent a 3-dimensional array of size $P \times Q \times R$, for example, a program would create tuples of the form {"x", p, q, r, v}, where p, q, and r would lie in the

```
procedure wait_turn()
  integer :: ticket
  in "ticket", ?ticket
  out "ticket", ticket+1
  rd "turn", ticket
end procedure

procedure signal_next()
  integer :: turn
  in "turn", turn
  out "turn", turn+1
end procedure
```

Program 6.1
A Generative Ticketing System

ranges $1\ldots P$, $1\ldots Q$, and $1\ldots R$ respectively, and v would be the current value of the $(p, q, r)^{\text{th}}$ element of the array x. Reading and writing would then be done with:

```
rd "name", i, j, k, ?val
```

and:

```
in "name", i, j, k, ?val
out "name", i, j, k, new_val
```

respectively, just as with scalars.

This representation is easy to use, but has one important drawback: storing the indices of each element explicitly greatly increases the memory required to represent the array. If processes usually access patches of arrays, rather than single elements, it may be more efficient to store sub-sections of the array in tuples. An $M \times N$ array, for example, could be stored as M tuples containing the array's name, a row index, and an array of N values, or as $\frac{M}{m} \times \frac{N}{n}$ tuples, each holding the indices identifying its least significant corner and an $m \times n$ sub-array, and so on. Such representations can be particularly useful in numerical operations such as matrix multiplication. A careful programmer will choose a format for storing arrays which permits all of these strategies as special cases. Users can then tune their programs simply by altering the shape and number of storage blocks, without re-writing all of their access operations. Optimizations of this kind will be discussed in greater detail in Section 6.5.

The reading and writing operations shown above all index the tuple-space representation of arrays in the same way that a serial program would, i.e., they specify indices, and

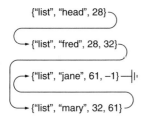

Figure 6.3
A Linked List in Tuple Space

either set or fetch the values associated with those indices. A program could, however, take advantage of tuple space's associative matching by specifying a value but giving formals in place of the corresponding indices, as in:

```
rd "name", ?i, ?j, ?k, some_val
```

This operation would try to match against a value in the array which had the value `some_val`, and return to the process that value's location. Essentially, this is the equivalent of the intrinsic function `dp_locate` in FORTRAN-KDP (Section 3.3.3). However, if no element of the array had the specified value, the calling process would block until it appeared. In addition, mixing access patterns in this fashion would almost certainly reduce the overall performance of the system, for reasons which will be discussed in Section 6.5.

6.2.2 Linked and Indexed Data Structures

More complicated data structures, such as graphs, queues, and stacks, can be implemented in tuple space using explicit indexing techniques that would be familiar to any 1960s FORTRAN programmer. Consider, for example, a linked list of strings. As shown in Figure 6.3, each tuple representing a list element has four fields: the list's name, its string value, an integer index which is unique within that list, and the index of the next element in the list (or some distinguished end-of-list value). The index identifying the head element of the list is stored separately in a 3-valued tuple whose fields are the list's name, a key word such as "head", and the index. Note that there is no danger of mistaking the head-of-list tuple for a list element, since the two have different numbers of fields.

How processes manipulate these tuples depends entirely on how much concurrency can safely be allowed. If a process simply wanted to read down the list to see if a particular string was present, it could use:

```
integer, constant :: EOL = -1                    ! marker for end of list
```

.
.
.

```
logical function gclist_str_present(list_name, key)
  type(string) :: list_name            ! name of list
  type(string) :: key                  ! key to search for
  type(string) :: list_str             ! string in current element
  integer      :: index                ! current and next index
  logical      :: result = .false.     ! result

  ! find head of list
  rd list_name, "head", ?index

  ! traverse list
  do while (.not. result) .and. (index /= EOL)
    rd list_name, ?list_str, index, ?index
    if str_cmp(list_str, key) = 0 then
      result = .true.
    end if
  end while

  ! report
  return result
end function
```

Note how the rd call inside the loop uses the old value of index to identify the next tuple to read, but simultaneously overwrites index with the value which identifies the next tuple.

Inserting and deleting elements would seem to be equally simple. A process which wanted to insert an element after an element with a known index could use:

```
procedure gclist_str_ins(list_name, pred, key)
  type(string) :: list_name            ! name of list
  integer      :: pred                  ! index after which to insert
  type(string) :: key                  ! key to insert
  type(string) :: str                  ! needed so that out will work
  integer      :: next_index            ! index of next element in list
  integer      :: new_index             ! index identifying new element
```

```
! get a unique new index
new_index = gclist_index(list_name)

! find which element is currently after pred
in list_name, ?str, pred, ?next_index

! change its pointer value
out list_name, str, pred, new_index

! insert new element
out list_name, key, new_index, next_index

end procedure
```

Here, the function `gclist_index` returns an integer index which is guaranteed not to be in use anywhere else in the list; its implementation is:

```
integer function gclist_index(list_name)
    type(string) :: list_name          ! name of list
    integer      :: index               ! index created

    in list_name, "index", ?index
    out list_name, "index", index+1

    return index
end function
```

The `in` which follows this function call removes the tuple which is to become the predecessor of the element being added. This `in` is necessary because there is no way to modify a tuple while it is in tuple space: the only way to make changes is to remove one tuple and install another. The first `out` then puts this element back in tuple space, having changed its next-element index value to point at the list element which is being inserted. The last `out` creates the new element, and includes a pointer to its successor in the list.

Deleting a list element is equally simple, and is left as an exercise. However, these simple functions have a serious flaw: they do not enforce mutual exclusion. Suppose one process A was trying to insert a new element in the list between the elements with indices x and y, while another process B was trying to delete element y. A could in element x, find that the next element had index y, and then create an element whose index was z, and whose "next" field pointed at element y. At the same time, however, B could delete

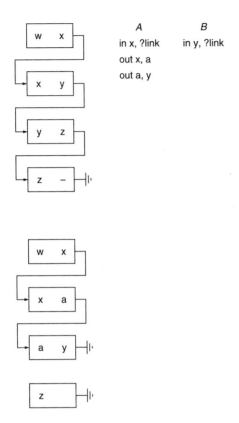

Figure 6.4
Accidental List Splitting

element y. The result would leave the list split in two (Figure 6.4). One way to prevent this would be to associate a semaphore tuple with the list, i.e., to enforce mutual exclusion on it. If every operation on the list had to acquire the semaphore before reading or modifying the list, all updates would be guaranteed to be consistent.

Doing things this way would be safe, but would also serialize all operations on the list. A less drastic solution would be to have processes `in` all of the tuples they were working with at any particular time. If, for example, `gclist_str_present` were to `in` list elements one by one, and then `out` them once the strings they contained had been checked, any process which tried to add or delete list elements would be blocked while the parts of the list it was trying to manipulate were being inspected by other processes. We can re-implement `gclist_str_present` along these lines as:

```
logical function gclist_str_present(list_name, ken)
    type(string) :: list_name              ! name of list
    type(string) :: key                    ! key to search for
    type(string) :: list_str               ! string in current element
    integer      :: index, next_index      ! current and next index
    logical      :: result = .false.       ! result

    ! find head of list
    rd list_name, "head", ?index

    ! traverse list
    do while (.not. result) .and. (index /= EOL)
      in list_name, ?list_str, index, ?next_index
      if str_cmp(list_str, key) == 0 then
        result = .true.
      end if
      out list_name, list_str, index, next_index
      index = next_index
    end while

    return result
end function
```

Note that in this implementation the order of the newly-inserted elements will be non-deterministic: if two processes are trying to insert new list elements after the same element, then one or the other process will manage to in that element first. However, the state of the modified list will be consistent with some serialization of the operations which created it.

A general directed graph can be implemented using this same technique, or one very similar to it. If the arity of each node in the graph is known to be bounded by a small integer N, the best way to implement the graph may be to include N fields in each tuple to hold the indices of the nodes on the other end of each of the edges connected to the node. If, on the other hand, the number of edges out of a node can be large, or cannot be bounded in advance, the best thing may be to store each node using two tuples. The first tuple of each pair holds the graph's name, the node's index, its value, and a count of the number of edges out of it. The second tuple holds an array containing the indices of the nodes on the other ends of those edges. This split representation allows a process to allocate enough memory to hold the array of edges between ining the node's tuple and ining the tuple

```
procedure add_edge(graph_name, node_1, node_2)
  type(string)     :: graph_name              ! graph being manipulated
  integer          :: node_1, node_2          ! node IDs
  type(value_type) :: value_1, value_2        ! values in nodes
  integer          :: count_1, count_2        ! edge counts
  integer          :: edge_1(:), edge_2(:)    ! neighbor arrays (edges)

  ! get nodes to be connected (allocating extra edge storage)
  if (node_1 < node_2) then
     call get_node(graph_name, node_1, value_1, count_1, edge_1, 1)
     call get_node(graph_name, node_2, value_2, count_2, edge_2, 1)
  else
     call get_node(graph_name, node_2, value_2, count_2, edge_2, 1)
     call get_node(graph_name, node_1, value_1, count_1, edge_1, 1)
  end if

  ! connect nodes
  edge_1(count_1 + 1) = node_2
  edge_2(count_2 + 1) = node_1

  ! restore
  call put_node(graph_name, node_1, value_1, count_1+1, edge_1)
  call put_node(graph_name, node_2, value_2, count_2+1, edge_2)
end procedure

procedure get_node(graph_name, node, value, count, edge, extra)
  type(string)     :: graph_name              ! graph being manipulated
  integer          :: node                     ! node ID
  type(value_type) :: value                    ! value in node
  integer          :: count, edge(:)           ! edge count and edges
  integer          :: extra                     ! extra storage to allocate

  in graph_name, node, ?value, ?count
  call allocate(edge, count+extra)
  in graph_name, node, ?edge
end procedure
```

Program 6.2
Adding an Edge to a Directed Graph in Tuple Space

```
procedure put_node(graph_name, node, value, count, edge)
  type(string)      :: graph_name        ! graph being manipulated
  integer           :: node              ! node ID
  type(value_type)  :: value             ! value in node
  integer           :: count, edge(:)    ! edge count and edges

  out graph_name, node, value, count
  out graph_name, node, edge(1:count)
end procedure
```

Program 6.2 *(continued)*
Adding an Edge to a Directed Graph in Tuple Space

holding its edges. Program 6.2 shows code which adds a new edge to connect two nodes. The code to remove edges, and to add and delete nodes, is similar.

A tuple which is used to store an index, like the one used to label list elements in the previous example, is called a counter tuple. Such tuples can be used for many other purposes as well. Queues, for example, can be implemented by using counter tuples to keep track of the head and tail index of the queue's elements. As with a one-dimensional array, each tuple representing an element of a queue contains the queue's name, the item's index, and the item's value. The head and tail tuples then store the indices identifying the current head and tail of the queue, just as the head index of a linked list identifies the first element in the list. To append an item to a queue, a process executes:

```
procedure gc_enqueue(queue_name, value)
  type(string) :: queue_name        ! name of queue
  integer      :: value             ! value to enqueue
  integer      :: index             ! new index

  ! update tail pointer
  in queue_name, "tail", index
  out queue_name, "tail", index+1

  ! add element
  out queue_name, index, value

end procedure
```

To take a value from the queue's head, a process performs the analogous operations on the queue's head tuple, *in*ing rather than *out*ing an item tuple.

One potential drawback of this implementation is that the dequeueing operation is committal. Because of the blocking nature of the final in, a process cannot back out of dequeueing a value if one is not available. Instead, dequeueing processes race ahead of enqueueing processes, creating "debts" which enqueueing processes must satisfy (Figure 6.5). If this is not desired, it can be prevented in one of two ways. The first is to introduce an extra tuple to count the number of values currently in the queue, and to have both enqueueing and dequeueing processes surround their actions with complementary ins and outs of this tuple. The second way to avoid trying to dequeue items which have not yet been enqueued is to store the head and tail indices in the same tuple. Since both approaches serialize operations on the queue to the same extent, but the latter requires fewer interactions with tuple space, it is generally preferred. Non-committal dequeuing then looks like:

```
logical function gc_dequeue_or_fail(queue_name, value)
   type(string) :: queue_name          ! name of queue
   integer      :: value                ! value dequeue
   integer      :: head, tail           ! head and tail indices
   logical      :: result               ! was something dequeued?

   ! check if operation possible
   in queue_name, "indices", ?head, ?tail
   if head >= tail then
     out queue_name, "indices", head, tail
     result = .false.
   else
     out queue_name, "indices", head+1, tail
     in queue_name, head, ?value
     result = .true.
   end if

   return result
end function
```

Stacks are more difficult to support. The simplest way to implement a stack would seem to be to record the index of the value at the top of the stack in a counter tuple, and to have pushing and popping processes increment and decrement this count respectively. However, consider a situation in which several attempts are made in a row to pop a value off an empty stack. These would build up debts of the sort shown in Figure 6.6. If subsequent

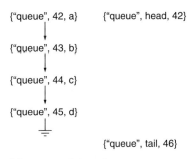

{"queue", head, 42}

{"queue", tail, 46}

(a) queue contains values

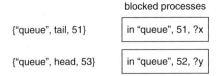

blocked processes

{"queue", tail, 51} | in "queue", 51, ?x |

{"queue", head, 53} | in "queue", 52, ?y |

(b) queue empty with 2-element debt

Figure 6.5
Creating "Debts" by Pre-Fetching Items from a Queue

pushes and pops were interleaved, some processes would be starved of tuples and trapped near the bottom of the stack. The source of this problem is that, unlike a queue, a stack re-uses index values.

6.2.3 Sets

Superficially, tuple space would seem a good medium in which to implement a set. Each set element could be represented by a binary tuple holding the set's name and the element's value, while members could be added to and deleted from the set using out and in respectively.

The reality is more complicated, and highlights some weaknesses in the standard generative model. Suppose we were to represent a set of integers using binary tuples of the form {"S", 0}, {"S", 29}, and so on. How would the three basic operations of addition, deletion, and membership testing be implemented? The first could not be done with a simple out, as this might lead to there being multiple copies of the element in tuple space at the same time. Conversely, we could not test for membership using in or rd, because these would block indefinitely if the element being looked for was not in the set. And even if a safe membership test member existed, we could not delete tuples using:

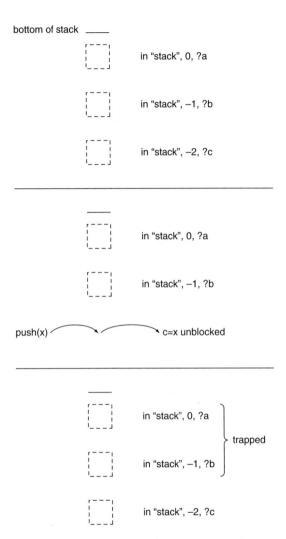

bottom of stack ____

in "stack", 0, ?a

in "stack", −1, ?b

in "stack", −2, ?c

in "stack", 0, ?a

in "stack", −1, ?b

push(x)   c=x unblocked

in "stack", 0, ?a ⎫
                  ⎬ trapped
in "stack", −1, ?b ⎭

in "stack", −2, ?c

Figure 6.6
Problems with Stacks

```
if member("S", i) then
  in "S", i
end if
```

because the operation would not be guaranteed to be atomic. If two processes A and B were trying to delete element i of the set, their operations could be interleaved so that A's membership test succeeded, but B then deleted the tuple, leaving A blocked on its in indefinitely.

A different method is to store the set as triples. For every value v that could possibly be in the set, there would be a tuple of the form {"S", v, present}, where present would be either .true. or .false.. This implementation is analogous to the bit-vector representation used to represent small sets in implementations of many languages, and suffers from the same drawback: the amount of storage required is proportional to the number of possible set elements, rather than to the number of elements actually in the set at any time. (Clearly, a lot of memory would be required to represent a set of arbitrary 32-bit integers.)

A compromise is to hash set elements, and to store each hash bucket in a tuple of its own. Suppose a function hash exists, which takes an arbitrary set element and returns a pseudo-random value h in the range $1 \le h \le H$, where H is reasonably small. The bucket holding elements whose hash code was h would be stored in two parts, just like the graph nodes on page 403. The first part would be a tuple of the form ("S", "size", h, ℓ), where h was the hash index and ℓ was the number of elements currently associated with that hash index. A second tuple of the form ("S", "vals", h, A) would then hold the elements in an array A, whose length would be no more than ℓ. This split representation is used so that a process can check that it has set aside enough space to hold a hash bucket before trying to in it. Program 6.3 shows a function which deletes an element from a set if it is present; the code to add an element is similar.

One shortcoming of using a hashed implementation is that operations on set elements which happen to have the same hash code are serialized. A more serious objection is the expense, both in programming and at run-time, of inserting and deleting elements in the arrays used to represent set fragments. There is therefore a tradeoff between the degree of concurrency an implementation permits and the amount of data copying which must be done to support it. The best compromise between these can only be found by considering the particulars of each application.

6.2.4   Barriers

Barrier synchronization is another common operation which is tricky to implement in the generative model. A barrier's purpose is to synchronize Π processes. Superficially, this is

```
procedure gc_set_delete(set_name, value)
  type(string)      :: set_name              ! set to work with
  type(value_type) :: value                  ! value to delete
  integer           :: hash_dex, len         ! tuple values
  type(value_type) :: old(:), new(:)         ! hash slices
  integer           :: i, j                  ! loop indices

  ! get old values
  hash_dex = hash_function(value)            ! determine slice
  in set_name, "size", hash_dex, ?len        ! find length
  call allocate(old, len)                    ! enough storage for current
  call resize(new, len-1)                    ! empty storage for result
  in set_name, "vals", hash_dex, ?old        ! get old values

  ! copy all but value to be deleted
  j = 1
  do i = 1, len
    assert j < len                           ! check for overflow
    if old(i) /= value then
      new(j) = value
      j = j + 1
    end if
  end do
  assert j == len-1                          ! check exactly one deleted

  ! create new values
  out set_name, "size", hash_dex, len-1
  out set_name, "vals", hash_dex, new
end procedure
```

Program 6.3
Deleting an Element from a Set

quite easy: each process ins a tuple containing the name of the barrier and the count of
processes which have reached the barrier so far, increments the count, and then rds a tuple
containing the barrier's name and the value Π:

```
procedure gc_bar(bar_name, quorum)
  type(string) :: bar_name                  ! name of barrier
  integer      :: quorum                    ! how many must arrive
  integer      :: n                         ! number so far
```

```
! register arrival
in bar_name, ?n
out bar_name, n+1

! wait
rd bar_name, quorum

end procedure
```

The `rd` in this function blocks its caller until the Πth process has incremented the barrier, which is exactly what is wanted.

But now suppose that this barrier is being used repeatedly, e.g., that the processes which are synchronizing are doing so during each iteration of a loop. After all Π process have passed their `rd`s, the barrier tuple is still in tuple space. Unless its value is somehow re-set, the next round of calls to `gc_bar` will increment its value from Π to 2Π. If this happens, no process will ever pass the barrier, as the `rd` call will never find a tuple containing the value Π.

One way around this problem is to add a generation number to the barrier tuple. Each process must then keep track of the number of times it has performed barrier synchronization. The nth time a process synchronizes, it waits on a barrier tuple whose generation number is n; after all of the processes have synchronized, that tuple is never accessed again. Only a small change to the synchronization function is required:

```
procedure gc_bar2(bar_name, generation, quorum)
     type(string) :: bar_name          ! name of barrier
     integer      :: generation         ! which barrier this is
     integer      :: quorum             ! how many must arrive
     integer      :: n                  ! number so far

     ! register arrival at generation'th barrier
     in bar_name, generation, ?n
     out bar_name, generation, n+1

     ! wait at generation'th barrier
     rd bar_name, generation, quorum

end procedure
```

Processes can then safely use loops like:

```
do index = start, end
  calculate
  call gc_bar2("some_barrier", index, num_processes
end do
```

There are, however, still two problems to be resolved. The first is that this implementation leaves "stale" tuples in tuple space, which represent barriers which have been passed by all processes. If a program performs many iterations of many loops, these stale tuples will eventually consume a considerable amount of memory.

More troubling is the problem of initializing barriers. In order to make the barrier work, someone must add a tuple containing a barrier's name, a generation number, and an initialized count to tuple space. One possibility is to make one of the synchronizing processes the barrier creator, and have it unilaterally out the initial tuple (with a count of one, to show that it has reached the barrier itself) rather than in and out a pre-existing barrier tuple.

This approach works, but is clumsy. Instead of being able to create workers by looping over a single eval, a program must make one worker special:

```
! create barrier creator
eval "worker", worker(params, .true.)
! create everything else
do i = 2, num_worker
  eval "worker", worker(params, .false.)
end do
```

Similarly, the worker function must not only keep track of the barrier at which to synchronize, but also whether to create the barrier tuple or look for one that someone else has created.

Another approach is to create a separate barrier manager process whose job it is to create new barrier tuples and clean up old ones. A barrier manager starts by creating the first two barrier tuples that its clients will require. Once it sees that barrier i has been passed, it deletes the tuple associated with that barrier and creates one to manage the $i + 2^{\text{th}}$ barrier. Barriers are created two steps ahead of their use, rather than one, to ensure that the barrier manager does not mistakenly delete a barrier tuple before every process that needs to rd it has done so. Code to implement a barrier manager which works this way is shown in Program 6.4. Note that gc_bar_man is a function, rather than a procedure, because eval only creates new processes for function calls.

```
integer function gc_bar_man(bar_name, quorum)
   type(string) :: bar_name            ! name of barrier
   integer      :: quorum              ! number of clients
   integer      :: generation          ! current generation

   ! create initial barriers: generation = 0, 1, count = 0
   out bar_name, 0, 0
   out bar_name, 1, 0

   generation = 1
   do while .true.
      ! make sure ith barrier reached
      rd bar_name, generation, quorum
      ! initialize i + 1th barrier
      out bar_name, generation+1, 0
      ! clean up i − 1th barrier
      in bar_name, generation-1, quorum
   end while

   return 0                            ! never executed
end function
```

Program 6.4
A Generative Barrier Manager

6.3   Active Data Structures

All of the examples shown so far have assumed that processes are relatively long-lived, like the processes in a message-passing system. However, the generative model supports another style of programming in which each process performs just enough calculation to create one element of a data structure, then turns into that element. Sets of processes doing this are called "active data structures", and programs which rely on them are often very similar to the futures-based programs of Section 4.3.

For example, consider the multiplication of two $N \times N$ matrices A and B, each of whose elements is stored in a separate tuple. Instead of fixing the number of processes doing the multiplication, and having each calculate many elements of the product, a program could eval one process to calculate each element of the result (Program 6.5). This program creates N^2 processes, each of which then executes gc_mmult_elt to calculate one element of the $N \times N$ result matrix C.

```
program
  integer :: i, j                                    ! loop indices
  real    :: A(N, N), B(N, N)                        ! multiplicands
  real    :: C(N, N)                                 ! result

  initialize A and B

  ! create evaluators
  do i = 1, N
    do j = 1, N
      eval "C", i, j, worker(A(i, :), B(:, j))
    end do
  end do

  ! collect results
  do i = 1, N
    do j = 1, N
      in "C", i, j, ?C(i, j)
    end do
  end do
end program

real function worker(row, col)
  real    :: row(:), col(:)                          ! to be multiplied
  integer :: i                                       ! index
  real    :: val                                     ! (i, j) value

  val = 0.0
  do i = 1, size(row, 1)
    val = val + row(i) * col(i)
  end do

  return val
end function
```

Program 6.5
Generative Matrix Multiplication

```
program
  logical :: patch(N, N)            ! to fill
  integer :: i, j                   ! traversal
  real    :: x, y                   ! coordinates

  ! calculate
  x = X0
  do i = 1, N
    y = Y0
    do j = 1, N
      eval i, j, mandel(x, y)
      y = y + Inc
    end do
    x = x + Inc
  end do

  ! fill
  do i = 1, N
    do j = 1, N
      in i, j, ?patch(i, j)
    end do
  end do
end program
```

Program 6.6
A Self-Evaluating Task Farm

Another way to use active data structures is to create a task farm in which every job simply becomes a result. Instead of creating some fixed number of workers, and distributing J jobs amongst them, a program can create J processes, each of which transforms a single job into a result tuple. The program can then in their results. A program which calculates the Mandelbrot Set in this fashion is shown in Program 6.6.

Example 6.1 (Adaptive Quadrature)   Because eval can be expensive compared to other tuple space operations, it is usually not cost-effective to use active data structures to perform regular computations, such as the matrix multiplication shown above. However, active data structures can be a very powerful way to express irregular computations, in which the work to be done cannot be known in advance. An example of this is the use of divide and conquer to perform numerical quadrature. Suppose a real function f and an interval $[a, b]$ have been specified, and a program is to calculate an approximation to $\int_a^b f$. One way to do this is to calculate two approximations to the integral, one finer than the other, and compare them. If their values are sufficiently close, and if f is reasonably smooth, then it is safe to assume that a still finer approximation would probably not yield a significant increase in accuracy. If their values are not sufficiently close, however, then the interval can be subdivided and this same procedure applied to each half recursively.

A pair of functions which use tuple space to hold the irregular tree of processes and results which are built up during divide and conquer is shown in Program 6.7; Figure 6.7 shows how quadrature might proceed in one particular case. Note that the string `name`, used to identify the tuples created during quadrature, is specified by the program which calls `gc_quad`. We do this so that many quadratures with different names can run concurrently without colliding with one another. Note also the recursive step in `gc_quad_recurse`, which either returns the better of the two values which have been calculated directly, or creates two new processes to improve on those values.

6.4   Message Passing Through Tuple Space

Many computations are naturally expressed as concurrent operations on shared data structures, or as active data structures, but many others seem more suited to the message-passing model. Simple message passing is easy to support in the generative model, but more sophisticated operations can be surprisingly difficult.

If two processes have agreed on the structure of the messages which are to pass between them, then a simple exchange of data can be accomplished using:

Sender	Receiver
`out "msg", data`	`in "msg", ?data`

A key feature of this example is that messages are anonymous—the receiver has no way of knowing where the message it has just received originated. This is adequate for those applications in which the origin of messages is implicit in their contents.

Example 6.2 (A Generative Message-Passing Task Farm)   Program 6.8 shows code for a simple task farm that uses message passing through tuple space, rather than active structures, to generate the Mandelbrot Set. Unlike earlier message-passing task farms in Examples 5.1 and 5.5, the source in this one does not have to keep track of which processes are ready to accept more work. Instead, it puts all of the work to be done into tuple space at the beginning of the program, then waits until it has retrieved the corresponding results. It then creates a single end-of-work tuple. When a worker `ins` this, it puts it back into tuple space (to terminate another worker) and fills in its own active tuple with the number of jobs it has done. The main program can then tidy up tuple space by `in`ing the workers'

```
real function gc_quad(name, x0, x1, tol)
  type(string) :: name                   ! name of quadrature
  real         :: x0, x1                  ! bounds on interval
  real         :: tol                     ! tolerance
  real         :: result                  ! value calculated
  ! start calculation
  eval name, x0, x1, gc_quad_recurse(name, x0, x1, tol)
  ! get and return result
  in name, x0, x1, ?result
  return result
end function

real function gc_quad_recurse(name, x0, x1, tol)
  type(string) :: name                    ! name of quadrature
  real         :: x0, x1, tol             ! parameters
  real         :: result                  ! value calculated
  real         :: y0, y1, y_mid           ! function values
  real         :: v_one, v_two            ! integral values
  real         :: x_mid = (x0 + x1)/2.0   ! calculate estimates

  y0    = f(x0)
  y1    = f(x1)
  y_mid = f(x_mid)
  v_one = (x1 - x0) * ((y0 + y1)/2.0)
  v_two = (x1 - x0) * ((y0 + (2 * y_mid) + y1)/4.0)

  ! accept or recurse
  if +(v_two - v_one) < tol then
    result = v_two
  else
    eval name, x0, x_mid, gc_quad_recurse(name, x0, x_mid, tol/2.0)
    eval name, x_mid, x1, gc_quad_recurse(name, x_mid, x1, tol/2.0)
    in name, x0, x_mid, ?y0
    in name, x_mid, x1, ?y1
    result = y0 + y1
  end if

  return result
end function
```

Program 6.7
Generative Quadrature

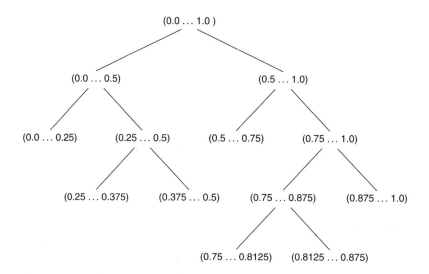

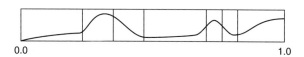

0.0   1.0

Figure 6.7
An Example of Adaptive Quadrature

tuples, and then in the end-of-work tuple itself. Note that the order of operations here is
very important: if the main program outs the end-of-work tuple before it has collected the
results from all of the jobs it has created, workers will start to terminate themselves before
all jobs have been done.

The first version of this program contained a serious error. In the loop labelled *retrieve
values*, the operation:

```
in "result", i, j, ?patch(i, j)
```

was mis-typed:

```
in "result", i, j, patch(i, j)
```

```
program
  logical :: patch(N, N)          ! to fill
  integer :: i, j                 ! traversal
  real    :: x, y                 ! coordinates

  ! create workers
  do i = 1, W
    eval "worker", worker(i)
  end do

  ! create jobs
  x = X0
  do i = 1, N
    y = Y0
    do j = 1, N
      out "job", i, j, x, y
      y = y + Inc
    end do
    x = x + Inc
  end do

  ! retrieve values
  do i = 1, N
    do j = 1, N
      in "result", i, j, ?patch(i, j)
    end do
  end do

  ! terminate workers
  out "job", 0, 0, 0.0, 0.0
  do i = 1, W
    in "worker", ?j
    write std_out, "%d jobs\n", j
  end do
  in "job", 0, 0, 0.0, 0.0

  ! display
  call print_patch(patch)
end program
```

Program 6.8
A Message-Passing Generative Farm

```
integer function worker(id)
  integer :: id                                    ! ID
  real    :: x, y                                  ! point location
  integer :: i, j                                  ! point indices
  integer :: num_done = 0                          ! number of jobs done

  in "job", ?i, ?j, ?x, ?y
  do while i > 0
    out "result", i, j, mandel(x, y)
    num_done = num_done + 1
    in "job", ?i, ?j, ?x, ?y
  end while
  out "job", i, j, x, y

  return num_done
end function
```

Program 6.8 *(continued)*
A Message-Passing Generative Farm

The missing question mark turned the formal parameter `patch` into an actual. As a result, most of the pattern matches failed, and the program deadlocked.

More sophistication than this is required to support general communication between many processes. For example, suppose that a server process S is to handle requests from an arbitrary set of client processes. If request and reply tuples contain only the name of the service, and the parameters describing the client's request or the server's reply to it, there is no way that a client can be sure that the reply it has `in`ed is the one corresponding to its request. Code which suffers from this flaw would look like:

```
procedure client(···, service_name, ···)
  type(string) :: service_name                     ! name of service being used

  do while working
  .
  .
  .
    out service_name, "request", request specification
    in service_name, "reply", reply values
  .
  .
  .
  end while
end procedure
```

```
procedure server(···, service_name, ···)
   type(string) :: service_name              ! name of service being used

   do while working
     .
     .

     in service_name, "request", request specification
     perform service
     out service_name, "reply", reply values
     .
     .

   end while
end procedure
```

This problem can be circumvented by introducing a counter tuple, and having each client obtain a unique index for each of its requests:

```
procedure client(···, service_name, ···)
   type(string) :: service_name              ! name of service being used
   integer      :: index                     ! value in counter tuple

   do while working
     .
     .

     in service_name, "index", ?index
     out service_name, "index", index+1
     out service_name, "request", index, request specification
     in service_name, "reply", index, reply values
     .
     .

   end while
end procedure

procedure server(···, service_name, ···)
   type(string) :: service_name              ! name of service being used
   integer      :: id                        ! ID of request

   do while working
     .
     .
```

```
    in service_name, "request", ?id, request specification
    perform service
    out service_name, "reply", id, reply values
      .
      .
      .
  end while
end procedure
```

Note that the server shown here does not necessarily handle requests in their indexed order; there is no guarantee, for example, that request i will always be handled before request $i + 1$. The index added to each request is simply a way of identifying that request. If such ordering was required, it would be easy for the server to make the id field in its in an actual, rather than a formal, and increment id after outing each reply. This would in effect re-create the ticketing algorithm shown earlier.

A cheaper indexing scheme which can be used in many applications is for each client to get an index the first time it makes a request of the server, and to re-use that index in each transaction. This scheme effectively assigns clients server-specific IDs according to the order in which they first interact with the server. Labelling processes this way eliminates the cost of accessing the index tuple associated with the server at the start of each transaction. However, an application which does this cannot permit a client to have more than one request outstanding at a time, i.e., cannot allow a client to start one transaction and then do other work which might involve further transactions before the reply to the first transaction has been received. To see why, suppose that a client generated requests with:

```
out "request", own_id, request-1
out "request", own_id, request-2
in "reply", own_id, reply-1
in "reply", own_id, reply-2
```

while the server handled these operations using:

```
do while .true.
  in "request", ?id, request
  process request
  out "reply", id, reply
end while
```

Nothing would prevent the server from picking up the client's second request first, processing it, and generating a reply which the client might then mistakenly interpret as being associated with its first request. The solution is for the client to index each request as it is generated, and then use that index when `ining` the reply, as in:

```
out "request", own id, 1, request-1
out "request", own_id, 2, request-2
in "reply", own_id, 1, reply-1
in "reply", own_id, 2, reply-2
```

and:

```
do while (true)
  in "request", ?id, ?serial, request
  process request
  out "reply", id, serial, reply
end while
```

Many more variations on this theme are clearly possible. In general, programmers should try to design protocols which involve the fewest tuple-space operations, but which enforce enough synchronization or matching to ensure correct behavior. When in doubt, it is always safest to start with a restrictive protocol (such as identifying each transaction with a unique index), and then modify it later.

Many-to-one communication is relatively straightforward to implement, since only one of the communicating processes needs to be identified. If any-to-any communication is to be supported, each message must identify both its sender and its receiver, so that processes can pick up only those messages intended for them, and can reply to those messages' originators. In general, generative programs may use as unsophisticated a naming scheme as they wish. If, for example, there is only one set of replicated processes, then each can be identified using a single integer, like the processes in the crystalline model discussed in Section 5.2. If the possible configurations of a program are more complicated, then something like the structured process groups of Section 5.3 may be needed. It would be easy to create a generative implementation of the task-farming harness introduced in Program 6.8 which used requests and replies like Example 5.5. While more complicated than its predecessor, it would have the advantage that job tuples would only generated as required, and so the amount of tuple space memory required to store them would be much less.

One obstacle to emulating the message-passing facilities of the previous chapter with generative communication is that the generative model does not allow a process to have several `in` or `rd` operations outstanding at the same time. In FORTRAN-KMP, for example, a process may initiate several non-blocking receives on different types of messages, then wait for one of them to complete. The only way to get the same functionality in FORTRAN-KGC is to require that all of the messages sent to a process have the same format, i.e., the same number and types of fields. If messages actually have different structures, this forces programmers to marshal and unmarshal data by hand. As has been pointed out before, this is complicated, tedious, and error-prone.

Another problem with using tuple space for messaging is that it does not guarantee that messages will arrive in the order in which they are sent. It is quite possible for a sending process to out two tuples and for their intended destination to pick them up in reverse order. For example, if two processes P and Q are managing neighboring sections of a decomposed grid, and each must send boundary values to its neighbors at the end of each iteration, then P could get so far ahead of Q that two successive boundary tuples from P wound up in tuple space at the same time. There would be no guarantee that Q would not pick up a boundary that was in its future, and do subsequent calculations incorrectly.

The third difficulty which must be faced when using tuple space for message passing is the difficulty of supporting broadcast. Broadcast can sometimes be emulated by having processes rd rather than in tuples, so that the message remains in tuple space for other processes to see. However, this requires receivers to know which messages have been sent to them directly, and which have been broadcast, which often complicates coding. In addition, since the tuple representing the broadcast message is left in tuple space, one message might be seen many times by a single process. The alternatives to this are either using repeated point-to-point sends (i.e., repeatedly outing the same message, with different identification fields), or including a count in the tuple representing the broadcast message, and having the message's source consume the tuple once all the members of the receiving group have seen it. This second option leads to broadcast code that looks like:

```
out "msg", ?int, 0, data
in "msg", ?int, group_size, ?data-type
```

and reception code like:

```
in "msg", id, ?count, ?data
out "msg", id, count+1, data
```

Note how the broadcaster outs a formal instead of an actual destination ID, so that every process can pick up the tuple as if it were a direct message.

Despite such cleverness (which is not allowed in FORTRAN-KGC), this approach is still unsatisfactory, as it serializes the receiving operations (which in a sensible system would be done concurrently), and allows race conditions. If one process ins and outs a broadcast tuple several times in succession, other processes may be starved of it. Allowing programs to do broadcasts more elegantly is one motivation for enhancing the basic generative model in the ways discussed in Section 6.6.

6.5   Implementing Generative Communication

While the generative model is elegant, it can only be considered useful if implementations of it can be as efficient as implementations of lower-level systems. This section describes some of the techniques which have been developed for implementing generative communication on both shared- and disjoint-memory computers.

6.5.1   Tuple Stores and Basic Operations

One of generative communication's strong points is that it is only a coordination language, not a new computing language. Its four basic operations can be (and have been) added to almost any existing serial language. The first step in implementing it is therefore to incorporate the four basic operations (in, rd, out, and eval) into a suitable host language. The usual way to do this is to build a pre-compiler which replaces each generative operation with a sequence of function calls to marshal data and either send messages or modify a shared region of memory; a similar pre-compiler was discussed in Section 5.3.4. This expanded program is then compiled by the normal compiler. Thus, the generative operation:

```
integer :: i, j
    .
    .
    .
in "tuple", ?i, j+5
```

might be translated into function calls such as:

```
call gc_open_tuple(str_len("tuple") + Formal_Len + Int_Len)
call gc_field_string_actual("tuple")
call gc_field_int_formal()
call gc_field_int_actual(j+5)
call gc_close_tuple()
call gc_op_in()
call gc_store_int(i)
```

gc_open_tuple checks to make sure that there is not some other tuple under construction (which should never happen), then initializes the support library's internal state. Its argument indicates how much storage space is needed to represent the tuple. Each field construction function then adds a single field to the tuple, incrementing a count of the number of fields in the tuple as it does so. Actual variables are passed by value; for formal fields, the system creates a formal marker in the tuple. The tuple is then closed, and the appropriate operation invoked.

If the operation is an `in` or a `rd`, and contains any formals, then when the operation completes, the tuple space manager must send values back to the process. When the process is re-scheduled, its first actions must be to bind these values to the appropriate variables. This is why the last function call in the list above stores an integer value in `i`: when the low-level `gc_op_in` call returns, it leaves a binding for `i` in a known location for this function to pick up.

One tricky aspect of this method is that there must be some globally-agreed coding which can identify the types of all values which may be stored in tuples. Without this, the process or processes responsible for managing tuple space cannot perform matching correctly, and might mistakenly allow (for example) a sequence of four null bytes and a 32-bit integer with the value 0 to match one another. One way to achieve such a coding is to restrict the types of tuple fields, e.g., to allow only intrinsic types, and arrays of intrinsic types, to be tuple fields. A better technique is to have the pre-compiler keep a record of the types of values it sees, and assign a unique tag to each new type as it is encountered. These tags can be stored in an auxiliary file, which can then be loaded and used by the run-time system. As Section 6.5.4 describes, there are many other uses for such a record of tuple space operations.

6.5.2   Process Creation

`eval` is relatively straightforward to provide in languages like Lisp and Prolog, which treat descriptions of functions as if they were data, and allow such descriptions to be copied and assembled at run-time. It is much more difficult to implement in imperative languages like C, FORTRAN, and FORTRAN-K. In most implementations of such languages, the pre-compiler must search through a program to determine what functions might be executed as free-standing processes. It must then create, compile, and link small executables containing the code for those procedures, and any procedures they call. The run-time system can then load one copy of each of these executables into each of the machine's address spaces. Each time an `eval` is encountered in the program's source, the system creates a record indicating which executable is to be run, and what parameters it is to be given. When the `eval` is executed, the system creates a new process block in the appropriate address space, and points it at the correct executable.

As mentioned in Section 6.1.2, a more serious problem with `eval` is what to do about references to global variables. Suppose that a process is created to `eval` a function `f`, which refers a variable `glbl` whose definition is outside `f`. If `f` is to be able to read `glbl`,

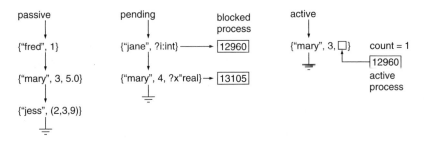

Figure 6.8
A List-Based Implementation of a Tuple Store Manager

then either the process created to execute f must be given a copy of glbl, or it must be allowed to read a variable in its parent. The first option can be expensive, particularly if glbl is a large data structure, but it is still preferable to the second because it is more modular. Forbidding the use of global variables in this way is one other possibility, as is throwing up one's hands and saying, "It's the user's responsibility."

Implementations also face the problem of what to do with parameters modified by evaled processes. When this happens, the system may either allow those changes to be reflected inside the parent of the process created by the eval, discard the changes, or simply signal an error. The first is easy to support in shared-memory systems, and the second on disjoint-memory machines. The last is what FORTRAN-KGC does, as it is the most consistent with the treatment of parameters to outed tuples.

6.5.3   Implementing a Tuple Store Manager

The simplest way to implement tuple space is to have a single server process manage all tuple space operations. Every in, out, rd, or eval operation sends a request of this manager, either by putting values in a known location and signalling the manager (on a shared-memory machine), or by sending a message to the manager (on one with disjoint memory). In either case, when the manager completes the operation it sends an acknowledgement and any bindings that may be appropriate back to the process. If the operation was an eval, the manager also signals the run-time system that a new process is to be created, and specifies the executable which is to be run.

A tuple store manager (TSM) such as this must do three things: it must store tuples, it must perform pattern matching on them, and it must ensure that processes are created, blocked, and terminated properly. The first two problems can be solved by storing tuples and anti-tuples in three linked lists (Figure 6.8). The first list holds tuples available for matching; the second holds anti-tuples which have not been matched, while the third holds active tuples whose fields are still being evaluated.

When a tuple is created by an `out`, the TSM searches the list of unmatched anti-tuples to see whether any of them can now be satisfied. Any number of `rds`, and one `in`, may be satisfied by the same tuple. As `rds` are matched, the TSM sends any appropriate values back to the corresponding process for binding. If an `in` is matched, the TSM sends back values and then stops searching. If no `ins` are found, the tuple is added to the passive tuple list.

When a `rd` or `in` occurs, the TSM performs a similar sweep on the list of passive tuples. If there is already a matching tuple in tuple space, then the appropriate bindings are sent back to the process immediately (and the passive tuple deleted if the operation was an `in`). If no match can be found, the anti-tuple is added to the list of pending anti-tuples, where it remains until a subsequent `out` or `eval` finds a match.

Finally, when an `eval` is executed, a dummy tuple is created in the active tuple list. The system gives each process which is evaluating a field of this tuple a reference to it, and to its particular field. When such processes terminate, they send their values to the TSM. Once the last value needed has been received, the TSM handles the new passive tuple as if it had just been `out`ed.

One drawback of this implementation is that that the time required to do an operation grows linearly with the number of tuples in tuple space, or with the number of processes which are waiting for operations to complete. A more efficient method is to use the pre-compiler's analysis of the kinds of tuples which processes will generate. As well as transforming generative operations into sequences of subroutine and function calls, the pre-compiler can record the *genus* of tuple involved in each operation. A tuple genus is defined by the cross-product of the types (and, for arrays, dimensions) of its fields. The tuples {"A", 3} and {"B", 29}, for example, both belong to the genus `string` × `integer`, while {"X", 3.14, (/.true., .false./)} belongs to the genus `string` × `real` × `logical(2)`.

Once the run-time system has classified each of the tuples and anti-tuples manipulated by a program, it can create a separate list for each genus. Since tuples of different genera can never match (either because they have a different number of fields, or because their fields are of different types), a TSM only has to look at tuples in the sub-list corresponding to the genus involved in a particular operation. Separating tuples in this way can dramatically reduce the amount of searching required.

If it is not possible to determine the genus of all possible tuples in advance (for example, if the host language being used allows tuple space operations to be created dynamically), another way to improve the efficiency of a TSM is to use hashing. As a tuple is generated, information about the types and sizes of its fields is fed to a hashing function, which generates a hash code for that tuple. So long as the values in the tuple's fields have no effect on this hash code, all tuples which could match one another will have the same code. Instead of using one list per genus, the TSM can simply use one list per hash code. If the hashing function is random enough, and the space of hash codes large enough, it is unlikely that tuples with different genera will be stored in the same list.

The second job of the TSM is to ensure that processes are created, blocked, and terminated at the right times. If, when a process is created, it is passed a reference to the active tuple into which its return value is eventually to be placed, then there is no need for multiple lists of active tuples. Instead, each time the last process contributing to an active tuple terminates, and the tuple becomes passive, it can just be inserted in the appropriate list. Process creation in languages in which programs can be represented as data, and constructed on the fly, is more difficult. If the body of the function to be executed is constructed at run time, it may be necessary to package that function's description into a message and include it along with the tuple being `evaled`. Clearly, the larger the function being `evaled`, the more expensive this will be.

6.5.4   Implementing a Distributed Tuple Space

Having one manager per genus can still lead to poor performance in both shared- and disjoint-memory implementations, as it only delays the onset of contention and serialization. Once enough processes are running, and enough operations are being done on tuple space, one genus's TSM will eventually become a bottleneck. The only scalable solution is to find a way to distribute tuples belonging to one genus. The obvious way to do this is to use several TSMs to manage each genus, and to distribute these TSMs as evenly as possible. However, this must be done very carefully. Tuple space must behave like a shared memory; all operations on it must appear to have taken place sequentially, although their order may be arbitrary. Any distributed implementation which allows programs to see some behavior which is inconsistent with this model is incorrect.

The key to solving this problem is to notice that many input operations can only ever match a small subset of the tuples belonging to a given genus. Consider, for example, a program which uses geometric decomposition and boundary value swapping to perform some calculation on a mesh. Each of Π processes has a unique ID p, $1 \leq p \leq \Pi$. During each iteration, process p outs the tuples:

{`"boundary"`, p, `"left"`, *data*}

and:

{`"boundary"`, p, `"right"`, *data*}

If tuples are only partitioned by genus, then all boundary value tuples will be sent to the same TSM. This will happen even though tuples with particular values of p are only ever generated in one place, and consumed in another.

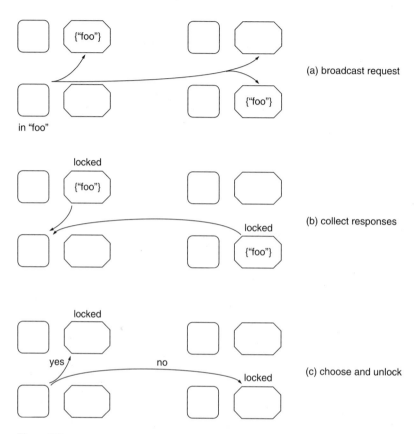

(a) broadcast request

in "foo"

(b) collect responses

(c) choose and unlock

Figure 6.9
Implementing Tuple Space Using Broadcast

A partial solution would be to store every tuple where it was created, or on some randomly-chosen processor. out would then be cheap, but rd and in would be expensive. Since an ining process would not know which processor or processors might contain possible matches, it would have to broadcast to all those which might. Since these processors could not know what replies would be sent by other processors, they would all have to respond to every broadcast. The broadcasting process would then have to select one of the replies, send a message to the processor whose tuple it wanted, and send its apologies to all the others (Figure 6.9).

This technique would generate an inordinate volume of network traffic, since each TSM would send or receive at least two messages every time an operation was performed. What is worse, all of the TSMs involved in the transaction would have to block until the

transaction was completed. To see why, imagine what would happen if a TSM was allowed
to start one operation on some genus of tuple before another on that genus had completed.
If both requesting processes decided that they wanted a tuple from the TSM, and it only
had one, it would have to send a follow-up message to one or the other process to back
out of the transaction. That process would then have to broadcast its request again.[1] As
the number of processes interacting with these TSMs increased, the protocol required to
ensure consistency would quickly drown the system.

A better way to distribute tuples of the same genus is to use the presence of any constants, or variables whose value can be known or bounded during compilation, to sub-
divide each genus into as many *species* as possible. Consider a boundary-swapping program again. The main loop for each process will resemble:

```
do i = 1, number of iterations
  out "boundary", "left",  ID, left boundary
  out "boundary", "right", ID, right boundary
  update interior points
  in "boundary", "left",  mod1((ID-1), num_wrkr), ?right boundary
  in "boundary", "right", mod1((ID+1), num_wrkr), ?left boundary
end do
```

If the compiler can determine that ID and num_wrkr are constant for each processor,
and can determine their values, the run-time system can create one TSM for each of the
species:

```
"boundary" × "left" × 0 × data format
"boundary" × "left" × 1 × data format
.
.
.
"boundary" × "left" × num_wrkr-1 × data format
```

and:

```
"boundary" × "right" × 0 × data format
"boundary" × "right" × 1 × data format
.
.
.
"boundary" × "right" × num_wrkr-1 × data format
```

---

1. This is analogous to the problems which would be encountered if a CSP-based system allowed processes to
alt on both input and output, as discussed in Section 5.1.2.

Once this is done, the actual implementation of tuple space looks more and more like that of a buffered message-passing system. Each TSM is a buffer of (theoretically) infinite size, whose contents are unordered; while any process may put a message in any buffer, or request a message from any buffer, in practice each buffer only has one reader and writer. If the number of workers cannot be known in advance, then the system can use a very simple hashing function to distribute boundary tuples among an arbitrary number of TSMs. This hashing function can be as simple as $i \bmod N$, where i is the integer index identifying the tuple's source, and N is the number of buffers. Since both the writing and the reading process specify a value for i, there is never any ambiguity about which TSM to use.

This idea can be pushed further still by eliminating some tuple space operations entirely. For a start, once the values of the strings which are usually included in tuples in order to help identify their contents (such as the strings "boundary" and "left" used above) have been used to divide tuples into species, they can then be eliminated, or replaced with integer constants. The point of this is not to economize on memory, but to reduce the amount of marshalling, matching, and unmarshalling which the run-time system has to do. Such replacement can be handled entirely by the pre-compiler, which can store the strings the program actually used in a table to allow comprehensible error-reporting.

Similarly, suppose that the pre-compiler finds that some process is executing the cliché:

```
in some_string, ?int_val
out some_string, int_val+1
```

Rather than pay the cost of actually ining and outing a tuple, the run-time system could replace this with a fetch&add operation (Section 4.2.2). This particular optimization, and the more general replacement of:

```
in some_string, ?val
out some_string, val ⊕ constant
```

with fetch&op, can have a dramatic effect on program performance. Since the tuple is never removed, many more operations can potentially be done on it in a fixed time, and less bandwidth used.

A further refinement of this is to optimize the larger cliché:

```
in some_string, ?val
out some_string, val ⊕ constant
in some other string, val, ?data
```

Code like this is often used to implement queues and other indexed structures, and can be replaced with a triangle of messages as shown in Figure 6.10. If a pre-compiler notices

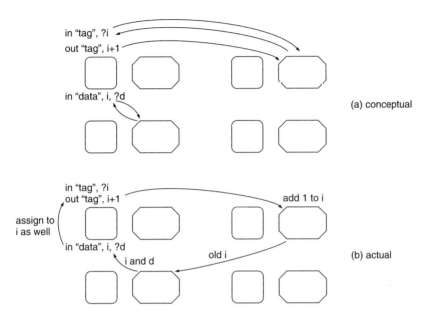

Figure 6.10
Triangular Messaging in a Generative System

that pattern matching is only done on some species of tuple in order to access the data in its members, not to select among them, tuples of that species can be stored in a simple queue or stack, and pattern-matching eliminated completely. In a task farm, for example, the most sensible place to put the TSM responsible for job tuples is the address space in which the source process resides. Even more sensible is to replace operations such as a worker process's call:

```
in farm_name, "job", ?keep_looping, job description
```

with a simple request message containing no pattern-matching information whatever, to which the source replies directly, without ever actually creating a job tuple [Carriero & Gelernter 1990a].

Taking this approach to its logical extreme, a very intelligent pre-compiler could analyze programs to determine whether it is cheaper to move tuples to processes, or operations to tuples. Replacing in-operate-out sequences with fetch&ops is a simple example of this, but if only a few different operations are ever performed on tuples, it may make sense to compile those operations into functions and store those functions with the appropriate TSMs. Allowing this level of sophistication blurs the run-time distinction between user processes and tuple store managers, although to the programmer they are still conceptually very different.

These transformations may be implemented either in the pre-compiler, or by allowing programmers to annotate their code using compiler directives like those used to describe data partitionings (Section 3.5). In either case, the tuple space operations which are being done must be analyzed very carefully. Suppose, for example, that the operations:

```
in "example", ?b0, false
```

and

```
in "example", true, ?b1
```

both occur in a single program, where b0 and b1 are logical variables. It is no longer possible to break the genus string × logical × logical into species based on the second field being .true., or the third field being .false., because tuples like {"example", .true., .false.} could match either of these templates. In this case, all tuples of the genus string × logical × logical would have to be stored in a single TSM so that pattern matching could be done correctly.

However, this does *not* mean that the generative model is intrinsically inefficient. Any program which wanted to allow processes to access records of this sort by value would also have to store all possible matches centrally, and perform some search to find matches. The secret to making distributed systems of any kind efficient is to allow fine-grained partitioning of data; one of the great strengths of the generative model is that it makes it easy to see what kinds of operations are being done on what kinds of data structures, which can make it easier for programmers to identify the causes of performance bottlenecks.

6.6 Enhancing Generative Communication

While the standard generative model described in the preceding sections is enough to support a wide range of parallel programming paradigms, it has, as we have seen, some annoying shortcomings. Many things which seem as though they ought to be easy to implement, such as sets, turn out to be difficult, while some of the model's most attractive features, such as its automatic marshalling of data, must be foregone by programs which use message passing in any non-trivial way.

Most implementations of generative communication include some non-standard operations [Jellingham 1990, Leler 1990, Anderson & Shasha 1991, Bakken & Schlichting 1991, Ciancarini 1991, Jagannathan 1991, Doberkat et al. 1992, Hasselbring 1994]. The aim of such enhancements is usually to increase the model's modularity, its efficiency, or its ability to support commonly-used data structures or paradigms. Modularity is an issue for the same reason that it is in message-passing systems: libraries written independently may use the same names for different entities, which can make it unsafe to build large programs by combining smaller ones. At the same time, a program which attempts to instantiate several instances of a single library at the same time can find that they interact, often with disastrous consequences. These problems are similar to those which must be faced in the design of message-passing systems, and the solution described below is similar to that used in the previous chapter.

Enhancements intended to increase efficiency are often proposed because present compilation techniques are often not adequate to find optimizations which programmers know to be possible. Allowing programmers to make these operations explicit may in fact make the compiler simpler, as it can concentrate on doing what it's told, rather than on trying to second-guess programmers. To counterbalance this, the run-time system must inevitably be more complex, as it must support more types of activity. As in all computer systems, the best balance between power and complexity is difficult to find.

Finally, some things simply cannot be done using the basic operations. A process cannot back out of an operation, for example, or ask for any one of several different types of tuple simultaneously. Several of the enhancements described below address issues such as these.

6.6.1 Predicate Operations

One way to sidestep many of the problems with the standard model is to provide conditional forms of the two input operations. In fact, most implementations contain so-called *predicate* forms of in and rd, which are called inp and rdp. These attempt to perform the same operations as their namesakes, but return a signal if they cannot find a tuple to match their anti-tuple. For example, when inp is invoked, it attempts to in a tuple matching its anti-tuple. If it finds such a tuple, it removes the tuple, performs any appropriate value binding, and returns .true.. If it cannot find such a tuple, it returns .false., and does not modify any of its arguments. rdp works in an analogous fashion.

Some data structure manipulations are much easier to implement when these operations are available. Testing set membership, for example, is exactly a rdp, in which it is the value returned by the rdp, rather than any binding which takes place, which is of interest. However, predicate operations are not a panacea; even with a membership test such as this it is not safe to add elements to a set in the obvious fashion, as there is no guarantee that the race condition identified in Section 6.2.3 will not occur.

Using predicate operations also makes it easier to trade off storage space, access granularity, and concurrency to create a reasonably efficient and robust implementation of many data structures. The key in doing this is to rely on a hashing scheme similar to the one outlined in Section 6.2.3, or the one which generative communication might use internally.

Suppose that, as before, we wish to implement a set of integers, and have defined some hashing function `hash` which takes an integer as an argument and returns a value h in the range $1 \ldots H$. We can consider all tuples whose values have the hash code h_i as belonging to some logical partition ℓ_i of the set, and create a set of lock tuples of the form:

```
{"S", "lock", h}
```

where $h \in \{1 \ldots H\}$. Each process must then in this lock tuple, and thereby lock the logical partition of the set it wishes to work on, before carrying out fragile operations. For example, to add an element to a set, a process would execute:

```
procedure gc_set_out(val)
   integer :: val                       ! value to add
   integer :: lock_id
   lock_id = h(i)                       ! determine which lock to use
   in "S", "lock", lock_id              ! lock
   inp "S", i                           ! removes i if it is in the set
   out "S", i                           ! put i (back) in the set
   out "S", "lock", lock_id             ! unlock
end procedure
```

Predicate operations must be implemented very carefully in order to make their behavior well-defined. Unlike non-predicate operations, their definition requires assertions about the global state of tuple space, which can be difficult or expensive to satisfy in a disjoint-memory environment. By definition, `in` and `rd` block until a matching tuple is found. This allows the way in which they search tuple space for such a tuple to be left undefined. In particular, if A, B, and C are processes, then the following sequence of operations is legal:

A	B	C
	out "fred", 0	
request in "fred", ?i		
		request in "fred", ?i
		satisfy in "fred",
		?i with $i \leftarrow 0$
	out "fred", 1	
satisfy in "fred",		
?i with $i \leftarrow 1$		

The semantics of the predicate operations are much more demanding. When a predicate operation returns `.false.`, then at some instant, there was no matching tuple anywhere in tuple space. If the `in` operations in the example above were `inp`s, the sequence shown would be illegal. As a result, if potentially-matching tuples are distributed, then some protocol must be used to maintain the semantics of a centralized store. Such protocols can make predicate operations significantly more expensive than their non-predicate counterparts. If, on the other hand, tuple space is centralized, or equivalently if there is only one tuple store in which a tuple matching an `inp` or `rdp` could be found, guaranteeing the correct behavior of the predicate operations is not problematic, but their performance is limited by access contention.

In practice, predicate operations are usually no less efficient than their non-predicate counterparts, as the partitioning tricks discussed previously can be used without compromising their semantics. Another way of looking at this is to say that both types of operations allow users to do things which will cause poor performance; it is therefore the programmer's responsibility to think carefully about when and how tuple space is used.

6.6.2 Multiple Tuple Spaces

One of the biggest problems programmers must face when using the standard generative model is name collision. Since a single tuple space is shared by all processes, each part of the program must make sure that the tuples it manipulates are distinct from the tuples manipulated by each other part. By itself, including the name of each library or program portion as a field in every tuple manipulated by that library is inadequate, as it prevents multiple instances of the same library from running concurrently.

One solution is to provide many independent tuple spaces. The simplest model for this is to make the structure of tuple spaces completely flat, i.e., to give each tuple space an absolute name, and allow any process to operate on any tuple space. However, if tuple space names are (for example) arbitrary strings, then such a flat naming scheme forces programmers to structure tuple spaces manually by structuring those tuple spaces' names. This is little improvement over the flat naming scheme for tuples themselves which was criticized above.

A second option is to make tuple spaces a new data type, and to allow tuple spaces to be manipulated like any other data. A tuple space T_1 could be included in another tuple space T_2 by putting a tuple containing T_1 in T_2. A process could create a copy of a tuple space, and of all the processes running in it, by `rd`ing and `out`ing that tuple, or suspend all the processes in it by `in`ing the tuple [Gelernter 1989].

While this model is attractive, it would be very difficult to implement efficiently. One particular problem would be defining the behavior of such operations if several tuples contained references to the same tuple space, and were being manipulated independently. A third, and more attractive, option is to structure tuple spaces hierarchically in a manner exactly analogous to the nesting of directories in UNIX. Every tuple space is identified by a name, which is interpreted relative to the name of its parent tuple space. Processes can look up tuple spaces using an intrinsic function lookup, which takes a single string argument and returns an object whose type is ts. Operations which are to be done in a particular tuple space can then include a reference to that tuple space, as in:

```
type(tuple_space) :: ts1, ts2, ts3
integer           :: value
   .
   .
   .
ts1 = lookup("one")
ts2 = lookup@ts1("two")
out@ts2 "name", value
ts3 = ts2
in@ts3 "name", ?value
```

Here, the first call to lookup does not contain a reference to a particular tuple space, so it returns a reference to the tuple space "one" located beneath the tuple space holding the process making the call. This convention is adopted for two reasons. First, it makes these extensions upwardly compatible with the standard generative model: any code which does not use tuple space identifiers will work entirely within the single, default tuple space (analogous to the root directory of a file system). Second, without this convention, processes would have to be passed at least one tuple space identifier as a parameter when they were created, so that they would have a context within which to look up any other tuple spaces they required. This would not be difficult, but could quickly become tedious. Finally, by reserving special names such as "." and ".." within each tuple space to mean that tuple space and its parent, and by defining the parent of the root tuple space to be itself, this scheme can emulate the directory tree structure with which most programmers are already familiar.

The second lookup call in the example above looks up the tuple space "two" nested below "one" (Figure 6.11). The out then puts a tuple in this tuple space. Finally, the assignment from ts2 to ts3 copies the reference to ts2, just as if it were any scalar value. The final in call is therefore applied to the tuple space "two".

Tuple space identifiers are joined to function or subroutine names using @, rather than included as arguments to those operations, in order to avoid mixing arguments to tuple space functions with fields of tuples. In the operation:

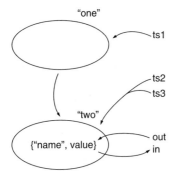

Figure 6.11
Nesting Tuple Spaces

```
type(ts) :: space
real     :: a, b, c
  .
  .
  .
out space, "name", a, b, c
```

for example, the nature and purpose of the first argument `ts` is qualitatively different from that of succeeding arguments, and should be kept separate in order to avoid confusion.

One important feature of this system is that tuple spaces may only be looked up directly through their parents; there is no direct equivalent of the multi-directory prefixes such as `/home/gvw/book` used in UNIX and other operating systems. Another important feature is that while tuple spaces may not be included in tuples, references to tuple spaces may. Thus, one process may execute:

```
type(tuple_space) :: ts1, ts2
integer :: value
  .
  .
  .
ts1 = lookup("top")
ts2 = lookup@ts1("bottom")
out@ts1 "look_at", ts2
out@ts2 "value", value
```

while another running in the same tuple space may call:

```
type(tuple_space) :: ts1, ts2
integer           :: value
```

```
        .
        .
        .
ts1 = lookup("top")
in@ts1 "look_at", ?ts2
in@ts2 "value", ?value
```

By ining and outing tuple space references in this way, processes can agree on where to put data for one another so that messages will not collide.

Finally, whenever a process lookups a tuple space which does not exist, that tuple space is created. Thus, if several processes have agreed on a name for a tuple space, they can all call lookup and get a correct result. The first lookup call creates the tuple space, while the subsequent ones simply return a reference to it. This behavior is like that of the mp_join function in Section 5.3.

One of the great advantages of using multiple tuple spaces is that an optimizing compiler only needs to know about patterns of reference within a single tuple space, rather than global reference patterns, in order to make decisions about eliminating fields, performing operations in place, and so on. This conceptual separation also means that large distributed systems can be constructed by using tuple spaces to separate processes which do not trust one another's behavior or longevity.

6.7   Some Other High-Level Alternatives

If nothing else, the generative model has served as a focus for (sometimes heated) discussion of the nature and aims of parallel programming systems [Carriero & Gelernter 1989, Davidson 1989, Kahn & Miller 1989, Kalé 1989, Shapiro 1989]. One of the strongest criticisms of it is that it is simultaneously too high-level—its associative matching seems intrinsically inefficient—and too low-level. The thrust of this latter argument is that the generative model only provides one type of data structure, out of which users must construct other, more useful, structures. This has been compared to FORTRAN (and OCCAM), which requires users to build record structures by hand using arrays.

An extension of this criticism is that it is more difficult for a compiler to optimize use of a single all-purpose data structure like tuple space than it would be for it to optimize use of several more specialized data structures. The question then is what those data structures should be, and how they should be presented to users. Each of the three systems discussed below provides a different answer.

6.7.1   Message Handlers and Shared Structures

The first system we consider is CHARM, developed by Laxmikant Kalé and his colleagues at the University of Illinois at Urbana-Champaign (UIUC) [Shu & Kalé 1991]. The organizing principle of CHARM is that a program consists of one or more processes, called chares, which can send and receive explicitly-typed messages. Each chare contains some local state, as well as one or more entry procedures (Program 6.9). Each entry procedure takes a single message structure as an argument; messages are declared using the same syntax as record structures. Chares communicate with one another by sending messages to particular entry procedures.

Every program must contain a single `main` chare, which must have an entry point called `init`. A single copy of this chare is created when the program is started. Further chares can then be created dynamically using:

```
type(id_type) function create_chare(chare_name, entry_point, init_msg)
  some_chare_type    :: chare_name
  procedure          :: entry_point
  some_message_type  :: init_msg
```

This function returns a unique ID for the chare being created, while creating a chare of the specified type on one of the available processors. The system then invokes the new chare's `entry_point` procedure with the specified message as an argument. Chares communicate using:

```
procedure send_msg(chare_id, entry_point, msg)
  some_chare_type    :: chare_name
  procedure          :: entry_point
  some_message_type  :: msg
```

to send a message to a particular entry procedure, and:

```
some_type function call_entry(chare_id, entry_point, msg)
  some_chare_type    :: chare_name
  procedure          :: entry_point
  some_message_type  :: msg
```

to invoke entry points that return a value. The return type of `call_entry` is determined by the return type of the `entry_point` function. Unlike the message-passing system of Section 5.3, messages for chares may be delivered in an arbitrary order.

Programs may also include a special type of chare called a branch office chare (BOC). When a BOC is created, one copy of it is installed on each physical processor. As well as the usual message-handling entry points, BOCs contain access functions which can be called directly by chares residing on the same processor. BOCs also contain private entry points which are used for communication between members of the same branch office

```
message_type msg_ctr_none                    ! message with no fields
end message_type

message_type msg_ctr_val                     ! message with value
  integer :: value
end message_type

chare counter
  integer :: state                           ! current state

  entry procedure init(msg)                  ! initialize or re-set
    message_type(msg_ctr_val) :: msg
    state = msg%value
  end procedure

  entry integer function fetch(msg)          ! fetch current value
    message_type(msg_ctr_none) :: msg
    return state
  end function

  entry integer function swap(msg)           ! swap with current value
    message_type(msg_ctr_val) :: msg
    integer :: old
    old   = state
    state = msg%val
    return old
  end function

  entry procedure incr(msg)                  ! increment current value
    message_type(msg_ctr_val) :: msg
    state = state + msg%value
  end procedure

end chare

    .
    .
    .
```

Program 6.9
A Simple Chare

```
procedure user(···)
  type(counter)                        :: counter_id
  messge_type(msg_ctr_none), auto :: msg_none
  message_type(msg_ctr_val), auto :: msg_val
  integer                              :: old_value
  .
  .
  .
  msg_val%value = initial value
  counter_id = create_chare(counter, init, msg_val)
  .
  .
  msg_val%value = another value
  old_value = call_entry(counter_id, swap, msg_val)
end procedure
```

Program 6.9 *(continued)*
A Simple Chare

group. BOCs are often used to implement system services: for example, processes access the file system through their local representative of the file system chare group. BOCs are also used to hide details of data distribution: a BOC might, for example, encapsulate a shared array. A chare would then access the array by calling one of the array BOC's local entry points. If the value needed was not stored locally, that BOC would request it from another BOC in the same group, then deliver the value to its caller.

This part of CHARM is a formalization of the structured message passing discussed in the previous chapter. Each chare can be thought of as a server, while entry procedures are analogous to the branches of the message-handling case statement which lies at the heart of most servers. However, CHARM also contains something which message-passing systems lack: shared data structures. Instead of requiring users to encapsulate shared structures inside processes, and invent access and modification protocols, CHARM provides five different mechanisms for sharing data. These can only be used in restricted ways, but because of that, their implementation can be optimized to take advantage of particular hardware. If users need a form of data sharing which is not supported directly by one of these mechanisms, they must fall back on the server-and-protocol approach of the lower message-passing level (although this is much easier to structure and build in CHARM than in a raw message-passing system).

The first sharing mechanism CHARM provides is read-only variables. These must be created during program initialization, i.e., during execution of the main chare's init entry procedure. A read-only variable is created using:

```
type(Id_Type) function create_rd_only(data)
  type(some_type) :: data
```

A chare reads its value using:

```
procedure read_shared(id, local_data)
  type(Id_Type)   :: id
  type(some_type) :: local_data
```

which copies the value(s) in the shared data structure into local memory. On disjoint-memory machines such as multicomputers and distributed computers, a read-only variable is implemented by giving each physical processor a copy of its value. Any process can then read the variable's value without performing communication. Since a read-only variable cannot be modified after its creation, there is no danger of these copies becoming inconsistent.

Write-once variables are similar to their read-only cousins, except that a program may create a write-once variable at any time using:

```
procedure create_wr_once(data, entry_point)
  type(some_type) :: data
  procedure       :: entry_point
```

This procedure creates the variable, assigns it a unique ID, and then sends a message containing that ID to the creating chare's `entry_proc` entry procedure. The creating chare can then share this ID with other chares so that they can access it using `read_shared`.

Two other types of shared data, accumulator and monotonic variables, can be modified by chares after their creation. An accumulator is a counter, which can be modified using one of two functions. The first combines a user-supplied value with the accumulator, while the second combines two accumulators. These functions must be commutative and associative; on disjoint-memory machines, the implementation of accumulators uses combining trees of the form discussed in Section 3.3.1. A monotonic variable is also a counter, but one whose value may only ever change in one direction (e.g., increase). The only function associated with a monotonic variable is the one which updates it based on a user-supplied value. The system guarantees that a change made to a monotonic variable by one chare will eventually be seen by all other chares, but does not guarantee when this will happen. Typically, monotonic variables are used to represent such things as the lower bound on cost found so far in a search problem, or the state of execution in a speculative problem. In the latter case, the variable's value only ever changes once, from 0 (no answer found) to 1 (answer found).

The last shared structure supported by CHARM is the most general. A dynamic table is a hash table containing zero or more entries, each comprised of a key and some data. Functions are provided to create a dynamic table, add an entry, examine an entry, and delete or modify entries. By default, keys are strings, and the system uses its own hashing function to distribute values among the available processors. However, there is nothing to prevent an implementation from allowing users to supply their own hash functions in order to control and optimize data distribution.

The CHARM model has several strengths. First, it can be implemented efficiently on a wide range of architectures without requiring genius-level compilers. Second, the model is well-grounded in existing practice: just as the process groups of Section 5.3 embodied the way programmers structured processes when given an unstructured message-passing system, chares embody the way programmers structure process internals. Branch office chares and CHARM's data-sharing mechanisms similarly capture common ways of managing data. Finally, CHARM can use *process migration* to perform load balancing automatically. If a processor notices that it is much less lightly loaded than one of its neighbors, it may request one or more chares. The donating processor then records forwarding information, so that messages intended for the relocated chares can be sent on (Figure 6.12). When such forwarding occurs, the forwarding processor also sends a signal to the message's originator, telling it where the chare has been moved to.

CHARM has weaknesses as well as strengths, however. One of these is that a chare may not acquire entry points by being linked to library software, in the way that processes could acquire membership in groups through library use in the structured message-passing model of Section 5.3. This inability makes it difficult to construct large applications by combining independently-written packages, since a chare must be a self-contained piece of code.

A second shortcoming is that its data-sharing mechanisms may not provide exactly the support needed for particular applications. In particular, data structures which are written to in arbitrary ways, such as shared arrays, must be encapsulated in chares, and an appropriate messaging protocol constructed. A more recent object-oriented version of CHARM called CHARM++ addresses many of these issues.

6.7.2 Shared Data-Objects

Where CHARM started with processes, and added shared data structures, ORCA [Bal 1991, Bal et al. 1992] starts with shared data-objects, and provides simpler mechanisms for structuring processes. Processes are defined using a syntax similar to that for procedures, and may take any number of parameters. A particular process is then created using a `fork` statement. This takes a process name and a list of actual arguments, and may optionally

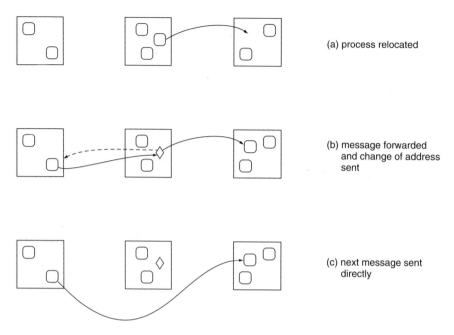

Figure 6.12
Message Forwarding in CHARM

include a processor number if the user wishes to manage process placement herself. (If a processor number is not provided, the system decides where to put the process.)

Formal parameters to processes are declared just like formal parameters to procedures. However, the formal parameters in a process may optionally include the keyword `shared` to indicate that the process is to inherit its parent's copy of the corresponding actual parameter, rather than a new copy. `shared` may not be applied to arbitrary parameters, but only to *data-objects*. These are system- and user-defined types which implement commonly-used data structures, and which the system can support efficiently.

Like chare definitions, data-object definitions include a mix of internal state and manipulating procedures, as in:

```
data_object counter
  integer :: count = 0

  integer function value()
    return count
  end function
```

```
integer function fetch_add(amount)
  integer :: amount
  integer :: tmp = count

  count = count + amount
  return tmp
end function

procedure reset()
  count = 0
end procedure
end data_object
```

Unlike the CHARM model, there is no notion of there being an active agent associated with a data-object. Instead, processes manipulate the data-object by calling its handling procedures, as in:

```
data_object(counter) :: c1              ! declare a counter
integer             :: tmp
  .
  .
  .
tmp = c1%fetch_add(3)                    ! tmp gets 0, counter now 3
tmp = c1%fetch_add(2)                    ! tmp gets 3, counter now 5
  .
  .
  .
tmp = c1%value()                         ! tmp gets 5
call c1%reset()                          ! counter now 0 again
```

Data-objects subsume records, in the sense that all user-defined data types are data-objects with manipulating procedures (similar to the packages or modules provided in many modern languages). The compiler decides whether to place a data-object within a process's private data area, or in the public shared area, by analyzing the use of that data-object. If it is ever passed as a shared parameter, then it is placed in shared memory; if it is only ever manipulated by one thread of control, the compiler optimizes its implementation by treating it like a private record variable.

The current implementation of ORCA offers users two kinds of synchronization. The simplest is mutual exclusion at the data-object level. If a process invokes one of a data-object's handler procedures, then other processes which try to manipulate the data-object are blocked until the first invocation completes. Thus, only a single operation can be in progress on any data-object at a time. Since data-objects are defined by users, this allows users to decide how much or how little synchronization a given data structure requires. Note that sequences of operations on a single object, and operations on two or more objects, are not guaranteed to be indivisible. In order to ensure that such operations execute atomically, users must guard them explicitly by constructing and acquiring locks.

Conditional synchronization, like the when statement of Section 4.1.2 or the guarded alts of Section 5.1.2, is more complicated. Conditional synchronization allows a process to block until a certain condition becomes true. Typically, this condition is an assertion about the state of a shared data-object, such as "the queue contains at least one item". Like alts, these are implemented using guards:

```
data_object object_type
    variables representing internal state
    .
    .
    .

    integer function operation(formal parameters)
      select
        guard condition 1
          body 1
        end guard
        guard condition 2
          body 2
        end guard
        .
        .
        .

        guard condition N
          body N
        end guard
      end select
      return result
  end function
end data_object
```

Each condition must be a logical expression depending only on the local variables of the data-object and the parameters to the operation. The operation blocks until at least one of these expressions is true, and then executes the code associated with one of the true conditions. (As with alts, more than one guard may be or become true simultaneously. In this case, the system may choose arbitrarily which body to execute.)

Handling conditional synchronization in nested objects is extremely difficult. Suppose that the definition of an object O_1 includes an instance of another object O_2, and that one of O_2's handlers is used in a guarded operation in O_1:

```
data_object object_2
    variables representing internal state
    .
    .
    .
    logical function op_on_2(formal parameters)
        .  .
        .
        .
        returns logical
    end function
end data_object

data_object object_1
    variables representing internal state
    data_object(object_2) :: instance_of_2
    .
    .
    .
    result type function op_on_1(formal parameters)
        select
            guard(op_on_2(actual parameters))
                body A
            end guard
            guard(condition B)
                body B
            end guard
        end select
        return result
    end function
end data_object
```

When a process tries to invoke the handler op_on_1, the system must invoke the handler op_on_2 to see whether *body A* can be executed. If neither it nor *condition B* is true, the system must suspend the process which invoked op_on_1 until something in the data-object's state changes, then re-evaluate the conditions.

But what if op_on_2 has side effects, so that the value it returns changes from invocation to invocation? In this case, the operation the calling process asked for may end up being applied to a different data-object than the one the caller thought it was dealing with, since repeated evaluation of operation guards might change the data-object's internal state. Matters are made even worse if the handler op_on_2 might block when invoked. If this was allowed, we could find ourselves in a situation in which a process trying to use the top-level object was blocked part-way through the evaluation of a set of operation guards, and never got to find out that the next guard would have been .true.. Deadlock would almost inevitably occur.

The ORCA implementation solves these problems by behaving as if it copied structures before trying to evaluate guards. When a conditional exclusion statement is encountered, the system acts as though it had made a complete copy of the object and all nested objects, and then evaluated the conditional expression's guards. The system then tries to execute the guarded statements; if any of these block, the entire copy is discarded and the whole operation re-tried. If several processes are trying to execute guarded operations concurrently, separate copies are made for each. The copy on which the operation can first proceed to completion then replaces the original, and all other copies are destroyed.

All of this copying would be tremendously expensive if it were actually done. In practice, side-effecting guards and blocking operations on nested data-objects are very rare. The compiler can almost always determine that these safeguards are not needed in practice, while giving the illusion that the copying rules described above were obeyed. This is similar to the way in which compilers for generative communication systems may eliminate run-time pattern matching, or indeed entire tuples, by analyzing usage.

The ORCA implementation of the shared data-object model relies on the fact that shared data structures are read more often than they are written. Accordingly, the disjoint-memory implementation replicates shared data-objects across processors, so that each process can read the object's current value from its local memory. Whenever a process writes to an object, the changes it makes are broadcast to other processors, which then update their local copies. In order to ensure consistency (i.e., in order to ensure that all processes see writes occurring in the same order), the system requires that broadcasts be both atomic and ordered. As a result, all broadcasts reach all processors in the same sequence, so that updates are performed in the same order everywhere.

ORCA's data-objects are much like the monitors of Section 4.2.4. The use of guards, rather than explicit waiting and signalling operations, is one important difference, as is the guarantee that operations execute atomically. Both differences make data-objects more difficult to implement efficiently, but in exchange make programming easier and safer.

Compared to the CHARM model, the shared data-object model relies much more heavily on clever compilation in order to achieve good performance. It also allows users to be much more expressive with shared passive data: along with sets, bags, arrays, and other commonly-used data structures (which are implemented directly to ensure efficiency without compromising the uniform semantics of shared data-objects), ORCA allows users to construct a wide variety of data types, and to control their synchronization. This can lead to inefficiency, however, as ORCA relies on a single update mechanism (broadcast) which can become a performance-limiting bottleneck on large machines. For example, suppose the most natural way to structure a computation is as a collection of communicating processes. One-to-one communication is intrinsic to the CHARM model, and very efficient; in early versions of ORCA, the only way to implement it was to create a shared mailbox, which one process wrote to and another process read from. Whenever a write occurred, the system had to broadcast the change to all processors, even though only one processor supported a process which actually needed to know. More recent versions of ORCA [Bal & Kaashoek 1993] perform extensive analysis during compilation to try to determine whether an object should be replicated, and changes to it broadcast, or stored in a single place, and read requests turned into non-local messaging operations.

6.7.3   Adaptive Cache Management

The best way to avoid the problems caused by ORCA's reliance on a single shared-data update mechanism is to provide several such mechanisms, each tailored for use in different circumstances. This idea is the basis of the MUNIN system developed at Rice University [Bennett et al. 1990b, Carter et al. 1991, Bennett et al. 1990a]. MUNIN is a *virtual shared memory* system, i.e., it manages data sharing using the paging and virtual memory mechanisms of the underlying operating system [Li & Hudak 1989]. Its novelty is that it relies on *adaptive caching*, a term its authors use to describe a policy which maintains memory coherence using techniques tailored to the observed or expected access patterns associated with particular objects.

The roots of the MUNIN work lie in the observation that parallel programs use individual shared objects in a small number of ways. The adjective "individual" is important here: if statistics are compiled at the whole-object level (e.g., at the level of a whole array, or entire list), then reading and writing patterns may be obscured. If such statistics are compiled at the level of individual scalar variables, then most variables can be classified as one of the following:

Write-once: variables which are assigned a value once (typically during program initialization), and only read thereafter. These can be supported through replication, like their counterparts in the CHARM model.

Write-many: variables which are written and read many times. If several processes write to the variable concurrently, they typically write to different portions of it. This has important implications for run-time support, which are discussed below.

Producer-consumer: variables which are written to by one or more objects, and read by one or more other objects. Entries in a shared queue, or a mailbox used for communication between two processes, are examples of this type.

Private: variables which are potentially shared, but actually private. The interior points of a mesh in a program which uses geometric decomposition fall into this category, while boundary points belong to the previous class.

Migratory: variables which are read and written many times in succession by a single process before ownership passes to another process. The structures representing particles in an N-body simulation are the clearest example of this category.

Result: Variables which are updated many times by different processes, but thereafter read. These correspond to the CHARM model's accumulators or monotonic variables, although there is no requirement that the updating function be associative, commutative, or monotonic.

Read-mostly: Any variable which is read much more often than it is written to. The best score so far in a search problem is a typical instance of this class; while any process might update it, in practice processes read its value much more often than they change it.

Synchronization: Variables used to force explicit synchronization in a program, such as semaphores and locks. These are typically ignored for long periods, and then the subject of intense bursts of access activity.

General read-write: Any variable which cannot be put in one of the above categories.

By now, the motivation for this taxonomy should be clear. The most efficient way to support a shared variable on a disjoint-memory machine is determined by its categorization as follows:

Write-once variables can be replicated.

Write-many variables can rely on a delayed update mechanism, which is discussed below.

Producer-consumer variables can be supported with eager movement, i.e., newly-written values can be moved immediately to where they are going to be needed. This eliminates any need for a request-reply protocol.

Private variables can be placed inside each process's private data, and any overheads associated with synchronization and remote access avoided.

Migratory variables can be moved from process to process on demand. At any time, the system contains a single copy of each variable; when a process wants the variable, it must send a message to a known address. That message is then forwarded until it reaches the object, and the object told to move to the processor supporting the requesting process.

Result variables can be supported using incremental combining, as discussed in Section 4.2.2.

Read-mostly variables can be replicated, and a centralized update mechanism similar to ORCA's atomic broadcasts used to ensure consistency. Provided the variable's read/write ratio is high, the overhead involved in this consistency mechanism will be low.

Synchronization variables in the present MUNIN implementation are handled using distributed locks. In the absence of hardware support for fetch&op operations, there is probably no better alternative.

General read-write variables are implemented using centralization. A single unique copy of the variable is stored in a known location; reads and writes are transformed into messages requesting its value or updating it.

The delayed update protocol alluded to in the description above of write-many variables relies on the use of explicit synchronization points, such as barriers. Between such points, writes to an object are stored locally; when synchronization is done, writes performed on different processors are merged. If two or more processors have written to the same part of a variable, e.g., the same element of an array, an error can be signalled. If, on the other hand, writes are disjoint, then the system has reaped the benefits of locality while giving the illusion of memory consistency. This technique is useful when structures are decomposed in different ways at different times. One example is sorting a large array: at any time, only one process has the right to modify any section, but over time, different processes may have rights to different sections.

Ideally, MUNIN would classify objects automatically during compilation, or during execution by noticing usage patterns. In practice, the former is unreasonably difficult, requiring as it does not only data dependence analysis but also an execution model good enough to predict the frequency of individual operations. The latter is more feasible, but inevitably incurs a run-time burden, and may not be effective at managing short-lived sections of a program. The most practical solution is to require users to annotate data structures, either by including compiler directives in their code or by providing such directives when linking code modules. This last approach has the advantage of allowing users to experiment with different classifications of variables without having to modify their programs.

6.8   Discussion

The high-level control-parallel systems discussed in this chapter all have their strengths and weaknesses. The buffering provided by the tuple space of the generative model, and the persistence of tuples, allow processes to be uncoupled from one another in both time and space, while the atomic nature of operations on tuple space allows simple implementations of many synchronization algorithms. It is also an extremely simple model, but one which allows a great deal of compile-time optimization. On the other hand, many parallel programming clichés are hard to express in the generative model, and it is not clear whether demanding that programmers express all of their operations on shared data using only associative operations on tuples makes optimization more difficult or less.

Each of the alternative models discussed in the previous section takes a different approach to the problem of providing the illusion of shared data in a disjoint-memory environment. Restricting what users can do with shared data, while providing customized support for those operations which are permitted, presently seems the best way to construct control-parallel programming environments which are both efficient and expressive.

A The FORTRAN-K Programming Language

A week of coding can sometimes save an hour of thought.
——Gregory V. Wilson

A.1 Introduction

There are already too many programming languages; why invent another just for the sake of this book? The simple answer is that no existing language seemed to be both popular and simple to emulate. Most scientists and engineers working today program in FORTRAN, but its most common dialect (FORTRAN-77) does not have records, pointers, or UNIX-style input and output. Its successor, FORTRAN-90, does have these features, but is so large that by the time I would have finished building an emulator for it, everything in this book would have become obsolete. C is becoming popular as a vehicle for scientific programming, but is often as obscure as it is powerful, and its (very) low-level memory model would have been difficult to emulate securely. PASCAL is too small and restrictive, MODULA-2 contains too many features which are interesting from a language design point of view, but which have nothing to do with parallelism, and ADA combines the weaknesses of MODULA-2 with those of FORTRAN-90. SCHEME would have been a good choice, except that its LISP-like syntax would have cut the readership of this book by at least 90%.

I chose to do the examples for this book using an emulator, rather than one or more "real" parallel programming systems, for three reasons. First, this emulator runs on a single workstation or personal computer, which allows students to do programming exercises even if they do not have access to a large parallel computer. Second, since the emulator controls process scheduling order, the behavior of a particular run of a program can be reproduced at will. This makes debugging *much* simpler, so that students can spend their time learning new ideas, instead of running their programs over and over until that once-in-a-million bug crops up again. Third, each real parallel programming system seemed to handle little issues, such as parameter copying during process creation, in a slightly different way, or use slightly different syntax to express the same idea. By building a system from scratch, I was able to ensure that (for example) the notation for iteration was the same in do-loops and `alt` branches.

I therefore chose to base this book on a FORTRAN-like language called FORTRAN-K. This is (mostly) a subset of FORTRAN-90, and includes its structured control constructs and record handling facilities. In order to allow all functions and procedures to be recursive, an explicit `return` statement is required in every function; in order to make my own life simpler, only UNIX-style input and output are supported. The sections below describe the basics of FORTRAN-K and its parallel dialects, and explain how to use its compiler and run-time system.

A.2   The Basics

A FORTRAN-K program consists of zero or more constant and record type definitions, global variable declarations, file inclusion specifications, and function and procedure definitions, and a declaration of a main program. These may be arranged in any order; however, when a program is run, these are processed in the following order:

1. constant definitions
2. record type definitions
3. global variable declarations
4. function and procedure definitions

File inclusion is permitted, and is specified by giving the keyword include, followed by a filename as a string constant. The use may specify that the compiler is to search for included files in directories other than the current directory using the −L flag (Section A).

A.2.1   Values

Constant value expressions, and all other expressions in FORTRAN-K, may be constructed from:

• decimal constants consisting of the digits 0-9;

• hexadecimal constants, consisting of a sequence of characters and digits in the ranges 0-9 and A-F enclosed in Z' . . . ';

• floating-point constants, consisting of a mantissa (which must have at least one digit before the decimal point), the character E or e, and an exponent (which must be signed);

• strings, which are sequences of printable characters or special escape sequences (see Table A.2.9); and

• the Boolean constants .true. and .false..

FORTRAN-K's intrinsic operators are shown in Table A.1. Note that there are five precedence classes: all unary operations; multiplicative, selective (maximum and minimum) and bitwise operations; additive operations; comparisons, and Boolean operations. == is used to test for equality; = is used for assignment. Remember: when in doubt (and even when not), parenthesize.

A.2.2   Scalar Variables

FORTRAN-K supports three atomic data types: integer (integer), floating point (real), and Boolean truth value (logical). A variable of one of these atomic types may be read

Table A.1
FORTRAN-K Operators

Group	Symbol	Operation
Unary	+	absolute value
	-	arithmetic negation
	.not.	Boolean negation
	.bitnot.	bitwise negation
Exponentiation	**	exponentiation
Multiplicative	*	multiplication
	/	division (integer quotient)
	.mod.	integer remainder
Selective	.max.	maximum
	.min.	minimum
Bitwise	.bitand.	bitwise and
	.bitor.	bitwise inclusive or
	.bitxor.	bitwise exclusive or
Additive	+	addition
	-	subtraction
Comparative	<	less than
	<=	less than or equal
	==	equal
	/=	not equal
	>=	greater than or equal
	>	greater than
Boolean	.and.	Boolean and
	.or.	Boolean inclusive or
	.xor.	Boolean exclusive or

or assigned to. No other operations are permitted; in particular, there is no way to take the address of an atom.

Variables are declared by giving a type name, the double-colon :: separator, and a comma-separated list of variable names. Initializers may be included, as in:

```
logical :: p, q = .false.
```

```
real   :: x, y = 1.212e-01
integer :: i, j = 2
```

A name in FORTRAN-K is made up of alphabetic characters, decimal digits, and the underscore _, and must begin with an alphabetic character. Like all sensible languages, FORTRAN-K is case insensitive (i.e., Bob and bob are the same thing).

Note that zero and non-zero are *not* equivalent to .false. and .true., as they are in C; except for automatic conversion between integer and floating-point values, all variables are strongly typed.

A.2.3   Arrays

Arrays are declared by adding a dimension specification to a variable. This is a list of one or more positive integers (or expressions using only intrinsic operators) contained in parentheses. Examples include:

```
integer :: A(3, 3), size = 2, B(size)
```

FORTRAN-K does not support FORTRAN's dimension specification, and there is no way to declare an array (or record) constant.

An array is indexed by giving its name, followed by a list of integer-valued expressions in parentheses. Unless the unsafe compilation option has been selected, all array indices will be checked at run-time. Unlike C, slices may not be taken out of arrays by giving an incomplete list of dimensions, i.e., if A has been declared as a 3×3 array as above, then A(2) is an illegal expression. The mechanisms used by FORTRAN-K to achieve a similar effect are described in Section A.3. Also unlike C (but like most other languages), array indexing starts at 1, not at 0.

A.2.4   Records

A new record type is defined in the outermost level of the program using the keyword type, followed by the type's name and a list of declarations specifying fields. Examples include:

```
! complex numbers
type complex
  real :: real, imag
end type
! for building linked list of screen points
integer, constant :: X = 1
integer, constant :: Y = 2
```

```
integer, constant :: XY = 1
type linked_pt
  integer   :: loc(XY)
  linked_pt :: next
end type
```

Variables of type `linked_pt` can then be declared using the keyword `type`, followed by a type name in parentheses:

```
type(linked_pt) :: lp, array_of_lp(10)
```

If `lp` is a variable of type `linked_pt`, then its fields are accessed using %, as in:

```
! initialize fields
lp%loc(X) = 0.0
lp%loc(Y) = 0.0
call nullify(lp%next)
```

These examples also show that FORTRAN-K comments are laid out as any characters between the symbol ! and the end of that line. The call to `nullify` is explained below.

The inclusion of a field of type `linked_pt` in the definition of `linked_pt` requires some explanation. All storage for records is allocated off the heap (to prevent aliasing problems in FORTRAN-K's parallel dialects). In addition, pointers and records are both strongly typed in FORTRAN-K; a pointer may only point to an object of its type. If a record contains record fields, then storage is not automatically allocated for those fields when a variable of that type is declared. Thus, the declaration:

```
type(linked_pt) corner
```

creates a structure containing an array of two integers and an unassociated pointer of type `linked_pt`. Another object of type `linked_pt` can be created using the intrinsic procedure `allocate`, as in:

```
call allocate(corner%next)
```

The compiler determines the type of `allocate`'s argument, and inserts this extra information into each call. Unwanted record storage can later be discarded by calling the procedure `deallocate`.

There is (sadly) no automatic garbage collection. However, to simplify record allocation, automatic pre-allocation can be specified using the variable property `auto`. The code:

```
type(linked_pt), auto :: a, b
```

has exactly the same effect as:

```
type(linked_pt) :: a, b
call allocate(a)
call allocate(b)
```

Unlike C and many other languages, but like FORTRAN-90, FORTRAN-K does not have a null pointer value. Instead, two functions are provided: `associated`, which takes a pointer as an argument and returns `.true.` if that pointer currently refers to something or `.false.` if it does not, and `nullify`, which changes the pointer's state to show that it no longer refers to anything. An unassociated pointer of a particular type can be created using the pseudo-function `nullptr`, which takes a type name as an "argument" and generates an appropriately-typed pointer to nowhere.

Finally, the term *shallow copying* is used in the description of several of the parallel dialects. This means that when pointers are copied, any subsidiary objects to which they refer are not copied. Thus, if a record of type `linked_pt` is shallow-copied, the new record will contain the same `loc` values, but its `next` field will be unassociated. Similarly, if an array of atoms is shallow-copied, the result will be an array of identical atoms; if an array of records is shallow-copied, the result is an array of records, each of which has individually been shallow-copied.

A.2.5   User-Defined Constants

New constants may be defined using constant definitions. A constant definition consists of a type name and the property `constant`, the separator `::`, and one or more pairs of definitions of the form `name = value`. Examples include:

```
logical, constant :: tidy = .true.
real,    constant :: mu_half = 1.22122/2.0
integer, constant :: a0 = 14, a1 = 3 * a0 + 1
```

A.2.6   Subroutines

Subroutines come in two flavors: procedures, which do not return a value, and functions, which do. Procedure definitions have the following form:

```
procedure swap_int(left, right)
  integer :: left, right
  integer :: tmp
  tmp = left ; left = right ; right = tmp
end procedure
```

Note how a semi-colon ; can be used as a statement separator. Both what precedes it and what comes after it must be properly-formed statements.

Function definitions are similar:

```
integer function average(x, y)
  integer :: x, y    ! to be averaged
  integer :: result
  result = (x + y) / 2
  return result
end function
```

or, more succinctly:

```
integer function average(x, y)
  integer :: x, y    ! to be averaged
  return (x + y) / 2
end function
```

Each program must also include a single definition of a starting point:

```
program
  .
  .
  .
end program
```

Note that function and procedure definitions may not be nested inside one another.

Procedure and function parameters must be defined in the order in which they appear in the subroutine header. A function may only contain one `return` statement, which must be the last statement in the function. It is important to note that all parameters are passed by reference during normal (sequential) calls, i.e., a subroutine (procedure or function) can always modify its parameters, and those modifications will always have effect in its caller. User-defined functions may only return scalar atoms or pointers; they may not return arrays.

A function which returns a value is invoked by giving its name and a list of expressions in parentheses. A procedure is invoked using `call`, as in:

```
call swap(x, y)
```

FORTRAN-K provides the usual intrinsic functions, listed in Table A.2. Note that all trigonometric functions work in radians, and that characters in strings are indexed like array elements, i.e., from 1 rather than from 0.

Table A.2
FORTRAN-K Intrinsic Functions

Function	Operation	Arguments	Result
associated	test pointer association	any pointer	logical
nullify	unassociate pointer	any pointer	none
acos	inverse cosine	real	real
asin	inverse sine	real	real
atan	inverse tangent	real	real
ishft	planar bitwise shifting	integer, integer	integer
ishftc	circular bitwise shifting	integer, integer	integer
ceiling	ceiling	real	integer
cos	cosine	real	real
exp	natural exponential	real	real
exp10	base-10 exponential	real	real
floor	floor	real	integer
log	natural logarithm	real	real
log10	base-10 logarithm	real	real
round	round off	real	integer
sin	sine	real	real
sqrt	square root	real	real
tan	tangent	real	real
str_cmp	string comparison	string, string	-1, 0, or 1
str_code	character code extraction	string, integer	integer
str_concat	string concatenation	string, string	string
str_const	test for constant string	string	logical
str_dup	duplicate string	string	string
str_empty	create empty string	none	logical
str_len	find length of string	string	integer
str_set_char	set character	string, integer, string	none
str_set_code	set character	string, integer, integer	none

A.2.7   Control Structures

FORTRAN-K provides the usual control structures: do-loops, while-loops, and if-then-else conditionals. A do-loop is laid out as follows:

```
do index = start, end, stride
  .
  .
  .
end do
```

The loop index may be any integer scalar variable; it is illegal to modify its value within the loop. If a stride is not specified, then either 1 or -1 is used, according to whether the starting value is less than or greater than the ending value. Note that this can sometimes have surprising effects, as a loop from (for example) N+1 to N will actually execute twice, rather than not executing at all. Note also that FORTRAN-K do-loops may execute zero times; this is an important difference between FORTRAN-K and some older dialects of FORTRAN.

FORTRAN-K's while loop is:

```
do while expression
  .
  .
  .
end while
```

The control expression must have Boolean type; the loop executes zero or more times. FORTRAN-K's conditional is the usual if – elseif – else – end if:

```
if expression then
  .
  .
  .
elseif expression then
  .
  .
  .
else
  .
  .
  .
end if
```

An end if is always required to prevent any ambiguity about nesting.

Finally, along with the features described above, FORTRAN-K's serial dialect contains three other statements: skip, which does nothing; stop, which immediately stops the program; and assert, which tells the run-time system to halt if a particular condition is not satisfied. These statements are laid out as:

```
skip
stop
assert Boolean
```

skip is usually used as a placeholder, while stop and assert can be used to freeze the program when an error is detected.

A.2.8 Strings

FORTRAN-K has two intrinsic record types: devices (which are covered in the next section) and strings. A string is declared like any other record variable:

```
type(string)        :: title          ! single null string
type(string), auto :: command        ! single auto-allocated string
type(string), auto :: text(100)      ! auto-allocated array of strings
```

As with other records, storage must be explicitly allocated for strings using either `allo-cate` or the `auto` property in the string's declaration. Table A.2 lists the intrinsic string-handling functions.

The most important difference between strings and other records is that constant strings can be created. A constant string consists of any legal character sequence enclosed in double quotes, such as:

```
"this is a string"
```

Table A.2.9 describes how special characters and escape sequences are interpreted. The FORTRAN-K compiler automatically converts this into a constant string, so that initializations of the form:

```
type(string) :: text = "initial text"
```

are possible. It is illegal to try to modify a constant string; the function `str_const` can be used to test whether a string is constant or not, while `str_dup` can be used to duplicate such a string to create a modifiable (non-constant) copy. Note, however, that it *is* legal to modify a pointer to a constant string. To continue the example above, the assignment:

```
text = str_dup("new text")
```

would duplicate the constant string `"new text"` to create a new string, and point `text` at that new copy.

Table A.3
FORTRAN-K I/O Formatting

Symbol	Output	Input
\\	print \	match \
%d	print decimal integer	read decimal integer
%e	—	read newline or EOF
%r	print real	read real
%l	print Boolean	read Boolean
\n	print newline	read to newline
\"	print "	match "
%s	print string	match up to newline
\t	print tab	match tab
%w	—	match white space
%z	print hexadecimal	match hexadecimal

A.2.9   Input and Output

Input and output are done in FORTRAN-K using `read` and `write`. Each requires a device or string, a format string, and a list of zero or more scalars to be read (`read`), or zero more scalars to be written (`write`). Examples include:

```
write output_file, "==== NEXT RUN ====\n"
write output_file, "last values: %d%d\n", i, j
read input_file, "%d%r\n", i, x
```

The rules for special formatting characters are given in Table A.2.9. Special characters are preceded by \, and format specifiers by %, as they are in C. Unlike formatted I/O in C, however, conformance between format specifiers and variables is checked at run-time.

Devices are record variables of type `device`, and are opened using the intrinsic function `f_open`. Its first parameter must be a string containing the name of the file, while its second must be a logical flag, indicating whether the file is to be opened for writing (`.true.`) or reading (`.false.`). If the file cannot be opened, an unassociated (null) file pointer is returned instead. The intrinsic function `f_close` is used to close a file; it takes a device variable as its single argument. A third function, `f_eof`, may be used to check for the end of an input file. Finally, four device constants called `std_in`, `std_out`, `std_err`, and `std_dbg` are defined which represent the standard input, standard output, standard error, and standard debugging channels respectively. The first three are automatically opened at the beginning of execution; depending on the machine being used, `std_out` and `std_err` may in fact be the same. An example of the use of these functions is:

```
procedure count_ints(filename)
  type(string) :: filename
  type(device) :: infile
  integer      :: num = 0, dummy

  infile = f_open(filename, .false.)
  assert associated(infile)
  do while .not. f_eof(infile)
    read infile, "%d%e", dummy
    num = num + 1
  end while
  call f_close(infile)
  return num
end procedure
```

The fourth standard device, std_dbg, is only opened for output if the -D option is given to the run-time system when the program is run. Writes to std_dbg are only executed if this has been done, which allows users to turn debugging output on and off.

A.2.10 Assignment

As mentioned earlier, FORTRAN-K uses = to indicate assignment. In all dialects except the data-parallel one, both the left and the right sides of this must evaluate to scalars or records. If the right side is a scalar, its value is copied into the variable referred to on the left; if the right side is a record (including a string), the left becomes another alias for it. Integer and floating-point values are automatically converted as needed; they may also be converted explicitly using the functions ceiling, floor, round, or frac (the last of which turns an integer into a real).

A.2.11 Explicit Critical Regions

The final language feature shared by all FORTRAN-K dialects is the explicit critical region. This takes the form:

```
critical
  .
  .
  .
end critical
```

Code inside a critical region is guaranteed to execute indivisibly, and to have no effect on the order of process scheduling in any of the parallel dialects. Note that it is very dangerous for code in critical regions to perform parallel operations such as waiting on a semaphore (Section A.3), or sending or receiving a message using a channel (Section A.3), as this can easily result in deadlock.

A.3 The Parallel Dialects

Five parallel dialects of FORTRAN-K are presently available. This section sketches the features of each; their features are discussed in more detail in the appropriate chapters.

A.3.1 Data Parallelism

The data-parallel dialect contains tools for manipulating whole arrays, or sections of arrays, with single statements. The most important of these is the range expression, which may contain from zero to three fields separated by colons. A two-valued range expression specifies a contiguous block of indices, i.e., $3:8$ is equivalent to the ordered list of indices $\{3, 4, 5, 6, 7, 8\}$. If a range expression contains a third field, that value specifies the stride, or separation between values, in the range specified by the first two fields. Thus, $3:8:2$ is equivalent to $\{3, 5, 7\}$. (Note that 8 does not appear, as it has been "stepped over".) A free-standing : may also be used as an index to indicate the whole of the corresponding axis—if A is a 10×10 array, then A(:, 3) indicates the whole of its third column, while A(:, :) is the same as A on its own. Finally, a range expression of the form :3 indicates that the whole range is to be used, with a stride of 3.

The data-parallel dialect allows whole-array assignment between conformant arrays, i.e., arrays with the same rank and the same extent along each dimension. One rule which is important in this context is that if an array has an extent of one along some dimension, it may be treated as a structure with one less dimension. Thus, A(:, 3) is actually a one-dimensional structure, so that both assignments in:

```
real :: v(10), a(5, 10)
    .
    .
    .
a(5, :) = v
v = a(3, :)
```

are legal.

Scalars are automatically promoted to arrays of the required shape when they are used in expressions. Arrays can be promoted to higher-dimensional structures using the intrinsic function dp_shape. This takes an array as its first argument, followed by a list of strings and integers. The strings must represent a permutation of the integers from 1 to R, where

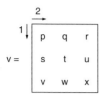

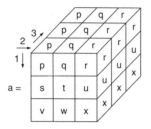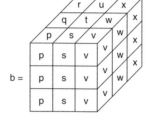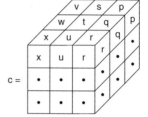

Figure A.1
Re-Shaping Arrays

R is the rank of the array being promoted; their order determines the re-ordering of the array argument's axes in the result. The remaining integer arguments are used to specify the extents of new dimensions, along which copying is done. Thus, the results of:

```
integer :: v(3, 3), a(3, 3, 3), b(3, 3, 3), c(3, 3, 3)
    .
    .
    .
a = dp_shape(v, "1", "2", 3)
b = dp_shape(v, 3, "1", "2")
c(1, :, :)  = dp_shape(v, "-1", "-2")
```

are as shown in Figure A.1. Note that a string argument can also represent the negation of an axis; in this case, the values along that axis are reversed.

Reduction operations may be performed on arrays using `dp_reduce`, which takes an array and a string representing the desired operation as arguments. For example:

```
biggest = dp_reduce(block, ".max.")
```

assigns `biggest` the maximum value in `block`.

A scan (parallel prefix) operation may be performed on a vector using `dp_scan`. This takes four arguments:

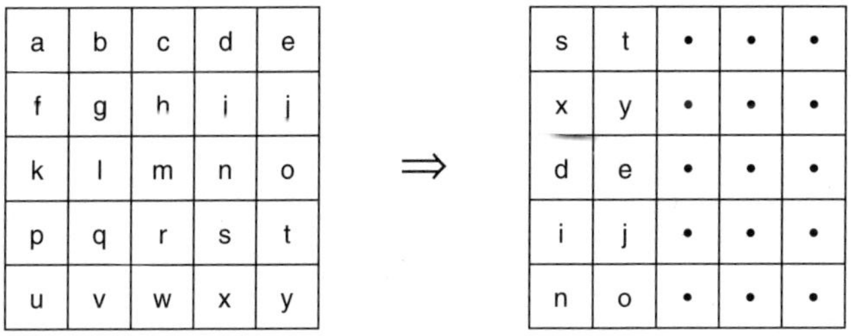

a	b	c	d	e
f	g	h	i	j
k	l	m	n	o
p	q	r	s	t
u	v	w	x	y

$\Rightarrow$

s	t	•	•	•
x	y	•	•	•
d	e	•	•	•
i	j	•	•	•
n	o	•	•	•

Figure A.2
Shifting Arrays

- the vector on which the operation is to be done;

- a string identifying the operation;

- a `logical` argument indicating whether the operation is inclusive (`.true.`) or exclusive (`.false.`); and

- a `logical` argument indicating whether the operation is upward (`.true.`) or downward (`.false.`).

There is also a segmented version of this function called `dp_scan_seg`, which takes a segment vector as a fifth argument. The details of their operation are explained in the main text.

Array values may be shifted using the `dp_shift` function. This takes an array as its first argument, and axis-ordered pairs of string and integer shift specifiers as its other arguments. The string portion of each specifier must be one of:

- `"c"` or `"C"`, indicating a circular shift;

- `"p"` or `"P"`, indicating a planar shift; or

- `"n"` or `"N"`, indicating no shift.

The integer amounts indicate how much to shift; this must be no greater than the extent of the array along the corresponding axis. Thus:

```
integer :: map(5, 5)
map = dp_shift(map, "C", 2, "P", -3)
```

shifts map's contents upward by two places along its first axis (filling with zeroes), and downward by three places along its second axis, wrapping values around (Figure A.2).

The other special functions of the data-parallel dialect are `dp_index`, which takes a single positive integer argument and returns a vector containing the integers from 1 up to this value (inclusive), and `dp_locate`, which takes an array, a value, and an integer vector whose length is equal to the rank of the array argument, and overwrites the vector with the indices of the least significant location in which the specified value can be found. This function returns `.true.` if the value was found, and `.false.` otherwise.

FORTRAN-KDP also includes parallel conditionals. These are implemented using `where`, which has the same format as the serial conditional `if`:

```
where expression do
  .
  .
  .
elsewhere expression do
  .
  .
  .
else
  .
  .
  .
end where
```

`where`s may be nested, but any operations within a `where`'s scope must conform to the shape of its control expression. In particular, an expression of the form:

```
real :: V(N)
  .
  .
  .
where V > 0 do
  V(1:N:2) = V(2:N:2)
end where
```

is *not* legal, since the sub-vectors selected on the right and left sides of the assignment statement have only half the extent of the controlling expression.

A.3.2 Shared Variables

The shared-variables dialect introduces one new syntactic construct, the `create` statement. This takes the form:

```
create
  NA of procedure_A(parameters)
  NB of procedure_B(parameters)
  .
  .
  .
  NZ of procedure_Z(parameters)
end create
```

Table A.4
Process Group Inspection Functions

grp_size	size of caller's process group
id_abs_grp	absolute group ID of caller's process group
id_abs_self	absolute process ID of caller
id_rel_grp	relative group ID of caller's process group
id_rel_self	relative ID of calling process within process group
id_parent	absolute process ID of caller's parent

and creates the specified number of processes. Those variables which are declared globally, and those which are passed as parameters to the functions, are shared; each receives private copies of all other variables (i.e., all variables declared locally in the subroutines, or in any subroutines they call). A process which executes a `create` is blocked until all of its children have finished executing.

Processes may use the functions listed in Table A.4 to determine who they are, what group they belong to, and so on. Process groups are numbered in the order in which they are created; each process is given both an absolute ID, and an ID within its group. All sets of IDs begin at 1.

Processes in the shared-variables model co-ordinate with one another using semaphores and barriers. A semaphore is a variable of type `semaphore`, and is initialized using the function `sem_init`. This takes as arguments the semaphore, the upper bound on the semaphore's value, and its initial value. Once a semaphore has been created, it may only be used as an argument to the intrinsic functions `sem_wait` and `sem_signal`. Similarly, a barrier is a variable of type `barrier`, and is initialized by calling `bar_init`, whose arguments are the barrier and the barrier's consensus number. A process waits at a barrier by calling `bar_arrive`, which takes the barrier as an argument.

A.3.3 Message Passing through Channels

The CSP-like dialect of FORTRAN-K includes several extensions. The first is the `create` statement outlined above, which allows users to create any number of concurrent processes. Even though FORTRAN-KCSP is a disjoint-memory model, parameters to child processes are shared, rather than copied; this is to allow channels and message buffers to be shared, as explained in the main text.

Channels are used for inter-process communication. Channels are represented using an intrinsic record type `chan`. The two operations permitted on channels are input, indicated by `->`, and output, indicated by `<-`. Each takes a channel on its left side, and a list of one or more variables (for input) or expressions (for output) on its right. Examples include:

```
a2b <- x, y                          ! send x and y
b2a -> msg_type, buffer(1:N)         ! receive msg type and buffer
```

The format of the last example shows how messages containing arrays of variable length may be sent by using non-striding index ranges. Thus, if two processes had both declared the variables

```
real :: A(10, 10), X, Y
```

and one sent its copy of A through a channel with:

```
c <- A(1:7, 1:3), 7, 3
```

while the other received using:

```
c -> A, X, Y
```

then the receiver's copy of X would have the value 7, its copy of Y would have the value 3, and the rectangle of values in the range $(1...7) \times (1...3)$ in the receiver's copy of A would be overwritten. Note that shallow copying is used when records and arrays are sent through channels.

The most complicated feature of FORTRAN-K's CSP dialect is the alt statement. alts are used to choose among several possible input operations. An alt consists of the keyword alt, followed by one or more choices:

```
alt
   ···choice···
   ···choice···
   .
   .
   .
end alt
```

Each choice can take one of several forms. The simplest uses the choose keyword to guard a single input operation:

```
alt
   choose channel -> variables
      statements
   end
   ···other choices···
   .
   .
end alt
```

This can be guarded by a Boolean expression using when:

```
alt
  choose channel -> variables
   when expression
    statements
  end
  ···other choices···
  .
  .
  .
end alt
```

The other major alternative is an iterated choose, which is used to select an input from any member of a vector of channels. This takes the form:

```
alt
  any index = start, end, stride
   choose channel(index) -> variables
     when expression
       statements
  end
  ···other choices···
  .
  .
  .
end alt
```

Finally, an alt branch may contain a when on its own. In this case, the branch is taken if no previous branch is ready, and the guard condition is satisfied.

A.3.4 Procedural Message Passing

In the other style of message passing, messages are sent to destinations rather than through channels. Most of this dialect is implemented as a library of functions, although some of these functions may take a variable number of parameters.

First, the message-passing dialect allows the program to contain a single create statement, of the sort seen before. All parameters are copied during process creation, so that changes made by one process are not reflected in other processes. Just to be sure users don't take the easy way out, global variables may not be declared in a message-passing program.

Once processes have been created, they may join one or more process groups, and then exchange messages. The functions which do this are:

`integer mp_grp_id(type(string) name)`: returns the caller's ID within the named process group.

`logical mp_grp_mem(type(string) name)`: returns `.true.` if the caller is a member of the named process group, and `.false.` otherwise.

`logical mp_grp_mem_live(type(string) name, int id)`: returns `.true.` if the named process group has a member with the specified ID, and `.false.` otherwise.

`integer mp_grp_size(type(string) name)`: returns the size of the named process group.

`integer mp_join(type(string) name, int req_id)`: join the named process group with the specified ID. If `req_id` is `MP_Any_Id`, a unique ID will be assigned to the process by the run-time system.

`type(msginfo) mp_pend(type(string) dst_grp, type(string) type, ⋯)`: create a message receipt buffer for messages of the specified type sent to the process as a member of the named process group `dst_grp`. This function allocates and returns a message information structure, which can later be tested to determine whether the buffer variables have been filled by an incoming message.

`mp_recv(type(string) dst_grp, type(string) type, ⋯)`: create a message receipt buffer for messages of the specified type sent to the process as a member of the named process group `dst_grp`, and block until that buffer is filled. This function acts as a combination of `mp_pend` nested inside a blocking `mp_test`.

`mp_send(type(string) src_grp, type(string) dst_grp, int dst_id, type(string) type, ⋯)`: send a message of the specified type to the specified destination. `src_grp` must be the name of a group to which the caller belongs; `dst_grp` may be the name of any other group, while `dst_id` must be either the ID of a process within that group, or the special value `MP_All_Id`, which signals that the message is to be broadcast to all group members.

`mp_synch()`: synchronize with other processes after group creation. Messages may not be sent or received before this function (which acts as a barrier) has been called by all processes; group membership may not be changed after its call has been passed.

`type(msginfo) mp_test(bool block, type(msginfo) msg)`: test to see whether a previously-pended message buffer has been filled. If `block` is `.true.`, the caller blocks until the buffer has been filled, and the message information structure given as an argument is returned; if `block` is `.false.`, the function returns the message information structure immediately if the buffer has been filled, or returns a null pointer if it has not. A process may also pass either of the special record structures `MP_Any_Id` or `MP_All_Id`. The former signals that the caller is testing for the completion of any outstanding transaction, while the latter indicates that the caller is testing for the completion of all of them.

A.3.5   Generative Communication

The generative dialect of FORTRAN-K is implemented through six operations: out, eval, in, inp, rd, and rdp. An out statement consists of the keyword out, followed by a comma-separated list of expressions. These expressions are evaluated, and a tuple created with their values as its field. The process performing the out then continues execution. eval is similar, except that a new process is created to evaluate each function call which appears as a top-level expression in the tuple. These processes execute concurrently with their parent; once they have all completed, a new tuple holding their values is created. Shallow copying is used when records and arrays are put into tuples, or passed as parameters to evaled functions.

The values given to in and rd may be either actuals or formals. Actuals are valued expressions on which value matching is done; formals are indicated by the prefix ?, and only type matching is done on them. When a formal matches an actual in a tuple, the formal's value is overwritten. in and rd are blocking operations, and cause calling processes to suspend until a matching tuple is available.

Array sections may be put into tuples, or retrieved from them, using mechanisms similar to those used in the CSP and message-passing dialects. If an array given as a field to an out or eval is subscripted using leading-colon notation, as in:

```
integer :: A(10, 10)
    .
    .
    .
out "example", A(1:5, 1:3), 5, 3
```

then only the indicated section of the array is included in the tuple. An array in an input operation matches any array of the same rank, whose dimensions are less than or equal to its dimensions. Thus, if:

```
integer :: A(10, 10), X, Y
in "example", ?A, ?X, ?Y
```

was performed after the out shown above, X and Y would have the values 5 and 3 respectively, and the lower 5×3 section of A would have been set.

Predicate versions of these operations, called inp and rdp, are also supported. These take a logical variable argument as well as a matching template. If a tuple matching the template can be found "immediately", the logical variable is set to .true. and the bindings returned; otherwise, the logical variable is set to .false. and the other variables are not altered. Thus, if a matching tuple can be found for the inp below, i and j will be

overwritten and `success` set to `.true.`; otherwise, `success` will be set to `.false.` and
i and j left undisturbed.

```
logical :: success
integer :: i, j
inp(success) "fred", ?i, ?j
```

A.4   fk: The FORTRAN-K Compiler

The FORTRAN-K compiler is called `fk`. In order to use it, you must have the shell environment variable `FORTK_DIR` defined to point to the directory containing the FORTRAN-K header and library files. On my system, this is presently `/h/f/gvw/fortk`; see your local guide for details on your own installation.

`fk` takes the following command-line arguments:

`+`: switch to C argument processing. Any arguments following the standalone + will be passed to the C compiler.

`-D . . .`: turn on some debugging output. The following characters, which must be part of the same argument as the `-D` flag, may be used to select debugging:

   `c`: parameters to the C compiler when it is forked.

   `l`: tokenization (lexing).

   `n`: line numbers in the source as it is read.

`-L directory-name`: add the specified directory to the search path for included files. Directories are searched in the order in which their names were specified on the command line.

`-M file-name`: turn on memory tracing. This causes a history of all dynamic memory allocation and de-allocation operations to be written to the specified file.

`-S stopping-point`: stop compilation after a certain point. Options are:

   `parse`: after parsing

   `check`: after semantic checking

   `generate`: after code generation

   `macros`: after macro expansion

`-T`: do not delete the temporary C file created during translation after compilation has completed.

-U: generate unsafe (but faster) code. At present, this only affects array indexing; array bounds are not checked in -U code.

-a: turn off assertions in the output program. This will make it run slightly faster, but less safely.

-d dialect: specify the dialect being compiled. If this flag is not given, only serial language features may be used. If it is present, exactly one of the following abbreviations may be used to specify the dialect being compiled:

csp: CSP

dp: data parallelism

gc: generative communication

mp: procedural message passing

sv: shared variables

-g: enable run-time tracing of variable references. This makes execution significantly slower, but permits symbolic run-time debugging.

-h: print a usage message and exit.

-i input-file: read input from the specified file. The -i flag is optional; any argument not preceded by a flag is interpreted as the name of the input file. The input file may only be specified once per invocation.

-l listing-file: creating a listing file for use in debugging.

-o output-file: put the output in the named file. If C compilation is not being done, this may be omitted, in which case the C translation of the FORTRAN-K program is sent to stdout.

A.5 The FORTRAN-K Run-Time System

Executable FORTRAN-K programs handle command-line arguments in a fashion similar to that used by C. In addition, the special argument + is used to introduce one or more arguments which are to be passed to the run-time system itself; thus, the command line:

```
k.out -W -d 12 + -TA -D k.trace
```

gives the run-time system the flags -TA, and -D k.trace while passing -W and 12 to the user's program.

The flags understood by the run-time system are:

`-D [filename]`: enable output to `std_dbg`. If a filename is specified, debugging output is put in it; otherwise, it is written to `stderr`.

`-T . . .` : Enable tracing. The characters immediately following the T are interpreted as follows:

A: all tracing

D: dialect-specific tracing

F: function calls

I: I/O

L: line numbers

R: variable references

S: scheduling

T: ticking

z: turns off ticking (note lower case)

Thus, `-TAz` traces everything except ticking. If a filename is specified along with the `-T` flag and its subflags, tracing output is put in that file; otherwise, it is written to `stderr`.

`-t default [seed]`: specify ticking controls. The first argument, which is mandatory, specifies the default interval (measured in ticks) between process scheduling operations. The second (optional) argument specifies the seed to use to generate randomized scheduling intervals. If this argument is not present, all intervals are of the specified fixed length.

All other flags are stored in the global string array `argv`, and the global integer variable `argc` is assigned the length of this array.

A.6 How and Where to Get FORTRAN-K

The easiest way to get the FORTRAN-K compiler and emulator is by anonymous FTP from `mitpress.mit.edu` (18.173.0.28). Log in using the name "guest", give your email address as a password, and then change directory to `pub/PPP`. This contains the source for the FORTRAN-K system, some example programs to supplement those given in this text, and some suggestions for practical exercises. If you would like to add your programs to this collection, or suggest other exercises, please send electronic mail to `PPP@mitpress.mit.edu`.

B A Short History Lesson

The greatest influence on the development of parallel programming has not been the development of conventional computer languages, but rather the rapidly-changing nature of parallel hardware.[1] In order to understand why the programming models presented in this book contain the features they do, it is necessary to understand the evolution of the hardware they were meant to run on. Accordingly, this section presents a short history of some of parallel computing's most influential projects and machines.

B.1 The Early Machines

Practical investigation of parallel computing can be said to date from 1964, when the Atomic Energy Commission (AEC) in the United States urged computer manufacturers to look at "radical" machine structures in order to deliver higher numerical performance at a lower cost. This call led directly to the CDC Star-100, to Texas Instruments' ASC, and to the most famous first-generation parallel computer, the ILLIAC-IV.

The ILLIAC-IV was commissioned in 1967 by the Advanced Research Projects Agency (ARPA) of the U.S. Department of Defense, who wanted a powerful engine for doing the matrix algebra and finite difference calculations required by aircraft and nuclear weapons designers. Each of its custom processors was to have had a peak performance of 4 MFLOPS, which was a tremendous speed for the time; the full 256-processor machine would have had a peak speed of over 1 GFLOPS [Barnes et al. 1968]. Each processor would also have had 16 kbyte of memory, organized as 2048 64-bit words. Measured against a rule of thumb which states that a machine needs at least 1 Mbyte per MFLOPS, this would have been grossly inadequate. However, a custom disk system with 128 read heads, capable of handling 500 Mbit/sec, would partly have compensated for the small size of the ILLIAC-IV's primary storage. This disk system was the fastest built before the mid-1980s, and neither the Cray-1 nor CDC's Cyber-205—contemporaries of ILLIAC-IV by the time it was completed—ever approached its I/O performance.

The ILLIAC-IV was to have contained four quadrants, each comprising 64 processing elements, or PEs. However, because of technological and political delays, the machine which was finally delivered to the NASA Ames Laboratory in California only had one quadrant. Each PE was driven by instructions from a single Central Unit. A PE could only access its own memory directly, but the Central Unit could read or write any part of memory. The machine was stitched together with a single global bus, and local 4-way

---

1. Put less stiffly, the history of parallel programming is the history of a few brave programmers trying to get good performance out of whatever the engineers have just inflicted on them.

interconnections between PEs. Finally, each PE contained an 8-bit mode register which determined whether the PE executed or ignored particular instructions.

One reason the machine was never completed was its size: each PE occupied 210 printed circuit boards, and even the quarter-sized machine cost $31 million. Another reason was that ILLIAC-IV's designers tried to push too many technologies too hard at the same time; it was, for example, the first large machine to use integrated circuit memory, and the difficulty of fabricating the required chips slowed the project down.

Software for the ILLIAC-IV was never as advanced as hardware. In fact, while the initial description of the ILLIAC-IV's hardware had six authors [Barnes et al. 1968], the first paper on its software had only one [Kuck 1968]. Effort was initially concentrated on developing a block-structured ALGOL-like language called Glypnir, which would give programmers a construct called doall. This construct implements the iterative decomposition strategy discussed in Section 2.4.2: while a conventional loop does one iteration at a time, a doall loop does all of its "iterations" simultaneously by giving different iterations to different processors. In fact, if there are fewer processors than iterations, either the compiler or the run-time system must allocate several iterations to each processor, while copying data and synchronizing as necessary in order to ensure that the final effect is the same. There were initially plans to write a parallelizing compiler for a FORTRAN-like language (which would have been called IVTran), but this last never worked properly, so a low-level facility called CFD was developed instead.

Another influential early parallel computer was C.mmp ("Carnegie multi-mini-processor computer"), which was built at Carnegie-Mellon University (CMU) in the 1970s. The aim of the C.mmp project was to build a large multiprocessor out of off-the-shelf components, and to develop an operating system for it which different users could customize in order to support their own research.

The most interesting architectural feature of the C.mmp was its use of a crossbar to connect processors to memory. Despite the cost of the large number of switches that this required, C.mmp's designers felt that using a crossbar would shorten cable lengths, and thereby reduce communication delays. They also hoped that giving each processor direct access to every memory unit would reduce the amount of memory contention by making it less likely that two or more processors would attempt to use the same memory simultaneously. Since each crossbar switch and memory unit could only handle a single request at a time, and automatically queued processors until their requests could be satisfied, such memory contention would have lowered the machine's performance dramatically.

On the software side, effort was concentrated on the development of an operating system called Hydra, which managed objects using "capabilities". A capability is a reference to an object which contains a description of how the owner is allowed to interact with that object, i.e., whether the owner can read, write, or delete the object. Since C.mmp's designers were not sure how people would want to program it, they hoped that if they built a small, capability-based kernel, users would be able to extend it to build file systems and run-time libraries appropriate to different styles of parallelism. Another operating system called StarOS was also developed, and later ported to CMU's second machine, the Cm* (discussed below).

Design of the C.mmp began in 1970, while hardware and software development started in 1972. The first version was running in 1973; by the time the machine was completed, in 1977, it contained 16 minicomputers (11 PDP-11/40s and 5 PDP-11/20s), connected through a 16×16 crossbar to 16 memory units containing a total of 2.5 Mbyte of memory. System software development was also completed by 1977, by which time C.mmp had schedulers, a file system, directory systems, and a debugger, and supported ALGOL-68, FORTRAN, C, and L*, a list processing language.

In their retrospective look at the C.mmp project [Wulf et al. 1981], the machine's designers identified several weaknesses in it. First, they had initially assumed that component reliability would not be a problem. As it turned out, while the crossbar switches did perform well, the cumulative unreliability of the PDP-11's was a continual headache. Second, while economics had dictated that 16-bit minicomputers be used for the machine's processors, their limited addressing capabilities meant that extra address translation hardware and page selection mechanisms had to be added to let each minicomputer access the whole of the machine's memory. Once again, this made using and maintaining the machine more difficult. Finally, although caches were designed for C.mmp, only one was ever implemented. As empirical studies showed that approximately 70% of all memory references were to read-only code pages, the use of caching might have improved C.mmp's performance greatly, not only by reducing the time required to access memory, but also by reducing memory contention.

One interesting feature of the C.mmp project was the relative amount of effort put into Hydra, and into applications development. Less than two chapters in [Wulf et al. 1981] are concerned with hardware; the others describe how to build an operating system capable of being extended by users for their own purposes. This work was one of the great successes of C.mmp, although it had its greatest influence in operating system design, not parallel computing.

The C.mmp was followed up by a second machine, the Cm*. Instead of separating processors and memory by a crossbar, the Cm* connected processor/memory pairs with a hierarchy of buses. Each processor was a DEC LSI-11 with up to 256 kbyte of memory. Processors were connected by a bus to make clusters with up to 14 elements, while clusters were connected by a higher-level bus. At its largest, the Cm* contained 50 processors.

While memory was physically local to a processor, the machine had a single 28-bit address space. Any processor could access any part of memory, although the time to do this depended on how many buses the request and reply had to traverse. In conjunction with direct message-passing facilities, this allowed programmers to treat the Cm* as either a large shared-memory multiprocessor or a tightly-coupled computer network. This style of use re-appeared a decade later on BBN's Butterfly multiprocessors. Interestingly, the 1:3:9 ratio of access times for local, in-cluster, and out-of-cluster memory in the Cm* is similar to the ratios in many of today's hierarchical-memory machines.

The Cm* was programmed using one of two different extensions of ALGOL-68. The first of these allowed programmers to run a computation whose result was not needed immediately in parallel with the main computation; this futures model was discussed in Section 4.3. The second model was the conventional fork-and-join found in operating systems such as UNIX. In this model, a process could split itself in two (or, from another viewpoint, spawn a single new child). The two processes could then run concurrently until being recombined at a later stage. In both models, a processor was selected automatically by the run-time system to run a process, rather than directly by the user.

B.2   The Evolution of Commercial Multiprocessors

By the late 1970s, several commercial groups were trying to develop new parallel computers by taking advantage of improved VLSI technology. One project, the Intel iAPX 432, or i432, did not lead to a commercial product, but members of the group went on to help found several other parallel computer firms.

Intel produced the world's first single-chip microprocessor, the 4004, in 1971. Ten years later, its Special Systems Operations group in Aloha, Oregon had designed a new microprocessor, the iAPX, to support a capabilities-based operating system called iMAX. The main aim of the project was to provide transparent multiprocessing, so that programmers could achieve high performance without having to know how many processors or memory units were in the system. To provide such transparency, each i432 computer could contain any number of processors, I/O units, and memories, connected by a single bus. The machine as a whole maintained a single queue of schedulable processes. As a process came to the head of this queue, it was assigned to an idle processor, which ran it for one time-slice, and then re-queued it. In order to reduce the cost of moving processes to processors, addresses were interleaved so that the machine appeared to have a single shared memory. Like the C.mmp's Hydra operating system, the i432's processors ensured that processes could not access segments of memory if they did not have appropriate permissions.

It is interesting to note that the book describing the i432 [Organick 1983] contains almost no discussion of parallelism, since it was supposed to be hidden from users. The only reason for incorporating parallelism was to get higher performance, and most programmers were not supposed to have to worry about it. On the other hand, system and application programmers who wanted to manage parallelism explicitly could do so by using the six communication instructions in the iAPX. These came in three pairs of send and receive: synchronous, conditional, and surrogate (now more commonly called asynchronous). A synchronous operation puts a request to send (or receive) in a queue associated with a process. If that queue was already full, the process performing the operation was suspended until the queue had space. Conditional messaging behaved in the same way, except that the interface functions signalled failure if the queue was full, rather than suspending the caller. Finally, the surrogate functions created a new "ghost" process which did nothing but send or receive the message, and allowed the main process to continue execution immediately.

Although the i432 never reached the marketplace, it did spawn many descendents. Sequent, which was one of the most successful computer manufacturers of the 1980s, built (and builds) shared-memory computers using many of the same ideas, and members of the i432 project helped to set up NCube and to build Intel's own iPSC multicomputers (discussed below). A joint venture between Intel and Siemens called BiiN, begun in 1982, was based on many of the same principles as the i432. However, like its predecessor, it was axed before it could produce a commercial product [Trew & Wilson 1991].

While Intel was experimenting with multiprocessors, established manufacturers were slowly introducing more and more parallelism into their product lines. One of the clearest examples of this is the continuing evolution of the machines built by Cray Research Incorporated (CRI).

CRI was founded by Seymour Cray. Having joined Control Data Corporation (CDC) in 1957, he had been the chief architect of its first commercial pipelined computer, the CDC 6600, and of its successor, the 7600. When CDC cancelled the 8600 development project in 1972, Cray left to set up his own company. Four years later, CRI delivered the first Cray-1 to the Los Alamos National Laboratory (LANL) in New Mexico. This machine had a peak performance of 160 MFLOPS, although for memory-to-memory vector multiplication this dropped to roughly 30 MFLOPS because of limited memory bandwidth. Even so, the Cray-1 was significantly more powerful than anything else on the market, and time on these machines was much sought after.

After enhancing the Cray-1 with extra I/O processors to create the Cray-1S, CRI's products went in two directions. The original plan had been to build a new machine, to be called the Cray-2, using gallium arsenide components instead of silicon. However, when it became apparent that the GaAs technology of the early 1980s was not going to be able to deliver reliable components in large quantities, Cray had to go back to the drawing board. To keep CRI in business while the Cray-2 was re-gestated, a group led by Steve Chen designed a multiprocessor version of the Cray-1 called the Cray-X/MP, which was brought out in 1982.

The X/MP was a shared-memory machine, originally having two processors, but later available with one or four as well. Each of these processors was a cleaned-up Cray-1 capable of up to 200 MFLOPS (although, as in all computers, typical performance was significantly less). Its instruction set was compatible with the Cray-1's, but also contained extra instructions to allow processors to co-ordinate their activities. Processors communicated through shared clusters of registers; each cluster contained address registers, scalar registers, and a single semaphore register. Any processor could busy-wait until a particular bit in the semaphore register was clear, and then immediately re-set it. Processors shared a single interleaved memory, to which they were connected by two read ports and one write port (i.e., one port for reading each of the operands of a binary operation such as multiplication, and a third port for writing the result).

Software for the Cray-1's descendents steadily improved over the years. A series of vectorizing FORTRAN compilers, which tried to turn loops into sequences of pipelined calculations, freed many users from the headache of assembly-level coding. In 1984, CRI introduced UNICOS, the first UNIX-compatible operating system to run on a supercomputer.

The X/MP was followed in 1988 by the eight-processor Y/MP, and in 1991 by the 16-processor Y/MP-C90. Each generation retained the basic structure and instruction set of the original X/MP, but used more sophisticated architectural tricks and fabrication technology to bring the per-processor speed up to a gigaFLOPS. Few users have ever taken advantage of these machines' multiprocessing capabilities. Instead, separate programs are typically run on each processor in order to improve overall throughput.

While all of this was going on, CRI was also developing the Cray-2, which was introduced in 1985. Each Cray-2 contained four background processors, whose internals were similar to those of a Cray-1 processor, and a single foreground, or control, processor. Each background processor had 16 kword of local memory, which it used as a scratchpad during calculations, and was connected to a shared memory of 256 Mwords. This shared memory was organized into four quadrants of 32 banks each; a processor could only access a particular quadrant during every fourth clock cycle. As in the X/MP line, processors in the Cray-2 synchronized by busy-waiting on single-bit semaphores.

What CRI did at the top end of the market, Digital Equipment Corporation (DEC) and other companies did further down. DEC more or less invented the minicomputer business in the late 1960s and early 1970s with its PDP-11 machines. The introduction of the VAX a decade later, and of networking technology to allow one VAX to talk to another, marked the beginning of the end for the traditional mainframe.

DEC introduced its first multiprocessor, the VAX 11/782, in 1981. The 11/782 was a two-processor machine which used the asymmetric model of multiprocessing shown in Figure 2.11: one processor was the master, and handled all operating system calls, while the other only handled user processes. Later versions of the machine added more slave processors, but, as with all heterogeneous architectures, this asymmetry made programming and performance tuning difficult. Eventually, DEC began producing machines that ran a *symmetric operating system*, in which processors shared a single queue of runnable processes like that in the Intel i432.

While existing firms' products evolved toward a few processors connected to a single memory by a high-speed bus, new companies were being formed to do this from scratch. Among these were Alliant (founded in 1982) and Sequent (1983). Alliant's first machines used proprietary processors, but the firm later moved to the Intel i860; Sequent began with National Semiconductor microprocessors, and then switched to Intel's 80286 and 80386 products. While Alliant concentrated on scientific and engineering markets, Sequent was more interested in commercial data-processing, particularly on-line transaction processing and database operations. For example, Alliant produced a variety of high-performance graphics hardware, so that users could visualize the results of their calculations, while Sequent established links with leading relational database software firms, such as Oracle. Both provided semi-automatic parallelizing tools for distributing loop iterations across processors, as well as lower-level mechanisms which allowed programmers to manage inter-process communication directly.

The Cray-X/MP and its descendents, the various multiprocessor VAXen, and the offerings of younger companies all evolved in response to market pressures. Customers wanted more power for their money, but did not want to have to re-write existing programs or make new programs dependent on a particular number of processors. Connecting processors and memory through a common bus, and having the operating system maintain a single queue of runnable processes, were the keys to ensuring that a collection of programs written for one size of machine would run unaltered on any other. Since the details of synchronization and message transfer were at least partially hidden by the compiler or run-time system, users did not need to know whether these activities were being performed by several co-operating processors, by software running on a single processor, or by some mix of the two. Programming a symmetric multiprocessor was thus (deliberately) similar to programming under a multi-tasking operating system; the only drawback was that the amount of hardware parallelism which could be used was limited by the speed of the single shared bus.

B.3 Hypercubes

The cure for the single-bus bottleneck was to introduce many more communication paths between processors and memories inside each computer. Many of the multicomputers which do this today are descended from work done at the California Institute of Technology (Caltech) in the first half of the 1980s; the different path taken by developments in Europe will be discussed in the next section.

In collaboration with a group headed by the physicist Geoffrey Fox, Charles Seitz and others in the computer science department at Caltech began to design a disjoint-memory multicomputer in the summer of 1981. This machine, the Mark I, contained 64 nodes arranged in a 6-dimensional binary hypercube. Each node was an Intel 8086 processor with an 8087 floating-point unit, 128 kbyte of memory, and six communication channels.

A 4-node prototype of the Mark I was in operation by the spring of 1982, and a 64-node version was running in the autumn of 1983. In the year that followed, the scientists involved in the cross-disciplinary Caltech Concurrent Computation Project (C^3P) that had formed around the machine used the Mark I to study acoustic wave equations, two-dimensional hydrodynamics, the evolution of the universe, the behavior of piles of sand, lattice gauge theory, the Travelling Salesrep Problem, and various sorting algorithms [Fox et al. 1988]. Many of these programs were built on top of a simple software environment called the Crystalline Operating System (CrOS). Originally developed in 1982 for handling matrix problems, CrOS supported programs in which all processes alternately computed and communicated. Many of the programming systems presently available for disjoint-memory multicomputers can be traced back to CrOS; the crystalline model it used is discussed in more detail in Section 5.2.

Buoyed by these successes, C^3P and the nearby NASA Jet Propulsion Laboratory (JPL) began work in 1983 on a Mark II machine. The Mark II used the same processors as the Mark I, but incorporated more memory, and gave each node its own connection to the outside world to allow direct I/O. A 256-node Mark II was in operation by the autumn of 1984. It was usually configured as four 32-node hypercubes and a single 128-node hypercube to allow up to five people to use the machine simultaneously.

In 1983, Intel, which had supported C^3P with hardware donations, sent a team under John Palmer to look at how their equipment was being used. Impressed by what he saw, Palmer left Intel to set up a company called NCube to make hypercubes commercially. Unlike C^3P's machines, NCube's used custom-built processors, although the software these ran was very similar.

The next team Intel sent, under Justin Rattner, was just as impressed. Under his guidance, Intel set up a new division called Intel Scientific Supercomputing Division to make hypercube computers itself. Its original iPSC/1 (the acronym standing for Intel Personal

SuperComputer) has since evolved into the iPSC/2 (which used 80386 processors), the iPSC/860 (which used i860s and wormhole routing), and more recently the Paragon, in which the hypercube topology has been dropped in favor of a mesh.

With these companies, and others like FPS and Ametek, manufacturing machines, the scientists at Caltech had to decide whether they would be better to continue building machines, or to rely on ones they could buy in. In the autumn of 1984, the C^3P group decided to carry on with a Mark III hypercube of their own. Their feeling was that Intel's machines had poor communication hardware (the Ethernet controller chips they used to manage messaging had very large latencies), while NCube's products had very little software support, and the FPS T-Node hypercubes, which were built out of a mix of Inmos transputers (discussed below) and Weitek floating point units, were extremely difficult to program. The C^3P group was also worried that the commercial manufacturers might concentrate on the super-minicomputer (or mini-supercomputer) market, i.e., build cost-effective number crunchers of only modest size rather than produce the high-performance machines the Caltech group needed to satisfy their users' ever-increasing demands.

The result of this decision, the Mark III, was the most complex machine the group ever built. Each node contained one Motorola 68020 microprocessor to do computation, another to handle communication, and a 68881 floating point unit. All three shared 4 Mbyte of memory. By the time the Mark III was finished in 1987, over 100 hypercubes had been sold commercially. What was more, the software environment on these machines had matured. CUBIX, developed by John Salmon and others, allowed programmers to make UNIX calls directly from any node of the hypercube. This environment simplified programming considerably, and freed programmers from switching back and forth between serial programming on a host machine and parallel programming on the hypercube's nodes.

B.4 The Transputer and Its Offspring

As American companies were building hypercubes in the 1980s, European companies began to experiment with a new microprocessor produced in the United Kingdom. In 1979, the British government financed the creation of a new semiconductor manufacturer called Inmos. Its aim was to get the U.K. back in the business of making electronic components. Inmos's strategy was to start by building memory chips, and then move into microprocessors.

In fact, the company's aims were more ambitious: its founders wanted to create an entirely new kind of microprocessor, one with on-board memory and communication capability so that it could be used as a building block for a wide variety of systems. This new chip, called the transputer, reached the market in 1985. Each carried 4 kbyte of RAM, four communication links, and a 32-bit CPU which could handle process scheduling and communication with single instructions. In theory, building a parallel computer was now simply a matter of soldering the appropriate pins together and providing a power source and a clock. In practice, the on-chip 4 kbyte of memory wasn't enough to store the code and data of most applications, so real machines had to contain much more than just transputers. In addition, it wasn't until 1988 that an on-board floating point unit was introduced, and memory management hardware never appeared at all (which made porting multi-tasking operating systems somewhat problematic).

The new chip's most significant shortcoming was software. In part, this was due to its newness. Most manufacturers of microprocessor-based parallel computers used chips that had been on the market for a long time, and which were supported by compilers, debuggers, and other utilities. All of these tools had to be created from scratch for the transputer. A greater reason for the transputer's lack of software was that in its early years Inmos put all of its marketing and support effort behind a new language called Occam, and a combined compiler/editor called the Transputer Development System (TDS). It didn't take long for people to start pronouncing the acronym "tedious"; the editor was difficult to use, the compiler was slow, and support for libraries and debugging was almost non-existent.

In the United States, Inmos's unwillingness to support standard languages such as C and FORTRAN, and the lack of a general-purpose message-passing system for the transputer, limited its uptake. In Europe, on the other hand, where there was a great deal of government support for the purchase of home-grown computer systems, the transputer flourished. Even as it was being launched, several members of the team which had implemented it left Inmos to found a new company to make transputer-based supercomputers. This company, called Meiko, produced its first Computing Surface in 1985, and started selling machines in 1986.

Like most transputer-based machines, the Computing Surface was highly modular. A generic board carried four transputers, each with 1 to 16 Mbyte of memory, and was plugged into a backplane which allowed the processors on one board to communicate with those on another. A variety of other boards provided graphics support, SCSI interfaces to disks, Ethernet connections, and so on. While users of Meiko's first machines had to knit these connections together by hand, later machines had an electronically-switchable backplane so that their topology could be changed on a program-by-program basis.

The Computing Surface initially had to be hosted by a VAX or a Sun workstation. Within two years, however, Meiko had produced a resource manager, which allowed the single physical machine to be partitioned into a number of disjoint *domains*, with a single user having sole access to each domain. This space sharing allowed programmers to develop and test code on a domain with a small number of processors while production runs were being done on larger domains, just as time sharing allows programmers to develop, test, and run code on a conventional machine concurrently.[2]

A more important software development was the introduction of a message-passing system called CS Tools, which quickly supplanted Occam and Meiko's re-worked version of the Inmos TDS. CS Tools was a library of functions, similar to those in CrOS and its descendents on hypercubes, which allowed any process to send a message to any other, no matter where each was located. After CS Tools was introduced in 1989, Meiko began producing boards using the SPARC and Intel i860 processors as well as transputers, with CS Tools being used to knit heterogeneous machines together. More recently, Meiko has abandoned the transputer altogether. The nodes in its CS-2 combine a SPARC microprocessor with a Fujitsu μVP vector processor and a custom-built communication chip. Nodes are connected through other custom switches in a multi-stage fat tree; the paths taken by messages through this network can be controlled by the user's software.

Meiko's history is more or less echoed by that of the other European manufacturers of large transputer-based machines, including Parsys, Telmat, and Parsytec. One important difference between these companies' products and Meiko's was that they provided a small UNIX-like operating system on each processor. Parsys did this with Idris, which was originally developed for the PDP-11 in the 1970s. The Idris kernel on each processor handled multi-tasking, and gave processes access to a shared file system. Telmat and Parsytec used a similar system, called Helios, which provided much of the same functionality.

B.5   Mixing Models

While the lack of a shared-bus bottleneck allowed engineers to make hypercubes and transputer-based machines which were much larger than conventional multiprocessors, most programmers found the latter much easier to use. Programmers working with shared memory only had to worry about synchronizing access to data structures; programmers working with disjoint memory, on the other hand, had to write explicit code to fetch or move remote data. As shown by the examples in [Babb 1988], this code was often long, error-prone, and tedious to construct. Many research groups and companies therefore experimented in the 1970s and 1980s with ways of making physically disjoint memory appear shared to programs. One early machine that provided this was the C.mmp, discussed above. However, the first commercial venture along these lines took a very different approach.

---

2. More recent systems use a technique called *gang scheduling* to allocate all the resources a program needs as a block. This makes for more efficient use of hardware, and simplifies scheduling.

In the 1960s and early 1970s, the Denver-based firm Denelcor was a manufacturer of analog computers, which were used primarily to solve systems of non-linear ordinary differential equations. Early in 1974, under contract from the U.S. Army Ballistics Research Laboratory, Burton Smith began work at Denelcor to design a shared-memory machine, which was eventually called the Heterogeneous Element Processor (HEP).

The HEP was a shared-memory machine, in which one or more Process Execution Modules (PEMs) were connected to one or more memory units through a multi-stage interconnection network. Unlike most supercomputers of its time, which pipelined the execution of arithmetic instructions on multiple operands, the HEP pipelined the execution of instructions taken from separate instruction streams. Each PEM maintained a queue of ready processes. In each cycle, an instruction from one of these, along with any operands and context that instruction required, was put into the PEM's execution pipeline. The various stages in this pipeline would then decode the instruction and execute it. Thus, the eight-stage pipeline could execute eight processes concurrently; once delays due to memory access times were taken into account, the actual degree of concurrency could rise to twelve or more.

As well as pipelining instruction execution, the HEP pipelined memory accesses. Each PEM contained some local program memory, and 4K of registers for storing constants, both of which could be accessed without using the PEM-to-memory switching network. When a process needed to read or write data, however, it injected a message into the switching network, then put itself in the memory reference queue to await a reply.

The switching network's role was to carry memory requests from the PEMs to the memory, and to carry values back. Each node in the network had three bi-directional ports, through which it could send or receive a single message in each time step. As these nodes did not have any internal queues, they had to forward every message immediately after receiving it. Whenever two messages actually wanted to exit by the same port, the switch would send one correctly, and mis-route the other in a different direction. In order to ensure that messages eventually reached their destinations, a 4-bit "age" was associated with each, and incremented every time the message was mis-routed. Older messages were always routed in preference to younger ones, and once a message's age reached the maximum possible value it was never mis-routed.

The HEP was programmed using a dialect of FORTRAN which incorporated two extensions. The first of these was a new keyword, CREATE, which could be used wherever a subroutine CALL could be used in standard FORTRAN. Instead of making a subroutine call, a CREATE statement spawned a new process, and gave it private copies of any variables declared local to that subroutine. When the subroutine's RETURN statement was reached, the process was terminated.

A more interesting feature of the HEP's FORTRAN was the inclusion of *asynchronous variables*. Every word in memory was tagged by a single bit, which showed whether the word was full or empty. If a variable's name began with a $, then the status of this bit was checked whenever the word was to be written or read. The rule used was simple: an asynchronous variable's value could not be read unless the variable was full, or written unless the variable was empty. Normally, when a full variable was read its status was re-set to empty, while writing an empty variable re-set its status to full.

Whenever a process tried to read an empty variable, or write a full one, it was suspended until the variable's status changed. This provided a very fine-grained synchronization mechanism, and allowed processes to communicate with one another cheaply and efficiently. More complicated mechanisms, such as the semaphores and barriers of Chapter 4, could easily be constructed on top of this mechanism.

After 1982, HEP-1's were installed at four sites in the United States, and two other machines were eventually installed in Germany and Japan. By then, however, the HEP hardware was slow by comparison with the recently-introduced Cray-X/MP. Although there were plans for a HEP-2 and HEP-3, these plans were put on hold following Denelcor's closure in 1985. They are now being resurrected at Tera Computers in Seattle.

Another firm that got into the supercomputer business at about the same time as Denelcor was Bolt, Beranek and Newman (BBN). BBN was founded in 1948 as a consulting firm specializing in underwater acoustics (i.e., submarine detection). Its first venture into parallel computing came in 1972, when it produced a multi-bus machine called Pluribus to act as a switching node in the ARPAnet (now Internet) computer network. Each of these machines contained several hardened PDP-11 minicomputers connected by a multi-stage interconnection network. A follow-on contract from the American government for a larger, more powerful version of this machine came in 1978. The new machine was given the name Butterfly because of the shape of the multi-stage interconnection network it used (page 76).

Each processing node in the original Butterflies, the first of which was delivered in 1981, contained a Motorola 68000 microprocessor with 512 kbyte of memory. After selling some forty of these machines, BBN produced an enhanced version, the Butterfly Plus, which used the Motorola 68020 and included 4 Mbyte of memory per node. Like the original hypercubes, both the Butterfly and Butterfly Plus required a front-end host to compile and down-load programs. Their successor, the GP1000, did away with this host, and instead ran a version of the UNIX-like operating system Mach on each node. This model was retained in the fourth and final generation of the Butterfly, called the TC2000. First delivered in 1989, the TC2000 used Motorola's 88000-series microprocessors, but retained the multi-stage interconnection network of its predecessors.

What made the Butterfly machines interesting was their use of the closely-coupled memory model introduced in Figure 2.9. Each Butterfly's memory was physically disjoint, but appeared to users to comprise a single address space. Whenever a processor referenced memory, the address it supplied was compared to the range of addresses in the memory directly connected to it. If the address was in range, the memory operation was done locally. If it was not, a request was automatically sent through the switching network to the appropriate node, and the processor blocked until the corresponding reply reached it.

While this allowed programmers to treat the memory of the Butterfly machines as if it were shared, the key to getting good performance was to ensure that most of a processor's memory references were to its own memory, thus minimizing network traffic and contention. For example, if processors were working on an array, then the best performance would be achieved by distributing the array's elements across the processors, and having each processor work as much as possible on its own portion. Another trick often used was duplicating data, so that each processor had its own copy; the story goes that this idea first occurred to someone who noticed that processors were spending 90% of their time waiting to access the value of π, which was stored in only one location in the whole machine. When data were duplicated in this way, the Butterfly hardware did not take steps to guarantee that cached copies of the same value were consistent with one another.

The differences between the Denelcor HEP and the BBN Butterfly are almost as instructive as the machines themselves. BBN's design used off-the-shelf microprocessors, on which switching between processes was very expensive. As a result, while it was important that memory appeared to be logically shared, it was equally important that processes be able to make most memory references without incurring the delays caused by non-local access. Denelcor's design, on the other hand, was predicated on the idea of hiding memory access latency by pipelining several different instruction streams within each processor. With such a technique in hand, it was not as important for most memory references to be local, so the machine's memory could be physically separated from the processors.

Several different parallel programming systems were produced for the Butterfly, both within BBN and at major user sites such as the Lawrence Livermore National Laboratory (LLNL). Among the former were the operating systems nX, a modified version of Mach, and pSOS, a much smaller kernel intended for real-time applications. In addition, several debugging and performance profiling tools were developed; one of these, the Totalview debugger, has since been ported to other machines, such as CRI's T3D multicomputer. While tools like debuggers and profilers are commonly available on serial machines, they are still relatively primitive on massively-parallel computers, and for a long time the Butterfly toolset was the best the industry had to offer.

The Canadian company Myrias never played in the same league as BBN, but from a programming point of view its SPS machines were just as interesting. Myrias was founded in

1983 by a group based at the University of Alberta, whose ambition was to build scalable, high-performance parallel computers. Myrias's staff spent their first two years designing an abstract architecture called the G machine, which was to serve as an intermediate vehicle for all future work. The model which it aimed to support was the same `doall` supported on the ILLIAC-IV, and on most other parallel supercomputers.

The G machine specification described an abstract set of instructions. Most of these were the conventional loads, stores, and arithmetic operations found in any machine. A few, however, did things like create new processes or wait for processes to terminate. The plan was that all compilers would output G machine instructions, which would then be translated into machine-specific instructions for particular parallel computers. The compiler writer's job would be simplified by having a fixed target to shoot at; the architect would have an exact specification of what had to be implemented, and could use whatever technology or tricks seemed appropriate, while users would have a simple, intuitive model of their machines' behavior which would be independent on any particular implementation.

Myrias did not start building hardware until 1985. In 1987, their first 68000-based Scalable Parallel Supercomputer (SPS) was up and running, and in 1989 they sold their first 68020-based SPS-2. Each processor had 4 Mbyte of RAM, and was controlled by a Parallel Applications Management System (PAMS) running on a single master processor. PAMS allocated tasks to processors, and directed the copying and merging of data images required to implement the machine's `doall` model. Whenever a processor executing part of a `doall` made a reference to memory, PAMS gave that processor a copy of the appropriate page. When the `doall` finished, these copies were merged by keeping one copy of each altered value. The rules used were simple:

- If no child had modified X, X was not changed.
- If exactly one child had modified X, that value was the final value of X.
- If several children had modified X, and all the new values were the same, that value was the final value of X.
- If several children had modified X, and the new values were not all the same, the final value was unpredictable, and might not even be one of the children's values.

This memory model was later extended so that different modifications could be accumulated in various ways, i.e., by being added, or by the largest being retained. PAMS also provided virtual memory by allowing processors to claim pages from one another's private memory stores.

B.6   Massively-Parallel, But Single-Bit

At the same time that the ILLIAC-IV was being developed in the United States, a group in the U.K. led by Stewart Reddaway was building the world's first thousand-processor computer. Preliminary paper studies of the Distributed Array Processor (DAP) were done in 1972 in an attempt to show that a machine made up of many small, slow processors would not be able to compete with conventional supercomputers. Perversely, the study convinced Reddaway that such a machine would be both powerful and cost-effective.

At the time, Reddaway was working for ICL, the UK's largest computer company. After several more paper studies, the company began to build a prototype in 1974. This machine contained 1024 single-bit processing elements, or PEs, arranged in a 32×32 mesh with wrap-around connections. Each PE initially had 1 kbit of memory, although this was later upgraded to 2 kbit. As in the ILLIAC-IV, a single control processor broadcast instructions to the PEs, while a single-bit control register in each PE determined whether that PE executed or ignored a particular instruction. However, as the DAP's PEs were much simpler than the ILLIAC-IV's, the instructions broadcast were much more elementary. For example, in order to add two 32-bit numbers, the controller would broadcast instructions to add the least significant bits of the numbers, then to add the carry to the sum of the next two bits, and so on. When doing division, the controller would first disable every processor on which the divisor was zero, in order to prevent an arithmetic error from occurring. The fact that PE memory was *bit-addressable* in this fashion also meant that programs could use non-standard data sizes (such as 12-bit integers) for applications such as signal processing.

By 1977, the British government had agreed to purchase at least one DAP for use at Queen Mary College in London. This machine was completed in 1979, and installed in 1980. Soon afterward, ICL's finances collapsed; the other five DAPs which had been constructed were sold off or given away, and the development project was in danger of dying. After ICL was bailed out, however, some work was done to develop a smaller MiniDAP for use in military and signal processing applications. This work kept the development group going until the mid-1980s, when they were spun off as a new company, Active Memory Technology (AMT). The DAP was then completely re-engineered using custom VLSI chips to produce a powerful co-processor which could be attached to a conventional workstation.

In retrospect, the DAP should have been much more important than it was. Many new algorithms and techniques were developed for it, and a great deal of software was produced, much of which is still in use on the younger AMT DAPs. However, a lack of support from within ICL, coupled with a failure to publicize the ideas embodied in the DAP, left it out of the mainstream of parallel computing.

In the end, it fell to Thinking Machines Corporation to bring massive bit-level parallelism to the forefront of supercomputing. The company was founded in 1983 to commercialize ideas coming out of research in artificial intelligence. Its first two products were a computer-aided design system and an index-generating tool, which would extract keywords from text. Its third, the CM-1 Connection Machine, was a massively-parallel computer whose design drew on the doctoral research done by Danny Hillis at the Massachussetts Institute of Technology (MIT).

Hillis had not been thinking of numerical applications when he designed the CM-1. Instead, he had wanted a vehicle for processing semantic networks, a formalism in vogue in artificial intelligence at the time. It wasn't until the spring of 1984, when Hillis gave a talk at Carnegie-Mellon University, that Guy Steele did a back-of-the-envelope calculation that showed that the CM-1 would be able to achieve 100 MFLOPS on floating-point operations, which was comparable to the performance of the most powerful machines of the time.

The first CM-1s were delivered in 1986. Like the DAP, the CM-1's simple bit-serial processors all executed the same instruction at the same time. The major differences between the two machines were the number of processors (the CM-1 contained 16k processors, rather than 4k), the interconnection topology (the CM-1 was a hypercube, rather than a torus), and the programming environment: unlike most supercomputers before and since, the CM-1 was primarily programmed in a variant of Lisp, and indeed the hosts for the first machines were Symbolics Lisp workstations. Only 10 CM-1s were ever produced, and most of these were sold to educational institutions.

A major re-design of the machine led to the production in 1987 of the CM-2, which proved much more popular. The CM-2 retained the hypercubic topology and bit-serial processors of the CM-1, but grouped the latter into 32's, and coupled a 14 MFLOPS Weitek floating-point chip with each group through a custom-built chip called the SPRINT. In most numerical programs, the single-bit PEs were used for moving data, while the bulk of the computation was done by the floating-point chips.

Programs for the CM-2 actually executed on a sequencer contained within the front-end host, which broadcast instructions to the PEs and floating-point units. Most programs were written in CM-Fortran, which extended FORTRAN-77 with whole-array operations. Other, more exotic, operations were provided to sum the elements of arrays, or to permute data in regular patterns. (In fact, one of the most important effects of the Connection Machine was to spur research into ways of implementing such permutations efficiently.)

In 1991, Thinking Machines began producing an upgraded CM-2 called the CM-200. A year later, it announced the CM-5, its first MIMD machine. Each CM-5 contained up to 1024 SPARC microprocessors connected in a fat tree topology. Each SPARC controlled four custom vector units, manufactured by Texas Instruments. While the bulk of these machines' users continued to program in the data-parallel style they had used on earlier Connection Machines, some groups began developing control-parallel software to take advantage of the independently-executing SPARCs. Many of these projects based other work on the Active Messages system developed by Thorsten von Eicken and others at the University of California at Berkeley (UCB), which supported low-latency communication by including a pointer to a message-handling function in each message. When the message reached a processor, that processor dealt with it simply by jumping to the specified location and executing the code found there.

B.7   A Quiet Success

One of the most successful parallel computer manufacturers of the 1980s was also one of the least well-known: Teradata. Founded in 1980 as a spin-off from the data processing wing of the American financial conglomerate Citibank, Teradata set out to capture the high end of the database market by building machines capable of processing queries on databases holding gigabytes of records. Since the only way to do this is in a reasonable time is to have many processors search and merge different parts of the database concurrently, Teradata set out to build a parallel machine.

The company sold its first Database Computer (DBC) in 1985. Each machine consisted of a tree-structured switching network, whose internal nodes were custom-built to route and collate messages. The processors at the leaves of this network had disks attached to them, or connected the machine to local area networks and mainframes. Teradata was very conservative with its technology—the network ran at only 6 MHz, for example, while the processor used for leaf nodes was originally the Intel 8086, and was only gradually upgraded to the 80286 and 80386. Teradata played it safe in other ways as well, by including a backup network in every machine and by making provision for users to duplicate data so that disk failures would not interrupt query processing.

The only way to program Teradata's DBC was to give it an SQL database query. Everything else, from the way records were examined to the way responses were merged and presented, was beyond users' control. In many ways, Teradata's success was achieved by hiding parallelism from users as much as possible, something which it could only do by restricting what its customers could do with its machines.

B.8   Today and Tomorrow

Fifteen years ago, a few visionaries believed that massive parallelism was the future of high-performance computing. Five years ago, that view had become commonplace; today, it is increasingly in doubt. Many scientists find that the overall time required to solve their problem on a conventional workstation is less than required on a parallel computer, since the increased performance of the latter is outweighed by the increased difficulty of programming it [Furht 1994]. In addition, many of the problems that parallelize easily will run as well on a network of workstations (which the company or department already has) as they will on a dedicated multicomputer.

Massively-parallel computing has also been hurt by the decline of "blank check" computing since the end of the Cold War. From the Second World War until the late 1980s, a handful of government laboratories in the United States were able to specify and purchase high-performance computer systems almost without regard to cost [Elzen & Mackenzie 1994, Mackenzie 1991]. Since then, manufacturers have not been able to depend on recouping their development costs from a small number of high-ticket sales. As a result, while firms such as Cray Research Incorporated have entered the market, others, such as Kendall Square Research and Thinking Machines Corporation, have been forced out.

The future of massively-parallel computing therefore depends the answers to two key questions: "Can large parallel computers be made cost-competitive with networks of workstations?" and "Can parallel programming be made time-competitive with sequential programming?" The first may well be moot, since the networks of the future will almost certainly have the low cost, low latency, multiple paths, and high bandwidth which characterize today's parallel machines. As for parallel programming becoming time-competitive with sequential programming, this will probably not happen until the languages used for each merge. The greatest hope for parallelism may ultimately lie in the sort of high-level language of which Sisal [Feo et al. 1990] is an example, in symbolic mathematical packages like Mathematica [Wolfram 1991], and, most importantly, in an increased willingness on the part of scientific and numerical programmers to use such modern tools.

C Recommended Reading

C.1 Books

1 Gregory R. Andrews. *Concurrent Programming: Principles and Practice*. Benjamin/Cummings, 1991. A thorough, readable introduction to the theory of concurrency. This book covers everything from low-level spinlocking to monitors and remote procedure call (RPC) mechanisms. The emphasis is on operating systems and distributed computing; many illustrations are given throughout, using the author's own SR language. Each chapter includes a short appendix summarizing the history and development of a particular set of ideas, with copious references to the literature.

2. Guy E. Blelloch. *Vector Models for Data-Parallel Computing*. MIT Press, 1990. An expanded version of the author's Ph.D. thesis, this is a careful exposition of the scan-vector model, an interesting alternative to the parallel random access machine (PRAM) model used by most theorists as a basis for analyzing parallel algorithms. The author presents and justifies the model, shows how it can be used, and describes an implementation of its primitives on the CM-2 Connection Machine.

3. Nicholas Carriero and David Gelernter. *How to Write Parallel Programs*. MIT Press, 1990. The title should really include the postscript "in C-Linda", as that is the only parallel programming system discussed, and the book's examples are problems which sit well on top of Linda. Despite that, this is a good introductory text; it describes different ways of exploiting parallelism while avoiding race conditions, deadlock, and low performance.

4. Garth A. Gibson. *Redundant Disk Arrays: Reliable Parallel Secondary Storage*. MIT Press, 1992. RAIDs (Redundant Arrays of Inexpensive Disks) are the mass-storage equivalent of microprocessor-based multicomputers. This book, which is an expanded version of the author's thesis, shows that one can achieve high performance and high reliability by combining a large number of mass-produced (i.e., small and cheap) hard disks. The book contains theoretical models, a discussion of the relevant coding theory, and experimental data drawn from prototype machines.

5. Vipin Kumar, Ananth Grama, Anshul Gupta, and George Karypis. *Introduction to Parallel Computing: Design and Analysis of Algorithms*. Benjamin-Cummings, 1994. An excellent text on parallel algorithms. The book's great strengths is that its authors invest little time in PRAM algorithms, preferring ones which can be implemented on machines which can actually be built. The chapters discussing architectures and programming languages are run-of-the-mill, but the bulk of the book describes and analyzes a wide variety of algorithms for mesh- and hypercube-based multicomputers (chosen as representative of sparsely-connected and densely-connected machines respectively).

6. Michael J. Quinn. *Parallel Computing: Theory and Practice*. McGraw-Hill, 1994. A good introductory text on parallel computing, which interleaves presentations of various parallel algorithms with discussions of their implementation and performance. The book also contains a good overview of the kinds of parallel programming systems which most parallel computer users are likely to encounter.

7. Arthur Trew and Greg Wilson, editors. *Past, Present, Parallel: A Survey of Available Parallel Computer Systems*. Springer-Verlag, 1991. Now out of date, but still a good survey of commercial parallel machines and the companies that build them. Each chapter covers a different company, living or deceased, traces the historical evolution of its machines, and describes its offerings circa 1991.

C.2 Algorithms and Techniques

1. Norbert S. Arenstorf and Harry F. Jordan. Comparing Barrier Algorithms. *Parallel Computing*, 12:157–70, 1989. This paper describes several algorithms for doing barrier synchronization and examines the pros and cons of each. A simple graphical notation for describing barriers is developed and used to show how some techniques lead to automatic self-synchronization, while others do not.

2. Guy E. Blelloch. Scans as Primitive Parallel Operations. *IEEE Transactions on Computers*, 38(11), November 1989. Introduces and analyzes the scan, or parallel prefix, operation. Given a vector $< v_1, v_2, v_3, \ldots >$ and an associative binary operator $\oplus$, parallel prefix generates the vector of partial sums $< v_1, v_1 \oplus v_2, v_1 \oplus v_2 \oplus v_3, \ldots >$. This operation turns out to be surprisingly powerful, and inexpensive to implement.

3. Richard M. Fujimoto. Parallel Discrete Event Simulation. *Communications of the ACM*, 33(10), October 1990. A comprehensive survey of techniques for parallelizing discrete event simulation. The paper describes and compares conservative and optimistic approaches, and discusses the performance which real systems have achieved, and the problems which these systems continue to encounter.

4. Leslie Lamport. Time, Clocks, and the Ordering of Events in a Distributed System. *Communications of the ACM*, 21(7), July 1978. The classic paper on the relativity of event ordering in distributed systems. Its author explains why it may not be possible to impose a complete ordering on events in a distributed system, then presents a simple algorithm for constructing a consistent partial order based on local virtual clocks.

5. John M. Mellor-Crummey and Michael L. Scott. Algorithms for Scalable Synchronization on Shared-Memory Multiprocessors. *ACM Transactions on Computer Systems*, 9(1), February 1991. Describes a technique for implementing spin-locking and barrier

synchronization which does not rely on opportunistic message combining. The algorithm distributes a linked list of activation records throughout a machine's memory, so that waiting processes need only examine their own local memory.

C.3   Architectures and Communications

1. Anant Agarwal, John Kubiatowicz, David Kranz, Beng-Hong Lim, Donald Yeung, Godfrey D'Souza, and Mike Parkin. Sparcle: An Evolutionary Processor Design for Large-Scale Multiprocessors. *IEEE Micro*, 13(3), June 1993. Describes a modified SPARC RISC microprocessor, called SPARCle, which has been developed for use in MIT's Alewife multiprocessor project. The SPARCle was designed with fast context switching, low communication start-up times, and cache consistency in mind, and is an indication of how the present generation of microprocessors might evolve in future.

2. Lionel M. Ni and Philip K. McKinley. A Survey of Wormhole Routing Techniques in Direct Networks. *IEEE Computer*, February 1993. A comprehensive survey of wormhole routing techniques, covering both the basic idea and many of the refinements which have been developed since the original presentation by Dally and Seitz in the mid-1980s.

3. B. Ramakrishna Rau and Joseph A. Fisher. Instruction-Level Parallel Processing: History, Overview, and Perspective. *Journal of Supercomputing*, 7:9–50, 1993. A retrospective look at the development of Very Large Instruction Word (VLIW) architectures, and compilers for them, written by two of the field's principals. VLIW system attempt to schedule computations statically (during compilation) by predicting branch directions and pipelining highly-probable execution traces. When this works, it allows VLIW computers to achieve very good performance on codes which are normally not considered vectorizable.

4. David B. Skillicorn. Architecture-Independent Parallel Computation. *IEEE Computer*, December 1990. A very readable presentation and critique of Valiant's scheme for emulating parallel random access machine (PRAM) model on realizable computers. The author explains why cost-optimal emulation is only possible on machines in which the proportion of hardware devoted to communication grows with machine size. The second half of the paper is more specialized, as it presents the author's own alternative model for parallel computation.

5. Lawrence Snyder. Type Architectures, Shared Memory, and the Corollary of Modest Potential. *Annual Review of Computer Science*, pages 289–317, 1986. A critique of the parallel random access machine (PRAM) model much-loved by theoreticians, wrapped up in a larger commentary on the nature and purpose of abstract models of computation. This

paper also includes a rather pessimistic discussion of the limits to what parallelism can be expected to deliver.

6. Per Stenström. Reducing Contention in Shared-Memory Multiprocessors. *IEEE Computer*, November 1988. An introduction to the difficulty of maintaining memory consistency in multiprocessor systems. The paper begins by presenting the simplest possible schemes, and analyzing their deficiencies, then moves develops more and more complicated alternatives.

7. Per Stenström. A Survey of Cache Coherence Schemes for Multiprocessors. *IEEE Computer*, June 1990. Discusses various ways of maintaining cache consistency in multiprocessor systems. The paper is not primarily concerned with performance analysis; instead, it examines the complexity of implementing various protocols under different assumptions.

C.4   Languages and Compilation

1. Arvind and Stephen Brobst. The Evolution of Dataflow Architectures: From Static Dataflow to P-RISC. *International Journal of High Speed Computing*, 5(2), 1993. The only paper on dataflow computing which a non-practitioner need ever read, traces the subject's evolution from theoretical work in the 1960s and 1970s through successive generations of experimental machines. The authors are fairly frank in describing the shortcomings and pitfalls of what has been tried. Both hardware and software are covered, although the emphasis is on the former.

2. David F. Bacon, Susan L. Graham, and Oliver J. Sharp. Compiler Transformations for High-Performance Computing. *ACM Computer Surveys*, 26(4), December 1994. An excellent survey of the state of the art in compile-time optimization and transformation of imperative languages. While most of the ideas and techniques described are intended for RISC uniprocessors, there is a lot of material on vectorization and parallelization. The paper's strongest point is its coherent organization and presentation; a method which might seem like magic in isolation makes a great deal more sense when presented beside several siblings.

3. Henri E. Bal, J. G. Steiner, and A. S. Tanenbaum. Programming Languages for Distributed Computing Systems. *ACM Computing Surveys*, 21(3), 1989. While this survey is now somewhat dated, no other of equal breadth and thoroughness has yet appeared. The authors restrict themselves to languages, rather than run-time libraries such as PVM, but still include references to approximately 300 different systems, and informative descriptions of one or two from each major category.

4. John K. Bennett, John B. Carter, and Willy Zwaenepoel. Munin: Distributed Shared Memory Based on Type-Specific Memory Coherence. In *Proceedings of the 1990 Conference on Principles and Practice of Parallel Programming*. ACM Press, 1990. Describes a virtual shared memory system which can use different protocols to maintain the consistency of different types of objects. A read-mostly object, for example, might be managed by replication, and locking and broadcast used to update it, while a many-writers, one-reader object would be stored on a single processor, which would handle all operations on it. The classification scheme that forms the basis of Munin is a generally useful way to think about the parallelization of data structures.

5. David Callahan and Burton Smith. A Future-based Parallel Language for a General-Purpose Highly-Parallel Computer. In David Gelernter, Alexandru Nicolau, and David Padua, editors, *Languages and Compilers for Parallel Computing*. Pitman, 1990. An interesting examination of the interplay between what users want, what compilers can do, and what hardware can support. The authors describe a way of incorporating futures, first introduced by Halstead in the context of functional languages, into traditional imperative languages such as C and FORTRAN. Their interest stems from the ability of the hardware they are building (the Tera context-flow machine) to support low-cost process creation and fine-grained process interleaving.

6. Nicholas Carriero and David Gelernter. Tuple Analysis and Partial Evaluation Strategies in the Linda Compiler. In David Gelernter, Alexandru Nicolau, and David Padua, editors, *Languages and Compilers for Parallel Computing*. Pitman, 1990. Describes how compile-time analysis of the pattern-matching operations done by a Linda system can be used to reduce the run-time costs of matching and messaging. The compiler can, for example, turn an in-modify-out sequence into a fetch&op operation, replace strings (and string-matching) with integer tokens (and equality testing), and so on. The paper is a good example of what can be done to squeeze efficiency out of a high-level parallel programming system.

7. David E. Culler, Andrea Dusseau, Seth Copen Goldstein, Arvind Krishnamurthy, Steven Lumetta, Thorsten von Eicken, and Katherine Yelick. Parallel Programming in Split-C. In *Proc. Supercomputing '93*, 1993. Describes a C-based parallel programming language called Split-C. The name is suggested by the way in which assignment operations involving remote memory references can be split, so that the computation begins at one point, and is only guaranteed to have completed after a later synchronization. The language is interesting not only as an attempt to integrate low-level message-passing into a high(ish)-level language, but also because the applications being supported involve irregular, linked structures.

8. Wayne Fenton, Balkrishan Ramkumar, Vikram Saletore, Amitabh B. Sinha, and Laxmikant V. Kalé. Supporting Machine-Independent Parallel Programming on Diverse Architectures. In *Proceedings of the 1991 International Conference on Parallel Processing*, 1991. Describes a C-based parallel programming system called CHARM, which supports both constrained data sharing and message passing. Processes are essentially message handlers, and may be created dynamically using messages; shared data structures managed by a small number of fixed protocols may also be used for inter-process communication and coordination.

9. I. Foster and K. M. Chandy. FORTRAN M: A Language for Modular Parallel Programming. *Journal of Parallel and Distributed Computing*, 25(1), 1995. The authors were principals in the development of Strand88 and PCN, two systems which allowed fragments of imperative code to be embedded in dataflow/parallel logic programming frameworks. FORTRAN M reverses this, and adds token-passing and synchronizing operations on channels to serial FORTRAN.

10. G. A. Geist and V. S. Sunderam. Network-Based Concurrent Computing on the PVM System. *Concurrency: Practice and Experience*, 4(4), June 1992. PVM (Parallel Virtual Machine) is a message-passing library which runs on many distributed and massively-parallel computers. It contains support for execution in heterogeneous environments, and is a strong influence on the emerging MPI (Message-Passing Interface) pseudo-standard. This paper describes PVM's interface and implementation, and gives a good idea of what most such systems do and do not contain.

11. Jonathan Schaeffer, Duane Szafron, Greg Lobe, and Ian Parsons. The Enterprise Model for Developing Distributed Applications. *IEEE Parallel & Distributed Technology*, 1(3):85–96, 1993. Describes a system which can be used to parallelize pre-existing sequential C programs by mixing several well-defined paradigms hierarchically. A graphical interface allows users to sketch out how parallelism is to be organized. The compiler then turns regular procedure calls into remote procedure calls (RPCs) as needed.

C.5   Performance Evaluation and Modelling

1. David H. Bailey. Twelve Ways to Fool the Masses When Giving Performance Results on Parallel Computers. *Supercomputing Review*, 4(8), August 1991. A brief jeremiad on the abuse of performance statistics. The author describes a dozen ways to mislead an audience about the performance of one's machine, and illustrates these techniques with examples drawn from the literature. Afraid of losing that all-important sale? Quote your own single-precision, assembly-level megafloppage; it's sure to look good against your competitor's double-precision, compiled-FORTRAN figures.

2. Guy E. Blelloch, Charles E. Leiserson, Bruce M. Maggs, Greg C. Plaxton, Stephen J. Smith, and Marco Zagha. A Comparison of Sorting Algorithms for the Connection Machine CM 2. Technical Report TMC-222, Thinking Machines Corporation, 1991. Describes several sorting algorithms for massively-parallel machines, and their performance on the CM-2 Connection Machine. The authors also describe some ways to optimize these algorithms, and explain why they believe parallel radix sort to be the best general-purpose sorting algorithm for the CM-2.

3. Ananth Grama, Anshul Gupta, and Vipin Kumar. Isoefficiency: Measuring the Scalability of Parallel Algorithms and Architectures. *IEEE Parallel & Distributed Technology*, 1(3), August 1993. The term "scalable" has been used in many different, and often meaningless, ways to describe parallel computer systems. This paper discusses a way of quantifying scalability by deriving an isoefficiency function for a particular combination of algorithm and architecture. This function measures the rate at which the problem size must grow as a function of the number of processors being used in order to maintain a specified efficiency.

4. Gary Graunke and Shreekant Thakkar. Synchronization Algorithms for Shared-Memory Multiprocessors. *IEEE Computer*, June 1990. A very hands-on paper which describes several techniques for implementing locks on a bus-based multiprocessor with coherent caching (the Sequent Symmetry), presents measurements of their performance, and explains why they behave as they do. .

5. Roger Hockney. Performance Parameters and Benchmarking of Supercomputers. *Parallel Computing*, 17:1111–30, 1991. Describes and justifies several performance metrics developed by the author. Two of these—r_∞ and $n_{1/2}$—quantify the peak performance and startup overhead of pipelined processors, and are widely used for both practical and pedagogic purposes. The other two, which are less widely known, quantify memory reference and synchronization overheads.

6. David M. Nicol and Paul F. Reynolds, Jr. Optimal Dynamic Remapping of Data Parallel Computations. *IEEE Transactions on Computers*, 39(2):206–19, February 1990. A thorough mathematical analysis of the tradeoff between the cost of re-mapping data in a parallel system, and the cost of wasted processor cycles due to load imbalance. Not for the mathophobic.

7. David M. Nicol and Joel H. Saltz. An Analysis of Scatter Decomposition. *IEEE Transactions on Computers*, 39(11):1337–45, November 1990. A thorough mathematical analysis of the costs and benefits of scattered spatial decomposition (SSD). SSD decomposes a mesh into many more fragments than there are processors, and makes each processor responsible for computations on several non-adjacent fragments in an attempt to avoid workload imbalance. Not for the mathophobic.

8. G. F Pfister and V. A. Norton. "Hot Spot" Contention and Combining in Multistage Interconnection Networks. In *Proceedings of the IEEE International Conference on Parallel Processing*, 1985. Describes how even small imbalances in memory reference patterns can degrade the performance of indirectly-switched multiprocessors. Read and write requests sent to a frequently-referenced memory location, or "hot spot", will have to queue up for service; once the queues in the switch nearest that memory bank become full, messages start spilling into the queues of neighboring switches, and so on. A paper written in the subsequent year extended this analysis and looked at the onset of contention of this kind.

9. Hanmao Shi and Jonathan Schaeffer. Parallel Sorting by Regular Sampling. *Journal of Parallel and Distributed Computing*, 14:361–372, 1992. Describes a general-purpose sorting algorithm for parallel machines, analyses its complexity, and presents performance figures for real implementations. The algorithm reduces data transmission costs and balances computational load by sampling each processor's data in order to estimate the likely distribution of the sorted result.

C.6   Tools and System Software

1. Michael L. Best, Adam Greenberg, Craig Stanfill, and Lewis W. Tucker. CMMD I/O: A Parallel Unix I/O. In *Proceedings of the Seventh International Parallel Processing Symposium*. IEEE Computer Society, 1993. It has been said that a supercomputer is something that turns a compute-bound problem into an I/O-bound problem. This is doubly true on most massively parallel systems, which have neither enough hardware to perform I/O, nor the system software needed to insulate users from that hardware. This paper describes one attempt to build a UNIX-like file system interface for a massively-parallel machine. The system described is representative of others which have been proposed or constructed.

2. Michael T. Heath and Jennifer A. Etheridge. Visualizing the Performance of Parallel Programs. *IEEE Software*, September 1991. An introduction to Paragraph, a performance monitoring and visualization system for parallel programs. The original implementation only worked with programs implemented using the PICL message-passing system, but its interface has since been ported to many other systems, and it is a good illustration of what such systems do and do not offer.

3. Barton P. Miller and Charles E. McDowell, editors. *Proceedings of the ACM/ONR Workshop on Parallel and Distributed Debugging (ACM SIGPLAN Notices)*, December 1991. An overview of parallel debugging systems which describes what they can do, both in general and in particular cases. The rest of the book in which this paper appears consists of more detailed descriptions of particular systems.

4. Michael Stumm and Songnian Zhou. Algorithms Implementing Distributed Shared Memory. *IEEE Computer*, May 1990. Compares four techniques for supporting distributed shared memory, i.e., for emulating shared memory in a disjoint-memory system. The paper includes performance analyses, and suggests two refinements to previously-proposed schemes.

D Glossary

active tuple see under *tuple*.

actual field see under *tuple*.

adaptive *(adj., p. 82)* Taking local surroundings or history into account. An adaptive *mesh*-generating algorithm generates a finer mesh near discontinuities such as boundaries and corners; an adaptive *routing* algorithm may send identical messages in different directions at different times, depending on the local density of message traffic, while adaptive *caching* maintains memory coherence using techniques tailored to the predicted or observed pattern of references to a data structure. See also: *oblivious*.

address space *(n., p. 13)* A region of a computer's total memory, within which addresses are contiguous and may refer to one another directly. A *shared-memory* computer has only one user-visible address space; a *disjoint-memory* computer can have several.

all-to-all personalized communication *(n., p. 336)* Communication in which each process sends a distinct message to each other. See also: *all-to-all replicated communication*; *all-to-one personalized communication*; *one-to-all personalized communication*; *one-to-all replicated communication*; *one-to-one communication*.

all-to-all replicated communication *(n., p. 336)* Communication in which each process sends the same message to each other. See also: *all-to-all personalized communication*; *all-to-one personalized communication*; *one-to-all personalized communication*; *one-to-all replicated communication*; *one-to-one communication*.

all-to-one personalized communication *(n., p. 336)* Communication in which each process sends a distinct message to a single collector. "Gather" is often used in this sense. See also: *all-to-all personalized communication*; *all-to-all replicated communication*; *one-to-all personalized communication*; *one-to-all replicated communication*; *one-to-one communication*.

Amdahl's Law *(n., p. 59)* A rule, first stated by Gene Amdahl [Amdahl 1967], which says that if σ is the proportion of a calculation that is serial, and $1 - \sigma$ is the portion that can be parallelized, then the *speedup* that can be achieved with $\mathcal{P}$ processors is:

$$S = \lim_{\mathcal{P} \to \infty} \frac{1}{\sigma + \frac{1-\sigma}{\mathcal{P}}}$$
$$= 1/\sigma$$

Thus, no matter how many processors are used, if 5% of a calculation must be done serially, the maximum speedup possible with any number of processors is 20. See also: *efficiency*; *Gustafson's Law*; *parallel balance point*.

anti-dependence   see under *dependence*.

anti-tuple   see under *tuple*.

architecture   *(n., p. 3)* The basic plan along which a computer has been constructed. Popular parallel architectures include *processor arrays*, *bus*-based *multiprocessors* (with *caches* of varying sizes), *disjoint-memory multicomputers*, and various *hierarchical architectures*. See also: *Flynn's taxonomy*.

arity   *(n., p. 69)* The number of arguments taken by a function: $f(x)$ has an arity of 1, while $g(v, w, x, y)$ has an arity of 4. Arity is also sometimes used to mean *valence*.

associative memory   *(adj., p. 9)* Memory that can be accessed by content rather than address; *content-addressable* is often used synonymously. An associative memory permits its user to specify part of a pattern, or key, and retrieve the values associated with that pattern. The *tuple space* used to implement the *generative communication* model is an associative memory.

asymmetric operating system   *(adj., p. 14)* An operating system which executes kernel operations on some processors, and user operations on others. See also: *symmetric operating system*.

asynchronous   *(adj., p. 371)* Not guaranteed to enforce coincidence in *clock time*. In an asynchronous communication operation, the sender and receiver may or may not both be engaged in the operation at the same instant in clock time; an asynchronous variable is one which may be in either a full or empty state. See also: *synchronous*.

atomic   *(adj., p. 198)* Not interruptable. An atomic operation is one that always appears to have been executed without interruption.

barrier   *(n., p. 237)* A point in a program at which *barrier synchronization* occurs. See also: *fuzzy barrier*.

barrier bit   *(n., p. 149)* A single bit associated with each operand in a *segmented parallel prefix* which indicates the start of a new segment. See also: *parallel prefix*.

barrier synchronization   *(n., p. 237)* An event in which two or more processes belonging to some implicit or explicit group *block* until all members of the group have blocked. No process in the group may pass a *barrier* until all processes in the group have reached it. See also: *fuzzy barrier*.

basic block   *(n., p. 164)* A section of a program that does not cross any conditional branches, loop boundaries, or other transfers of control. Most *compiler optimization* is done within basic blocks.

Bernstein's Condition   *(n., p. 164)* A sufficient condition for the independence of two sections of a program [Bernstein 1966]. If R_i (W_i) is the set of variables read (written) by a section i, then Bernstein's Condition states that sections i and j may be executed in an arbitrary order, or concurrently, if:

$$(R_i \cap W_j) \cup (R_j \cap W_i) \cup (W_i \cap W_j) = \emptyset$$

that is, if there is no *true dependence*, *output dependence*, or *anti-dependence* among the statements in the sections.

bisection bandwidth   *(n., p. 70)* The rate at which communication can take place between one half of a computer and the other. A low bisection bandwidth, or a large disparity between the maximum and minimum bisection bandwidths achieved by "cutting" the computer's elements in different ways, is a warning that communication bottlenecks may arise in some calculations.

bit-addressable   *(adj., p. 494)* Allowing direct access to individual bits, rather than requiring bits to be selected by applying arithmetic or other operations to whole words. The local memory of each processing element in many *processor arrays* is bit-addressable.

block   *(v., p. 189)* To suspend one's own operation, or the operation of another. A process may block itself, or be blocked by the system, until some event occurs; if all processes are simultaneously blocked, and no external event can cause any to be unblocked, then *deadlock* has occurred.

blocking   *(adj., p. 189)* Describes an operation that causes the process executing it to *block*. Usually applied to communication operations, where it implies that the communicating process cannot perform any other operation until the communication has completed. See also: *asynchronous*; *non-blocking*; *synchronous*.

boundary value swapping   *(n., p. 263)* A technique used when performing calculations on a *mesh* on which *geometric decomposition* has been used. During a boundary value swap, each process exchanges values on the edges of its tile or tiles for the complementary values of its neighbors. See also: *fluff*; *indirect method*.

broadcast   *(v., p. 335)* To send a message to all possible recipients. Broadcast can be a single operation on a *bus*, but is most efficiently implemented on a *multicomputer* by having each node in a *spanning tree* propagate the message to its descendents. See also: *multicast*; *one-to-all replicated communication*; *process group*.

buffer   *(n., p. 80)* A temporary storage area in memory. Many methods for *routing* messages between processors use buffers at the source and destination, or at intermediate processors. See also: *packet switching*; *virtual cut-through*; *wormhole routing*.

bus   *(n., p. 7)* A single physical communication medium shared by two or more devices. The network shared by processors in most *distributed computers* is a bus, as is the shared data path in most *multiprocessors*. See also: *contention*; *link*.

butterfly   *(n., p. 76)* A *topology* in which nodes are organized into levels, and there is a unique path from any node in the first level to any node in the last. A butterfly with ℓ levels has $(\ell + 1)2^{\ell}$ nodes, each of which can be labeled (i, j), where $0 \leq i \leq \ell$ indicates the level and $0 \leq j < 2^{\ell}$ identifies the node within a level. Two nodes (i, j) and (i', j') are only connected if $i' = i + 1$ (that is, the second node is in the layer above the first) and either $j = j'$ or the bitwise representations of j and j' differ in only bit i'. See also: *hypercube*; *shuffle-exchange network*.

cache   *(n., p. 8)* A high-speed memory, local to a single processor, whose data transfers are carried out automatically in hardware. Items are brought into a cache when they are referenced, while any changes to values in a cache are automatically written when they are no longer needed, when the cache becomes full, or when some other process attempts to access them. See also: *hit rate*.

cache   *(v., p. 8)* To bring something into a cache.

cache consistency   *(n., p. 9)* The problem of ensuring that the values associated with a particular variable in the *caches* of several processors are never (visibly) different. Cache consistency is also called cache coherency.

cache line   *(n., p. 9)* The smallest unit of memory in a *cache* on which reading and writing are done independently. A typical cache line holds 16 bytes.

cache protocol   *(n., p. 265)* The rule used to maintain *cache consistency*. If a "write-invalidate" policy is used, a processor which writes to cached data signals other processors that it has done so. If a "write-update" policy is used, the writing processor sends the new data values to those other processors.

centralized memory   *(n., p. 20)* Memory that is organized as a single physical unit. The term is used in contrast with *distributed memory*.

chain   *(n., p. 71)* A *topology* in which every processor is connected to two others, except for two "end" processors that are connected to only one other. See also: *ring*.

channel   *(n., p. 87)* A point-to-point connection between two processes through which messages can be sent. Programming systems that rely on channels are sometimes called "connection-oriented," to distinguish them from the more popular "connectionless" systems in which messages are sent to named destinations, rather than through named channels. See also: *CSP*.

circular shifting   see under *shifting*.

clock time   *(n., p. 371)* Physical or elapsed time, as seen by an omniscient observer external to a system; nonrelativistic time. In small computer systems, all components can be synchronized, so clock time and *logical time* may be the same everywhere. In large systems it may be difficult for a processor to correlate the events it sees with the clock time an external observer would see. The clock times of events define a complete order on those events.

closely-coupled multiprocessor   *(adj., p. 12)* A *multiprocessor* in which all memory is the same distance from each processor.

coarse-grained   see under *granularity*.

communicating sequential processes   see under *CSP*.

compiler directive   *(n., p. 170)* A special comment added to a program's text which directs the compiler to perform certain actions, such as *vectorization* or *data layout*. See also: *HPF*.

compiler optimization   *(n., p. 161)* Rearranging or eliminating sections of a program during compilation to achieve higher performance. Compiler optimization is usually applied only within *basic blocks* and must account for the possible *dependence* of one section of a program on another. See also: *constant replacement*; *loop normalization*; *loop unrolling*.

computation-to-communication ratio   *(n., p. 54)* The ratio of the number of calculations a process does to the total size of the messages it sends. A process that performs a few calculations and then sends a single short message may have the same computation-to-communication ratio as a process that performs millions of calculations and then sends many large messages. The ratio may also be measured by the ratio of the time spent calculating to the time spent communicating, in which case the ratio's value depends on the relative speeds of the processor and communication medium, and on the startup cost and *latency* of communication. See also: *granularity*.

configuration   *(n., p. 339)* A particular selection of the types of processes that could make up a parallel program. Configuration is trivial in the *SPMD* model, in which every processor runs a single identical process, but can be complicated in the general *MIMD* case, particularly if user-level processes rely on libraries that may themselves require "extra" processes. See also: *mapping*.

conform   *(v., p. 97)* Having the same number of dimensions, and the same size in each dimension. If two arrays conform, their values have a natural one-to-one correspondence with one another.

constant replacement   *(n., p. 164)* A step in *compiler optimization* in which variables whose values can be determined during compilation are replaced by those values.

content-addressable   see under *associative*.

contention *(n., p. 8)* Conflict that arises when two or more requests are made concurrently for a resource that cannot be shared: Processes running on a single processor may contend for CPU time, or a network may suffer from contention if several messages attempt to traverse the same *link* at the same time.

context switching *(n., p. 25)* The act of saving the state of one process and replacing it with that of another that is *time sharing* the same processor. If little time is required to switch contexts, *processor overloading* can be an effective way to hide *latency* in a *message-passing* system.

control parallelism *(n., p. 21)* Any model of parallel computing in which many different operations may be executed concurrently. See also: *generative communication*; *MIMD*; *multicomputer*; *multiprocessor*; *SPMD*.

control processor *(n., p. 17)* A processor primarily responsible for fetching, decoding, and issuing instructions in a *processor array*.

COW *(n., p. 70)* Cluster Of Workstations; see under *distributed computer*.

critical region *(n., p. 208)* A portion of a program which must never be executed by two or more processes concurrently. See also: *Mutual exclusion*.

crossbar *(n., p. 11)* A *topology* which connects one set of A nodes to another set of B nodes using AB *switches* to join $A + B$ *buses*.

crystalline model *(n., p. 331)* A model of parallel computation in which processes may calculate independently, but must communicate collectively. It may be viewed as a special case of the *SPMD* model.

CSP *(n., p. 283)* Communicating sequential processes; an approach to parallelism in which anonymous processes communicate by sending messages through named point-to-point *channels* [Hoare 1985]. All communication is *synchronous*—the process that reaches the communication operation first is *blocked* until a complementary process reaches the same operation. See also: *guard*.

cube-connected cycles *(n., p. 74)* A *topology* in which processors are first connected in *rings*, and those rings then connected to form a *hypercube*. See also: *k-ary n-cube*.

DAG *(n., p. 269)* Direct Acyclic Graph; a graph whose edges have directions, but which does not contain any closed paths (cycles). DAGs are often used to encode *dependence* information in *basic blocks* for use in *compiler optimization*.

data dependence *(n., p. 6)* Any form of *dependence* other than control dependence.

data layout *(n., p. 170)* A user-specified mapping of data (usually arrays or array sections) to a *logical processor array*, which is then mapped to the physical processors in a machine. Data layout is usually specified using *compiler directives*. See also: *HPF*.

data parallelism   *(n., p. 21)* A model of parallel computing in which a single operation can be applied to all elements of a data structure simultaneously. Typically, these data structures are matrices, and the operations act independently on every matrix element. See also: *control parallelism*; *processor array*; *reduction*; *SIMD*; *vector processor*.

data processor   *(n., p. 17)* A processor primarily responsible for executing instructions in a *processor array*.

dataflow   *(n., p. 268)* A model of parallel computing in which programs are represented as *dependence graphs*, and each operation is automatically *blocked* until the values on which it depends are available.

dead code   *(n., p. 164)* A portion of a program that will never be entered, or does not have to be executed because the values it calculates are never used. *Compiler optimization* usually removes sections of dead code. See also: *dependence*.

deadlock   *(n., p. 85)* A situation in which each possible activity is *blocked*, waiting on some other activity that is also blocked. If a directed graph represents how activities depend on others, then deadlock arises if and only if there is a cycle in this graph. See also: *dependence graph*.

decomposition   *(n., p. 46)* A division of a data structure into substructures that can be distributed separately, or a technique for dividing a computation into subcomputations that can be executed separately. Common decomposition strategies include:

    functional decomposition: Breaking a calculation into qualitatively different subcalculations, such as the transformation, shading, z-buffering, and rendering portions of a polygon display algorithm.

    geometric decomposition: Breaking a calculation into sections that correspond to some physical subdivision of the system being modeled, such as *tiling* a *mesh*. To achieve good *load balance*, such sections may be either distributed according to some regular rule or "scattered" randomly.

    iterative decomposition: Breaking down a calculation in which one or more operations are repeatedly applied to one or more data values by executing those operations on those data simultaneously. In a "deterministic" decomposition, the data to be processed are fixed, and the same operations are applied to each. In a "speculative" decomposition, different operations are applied simultaneously to the same input until at least one has completed.

recursive decomposition: Breaking down a problem into parts whose values can either be calculated directly, or which can themselves be broken down into smaller parts.

speculative decomposition: Performing many independent calculations concurrently, using the results of the first to complete and discarding (and if possible terminating) the others.

dependence *(n., p. 6)* The relationship of a calculation B to a calculation A if changes to A, or to the ordering of A and B, could affect B. If A and B are calculations in a program, for example, then B is dependent on A if B uses values calculated by A. There are four types of dependence:

true dependence: B uses values calculated by A.

anti-dependence: A uses values overwritten by B.

output dependence: A and B both write to the same variables.

control dependence: B's execution is controlled by values set in A.

Dependence is also used in message *routing* to mean that some activity X cannot proceed until another activity Y has completed. For example, if X and Y are messages attempting to pass through a region with limited *buffer* space, and Y currently holds some or all of the buffer, X may depend on Y releasing some buffer space before proceeding.

dependence graph *(n., p. 163)* A directed graph whose nodes represent calculations and whose edges represent dependencies among those calculations. If the calculation represented by node k depends on the calculations represented by nodes i and j, then the dependence graph contains the edges $i \to k$ and $j \to k$. See also: *compiler optimization*; *dataflow*; *dependence*.

deterministic *(adj., p. 56)* Always evolving in the same manner. A deterministic program is one which always executes the same way for any particular set of inputs. Most correct serial programs are deterministic. See also: *non-deterministic*.

diameter *(n., p. 69)* The distance across a graph, measured by the number of *links* traversed. Diameter is usually taken to mean "maximum diameter" (the greatest internode distance in the graph), but it can also mean the average of all internode distances. Diameter is sometimes used as a measure of the goodness of a *topology*.

direct method *(n., p. 35)* Any technique for solving a system of equations which relies on the algebraic properties of the system, rather than successive approximation. LU-decomposition with back-substitution is an example of a direct method. See also: *indirect method*.

directed acyclic graph see under *DAG*.

disjoint memory   *(n., p. 20)* Memory that appears to the user to be divided among many separate *address spaces*. In a *multicomputer*, each processor typically has its own *private memory* and manages requests to it from processes running on other processors. Disjoint memory is more commonly called *distributed memory*, but the memory of many *shared-memory* computers is physically distributed.

distributed computer   *(n., p. 70)* A computer made up of many smaller and potentially independent computers, such as a network of workstations. This *architecture* is increasingly popular because of its cost-effectiveness and flexibility. Distributed computers are often *heterogeneous*. See also: *COW*; *multiprocessor*; *multicomputer*.

distributed memory   *(n., p. 20)* Memory that is physically distributed among several modules. A *distributed-memory architecture* may appear to users to have a single *shared memory* and a single *address space*, or may appear as *disjoint memory* made up of many *address spaces*.

divide and conquer   see under *decomposition, recursive*.

doall   *(n., p. 480)* A programming construct that specifies a set of loop iterations and further specifies that these iterations can be done in any order. *data-parallel* and *shared-variable* programs are often expressed using doall loops.

domain   *(n., p. 488)* That part of a larger computing resource allocated for the sole use of a specific user or group of users. See also: *space sharing*.

e-cube routing   *(n., p. 87)* A message routing algorithm used on binary *hypercubes*. If $\langle |s_{n-1} \ldots s_0| \rangle$ and $\langle |d_{n-1} \ldots d_0| \rangle$ are the binary coordinates of the source and destination of the message, and $\langle |x_{n-1} \ldots x_0| \rangle$ their difference, then the e-cube algorithm routes the message along *links* parallel to the axes corresponding to 1's in $\langle |x_{n-1} \ldots x_0| \rangle$, in order from highest to lowest. See also: *Metropolis routing*; *randomized routing*.

eager evaluation   *(n., p. 261)* A scheduling policy under which each computation begins as soon as its inputs are ready or its necessary preconditions have been satisfied. This scheduling policy is used in most programs, but contrasts with the *lazy evaluation* policy often used in functional and logic programming. See also: *dataflow*; *dependence*; *dependence graph*.

efficiency   *(n., p. 57)* A measure of hardware utilization, equal to the ratio of *speedup* achieved on $\mathcal{P}$ processors to $\mathcal{P}$. If the time taken by a program to execute on 1 processor is τ_1, and the time taken by it to execute on $\mathcal{P}$ processors is $\tau_{\mathcal{P}}$, the efficiency ε is:

$$\varepsilon = \frac{\tau_1}{\mathcal{P}\tau_{\mathcal{P}}}$$

See also: *isoefficiency*; *optimality*.

embarrassingly parallel *(adj., p. 32)* Trivial to parallelize. Any problem which contains a large amount of independent computation, and very little communication, is embarrassingly parallel.

exclusive parallel prefix see under *parallel prefix*.

explicit method *(n., p. 34)* A technique for determining the state of a physical system, or the evolution of a system's state, which simulates the behavior of the system's components. See also: *implicit method*.

fairness *(n., p. 205)* A property of a concurrent system. A system is "unconditionally" fair if every process which can run is eventually scheduled. A system is "weakly" fair if every *guarded* action which is enabled, and stays enabled, is eventually executed. A system is "strongly" fair if every guarded action whose guard is enabled an infinite number of times is eventually executed. See also: *deadlock*; *livelock*.

fat tree *(n., p. 74)* A *topology* in which nodes are arranged in a tree, and the bandwidth between a node and its children is proportional to the height of the node.

fetch-and-add *(n., p. 212)* An operation which *atomically* fetches the previous value of a counter, while incrementing it by a user-specified amount. For example, fetch-and-add on 3 with an argument of 2 would return 3, and set the counter's value to 5. Fetch-and-add is often used to ensure *fairness*.

fine-grained see under *granularity*.

flit *(n., p. 88)* A flow control unit – the basic unit of information sent through a *message-passing* system that uses *virtual cut-through* or *wormhole routing*.

fluff *(n., p. 30)* The duplicate values stored by a processor in a *disjoint-memory* system in a program which is performing *boundary value swapping*.

FLOPS *(n., p. 15)* Floating-point operations per second; a measure of numerical performance, equal to the rate at which a machine can perform single-precision floating-point calculations. See also: *WARPS*; *WASPS*.

Flynn's taxonomy *(n., p. 16)* A classification scheme for *architectures* that has two axes: the number of instruction streams executing concurrently, and the number of data sets to which those instructions are being applied [Flynn 1966]. See also: *architecture*; *MIMD*; *SIMD*; *SISD*.

forall see under *doall*.

fork *(v., p. 181)* To create a new process that is a copy of its immediate parent. See also: *join*.

formal field see under *tuple*.

FPMD *(adj., p. 20)* A few programs, multiple data; a category sometimes added to *Flynn's taxonomy* to describe programs made up of many instances of a small number of types of process. FPMD can be viewed either as an extension of of *SPMD*, or as a restriction of *MIMD*. See also: *process group*; *SISD*; *SIMD*.

fully-connected network *(n., p. 71)* A *topology* in which every node is directly connected to every other. See also: *crossbar*, *star*.

functional decomposition see under *decomposition*.

futures *(n., p. 256)* A programming construct specifying that the value of some computation will be needed at some later point, but allowing the system to schedule that computation to run at any arbitrary time. Futures are one way to present *lazy evaluation* in *shared-variable* programs. See also: *eager evaluation*.

fuzzy barrier *(n., p. 238)* A pair of points in a program such that no process may pass the second point before all processes have reached the first. Fuzzy barriers are often used inside loop iterations to ensure that no changes are made in the $(i + 1)^{\text{th}}$ iteration before all values needed in the ith iteration have been read. See also: *barrier*; *barrier synchronization*; *dependence*.

gang scheduling *(n., p. 489)* A time-scheduling policy on multi-user parallel computers under which all the resources an application currently has (such as processors) are given and taken away as a group. Gang scheduling prevents livelock and allows efficient use of spin-waiting for events. See also: *scheduling*.

gather see under *all-to-one personalized communication*.

generative communication *(n., p. 387)* A model of parallel computing in which processes that have been spawned dynamically turn into data upon completion, and data may be stored in *tuples* in one or more shared *tuple spaces*. A process may add tuples to a tuple space, or remove them by matching against their contents. See also: *associative*; *shared variables*; *virtual shared memory*.

geometric decomposition see under *decomposition*.

gigaFLOPS (GFLOPS) *(n., p. 66)* 10^9 FLOPS.

granularity *(n., p. 50)* The size of the operations done by a process between communication events. A "fine-grained" process may perform only a few arithmetic operations between processing one message and the next, while a "coarse-grained" process may perform millions. See also: *computation-to-communication ratio*.

Gray code *(n., p. 77)* A cyclic ordering of the values $0 \ldots 2^n - 1$ such that each value differs from its predecessor and successor in exactly one bit location.

guard *(n., p. 199)* A logical condition that controls whether a communication operation can take place. Guards are usually defined as part of the syntax and semantics of *CSP*-based languages.

Gustafson's Law *(n., p. 61)* A rule stating that if the size of a problem is scaled up sufficiently, then any required *efficiency* can be achieved on any number of processors [Gustafson et al. 1988]. See also: *Amdahl's Law*; *efficiency*; *isoefficiency*.

halo *(n., p. 46)* The region around a point in a *mesh* whose values are used when updating the value of the central point. In an *indirect method*, the halo is the set of points around some point x whose values are used to update x. See also: *stencil*.

heavyweight process *(n., p. 179)* A process which contains all of its own operating system information, such as file descriptors, heap, interrupt handlers, and so on. See also: *lightweight process*.

heterogeneous *(adj., p. 70)* Containing components of more than one kind. A heterogeneous *architecture* may be one in which some components are processors, and others memories, or it may be one that uses different types of processors together. See also: *distributed computer*; *homogeneous*.

hierarchical architecture *(n., p. 14)* An *architecture* built up recursively, so that one or more processors are connected by one bus to a single memory, clusters of such nodes are connected by another bus (and possibly to more memory as well), and so on.

hierarchical memory *(n., p. 21)* A memory system built up recursively, so that successive layers are larger, but have greater access times. See also: *NUMA*.

High-Performance FORTRAN *(n., p. 170)* A set of extensions to FORTRAN-90 which standardizes *data layout* directives, parallel looping constructs, and so on. HPF uses the *SPMD* model.

hit rate *(n., p. 9)* The frequency with which values required from memory are found in the *cache*.

homogeneous *(adj., p. 70)* Made up of identical components. A homogeneous *architecture* is one in which each element is the same; *processor arrays* and *multicomputers* are usually homogeneous. See also: *heterogeneous*.

HPF see under *High Performance Fortran*.

hypercube *(n., p. 72)* A *topology* in which each node is the vertex of an $\mathcal{D}$-dimensional cube. In a binary hypercube, each node is connected to n others, and its coordinates are one of the 2^n different n-bit sequences of binary digits. Because most early American *multicomputers* used hypercubic topologies, the term hypercube is sometimes incorrectly used as a synonym for multicomputer. See also: *butterfly*; *e-cube routing*; *shuffle-exchange network*.

implicit method *(n., p. 34)* A technique for determining a system's state which represents that state as a matrix equation, and then finds or approximates a solution to the equation. See also: *explicit method*.

inclusive parallel prefix see under *parallel prefix*.

indirect method *(n., p. 35)* Any technique for solving a system of equations that uses successive approximation. Successive over-relaxation is an example of an indirect method. Such techniques are sometimes called "relaxation" methods. See also: *direct method*.

interval routing *(n., p. 89)* A routing algorithm that assigns an integer identifier to each possible destination and then labels the outgoing *links* of each node with a single contiguous interval, or window, so that a message can be routed simply by sending it out the link in whose interval its destination identifier falls.

isoefficiency *(n., p. 62)* A way to quantify the effect of scaling problem size on an algorithm's *efficiency*. For a given efficiency, the isoefficiency function for an algorithm A specifies what size of problem must be solved on P processors to achieve that efficiency.

iterative decomposition see under *decomposition*.

join *(v., p. 181)* To wait for the termination of one or more descendent processes that were *forked* at some earlier time.

k-ary n-cube *(n., p. 77)* A *topology* in which processors are laid out along the axes of an n-dimensional mesh with extent k in each dimension. This topology generalizes the *mesh* and *hypercube*.

latency *(n., p. 5)* The time taken to service a request, deliver a message, and so on, which is independent of the size or nature of the operation. The latency of a *message-passing* system is the minimum time to deliver a message, even one of zero length that does not have to leave the source processor; the latency of a file system is the time required to decode and execute a null operation.

lazy evaluation *(n., p. 256)* A scheduling policy under which no calculation is begun until it is certain that its result is needed. This policy contrasts with the *eager evaluation* used in most programs, but is often used in functional and logic programming. See also: *dataflow*; *dependence*; *dependence graph*; *futures*.

lightweight process *(n., p. 180)* A process which has its own registers, stack, and program counter, but which inherits other information (such as a heap or file descriptors) from a *heavyweight process*. Lightweight processes are often called "threads."

linear speedup   *(n., p. 58) Speedup* that is directly proportional to the number of processors used. According to *Amdahl's Law*, linear speedup is not possible for a problem that contains any sequential portion, no matter how small; *Gustafson's Law*, however, states that linear speedup can be achieved if the problem size increases as the number of processors increases. See also: *superlinear speedup.*

link   *(n., p. 13)* A one-to-one connection between two processors, usually in a *multicomputer.* See also: *bus.*

link loading   *(n., p. 70)* The amount of communication traffic carried by a link, or by the most heavily loaded link in the system. As link loading increases, both *latency* and *contention* are likely to increase. A topology's "worst link loading" is its maximum link loading value; its "link loading ratio" is the ratio between its maximum and minimum link loading values. See also: *bisection bandwidth.*

live variable   *(n., p. 198)* A variable visible to a process and whose value can be changed by actions taken outside that process. For example, if a variable v is shared by two processes, one of which can write to it at some point, then that variable is live within the other process. See also: *race condition*; *shared variables.*

livelock   *(n., p. 397)* A situation in which a process A is forever *blocked* because a process B has preferential access to a resource needed by both.

load balance   *(n., p. 50)* The degree to which work is evenly distributed among available processors. A program executes most quickly when it is perfectly load-balanced, that is, when every processor has exactly the same amount of work to do. One measure of this is $\mathcal{L}$: if τ_i is the completion time of processor i, and τ_{max} is the maximum value of τ_i (i.e. the overall completion time), then:

$$\mathcal{L} = \frac{\Sigma(\tau_{max} - \tau_i)}{\mathcal{P}\tau_{max}}$$

quantifies load imbalance as a percentage of wasted processor cycles.

locality   *(n., p. 50)* The degree to which the computations done by a processor depend only on values held close to that processor, or the degree to which computations done on a point in some data structure depend only on values near that point. Locality can be measured by the ratio of local to nonlocal data accesses, or by the distribution of distances of, or times taken by, nonlocal accesses. The term is also used to explain why *caches* are effective: a program shows "spatial" locality if a reference to an address a implies that addresses near a are also likely to be referenced, while it shows "temporal" locality if there is a high probability that the next address accessed will be one which has been accessed recently. See also: *halo*; *stencil.*

location *(n., p. 152)* An operation which tries to find where a value occurs in an array, and returns either its indices or an indication that the value is not in the array. See also: *data parallelism*.

lock *(n., p. 207)* Any device or algorithm whose use guarantees that only one process can perform some action or use some resource at a time.

lock *(v., p. 207)* To acquire exclusive permission to perform an action or use a resource.

logical processor array *(n., p. 173)* A notional set of processors to which data are mapped during *data layout*; the logical processor array is then mapped to the physical processors in a machine. This two-step process helps make data layout less machine-dependent. See also: *HPF*.

logical time *(n., p. 371)* Elapsed time as seen from within processes. Logical time may differ from *clock time* because processes can *block* or be suspended during *multitasking*, and because they can run at different speeds. The logical times of events only define a partial order on those events.

loop normalization *(n., p. 164)* A step in *compiler optimization* in which a loop's index is adjusted so that it starts at 1 and proceeds upward with a unit *stride*. Indexing operations inside the loop are then altered to ensure that the same data values are accessed.

loop unrolling *(n., p. 7)* A *compiler optimization* technique in which the body of a loop is replicated ℓ times, and the number of iterations of that loop reduced by a factor of ℓ. By lengthening the *basic block* inside the loop, this can increase the scope for *vectorization* and other optimizations.

loosely-coupled multiprocessor *(adj., p. 12)* A *multiprocessor* in which the "distance" between portions of memory and individual processors may vary.

mapping *(n., p. 268)* An allocation of processes to processors; allocating work to processes is usually called scheduling. See also: *load balance*.

marshal *(v., p. 295)* To compact the values of several variables, arrays, or structures into a single contiguous block of memory; copying values out of a block of memory is called "unmarshalling". In most *message-passing* systems, data must be marshalled to be sent in a single message.

mask *(n., p. 109)* A logical array or array-valued expression used to control where a *data-parallel* operation has effect; the operation is only executed where array elements are true.

mask *(v., p. 109)* To control where a *data-parallel* operation has effect using a logical array or array-valued expression; the operation is only executed where array elements are true.

megaFLOPS (MFLOPS) *(n., p. 66)* 10^6 FLOPS.

mesh *(n., p. 72)* A *topology* in which nodes form a regular acyclic $\mathcal{D}$-dimensional grid, and each edge is parallel to a grid axis and joins two nodes that are adjacent along that axis. The *architecture* of many *multicomputers* is a two- or three-dimensional mesh; meshes are also the basis of many scientific calculations, in which each node represents a point in space, and the edges define the neighbors of a node. See also: *hypercube*; *torus*.

message combining *(v., p. 216)* Joining messages together as they traverse a network. Combining may be done to reduce the total traffic in the network, to reduce the number of times the start-up penalty of messaging is incurred, or to reduce the number of messages reaching a particular destination.

message passing *(n., p. 283)* A style of interprocess communication in which processes send discrete messages to one another. Some computer *architectures* are called "message-passing" *architectures* because they support this model in hardware, although message passing has often been used to construct operating systems and network software for *uniprocessors* and *distributed computers*. See also: *routing*.

message port *(n., p. 339)* A connection between a process and the *message-passing* system which it is using to communicate with its peers. Some systems require processes to specify which of its recipient's ports a message is to be sent to, and allow processes to select messages based upon their port of arrival.

message tagging *(n., p. 297)* The association of information with a message that identifies the nature of its contents. Most *message-passing* systems automatically transfer information about a message's sender to its receiver. Many also require the sender to specify a tag (or type) for the message, and let the receiver select which messages it is willing to receive by specifying a tag or range of tags.

Metropolis routing *(n., p. 87)* A routing algorithm for *meshes*, in which an ordering is imposed on axes, and messages are sent as far along the most significant axis as they need to go, then as far along the next most significant, and so on. See also: *e-cube routing*; *randomized routing*.

MIMD *(adj., p. 19)* Multiple Instruction, Multiple Data; a category of *Flynn's taxonomy* in which many instruction streams are concurrently applied to multiple data sets. A MIMD *architecture* is one in which *heterogeneous* processes may execute at different rates.

MIN *(n., p. 11)* Multistage Interconnection Network; a *topology* in which several layers of *switches* connect N objects of one type to N objects of another type.

Monte Carlo *(adj., p. 32)* Making use of randomness. A simulation in which many independent trials are run independently to gather statistics is a "Monte Carlo simulation."

A search algorithm that uses randomness to try to speed up convergence is a "Monte Carlo algorithm."

multicast *(n., p. 343)* To send a message to many, but not necessarily all, possible recipient processes. See also: *broadcast*; *process group*.

multicomputer *(n., p. 13)* A computer in which processors can execute separate instruction streams, have their own private memories, and cannot directly access one another's memories [Athas & Seitz 1988]. Most multicomputers are *disjoint-memory* machines, constructed by joining nodes (each containing a microprocessor and some memory) via *links*. See also: *architecture*; *distributed computer*; *multiprocessor*; *processor array*.

multiprocessor *(n., p. 7)* A computer in which processors can execute separate instructions streams, but have access to a single *address space*. Most multiprocessors are *shared-memory* machines, constructed by connecting several processors to one or more memory banks through a *bus* or *MIN*. See also: *architecture*; *distributed computer*; *multicomputer*; *processor array*.

multi-stage interconnection network   see under *MIN*.

multitasking *(n., p. 7)* Executing many processes on a single processor. This is usually done by time-slicing the execution of individual processes and performing a context switch each time a process is *swapped* in or out, but is supported by special-purpose hardware in computers such as the Denelcor HEP [Kowalik 1985]. Most operating systems support multitasking, but it can be expensive if the need to flush large *caches* or execution *pipelines* makes *context switching* expensive.

mutual exclusion *(n., p. 199)* A situation in which at most one process can be engaged in a specified activity at any time. Semaphores are often used to implement this. See also: *contention*; *critical region*; *deadlock*.

$n_{1/2}$ *(n., p. 66)* The minimum vector length on which a *pipelined architecture* delivers half its theoretical peak performance [Hockney & Jesshope 1988]. The larger $n_{1/2}$ is, the longer calculations must be to amortize the startup cost of the pipeline. See also: r_∞.

non-blocking *(adj., p. 338)* An operation that does not *block* the execution of the process using it. Usually applied to communication operations, where it implies that the communicating process may perform other operations before the communication has completed. See also: *blocking*.

non-deterministic *(adj., p. 56)* Not guaranteed to evolve in a particular manner. A non-deterministic program is one which may execute in different ways even when given the same input; many control-parallel programs are non-deterministic because the order of concurrent events is unpredictable. See also: *deterministic*.

non-uniform memory access   see under *NUMA*.

NUMA   *(adj., p. 21)* Non-Uniform Memory Access; not supporting constant-time read and write operations. In most NUMA *architectures*, memory is organized hierarchically, so that some portions can be read and written more quickly by some processors than by others. See also: *UMA*.

oblivious   *(adj., p. 89)* Working in the same fashion regardless of surroundings or history. An oblivious scheduling strategy always schedules processes in the same way, no matter how much work they have done in the past; an oblivious *routing* algorithm always routes messages in the same direction, regardless of local load. See also: *adaptive*.

one-to-all personalized communication   *(n., p. 335)* Communication in which one process sends a distinct message to each other process. "Scatter" is often used in this sense. See also: *all-to-all personalized communication*; *all-to-all replicated communication*; *all-to-one personalized communication*; *one-to-all replicated communication*; *one-to-one communication*.

one-to-all replicated communication   *(n., p. 335)* Communication in which one process sends the same message to each other process. "Broadcast" is often used in this sense. See also: *all-to-all personalized communication*; *all-to-all replicated communication*; *all-to-one personalized communication*; *one-to-all personalized communication*; *one-to-one communication*.

one-to-one communication   *(n., p. 336)* Communication in which one process sends a single message to one other. This is the normal case in most *message-passing* systems, but may not be possible in some *crystalline* or *SPMD* systems. See also: *all-to-all personalized communication*; *all-to-all replicated communication*; *all-to-one personalized communication*; *one-to-all personalized communication*; *one-to-all replicated communication*.

output dependence   see under *dependence*.

owner-computes rules   *(n., p. 185)* A *scheduling* policy used in many *data-parallel* and *SPMD* systems, in which the processor on which data are located performs computations on those data. See also: *data layout*, *HPF*.

packet switching   *(n., p. 80)* A *routing* technique in which intermediate nodes wait until they have received the whole of a message before forwarding any of it. Packet switching often requires a large amount of *buffer* space, and *contention* for access to this space can lead to *deadlock*. See also: *virtual cut-through*; *wormhole routing*.

parallelization   *(n., p. 161)* Turning a serial computation into a parallel one. This may be done automatically, by a "parallelizing compiler," or (more usually) by rewriting the program so that it uses some parallel paradigm. See also: *dataflow*; *data parallelism*; *futures*; *generative communication*; *message passing*; *shared variables*.

parallel balance point *(n., p. 65)* The point at which using more processors to do a calculation increases the time taken to complete that calculation. On any realizable *architecture*, the time taken to perform some calculation of size $\mathcal{N}$ on $\mathcal{P}$ processors is $\tau = f_r(\mathcal{N}, \mathcal{P}) + f_c(\mathcal{N}, \mathcal{P})$, where the execution time function f_x is a decreasing function of $\mathcal{P}$, while the coordination time function f_c is an increasing function of $\mathcal{P}$. Unless $f_x \mathrel{\rlap{\raise.5ex{<}}{\lower.5ex{}}} f_c$ for all $\mathcal{P} > 1$, there will be some finite number of processors $\mathcal{P}^{\star}$ that minimizes the total execution time for a particular problem size. See also: *Amdahl's Law*; *efficiency*; *Gustafson's Law*; *isoefficiency*; *speedup*.

parallel prefix *(n., p. 141)* An operation applying an associative binary operator $\oplus$ to an n-vector v to produce

$$\langle (v_0)(v_0 \oplus v_1)(v_0 \oplus v_1 \oplus v_2) \ldots (v_0 \oplus v_1 \oplus \ldots \oplus v_{n_1}) \rangle$$

An "inclusive" parallel prefix leaves the value of the original vector's first element in that element; an "exclusive" prefix replaces that value with the operation's identify element. Other variations apply the operation downward from the last element of the vector, and so on. See also: *reduction*; *scan-vector model*; *segmented parallel prefix*.

parallel random access machine see under *PRAM*.

parallel slackness *(n., p. 90)* Hiding the *latency* of communication by giving each processor many different tasks, and having it work on the tasks that are ready while others are *blocked* (waiting on communication or other operations).

passive tuple see under *tuple*.

permutation *(n., p. 123)* An operation in which every value in an array is moved to a new location. The normal case is for this relocation to be a one-to-one mapping, but many systems allow many-to-one or one-to-many mappings as well. Permutation can be specified as a "push", which is equivalent to:

```
do i = 1, N
  dst(i) = src(map(i))
end do
```

or as a "pull", which is equivalent to

```
do i = 1, N
  dst(map(i)) = src(i)
end do
```

See also: *reduction*.

pipelining *(n., p. 5)* Overlapping the execution of two or more operations. Pipelining is used within processors by prefetching instructions on the assumption that no branches are going to preempt their execution; in *vector processors*, in which application of a single operation to the elements of a vector or vectors may be pipelined to decrease the time needed to complete the aggregate operation; and in *multiprocessors* and *multicomputers*, in which a process may send a request for values before it reaches the computation that requires them. A "pipeline" is any piece of hardware, or collection of processes, which does pipelining. See also: *architecture*.

planar shifting see under *shifting*.

polarity *(n., p. 390)* A property of a *tuple* field in the *generative communication* model. A field may have either *actual* or *formal* polarity.

PRAM *(n., p. 89)* Parallel Random Access Machine; a theoretical model of parallel computation in which an arbitrary but finite number of processors can access any value in an arbitrarily large *shared memory* in a single time step. Processors may execute different instruction streams, but work *synchronously*. The three most important variations of the PRAM are:

EREW: Exclusive Read, Exclusive Write; any memory location may only be accessed once in any step.

CREW: Concurrent Read, Exclusive Write; any memory location may be read any number of times during a single step, but only written to once, with the write taking place after the reads.

CRCW: Concurrent Read, Concurrent Write; any memory location may be written to or read any number of times during a single step. A CRCW PRAM model must define some rule for resolving multiple writes, such as giving priority to the lowest-numbered processor or choosing among processors randomly.

The PRAM is popular because it is theoretically tractable and because it gives algorithm designers a common target. However, PRAMs cannot be emulated optimally on all *architectures* [Skillicorn 1990, Valiant 1990].

predicate operation *(n., p. 435)* A *non-blocking* operation in the *generative communication* model, which either matches a *tuple* or signals that no match can be found.

private memory *(n., p. 20)* Memory that appears to the user to be divided among many *address spaces*, each of which can be accessed by only one process. Most operating systems rely on some *memory protection* mechanism to prevent one process from accessing the private memory of another; in *disjoint-memory* machines, the problem is usually to find a way to emulate *shared memory* using a set of private memories. See also: *virtual shared memory*.

probe effect   *(n., p. 375)* The way in which collecting information about the execution of a parallel system may alter that system's behavior.

process group   *(n., p. 341)* A set of processes that can be treated as a single entity for some purposes, such as *synchronization* and *broadcast*. In some parallel programming systems, there is only one process group, which implicitly contains all processes; in others, programmers can assign processes to groups statically when configuring their program, or dynamically by having processes create, join, and leave groups during execution. See also: *multicast*.

process migration   *(n., p. 445)* Changing the processor responsible for executing a process during the lifetime of that process. Process migration is sometimes used to dynamically *load balance* a program.

processor array   *(n., p. 17)* A computer that consists of a regular *mesh* of simple processing elements called *data processors*, under the direction of a single *control processor*. Processor arrays are usually *SIMD* machines, and are primarily used to support *data-parallel* computations. See also: *vector processor*.

processor overloading   *(n., p. 52) Mapping* many processes to a single processor, so that *parallel slackness* can be exploited.

producer-consumer problem   *(n., p. 200)* A paradigmatic problem in concurrent systems, in which one process produces values which another consumes. The problem is to ensure that their interaction is correct, i.e. that every value that is produced is eventually consumed.

program transformation   *(n., p. 167)* Any technique which translates one program into an equivalent in the same language. Program transformation is often used as part of *parallelization* or *vectorization*, and is equivalent to compilation in which the source and target languages are the same.

pull mapping   see under *permutation*.

push mapping   see under *permutation*.

r_∞ *(n., p. 66)* The performance a *pipelined architecture* would deliver on an infinitely long vector; that is, the performance of such an *architecture* when *startup costs* are not considered [Hockney & Jesshope 1988]. See also: $n_{1/2}$.

race condition   *(n., p. 198)* A situation in which the final result of operations being executed by two or more processes depends on the order in which those processes execute. For example, if two processes A and B are to write different values v_A and v_B to some variable, then the final value of that variable is determined by the order in which A and B are scheduled. See also: *non-deterministic*; *output dependence*.

RAID   *(n., p. 275)* Redundant Array of Inexpensive Disks; a file system containing many disks, some of which are used to hold redundant copies of data or error-correction values to increase reliability. RAIDs are often used as parallel-access file systems.

random graph   *(n., p. 75)* A *topology* in which nodes are connected to each other randomly, with no two nodes being connected twice.

randomized routing   *(n., p. 89)* A routing technique in which each message is sent to a randomly chosen node, which then forwards it to its final destination. Theory and practice show that this can greatly reduce the amount of *contention* for access to *links* in a *multicomputer*. See also: *e-cube routing*; *Metropolis routing*.

readers-writers problem   *(n., p. 225)* A paradigmatic problem in concurrent systems, in which either many processes are allowed to read a database concurrently, or one process is allowed to write it exclusively. See also: *mutual exclusion*; *producer-consumer problem*.

recursive   see under *recursive*.

reduction operation   *(n., p. 137)* An operation applying an associative and commutative binary operator $\oplus$ to a list of values $\{v_0 v_1 \ldots v_{n-1}\}$ to produce $\{v_0 \oplus \ldots \oplus v_{n-1}\}$. See also: *parallel prefix*.

redundant array of inexpensive disks   see under *RAID*.

redundant computation   *(n., p. 273)* Calculations that are carried out more than once or by more than one processor. Computations may be done redundantly because it is cheaper to have every processor calculate a value for itself than to have one processor calculate the value and then *broadcast* it, or because processes may not have enough memory to store all the values they calculate and may need to overwrite some during execution.

relaxation method   see under *indirect method*.

remote procedure call   see under *RPC*.

reproducibility   *(n., p. 56)* A property of computations which are guaranteed to generate the same result, regardless of the order in which their components are executed. Integer calculations are reproducible on most computers, but floating-point calculations are not due to round-off effects. See also: *non-determinism*.

ring   *(n., p. 71)* A *topology* in which each node is connected to two others to form a closed loop. See also: *chain*.

routing   *(n., p. 80)* The act of moving a message from its source to its destination. A "routing algorithm" is a rule for deciding, at any intermediate node, where to send a message next; a "routing technique" is a way of handling the message as it passes through individual nodes. See also: *e-cube routing*; *interval routing*; *Metropolis routing*; *packet switching*; *randomized routing*; *virtual cut-through*; *wormhole routing*.

RPC   *(n., p. 255)* Remote Procedure Call; an operation in which one process executes a procedure on behalf of another. Normally, the calling process *marshals* the parameters to the call and sends them to the executor, which then returns the call's results. RPC may be *blocking* or *non-blocking*, and is widely used to structure client-server systems.

RTI   *(n., p. 344)* Run-Time Initialization; importing information about a program *configuration* using explicit function calls within each process. Most *message-passing* systems use RTI. See also: *SPB*.

run-time initialization   see under *RTI*.

scalable   *(adj., p. 62)* Capable of being increased in size, or more accurately, capable of delivering an increase in performance proportional to an increase in size. A scalable *architecture* is one that can be used as a design for arbitrarily large machines, or one whose increase in performance is linear in the amount of hardware invested. The term is also applied to programming systems, although its meaning is less clear in these cases. See also: *Gustafson's Law*.

scalar promotion   *(n., p. 97)* The operation of replicating a scalar value so that it *conforms* with an array. Scalar promotion is often done in *data-parallel* systems in which mixed scalar-array operations are permitted. See also: *reduction*.

scan-vector model   *(n., p. 141)* A theoretical model of parallel computing in which a scalar processor and a *vector processor* have access, respectively, to a memory holding scalar values and a memory holding vectors of arbitrary length. Vector operations take either a single time step or a time proportional to the logarithm of the number of elements [Blelloch 1989]. See also: *data parallelism*; *parallel prefix operation*; *reduction operation*.

scatter   see under *one-to-all personalized communication*.

scattered decomposition   see under *decomposition, geometric*.

scheduling   *(n., p. 268)* Deciding the order in which the calculations in a program are to be executed, and by which processes. Allocating processes to processors is usually called *mapping*. See also: *gang scheduling*; *load balance*.

segmented parallel prefix   *(n., p. 149)* A *parallel prefix operation* in which the vector being operated on, $\langle v_0 v_1 v_2 \ldots v_{n-1} \rangle$, is divided into segments, and the operator $\oplus$ is applied to each segment as if it were a separate vector. Segmented parallel prefix is usually implemented by supplying a k-vector of segment lengths $\langle s_0 s_1 s_2 \ldots s_{k-1} \rangle$, such that $0 \leq s_i \leq n$ and $\sum_{i=0}^{k} s_i = n$.

self-scheduling   *(adj., p. 275)* Automatically allocating work to processes. If T tasks are to be done by $\mathcal{P}$ processors, and $\mathcal{P} < T$, then they may be self-scheduled by keeping them in a central pool from which each processor claims a new job when it finishes executing its old one. See also: *task farming*.

semaphore *(n., p. 220)* A data type for controlling concurrency. A semaphore can be initialized to any nonnegative integer value. After that, only two operations may be applied to it: signal, which increments the semaphore's value by one, and wait, which *blocks* its caller until the semaphore's value is greater than zero, then decrements the semaphore. The value of a semaphore typically represents the amount of some resource that is currently available, while waiting on a semaphore forces processes to block until some of that resource can be claimed. A "binary semaphore" is one that can only take on the values 0 and 1.

serialize *(v., p. 221)* To put potentially concurrent operations in a strictly sequential order. If concurrent processes must claim a *lock* before doing some operation, for example, then their operations will be serialized.

shallow copying *(n., p. 189)* The act of duplicating data non-recursively. A shallow copy of a linked structure contains only the top-most element; other elements referenced through pointers are not copied. A sensible system will nullify the pointers in the copied value to show that they are invalid.

shared memory *(n., p. 20)* Memory that appears to the user to be contained in a single *address space* and that can be accessed by any process. In a *uniprocessor* or *multiprocessor* there is typically a single memory unit, or several memory units interleaved to give the appearance of a single memory unit. See also: *centralized memory*; *disjoint memory*; *distributed memory*.

shared variables *(n., p. 179)* Variables to which two or more processes have access, or the model of parallel computing in which interprocess communication and *synchronization* are managed through such variables. See also: *data parallelism*; *futures*; *generative communication*; *live variable*; *message passing*.

shifting *(n., p. 107)* Moving every value in an array in the same direction and by the same amount. "Circular" shifting wraps values around, i.e. treats the axis as a ring, while "planar" shifting discards values which have been shifted off one end of the axis, and fills the corresponding space at the other end with some default or user-defined value. See also: *permutation*.

shuffle-exchange network *(n., p. 76)* A *topology* containing $N = 2^\ell$ nodes, each of which is labelled by a unique ℓ-bit binary integer. If two nodes have labels $\langle |i_{\ell-1} \ldots i_0| \rangle$ and $\langle |j_{\ell-1} \ldots j_0| \rangle$, then i and j are connected if $i_k = j_k$ for $1 \le k < (\ell - 1)$ and $i_0 \ne j_0$, or if j is a left or right cyclic shift of i. See also: *butterfly*; *hypercube*.

SIMD *(adj., p. 18)* Single Instruction, Multiple Data; a category of *Flynn's taxonomy* in which a single instruction stream is concurrently applied to multiple data sets. A SIMD *architecture* is one in which *homogeneous* processes *synchronously* execute the same instructions on their own data, or one in which an operation can be executed on vectors of fixed or varying size. See also: *processor array*; *vector processor*.

single instruction, multiple data see under *SIMD*.

single instruction, single data see under *SISD*.

single program, multiple data see under *SPMD*.

SISD *(adj., p. 17)* Single Instruction, Single Data; a category of *Flynn's taxonomy* in which a single instruction stream is serially applied to a single data set. Most *uniprocessors* are SISD machines.

skewing *(n., p. 128)* Shifting the values in each row or column of a matrix by an amount proportional to that row or column's index. For example, the first row might not be shifted at all, the second row shifted by one place, the third by two places, and so on.

snoopy cache *(n., p. 265)* A *cache* which constantly monitors the memory *bus* to see when values it is caching are modified.

space sharing *(n., p. 66)* Dividing the resources of a parallel computer among many programs so they can run simultaneously without affecting one another's performance. The processors given to one program are sometimes called a *domain*. See also: *time sharing*.

spanning tree *(n., p. 335)* A tree containing a subset of the *links* in a graph which reaches every node in that graph. A spanning tree can always be constructed so that its depth (the greatest distance between its root and any leaf) is no greater than the *diameter* of the graph. Spanning trees are frequently used to implement *broadcast* operations.

spatial locality see under *locality*.

speculative decomposition see under *decomposition*.

speedup *(n., p. 56)* The ratio of two program execution times. If τ_1 is the time to run a program on one processor, and τ_P the time to run it on P processors, then the speedup is $S = \tau_1 / \tau_P$. Speedup is usually discussed as a function of the number of processors, but also depends on problem size. See also: *Amdahl's Law*; *efficiency*; *Gustafson's Law*; *isoefficiency*; *optimal*.

spin lock *(n., p. 208)* A *lock* which is implemented by having processors repeatedly test its value, often using *test-and-set*.

SPB *(n., p. 344)* Static Parameter Binding; importing information about a program's *configuration* automatically through specially-designated parameters or structures, rather than by using explicit procedure calls. See also: *RTI*.

SPMD   *(adj., p. 19)* Single program, multiple data; a category sometimes added to *Flynn's taxonomy* to describe programs made up of many instances of a single type of process, each executing the same code independently. SPMD can be viewed either as an extension of *SIMD*, or as a restriction of *MIMD*. See also: *process group*; *SISD*.

star   *(n., p. 71)* A *topology* in which a single central node is connected to all other nodes, which are in turn only connected to the central node.

static parameter binding   see under *SPB*.

static scheduling   *(n., p. 185)* Determining the location and order of events during compilation, rather than dynamically at run-time.

stencil   *(n., p. 365)* A pattern of data accesses used when updating the values in a *mesh*. A stencil is usually represented as a grid around a central point, which indicates the location of the value being updated. See also: *halo*.

stride   *(n., p. 99)* The difference between successive index values of a loop, or the separation between successive elements of an array.

strong fairness   see under *fairness*.

superlinear speedup   *(n., p. 58)* *Speedup* that is greater than the number of processors used. While superlinear speedup is theoretically impossible, in practice it may occur because distributing a problem among many processors may increase the effective total size of the *cache* being used, or because distribution may change the order in which non-deterministic operations are carried out, which can lead to earlier termination of the program.

superscalar   *(adj., p. 69)* A processor which can overlap the execution of several different instructions.

switch   *(n., p. 11)* Either a monolithic communication medium, or a single node in such a medium. Examples include *crossbar* switches and the individual *switches* in a *multi-stage interconnection network*. See also: *bus*; *butterfly*; *message combining*; *shuffle-exchange network*.

symmetric operating system   *(adj., p. 485)* An operating system in which both kernel and users processes may run on any processor. See also: *asymmetric operating system*.

synchronization   *(n., p. 21)* The act of bringing two or more processes to known points in their execution at the same *clock time*. Explicit synchronization is not needed in *SIMD* programs (in which every processor either executes the same operation as every other or does nothing), but is often necessary in *SPMD* and *MIMD* programs. The time wasted by processes waiting for other processes to synchronize with them can be a major source of inefficiency in parallel programs. See also: *asynchronous*; *barrier synchronization*; *synchronous*.

synchronous   *(adj., p. 371)* Occurring at the same *clock time*. For example, if a communication event is synchronous, then there is some moment at which both the sender and the receiver are engaged in the operation. See also: *asynchronous*.

systolic   *(adj., p. 309)* Driven by the availability of data or other resources. In a systolic system, processes execute operations *synchronously* as their inputs become available.

task farming   *(n., p. 47)* A technique for implementing *self-scheduling* calculations. In a task farm, a "source" process generates a pool of jobs, while a "sink" process consumes results. In between, one or more "worker" processes repeatedly claim jobs from the source, turn them into results, despatch those results to the sink, and claim their next jobs. If the number of jobs is much greater than the number of workers, task farming can be an effective way to *load balance* a computation.

temporal locality   see under *locality*.

teraFLOPS (TFLOPS)   *(n., p. 66)* 10^{12} FLOPS.

test-and-set   *(n., p. 207)* A *synchronization* mechanism which *atomically* fetches the value of a variable, while setting it to a new value. *Spin locks* are often implemented using *test-and-set*.

thread   see under *lightweight process*.

tiling   *(n., p. 46)* A regular division of a *mesh* into patches, or "tiles." Tiling is the most common way to do *geometric decomposition*.

time-processor product   *(n., p. 24)* The product of the time taken to execute a program and the number of processors used to achieve that time, often used as a measure of goodness for parallel algorithms. See also: *Amdahl's Law*; *efficiency*; *Gustafson's Law*; *speedup*.

time sharing   *(adj., p. 66)* Dividing the effort of a processor among many programs so they can run concurrently. Time sharing is usually managed by an operating system. See also: *space sharing*.

topology   *(n., p. 69)* A family of graphs that share certain properties or are created using the same general rule. The processors in a *multicomputer*, and the circuits in a *multi-stage interconnection network*, are usually laid out using one of several topologies, including the *mesh*, the *hypercube*, the *butterfly*, and the *shuffle-exchange network*. See also: *bisection bandwidth*; *diameter*.

torus   *(n., p. 72)* A *topology* in which nodes form a regular cyclic $\mathcal{D}$-dimensional grid, and each edge is parallel to a grid axis and joins two nodes that are adjacent along that axis.

The *architecture* of some *multicomputers* is a two-dimensional torus. See also: *hypercube*; *mesh*.

trace   *(n., p. 170)* A single execution path through a program; a potential "life history" for that program. Traces are often identified for use in *compiler optimization*, particularly by *trace scheduling* compilers.

trace scheduling   *(n., p. 170)* A *compiler optimization* technique that *vectorizes* the most likely path through a program as if it were a single *basic block*, includes extra instructions at each branch to undo any ill effects of having made a wrong guess, vectorizes the next most-likely branches, and so on.

tree saturation   *(n., p. 217)* A phenomenon observed in *multiprocessors* built around *multi-stage interconnection networks*, in which the presence of even a single "hot spot", or frequently-referenced memory location, will cause switch queues to become full, and degrade the overall performance of the system [Pfister & Norton 1985, Kumar & Pfister 1986]. See also: *contention*.

true dependence   see under *dependence*.

tuple   *(n., p. 388)* An ordered sequence of fixed length of values of arbitrary types. Tuples are used for both data storage and interprocess communication in the *generative communication* paradigm. A "passive" tuple is one which contains only *actual fields*; an "active" tuple is a place-holder for which some processes are still evaluating. An "actual" field in a tuple is one that has both a type and a value; a "formal" field is one with only a type, and is used for pattern-matching. A tuple template containing formal fields is called an "anti-tuple". A tuple's "genus" is the cross-product of its fields' types; its "species" is determined by partitioning tuples into disjoint sets according to genus and the presence of known field values. See also: *tuple space*.

tuple space   *(n., p. 387)* A repository for tuples in a *generative communication* system. Tuple space is an *associative memory*.

unconditional fairness   see under *fairness*.

uniform memory access   see under *UMA*.

UMA   *(adj., p. 21)* Uniform Memory Access; permitting any memory element to be read or written in the same, constant time. See also: *NUMA*.

uniprocessor   *(n., p. 3)* A computer containing a single processor.

valence   *(n., p. 69)* The number of edges connected to a vertex in a graph; for example, every node in a regular square *mesh* has a valence of 4. Confusingly, valence also means the number of branches below a tree node, which is one fewer than the number of edges incident to that node—every node in a binary tree has a valence of 2. The term *arity* is sometimes used in this sense.

vector processor   *(n., p. 5)* A computer designed to apply arithmetic operations to long vectors or arrays. Most vector processors rely heavily on *pipelining* to achieve high performance.

vectorize   *(v., p. 7)* To transform a sequence of identical arithmetic operations into a single instruction. See also: *vector processor*.

Very Long Instruction Word   *(adj., p. 170)* A style of architecture in which instructions for many separate functional units are packed into a single instruction word, which may be from 128 to 1024 bits long.

virtual channel   *(n., p. 88)* A logical point-to-point connection between two processes. Many virtual channels may *time-share* a single *link* to hide *latency* or avoid *deadlock*. See also: *wormhole routing*.

virtual cut-through   *(n., p. 82)* A technique for *routing* messages in which the head and tail of the message both proceed as rapidly as they can. If the head is *blocked* because a *link* it wants to cross is being used by some other message, the tail continues to advance, and the message's contents are put into *buffers* on intermediate nodes. See also: *packet switching*; *wormhole routing*.

virtual processor   *(n., p. 25)* A logical execution unit which may be thought of during compilation as being mapped to a unique physical processor, but which may share a processor with other virtual processors during actual execution. Many *data-parallel* systems rely on virtual processors to simplify compilation.

virtual shared memory   *(n., p. 451)* Memory that appears to users to constitute a single *address space*, but that is physically disjoint. Virtual shared memory is often implemented using some combination of hashing and local caching.

VLIW   see under *Very Long Instruction Word*.

WARPS   *(n., p. 69)* Words accessed randomly per second; a measure of memory access performance, equal to the rate of uniformly random accesses across the whole of the *address space* visible to a process that a machine supports. See also: *FLOPS*; *WASPS*.

WASPS   *(n., p. 69)* Words accessed sequentially per second; a measure of memory access performance, equal to the rate of sequential accesses across the whole of the *address space* visible to a process that a machine supports. See also: *FLOPS*; *WARPS*.

weak fairness   see under *fairness*.

wormhole routing   *(n., p. 83)* A technique for *routing* messages in which the head of the message establishes a path, which is reserved for the message until the tail has passed through it. Unlike *virtual cut-through*, the tail proceeds at a rate dictated by the progress of the head, which reduces the demand for intermediate *buffering*. See also: *packet switching*.

worst link loading   see under *link loading*.

write-invalidate   see under *cache protocol*.

write-update   see under *cache protocol*.

E A Little Bit of Sarcasm

Anyone who has ever programmed a highly parallel computer knows that parallel programming is more difficult than sequential programming. In order to keep ourselves employed, we should make sure it stays that way. Therefore, if you are thinking of adding to the hundreds of parallel programming systems already in existence, please follow the rules given below to ensure that the software you produce does not make the rest of us look stupid, or put us out of a job.

1. **Do not allow users to think about the logical and physical structure of their programs separately.** For example, you should:

• Require users to do index calculations for distributed arrays by hand; it will encourage efficiency.

• Require that array dimensions be some multiple of the number of processors in the machine, or a power of two.

• Discourage users from putting more than one process on each processor by providing a message-passing system in which addresses are (processor, local-process-id) pairs.

• Use point-to-point channels as the basis for your programming model. Most users enjoy drawing plumbing diagrams for their programs (it reminds them of the good ol' days of unstructured flow charts), and are stimulated by the intellectual challenge of determining whether process (i, j) is supposed to use channel $(i + j)$, and pass channel $(i - j + 1)$ to its first-but-one child, or *vice versa*. Point-to-point channels also complicate the implementation of group operations (discussed below). If you are really keen, you can build a graphical user interface to help users draw plumbing diagrams for their programs. However, you should make sure that you limit its usefulness by (a) not checking the consistency of the plumbing created, or (b) require the user to include physical layout information right from the beginning.

2. **Do not include group operations**, such as barrier synchronization and broadcast. If you do, you will ruin the academic career of at least one graduate student at every user site, who would otherwise have been able to write an entire thesis on how s/he implemented these operations using spanning trees. If you cannot avoid including group operations, try to follow the first rule in this list by making sure that they require the participation of all of the processors in the machine.

3. **Do not support I/O.** Well, `printf` to `stdout` is probably OK, but whatever you do, don't give every process direct access to the file system. I/O just slows programs down, and

let's face it: the more test files a program is run on, the more likely it is to turn up a bug in your run-time system. If you do provide I/O facilities, make it the user's responsibility to ensure that input and output are interleaved sensibly. Real users enjoy looking at the detailed workings of systems buffers.

4. **Do not marshal message data automatically.** Packing and unpacking non-contiguous array elements or heterogeneous data doesn't really have anything to do with parallelism, so why waste time implementing it? It is much better to require users to pack data into messages manually, since this will encourage them to use only small, simple data structures. If you have the nerve, you can even make this sound like an advantage ("Unlike System Splodge, our system does not incur the overhead of automatic data marshalling … ").

5. **Do not support interactive use or timesharing, particularly not on a full-sized machine.** Remember the thrill of sending a box of punched cards down to the Burroughs in the basement for the first time? You can recapture some of that feeling for your users by putting a 1960s-style job queue between them and the machine. Requiring them to wait for their job to come up before they can start debugging re-creates that "old time" atmosphere even more. The lack of time-sharing, and the difficulty of getting the full machine when space-sharing, will also ensure that the only applications which are ever run will be those which were easy to parallelize. Your only users will therefore be ones who think your programming system is great, which is obviously better than having to deal with a mob of ungrateful whiners.

6. **Make sure your system's behavior is as variable as possible.** After all, if a program generates the same result twice, then obviously at least one of those runs has been wasted. One proven technique is not guaranteeing the order of floating-point operations. Another is requiring processes to handle messages in the order of their arrival, rather than allowing them to select messages according to their own criteria. Debugging non-deterministic programs is a rite of passage akin to toggling bootstrap code into a DEC-10, and just as important a part of a programmer's education.

7. **Make it difficult for users to determine what is going on inside their programs.** You would be embarrassed if users ever found out that 72% of their total execution time was spent loading the same executable binary N times, so make damn sure they can't find out. Corollaries of this rule include:

• Vendors shouldn't include hard-wired LEDs on their machines, since they might show everyone what isn't happening inside. Programmable LEDs are better, since they can be set to flash on and off a lot to simulate a much more desirable "reality".

• Do not build a debugger for your system. This will not only encourage programmers to write bug-free code, but will also keep the total number of users down, so that you won't have to spend a lot of time doing support work. Note that it is OK to provide dbx-on-a-node, since that won't actually help anyone. It is also OK to provide trace visualization tools, since these are much better at displaying data than at giving programmers useful information.

Remember, all users really want for their papers are speedup figures; absolute performance is unimportant, particularly if you keep repeating:

8. **"A more intelligent compiler could easily optimize this case."** This phrase is very useful, and you should trot it out whenever you are discussing your system's (lack of) performance. It is naïve to think that you should include some discussion of whether anyone actually knows how to implement such optimizations, or how effective they would be. Your users will trust you.

9. **Shared object or address spaces are a bad idea.** In fact, shared data structures of any kind are a bad idea. One particularly bad thing about them is their usefulness: users will exercise them in so many different ways that your system is bound to break. Tell them what real FORTRAN (and OCCAM) programmers told advocates of recursion: it's unsafe, and anyway you can emulate it by hand if you really want it.

10. **Keep adding features to your system until any single user can only ever understand a small sub-set of it.** If properly handled, each new feature can be good for at least two conference papers, or another page in the standard with your name on it. Building your system this way will also give implementors lots of places to lay the blame for poor performance. And keep pushing the entire set of features, rather than making simplifications for new users. After all, the fewer people who know how to do this stuff, the more secure our jobs will be.

11. Natural languages, such as Journal English, are ambiguous for a reason. **Be as fuzzy as possible** when describing the status of your system in order to give the impression that something you've been thinking about has in fact been implemented in some version of your system other than whichever one you are presently discussing. Vendors do this sort of thing all the time; why should they have all the fun?

12. Finally, **do not write any non-trivial applications** on top of your system, and try to discourage users from doing it either. Deep down, you intuitively know that your system is a good one; time spent double-checking that intuition is just time taken away from writing the next version. Anyway, the Mandelbrot set (a heavy user of CPU cycles in industry), the Game of Life, matrix multiplication (or LU decomposition without pivoting if you really must show off), and the N-queens problem were good enough for your supervisor; they should be good enough for you.

References

[Accetta et al. 1986] Mike Accetta, Robert Baron, David Golub, Richard Rashid, Avadis Tevanian, and Michael Young. Mach: A New Kernel Foundation for UNIX. In *Proceedings of the Summer 1986 USENIX Conference*, July 1986.

[Agarwal et al. 1993] Anant Agarwal, John Kubiatowicz, David Kranz, Beng-Hong Lim, Donald Yeung, Godfrey D'Souza, and Mike Parkin. Sparcle: An Evolutionary Processor Design for Large-Scale Multiprocessors. *IEEE Micro*, 13(3), June 1993.

[Akl 1985] Selim G. Akl. *Parallel Sorting Algorithms*. Academic Press, 1985.

[Akl 1989] Selim G. Akl. *The Design and Analysis of Parallel Algorithms*. Prentice-Hall, 1989.

[Amdahl 1967] G. Amdahl. Validity of the Single Processor Approach to Achieving Large-Scale Computer Capabilities. In *AFIPS Conference Proceedings*, volume 30, 1967.

[Anderson & Shasha 1991] Brian G. Anderson and Dennis Shasha. Persistent Linda: Linda + Transactions + Query Processing. In J. P. Banâtre and D. Le Métayer, editors, *Research Directions in High-Level Parallel Programming Languages*. Springer-Verlag, 1991.

[Andrews 1991] Gregory R. Andrews. *Concurrent Programming: Principles and Practice*. Benjamin/ Cummings, 1991.

[Arenstorf & Jordan 1989] Norbert S. Arenstorf and Harry F. Jordan. Comparing Barrier Algorithms. *Parallel Computing*, 12:157–70, 1989.

[Arvind & Brobst 1993] Arvind and Stephen Brobst. The Evolution of Dataflow Architectures: From Static Dataflow to P-RISC. *International Journal of High Speed Computing*, 5(2), 1993.

[Athas & Seitz 1988] W. C. Athas and C. L. Seitz. Multicomputers: Message-Passing Concurrent Computers. *IEEE Computer*, 12(8), August 1988.

[Babb 1988] Robert G. Babb, editor. *Programming Parallel Processors*. Addison-Wesley, 1988.

[Bacci et al. 1994] B. Bacci, M. Danelutto, and S. Pelagatti. Resource Optimisation via Structured Parallel Programming. In *Proceedings of the IFIP Working Conference on Programming Environments for Massively Parallel Distributed Systems*. Birkhäuser Verlag AG, April 1994.

[Bacon et al. 1993] David F. Bacon, Susan L. Graham, and Oliver J. Sharp. Compiler Transformations for High-Performance Computing. *ACM Computing Surveys*, 26(4), December 1994.

[Badouel & Priol 1990] Didier Badouel and Thierry Priol. An Efficient Parallel Ray Tracing Scheme for Highly Parallel Architectures. In *Proceedings of the Fifth Eurographics Workshop on Graphics Hardware*, September 1990.

[Badouel et al. 1990] Didier Badouel, Kadi Bouatouch, and Thierry Priol. Ray Tracing on Distributed Memory Parallel Computers: Strategies for Distributing Computations and Data. In *Siggraph '90*, September 1990.

[Bakken & Schlichting 1991] David E. Bakken and Richard D. Schlichting. Tolerating Failures in the Bag-of-Tasks Programming Paradigm. In *Proceedings of the 19th International Symposium on Fault-Tolerant Computing*, June 1991.

[Bal & Kaashoek 1993] Henri E. Bal and M. Frans Kaashoek. Object Distribution in Orca using Compile-Time and Run-Time Techniques. In *Proceedings of OOPSLA'93*, 1993.

[Bal 1991] Henri Bal. *Programming Distributed Systems*. Prentice Hall, 1991.

[Bal et al. 1992] Henri E. Bal, M. Frans Kaashoek, and Andrew S. Tanenbaum. Orca: A Language for Parallel Programming of Distributed Systems. *IEEE Transactions on Software Engineering*, 18(3), March 1992.

[Barnes et al. 1968] George H. Barnes, Richard M. Brown, Maso Kato, David J. Kuck, Daniel L. Slotnick, and Richard A. Stokes. The ILLIAC-IV Computer. *IEEE Transactions on Computers*, 17(8), August 1968.

[Benkner et al. 1990] Siegfried Benkner, Barbara M. Chapman, and Hans P. Zima. Vienna Fortran 90. In Robert Voigt and Joel Saltz, editors, *Proceedings of the Scalable High-Performance Computing Conference*, pages 51–59. IEEE Computer Society Press, 1992.

[Bennett et al. 1990a] John K. Bennett, John B. Carter, and Willy Zwaenepoel. Adaptive Software Cache Management for Distributed Shared Memory Architectures. In *Proceedings of the 17th International Symposium on Computer Architecture*, 1990.

[Bennett et al. 1990b] John K. Bennett, John B. Carter, and Willy Zwaenepoel. Munin: Distributed Shared Memory Based on Type-Specific Memory Coherence. In *Proceedings of the 1990 Conference on Principles and Practice of Parallel Programming*. ACM Press, 1990.

[Bernstein 1966] A. J. Bernstein. Analysis of Programs for Parallel Processing. *IEEE Transactions on Electronic Computers*, 15:757–62, 1966.

[Best et al. 1993] Michael L. Best, Adam Greenberg, Craig Stanfill, and Lewis W. Tucker. CMMD I/O: A Parallel Unix I/O. In *Proceedings of the Seventh International Parallel Processing Symposium*. IEEE Computer Society, 1993.

[Blelloch 1989] Guy E. Blelloch. Scans as Primitive Parallel Operations. *IEEE Transactions on Computers*, 38(11), November 1989.

[Blelloch 1990] Guy E. Blelloch. *Vector Models for Data-Parallel Computing*. MIT Press, 1990.

[Boghosian & Levermore 1988] B. M. Boghosian and C. D. Levermore. A Deterministic Cellular Automaton with Diffusive Behavior. In *Proceedings of the Workshope on Discrete Kinetic Theory, Lattice Gas Dynamics, and Foundations of Hydrodynamics*. World Scientific, 1988.

[Brawer 1989] Steven Brawer. *Introduction to Parallel Programming*. Academic Press, 1989.

[Carriero & Gelernter 1989] Nicholas Carriero and David Gelernter. Linda in Context. *Communications of the ACM*, 32(4), April 1989.

[Carriero & Gelernter 1990a] Nicholas Carriero and David Gelernter. Tuple Analysis and Partial Evaluation Strategies in the Linda Compiler. In David Gelernter, Alexandru Nicolau, and David Padua, editors, *Languages and Compilers for Parallel Computing*. Pitman, 1990.

[Carriero & Gelernter 1990b] Nicholas Carriero and David Gelernter. *How to Write Parallel Programs*. MIT Press, 1990.

[Carter et al. 1991] John B. Carter, John K. Bennett, and Willy Zwaenepoel. Implementation and Performance of Munin. In *Proceedings of the 13th Symposium on Operating Systems Principles*, 1991.

[Chaiken et al. 1990] D. Chaiken, C. Fields, K. Kurihara, and A. Agarwal. Directory-Based Cache Coherence in Large-Scale Multiprocessors. *IEEE Computer*, June 1990.

[Ciancarini 1991] Paolo Ciancarini. Parallel Logic Programming Using the Linda Model of Computation. In J. P. Banâtre and D. Le Métayer, editors, *Research Directions in High-Level Parallel Programming Languages*. Springer-Verlag, 1991.

[Clarke & Wilson 1991] Lyndon J. Clarke and Greg Wilson. Tiny: An Efficient Routing Harness for the Inmos Tranpsuter. *Concurrency: Practice and Experience*, 3(3), June 1991.

[Clarke et al. 1994] Lyndon J. Clarke, Robert A. Fletcher, Shari M. Trewin, R. Alasdair A. Bruce, A. Gordon Smith, and Simon R. Chapple. Reuse, Portability and Parallel Libraries. In *Proceedings of the IFIP Working Conference on Programming Environments for Massively Parallel Distributed Systems*. Birkhäuser Verlag AG, April 1994.

[Coffman and Graham 1972] E. Coffman, Jr. and R. Graham. Optimal Scheduling for Two-Processor Systems. *Acta Informatica*, 1:200–13, 1972.

[Cole 1989] Murray Cole. *Algorithmic Skeletons: Structured Management of Parallel Computation*. MIT Press, 1989.

[Crovella & LeBlanc 1993] Mark E. Crovella and Thomas J. LeBlanc. Performance Debugging using Parallel Performance Predicates. *ACM SIGPLAN Notices (Proc. Third ACM/ONR Workshop on Parallel and Distributed Debugging)*, 28(12), December 1993.

[Crowl 1994] Lawrence A. Crowl. How to Measure, Present, and Compare Parallel Performance. *IEEE Parallel & Distributed Technology*, 2(1), Spring 1994.

[Culler et al. 1993] David E. Culler, Andrea Dusseau, Seth Copen Goldstein, Arvind Krishnamurthy, Steven Lumetta, Thorsten von Eicken, and Katherine Yelick. Parallel Programming in Split-C. In *Proc. Supercomputing '93*, 1993.

[Dally & Seitz 1987] William J. Dally and Charles L. Seitz. Deadlock-Free Message Routing in Multiprocessor Interconnection Networks. *IEEE Transactions on Computers*, 36(5), May 1987.

[Davidson 1989] Craig Davidson. Technical Correspondence in Response to *Linda in Context*. *Communications of the ACM*, 32(10), October 1989.

[Dijkstra 1968] Edsger Dijkstra. Cooperating Sequential Processes. In F. Genuys, editor, *Programming Languages*. Academic Press, 1968.

[Doberkat et al. 1992] E. E. Doberkat, W. Franke, U. Gutenbeil, W. Hasselbring, U. Lammers, and C. Pahl. PROSET—A Language for Prototyping with Sets. In *Proceedings of the 3rd International Workshop on Rapid System Prototyping*. IEEE, June 1992.

[Duato 1991] José Duato. On the Design of Deadlock-Free Adaptive Routing Algorithms for Multicomputers: Design Methodologies. In E. H. L. Aarts, J. van Leeuwen, and M. Rem, editors, *Proceedings of Parallel Architectures and Languages Europe 1991*. Springer-Verlag, 1991.

[Ellis 1985] J. R. Ellis. *Bulldog: A Compiler for VLIW Architectures*. MIT Press, 1985.

[Elzen & Mackenzie 1994] Boelie Elzen and Donald MacKenzie. The Social Limits of Speed: The Development and Use of Supercomputers. *IEEE Annals of the History of Computing*, 16(1), 1994.

[Faber et al. 1986] V. Faber, Olaf M. Lubeck, and Andrew B. White, Jr. Superlinear Speedup of an Efficient Sequential Algorithm is Not Possible. *Parallel Computing*, 3:259–260, 1986.

[Felten & Otto 1988] E. W. Felten and S. W. Otto. A Highly Parallel Chess Program. In *Proc. International Conference on 5th Generation Computer Systems*, pages 1001–9, 1988.

[Feo et al. 1990] John T. Feo, David C. Cann, and Rodney R. Oldehoeft. A Report on the Sisal Language Project. *Journal of Parallel and Distributed Computing*, 10:349–66, 1990.

[Fidge 1991] Colin Fidge. Logical Time in Distributed Computing Systems. *IEEE Computer*, August 1991.

[Flynn 1966] Michael J. Flynn. Very High-Speed Computing Systems. *Proceedings of the IEEE*, 54(12): 1901–09, 1966.

[Foley et al. 1990] James Foley, Andries van Dam, Steven Feiner, and John Hughes. *Computer Graphics: Principles and Practice*. Addison Wesley, third edition, 1990.

[Fortune & Wyllie 1978] Steven Fortune and James Wyllie. Parallelism in Random Access Machines. In *Proceedings of the Tenth ACM Symposium on the Theory of Computing*, 1978.

[Foster & Chandy 1995] I. Foster and K. M. Chandy. FORTRAN M: A Language for Modular Parallel Programming. *Journal of Parallel and Distributed Computing*, 25(1), 1995.

[Fox et al. 1988] G. Fox, M. Johnson, G. Lyzenga, S. Otto, J. Salmon, and D. Walker. *Solving Problems on Concurrent Processors, Volume 1*. Prentice-Hall, 1988.

[Furht 1994] Borko Furht. Parallel Computing: Glory and Collapse. *IEEE Computer*, 27(11), November 1994.

[Gardner 1983] Martin Gardner. *Wheels, Life and Other Mathematical Amusements*. W. H. Freeman, 1983.

[Geist & Sunderam 1992] G. A. Geist and V. S. Sunderam. Network-Based Concurrent Computing on the PVM System. *Concurrency: Practice and Experience*, 4(4), June 1992.

[Geist et al. 1994] Al Geist, Adam Beguelin, Jack Dongarra, Weicheng Jiang, Robert Manchek, and Vaidyalin- gam S. Sunderam. *PVM (Parallel Virtual Machine): A Users' Guide and Tutorial for Network Parallel Computing*. MIT Press, 1994.

[Gelernter 1989] David Gelernter. Multiple Tuple Spaces in Linda. In *PARLE '89: Parallel Architectures and Languages Europe*. Springer-Verlag, June 1989.

[Gibson 1992] Garth A. Gibson. *Redundant Disk Arrays: Reliable Parallel Secondary Storage*. MIT Press, 1992.

[Gottlieb et al. 1983] Allan Gottlieb, Ralph Grishman, Clyde P. Kruskal, Kevin P. McAuliffe, Larry Rudolph, and Marc Snir. The NYU Ultracomputer—Designing and MIMD Shared Memory Parallel Computer. *IEEE Transactions on Computers*, 32(2), February 1983.

[Grama et al. 1993] Ananth Grama, Anshul Gupta, and Vipin Kumar. Isoefficiency: Measuring the Scalability of Parallel Algorithms and Architectures. *IEEE Parallel & Distributed Technology*, 1(3), August 1993.

[Graunke & Thakkar 1990] Gary Graunke and Shreekant Thakkar. Synchronization Algorithms for Shared-Memory Multiprocessors. *IEEE Computer*, June 1990.

[Gropp et al. 1994] William Gropp, Ewing Lusk, and Anthony Skjellum. *Using MPI: Portable Parallel Programming with the Message-Passing Interface*. MIT Press, 1994.

[Grunwald & Vajracharya 1994] Dirk Grunwald and Suvas Vajracharya. Efficient Barriers for Distributed Shared Memory Computers. In Howard Jay Siegel, editor, *Proc. Eighth International Parallel Processing Symposium*. IEEE Computer Society Press, April 1994.

[Grunwald et al. 1990] Dirk C. Grunwald, Bobby A. A. Nazief, and Daniel A. Reed. Empirical Comparison of Heuristic Load Distribution in Point-to-Point Multicomputer Networks. In *Fifth Distributed Memory Computing Conference*. IEEE, 1990.

[Gupta & Kumar 1993] Anshul Gupta and Vipin Kumar. Analyzing Performance of Large Scale Parallel Systems. In *Proc. 26th Hawaii INternational Conference on System Sciences*, 1993.

[Gustafson et al. 1988] John L. Gustafson, Gary R. Montry, and Robert E. Benner. Development of Parallel Methods for 1024-Processor Hypercube. *SIAM Journal on Scientific and Statistical Computing*, 9(4), July 1988.

[Gustavson 1992] David B. Gustavson. The Scalable Coherent Interface and Related Standards Projects. *IEEE Micro*, February 1992.

[Halstead 1985] Robert Halstead. Multilisp: A Language for Concurrent Symbolic Computation. *ACM Transactions on Programming Languages and Systems*, October 1985.

[Hasselbring 1994] W. Hasselbring. *Prototyping Parallel Algorithms in a Set-Oriented Language*. Dissertation (University of Dortmund, Dept. Computer Science). Verlag Dr. Kovac, Hamburg, 1994.

[Hatcher & Quinn 1991] Philip J. Hatcher and Michael J. Quinn. *Data-Parallel Programming on MIMD Computers*. MIT Press, 1991.

[Hillis 1985] W. D. Hillis. *The Connection Machine*. MIT Press, 1985.

[Hiranandani et al. 1991] Seema Hiranandani, Ken Kennedy, Charles Koelbel, Ulrich Kremer, and Chau-Wen Tseng. An Overview of the Fortran D Programming System. Technical report, Center for Research on Parallel Computation, Rice University, 1991.

[Hoare 1985] C. A. R. Hoare. *Communicating Sequential Processes*. Prentice-Hall, 1985.

[Hockney & Jesshope 1988] R. W. Hockney and C. R. Jesshope. *Parallel Computers 2*. Adam Hilger, 1988.

[Hockney 1982] Roger Hockney. Untitled article. *Computer Physics Communications*, 26:285, 1982.

[Hockney 1991] Roger Hockney. Performance Parameters and Benchmarking of Supercomputers. *Parallel Computing*, 17:1111–30, 1991.

[Hu 1961] T. Hu. Parallel Sequencing and Assembly Line Problems. *Operations Research*, 9:841–48, 1961.

[Inmos 1988a] Inmos Ltd. *Occam 2 Reference Manual*. Prentice Hall, 1988.

[Inmos 1988b] INMOS Limited. *Transputer Reference Manual*. Prentice Hall, 1988.

[ISO/DP 8485] International Standards Organisation TC97/SC5. Draft Proposal Standard for the Programming Language APL. *APL Quote Quad (Proceedings of ACM SIGAPL)*, 14(2), December 1983.

[Jagannathan 1991] Suresh Jagannathan. Expressing Fine-Grained Parallelism Using Concurrent Data Structures. In J. P. Banâtre and D. Le Métayer, editors, *Research Directions in High-Level Parallel Programming Languages*. Springer-Verlag, 1991.

[Jellingham 1990] Robert Jellingham. Eiffel Linda: An Object-Oriented Linda Dialect. *ACM SIGPLAN Notices*, 25(12), December 1990.

[Kahn & Miller 1989] Kenneth M. Kahn and Mark S. Miller. Technical Correspondence in Response to *Linda in Context. Communications of the ACM*, 32(10), October 1989.

[Kalé 1989] L. V. Kalé. Technical Correspondence in Response to *Linda in Context. Communications of the ACM*, 32(10), October 1989.

[Kermani & Kleinrock 1979] Parviz Kermani and Leonard Kleinrock. Virtual Cut-Through: A New Computer Communication Switching Technique. *Computer Networks*, 3:267–86, 1979.

[Knuth 1981a] Donald Knuth. *The Art of Computer Programming: Vol II (Seminumerical Algorithms)*. Addison-Wesley, 1981.

[Knuth 1981b] Donald Knuth. *The Art of Computer Programming: Vol III (Sorting and Searching)*. Addison-Wesley, 1981.

[Koelbel et al. 1994] Charles H. Koelbel, David B. Loveman, Robert S. Schreiber, Guy L. Steele Jr., and Mary E. Zosel. *The High Performance Fortran Handbook*. MIT Press, 1994.

[Kohn & Williams 1993] James Kohn and Winifred Williams. ATExpert. *Journal of Parallel and Distributed Computing*, 18:205–22, 1993.

[Kowalik 1985] J. S. Kowalik, editor. *Parallel MIMD Computation: The HEP Supercomputer and Its Applications*. MIT Press, 1985.

[Kruskal et al. 1988] Clyde P. Kruskal, Larry Rudolph, and Marc Snir. Efficient Synchronization on Multiprocessors with Shared Memory. *ACM Transactions on Programming Languages and Systems*, 10(4), October 1988.

[Kuck 1968] David J. Kuck. ILLIAC-IV Software and Application Programming. *IEEE Transactions on Computers*, 17(8), August 1968.

[Kuck et al. 1972] David J. Kuck, Y. Muraoka, and S. C. Chen. On the Number of Operations Simultaneously Executable in Fortran-Like Programs and Their Resulting Speed-Up. *IEEE Transactions on Computers*, 21, 1972.

[Kumar & Pfister 1986] Manoj Kumar and Gregory F. Pfister. The Onset of Hot Spot Contention. In *Proceedings of the 1986 International Conference on Parallel Processing*, 1986.

[Kumar et al. 1993] Vipin Kumar, Ananth Grama, Anshul Gupta, and George Karypis. *Introduction to Parallel Computing: Design and Analysis of Algorithms*. Benjamin-Cummings, 1994.

[Lamport 1978] Leslie Lamport. Time, Clocks, and the Ordering of Events in a Distributed System. *Communications of the ACM*, 21(7), July 1978.

[Lawrie 1975] Duncan Lawrie. Access and Alignment of Data in an Array Processor. *IEEE Transactions on Computers*, December 1975.

[Lee & Gannon 1991] J. K. Lee and D. Gannon. Object Oriented Parallel Programming: Experiments and Results. In *Proceedings of Supercomputing '91*. IEEE Computer Society and ACM SIGARCH, 1991.

[Lee et al. 1986] Gyungho Lee, Clyde P. Kruskal, and David J. Kuck. The Effectiveness of Combining in Shared Memory Parallel Computers in the Presence of 'Hot Spots'. In *Proceedings of the 1986 International Conference on Parallel Processing*, 1986.

[Lee et al. 1988] Chung-Yee Lee, Jing-Jang Hwang, Yuan-Chieh Chow, and Frank Anger. Multiprocessor Scheduling with Interprocessor Communication Delays. *Operations Research Letters*, 7(3), June 1988.

[Leighton 1991] F. Thomson Leighton. *Introduction to Parallel Algorithms and Architectures: Arrays · Trees · Hypercubes*. Morgan Kaufmann, 1991.

[Leiserson 1985] Charles E. Leiserson. Fat-trees: Universal Networks for Hardware-Efficient Supercomputing. *IEEE Transactions on Computers*, 34(10), October 1985.

[Lcler 1990] Wm Lcler. Linda Mccts UNIX. *IEEE Computer*, February 1990.

[Lenoski et al. 1992] D. Lenoski, J. Laudon, K. Gharachorloo, W.-D. Weber, A. Gupta, J. Hennessy, M. Horo- witz, and M. S. Lam. The Stanford Dash Multiprocessor. *IEEE Computer*, March 1992.

[Levy 1988] David Levy, editor. *Computer Chess Compendium*. Batsford, 1988.

[Li & Hudak 1989] Kai Li and Paul Hudak. Memory Coherence in Shared Virtual Memory Systems. *ACM Transactions on Computer Systems*, 7(4), November 1989.

[Liskov 1979] Barbara Liskov. Primitives for Distributed Computing. In *Proceedings of the 7th Symposium on Operating Systems Principles*, December 1979.

[Lo 1992] Virginia M. Lo. Temporal Communication Graphs: Lamport's Process-Time Graphs Augmented for the Purpose of Mapping and Scheduling. *Journal of Parallel and Distributed Computing*, 16:378–84, 1992.

[MacDonald 1993] Neil B. MacDonald. A Framework for Parallel Applications. In *Proceedings of the Second British Computer Soceity Workshop on Abstracts Models for Highly Parallel Computers*. Oxford University Press, 1993.

[Mackenzie 1991] Donald Mackenzie. The Influence of the Los Alamos and Livermore National Laboratories on the Development of Supercomputing. *IEEE Annals of the History of Computing*, 13:179–201, 1991.

[McDowell & Helmbold 1989] Charles E. McDowell and David P. Helmbold. Debugging Concurrent Programs. *ACM Computing Surveys*, 21(4), December 1989.

[Mehlhorn & Vishkin 1984] Kurt Mehlhorn and Uzi Vishkin. Randomized and Deterministic Simulations of PRAMs by Parallel Machines with Restricted Granularity of Parallel Memories. *Acta Informatica*, 21, 1984.

[Mellor-Crummey & Scott 1991] John M. Mellor-Crummey and Michael L. Scott. Algorithms for Scalable Synchronization on Shared-Memory Multiprocessors. *ACM Transactions on Computer Systems*, 9(1), February 1991.

[Metcalf & Reid 1989] Michael Metcalf and John Reid. *Fortran 90 Explained*. Clarendon Press, 1989.

[Miller & McDowell 1991] Barton P. Miller and Charles E. McDowell, editors. *Proceedings of the ACM/ ONR Workshop on Parallel and Distributed Debugging (ACM SIGPLAN Notices)*, December 1991.

[Milner 1989] Robin Milner. *Communication and Concurrency*. Prentice Hall, 1989.

[Nakanishi et al. 1992] H. Nakanishi, V. Rego, and V. Sunderam. Superconcurrent Simulatino of Polymer Chains on Heterogeneous Networks. In *Proceedings of Supercomputing '92*, 1992.

[Netzer 1994] Robert H. B. Netzer. Trace Size vs. Parallelism in Trace-and-Replay Debugging of Shared-Memory Programs. In Utpal Banerjee, David Gelernter, Alex Nicolau, and David Padua, editors, *Languages and Comilers for Parallel Computing 6*. Springer Verlag, 1994.

[Ni & McKinley 1993] Lionel M. Ni and Philip K. McKinley. A Survey of Wormhole Routing Techniques in Direct Networks. *IEEE Computer*, February 1993.

[Nickolls 1994] John R. Nickolls. The MasPar Scalable Unix I/O System. In Howard Jay Siegel, editor, *Proc. Eighth International Parallel Processing Symposium*. IEEE Computer Society Press, April 1994.

[Nielson 1991] Gregory M. Nielson. Visualization in Scientific and Engineering Computation. *IEEE Computer*, September 1991.

[Nikhil 1991] Rishiyur S. Nikhil. Id Language Reference Manual (Version 90.1). Technical report, Laboratory for Computer Science, MIT, 1991.

[Organick 1983] Elliott I. Organick. *A Programmer's View of the Intel 432 System*. McGraw-Hill, 1983.

[Osterhaug 1989] Anita Osterhaug. *Guide to Parallel Programming*. Sequent, 1989.

[Parkinson 1986] D. Parkinson. Parallel Efficiency Can be Greater than Unity. *Parallel Computing*, 3:261–62, 1986.

[Pfister & Norton 1985] G. F Pfister and V. A. Norton. "Hot Spot" Contention and Combining in Multistage Interconnection Networks. In *Proceedings of the IEEE International Conference on Parallel Processing*, 1985.

[Pfister et al. 1985] G. F Pfister, W. C. Brantley, D. A. George, S. L. Harvey, W. J. Kleinfelder, K. P. McAuliffe, E. A. Melton, V. A. Norton, and J. Weiss. The IBM Research Parallel Processor Prototype (RP3): Introduction and Architecture. In *Proceedings of the IEEE International Conference on Parallel Processing*, 1985.

[Polychronopoulos & Kuck 1987] Constantine D. Polychronopoulos and David J. Kuck. Guided Self-Sched- uling: A Practical Scheduling Scheme for Parallel Supercomputers. *IEEE Transactions on Computers*, 36(12), December 1987.

[Polychronopoulos et al. 1990] Constantine D. Polychronopoulos, Milind B. Girkar, Mohammad R. Haghighat, Chia L. Lee, Bruce P. Leung, and Dale A. Schouten. The Structure of Parafrase-2: an Advanced Parallelizing Compiler for C and Fortran. In David Gelernter, Alexandru Nicolau, and David Padua, editors, *Languages and Compilers for Parallel Computing*. Pitman (London), 1990.

[Prior et al. 1990] Dominic M. N. Prior, Michael G. Norman, Nicholas J. Radcliffe, and Lyndon J. Clarke. What Price Regularity? *Concurrency: Practice and Experience*, 2(1), March 1990.

[Quinn 1994] Michael J. Quinn. *Parallel Computing: Theory and Practice*. McGraw-Hill, 1994.

[Ranade 1991] Abhiram G. Ranade. How to Emulate Shared Memory. *Journal of Computer and System Sciences*, 42(3), June 1991.

[Rao & Kumar 1989] V. Nageshwara Rao and Vipin Kumar. Analysis of Scalability of Parallel Algorithms. Technical report, Department of Computer Science, University of Texas at Austin, January 1989.

[Rau & Fisher 1993] B. Ramakrishna Rau and Joseph A. Fisher. Instruction-Level Parallel Processing: History, Overview, and Perspective. *Journal of Supercomputing*, 7:9–50, 1993.

[Reed et al. 1991] Daniel A. Reed, Robert D. Olson, Ruth A. Aydt, Tara M. Madhyastha, Thomas Birkett, David W. Jensen, Bobby A. A. Nazief, and Brian K. Totty. Scalable Performance Environments for Parallel Systems. In *Proceedings of the Sixth Distributed Memory Computing Conference*, pages 562–69, April 1991.

[Reppy 1991] John H. Reppy. CML: A Higher-order Concurrent Language. In *Proceedings of the SIGPLAN'91 Conference on Programming Language Design and Implementation*, 1991.

[Ritchie & Thompson 1974] D. M. Ritchie and K. Thompson. The UNIX Time-Sharing System. *Communications of the ACM*, 17(7), July 1974.

[Rover & Wright 1993] Diane T. Rover and Charles T. Wright Jr. Visualizing the Performance of SPMD and Data-Parallel Programs. *Journal of Parallel and Distributed Computing*, 18:129–46, 1993.

[Schaeffer et al. 1993] Jonathan Schaeffer, Duane Szafron, Greg Lobe, and Ian Parsons. The Enterprise Model for Developing Distributed Applications. *IEEE Parallel & Distributed Technology*, 1(3):85–96, 1993.

[Schimmel 1994] Curt Schimmel. *UNIX Systems for Modern Architectures*. Addison-Wesley, 1994.

[Shapiro 1989] Ehud Shapiro. Technical Correspondence in Response to *Linda in Context*. *Communications of the ACM*, 32(10), October 1989.

[Shirazi et al. 1990] Behrooz Shirazi, Mingfang Wang, and Girish Pathak. Analysis and Evaluation of Heuristic Methods for Static Task Scheduling. *Journal of Parallel and Distributed Computing*, 10:222–32, 1990.

[Shi & Schaeffer 1992] Hanmao Shi and Jonathan Schaeffer. Parallel Sorting by Regular Sampling. *Journal of Parallel and Distributed Computing*, 14:361–372, 1992.

[Shu & Kalé 1991] Wei Shu and L. V. Kalé. Chare Kernel—a Runtime Support System for Parallel Computations. *Journal of Parallel and Distributed Computing*, 11, 1991.

[Sipelstein & Blelloch 1991] Jay M. Sipelstein and Guy E. Blelloch. Collection-oriented languages. *Proceedings of the IEEE*, 79(4):504–523, April 1991.

[Skillicorn 1990] David B. Skillicorn. Architecture-Independent Parallel Computation. *IEEE Computer*, December 1990.

[Smith 1981] Burton Smith. Architecture and Applications of the HEP Computer System. In *Real Time Processing IV, Proc. SPIE*, 1981.

[Stenström 1990] Per Stenström. A Survey of Cache Coherence Schemes for Multiprocessors. *IEEE Computer*, June 1990.

[Stone 1971] Harold S. Stone. Parallel Processing with the Perfect Shuffle. *IEEE Transactions on Computers*, C-20:153–61, 1971.

[Stone 1977] Harold S. Stone. Multiprocessor Scheduling with the Aid of Network Flow Algorithms. *IEEE Transactions on Software Engineering*, 3(1), January 1977.

[Tannenbaum 1987] Andrew S. Tannenbaum. *Operating Systems: Design and Implementation*. Prentice-Hall, 1987.

[Trew & Wilson 1991] Arthur Trew and Greg Wilson, editors. *Past, Present, Parallel: A Survey of Available Parallel Computer Systems*. Springer-Verlag, 1991.

[Tufte 1983] Edward R. Tufte. *The Visual Display of Quantitative Information*. Graphics Press, 1983.

[Tufte 1990] Edward R. Tufte. *Envisioning Information*. Graphics Press, 1990.

[Upson et al. 1989] Craig Upson, Thomas Faulhaber Jr, David Kamins, David Laidlaw, David Schlegel, Jeffrey Vroom, Robert Gurwitz, and Andries van Dam. The Application Visualization System: A Computational Environment for Scientific Visualization. *IEEE Computer Graphics and Applications*, pages 30–42, July 1989.

[Valiant 1988] Leslie G. Valiant. Optimally Universal Parallel Computers. *Philosophical Transactions of the Royal Society of London*, A326, 1988.

[Valiant 1990] Leslie Valiant. A Bridging Model for Parallel Computation. *Communications of the ACM*, 33(8), August 1990.

[Van Leeuwen & Tan 1987] J. Van Leeuwen and R. B. Tan. Interval Routing. *The Computer Journal*, 30(4), 1987.

[Vitter & Nodine 1993] Jeffrey Scott Vitter and Mark H. Nodine. Large-Scale Sorting in Uniform Memory Hierarchies. *Journal of Parallel and Distributed Computing*, pages 107–14, 1993.

[Wolfe 1989] Michael Wolfe. *Optimizing Supercompilers for Supercomputers*. MIT Press, 1989.

[Wolfram 1991] Stephen Wolfram. *Mathematica: A System for Doing Mathematics by Computer*. Addison Wesley, second edition, 1991.

[Wulf et al. 1981] William A. Wulf, Roy Levin, and Samuel P. Harbison. *HYDRA/C.mmp: An Experimental Computer System*. McGraw-Hill, 1981.

[Yew et al. 1986] Pen-Chung Yew, Nian-Feng Tzeng, and Duncan H. Lawrie. Distributing Hot-Spot Addressing in Large-Scale Multiprocessors. In *Proceedings of the 1986 International Conference on Parallel Processing*, 1986.

[Zima 1990] Hans Zima. *Supercompilers for Parallel and Vector Computers*. Addison Wesley, 1990.

Index

4004. *See under* Intel.

6600. *See under* Control Data Corporation.
68000. *See under* Motorola.
68020. *See under* Motorola.
68881. *See under* Motorola.

7600. *See under* Control Data Corporation.

80286. *See under* Intel.
80386. *See under* Intel.
8086. *See under* Intel.
8087. *See under* Intel.
8600. *See under* Control Data Corporation.
88000. *See under* Motorola.

$\alpha\beta$ search, 44

Active Memory Technology (AMT), 494
 DAP, 120, 122, 494, 495
 MiniDAP, 494
Active Messages, 496
active tuple. *See under* tuple.
actual field. *See under* tuple.
ADA, 455
adaptive caching, 451
adaptive routing. *See under* routing.
address space, 13, 20, 328, 426, 433, 492
Advanced Research Projects Agency (ARPA), 479
AEC. *See* Atomic Energy Commission.
AI. *See* artificial intelligence.
Alewife, 281
ALGOL, 125, 480
ALGOL-68, 481, 482
algorithmic decomposition. *See under* decomposition.
algorithmic skeleton, 364
all-to-all personalized communication. *See under* communication patterns.
all-to-all replicated communication. *See under* communication patterns.
all-to-one personalized communication. *See under* communication patterns.

Alliant, 181, 485
Amdahl's Law, 59, 60
Amdahl, Gene, 15, 59
Ametek, 487
AMT. *See* Active Memory Technology.
anti-dependence. *See under* dependence.
anti-tuple. *See under* tuple.
APL, 93
Application Visualization System (AVS), 380
architecture, 3, 50, 62, 63, 68, 69, 90, 118, 120, 164, 166, 167, 170, 176, 268, 445, 493
 heterogeneous, 269, 341, 343, 352, 485, 489
 hierarchical, 14
 hypercube, 80, 88, 92, 283, 331, 487, 489, 491
arity, 69, 403
ARPA. *See* Advanced Research Projects Agency.
ARPAnet, 491
artificial intelligence (AI), 495
ASC. *See under* Texas Instruments.
associative matching, 399, 440
associative memory. *See under* memory.
asymmetric operating system. *See under* operating system.
asynchronous
 event, 371
 variable, 491
asynchronous communication. *See under* communication.
atomic, 198, 207, 212, 220, 397, 409, 448, 450, 453, 454
Atomic Energy Commission (AEC), 479
automatic parallelization, 151, 161, 167
AVS. *See* Application Visualization System.

barrier, 237, 266, 346, 381, 453, 491
 bit, 149
 fuzzy, 238
 synchronization, 237, 266, 276, 280, 332, 345, 346, 365
basic block, 164
BBN. *See* Bolt Beranek and Newman.
Bernstein's Condition, 164
Best, Michael, 280, 281